David Hume's Political

Hume's *Political Discourses* (1752) won immediate acclaim and positioned him as an authoritative figure on the subject of political economy. This volume of thirteen new essays definitively establishes the central place of political economy in Hume's life and work, as well as the profound and far-reaching influence of his theories on Enlightenment discourse and practice. A major strength of this collection is that the contributors come from a diverse set of fields – philosophy, economics, political science, history and literature. This promotes a comprehensive reading of Hume's political economy, taking into account his entire set of writings and correspondence, in a way that captures his polymathic genius. Hume's analyses of trade and commerce not only delve into the institutions of money and markets, but also human agency, the role of reason and the passions, manners and social mores. Hume sought general principles but also concrete applications, whether he grappled with the problem of economic development (Scotland and Ireland), with the debates on luxury consumption (France), or with the mounting public debt (England).

This book is an important resource for students and researchers in the areas of economic and political philosophy, history of economic and political theory, and the history of ideas.

Carl Wennerlind is Assistant Professor of History at Barnard College.

Margaret Schabas is Professor of Philosophy at the University of British Columbia.

Routledge Studies in the History of Economics

David Hume's Political Economy

Edited by Carl Wennerlind
and Margaret Schabas

LONDON AND NEW YORK

First published 2008
by Routledge
2 Park Square, Milton Park, Abingdon, OX14 4RN

Simultaneously published in the USA and Canada
by Routledge
270 Madison Ave, New York, 10016

Routledge is an imprint of the Taylor & Francis Group, an informa business

Transferred to Digital Printing 2009

© 2008 Selection and editorial matter, Carl Wennerlind and Margaret
Schabas; individual chapters, the contributors

Typeset in Times NR MT by
Taylor & Francis Books

British Library Cataloguing in Publication Data
A catalogue record for this book is available from the British Library

Library of Congress Cataloging in Publication Data
A catalog record for this book has been requested

ISBN10: 0-415-32001-1 (hbk)
ISBN10: 0-415-49413-3 (pbk)
ISBN10: 0-203-32447-1 (ebk)

ISBN13: 978-0-415-32001-6 (hbk)
ISBN13: 978-0-415-49413-7 (pbk)
ISBN13: 978-0-203-32447-9 (ebk)

Contents

Author Biographies

Christopher J. Berry is Professor of Political Theory at the University of Glasgow and the author of *Hume, Hegel and Human Nature* (1982), *Human Nature* (1986), *The Idea of a Democratic Community* (1989), *The Idea of Luxury* (1994), *Social Theory of the Scottish Enlightenment* (1997), as well as many articles in political theory and the history of ideas. He is currently writing a book on the philosophical anthropology of politics. He is an elected Fellow of the Royal Society of Edinburgh.

Richard Boyd is Associate Professor of Government at Georgetown University. He is the author of *Uncivil Society: The Perils of Pluralism and the Making of Modern Liberalism* (2004) and of numerous journal articles and book chapters on 17th- and 18th-century social and political theory. He is currently completing a book manuscript dealing with questions of membership and belonging in the classical liberal tradition.

C. George Caffentzis is Professor of Philosophy at the University of Southern Maine. He is the author of *Clipped Coins, Abused Words and Civil Government: John Locke's Philosophy of Money* (1989) and *Exciting the Industry of Banking: George Berkeley's Philosophy of Money* (2000). He is now working on a book about David Hume's philosophy of money.

Loïc Charles is Associate Professor of Economics at the University of Paris II. He is working on the history of French political economy during the Enlightenment. He has published articles in *History of Political Economy*, *The European Journal of the History of Economic Thought*, and co-edited, with C. Théré and J.-C. Perrot, the *Œuvres économiques complètes et autres textes de François Quesnay* (2005). He received the History of Economics Society's Best Article Award for 2004.

Paul Cheney is Assistant Professor of French History at the University of Chicago. He studied history at Columbia University and political economy at the New School for Social Research. His principal domain of interest is the problem of globalization and its discontents in eighteenth-century

France, and articles on this subject appear in *Historical Reflections, Dix-Huitième Siècle* and *The William and Mary Quarterly*.

Robert W. Dimand is Professor of Economics at Brock University, St. Catharines, Ontario, Canada. He is the author of *The Origins of the Keynesian Revolution* (1988) and the co-editor, with C. Nyland, of *The Status of Women in Classical Economic Thought* (2003).

Roger L. Emerson is Professor Emeritus of History at the University of Western Ontario where he taught from 1964 until his retirement in 1999. He is the author of a volume on the Universities in Aberdeen 1690–1800, an associate editor of the *Oxford Encyclopedia of the Enlightenment* and the author of many papers on the Scottish Enlightenment. He is presently writing a biography of the 3rd Duke of Argyll, the founder of the Royal Bank of Scotland.

Till Grüne-Yanoff is Postdoctoral Researcher at the Royal Institute of Technology in Stockholm. He received his PhD from the London School of Economics with a thesis on the concept of preferences in the social sciences. He has published articles on decision and game theory, philosophy of economics, and policy analysis.

Istvan Hont is University Lecturer in the History of Political Thought at the University of Cambridge, and a Fellow of King's College, Cambridge. He is the author of numerous articles on political and economic thought and co-editor of *Wealth and Virtue: The Shaping of Political Economy in the Scottish Enlightenment* (1983). Most recently, he published an essay on luxury in *The Cambridge History of Eighteenth-Century Political Thought* (2006) and the book *Jealousy of Trade: International Competition and the Nation-State in Historical Perspective* (2005).

Edward F. McClennen is Professor of Political Philosophy at Syracuse University, and Visiting Centennial Professor of Philosophy at the London School of Economics and Political Science. His publications include *Rationality and Dynamic Choice: Foundational Explorations* (1990); "Pragmatic Rationality and Rules," *Philosophy and Public Affairs* Vol. 26 (1997); and "The Rationality of Being Guided by Rules," in Mele, Alfred R. and Piers Rawling (eds.) *The Oxford Handbook of Rationality* (2004).

Ian Simpson Ross is Professor Emeritus of English, University of British Columbia, and Fellow of the Royal Society of Canada. He is the author of *Lord Kames and the Scotland of his Day* (1972), *William Dunbar* (1981), and *The Life of Adam Smith* (1995); co-editor with E.C. Mossner of *The Correspondence of Adam Smith* (2nd edn. 1987); and editor of *Contemporary Responses to Adam Smith: On the Wealth of Nations* (1998). He is preparing a second edition of the Smith biography.

Margaret Schabas is Professor of Philosophy at the University of British Columbia. She is the author of two monographs, *A World Ruled by Number* (1990) and *The Natural Origins of Economics* (2005). She is also co-editor, with Neil De Marchi, of *Oeconomies in the Age of Newton* (2003), and the author of over 40 articles.

John Shovlin is Assistant Professor of History at New York University. He is the author of a recent book exploring French political economy and its articulation with politics in the latter half of the eighteenth century: *The Political Economy of Virtue: Patriotism, the Luxury Debate, and the Origins of the French Revolution* (2006).

Carl Wennerlind is Assistant Professor of History at Barnard College. He has published articles on Hume's political economy in *History of Political Economy*, *Hume Studies*, and *Journal of Political Economy*. His work on Hume has been awarded the Best Article Prize from both the History of Economics Society and the European Society for the History of Economic Thought. He is currently working on a monograph about the English Financial Revolution.

Introduction

Carl Wennerlind and Margaret Schabas

It is now approximately 250 years since David Hume published his celebrated essays on political economy as part of his *Political Discourses* (1752).
His work won immediate acclaim and was absorbed directly into the work
of several prominent economic thinkers of the period, most notably Adam
Smith and A.R.J. Turgot. For several decades thereafter, numerous editions
and translations of his essays were issued, leaving a definite imprint on economic discourse on both sides of the Atlantic. For much of the twentieth
century, however, Hume was treated as a relatively minor figure in the history
of economics, occupying the nebulous territory between mercantilism, physiocracy, and classical political economy. Joseph Schumpeter's *History of
Economic Analysis* (1954), for example, addressed Hume's contributions *en
passant*, and positioned Richard Cantillon and Turgot as the superior con-
temporaneous economic analysts. Another leading overview, Mark Blaug's
Economic Theory in Retrospect (1978 [1962]), contains about a dozen references
to Hume in his opening chapter on "Pre-Adamite Economics," but because
Hume does not fit within a distinct school he is treated incidentally.[1]

The modern philosophical literature has also paid scant attention to
Hume's writings on political economy. While the *Political Discourses* is
often acknowledged as an important text, few philosophers, including political philosophers, engage seriously with Hume's economic thought.
Duncan Forbes's *Hume's Philosophical Politics* (1975) remains the most
authoritative account of Hume's political thought, yet it neglects almost
entirely the subject of Hume's economics. To his credit, Forbes acknowledges that Hume's economics was central to his "science of politics" and
warrants a "full-scale serious study," but then offers the disclaimer that this
subject is better "left to economists" (Forbes 1975, vii). A similar apology is
offered on the first page of Barry Stroud's watershed study, *Hume*, noting
that he will not "consider any of his [Hume's] philosophical writings about
economics" (Stroud 1977, ix). Amongst philosophers who do comment on
Hume's economic thought, the coverage is always subordinate to political
and philosophical considerations. For example, while political philosopher
John B. Stewart (1992) makes promising forays into Hume's economic
thought, his concern with economic ideas is overshadowed by issues

pertaining to political stability. Annette Baier's *Progress of Sentiments* (1991) is one of the few leading general monographs on Hume that addresses economic concepts such as consumption, utility, and money. Nevertheless, it would be a serious overstatement to say that one can extract a reading of Hume the political economist from her book.

The marginalization of Hume's economic thought in the modern literature on economics and philosophy is a curious fact in light of the significant role that Hume's political economy played both during his own lifetime and well into the early nineteenth century in the works of the American Federalists (see Pocock 1985c and Fleischacker 2003). Moreover, it is well known that Hume's initial attempt at philosophical prominence, *A Treatise of Human Nature*, "fell *dead-born from the Press*," and that his subsequent efforts to repackage and revise these ideas as the *Enquiry Concerning Human Understanding* (1748) and the *Enquiry Concerning the Principles of Morals* (1751) did not encounter the success he had hoped for (Mossner 1980, 612). Hume's rise to intellectual eminence only commenced with his decision to start publishing in the more popular genre of polite essays. While he wrote on a wide array of topics, as diverse as polygamy, prose style, suicide and tragedy, the majority of his essays have a distinct bearing on the discipline of political economy.[2] This is true, we believe, not only for the dozen or so essays that are explicitly about economic topics, such as *Of Money* or *Of Interest*, but for many of the essays on human nature, such as *Of National Character* and *Of the Standard of Taste*, as well as those essays on topics pertaining to politics, such as *Of the Original Contract*. This overriding attention to political economy also framed his next endeavor, the hugely popular *History of England* (1894 [1754–62]). Hence, the body of work that transformed Hume into an intellectual avatar of the Enlightenment was either explicitly about political economy or was deeply informed by his political economy. Scholars of Enlightenment thought, it seems, would be wise to avail themselves of this facet of Hume.

Our admonition is in an important sense outdated, since the case was already made over thirty years ago by J.G.A. Pocock's *Machiavellian Moment* (1975), and further endorsed by his essays in *Virtue, Commerce, and History* (1985a). These works explicitly recognized Hume's pivotal role in the history of political economy, by appreciating Hume's profound understanding of how economic institutions and phenomena fit within the larger political and cultural context. Pocock situated Hume in the larger conversation about commerce and politics such that an understanding of the *Political Discourses* became central to accounts of eighteenth-century British intellectual history. Two additional works inspired by Pocock's contribution also sustained the importance of Hume qua political economist, namely Albert O. Hirschman's *The Passions and the Interests* (1977) and Istvan Hont and Michael Ignatieff's edited collection, *Wealth and Virtue* (1983).

Studies of Hume's political economy have also benefited from a concurrent growth of scholarship on Adam Smith. Hume and Smith were close friends and, the dearth of correspondence between them notwithstanding, there is considerable evidence that Smith drew heavily on the work of Hume and possibly vice versa.[3] More importantly, Smith scholarship, from Donald Winch's *Adam Smith's Politics* (1978) to Emma Rothschild's *Economic Sentiments* (2001), has highlighted the common ground between Smith's political economy and moral philosophy. This has inspired scholars to pursue similar couplings in the works of Hume (see Young 1990; and Levy and Peart 2004). While Smith scholars have moved from the economic toward the moral, Hume scholars, conversely, have moved from the moral toward the economic. Hence, students of Hume's economics are now much more likely to read his *Political Discourses* in conjunction with his *Treatise of Human Nature* than was hitherto the case (see Wennerlind 2001b; Sturn 2004).

Despite the resurgence of interest in Hume's political economy over the last thirty years, we still await the first monograph in English dedicated exclusively to this topic.[4] The most substantial and influential general treatment in English is Eugene Rotwein's *Introduction* (1955) to his edition of Hume's nine economic essays.[5] It is remarkable for its breadth of coverage, assimilating Hume's "psychology" with his "economic philosophy." More recently, Andrew Skinner's essay in the *Cambridge Companion to Hume* (Norton 1993a), provides the most comprehensive portrait and is particularly strong on the historical and cosmopolitan dimensions of Hume's work.[6] Knud Haakonssen (1994) weaves economic threads into his "Introduction" to a new edition of Hume's *Political Essays* but subordinates them to the political material. All of these are valuable contributions, but there is still no full-length study of the subject in English.

The majority of scholarly articles on Hume's political economy focus on a specific topic, such as money, commerce, or foreign trade. Apart from the overviews by Rotwein and Skinner, there are virtually no general interpretations of Hume's political economy.[7] By far the most attention has been devoted to Hume's analysis of money, in part because it is widely asserted that Hume laid the groundwork for modern monetary thinking.[8] Both Keynesians and Monetarists claim Hume as their intellectual progenitor, arguing that Hume's discussion of money corroborates their respective views on whether an increase in the money supply has real or nominal effects.[9] This debate goes far beyond technical details insofar as it confronts the deeper political question of the role of the government in managing the money supply and the issue of fiduciary money. Since Hume's discussion of this topic is notoriously subtle, scholarly attention has been directed primarily at unearthing Hume's underlying theoretical assumptions as a means of sorting out his policy prescriptions.[10]

Partisanship has also come to pass over Hume's analysis of the specie-flow mechanism, a term that Jacob Viner rendered synonymous with Hume (see Viner 1937). Two giants of twentieth-century economics, Paul Samuelson (1971) and Milton Friedman (1975), both entered the debate, one to condemn, the other to praise Hume. Indeed, while Friedman suggests that twentieth-century monetary theory is a technical footnote to Hume, Samuelson reproves Hume for not distinguishing between the nominal and real balance of payments, or grasping the law of one price.[11] Many others have also taken on the task of judging Hume's analysis with reference to contemporary economic theory.[12]

Hume also sketched a philosophical account of money, delving into the nature of convention, the role of property and markets and, most fundamentally, the role of trust in a monetized society.[13] This strand of Hume's analysis provides important links to other topics in his political philosophy, such as the nature of property, justice, and political authority.[14] In addition to linking up with his broader philosophical objectives, Hume's political economy also meshed closely with his historical writings, both his *History of England* and his essays that adopt a historical framework, such as "Of the Populousness of Ancient Nations."[15] Not only does Hume extend his economic analysis by providing historical evidence on a continuous basis, but he emphasizes the extent to which political history is itself moved by material forces, the "interplay between economic growth and liberty" (Skinner 1993, 230).

Hume sought to illuminate the behavioral dynamics of commercial societies and, conversely, to understand human behavior in terms of commercial development.[16] This historical bootstrapping is also manifest in his profound account of the passions in Book Two of his *Treatise*. Whether examining the questions of esteem, compassion, jealousy or benevolence, economic material enters into the account, both as cause and effect (see Davis 2003 and Mankin 2005). One of the primary passions, to be industrious, has been shown to satisfy an array of intrinsic and extrinsic ends (see Hundert 1974 and Marshall 2000). Likewise, the desire for luxuries, fueled by envy, incites merchants to promote commerce and thus to set in motion a process of ever-expanding wealth. Hume's emphasis on the role of manufacturing as the key to economic growth was in sharp contrast to the physiocrats or even Adam Smith, who still arguably privileged the agrarian sector.[17]

Hume was no friend of the lower orders, but his picture of the underlying dynamic of the modern era implied improved economic standards for laborers and merchants alike. Moreover, as has been widely observed, modern commercial society was thought to bring about greater sociability, enhanced politeness, and softer manners (see Berry 1994). Commercial eras are also characterized by greater philosophical excellence, which in turn enters the social fabric in ways that not only improve polite conversation, but also the standards of literary discourse and hence learning writ large. Additionally, the growth of commerce and industry transforms the distribution of wealth and this in turn tends to promote greater political liberty and stability. The lower orders are not as rebellious as they were in rude and barbarous ages, because they are now disciplined by regular labor and by overriding desires for material affluence. The barons and lords who had previously exercised arbitrary control over their subjects, have now lost power in proportion to their relative decline in wealth, while the up-and-coming merchants—the greatest advocates of justice for Hume—were able to translate their economic prosperity into political clout.

Refinement and emulation also play central roles in the dynamic of global economic and political change (see Berdell 1996; Waterman 1998). As nations look to each other for novel fashions in consumption and new methods of production, an overall expansion in both commerce and industry ensues. Beyond the resulting expansion in material wealth, the increased flow of goods and ideas between countries brought people of different nationalities, religions, and political persuasions together, thus fostering greater mutual understanding and respect. Following Montesquieu, it was Hume's great hope that this increased familiarity and trust would reduce the friction between neighboring countries that had previously instigated so many conflicts and wars (see Hirschman 1977).

Another question relating to Hume's discussion of international commerce is whether free trade tends to generate a convergence between rich and poor nations (see Elmslie 1995 and Hont, this volume). More specifically, this question hinges on whether the higher wages in richer nations provide poorer nations with the opportunity to catch up. Istvan Hont (2005e [1983]) argued persuasively that there is no such inherent tendency for convergence to occur. He has shown that the richer nations will maintain their competitive advantage in the capital- and skill-intensive manufacturing sectors, while the poorer nations will enjoy an advantage in the more labor-intensive industries, where their lower wages give them an advantage. The question of whether these separate growth paths will eventually merge is treated by Hume in much the same way as the inequality between people. Just as Hume did not entertain the possibility or desirability of individual equality, nor did he think that there was an inbuilt tendency toward the equality of nations. Hence, the benefits of commerce for individuals and nations alike, is not that it tends toward equality, but rather that it enriches everyone in an absolute sense.

Hume's analyses of money, luxury, growth, trade and commerce engross most of the scholarly literature on his economics. Hume, however, wrote on several other economic subjects that have received significantly less scholarly attention. Among these are such subjects as the interest rate, population growth and reproduction, consumption, taxation, public finance, and distributive justice. It would take us too far afield to do more than highlight a few leading contributions to these other dimensions of Hume's economic thought. On the question of the public debt one can do no better than read Pocock (1979) and Hont (2005f [1993]). On the broader political context of Hume's political economy, preliminary ground was broken by Phillipson (1988) and Venning (1991). More recently, Caffentzis (2005) has shown the links between Hume's political economy and the managed or, in some readings, forced civilization of the Highlanders after the rebellion of 1745. Many of the essays contained in this volume will also advance the view that

Hume's political economy provided an accurate and apposite prism to the social, economic and political currents of his day.

Readers of edited volumes have come to expect an introduction to provide a brief synopsis of the contents, and we are loath to disappoint. But we will be brief here, since it is our firm belief that the papers read well together and that the whole is greater than the sum of the parts. Our intent is to pique the curiosity of the reader rather than provide a proper summary.

Our volume commences with two essays on Hume's life and times, with an emphasis on economic themes. Roger Emerson's essay addresses the relevance of Hume's Scottish heritage and argues that it made a significant difference to his political economy. The Darien Scheme of 1699, the Union of 1707, the monetary policies of John Law and Lord Ilay and, most importantly, the economic underdevelopment of the Scottish Highlands, all figured implicitly or explicitly in Hume's political economy. Ian Simpson Ross's biographical sketch identifies a number of episodes in Hume's life, the South Sea bubble, his many travels on the Continent, and his friendship with Isaac de Pinto, to name but a few, that may also have shaped his economic thought. Both essays point to Hume's strong empiricism and bolster the view that his theoretical claims, in his mind at least, were congruent with the empirical record. As Hume observes in the opening chapter of his *Enquiry Concerning Human Understanding*, "let your science be human, and such as may have a direct reference to action and society" (Hume 2000b [1748], 7–8).

The next group of three essays, by Christopher Berry, Richard Boyd, and co-authors Till Grüne-Yanoff and Edward F. McClennen, enlarge our understanding of Hume on the broader dimensions of human motivations. Christopher Berry's paper establishes the extent to which Hume cast luxury goods in a positive light, as contingent and morally neutral, in contrast to ancient and medieval thought. Even in the case where the pursuit of luxuries might promote vicious behavior, we would benefit from more industry and thus a reduction in poverty. Berry sees this new approach as an added endorsement of the modern commercial world where sumptuary laws were no longer in vogue. Richard Boyd unpacks the means by which commerce had come to foster civility, and a civility that was not feigned but deeply democratic, particularly a respect for different ranks, ethnicities, and religious beliefs. This fits with Hume's overarching cosmopolitanism and skepticism regarding religious sects. Finally, Till Grüne-Yanoff and Edward McClennen argue that Hume's natural history of the passions serves as a fundamental component of his political economy. Moreover, new passions can emerge or transmute as commerce takes hold. This in turn challenges the concept of interest put forth by Hirschman (1977) and sheds light on the role of reason as the mechanism that constrains our passions. Taken broadly, these three papers suggest that Hume's political economy is far-reaching, that he envisioned commercial development as part and parcel of a broader human narrative of the evolution of manners and morals, and that the predilection in modern times for luxuries are not antithetical to these ends (see also Cunningham 2005).

The next cluster of four essays, by Carl Wennerlind, Margaret Schabas, George Caffentzis, and Robert Dimand, explore the topic of Hume's political economy for which he is best known, namely money. The common themes help to serve the emergent consensus that may now exist about Hume's monetary theory and practice. Carl Wennerlind provides a synthetic reading of Hume's monetary theory by drawing on both his philosophical and economic writings. He also compares Hume's analysis to that of his immediate predecessors and thereby ferrets out Hume's unique contributions to eighteenth-century monetary thought. Margaret Schabas challenges the received view that Hume had the short run/long run distinction in mind when asserting his two central tenets about growth and specie-flow; the temporal dimensions to Hume's political economy are not precise, and the framework if anything is one of centuries not years. She also argues that Hume's equivocation toward the treatment of money as a veil can be viewed as a strength, not a weakness. George Caffentzis offers a novel reading by showing the congruence between the fiction/counterfeit distinction that Hume posits in his epistemology and moral philosophy, and his predilection for metallic currency over paper issue. He suggests that deep beneath the textual and semantic similarities lie profound unities to Hume's philosophy. Finally, Robert Dimand provides us with an account of Hume the practical economist, for his work in reforming the Canadian monetary system while serving as Secretary for the British Embassy in Paris from 1765 to 1766. Lower Canada (now Quebec) was notorious for using playing cards in place of hard currency, but what was not known until now (apart from a brief reference in Mossner's biography), was the central role Hume played in that reform.

The next group of three essays, by Loïc Charles, John Shovlin, and Paul Cheney, address different but consonant aspects related to the reception and dissemination of Hume's political economy in France. What unites all three accounts are the strong political applications made of Hume's analyses, even though, ironically, the term *les économistes* without the adjective 'political' was first coined in France at this very time. Hume's *Political Discourses* was immensely popular and over a dozen translations were made into French before 1760. Loïc Charles argues that the translations varied quite a lot and that almost none were politically neutral or entirely faithful. A close reading of one of the most influential translations and accompanying commentary by abbé Jean-Bernard Le Blanc (1755) points to a distinctive bias toward the political views of Jacques-Claude-Marie Vincent de Gournay and his circle. As a result, certain segments of Hume's analysis, notably his views on trade and luxury, were absorbed into French policy, while others, notably Hume's monetary theory, were not, despite Vincent de Gournay's own predilection for fiduciary notes.

John Shovlin argues, like Christopher Berry, that Hume's analysis of luxury rendered it morally neutral, but Shovlin embeds his argument in a different context, first by opposing it to Bernard Mandeville's position and, then, by studying the reception of Hume in France. Luxury was especially pejorative in France, given the shadow cast by Versailles and the rigidities of the ancien régime. But the French also appropriated only parts of Hume's analysis and, for that reason alone, Shovlin speculates, Hume may have been prompted to revise his position on the subject with the 1760 edition of his essays, whereby the term luxury was dropped from the title of his essay. Finally, Paul Cheney positions Hume within a broader movement that took the system of modern commerce as privileging the modern republican constitution. Cheney argues that Hume went one step further by demonstrating that "civilized monarchies" were coming to resemble republics, at least for the central legal and social norms that matter most. This appreciation for the overarching convergence of European nations adds to the portrait of Hume as a true cosmopolitan. All three essays pave the way toward reaping more gains from trade between Hume's political theory and Hume's political economy, in France and beyond.

The final essay, by Istvan Hont, ties together the themes of most of the preceding essays. He embeds Hume in the intellectual context of his time, addresses the importance of the luxury debates, shows the uneasy place of money in Hume's economics, and has much to say about Hume's standing among his contemporaries. Hont is all the more persuaded that the rich country–poor country debate was of seminal importance to Hume, both in the genesis and reception of his political economy. In addressing Scotland's commercial development, Hume drew important insights from the earlier debates about the economic future of Ireland. Hont also investigates how Hume's ideas were situated in the French debates, initially between Melon and Montesquieu and later between the Gournay-group and Mirabeau. This in turn sheds light on the distinctions between Hume and Smith on the subjects of trade, money, and economic growth.

The essays in this volume were, with one exception, first presented at a workshop we organized at Barnard College in May of 2003. We would like to express our sincerest gratitude to the Columbia University Seminars, under the direction of Amanda Roberts and Robert Belknap, for their generous financial and administrative support. We also wish to thank the Provost of Barnard College, Elizabeth Boylan, for providing additional funds and, something rare among university leaders, for her visible enthusiastic support. We owe the Special Events staff at Barnard College a heartfelt thanks for putting together such a successful gathering. It is a truism that books of collected essays are much improved if the authors can interact in person, ideally by preliminary gatherings, and this volume is no exception. Many scholars met for the first time, but even those well indentured to Hume studies were pleased to break bread together once more.

Lastly, there are a number of Hume scholars whom we would like to thank for their extensive comments and contributions, notably Sheila Dow, Christopher Finlay, Antoin Murphy, Nicholas Phillipson, David Raynor,

Paul Russell, Tatsuya Sakamoto, Eric Schliesser, and Andrew Skinner. Most of the essays benefited from the superb copyediting of James Kelleher and Jennifer Barager. We also wish to thank Robert Langham, Terry Clague, and Tom Sutton at Routledge for their unwavering support for this project from its very inception. Our deepest thanks are to our respective families, to Joel Schabas, Monica Miller and Langston Wennerlind for providing laughter and enthusiasm.

Notes

1 Blaug, to his credit, is the only scholar who has compiled a collection of previously published articles on Hume's economics, so his textbook is not representative of his own high esteem for Hume. See Blaug (1991).
2 Hume's essays (1777 edition) are conveniently available in *Essays Moral, Political, and Literary*, edited by Eugene Miller (1985).
3 See, for example, Haakonssen (1981), Raynor (1984), Wennerlind (2000), and Schliesser (2003).
4 Tatsuya Sakamoto (1995), Marialuisa Baldi (1983), and Didier Deleule (1979) have published books on David Hume's political economy in Japanese, Italian, and French respectively. There is also a very dated account by Albert Schatz (1902).
5 The essays he includes are 'Of Commerce,' 'Of Refinement in the Arts,' 'Of Money,' 'Of Interest,' 'Of the Balance of Trade,' 'Of the Jealousy of Trade,' 'Of Taxes,' 'Of Public Credit,' and 'Of the Populousness of Ancient Nations.'
6 Both Rotwein (1987) and Skinner (2003) offer a revised version of their initial essays.
7 The best approximations can be found in Arkin (1956), Hutchison (1988), McGee (1989), Dow (2002), and Wennerlind (2006).
8 See Mayer (1980), Blaug (1995), and Wood (1995). Rashid (1984) downplays Hume's originality.
9 See Samuelson (1980), Friedman (1987), and Lucas (1996).
10 See Humphrey (1974), Duke (1979), Velk and Riggs (1985), Cesarano (1998), and Wennerlind (2005).
11 Friedman (1975), in his address "25 Years After the Rediscovery of Money: What Have We Learned?" asserts that, apart from adding a second derivative to the velocity of money, we have learned very little since Hume. Much the same sentiment is echoed in his Palgrave entry (1987).
12 See Staley (1976), Fausten (1979), Berdell (1995), and Cesarano (1998).
13 See Schabas (1994), Gatch (1996), Bruni and Sugden (2000), and Caffentzis (2001).
14 See Haakonssen (1981) and Moss (1991).
15 See Stockton (1976), Phillipson (1989), Wootton (1993), Berry (1997), Brewer (1998), Pocock (1999), Wennerlind (2002), and Schmidt (2003).
16 For a recent debate on the presence or absence of a nascent rational choice theory in Hume, see Diaye and Lapidus (2005) and Sugden (2005).
17 See McNally (1988), Brewer (1997), and Schabas (2005).

1   The Scottish Contexts for David Hume's Political-Economic Thinking

Roger L. Emerson

1. Introduction

Scholarship on David Hume's political economy generally positions him in the broader context of his European and English predecessors. Hume's essays themselves give little indication that he wrote as a Scot with Scotland in mind. His political-economic essays, excluding the essay on population, contain explicit references to 30 ancient authors, at least a dozen English writers, and nearly as many from the continent. Hume cited only two Scots—John Law and Dr. John Arbuthnot.[1] Hume preferred to make general statements unrelated to specific social contexts and often cited an ancient example in preference to a modern one. He seldom mentioned a contemporary case if he could find an older one. This approach facilitated understanding of his works abroad, but also made them look far less rooted in Scottish discussion than I believe they were. There is a very Scottish orientation to much of the practical and theoretical material he wrote, but it was masked by the generality with which Hume thought and the discretion with which he wrote.[2] The evidence for this claim is largely circumstantial but nevertheless abundant. There was of course much in the essays that did not pertain to Scotland, but there is enough material to support the view that Hume had Scots in mind for significant portions of his theoretical analyses and policy recommendations.

Before turning to those recommendations, we should take notice of another fact about Hume. Throughout his career, Hume sought to influence public, particularly Scottish, affairs. This was perfectly natural for the son of a laird who believed that opinion ruled the world and that it might be shaped by a literary man. The "Advertisement" and "Introduction" to Hume's *Treatise of Human Nature* (2000a [1739–40]) convey the impression that Hume harbored hopes of making men more skeptical of the claims of organized religion. In the late 1730s, he, Henry Home (later Lord Kames), and others planned to publish a periodical that was to resemble Lord Bolingbroke's *The Craftsman*, one of the most successful political journals of the time and one that had been highly critical of the government. In the early 1740s, Hume's two-volume *Essays, Moral and Political* (1741, 1742) sought to change opinion about government, freedom of the press, and religious beliefs and practices, a cause he continued in the *History of England* (1754–62). His anonymous pamphlet for Lord Provost Archibald Stewart (1748) was another effort to affect the course of political events (Hume 2004 [1748], 223–66). So too was his squib, the *Bellman's Petition* (1751), which argued against raising the salaries of clergymen and teachers. The *Political Discourses* (1752) were, I believe, another instance of this.[3] Hume was partly bent on affecting public policy with regard to the Highlands. The work was published at the end of a long debate in Parliament and Britain generally about the Highlands. Policies had been established but men named to implement them had not yet been chosen. Thus Hume could hope to affect the way in which policies were applied and to warn of the likely failure of various measures.

2. Scottish Conditions

One can profitably consider what Hume has to say about political economy by looking at his family's estate in Berwickshire. His brother John's improvements at Ninewells, the family estate, and the changes in the regional economy had been stimulated in part by the expansion of Edinburgh and neighboring towns. What Hume has to say in the *Political Discourses* and in the *History of England* about the interdependence of towns and countryside, of industry and agriculture, about the need for transportation and market facilities, and for the improvement of many facets of economic life all at once, was fully borne out by the experience of Border farmers. It is not altogether surprising that Hume should have left money in his will for the repair of Chirnside bridge.

Some of those ideas had been discussed in 1743 in a much read collection of essays edited by Robert Maxwell (1743), secretary to the Honourable the Society of Improvers in the Knowledge of Agriculture (1723–46). Maxwell's introduction was largely devoted to practical improving proposals about farming, but he did state a few ideas that were probably common in the club from its inception. Maxwell saw an important place for science in agriculture and called for the creation by the government of a public professor of agriculture who would be "a General inspector of improvements, who should be obliged to report annually the Husbandry of each County, that Errors might be known and rectified."[4] Education and the application of new knowledge would improve productivity. Such ideas, in the short run, made clubs like the Edinburgh Philosophical Society (1737–83) more attentive to improving schemes than they might otherwise have been.[5] Hume himself was interested in new plows and acted almost as an agent for one maker.[6] Maxwell found all surpluses to arise only from the land and from labor expended on it and its products. Hume similarly expressed that "Every thing useful to the life of man arises from the ground; but few things arise in that condition which is requisite to render them useful" (1985v [1752d], 299).

Hume accepted another idea of Maxwell's, which had been stated earlier by John Law:

> The Success of the Fisheries and Manufactures depends upon the Cheapness of Provisions and Materials; this also depends upon the progress made in Agriculture: And the encouragement of the Husbandman relies upon the ready Consumpt, and the Value of the several Products of his Farm bear in the Market, which must rise in proportion as our People shall be encouraged to stay at home, and Foreigners to come and reside among us.
>
> (Maxwell 1743, iii–iv)

Notions of this sort had long circulated in Scotland and had become the common stock of improvers and those interested in their schemes. While Hume was less attentive to agriculture in his economic essays, he nonetheless recognized, like Law and Maxwell, that there was an unbroken chain between agriculture, industry, trade, and population.

Hume also would have remembered the hard years of 1739 and 1740. Near-famine conditions in many towns and in the countryside of Scotland had been relieved by the importation of meal, which was then sold at a subsidized rate.[7] No one had starved in Scotland during those years and there were no major riots. Market conditions had not been allowed to operate freely, but they had not quite been ignored either. Hume never advocated free trade if it meant widespread starvation. Order and the safety of the people were more important than a free market (Hume 1998 [1751], 3.8.15f).[8] The Scots' long-term solution to food shortages was to improve agricultural practices and introduce new crops, as Hume's brother was doing. Scottish economic conditions were also changing outside the agrarian sphere. There had been a continual breakdown of the regulations affecting economic life in Edinburgh since before Hume was born, as R. A. Houston has noted (1994).[9] The freedom of the city had become easier to obtain, thus freeing trade from one restraint that tended to restrict the movement of labor and the capital that accompanied people who could afford to buy the freedom of the city. More economic freedom came in the burgh as quality controls on some items effectively lapsed and the regulation of industry beyond the walls lessened and even ceased in some trades. Luxury goods and ordinary utensils were produced in greater volume and sold to a larger market. Greater output was accompanied by generally higher wages paid to some artisans in the expanding population, which had increased its demand for many items. Hume's arguments about the value of luxury and greater economic freedom reflected the world in which he lived. The consumption of goods increased among some of the working classes, but they may have worked harder to attain it.[10]

By the time he wrote *Political Discourses*, Hume also knew many merchants and bankers. Archibald Stewart of Allanbank was his Berwickshire neighbor. John Coutts, whose family a bit later was to give its name to one of the largest of the London private banks, headed the bank that Hume himself later used. William and Robert Alexander not only ran a large and innovative business dealing in tobacco and other commodities shipped through Glasgow, but they also carried on banking operations, as did Hume's friend Adam Fairholm (Price 1973). Fairholm's was a commodity and banking firm, which by 1760 could issue letters of credit that were honored from Riga to Naples. It was to his friend, James Oswald, a member of Parliament from a merchant family, that Hume showed a draft of the essay "Of the Balance of Trade" (1985x [1752e]) and from whom he received comments and criticisms (1969, 2:142).[11] Hume knew others involved with commercial and banking operations in Scotland. Besides Henry Home, who after 1743 was a lawyer for the British Linen Company, there was Kames's patron Archibald Campbell, third duke of Argyll and founder of the Board of Trustees for Fisheries and Manufactures; the Royal Bank; and the British Linen Company. His protégés Andrew Fletcher (Lord Milton) and Charles Erskine (Lord Tinwald) were governors of the Royal Bank. Many of Hume's friends owned stock in the latter institutions or in the Bank of Scotland. Lord Elibank's wealth was largely in stocks, including some in banks and merchant houses abroad. These men knew quite well that capital moves to the areas of highest profit, since they lived partially on such returns. Landowners like Argyll tried to sell their grains where prices were highest and speculated in stocks and currency in at least three markets—London, Paris, and Amsterdam.

Such men tended not to be free-traders. They believed in tariffs on imported goods to protect their own markets while they sought unprotected markets for the produce and manufactured items from their own state and estates. The British Navigation Laws insured that their goods were sheltered and protected. Scottish producers of linen, sugar, and rum, like importers of tobacco, benefited from that system.[12] It was clear to such men that Scots had gained much from their union with England, which had created the largest free-trade area in Europe. Anyone who thought about this problem would have found contradictions here, as Hume did, but he was not immune to the contradictory impulses himself. He was willing to allow tariffs to encourage Scottish industries, and thus employment, which he always—and correctly—tended to assume was less than full:

> All taxes, however, upon foreign commodities, are not to be regarded as prejudicial or useless. ... A tax on GERMAN linen encourages home manufactures, and thereby multiplies our people and industry. A tax on brandy encreases the sale of rum, and supports our southern colonies. And as it is necessary, that imposts should be levied, for the support of the government, it may be thought more convenient to lay them on foreign commodities, which can be easily intercepted at the port, and subjected to the impost. We ought, however, always to remember the

maxim of DR. SWIFT, that in the arithmetic of customs, two and two
make not four, but often make only one.

(Hume 1985x [1752e], 324)

These remarks appear to be a direct comment on the policies of the third
duke of Argyll, who had helped to secure protection and subsidies for Scottish
linen. Trade, both domestic and international, was a topic of discussion as
the debate lists of the Select Society of Edinburgh show.[13] In Hume's day
those issues were complicated by the fact that the principal European
powers were at war.

Hume and his friends knew that war benefited those who supplied armies
and navies but that it often injured some farmers, manufacturers, merchants, and their workers. It upset the normal circulation of money in the
economy. It made moneyed men richer because they were the ones who
issued, handled, and bought the government's debts and generally were well
placed to benefit from the financial opportunities that conflicts produced.
Their gains came at the expense of the ordinary taxpayers, however, since
every penny of war profit translated into someone being taxed or suffering
from inflation or economic dislocation. The ordinary small merchant trading overseas found that his risks and costs went up while his profits were as
likely to go down as to improve. All that had been much canvassed by
Opposition and Country Party writers.[14] Hume would have been familiar
with their arguments from 25 years of reading essays republished from the
Craftsman, the *London Journal*, and their numerous successors. Hume's
advocacy of peace was also rooted in economic realities, which he had had
ample time to study. Britain had been at war most of the time from 1739 to
1752 and would again be engaged in conflicts after 1753. To make clear the
economic consequences of war for Scotland and other nations was one
objective of Hume's essays; another was to show that, with a balance of
political and diplomatic power in Europe now fairly securely established,
one needed a trading regime that was not based on beggar-your-neighbor
policies. They might work in the short run or in wartime, but in peacetime
they made for inefficient uses of resources, lowered general employment
rates, and created difficulties in finding markets for all of one's goods. His
work resonated among the men with whom he associated because they too
had reflected on the subject of war, which had affected many of them.

3. Scottish Political Economy Before Hume

Scottish economic pamphleteering effectively began at the end of the
seventeenth century when the pressures to reunite with England began to build,
and intensified in the 1690s when famine made Scots consider various schemes
to improve their economic well-being.[15] The improvers wrote on fisheries,
agriculture, mining, welfare schemes, banking, and much else. Their discussions persisted through the debates over the Treaty of Union (1707), indeed,

well past that time, because the benefits of the union were not quickly felt. While Hume never specifically mentioned this literature, it is hard to believe that he was ignorant of it, if only because his works seemed to respond directly to the mercantilist arguments advanced by the pamphlet literature.

The crises of the period 1690–1715 left deep impressions on most Scots who lived through them or who thought deeply about them afterward. Was Scotland to have some closer union with England or was it to be more independent? If the latter, how? Some of those who wanted Scots to pursue an independent path were concerned in the Darien scheme, which involved the planting of a colony on the Isthmus of Panama. This scheme addressed the problems faced by small weak countries trying to trade in a world increasingly divided by large imperial powers. Darien was envisioned as an entrepôt open to all, a free port that would permit small nations to benefit from trades from which they had been barred (Armitage 1995, 97–120). John Robertson has found echoes of the Darien scheme in Hume's views of "a more general system of free trade"(Robertson 1997, 678).[16]

What many of the Darien projectors thought and wanted can be seen in William Paterson's *Proposals and Reasons for Constituting a Council of Trade* (1701), a pamphlet that excited many of his contemporaries and remained of interest for a long time. This founder of the Bank of England wished to improve Scotland, rationalize its government and fiscal regime, and make it a trading nation able to sustain its independence. His reforms aimed to solve social problems, such as poverty and under-employment, and to improve the administration of justice, which was to become less brutal. In those respects Paterson's pamphlet was typical of others written around the same time (1968 [1859], 1:16).

Paterson's national improvements scheme required a virtuous national effort on the part of the talented and patriotic (1968 [1859], 1:28). He viewed it as a religious obligation and a moral necessity, dictated by prudence. It was also a task to be undertaken in good humor. Paterson was a man of irenical temper who tried to convince his compatriots "that those who are violent in everything will be constant in nothing, and [we] have had reason to know that angry men are never fit for business, but least of all in angry times" (1968 [1859], 1:102). His peroration resembled the views of later men, including Hume. Paterson held that trade civilizes and increases polite behavior,[17] and allows the accumulation of riches for use in wars should they come. He further argued that trade will make us free, and that it is at the root of all we can do and hope for in this world. It can and will transform the world as it has already done. We are called to promote trade; we should not ignore this calling but we should ignore those who fear that it will produce luxury and nonmartial men.[18] Rich and luxurious states need not be effete. Hume agreed with most of these views, but he could never share such optimism about a visionary scheme that required such disinterestedness among men and that assumed their ability to calculate the results of their actions. Experience had shown the opposite.

Paterson also advocated the creation of a number of institutions as a means to transform a backward, impoverished kingdom into a prosperous one. Despite all the jobbery involved in the creation of such institutions—the Board of Police (1714); the Board of Trustees for Fisheries and Manufacturers (1727); the Edinburgh Linen Co-Partnery (1727); the Commissions for Forfeited and Annexed Estates (1715, 1747); and even the Royal Bank (1727) and the British Linen Company (1746)—some idealism remained. Those institutions, designed to increase output, enhance trade, and provide employment, were also expected to increase tax revenues and provide larger incomes to the propertied. Their promoters shared some of Paterson's spirit as well as his belief in the efficacy of state interference in the economic sphere. In those respects they were not unlike John Law, whom Hume cited in his "Early Memoranda" (1948 [1729–40], 507).

Law is usually remembered as the man who caused the speculative "bubbles" that burst in 1720, first in France and then in Holland and England, but Law also published pamphlets such as *Money and Trade* (1720), which summarized his thinking from approximately 1703 forward (Murphy 1997). Hume read Law sometime before 1752. Law, like Hume, tended to see money as a medium of exchange lubricating the economic machine. How it was denominated and backed mattered. Land would do better than gold, Law argued, because land values were more stable than gold. A currency based on land would be subject to less inflation than a system based on precious metals. Hume seemed to agree. In the *History of England*, he showed how gold had fluctuated against silver, wheat, and land.[19] Law thought land-backed money could increase the circulating funds of a state like Scotland without the risk of over-issuance.[20] Land-backed paper money would be guaranteed by the stability of the value of land against which it had been issued. The notes measured the value of the land and thus all that might be exchanged for it. Law imagined the institution that would manage all this might be a body chartered by parliament or a joint-stock company open to any who had land worth £1,000. In exchange for a pledge of this sum, supporters would receive stock or notes (Murphy 1997, 40). The state would make these notes legal tender and they would serve in commerce just as well as gold, at least within the realm. The value of the money would fluctuate as the demand for land and as the quality of it varied. In the short run it would fluctuate very little, and in the long run certainly not as much as commodities like gold and silver. It would not shrink in value as had the Scottish pound, which in 1707 was worth only one-twelfth of the English pound. Whereas other forms of money, such as stocks and bills of exchange, constantly changed in value as the markets decided their worth, the land-backed currency would provide the Scots with a more stable currency.[21]

In 1705, Law may have gone beyond his earlier proposals for paper money based on land.[22] In one document attributed to him, which contained imaginative variations of older visions of a land bank, he proposed to increase the Scottish money supply through the issuance of interest-bearing unbacked paper currency forced on the country and controlled by the government. The government was also to create the Commission of Trade—a body of merchants, nobles, and gentlemen that would "employ these notes so struck in erecting a fisherie, and in improving our manufactories" (Paterson 1968, 2:xlii–v). The commission was to become the sole foreign trader for the country, which would benefit from the gold it accumulated for the state in its transactions. The portion of the national debt held in the kingdom was to be paid off in the notes issued by the commission. Law even proposed to pay the arrears of the Scottish troops in the same paper bearing three-percent interest and circulating as would other government-backed notes (Paterson 1968, 2:xlvif). That money would not stay long in the pockets of its recipients but would be spent and thus set to work the artisans and laborers of Scotland to the benefit of all (Paterson 1968, 2:xlvii).

Law believed it was within the means of the government, at least partially, to control the money supply. States would not issue too much money because the supply of money would only equal the demand for it. The price level, determined by the issue of money, should not be inflationary, although prices might be modestly raised to stimulate the economy and bring about recovery and progress in the short run (Murphy 1997, 26–42). Law saw domestic prices, all things being equal, varying directly with the amount of money of all sorts in circulation. Law in 1705 envisioned Scots spending their way out of the deep recession to which bad luck and the English had condemned them.

Hume appears to have agreed with Law that, in the short run, an increase in the money supply would act as an economic stimulus. He believed, however, that banks ought not to have the power to provide an increase in the money supply (Hont 2005e [1983], 273–6). Hume thought that neither political leaders nor bankers would ever be able to discipline themselves; the political expediency of increasing paper money would always be too tempting (1985u [1752c], 284; 1985aa [1752h], 352). Unlike Law and Paterson, Hume distrusted giving so much power to any set of men and he was skeptical about fiat money. Also, contrary to Law, he believed that not having a currency backed by gold or another precious metal would hamper foreign trade. But, Hume in 1752 was still arguing in an old Scottish debate that went back to the 1690s.

While Hume never cited Law in his published works, there is ample evidence of Law's influence in Italy, France, and Britain and on writers and politicians Hume knew.[23] The Scottish Parliament as a whole did not support Law's scheme in 1705 for a land bank, but two sets of politicians did. Some of the Squadrone men supported it as did John Campbell, second duke of Argyll, and his brother, Archibald, first earl of Ilay (Wood 1791, 5). Those men would control Scottish politics from 1714 to 1761. The most influential of them was Ilay, who became the third duke of Argyll in 1743. He possessed all of Law's works, including a manuscript copy of the "Essay on a Land Bank."[24] Ilay dealt with Law in financial transactions and he and his brother protected Law after 1720, perhaps because Ilay had made money on the French bubble. The earl of Ilay was said to have written the preface to the London edition of the republication of Law's book in 1720 (Bannister 1968, 1:xciii). From about 1725 until his death in 1761, Ilay was the premier improver in Scotland and the government's chief political manager of the country for most of that time. He was also active in the economy as a banker, an investor, and a manager of a huge estate, which he worked to transform. Ilay's career in a sense embodied Law's beliefs. Thus, it is no wonder that Hume felt he should give the third duke a copy of his essays (Hume 1969, 1:113).[25] In the early 1750s, if a philosopher such as Hume hoped to affect Scottish affairs, he would have to secure the duke's agreement.

In 1727, Lord Ilay and his friends had a chance to expand the money supply in order to promote industry and trade in ways Law would have approved. Their opportunity took two forms. The government, advised by Ilay, formed the Board of Trustees for Fisheries, and Manufactures to disburse in Scotland an annual sum of £6,000. This was a means of giving back to Scots some of the losses they had incurred when, at the beginning of the century, the Darien Company had failed. It also compensated them for the interest they now paid on the portion of the English national debt that had been incurred before the Union of 1707. The £6,000 was used to provide direct grants to some establishments and individuals and to fund annual premiums for which producers were to compete. In that way it was hoped that the impact of small sums might be multiplied in the economy. The other thing Ilay and his friends did was to create the Royal Bank of Scotland.[26] This initiative, in 1727, provided an important adjunct to their political machine, but it also fulfilled Ilay's dream, dating back to 1705, of increasing the money supply, circulating money in the country at a faster rate, and thus stimulating the economy. Hume was unlikely to have recommended either measure but he clearly understood them and the attraction they had for Scots.

The Board of Trustees, reminiscent of the Council of Trade of a generation earlier, functioned principally as a device to improve the country by promoting the linen trade through grants to bleachers and premiums awarded to spinners and weavers. It helped to establish spinning schools and bought spinning wheels to employ idle hands. It inspected, stamped, and thus controlled the quality of cloth to be sold (Durie 1996, 3). Ilay was much involved with these developments, which allowed the Scottish linen industry to flourish behind the protective walls of tariffs, which he had helped to erect. What was needed, he and his friends thought, was a corporation to organize the trade, market its product, and finance it with small sums distributed over larger areas of the country than the two chartered national banks reached. He supported schemes to create one, which led first in 1727 to the formation of a linen copartnery and then to the British Linen Company (1746), which became the British Linen Bank in 1839. Their functions—funding and organizing the production and marketing of linen—remedied problems, which Law had presciently described in *Money and Trade*:

> If the Country People about *Perth* and *Sterling*, have to the value of 20000 L. of Linen, Serges, and other Manufacture more than is bought up; tho these Goods exported will yield 20 or 30 *percent*. Profit, yet the Owners can't export them, the Goods being in so many different Hands, and not having Correspondents Abroad to whom they could trust the Sale of them. A. B. and C. are satisfied for that Profit to take the Trouble and Hazard of exporting them, but Money being scarce they cannot get any to borrow, tho their Security be good; Nor cannot well have Credit for the Goods from so many different People they are Strangers to. If they could have Credit for them, yet these Country People must be idle till A. B. and C. pay them out of their Returns from Abroad. So for the want of Money to Exchange by, Goods fall in value, and manufacture decays.
>
> (Law 1705, 116)

The British Linen Company cured those problems. The effort to realize those ends was largely a product of the decade before Hume published his economic essays. It involved many of Hume's friends—Charles Erskine, Henry Home, and Hume's merchant-banker friends in Edinburgh; others well known to him were among the Linen Company's stockholders. The improvers of the linen trade imported flaxseed, lint, and yarn; they subsidized spinning and weaving, built bleach-fields, employed chemists—such as William Cullen and Francis Home—to find better bleaches, funded the trade, and helped market the stamped and quality-controlled cloth. All this was normal mercantilist practice and it worked brilliantly without interfering with any important English trade. By the end of the eighteenth century, about a third of the Scottish labor force was employed for at least part of the year in the linen trade. Of course, it operated at the expense of the linen producers in Ireland, Holland, and the Baltic. It was just the sort of venture a free-trader would object to, but the eminence of the industry's backers tended to stifle open criticism. Ilay remained the principal dispenser of patronage in Scotland from 1723 to 1761, partly because so many benefited from his schemes. On the few occasions Hume praised the introduction or protection of new industries, he perhaps had such schemes as this in mind.[27] When he thought about freer trade, he considered the cost of this to consumers.

4. Hume and the Highland Problem

Ilay all his life had been involved in another pressing debate—what to do with the Highlands and Highlanders. How could he civilize his tenants and his Highland neighbors, and at the same time improve the value of his estates? This was hardly a new topic for Scots, but the uprising of 1745 made it an urgent question. There seemed to be a need for the government to intervene decisively in the political and economic affairs of the Highlands to prevent similar rebellions in the future. This meant restructuring Highland society or "civilizing" the Highlanders, whom Hume in the 1740s, like many Lowlanders, regarded as still "barbarous" and living "chiefly by Pasturage" (Box et al. 2003, 236).[28] The usual prescriptions for civilizing the Highlanders were again intensely discussed in Scotland from the mid-1740s until the mid-1750s. There was little novel in the discussions of those measures but now they could be forced on Highlanders by a stronger British state. The government's response to the uprising of 1745 had been repressive, including the passage of the Disarming Act (1746), which prohibited not only the possession of guns and swords by all Highlanders but also dirks and shields. Another act of the same year, the Tenures Abolition Act, abolished military tenures, turning them into ordinary feus or into blench holdings, for which the holder paid a nominal quit-rent to the Crown. In 1747, the Highland jurisdictions, to which Hume referred in a letter to Montesquieu (Hume 1969, 1:134), were abolished save for the courts baron, which lost some powers.[29] Those loyal Highlanders who surrendered jurisdictions, a form of property, were compensated for their losses of revenue; few thought they received enough in the way of compensation. Because many believed those acts were not sufficient to settle the Highlands so as to prevent future rebellions, discussions of further actions continued well into the 1760s. Nearly every important collection of Scottish papers from this period has material relating to this set of topics. Hume would have read arguments about the Highlands in the papers and in numerous pamphlets or heard them at his clubs and while dining out. We must assume Hume participated in those debates and stated opinions that he need not have recently formulated since the issues were all long-standing. Further, many of the topics Hume addresses in the *Political Discourses* pertain to this Scottish social context, as well as to European and English economic trends and theories, which are the usual focus of discussions of Hume's political economy.

Most Lowlanders assumed that government intervention in the Highland society and economy was the only way to remedy the situation and to bring the Highlanders into the modern world.[30] They held that more money should be spent for roads and forts, towns and schools, and on coercive measures to force the region into conformity to new ways. All this, as the lord chancellor told the House of Lords in February 1748, would result in "Civilizing the Highlands."

Two of Hume's colleagues in the Philosophical and Select Societies discussed the chancellor's speech. The earl of Seafield and Findlatter summarized the plans for the earl of Hopetoun, in a letter dated 20 February 1748: Clan chieftainships were to be abolished and no further subsidies paid to any of the clans. The tacksmen and tenant farmers on the estates confiscated or bought would be changed. New tenants, such as disbanded soldiers, were to be imposed and settled on the farms vacated by the unreliable clansmen loyal to the dispossessed owners. The new men were to be given restrictive leases and forced to farm in particular ways but with subsidized supplies of lime and marl. This would insure that men loyal to King George would hold and work the lands and oversee ordinary clansmen. English was to be the language of instruction for the Gaelic-speaking children in Highland schools. No kirks served by Episcopalian nonjurors were to be allowed, but more Presbyterian churches and schools were to be built. It was urged that the linen trade should be introduced and other manufactures set up and mines found and opened. To safeguard those changes, forts and garrisons would be established and the Highlands drained of possible rebels by raising regiments in that area. To oversee all this, a special commission and more sheriffships (county courts) would have to be created (Linlithgow Manuscripts, box 122, bundle 1520). Hopetoun replied, in a letter dated 10 March 1748, that the farms would have to be stocked at government expense and that nothing could really be done until roads and forts were built to give security in the area to the new tenants:

> It is no easy Matter to lay down a right Plan for civilizing the Highlands, but it will be infinitely more difficult to carry into Execution. That will require a closer Attention from the Administration than any other publick Affairs will often permit of, and a greater Degree of Application, Disinterestedness, Resolution, Moderation in those to whom the immediate Execution shall be committed than we meet with on every occasion & few that are qualified will I'm afraid be public spirited enough to undertake the Task.
>
> (Linlithgow Manuscripts, box 122, bundle 1520)

Hopetoun was a respected intellectual, an active improver, and a mine owner who employed men like James Stirling and Joseph Black. His opinions were but variations on those of most of his and Hume's friends. They all called for the government to confiscate land, to forfeit disloyal clan chiefs, and then manage their partially restructured estates through state agencies. Significant amounts of capital were to be invested in the Highlands; new managers and new techniques were to be introduced to further the productive activities of the people. More artisans were to be introduced. This would aid the development of agriculture and also mining and fishing. Increased employment in public works projects, such as roads, bridges, and ports, would keep idle Highlanders from thinking about rebellion. Military expenditures would enable the government to overawe the Highlanders. Their newfound wages would bring them into a consumer society where they would hesitate to jeopardize their prosperity and future consumption. Such views were all reminiscent of discussions about the Highlands that had taken place for 200 years. Hume, who always advocated slow change, without shock to people, did not think such proposals were likely to succeed.[31]

Most of the chancellor's scheme was enacted. The Crown annexed 13 of the confiscated estates—about a quarter of those forfeited—in 1752. Others were sold to pay their debts. A third of the land of the Highlands, an area the size of Connecticut, was affected in these ways. The annexation act, passed in March 1752, set up the Commission of Annexed Estates whose members were to serve without pay and under the supervision of the Scottish Court of Exchequer and the Treasury. Those bodies were to handle the finances of the estates. The commissioners, however, were not appointed until 1755, when they included the earls of Hopetoun, Findlatter, Morton, and Marchmont, as well as Charles Erskine, Gilbert Elliot of Minto, James Oswald, Andrew Mitchell, and Robert Alexander—all men Hume knew well.[32] Collectively, this body was dominated by the duke of Argyll's men, whose policies, like his, were mercantilist and interfering. The commissioners had only about £4,500 annually to distribute for the support of industry, agriculture, and the fisheries, for schools and roads, and for all the other things it seemed desirable to fund. It was not enough. This Highland Development Agency was but the first that proved to be inadequate.

Hume wrote and published *Political Discourses* (1752) before the Commission of Annexed Estates had been struck and while the policies it would actually carry out were still under discussion. He could hope that what he had to say might have some effect on the commissioners' activities and thus on the course of future developments in the Highlands. Almost all that the commissioners were supposed to do Hume implicitly criticized in his essays dedicated to promoting the freer movement of goods, money, and people, and to *laissez-faire* policies generally.

Hume's advice begins with the opening essay "Of Commerce" (1985s [1752a]), which can be read as an indictment of the Highland policy that the government and even his own friends were pursuing (and would continue to pursue throughout his lifetime). They were treating as modern a people who were not yet in the same stage of civility as most of those in Britain. They were going to use public monies to try to force development where conditions were unripe. Confiscations were unwise. Sending in outsiders to run the forfeited estates would not work well. Should the state employ its superfluous people in the public sector? This was then equivalent to asking if the new schemes to raise Highland regiments were well founded.[33] He may have regarded those schemes as "merely chimerical" (1985s [1752a], 257), since they would allow the recruited soldiers to contribute nothing to the national wealth created by husbandmen, manufacturers, and traders. Perhaps it would be better to adopt other courses and not interfere in the area and with its people:

> Sovereigns must take mankind as they find them, and cannot pretend to introduce violent change in their principles and ways of thinking. ... It

is the best policy to comply with the common bent of mankind, and to give it all the improvements of which it is susceptible. Now, according to the most natural course of things, industry and the arts and trade encrease the power of the sovereign as well as the happiness of the subjects; and that policy is violent, which aggrandizes the public by the poverty of individuals.

(Hume 1985s [1752a], 260)

Read in the Scottish social-political context in which it was written, this passage suggests that Hume was unwilling to see Highland life disrupted by confiscations and evictions, or even by the gross interference in the economy of the region that recruitment caused. To confiscate land and impose new tenants and overseers from outside would not be to "comply with the common bent of mankind." If one wanted to civilize Highlanders, making them more productive was a better way of doing so than sending them off to fight in North America and elsewhere. Let time teach the Highlanders the skills and arts that would give them surpluses to spend on new consumer items. Their growing needs and delight in luxuries, which would soon become necessities, would drive Highlanders from the "habit of indolence [that] naturally prevails" (Hume 1985s [1752a], 260). That view was consonant with what he expressed elsewhere about "plans of government, which suppose great reformation in the manners of mankind," plans he regarded as "plainly imaginary" (Hume 1985cc [1752j], 514).

In other passages, Hume seems to defend some modest interferences. For example, he suggests that introducing into the region more wealth in the form of subsidies to those living there might produce higher incomes for laborers.

Furnish him with the manufactures and commodities, and he will do it [labor and improve] himself. Afterwards you will find it easy to seize some part of his superfluous labour,[34] and employ it in the public service, without giving him his wonted return. Being accustomed to industry, he will think this less grievous, than if at once, you oblige him to an augmentation of labour without reward.

(Hume 1985s [1752a], 262)

Here Hume seems to favor the subsidies his friends would direct to the Highland areas to encourage and improve agriculture and the cattle trade with the south—the Highland equivalent of foreign trade. We should remember that the British army in repressing the Highlanders had slaughtered much of the livestock in the region. Trade in cattle outside the area, "foreign trade," gave larger profits and brought in the pleasures of luxurious spending, which then fueled the desires for more of the same. "Industry, knowledge and humanity" would certainly follow (Hume 1985s [1752a], 271).

If one sees the Highlands as a poor nation, and the Lowlands as a rich one, Hume's arguments concerning rich nations and poor nations apply here too (1985u [1752c], 283–84; 1985s [1752a], 265). Highlanders need the arts and sciences, luxuries, and refinements—with which will come liberty, commerce, and a complex social world. The pace of these developments, however, cannot be greatly forced. For the moment, one should not expect Highlanders to participate in modern industry but to work at labor-intensive activities that will allow them to trade with areas that are more advanced. In the essay "Of Refinement in the Arts," originally entitled "Of Luxury," Hume restates the value of luxuries as incentives to work and obtain knowledge, which bring in their wake freedom without the loss of "martial spirit" (1985t [1752b], 274). In a following passage (277f) he describes the ordinary Highlanders, but without naming them, as "rude" and subject to "petty tyrants," who in the early editions of the *Political Discourses* are described as "Gothick barons" (1994 [1752], 631). Highland society is poor, confused, unfree, and ignorant. What it really needs is trade and "equal laws, which may secure their property, and preserve them from monarchial, as well as aristocratical tyranny"(1985t [1752b], 278).

Hume could never have written explicitly about the Highlanders without giving offense to many of his Jacobite friends and to others made during his army service. Stated more generally, his remarks were acceptable and show that he would have favored the ending of chieftainships, Highland tenures and, most likely, anything which would civilize people who had missed out on the course of development that had been normal for the Lowlands, for England, and much of Europe. His *History of England* took the same line when it traced the progress of barbarous Saxons into the polished men of his own time; unbridled license evolved into ordered liberty.

In "Of Interest" (Hume 1985v [1752d]) he also addressed what looks like a Highland problem. In this essay he explains why interest rates are high in underdeveloped regions of the world. The principal reason (298) seems to be that different "habits and manners" exist in rude societies, in which there is great demand for money but little industry and much idleness. Prices are generally higher; everything is in short supply. Interest rates will fall if wealth increases and industry produces more lenders (302). The Highlands were in an infantile state of society, one that lacked merchants, the arts, and law. Only with time will such societies improve and become civilized, refined, and peaceful. Disrupting interferences generally will not be helpful but, as he noted in "Of Money," a constant infusion of money has good effects in the short run (Hume 1985u [1752c], 286, 288). That was also part of the government's plan.

The essays in *Political Discourses* do not exclusively concern problems of the Highlanders, but there are many places where one can discern Hume addressing then-current Scottish issues. This makes sense given his other attempts to shape public opinion. We can infer what he might have said in the debates over the Highlands and we see his warnings about the likelihood and reasons for failure as government policy was set. As usual, his arguments are general and his examples non-Scottish. Unlike many Scots, he was unwilling to openly slight the now-defeated Highlanders.

5. Scottish Elements in Other Political-Economy Essays

Two other essays by Hume, "Of the Populousness of Ancient Nations" (1985bb [1752i]) and "Idea of a Perfect Commonwealth" (1985cc [1752j]), also have Scottish contexts. Population questions were multifaceted ones and had been discussed for over a hundred years when Hume came to them. In Scotland they had first arisen in a variety of religious concerns discussed after about 1660 and then in literary and political-economic arguments discussed from the early 1700s to the 1740s.[35] Population was also an improving topic, related to actuarial problems, such as those encountered by the Reverend Robert Wallace when in 1742 and 1743 he acted as an actuary for the Widows and Orphans Fund, a life-insurance scheme for ministers and university professors.[36] Hume responded to Wallace's manuscript essay on the topic of ancient populations (1744?) showing his own great command of ancient literary sources. In the essay Hume asks for a more realistic look at the ancient world in which men were like us but societies and the values they sheltered were not. After Hume, demography would be included more prominently in social theories and the learned would be less tempted to think that the ancients were more numerous and better governed than people in their own world. Beginning in 1767, with Hume's friend Sir James Steuart, demography would be included in most systematic discussions of political economy.

Hume's "Idea of a Perfect Commonwealth" (1985cc [1752j]) picks up themes that had appeared in James Harrington's *The Commonwealth of Oceana* (1656) but also in the pre-Union works of Andrew Fletcher of Saltoun.[37] It is not usually included among Hume's economic essays but it should be. Here a somewhat whimsical Hume appears as a constructive thinker and not just as a skeptical critic of ideas. The essay contains some of Hume's strongest objections to political projects and revolutionary changes in states, yet it also provides long-term guidance on radical political-economic transformations. He thought such changes would be desirable in Great Britain, if implemented slowly. In the long run, Hume's imagination was that of a quiet revolutionary, not so unlike the imaginations of some of his Parisian friends. Hume's essay envisions an incorporating union of the kingdoms of England, Scotland, and Ireland, and the elimination of all the liberties and franchises of whatever sort. All would be assimilated into a federal system and into one large free market. Laws would no longer favor the trade of the English and the Scottish. Equality would come to the Celtic fringe.

Hume in this essay is at his most republican and his strictures on republican government elsewhere should be read against this description of an ideal, but not permanent, government and state. Hume imagined a world in which the franchise, while still severely restricted, would be extended to £20 freeholders and "householders worth 500 pounds" (1985cc [1752j], 516). The first Reform Bills in 1832 and 1833 offered little more than this. Hume's republic was to be a virtuous place in which the freeholders of the country would gradually gain more and more power and the 100 regional governments would have many functions. Places in "Humeland" would be filled by those whom John Adams called "the rich, the well born, and the able." In Hume's world, as in America, no one would have an inherited title. Important statuses would be earned. The goodness of this republic would be "a sufficient incitement to human endeavours" (529). Hume was even prepared to grant a Leveller demand—annual elections—which in reality would have produced chaos, and which even he felt he had to supplement with a provision for a six-month dictatorship in the case of emergencies. He institutionalized a political opposition but one that would not have power to obstruct the government's business or to support a faction, only to appeal to the people to decide against a policy. Republicans needed and got representation in their civil establishments, but also in their churches. Humeland would be a somewhat turbulent society in which "the natural equality of property" would promote liberty and prosperity as would the representative elements in his imagined polity, which were made possible by them. Hume's politics, when it came to wishes and desires, were radical and Whiggish, but his practical politics were those of a cautious Tory. That was often the case with enlightened Scots. This society was expected to flourish as had the Dutch Republic, on which it was modeled, and for the same reasons—its lack of territorial ambitions, its pacifism, its decentralized powers, and the wisdom of the six councils, which would advise its government. The Council of Trade, however, was subject in all matters to the Senate. Economic issues even in this ideal world would still be shaped and partly determined by magistrates and politicians and not just by market forces.

6. Conclusion

Hume's political-economic essays rejected many of the shibboleths of his age. In the *Political Discourses* Hume attempted to test by experience then-popular economic and political beliefs and to correct them. His references to history and his eagerness to place problems—like population levels, the changing value of money, and interest rates—in historical contexts partly demonstrate that. The essays as a whole reflect his already intense interest in history just as the later *History of England* reflected his continuing interest in topics such as prices and the value of money. *Political Discourses* alludes to, even embodies, a sophisticated conjectural history in which he traces the progress of mankind from the necessitous state of barbarous hunter-gatherers, through stages involving pastoral and subsistence agriculture, to complex but primitive societies that were made possible by the first agricultural surpluses.[38] Those societies had evolved through the development of the arts, industry, and commerce to the present. Every topic is in one way or another holistically related to this scheme and to the social institutions the various stages possess. His essays about social change and its causes suggest that his essays addressed Scottish conditions and were relevant to what was going on in Scottish thought and practice. Hume's discussions contained pertinent comments on the nature of political economy in a developing but uncertain world—such as the one in which Scots lived.

Hume also seems to have written *Political Discourses* with an eye to the improving activities and theoretical views expressed by earlier Scottish writers and in reaction to contemporary improvers such as his friends. Most of those men were in favor of government interventions of various sorts to promote improvements. Those seemed to work. Greater freedom of trade within Britain came with a judicious protectionism that had benefited Scotland. Improving and protectionist policies had been pushed by politicians such as the third duke of Argyll. All that serves as an immediate background to the *Political Discourses*; all that would have been in the minds of his local audience, although it has largely vanished from the minds of his modern readers and commentators. Market forces could do much but not all could be left to markets. Hume wanted freer trade and markets operating without interference, but suspected that such policies would not work in the linen trade. Further, he believed that during famines food must be provided for those with no money, or else intolerable violence would result. The rebellion of 1745 also made apparent the need for some government interventions in the economy to realize political ends.

Throughout his career, Hume, like Paterson and Law, thought that government was essential to well-run economies. To protect the nation, pay the public debts, and realize whatever social goods they need to pursue, governments will and must intervene in their state's economy if only through taxation, without which they could not exist:

> Though a resolution should be formed by the legislature never to impose any tax which hurts commerce and discourages industry, it will be impossible for men, in subjects of such extreme delicacy, to reason so justly as never to be mistaken, or amidst difficulties so urgent, never to be seduced from their resolution. The continual fluctuations in commerce require continual alterations in the nature of the taxes; which exposes the legislature every moment to the danger of both wilful and involuntary error. And by any great blow given to trade, whether by injudicious taxes or other accidents, throws the whole system of government into confusion.
>
> (Hume 1985aa [1752h], 358)

Hume's economics is always political, and always related to legal and constitutional regimes, manners, customs, laws, religions, and the physical setting in which a given economy is located. His *laissez faire* was one with qualifications. The theory he deploys is ultimately for the statesman who should be skeptical, guided by experience and always proceeds with caution when making changes. He must be wary of unintended consequences. For those reasons Hume is still readable and his ideas applicable to modern discussions of political economy.

Notes

1 His *History of England* (Hume 1983a [1754–62]) adds to this short list Adam and James Anderson, and incidental information found in many other sources. The *History of England* is not well footnoted and the volumes devoted to the most recent period initially lacked notes and contain the fewest sources. For more on his sources see Stockton (1976, 300–303).

2 This has been noticed by others—e.g., C. George Caffentzis has interpreted the *Political Discourses* in relation to the Highlands, and Istvan Hont has found Hume addressing the ways in which Scots could participate in and benefit from international trade. See Caffentzis (2001, 301–35) and Hont's essay in this volume.

3 See Haakonssen (1994, xvii); Hume to Henry Home, 4 June 1739 (Hume 1983b [1954]); Hume to Henry Home, 1 July 1739 (Hume [1932] 1932; 1969, 31f); and Emerson (1997, 9–28).

4 The model for this agricultural scheme was possibly the old office of the Master of the Metals, which in the early 1740s Sir John Clerk had wanted restored in Scotland. The master was supposed to prospect for minerals and then mine them if landowners were reluctant to open on their lands deposits of use to the kingdom. See Clerk (c. 1742, MS GD18\1144). This memorandum dates from about 1742 and discusses opening mines in the Highlands as part of a scheme to "establish Liberty, Property, Industrie and Independence of clanships, the best Security against Insurrection and Rebellion." It is typical of the long-standing attitudes and discussions that led to the Highland settlement acts of the 1740s and early 1750s.

5 In 1743, the Philosophical Society discussed agriculture, some industrial processes, and mining; and it offered to analyze any ore samples sent to it by landowners throughout the kingdom. See Emerson (1979, 179) for one of a series of four articles about a society of which Hume became a secretary.

6 The Edinburgh Society (1755–63) announced a prize for the best plow design. The theoretical problems were to create an efficient cutting blade, a durable sock, and a mould board that would completely turn over the plowed sod.

7 Hume commented on those years during which he seems to have thought scarcity was not extreme; others, including magistrates, thought it was. See Hume (1985, 347) and Clerk (1892, 159). Hume's attitude presages the later hardening of social attitudes toward the poor; see Mitchison (1989, 199–224).

8 This passage survived unaltered through many editions of his favorite work. It gives to political considerations a priority contradicted by the essay "Of Commerce," in which Hume argued for the better provisioning provided by trade and an open market (262f) and in the *History of England*, in which he praised Elizabeth for "encourag[ing] agriculture by allowing a free exportation of corn" (1983a, 4:48). Hume also criticized the abandonment of this policy (1983a, 3:78 and 5:4.138f). At about the same time those volumes of the *History of England* were printed, Hume defended a free market in corn in the advertisement to a pamphlet republished in Edinburgh in 1758. Again, his consideration of the

question there is an economic one dealing with high prices but not with starvation. See Raynor (1998, 2).

9 See also Rotwein (1955, xi).

10 Such progress was not true for all in the working classes; see Gibson and Smout (1995), and Whatley (2000, 76–78).

11 Hume to James Oswald, 1 November 1750, in Hume (1932, 2.142).

12 For linen see Durie (1979); for tobacco see Price (1973) and Devine (1975).

13 See Emerson (1973, 291–329). This article lists the members of the Select Society of Edinburgh, including most of the men mentioned in earlier paragraphs. The society's debate topics are contained in the society's minutes ("Book of Rules and Minutes," ADV MS 23.1.1); see also the Select Society of Edinburgh (NLS MS 98\70), and Emerson (2004). A few more (or variants) are to be found in the newspapers of the time.

14 The general arguments were presented in various much-read texts cited by Kramnick (1968) and by others in numerous works.

15 A convenient if partial list of these is contained in McLeod and McLeod (1979). See also Robertson (1995b, 198–227).

16 Arguments for freer trade were not uncommon among the economic writers of c. 1700.

17 Hume often put similar arguments in terms of the increase of luxury, particularly in the *History of England* (1983a [1754–62], 3:76). Luxury can be "vicious" but it is generally not so for Hume and seldom is in the *History of England*.

18 Charles Du Tot was later to argue that point at some length and to set it in the context of the honorableness of the merchants' calling. See Du Tot (1974 [1739], 264–72, 304).

19 See, e.g., Hume's *History of England* (1983a [1754–62]), 1:183f, 497; 3:330f, 369f, 35; 4:381. Hume's discussion of these topics may owe something to Charles Du Tot but it also relates to a Scottish preoccupation of the times—tracing the changes in measures of all sorts. Hume's colleague in the Philosophical Society, James Stirling of Keir, was an obsessive writer on this topic. His surviving manuscripts at Garden House, Stirlingshire, contain several drafts of a work comparing the coinage, weights, and measures of peoples since Tubal Cain made brass and Noah built the Ark.

20 The value of land was worth more than the circulating money in currency-poor Scotland, which had less money in circulation than it needed.

21 Monetization of landed estates was something Hume's friends called for when they asked for reform of the Scottish laws of entail. Those prevented owners from freely alienating or borrowing against their estates to make improvements or to invest in other things. This seems not to have much interested Hume who seldom mentions entails.

22 The arguments over this resemble the debates of the 1750s over a bill to repeal entails and those in the 1770s when the Douglas and Heron Bank (the Ayr Bank) was created. See Checkland (1975, 124–35).

23 I thank Istvan Hont for pointing out to me that the French economists cited by Hume all had some relation to John Law. See Murphy (1986a, 1997). Hume never cited Cantillon, Quesnay, Galieni, Morrellet, or Sir James Steuart, just as he never mentions Law or Paterson in his published works.

24 The manuscript is reprinted in Law (1994), edited by Murphy, who thinks the manuscript was written c. 1702–5 (Law 1994, 23).

25 The duke's library catalog shows that he possessed the 1753 edition of *Essays and Discourses*, which contained the *Political Discourses*. See Campbell (1758, misc. octavos**).**

26 Hume commented on this bank and its policies in "Of the Balance of Trade" (1985x [1752e], 319). All of the bank's notes still bear the duke's picture.

27 It was one of King Alfred's glories that in his reign learning and humanity were followed by arts introduced by him for the benefit of all (Hume 1983a [1754–62], 1:81).

28 See also Hume (1983a [1754–62], 6:329).

29 Hume approved of this (1932), 1:134; 1985t [1752b], 277f.

30 See A. J. Youngson (1973) and Eric Richards (1982).

31 See, e.g., Hume (1983a [1754–62]), 2:460f.

32 The political nature of the Commission of Annexed Estates is discussed by John Stuart Shaw (1983, 77–82).

33 See the recent discussion of these issues by Andrew Mackillop (2000).

34 Hume makes the same point in "Of Money" (1985u [1752c], 293) when he notes that only in fairly developed economies can taxes paid in money be raised in the countryside.

35 See the discussion of the seventeenth-century background to all this by Richard H. Popkin (1987). For a discussion of the eighteenth century, see Sylvana Tomaselli (1989, 7–29). Yasuo Amoh has recently seen the debate as principally belonging to controversy between "ancients" and "moderns" (2003, 69–86).

36 He worked with figures provided by Alexander Webster who published a Scottish census in 1755. See Kyd (1975, xii–xv; 1977, 60).

37 See especially Fletcher (1979 [1698]; 1997b [1704]).

38 Of course, one needs to add to these essays the materials in the *Natural History of Religion* (1757).

2 The Emergence of David Hume as a Political Economist: A Biographical Sketch

Ian Simpson Ross

> There is a word, which is here in the mouth of every body, and which, I find, has also got abroad, and is much employed by foreign writers, in imitation of the ENGLISH; and this is, CIRCULATION. This word serves as an account of everything; and though I confess I have sought for its meaning in the present subject, ever since I was a school-boy, I have never yet been able to discover it.
>
> (David Hume 1985aa [1752h], 636)[1]

This intriguing admission by David Hume appeared from 1752 until 1768 in the essay, "Of Public Credit," in *Political Discourses*. Biographical interest in Hume as an economic theorist and analyst prompts inquiry into the chronology attached to this statement, and the unfolding of its conceptual implications. This paper aims to establish what early impressions of this kind and from later stages of his career probably influenced Hume's thinking about economics, especially as these are revealed in his correspondence.[2]

He was a student at Edinburgh from 1721 to 1725, so let us say his puzzlement over the widespread use of the term *circulation*—which we understand in the broad, commercial sense of transmission of products and values, and in the narrower sense of issuance of negotiable paper: stocks, bonds, notes, bills, and receipts (Littré 1889, "circulation")—began in the early 1720s. He was 12 years old or so then, and no doubt precocious,[3] therefore likely to have been inquisitive about a farming and business world in which his elders transferred objects for cash, and negotiated over pieces of paper that somehow represented values and cash, while meantime a distant government collected taxes and incurred debt by borrowing money on promises to make timely repayments. This world of commerce, and to some extent its problems, was delineated in the *Spectator* papers that were popular reading of the period, such as issue 174 by Steele, presenting Sir Andrew Freeport's defense of commerce (Addison and Steele 1982 [1711–12], 447–54).

Seen in the long-term, Britain was undergoing a financial revolution during Hume's youth, with economic growth funded through private and government stock circulation, and the fiscal-military state functioning and expanding on the basis of public debt (Dickson 1967; Brewer 1990; Roseveare 1991; Brewer and Hellmuth 1999; Winch 1996). In the short-term, however, this was the era following the bursting of the South Sea Bubble in September 1720 caused by stock swindling and speculation mania. This was also the era in which Robert Walpole assumed political leadership in Britain, and achieved relative success in managing the fall-out from the Bubble crisis. Walpole's restructuring of the national debt had two outcomes. First, a significant part of the British national debt caused by the French wars was converted to redeemable government stock and, second, responsible management of the debt was an issue for every government thereafter (Roseveare 1969, 111).[4]

Reactions to Walpole's policies in Britain were mixed from the start, as witnessed by the highly critical publication, *Cato's Letters* (Trenchard and Gordon 1995 [1720–23]). Hume came to share this critical perspective on Walpole's administration, commenting as follows: "During his Time, Trade has flourish'd, Liberty declin'd, and Learning has gone to Ruin. As I am a man, I love him; as I am a scholar, I hate him; as I am a Briton, I calmly wish his fall." This passage was part of "A Character of Sir Robert Walpole," an essay in the second volume of *Essays, Moral and Political* (1742), published on the eve of Walpole's resignation as prime minister; from 1748 to 1768 this comment appeared as a footnote to the essay, "That Politics May Be Reduced to a Science" (originally published in 1741), and was dropped from the 1770 edition of the *Essays* (Hume 1985c [1741c], 27 n. 20; 1985o [1742e], 574–76). After Walpole faded from the public eye and the *Essays*, Hume modified his stance on the growth and management of Britain's public debt. This occurred when his understanding of *circulation* was sharply challenged by the financier Isaac de Pinto, discussed below as an acquaintance of Hume in the 1760s. He is presented in the guise of an advocate of government stock circulation and prudent continuance, also management, of the national debt, who criticized Hume's views and claimed to have changed Hume's mind.

In the aftermath of the South Sea Bubble, there was a belief that *circulation*, as defined above, had stopped because of a collapse of public and private credit, which for a hundred years in England rested on these paper instruments. People also felt an urgent need to get the financial system moving again, through increases in the interest on Exchequer Bills and minting more coins, since paper currency was for a time non-negotiable (Carswell 1993, 159–61). The schoolboy Hume must have heard his elders express alarm about the rash of bankruptcies caused by the bursting of the Bubble,[5] perhaps coupled with discussion of technical details about the need for *circulation* in the economy. We can surmise this would be one stimulus for his later inquiries into financial systems.

As he grew older, Hume seems to have been impressed by Country Whig criticism of the dishonesty of the financial wheeling and dealing in London that helped to maintain the Court Whigs in government under Walpole. The system of managing public debt which Walpole bequeathed would have an aura of corruption, coloring Hume's subsequent opinions. His adult view that the prime minister was disingenuous in arguing that increasing the national debt through stock issues was beneficial is expressed in another paragraph appearing in "Of Public Credit," from 1752 to 1768:

> And these puzzling arguments, (for they deserve not the name of specious) though they could not be the foundation of [Walpole's] conduct, for he had more sense; served at least to keep his partisans in countenance, and perplex the understanding of the nation.
>
> (Hume 1985aa [1752h], 636, n. c)

Hume's admission of puzzlement (which remained in his text until 1768) over the meaning of *circulation* leads into an outburst against the London traders in stocks:

> But what production we owe to CHANGE-ALLEY, or even what consumption, except that of coffee, and pen, ink, and paper, I have not yet learned; nor can one foresee the loss or decay of any one beneficial commerce or commodity, though that place and all its inhabitants were forever buried in the ocean.
>
> (Hume 1985aa [1752h], 637)

Hume's sharp reflection on a modern economy of producers and consumers, and the usefulness or not of the stock market, echoes the rage vented in London by pamphleteers and satirists around 1720, against the gambling stock-jobbers to be found in "Change Alley." This was a labyrinth of lanes in the acute angle formed by Lombard Street and Cornhill, where the jobbers had taken refuge when formally excluded from the Royal Exchange on the other side of Lombard Street. A satirical account of the drowning of speculators succumbing to circulation is found in a frequently reprinted poem— "The Bubble" or "Upon the South Sea Project" (1720)—by Jonathan Swift, one of Hume's favorite authors:

> There is a gulf where thousands fell,
> Here all the bold adventurers came,
> A narrow sound though deep as hell,
> 'Change Alley' is the dreadful name.

> Subscribers here by thousands float,
> And jostle one another down
> Each paddling in his leaky boat,
> And here they fish for gold and drown.
>
> (Swift 1983, 212)[6]

To be sure, in his essay, "Of Public Credit," Hume admitted (at least from 1752 to 1768) that some economic good arises from stock "circulation," just as some good arises from that other evil, the "incumbrance" arising from governments mortgaging the future of their people to fund domestic and foreign policies in the present. Still, the conclusion he presented in 1752 and retained is dire: "either the nation must destroy public credit, or public credit will destroy the nation" (Hume 1985aa [1752h], 352, 360–61).[7]

Focusing now on Hume's career, it is notable that a nervous breakdown in 1729, then recovery at home, and consciousness of his slender means as a laird's younger brother, forced Hume to turn from the reflective life of a philosopher he preferred to an active life abroad (Mossner 1980, 611–15). This meant he suspended a far-reaching inquiry into "human Nature, upon which every moral Conclusion must depend," that had involved by 1732 the planning of the *Treatise of Human Nature*, finally published in 1739–40 (Hume 1969 [1932], 1:158; Hume 2000a). He comments on his situation in a letter provisionally dated March or April 1734, addressed to an unknown physician.[8] Hume recounts that he had emigrated from Scotland, and was hastening from London to Bristol, to become a merchant. He envisioned a career of "toss[ing] about the world from pole to pole," presumably as a supercargo, that is, an agent sent on a voyage to manage commercial transactions. Did Hume know that the merchant voyages he anticipated might take him across the Atlantic, where Bristol ships were in the forefront of sugar and tobacco trading with Britain's colonies in North America and the Caribbean? These ships were also heavily involved in the infamous traffic in West African slaves seized to work the plantations. Bristol was the premier organizing port in Britain for the slave trade from 1728 to 1732, and then was overtaken by Liverpool and London (Morgan 1993, 132–33).

In the event, Hume became a clerk in the counting-house of a sugar-importer, Michael Miller, an agent trading on commission with Jamaica plantations from 15 Queen Square, Bristol. Owners or managers of plantations or traders in that commodity would consign sugar for sale by Miller, and order goods in return from him. Miller would receive something like a 2.5 percent commission for his sales, for performing services such as buying supplies and provisions for the trading ships, and for acting as a quasi-banker by providing credit and accepting bills of exchange. His clerks would be involved in paying customs duties and freight charges on the ships, arranging for cargoes to be placed in warehouses, and perhaps passing on market information to the planters' lawyers, as well as in arranging for insurance on cargoes and ships, with a half-percent extra commission for their employer (Morgan 1993, 128–40, 193–96,). Miller apparently made £20,000 from his business— at least this is reported in an anecdote about his unwillingness to have his English corrected by Hume, since it was apparently good enough to enable him to realize a fortune of this size (Mossner 1980, 88–91).

One indication, perhaps, of Hume's interest in his work is that he owned a copy of John Ashley's pamphlet, "Some Observations on a Direct Exportation of Sugar from the British Islands, London," 1735 (Norton and Norton 1996, 146 n. 72). In the 1730s, Ashley, a former Barbados planter and colonial administrator, was a leading spokesman in England for West Indies' interests, strongly advocating direct trade between the British islands and Europe. Sugar is believed to have been the "most valuable of all British imports" from 1670 to 1820, after it passed from being a luxury item to a regular household one, and Bristol had a major share of this trade (Morgan 1993, 1–2, 184). Hume probably derived economic information and insights from the business of Miller's counting-house and its connection with Atlantic seaboard trade. For example, he cites with assurance the interest rate in Jamaica ("Of Interest," Hume 1985v [1752d], 296). In addition, he must have been conscious of the racist attitudes of Bristolians involved in, or benefiting from, the slave trade. Did this contribute to his position on the "natural" inferiority of black people, so offensive to modern readers ("Of National Characters," note as amended in 1776, 1985q [1748a], 629–30)? Despite his thesis on racial superiority, however, Hume condemns the imposition of slavery as a moral wrong to the victims that also brutalizes the masters. Further, going into the economics of modern slavery, he concludes that it was not a profitable enterprise. The verdict from the West Indies, where Bristol merchants principally traded, was that the stock of slaves decreased 5 percent each year unless new ones were brought in, and that the fear of punishment did not bring out as much work from a slave as the dread of dismissal from a hired servant ("Of the Populousness of Ancient Nations," Hume 1985bb [1752i], 383–84, 389–90, n. 23; Immerwahr 1992, 481–86; Palter 1995, 3–4, 6–10).

On the point of socioeconomic organization, a quick-witted young man like Hume would find much to interest him in Bristol. It was the second-largest city of England, a crowded, dirty port with a population in 1700 of 20,000, small compared to London's 687,000, which was a tenth of England's population at that date. Nevertheless, Bristol possessed a thriving, affluent merchant community, often led by younger sons of the landed and clerical classes, with intellectual and charitable interests, represented, for example, by the founding of the Free Library in 1613, and the Merchants' Almshouses beginning in 1699 (Wilson 1971, 179; Mathias 1979, 98, 118; Marcy 1972, 14).

A tradition of economic analysis in Bristol is suggested by the work of John Cary (d. 1720 ?), a vicar's son who became a West Indies sugar merchant in Bristol, and published successful pamphlets on industry as the main engine of wealth, for example, "An Essay on the State of England in Relation to its Trade, its Poor, and its Taxes" (1695, with several reprints up to 1745).[9] Cary also wrote "Essay Towards the Settlement of a National Credit in the Kingdom of England" (1696) and literature on the balance of trade and currency issues, advancing doctrines of the mercantilist cast that Hume would challenge in *Political Discourses* (Schumpeter 1986, 197, 365–367; Appleby 1978, 155, 170, 226). Likely to have influenced Hume's viewpoint in a positive way was Jacob Vanderlint's pamphlet, *Money Answers All Things* (1914 [1734]), an explanation of the mechanisms and benefits of a money economy and free trade, extensively quoted in the leading monthly periodical, the *Gentleman's Magazine*, in March 1734, about the time Hume reached Bristol.

In that city, to be sure, the young man had an opportunity to observe or even deal directly with interest rates, credit arrangements, and tax problems. Bristol's banking, credit, and capital-accumulation systems were well developed, involving remittances by metal and paper instruments. Traders and bankers, also commission agents like Miller, were involved in discounting bills of exchange and handling foreign currency, requiring awareness of specie movement and the balance of trade (Wilson 1971, 51, 330–31). It is possible, of course, that Hume encountered ill will as a Scot in Bristol, since its merchants were so incensed about Scottish success in the tobacco trade that they petitioned Parliament to strangle Glasgow's enterprise in that sector (Hamilton 1963, 255–61; Morgan 1993, 153–57). Nevertheless, Hume went on record in the *Political Discourses* with a positive view of merchants: "one of the most useful races of men, who serve as agents between those parts of the state, that are wholly unacquainted, and are ignorant of each other's necessities" (Hume 1985v [1752d], 300).[10] It is worth remembering that his four months' employment with Miller represented Hume's only concentrated exposure to merchants and commercial activity, in a city where the inhabitants were fond of saying that the "very parson thinks of nothing but turning a penny" (Lamoine 1990, 113).

However, the memory of the "knavery and extravagance" of the stock-jobbing projectors of the South Sea Company[11] and their like was still obnoxious in Britain, and as Hume was leaving his country in 1734, the government put through Parliament an act against the "wicked, pernicious, and destructive Practice of Stock-jobbing" (7 Geo. II, c.8). Though no doubt glad to proceed to France and follow his true vocation as a philosopher, Hume took with him his memories of transatlantic commerce conducted from Bristol. His aim was to continue with his *Treatise of Human Nature*, within which there was to be a place for "Politics" (as indicated on the advertisement for the first volume in 1739 [2000a]), comprised by history and political economy. But this project was now advanced against the backdrop of a metropolitan economy in Paris and two regional economies, first, that of Champagne, where his base was Reims (1734–35), and then Anjou, where his base was La Flèche (1735–37). These settings varied greatly from what he had experienced in Britain, and therefore offered useful comparative material. As for the scene in the realm of finance, however, there were some similarities, since the French were still feeling keenly the effects of the bursting of their Mississippi Company bubble in the spring of 1720 (Kindleberger 2000, 208). The revolutionary Mississippi scheme had been launched in August 1717, in the time of the Regent Orléans, by another Scot with a highly original mind, the economic theorist and gambler John Law (Murphy 1997; Gleeson 2000), who was greatly concerned with the two themes that seem to have interested Hume from his early student years: circulation of money as a stimulus to the economy, and establishment of sound public credit.

Law had two major aims in mind for the Mississippi scheme: first, solving the shortage of money in France, by replacing specie with paper-note circulation underwritten by a central bank; and second, managing French finances, ruined as the result of Louis XIV's wars, by substituting for the national debt the circulation of shares in the Mississippi Company, which had been granted the authority to trade in and colonize the vastly expanded territory of Louisiana. Facing the opposition of those with vested interests, Law had to push his scheme too hard and too fast, and it collapsed after a mania of speculation, which created a financial disaster even more appalling than the bursting of the South Sea Bubble that soon followed.

When Hume expressed his skepticism about there being any fixed meaning for the word *circulation*, he stated that foreign writers employed it, imitating the English, and he cited in a note: "Melon, Du Tot, Law, in the pamphlets published in France" (1985aa [1752h], 636, n. 1). Hume expressed a negative view of Law in his essay "Of Public Credit," and did not do justice to him as a seminal monetary theorist:

> when the nation becomes heartily sick of their debts, and is cruelly oppressed by them, some daring projector may arise with visionary schemes for their discharge. And as public credit will begin, by that time, to be a little frail, the least touch will destroy it as happened in FRANCE during the regency; and in this manner it will *die of the doctor.*
> (1985aa [1752h], 361; italics in the original)[12]

In three other essays included in *Political Discourses*: "Of Commerce," "Of Money," and "Of the Balance of Trade," as well as in "Of Public Credit," Hume reveals awareness of economic theories expressed in Law's book, *Money and Trade Consider'd with a Proposal for Supplying the Nation with Money* (1720), which he retained in his library in an English edition published at Glasgow in 1760 (Norton and Norton 1996, 107 n. 751). In general, it seems that some knowledge of French financial history reinforced features of Hume's thinking about money, such as his concern over inflation, and his preference for an open economy, as recent scholars have explained (Wennerlind 2000, 2001b, 2002, 2005; Caffentzis 2001; Sakamoto 2003).

As well, Hume reflects awareness of three other writers who began debating Law's ideas in print within 20 years of the collapse of the Mississippi scheme. Two were connected with Law himself. Jean-François Melon was the great man's private secretary from 1718 to 1720, and Charles de Ferrare Du Tot was manager of the cash account in the French Royal Bank under

Law. Melon (1734) argued that money is the life-blood of the economy, and should be kept in plentiful supply (circulation), and held that contracting a national debt was a transfer from the right hand to the left. As far as Hume was concerned, this was a doctrine based on "loose reasonings and specious comparisons" (1985x [1752e], 356; Larrère 1992, 107–15). It has been suggested by John Robertson that Melon's stress on agriculture as the chief productive sector of an economy prompted Hume to argue in the *Political Discourses* that commerce best promoted economic growth, and that this was frustrated for the most part by jealousy of trade and the mishandling of the instruments of commerce—money and credit (Robertson 2000, 51). Du Tot (1738) debated Melon's views on the effects of changes in the domestic currency rates, and provided the favorable assessment of an insider on the rise and fall of Law's system of paper currency and state finance, funded through investment in colonial trade (Murphy 1998, 57–77). Hume refers to Du Tot's criticisms of Law approvingly in "Of the Balance of Trade" (1985x [1752e], 315 n. 11), and wrote out 11 extracts from his *Réflexions politiques sur les finances et le commerce* (1738) in the "Early Memoranda" (Mossner 1948, discussed below).

The third writer mentioned by Hume was Joseph Pâris-Duverney, significant for countering Du Tot's positive view of Law by stating bluntly that, after December 1720, Law's policies had left France "more drained than it had been by twenty-five years of war and the almost total losses at the end of the reign of Louis XIV" (1740, 2:132). In "Of the Balance of Trade," Hume seems to echo Pâris-Duverney's negative view of Law's innovations, commenting that an increase in "paper-credit" may have a good effect on the economy in the interval between an increase in money in this form and the subsequent rise in price, "but it is dangerous to precipitate matters, at the risk of losing all by the failing of that credit, as must happen upon any violent shock in public affairs" (1985x [1752e], 317 n. 13).[13] To be sure, Pâris-Duverney was far from objective in his criticism of Law, since his livelihood was threatened by Law's drive to rid the French taxation system of tax-farmers like himself (Murphy 1997, 4).

The English writings imitated by the French in their discussions of *circulation* may well have included, in addition to Law's "Essay on Money and Trade" (1720), Sir Josiah Child's *Discourse about Trade* (1690), Joshua Gee's *Trade and Navigation of Great-Britain Considered* (1730), and Bishop Berkeley's *Querist* (1901 [1735]). Thus Dugald Stewart, intellectual heir of Hume and Adam Smith, cited these sources as inspiring French analysis of commerce (1982 [1811], 348 n. 1). Hume's library included an edition of the Berkeley title dated 1751 (Norton and Norton 1996, 75 n. 134).

In addition to following up ideas about monetary policy in France and Britain when he crossed the Channel, Hume took an interest in economic data. This topic comes up in his correspondence with a young English friend involved in commerce, James Birch, employed or lodging in Bristol's Old Market in September 1734 (Hume 1969 [1932], 1:23), and the next May residing at "Mr Emory's Grocer in Taunton," Somerset (Mossner 1958, 31). Birch wished to come over to France for "Study & Diversion," and Hume provided some economic information about Reims, where he had settled first. Writing from Reims on 12 September 1734, Hume estimated the population at 40,000, and claimed that thirty families kept coaches, though none had an income of more than £500 a year. Reims's population actually did not reach 40,000 for many years after that—it was recorded as only 30,602 in 1787–89—but Hume may have judged it to be about the size of Edinburgh, where he had been educated. As for Paris, at this time it had possibly 524,186 inhabitants, between a fiftieth and sixtieth part of the total population of France, and was a very expensive place to live compared to the provinces (Hume 1985aa [1752h], 354–55; Hamilton 1963, 22; Braudel 1990, 248). It is likely that Reims's economic strength was observed by Hume, since it was an important centre of the wine industry, principally champagne, named after the region, no doubt a factor in what Hume said the French did best, cultivating "*l'Art de Vivre*, the art of society and conversation" (Hume 1985i [1741i], 91).

But Reims also had a woolen industry, fostered by Colbert, a native son elevated to become the controller general of France under Louis XIV. He is depicted by Smith, Hume's more zealous follower in advocating free-market economics, as an arch-interventionist, who was prepared to restrain some branches of industry drastically, and privilege others to an extraordinary degree. Colbert was also ready to depress the industry of the country to support that of the town, rather than allow "every man to pursue his own interest in his own way, upon the liberal plan of equality, liberty, and justice" (Smith 1976 [1776], 4.9.3).

Hume's reflections on the link between public policy and economic advantage for France took a more conservative form. In the last section of *Essays, Moral and Political* (1741), namely, "Of Liberty and Despotism" (later "Of Civil Liberty" from 1758), written not too long after Hume left France, he dealt with the theme of amelioration of government in modern times, both of the free and the autocratic kind, and announced: "It has become an established opinion, that commerce can never flourish but in a free government" (1985i [1741i], 92). Hume departed from this "vulgar Whig" position in suggesting that the monarchy of France, if it sank under an oppressive tax system, could rise through tax reform undertaken by a wise prince or minister, "endowed with sufficient discernment to know his own and the public interest." This kind of reform could certainly extend to economic initiatives *à la* Colbert, while free governments in a flourishing state sank under the burden of taxes raised to pay down national debt (ibid., 95–96). In this passage, to be sure, Hume is addressing a central issue in his *Political Discourses*: under what conditions do nations flourish and decline? Here, indeed, is the opening for his enquiries into commerce as the engine of economic growth, with money, interest, taxes, and public credit as its instruments.

However, the immediate attraction of Reims for Hume was that he had an introduction to its chief man of letters: the abbé Noël-Antoine Pluche (1688–1761), noted for his poetry, tragedies, and histories, and also for publishing a popular textbook on life and creation, the eight-volume *Le Spectacle de la nature* (1732–51), which paid some attention to commerce. Pluche opened his fine library to Hume, who reported on 29 September 1734 to a Scottish friend, Michael Ramsay, that he was reading Berkeley's *Principles of Human Knowledge* there in English and French, and re-reading Locke. Hume mentioned that new works of "Learning & Philosophy" arrived from London and Paris each month, so he did not feel the want of the latest books (Morrisroe 1973, 314–15). Melon's "Essai politique sur le commerce" (1734) fits this category, and Berkeley's *Alciphron*, published in a second edition in London in 1734, then in French at The Hague the same year. The "Second Dialogue" of the *Alciphron* contains a discussion of *circulation*, satirizing the enthusiasm of Mandeville (1988, 1:86–147) for this principle as explaining economic growth through luxury demand. Hume, of course, tended to endorse Mandeville's views on this subject (Hume 1985t [1752b], 280; Berry 1994, 101–25, 126–76).

In Reims, Hume settled down to the philosophical reading, or re-reading, that contributed to the composition of the *Treatise*, but he stayed only one year, acquiring some proficiency in French, then moved for two years to La Flèche—in Anjou, also noted for its wines—a small, quiet town of 5,000 souls or so. It had the advantage of offering access to the library of a Jesuit college, reputed to have had 40,000 volumes when Louis XV dissolved the college in 1762. Hume is known to have debated the issue of proof of miracles with the church fathers (Hume 1969 [1932], 1:360–61). One wonders, however, did he reason with them on economic topics such as the *just price* constituted by the naturally exchange-established price, and the *quantity theory of money*? Before Jean Bodin, Jesuit thinkers such as Luis Molina, Juan de Lugo, and Leonard de Leys (Lessius) had developed these concepts to explain the inflation resulting from the influx of precious metals from Latin America, and in an attempt to balance the conflicting claims of acceptable commercial practice and the public good. F. A. von Hayek (1968), who found inspiration in Hume's writings, took this neoscholastic material seriously, inclining to the belief that Max Weber was wrong, and that the Jesuits rather than the Calvinists laid down the basis for capitalism (see Grice-Hutchinson 1952; 1993).

From his correspondence, we learn of Hume in August 1737, en route to London to publish the *Treatise*, advising Michael Ramsay what to read to understand the metaphysical part, that is, book 1, "Of the Understanding" (Kozanecki 1963, 133). Hume believed that the more original part of his work dealt with "Morals," his analysis of motives and actions underscoring his views on human behavior as recorded in history in its social stages, and finding expression in politics and economics. In January 1739, he published as part of his "science of man," the first two Books of the *Treatise*, "Of the

Understanding" and "Of the Passions," and the advertisement for them stated that if he was fortunate enough to be successful, he would "proceed to the examination of Morals, Politics, and Criticism; which will compleat this Treatise of Human Nature" (2000a). The third book, "Of Morals," duly appeared on 5 November 1740, with its novel teaching about the "conventions of property, exchange, and money" as a theory of the "emergence of modern commercial society" (Wennerlind 2002), in essence a basis for an innovative exploration of political economy. Sad to relate, the enterprise on the whole met with indifference or contempt. Further elucidation of the new explanatory principles of thought, and analysis of the relevant emotions, motivations, and values, with a view to applying them systematically to the field of political economy, seemed indefinitely postponed.

Hume's strategy, however, was to change his approach to writing, and launch what became a profitable career as a man of letters, with an expanding market for his books. At this period, he continued with his plan for the "science of man," through writing on "moral and political" topics, but in the form of essays (1741–42) rather than philosophical treatises. To deal with the problem of style, he adopted the approach of Addison and Steele in their highly successful periodicals, *Tatler* and *Spectator*. As Hume points out in "Of Essay Writing" (1985p [1742f]), he viewed himself as a sort of ambassador, representing the "Dominions of Learning" separated for too long from "those of Conversation." What was needed, he wrote, using an economic metaphor, was the establishment of a healthy balance of trade between the two realms, to ensure that sound reasoning would draw its materials from the experience available only in the "conversible world" (Hume 1985aa [1742a], 535). This explains that Hume never wrote a treatise on economics, unlike his successors Sir James Steuart and Adam Smith, but gave his readers *Political Discourses* in the form of a series of essays.

But we have further evidence for thinking that Hume was also collecting materials for, and developing his ideas on, the subject of "politics," including economics, intended for inclusion in the "science of man." This is to be found in his "Early Memoranda" (Mossner 1948), which M. A. Stewart (2000, 276–88) and Tatsuya Sakamoto (2004), going back to the conclusion of John Hill Burton (1846, 1:125), suggest have a later date than Mossner accepted, because a link can be made between certain extracts and the precisely datable first volume of *Essays* of 1741. Of great methodological interest is number 257 of Section III: "The Moderns have not treated Morals so well as the Ancients merely from their Reasoning turn, which carry'd them away from Sentiment." This is surely a guide for Hume in coming to terms with the sentiment (passion) whose constant pressure drives economic activity: "Avarice, or the desire of gain, is the universal passion, which operates at all times, in all places, and upon all persons" (Hume 1985k [1742a], 113). Sakamoto notes that the Memoranda entries prior to number 145, Section III, for the most part concern economic subjects, which Hume had already classified into topics concerning "taxation, foreign trade, interest rates, and public finance." Also, Hume recorded items about money, interest, and population from his inquiries into the history of ancient Greece and Rome. As well, his comparative approach to economics is further in evidence from assembling facts and identifying issues from a broad range of contemporary British, French, and Dutch sources. A basis for the subject matter of separate essays in *Political Discourses* is thus clearly established in these Memoranda.

Reflections on his reading and composition, however, were not the sole activities that contributed to the making of the *Political Discourses*. We also have to think of Hume's career experience in the period 1746–48: "almost the only Interruption which my Studies have received in the Course of my Life" (Mossner 1980, 612). Unexpectedly, in the spring of 1746, he was whirled off by a distant relation, Lt.-General James St. Clair, to be his secretary and act as the judge advocate for a military expedition, designed first as a descent on Canada, and then diverted to be a blow at France's economic empire, namely, an ill-fated attack on the French East India Company's home port at Lorient in Brittany. Hume recorded these adventures in his notebooks for the years 1746–47 (National Library of Scotland, Hume Papers, MSS 25689–91). As an analyst of politics and economics, also the future historian of England, Hume gained invaluable lessons from this episode, and saw firsthand how the public debt contracted for Britain's foreign wars was actually spent or misspent.

General St. Clair also invited Hume to travel across Europe in 1748–49 as his secretary and aide-de-camp on a secret military-diplomatic mission to the court of the Empress Maria Theresa at Vienna and that of the king of Sardinia at Turin. Hume wrote a journal of his travels in the form of a running letter, dated from 3 March 1748 at The Hague to 16 June at Turin (Hume 1969 [1932], 1:114–33), maintained for the "Amusement" of his brother, the stay-at-home but avid reader John. In the main, it offers shrewd commentary on the different societies through which he passed. In a sense, it is also an important subtext to the essay, "Of National Characters," separately published in November 1748 as one of *Three Essays, Moral and Political*, and simultaneously as part of the third edition of *Essays, Moral and Political* (Todd 1974, 193; Chamley 1975, 287–91). Further, it has a relationship to *Political Discourses*, since it offers case studies of societies and human types under different constitutions and economic dispensations.

In Holland, Hume found an insurrection in progress against war taxes and the patriciate that levied them, or farmed them out. This uprising was a violent challenge to the orthodoxy established by Hugo Grotius that "True Liberty" consisted in entrusting sovereignty to an oligarchy (Schama 1988, 601). Hume's summing up of the situation was succinct: "Holland was undoubtedly ruin'd by its Liberty; & now has a Chance of being sav'd by its Prince [William IV of Orange]: let Republic make the best of this example that they can." He was also satisfied this was not the result of mob rule: "It was not the Mob, properly speaking, that made the Revolution but the middling & substantial Tradesmen." Hume's interpretation of this episode, which he personally observed, corresponds with the views he had expressed on free governments and autocratic ones in the essay "Of Liberty and Despotism" (1741), mentioned above. It corresponds as well with his views about the importance of political stability for the economic health of a country.

Hume was not impressed with Vienna, and thought the Empress Maria Theresa prudish, though a woman of spirit. It is possible he met at this time Count L. F. J. von Zinzendorf, an expert on finance and commerce in the imperial administration, who provided him with an account of money (specie) imported into Spain. Hume passed this account on to Adam Smith in 1772 while he was composing the *Wealth of Nations* (Smith 1987a, 415–16). The journal ended in Turin, in an Italy that according to Hume was excessively taxed, and where news of the Treaty of Aix-la-Chapelle reached St. Clair's embassy group. It is likely that Hume's international perspective on politics and economics was given focus by his travels, resulting in his condemnation of the "narrow and malignant politics" of his country, and the declaration that ends "Of the Jealousy of Trade":

> as a British subject, I pray for the flourishing commerce of Germany, Spain, Italy, and even France itself. I am at least certain, that Great Britain, and all these nations, would flourish more, did their sovereigns and ministers adopt such enlarged and benevolent sentiments towards each other.
>
> (1985ee [1758], 331)

Though he had little time for authorship during this active interlude in his life, Hume kept up his interest in books, and secured a copy of Montesquieu's masterwork, *De l'Esprit des lois* (1748), before he left Italy. Reading and annotating it, and then corresponding with Montesquieu (Hume 1969 [1932], 1:33–38), was part of the enterprise of pulling together in the years 1749–51, in retirement at Ninewells, the elements that comprise the *Political Discourses* of 1752.

Identifying the capstone to this period in "My Own Life," Hume observed that, "In 1752, were published at Edinburgh, where I then lived, my *Political Discourses*, the only work of mine that was successful on the first publication." Writing from the point of view of a historian of the book as an artifact and commodity, Richard B. Sher has recently argued that Hume's account of his success at this time in his brief autobiography is "misleading," and claims that by 1752 Hume had little to show for his literary efforts in terms of financial reward and professional standing (Sher 2000, 44–47). Sher thinks that Hume's works were successful commercially through adoption of "brilliant marketing strategy," when they were "repackaged" in a first collected edition, namely, the Essays and Treatises of 1753, in which the Political Discourses were presented in the fourth volume. In this way, according to Sher, Hume "repackaged" himself as an author with a "coherent identity as a philosophical writer," and truly began to achieve fame and success in the literary marketplace. However, a simpler explanation is that *Political Discourses* appears in the fourth and last volume of the *Essays and Treatises*, ostensibly in 1753, because it was the most recent of Hume's books to be published.[14]

In the years after the publication of his book, Hume corresponded on monetary theory with the witty and, at times, highly irascible, pro-Jacobite peer, Lord Elibank, author of *Thoughts on Money, Circulation, and Paper Currency*, published in May 1758. Writing to Elibank the month before, on 6 April 1758, Hume clarified his opinion, that "Multiplication of Money" was advantageous neither to an industrious country nor to an idle one, because "it seems to prevent the Importation of as much Bullion (which has a real intrinsic Value) as the paper amounts to" (Mossner 1962, 441–42). He also pointed out that while an increase in the money supply increases demand, prices will remain the same if the increase of the demand goes along with an increase in "Industry" (production). Hume also recollected to Elibank that provisions in La Flèche, where he resided after moving from Reims, according to a Catholic English woman he knew there, cost a "third of the price, which they bore in Suffolk, where she usually liv'd." Hume believed this was the case because of the "greater Encrease of Money in England" (Mossner 1962, 446). This anecdote reveals Hume interpreting comparative French/English experience in the light of the quantity theory of money.[15]

The letters to Elibank date from the same time as his correspondence with James Oswald (10 October 1749, 1 November 1750), Lord Kames (4 March 1758), and Morellet (10 July 1769) (Hume 1955, 190–99, 199–202, 214–16), thus constituting a rich quarry for this concern of Hume's with monetary theory (Wennerlind 2005, 6, 10, 11). Hume was not entirely consistent, however, in developing his views on money in his essays and correspondence. Though genial in acknowledging errors (Hume 1955, 190–98), perhaps he did not rise above the standards of his age in identifying contemporary sources (Rashid 1984, 158–59). These possibly included Vanderlint's pamphlet on money of 1734, already discussed, and Cantillon's *Essai sur la nature du commerce* (n.d. [1755]), which circulated in manuscript before it was published in the version found in Hume's library (Norton and Norton 1996, 83 n. 289).

Following the years given over to writing his *History of England* (1754–62), in which economic theory and economic history play a considerable role, Hume returned to diplomatic service, becoming British embassy secretary and finally chargé d'affaires in Paris (1763–66), where he received acclaim suggesting he was regarded as the foremost man of letters in Europe. While in Paris at this time, Hume encountered the Jewish financier Isaac de Pinto, scion of one of the wealthiest Portuguese Sephardic families in the Netherlands. Pinto had been an adviser to the Stadtholder, William IV, whom Hume regarded as the hero of a bourgeois revolution. Pinto had also been deeply involved in the affairs of the Dutch West India Company, and was active in the London money market on the eve of the Seven Years War in 1759, raising for the British government a loan of £6,600,000 (Popkin 1970; 1974). When his financial situation in the Netherlands altered for the worse, he settled at Paris from 1761 until 1764, acting as a tax consultant, and passing around to various readers including Hume his manuscript *Traité de la circulation et de crédit*. With Hume's encouragement, he revised it for publication (Pinto 2000 [1771], 122), and it proved to be the most knowledgeable response to Hume's views on and concerns about circulation (Fieser 2001).

Pinto's stay in Paris overlapped with the period of Hume's involvement in negotiations for the conclusion of the Seven Years War. Soon after the signing of the Treaty of Paris in March 1763, Pinto learned that concessions given to the French East Company were very costly for its British counterpart, and he found a way for pressure to be put on the French to change the treaty in favor of the British East India Company. Hume helped him secure a reward in the form of a British pension in 1767–68. This success was duly celebrated, "chez Mr David Hume" in London, and at this time the two men discussed their divergent views on economics.

In due course, Pinto's *Traité de la circulation et de crédit* (1771) was translated into English, ostensibly by the Reverend Stephen Baggs, but in fact by his cousin, Sir Philip Francis, reputed author of the *Letters of Junius* (1768–73). The resulting *Essay on Circulation and Credit, in Four Parts; and a Letter on the Jealousy of Commerce* was published in London in 1774 (Popkin 1974, 117). Francis hid his involvement in the translation, as he did not want to damage his chances of a patronage appointment from Prime Minister North, by praising too enthusiastically the advantages of public debt (Cardoso and Nogueira 2005, 19).

Pinto himself had highly positive views on the national debt and speculating in government securities in the stock market. He asserted that the debt supported credit and promoted increases in the circulation of money and goods. According to Pinto, "M. Hume, quand il écrivit cet Essai, n'avoit pas fait encore un analyse exacte & commerçante de la circulation, de la Nature des fonds & des rentes" (2000 [1771], 124).[16] Pinto alleged, however, that his explanation of proper management of the national debt through refinancing and conversion into annuities satisfied Hume that it was not the menace he considered it to be. Pinto's chief argument was that each new loan to the government created "un Capital artificial & nouveau, qui n'existoit pas auparavant, qui devient permanent, fixe & solide, & qui, au moyen du credit, circule à l'avantage du public, comme si c'étoit un trésor effectif en argent dont le Royaume se fut enrichi."[17] This process of "circulation" had real outcomes that made the nation richer, making the burden of interest that much easier to bear (ibid., 44, 48).

Pinto was deeply perturbed by Hume's "voluntary bankruptcy" answer to the debt problem (2000 [1771], 122–23), since he reckoned that the fate of the 17,000 creditors Hume was prepared to sacrifice in a public bankruptcy would in turn affect through consequent deflation the millions in the population that Hume wished to safeguard (Hume 1985aa [1752h], 361–65; Winch 1996). Pinto wrote that his account of circulation and public debt had satisfied Hume: "Je crois l'avoir tranqilleté là-dessous" (2000 [1771], 122).[18] In the event, however, Hume never gave up on this stand on the alarming expansion of national debt (Murphy 2000, 76–77). Nevertheless, he did withdraw from the 1768 edition of his essay "Of Public Credit" his admission of skepticism about the claims for the benefits of circulation in bringing to debtor governments the means for carrying out their business, and to creditors the returns for supporting and possibly enriching their lives.

Donald Winch (1996, 14 n. 31) suggests that Pinto's arguments about "circulation" caused Hume to curtail his essay in this fashion. At the least, it is possible that Pinto with his informed viewpoint about the role of paper money and futures transaction on the stock market, as essential element of the modern world's financial system (Nijenhuis 1992, 75–78, 199), made an impression on Hume, and reinforced the effort of Melon and Du Tot to clarify the nature of circulation in the economic domain. Approaching the end of his life, however, Hume the philosophical economist was more concerned about the politics of public debt as he assessed the problems of his time, with a Country Whig bias (Pocock 1985c, ch. 7; Winch 1996, 2), than about the theories of the financier Pinto. It remained for Dugald Stewart, when he was professor of moral philosophy at Edinburgh (1785–1810), to pronounce in his lectures on political economy that Pinto was the "most ingenious and best informed writer who has hitherto appeared as an advocate for the policy of our national debt" (Stewart 1994 [1855–56], 9:218).

In summary, this paper argues that Hume's ideas on political economy can be associated with distinct episodes in his life. His early problem over the meaning of *circulation*, in the aftermath of the bursting of the South Sea Bubble, seems to have awakened an interest in problems of economic analysis and their political implications. This interest may have been deepened through actual experience of international commerce in Bristol. Hume's ambitious scheme for a "science of man," which included economics, was advanced in the novel setting of France, then recovering from financial collapse caused by a frenzy over circulation. His awareness of contemporary economic debate in Europe is recorded both in his "Early Memoranda" and early essays. Subsequently, he investigated the resource base, human potential, allocation strategies, rivalry, wars, and diplomacy of the major European powers of his time, all of which informed his *Political Discourses* of 1752. Thereafter, an encounter with a new man on the economic scene, Isaac de Pinto, seems to have made Hume revise his thinking about public debt and circulation. These experiences and challenges are mirrored to a remarkable extent in his correspondence. When this story is put together, we can chart the emergence of the persuasive and cosmopolitan economic theorist, David Hume.

Notes

I am very grateful to Herr Michael Tochtermann, former director of Verlag Wirtschaft und Finanzen (Düsseldorf), for providing books by and about Isaac de Pinto; also to Professors José Luís Cardoso (Lisbon) and António Vasconcelos Nogueira (Aveiro), and Professor Tatsuya Sakamoto (Tokyo), for sending, respectively, copies of their papers on Pinto and Hume's "Early Memoranda."

1 Citations are taken from the 1985 edition of Hume's *Essays: Moral, Political, and Literary*, edited by Eugene F. Miller, but I have also made use of Hume's *Political Essays*, edited by Knud Haakonssen (1994), which contains valuable notes and commentary, as does Gilles Robel's translation of the *Essays* (2001).

2 Since Raymond Klibansky and Ernest Campbell Mossner published *New Letters of David Hume* in 1954, much more of Hume's correspondence has been discovered, and this paper draws on letters to Jeremy Birch, Michael Ramsay, Lord Elibank, and Isaac de Pinto, which shed new light on Hume's economic concerns.

3 In Hume's time, boys were sent to Scottish universities in their early teens (Hume 1969 [1932], 1:13; Barfoot 1990, 151 n. 2).

4 The directors of the South Sea Company devised plans in 1722 to manage publicly the effects of the "scandalous transfers" of their predecessors, and accede to the preeminence of the Bank of England in taking over the national debt. They recorded their schemes in the "Minutes of the General Court" for the years 1721–33 (British Library, South Sea Company Papers: MS. 25544).

5 In Hume's boyhood, there was an alarming cycle of English bankruptcies—220 in 1720, 288 in 1721, 240 in 1722—due to the collapse of the South Sea Bubble (Ashton 1959, 172). As well, many Scottish peers, for example, the Duke of Montrose, also Lords Rothes, Dunmore, Hyndford, Irvine, and Belhaven (a notorious plunger in stock schemes in Paris and London), suffered in the crash, which was said to have diminished their political power thereafter (Carswell 1993, 162–63).

6 In Edinburgh, Allan Ramsay satirized the bubble with a "South Sea Sang," printed in 1720, and followed this up with other topical pieces in the *Collected Poems* of 1721, whose large subscription list included virtually all the Scottish nobility. Ramsay sold his poetry from a bookshop close to Hume's Edinburgh home. See Ramsay (1954, 1:153–82; 2000, vol. 3).

7 Hont (2005f [1993]) discusses six paragraphs added to "Of Public Credit" in 1764 (Hume 1985aa [1752h], 358–60) as being responsible for the essay's notoriety as a "jeremiad which can be read as the worst of eighteenth-century Country tracts," directed against immoderate contraction of public debt, and consequent delivery of power in Britain to moneyed interests at the expense of the landed gentry. Curiously, Hont overlooks Hume's decision in 1768 to omit the passage about circulation featured in this paper.

8 Perhaps this was Swift's friend, Dr. Arbuthnot, or perhaps another Scottish physician practicing in England, Dr. George Cheyne: Hume ([1932], 2:18); Mossner (1944, 135–52; 1980, 84–88); Wright (2003).

9 Locke admired this book, according to Schumpeter (1986, 197 n. 5).

10 In some ways this echoes Addison's *Spectator* no. 69(1982, 438).

11 Adam Smith's phrase in the *Wealth of Nations* (1976 [1776], 5.1.e.22).

12 Antoin Murphy (1997, 5, 335 n. 10) thinks that Hume refers in this passage to Law operating during the regency of Orléans. Eugene Miller seems to be wrong in citing the period of the ascendancy of Mazarin, 1643–61 (Hume 1985aa [1752h], 361 n. 15).

13 But Hume on occasion was prepared to argue that England's financial reserves could hold up against shocks, explaining in his *History of England*, with reference to Charles II's ability to borrow money even after the Stop of the Exchequer in 1672, that "public credit, instead of being so delicate a nature, as we are apt to imagine, is, in reality, so hardy and robust, that it is very difficult to destroy it" (1792, 8:326).

14 See Todd (1974, 194–96): the first collected edition of Hume's works (1753) involved the resetting of "all the separate volumes previously issued, the reissue of the earlier volumes with cancel titles and, where the cancels were not prepared in sufficient numbers, the further reissue of certain volumes with original volumes still intact." The two-volume, quarto edition of Hume's *Essays and Treatises* of 1772, the last he saw through to press, established the canon of his writings, other than his *History of England* and posthumously published writings. The various works are grouped thus: Vol. 1, *Essays, Moral, Political, and Literary*; Part 1, the *Essays* except for *Political Discourses*; Part 2, *Political Discourses*; Vol. 2, the first *Enquiry*, *Dissertation on the Passions*, the second *Enquiry*, and *Natural History of Religion*. The order here is in part generic and in part chronological, perhaps acknowledging that Hume's writings on religion excited most contemporary interest.

15 Hume presents the kernel of the quantity theory of money, namely, that the price level is related to the nation's money stock, in "Of Interest" (Hume 1985v [1752d], 295–97). He was probably responding to Locke's version of the theory in *Some considerations of the consequences of the lowering of interest, and raising the value of money* (1692), which suggested, incorrectly, that money's value was inversely related to the quantity of money in circulation (Locke 1991, vol. 1). Hume argued that flows of gold could not get out of line with flows of trade, since if too little gold flowed into Britain, relative to flows elsewhere, then British goods would become cheaper than those abroad, and more gold would come to Britain to buy them for export.

16 "Hume, when he wrote this essay ["Of Public Credit"], had not yet made an exact and commercial analysis of the circulation, of the Nature of funds and annuities." (This and the next two notes translated by the author.)

17 "An artificial and new Capital, which did not exist before, which becomes permanent, fixed, and solid, and which, in the medium of credit, circulates to the advantage of the public, as if this were an effective treasure in silver, from which the Kingdom grew rich."

18 "I believe him to have peace of mind on that subject."

3 Hume and Superfluous Value (or the Problem with Epictetus' Slippers)

Christopher J. Berry

1.

Hume opens "Of Refinement in the Arts" by stating that "luxury" is a word of "uncertain signification" (Hume 1985t [1752b], 268). He knows full well the position of, on the one hand, those "severe moralists" (Sallust is named as an example) who berate "luxury" as a vice and, on the other, those men of "libertine principles" (Mandeville is his unnamed exemplar) who treat luxury as advantageous even when "vicious." As he is wont, Hume states that this essay is designed to correct these opposed extremes. It is clear, however, if only from the relative attention paid to it, that it is the former position that is principally in his sights. That focus is unsurprising because it is central to a particular animus within his political economy. It is this animus—his engagement with a distinctive but well-established and still well-entrenched moral stance—that is the concern of this paper. While to look on Hume from this perspective is not novel, its ramifications are more extensive than might be supposed. I here give an indication of this extent and limit the discussion to a key central argument. This argument I seek to capture in the notion (or conceit) of "superfluous value."[1]

The late Stoic philosopher Epictetus is recorded as saying that the measure for a slipper or sandal is the foot. "Measure" (*metron*) here means not merely that size-eight slippers fit size-eight feet, but, more significantly, that a slipper's purpose is to protect the foot. Once that appropriate measure is forsaken then there are no limits; there is nothing inappropriate about, successively, a gilded, a purple, and an embroidered slipper (Epictetus 1928, par. 39). The clear message is that these are superfluous refinements that should be eschewed. It follows, moreover, that there is no poverty in possessing "merely" an unadorned sandal; indeed, the converse is true.

The meaning of *poverty* here needs unfolding. There is a long-standing discourse within which poverty has a positive moral connotation. Within this discourse two emphases can be identified. The first of these is exemplified by Epictetus' Stoicism but is equally manifest in the ascetic tradition in Christianity, with its notion of apostolic or voluntary poverty. Here, like its contextual close relations, *simplicity* and *austerity*, as well as *severity*, poverty refers to the estimable practice of temperance and continence. To be severe in this sense is to be in control of oneself and thus of one's actions; it is to know the true and proper value of things and to be in a position of for-swearing temptations, that is, things of illusory value or luxurious super-fluities like embroidered slippers. The second emphasis is more civic and is embodied in Sparta and "ancient Rome." Of the latter Hume explicitly says that (according to the severe moralists) it combined its "poverty and rusti-city" with "virtue and public liberty" (Hume 1985t [1752b], 275). This virtue is undermined once luxury goods for private consumption (like embroidered slippers) are available; in the words of the seventeenth-century civic moral-ist, Algernon Sidney, poverty is "the mother and nurse of . . . virtue" (1990, 254).[2] Hume reflects this duality of emphasis when he states he will consider the "effects of refinement both on private and on public life" (269). One consequence, common to both emphases, of situating poverty in this lexicon is that it is a product of choice or will or reason. Thus understood it is possible to draw a conceptual distinction between poverty and being impo-verished (or necessitous, that is, having no choice). As we will see, this dis-tinction is a significant ingredient in Hume's political economy.

There is an accompanying philosophical anthropology to this moralized use of poverty. This can be expressed variously but, at its core, is the hier-archical division between reason and desire. In its paradigmatic Aristotelian form, the *enkratic* man acts from choice, not from "desire" (*epithumia*) (Aristotle 1976, 1111b15). All humans properly aim at (*hairetos*) *eudaimonia*, which is a "perfect and self-sufficient end" (Aristotle 1097b15–20). Those who attain *eudaimonia* are living life as it should be led; it is a complete life and, as such, one without "desire." (Epictetus has no "craving" for a slipper beyond what is necessary to protect his feet.) There are, it is true, "natural desires" (*phusikais epithumiais*) but these are naturally (*kata phusin*) limited (Aris-totle 1118b15–18) and it is a hallmark of the *akratic* that they pursue bodily pleasures excessively and *para . . . orthon logon* (Aristotle 1151a10–12).[3]

In line with this anthropology, the virtue of poverty is expressed by the individual who, in the light of a rational apprehension of the natural order, self-disciplines desires so that indulgence is forsworn. Just as Epictetus appreciates the appropriate measure of slippers, so the Stoic sage will drink but not get drunk; likewise, one informed with Patristic teaching will forgo sex with—or as—a pregnant woman. Similarly, in the civic emphasis, the virtuous citizens of Rome's early years were portrayed as forgoing indulging themselves with the spoils of victory, such as by banqueting sumptuously and building magnificent villas, and, instead, as dedicating the resources to public monuments.[4] These examples underwrite the fact that this anthro-pology has a particular focus on the body. Of course, the body has needs that must be satisfied, but there is also a natural or rational limit to this satisfaction—hence drink only when thirsty and have sex only for the sake of conception and wear on one's feet only what is functionally needed for protection.

Here in the meeting of functional needs we have classically the place of economics—it deals literally with the order or rule of the household. Once again Aristotle lays down the basic model. The household is geared to the meeting of "everyday needs" (Aristotle 1977 1252b) and what makes them quotidian is their reference to the recurring somatic satisfactions—food, clothing, and shelter for warmth, protection, and nurture. The activity of meeting these needs is for Aristotle a finite task, that is, though they ceaselessly recur there is an inherent, natural (*kata phusin*) limit that identifies proper satiation (Aristotle 1977, 1256b). In this context exchange can take place, but this too is properly finite. Hence a shoe may be exchanged for food but only so long as the recipients use them for their proper ends— meeting the need for foot protection and hunger. What is not permissible is to produce the shoe for the sake of exchange (rather than need) (Aristotle 1257a). Aristotle is particularly exercised that those (*hoi kapeloi*) who spend their time exchanging will come to regard money-making (*chrēmatistikē*) as an end in itself rather than an instrumental activity. This inversion of means/end is a perversion, or corruption, for Aristotle, and one marker of this is that once the natural/rational limit of need-satisfaction is overstepped then the unnatural/subrational limitlessness of desire can take over.

Those who are taken over—who become "slaves" to desire, to bodily pleasures (see Epictetus 1928, par. 1; Sidney 1990, 254)—no longer live the simple, natural life of virtuous poverty; instead they are prone to a life of luxury. Epictetus' embroidered slippers would qualify as an item of luxury. It would be consistent for the "corrupted" owner of gilded purple slippers to feel poor when she (the gender is not incidental) sees an embroidered pair. This is an emotional issue (a "feeling"); it is certainly not a matter of rational judgment. Once the rationally determined natural limit is transgressed there is no resting place and, viewed from that perspective, life will always appear too short. Those who see matters in this light will become "soft through a life of luxury" and, accordingly, afraid of death (Seneca 1932, no. 78). Such fear is unmanly and it is here that we can discern the long-running association between luxury and softness and effeminacy. On an individual level, men who live a life of luxury become effeminate. That is to say they become "soft," unable to endure hardship and act courageously in the etymologically definitive masculine fashion.[5] To live luxuriously is thus to the detriment of both the resolve of individuals and the strength of their *patria*.

It follows that such a life is to be morally censured. Within this discourse, poverty and luxury exist as categorical opposites—as virtue and vice. However, it will follow that if the former term is displaced then the latter too is uprooted. If, that is, poverty is understood not as virtuous austerity but as necessitousness, then luxury can lose its moralized (categorical) meaning. This reconfiguration is Hume's radical agenda, his animus.

Implicit in this reconfiguration is a double shift. First, Hume associates poverty with a pre-existing sense of destitution,[6] linked traditionally to the plight of orphans, widows, the aged, and so on, who were the proper recipients of alms. This is a compassionate, not a severe, morality.[7] Secondly, he associates the necessity of labor (the traditional, specific lot of the poor) with the universal virtue of industry. In Hume this virtue is one of those qualities the purpose of which is to make mankind cheerful and happy and which are, as such, opposed to the severe or austere demands exacted by reason in order to control appetites, as enjoined by "the perpetual cant of the Stoics and Cynics" (Hume 1998, 6:21).[8] Luxury/commerce, as we will see, increases industry and thus both reduces destitution and augments the resources available for amelioration.

The reason why this can be an "agenda" for Hume is (sweepingly) because "luxury" had come again to the fore of debate in the later seventeenth and throughout the eighteenth century. The short-hand explanation for luxury's recrudescence is that its longevity gave to it a ready-made quality that enabled it to encapsulate the range of disquiet that had been generated by the pace of social change—by the emergence of a commercial society of private market relations as well as of public credit and national debt.[9] To debate "luxury" was to debate this emergence. The worries about commerce intensified—as is evident from the scale of the literature. The popularity of John Brown's *Estimate*, which went through six editions in its year of publication (1757), and which sums up the "character of the times" as manifesting "a vain, luxurious and selfish effeminacy," is merely an indicative case (Brown 1758, 1:29, 67, 129). A similar avalanche of literature is evident in France.[10] It is not that the articulation of these worries was particularly profound—there was a predictable sameness about them, with the moralized fate of Rome being a favorite *topos*. Though this might comprise a "tired litany" (Hont 2005e [1983]), it nonetheless had sufficient energy to warrant Hume taking issue.[11]

In an attempt to bring out an aspect of Hume's agenda in his "economic" essays, I employ as a term of art the idea of *superfluous value*. What Epictetus (and those severe and civic moralists who share his perspective on poverty) would consider to be an oxymoron is rather for Hume an expression of his repudiation of that outlook. He rejects the philosophical anthropology that privileges reason and he displaces the ethic of poverty. For Hume, to be poor is to be necessitous—it is to lack the basics. What commerce holds out is the way to improve that condition, and integral to that improvement is giving value to the production of luxury goods such as exquisitely embroidered slippers. There are two aspects to giving a positive evaluation of that footwear. First, they represent a source of pleasure or enjoyment that is intrinsically valuable in its own right—consumption is a good. Second, as consumption goods, their production and participation in a system of commerce has instrumental benefits that redound generally. I examine these in turn.

2.

This examination commences with a return to the beginning. In "Of Refinement in the Arts," having declared "luxury" to have an uncertain signification, Hume gives his own definition: luxury is "great refinement in the gratification of senses" (1985t [1752b], 268). This is not to be read censoriously as an endorsement of the moralists, because he goes on to declare, as a generalization, that "ages of refinement" are "both the happiest and most virtuous" (269). In a clear break, therefore, from the moralist tradition, Hume is coupling luxury/refinement with happiness/virtue, *not* opposing them.

Hume can now put forward arguments that would be anathema to the severe moralists. For current purposes we can focus on how Hume is able to give a positive gloss to the "superfluous"—why there is no inherent vice in those embroidered slippers. Such slippers would qualify as one of those "commodities which serve to the ornament and pleasure of life"; they represent an "innocent gratification" (272). Hume, indeed, scarcely bothers to argue for this innocence. He affirms that it would not occur to anyone that "indulging of any delicacy in meat, drink or apparel" is of itself a vice; unless, that is, they were "disordered by the frenzies of enthusiasm" (268). A little later, Hume reasserts the point by remarking that "refinement on the pleasures and conveniencies of life has no natural tendency to beget venality and corruption" (276). The fact that Hume is so disdainful reflects his animus, that his chief target is the moralized poverty/luxury pairing.

Underpinning this disdain is his rejection of the philosophical anthropology that underlies that moralism. The "modern" view, to which Hume subscribes, rejects the idea that desires can be limited to some fixed end. As Hobbes pointed out, the only way to be "free" of desire is to be dead. Desire, or "uneasiness of the mind" (Locke 1854, 2.21.31), *is* the spring or spur of action as humans move toward what they imagine will please and away from what they imagine will occasion pain. For Aristotle such mutability was characteristic of normative imperfection. It was this judgment that established the basic classical/Christian distinction between, on the one hand, the tranquil/ascetic life, devoted to the contemplation of the immutable First Cause or the eternal perfection of God, and, on the other, the mundane life, which is unceasingly at the beck and call of the demands of bodily desires.

According to Hume, the "arts of luxury" add to the "happiness of the state *since* they afford to *many* the opportunity of receiving enjoyments with which they would otherwise have been unacquainted" (1985s [1752a], 256; my emphasis). Humans, he continues, are roused to activity or industry by the presence of "objects of luxury" and by, consequently, a "desire of a more splendid way of life than what their ancestors enjoyed" (264). Hume does not specify the content of this splendor but we know from his definition that it encompasses sensual gratification and thus it is reasonable to suppose it refers to those same sorts of goods that were deprecated by the moralists—fine homes, fine food, and fine apparel like embroidered slippers. In addition, there is a dynamism to this desire—my ancestors may have thought gilded slippers the very acme of luxury; I know that hand-embroidered ones are far more desirable. Hume reinforces the anthropological fact that desire moves humans, and signals further his dismissal of the moralized perspective, when he also refers to "men's luxury" making them "covet" commodities (261) and, perhaps most strikingly of all, when he then enumerates as effective human motivations "avarice and industry, art and luxury" (263). Since "avarice" was uniformly condemned by the civic and severe moralists,[12] this statement alone effectively signals the switch in evaluations that has occurred. It is, moreover, not the only such statement. Elsewhere, Hume depicts avarice as a "constant and insatiable" "craving" (1985v [1752d], 149), as "universal" and thus operating "at all times on all persons" (1985k [1742a], 113), and as "obstinate" and thus "the spur of industry" (1985i [1741i], 93). As I will develop later, this spur is central to the benefits that flow from the recognition of superfluous value. When industry abounds then individuals will be not only opulent but happy as they "reap the benefit of . . . commodities so far as they gratify the senses and appetite" (1985s [1752a], 263).

Against the back-cloth of Epictetus' slippers, it is worth underlining the import of this remark. Sensual gratification is a source of happiness; to indulge one's appetites by delighting in a pair of embroidered slippers is not something to be severely censured. Furthermore, the inhabitants of opulent nations will "desire to have every commodity in the utmost perfection" (1985ee [1758], 329; cf. 1985s [1752a], 264). Epictetus' downward spiral of gilded, purple, and embroidered slippers is rather the upward thrust for more and better. And because this is comparative, and because this is rooted in the anthropology of infinite desire (cf. 264), then this "utmost perfection" is ever evanescent. One implication of this is the recognition of qualitative differences. The Epictetean view treats all these "departures" from functionality as superfluous. For Hume they are the essence of refinement. He aptly compares the gluttonous Tartars, who feast on dead horses, to the "refinements of cookery" experienced in the contemporary courts of Europe (1985t [1752b], 272). To develop refinement—as manifest both in the presence of qualitatively differentiated goods and in the ability to appreciate both the skill and the beauty of a fine meal or splendid slippers— is not to indulge in excess. Excess, as exhibited by the Tartars, is mere quantitative increase beyond some fixed sum but, as such, it is conceptually distinct from qualitative refinement. To recognize that goods possess superfluous value is to recognize and endorse that distinction.[13]

To own an elegant (refined) pair of slippers, with their "superfluous" stitchery, is not only satisfying but also makes a "statement"; their possession is an object of pleasurable pride. In an image that Smith adopts (Smith 1982, 4.1.10), Hume refers to men's minds as "mirrors" in which the owner of the slippers will see reflected the esteem of others and which, in its turn, supplies him with further satisfaction (Hume 2000a, 2.2.5.21; cf. Hume 1998, 6:30). This recognition of deep sociality, which Hume along with his compatriots regards as a foundation of the science of man (see Berry

2003a), affords another reason to dismiss the Epictetean perspective. The essence of the austere poverty prescribed by Epictetus was to be self-sufficient, not dependent on the views of others. It is the same outlook that sustains Christian asceticism and makes the hermit "saintly." For Hume these are "monkish virtues," which for him means they are really not virtues at all—recall that ages of refinement are the "most virtuous."[14]

This basic sociality is enhanced in commercial societies. In them there is both more sociability (as they "flock into cities" [1985t (1752b), 271]—recall ancient Rome's "rusticity") and a variety of differentially refined goods, so that their consumption takes place under the gaze of others. This "public" consumption imparts, once more, a dynamic to such societies. These "others," seeing how the owner of splendid slippers enjoys both the slippers and the social esteem that goes with their ownership, will seek to desire them also. This desire (though this is implicit in Hume, Smith makes it explicit) becomes one of the "passions" causing labor and thus increases both the quantity and quality of consumables (cf. 1985s [1752a], 261). In consequence, as I will develop in the next section, those who live in non-opulent states will be less "happy" because they will consume fewer and inferior commodities; they will be poor in the sense of being impoverished.

This recognition of the social context means that it would be misleading to think that Hume was crudely Epicurean. In his "economic" essays he treats happiness as more than passive (hedonistic) consumption. In "Of Refinement in the Arts" he analyses happiness into three inter-related components—repose, pleasure, and action (1985t [1752b], 269–70). Of these the last is given most weight. Repose or indolence is agreeable only in the short-term, as a necessary recuperative interlude, but if prolonged it subsides into lethargy and, in fact, "destroys all enjoyment." Pleasure, Hume thinks, is attained as much from the activity itself as it is from the enjoyment of its fruits. There is, he affirms, "no craving or demand of the human mind more constant and insatiable than that for exercise and employment"; this "desire" seems, as a result, to be the "foundation of most of our passions and pursuits" (1985v [1752d], 300). Action, industry, and employment or labor enlarge mental powers and faculties and, crucially, produce great social benefits.

3.

There are both political and economic benefits that ensue from the recognition and acceptance of superfluous value. As we have seen, an opulent nation is also a happy and industrious one. However, while that view might be accepted, there was a long-standing argument that such opulence represented the weakness of the nation, that is, a commercial nation given over to luxury would be soft (cf. Hirschman 1977, 64).

Hume rebuts this argument. A key part of his strategy is to develop a contrast between the civilized or refined on the one hand and the barbarous or rude on the other. (This contrast we have already met in the form of the contrast between Tartars and the European courts as well as between the rustic and the urban[e].) He declares that it is "peculiar" to "polished or . . . luxurious ages" that "industry, knowledge and humanity are linked together by an indissoluble chain" (1985t [1752b], 271). The converse, as neatly expressed in a later essay, is that rude states "are buried in ignorance, sloth and barbarism" (1985ee [1758], 328). Further, by extension, from what we ascertained in the previous section, its inhabitants will be unhappy and impoverished, unappreciative of "the pleasures of the mind as well as those of the body" (1985t [1752b], 271). Nonetheless, this positive argument in favor of "civilization" might still fall foul of the severe moralist's claim that "hardiness" is vital to national greatness, given that such greatness is measured by military strength. It is, accordingly, important to the argumentative success of Hume's ("political") defense of a commercial society that this view of "greatness" and its associated virtues is undermined.

A mark of the growth in "humanity," within civilized states, is that the "tempers" of men are "softened," and one manifestation of this softening of manners is that wars are less cruel and the aftermath more humane (274). Despite this Hume denies (here echoing Mandeville [1988, 1:122–23]) that this softening has enervated "the martial spirit." The supposed causal link between luxury and military weakness is undermined by the cases of France and England, that is, of the two most powerful *and* most polished and commercial societies (Hume 1985t [1752b], 275, cf. Hume 1894 [1754–62], 2:598–99).

Hume elaborates on this latter causal link. It is for him "according to the most natural course of things" that "industry and arts and trade encrease the power of the sovereign" *and* do so without impoverishing the people (1985s [1752a], 260). This combination is made possible by the very "superfluity" that industry in the pursuit of luxury has created. In times of peace this superfluity goes to the maintenance of manufactures and the "improvers of liberal arts" (hallmarks of civilization), but when an army is needed the sovereign levies a tax, the effect of which is to reduce expenditure on luxuries. This frees up, for the military, manpower that was previously employed in luxury-good production (261). In both "Of Commerce" (1985s [1752a], 262) and "Of Refinement in the Arts" (1985t [1752b], 272), Hume declares that the more labor is employed beyond "mere necessaries" the more powerful is the state due to the ease with which that labor (as a sort of "storehouse") may be converted to the "public service." Nor does it follow that these will be inferior troops. On the contrary, recalling the "indissoluble chain," these fighters will benefit not only from the technology that a civilized society can command but also from the overall higher level of intellectual competence.[15] All that the "ignorant and unskilful" soldiers of rude nations can achieve are "sudden and violent conquests" (1985s [1752a], 261; cf. Hume 1894 [1754–62], 1:627). As Culloden testified, they are ineffective against trained troops armed with sophisticated weaponry.[16] A further consequence of this is that the quintes-sentially male virtue of courage is now passé. The fact that Hume calls luxurious ages "most virtuous" signifies that he sees no loss—rather a gain—in the fact that this virtue is largely absent. Equity and justice have taken its place.[17]

Incidentally this argument also enables Hume to dispel, in effect, the classical prejudice against *hoi kapeloi*. Once the military virtues are down-graded then the accusations of effeminacy and commitment to their own private—rather than the common public—good leveled at merchants can be dismissed as untenable. This opens the way for an endorsement of their role. Hume thus unambiguously declares that "merchants are one of the most useful races of men." They "beget industry" and, in contrast to the landed gentry and peasantry, they accumulate capital that can be lent competitively at a rate to stimulate further commerce and consumption (1985v [1752d], 300–303). What is equally (if not more) significant about this vindication of merchants is its link with the virtues of a commercial society.

Merchants, as the "middling rank of men," are "the best and firmest basis of public liberty" (1985t [1752b], 277).[18] In essence, this is because they "covet equal laws." This linkage between liberty and equality under law (what he calls "true liberty" [Hume 1894 [1754–62], 1:115; cf. 1:175; 1:320; 2:602]) is a prerogative of commercial states—"progress in arts is rather favourable to liberty and has a natural tendency to preserve ... free government" (1985t [1752b], 277). Accordingly, one background condition of the happiness enjoyed by the citizens of such states is that they are "free." But this is a (private) liberty to receive securely what their art or industry has produced. There is a polemical bifocality to Hume's argument. We have already seen how he contrasts the rule-governed liberty of a com-mercial society (government of laws) with the licentious anarchy of pre-commercial eras (government of men), but here Hume is also, more subtly, subverting the "republican" or civic case for free government, in which public liberty is conceived of as embodying, and sustained by, active civic virtues.

In "Of Civil Liberty," Hume comments that ("notwithstanding the French") "there is something hurtful to commerce inherent in the very nature of absolute government" (1985i [1741i], 92). Though in this essay Hume puts this down to the lack of "honour" socially attributed to it, he is aware of the more common argument that absolutism breeds insecurity and is thus harmful to commerce. This latter argument Hume does address in "Of Taxes." There the most "pernicious" taxes are identified as "the arbi-trary" and a sovereign can easily convert these (such as a poll-tax) to "punishments on industry," so that they become "oppressive and intoler-able" (1985z [1752g], 345–46). A "natural if not an infallible effect of abso-lute government" is that the "common people" are "in poverty" (1985s [1752a], 265). For Hume the connection between liberty and opulence is a definitive characteristic of a civilized nation (in which industry, knowledge, and humanity cohere). Moreover, "honour" itself "acquires a fresh vigour" with the advance of knowledge and good education and one effect of this is to "restrain" the "love of money" (1985t [1752b], 274, 276).[19] Accordingly, refinement does *not* have a "natural tendency" to venality; once again, excess characterizes rude rather than civilized societies. This is reinforced by his notion of a civilized monarchy (1985i [1741i], 94; cf. 1985k [1742a], 125; 1894 [1754–62], 2:15). The decisive factor is not the type of regime but the presence of civilization, since it brings free government and does so without any recourse to the possession of civic virtues.

The prime embodiments of such virtues were Sparta and the Roman republic. Though beloved of the moralists (whom "we peruse in our infancy" [1985t (1752b), 275]), for Hume, these poleis were unworthy of emulation. Their much-vaunted poverty, supposedly the basis of their civic virtue and military prowess, rested on slavery, and slavery, at the very least, is "disadvantageous" to "happiness" (1985bb [1752i], 396).[20] Slaves are impoverished. Note here how Hume's reconfiguration has shifted the argument. Once the moralistic perspective—with its "idealised" advocacy of poverty as the transcendence of bodily desire—is displaced, then a more "realistic" assessment of the actual "experience" of being poor is possible. From that latter perspective slavery, not liberty, is the more likely outcome; peasants, he says explicitly, submit to slavery "from poverty" (1985t [1752b], 277). From that same realistic perspective, Spartan policy goes against the "natural bent of the mind" (1985s [1752a], 263), so that to govern along Spartan lines would require a "miraculous transformation of mankind" (1985t [1752b], 280).[21] Government, however, is not in the business of miracles; it must deal with the world and human nature as it is. (In his introduction to the *Treatise*, Hume declares "politics" to be a subject belonging to the "science of man" [Hume 2000a, 5].) All a government can do is channel human passions so that their effects minimize social disharmony. From the perspective of a grand simplifier, Hume's position is in stark contrast to the classical framework and its influential early-modern embodiment in the neo-Stoicism of, for example, Lipsius, for whom the proper response to unruly bodily passions was the cultivation and application of reason.[22] Rather, for Hume, the "magistrate" can "very often" only cure one vice by encouraging another, the effects of which are less damaging than the former's. It makes no sense to criticize the magistrate for not imposing in line with "classical" principles some objective, rational doctrine of the "good life." Instead the appropriate judgment is whether a particular policy promotes the material well-being of those individuals subject to it.

This is the crux of the "benefits" argument for superfluous value. This argument is a form of utilitarianism—"*Le superflu chose très nécessaire.*"[23] Understood in this way luxury can be justly cultivated because it is superior to sloth. The stimulus for such cultivation is initially external, since foreign trade has "given birth to domestic luxury" (1985s [1752a], 263–64). This has the effect of acquainting men with both the "pleasures of luxury" and the "profits of commerce." The latter are attained by exporting what is "superfluous at home" to nations where that commodity is in short supply. The appreciation of such "great profits" stimulates more merchants to set up in competition. This dynamic is replicated by domestic manufacturers, as they seek to "emulate the foreign in their improvements." Industry is thus advanced to the benefit of all. But "delicacy" is also stimulated by the pleasures of luxury and, as we have seen, desires for a more splendid way of living ensue. Delicacy and industry come together, as noted above, to work up commodities to "utmost perfection." Hence the happiness of those who live in refined societies, able to wear elegant ("the last word" in) slippers.

Hume's defense of luxury still enables him to allow that it can be "vicious" as well as innocent (virtuous). What he means by vicious is nonbeneficial or without advantage to the public (1985t [1752b], 269, 278).[24] His argument is exiguous and is little more than a jibe at Mandeville's supposed casuistry— Hume sees no need to deny that pernicious luxury is poisonous (279).[25] However, this brevity is to be expected once it is appreciated that Hume's animus is directed at the moralist critique of luxury. In effect, "vicious luxury" for Hume describes an individual who, by confining gratification to himself, is unable to execute those "acts of duty and generosity" that his station and fortune require. Even here the thrust is that the virtue of relieving the poor and the necessitous (279) disperses gratifications more widely to public advantage. Hume's argument is casual precisely because he has already displaced the ethic of poverty and its counterpart deprecation of luxury. Once poverty becomes thought of as necessitousness or impoverishment, then luxury, as its counterpart, is so only contingently, rather than categorically. That is, if we criticize someone for purchasing embroidered slippers ahead of a staple, our criticism represents a judgment on the buyer's priorities.

Such a judgment, however, is relative (contingent) and not absolute (categorical) in at least two respects. First, what counts as a staple is not necessarily fixed (poverty is relative). Hume recognizes, as his contemporaries did, that one-time luxuries become necessities,[26] which implies that the relation between them is temporally contingent. Second, "value" is not intrinsic but relative. Hume himself says the "value which all men put upon any particular pleasure depends on comparison and experience" (276; cf. Hume 2000a, 2.1.6.2) (recall the inadequacy with which a pair of "merely" gilded slippers is now viewed). It is at least feasible that I might "set my heart on" owning such slippers to the extent that I deliberately skew my expenditures to afford them—you might think I am foolish but for me it is a sacrifice worth making; the slippers truly have superfluous value. Regardless, what Hume is at pains to reaffirm is that, though luxury "when excessive" can generate both private and public ills, nevertheless, it is still better to accept it than attempt vainly to eradicate it (1985t [1752b], 279–80). It is a trade-off. Without the spur to industry that luxury supplies, individuals (and thence their society) will fall into sloth and idleness. The social and individual cost of such outcomes outweighs any benefits that might conceivably accrue from a proscription on "luxury"—a circumstance the historical record bears out.[27]

In other words, once luxury is detached from its moralistic anchorage, then it can be viewed "positively." Of course, the evolution of ideas is not smooth, and luxury as the prerogative of the "idle rich" continued (and perhaps continues) to be criticized, though even here it is Hume's bugbear of "sloth" rather than luxury itself that is the real target. Rather more symptomatic is that, once luxury was detached from a moralistic context and "economics" developed as a discipline, luxury came to attain a technical neutral meaning as high-income elasticity of demand.

The shift away from moralism that Hume's account exemplifies means that luxury can be understood as the (contingent) opposite of necessity. It can be assessed by the extent to which it promotes employment, industry, population, and all-around national strength (and by the opportunity costs of its absence). And central to this enhancement is its improvement of the conditions of the poor. As we noted above, Hume explicitly states that in ages of refinement "many" can now "enjoy" the "finer arts"; such pleasures are not the pre-rogative of the (few) rich. The more people are employed in the "mechanical arts," then the more an appropriate equality will be enjoyed, that is, when every person "ought to enjoy the fruits of his labour, in full possession of all the necessaries and many of the conveniencies of life" (1985s [1752a], 265). This enjoyment adds more to the happiness of the poor than it diminishes that of the rich. Moreover, this "equality" inhibits the rich from increasing burdens "on the poor" and oppressing them still further (265; cf. Hume 1998, 3:25). A life confined to "necessity" now signifies not the austere life of poverty but an impoverished one, a life of misery. There is nothing ennobling or redemp-tive about *this* poverty. Hume spells this out unambiguously in an earlier essay, "Of National Characters," when he exclaims that "poverty and hard labour debase the minds of the common people" (1985q [1748a], 198).[28]

His rejection of the virtue of poverty exemplifies Hume's rejection of the mercantilist and Mandevillean advocacy of "low wages."[29] In order for the manufacture of slippers (beyond Epictetus' severe criterion) to act as a "spur" to industry, sufficient "spending power" has to be present in the economy. While Hume's dismissal of the "utility of poverty" (Furniss 1920, chap. 6) is based on economic considerations, it also reveals a loosely con-strued utilitarian ethic—to be poor is to be unhappy and that "painful" state is "bad." Again, just as the degree of "civilization" is more decisive than political form when it comes to liberty, so the "poverty" which accompanies the absence of industry, will occur whether the government be republican or monarchical (1985s [1752a], 267).

4.

From the perspective of the simple/poor life, any alteration to Epictetus' functional slipper is unwarranted, for, as noted earlier, the mutable is the imperfect. There is seemingly no place for change or innovation; a slipper simply does what a slipper does—keep feet warm indoors. This fixity is a corollary of the categorical opposition between poverty and luxury. But once poverty becomes impoverishment then its relation with luxury becomes contingent and potentially dynamic.

One of the striking things about the moral critique of luxury is that in practice it has often served to underwrite a hierarchical status quo. Politically, Hume is no egalitarian, but his recognition of superfluous value does betoken implicitly a rejection of the precommercial world in which, for example, sumptuary laws operated. This legislation sought to preserve the pecking order, to attempt to maintain "distance"[30] through an ostentatious display of wealth, and thus to confine the incidence of a good and prevent its diffusion. Luxury, "new" wealth, always threatened to overturn such regulations. Those in the lower ranks of these societies may well have wanted some of those privileged goods, like embroidered slippers, but that desire was a mark of their unworthiness. Intrinsic to Hume's animus is the rebuttal of that disparagement. This egalitarianism should not be misinterpreted—Hume is no more an "economic" egalitarian than he is a political one. Rather, what his view represents is closer to what Werner Sombart called *Versachlichung*, the wish to enjoy the tangible reality of magnificent clothes and comfortable homes (Sombart 1913, 112).[31] It is the enjoyment of such goods that intrinsically—and the motivating desire to attain them that instrumentally—gives "value" to the "superfluous." And since the presence of that enjoyment and that motivation in an age of refinement makes us at once happy and virtuous, then the desire on the part of the "have-nots" to those goods currently possessed by the "haves" is legitimate.[32] Indeed this desire exemplifies the "natural bent of the mind"; it is the view of human nature that the science of man underwrites (endorses).

To offer a generalizing conclusion, one consequence of rejecting the normative superiority of the eternally immutable is the acceptance of the worth of the mundanely mutable, of what has been called "the affirmation of ordinary life" (Taylor 1989, pt. 3). Life, from being for Epictetus a "thing indifferent" or for civic moralists a "thing" that can be nobly sacrificed (*dulce et decorum est pro patria mori*), attains value for its own sake. Politically this means that desires are to be accommodated, not proscribed, as the sovereign's interest lies not in the specific content of the desires, but only in the likelihood of their peaceful co-existence. This is the view that comes to be called "liberalism." In effect, liberalism valorizes the mundane. When seen against this admittedly broadly drawn backcloth, Hume's recognition of what has here been called "superfluous value" is an endorsement of that valorization and a key ingredient of his political economy.

Notes

1 I used this term (without specific reference to Hume) in passing in Berry (1999). This paper develops some points made therein.

2 This is not a novel distinction; it occasioned considerable debate in the Middle Ages. The canon lawyer Huguccio (of Pisa) (d. 1210), for example, in his commentary (1188) on Gratian's *Decretum* (1140), elaborated on this distinction between voluntary and involuntary poverty. He divided the poor into three categories. There were those who while born poor willingly endured it as an expression of their love of God, and there were those who deliberately surrendered their possessions that they might live a virtuous Christian life. Both of these exemplified voluntary poverty. The third category, however, comprised those who were destitute and liable to be inhibited from achieving the higher moral values. This was involuntary poverty. However, the thrust here is on the involuntary poor being inhibited; as the first category demonstrates, the dominant sensibility was that poverty was not of itself an evil to be extirpated. Indeed, Stoic echoes can still be heard in Huguccio's explicit identification of this category with those who are poor because they are filled with the "voracity of cupidity" (quoted in Tierney 1959, 11). It is that "sensibility" that changes and is expressed by Hume.

3 Aristotle links incontinence (*akrasia*) with softness and luxury (*malakia, truphē*), where the latter is sometimes revealingly translated as "effeminacy" (Aristotle 1976, 1145a35).

4 Cf. Sallust (1930, par. 9). Of course, this is a rhetorical ploy but that presupposes established judgments. For commentary on the practice of public endowment ("evergetism") see Veyne (1976).

5 The pagan/classical roots of this were exploited by early Christians. Tertullian (1951, 2:13), for example, talked of *fidei virtus* being rendered effeminate (*effeminari potest*) by the softening of luxury (*deliciae*).

6 Cf. his characterization, "when a poor man appears, the disagreeable images of want, penury, hard labour, dirty furniture, coarse or ragged cloathes, nauseous meats and distasteful liquor, immediately strike our fancy" (Hume 1998, 6:33). The references to apparel, furnishing, and food recall the focus on bodily needs.

7 In one of his few explicit references to Epictetus, Hume remarks that "he scarcely ever mentioned the sentiment of humanity and compassion but in order to put his disciples on their guard against it" (1998, app. 4.14).

8 The critique of "austere pretenders" who talk of "useless austerities and rigours, suffering and self-denial" is a recurrent theme; see Hume (1998, 9:15).

9 There is now an extensive literature on the growth of "luxury trade/goods" and patterns of consumption. A recent collection that reviews (and adds to) that literature is M. Berg and E. Eger (eds.) (2003).

10 Cf. E. Ross (1976), S. Maza (1997), D. Roche (1993, 507–20), M. Labriolle-Rutherford (1963), and J. Shovlin (2000).

11 I forgo discussion/speculation as to his motives, but see the papers of R. Emerson and I. Hont in this volume.

12 Cf. Sallust's remark that public mores had been corrupted by luxury and avarice, as poverty became a disgrace rather than a virtue and *corpus animumque virilem effeminat* (1930, pars. 5, 11, 12).

13 Hume does on occasion employ the term "refinement" less positively (see, for example, his early essay "Of Simplicity and Refinement in Writing," but it recurs in "Of Commerce" (254), where he comments, à propos modes of thinking, that "an extraordinary refinement affords a strong presumption of falsehood"). I am grateful to Eric Schliesser for drawing my attention to this more negative usage.

14 It is not merely circumstantial that, at the very start of "Of Refinement in the Arts," Hume chooses a monk to exemplify someone who is disordered by the frenzies of enthusiasm as he covenanted with himself never to look out of his cell window on to the "noble prospect." Cf. Hume (1998, 9:3).

15 In his *History* Hume implicitly connects the development of artillery with humanity (the third link on the chain) when he observes that, though "contrived for the destruction of mankind," it has "rendered battles less bloody" (Hume 1894 [1754–62], 1:498).

16 Not that Hume was starry-eyed about the competence of contemporary military conduct. He witnessed first-hand the disastrous campaign in Brittany of St. Clair (Mossner 1980, chap.15).

17 Cf. Hume (1998, 7:15), "it is indeed observable that among all uncultivated nations who have not as yet had full experience of the advantages attending beneficence, justice and the social virtues, courage is the predominant excellence." (A little later the "social virtues" are identified as "humanity, clemency, order, tranquillity.") A particular case is sixteenth-century Scotland when "arms" prevailed over "laws" so that "courage preferably to equity or justice was the virtue most valued and respected" (1894 [1754–62], 2:82). See also the Anglo-Saxons (1894 [1754–62], 1:10,115).

18 See Forbes (1975, 176ff), however, for further (complicating) comment.

19 It is true that Hume remarks that "it is an infallible consequence of all industrious professions, to beget frugality, and make the love of gain prevail over the love of pleasure" (1985v [1752d], 301). But two comments are in order. First, this itself expresses the differentiation of a commercial society since Hume uses *industrious* in a narrow sense to refer to merchants in distinction from lawyers and physicians as well as the landed gentry. Second, these frugal merchants are nonetheless beneficial because they use their wealth to stimulate industry through investment.

20 Hume makes a telling *ad hominem* critique of Seneca, who is quoted as complaining about the beating of servants not as an example of cruelty but of the disorders attendant on luxury (1985bb [1752i], 386).

21 For an examination of Hume's treatment of Sparta see Berry (1994, 142–52).

22 Lipsius (1586, bk. 1, chap. 5) distinguishes *ratio* (from obedience to which flows command of all lusts [*cupidines*]) from *opinio* (through which, as the offspring of the body, the vices rule).

23 Voltaire's *Le Mondain* (2003 [1763], l:22). There is here detectable a critique of Fénelon (1962 [1699], 453–54), the most influential critic of luxury in early eighteenth-century France who had contrasted *les arts superflus* to *les vrais besoins* that were imposed by nature (cf. Bonolas 1987). Voltaire was directly influenced by Melon and indirectly (probably) by Mandeville. Hume knew Melon's *Essai politique sur le Commerce* (1734) and cites him in "Of Commerce" and "Of Money." For discussions of Hume's reception in France see the papers by L. Charles, I. Hont, and J. Shovlin in this volume.

24 Hume had called luxury (along with prodigality, irresolution, and uncertainty) "vicious" in the *Treatise*, the fault being that these characteristics "incapacitate us for business and action" (Hume 2002a, 3.3.4.7). In line with Hume's later account in "Of Refinement in the Arts," this fault is consequential, not intrinsic. I am grateful to Carl Wennerlind for drawing my attention to this passage.

25 Sallust (1930, par. 11) had declared avarice a *venenis malis*.

26 Melon (1842, 742), for example, "*ce qui était luxe pour nos pères est à présent commun, et ce qui l'est pour nous ne le sera pas pour nos neveux.*" Also Mandeville (1988, 1:169–72).

27 Cf. his account of England under Elizabeth when the "nobility were by degrees acquiring a taste for elegant luxury"; though this led to the decay of "glorious hospitality," yet it is "more reasonable to think that this new turn of expense promoted the arts and industry, while the ancient hospitality was the source of vice, disorder, sedition and idleness" (Hume 1894 [1754–62], 2:601).

28 He is similarly explicit when he depicts the era of the Normans as one during which the "Languishing state of commerce kept the inhabitants poor and contemptible; and the political institutions were calculated to render that poverty perpetual" (Hume 1894 [1754–62], 1:320; cf. 1:2, 127).

29 There has been some debate over this. The text most quoted as indicating Hume was an advocate of low wages is his report that "'tis always observed in years of scarcity, if it be not extreme, that the poor labour more and really live better than in years of great plenty" (1985z [1752g], 635). This is cited by Johnson who treats Hume as "partially" accepting low wages as incentive (1937, 287), by Himmelfarb (1984, 51), and by Furniss (1920, 122). However, Furniss later identifies Hume as urging the utility of increasing real wages so that the standard of living might rise (189). According to Coats (1958), Hume presents both sides but the main weight of his case was against restrictions on the expansion of labourers' wants and improvement of their living standards. (Coats (1992, 1:90) elsewhere is more emphatic in aligning Hume with the view that a rising standard of living was a good for all.) The passage from "Of Taxes" was omitted from the 1768 and subsequent editions of the essays (note also the conditional clause). However, see Hume (1894 [1754–62], 2:259), where "necessity" is cited as required to shake people from "habits of indolence." Hume is noncommittal about the Elizabethan Poor Law. It is, however, consistent with his stress on action and the virtue of industry that labourers are more deserving than sturdy beggars (though he is contemptuous of Elizabeth's declaration of martial law to rid London of "idle vagabonds" (1894 [1754–62], 2:583)).

30 Cf. Bourdieu (1979, 58), "*le pouvoir économique est d'abord un pouvoir de mettre la nécessité économique à distance; c'est pourquoi il s'affirme universellement par le destruction de richesses, le dépense ostentoire, le gaspillage et toutes les formes de luxe gratuit.*" Compare Hume's comment on the process historically, "High pride then [during the reign of James I] prevailed; and it was by a dignity and stateliness of behaviour, that the gentry and the nobility distinguished themselves from the common people. Great riches acquired by commerce were more rare and had not yet been able to confound all ranks of men and render money the chief foundation of distinction. Much ceremony took place in the common intercourse of life and little familiarity was indulged in by the great. The advantages which result from opulence are so solid and real, that those who are possessed of them need not dread the near approach of their inferiors. The distinctions of birth and title, being more empty and imaginary, soon vanish upon familiar access and acquaintance" (Hume 1894 [1754–62], 3:97). In his usual forthright manner Hume called the sumptuary legislation of Edward III "ridiculous" (1894 [1754–62], 2:259).

31 This coincides with the decline in luxury as "display," especially by rulers to signify their "majesty"; a function necessarily undermined by the diffusion of such "signifiers," Hume himself remarks on how the nobility moved from vying with each other over the number of retainers to "a more civilized species of emulation, and endeavoured to excel in the splendour and elegance of their equipage, houses and tables" (Hume 1894 [1754–62], 2:53).

32 Cf. E. Hundert (1974, 139–43) who refers to Hume's "psychological egalitarianism," and his conviction that "the lower orders" were "the psychic equals of all men."

4 Manners and Morals: David Hume on Civility, Commerce, and the Social Construction of Difference

Richard Boyd

Introduction: Commerce and Civility

Seventeenth- and eighteenth-century political economy has been the subject of a large and influential body of scholarship by historians, sociologists, political theorists, and economists. It is now widely recognized that figures as diverse as Locke, Montesquieu, Hume, Smith, Ferguson, and Burke all expected the extended market order to soften or polish away the barbarism, rudeness, superstition, and enthusiasm of premodern societies. Eighteenth-century thinkers in particular focused on "civil society" as the moral antonym of "barbarism"; "civilization" as the broader description of the gradual progress of Enlightenment; commerce as the most likely engine of this transformation; and "civility" as the distinctive virtue associated with the social conditions of an extended economic order (Pocock 1985b; Langford 1989; Gellner 1994; Sally 1997; Shils 1997). This vision of political economy has variously come to be known as the *doux commerce* thesis or "commercial republicanism" (A. Hirschman 1977; Lerner 1987, 195–221).

Less often noted is that even those figures most optimistic about the prospects of commercial civilization had their doubts (A. Hirschman 1986; Hont and Ignatieff 1983). Adam Smith expressed concerns about whether the triumph of commercial society was compatible with the more elemental virtues of compassion and human sympathy; Adam Ferguson worried that the triumph of commerce might extinguish the participatory virtues of citizenship; and Edmund Burke had misgivings about the kind of human beings the market order was likely to form (Smith 1976 [1776], 302–9; Ferguson 1966 [1767], parts 4 and 5; Burke 1871).[1] Even so, the eighteenth century was largely committed, however ambivalently, to the extended market order as a solution to some of the most vexing problems of society and politics.[2]

In contrast to the ambivalent views of some of his contemporaries, David Hume's position on the relationship between commerce and civility seems relatively straightforward.[3] Because Hume entertains no romanticized notions of antiquity's alleged "virtue," he has few concerns about anything much being lost along the way: "We may observe, that the ancient republics were almost in perpetual war, a natural effect of their martial spirit, their love of liberty, their mutual emulation, and that hatred which generally prevails among nations that live in close neighborhood" (1985bb [1752i], 404).[4] Nor does Hume seem unduly worried—as were Smith, Ferguson, Burke, and others—about the caustic side effects of this economic revolution on the social cohesion of modern commercial societies. As he notes, "Nor are these advantages [of commercial society] attended with disadvantages that bear any proportion to them" (Hume 1985t [1752b], 271). Republican laments about the dangers of civic enervation, the corruption of taste, and the morally corrosive effects of luxury on the citizens of commercial republics overstate the case against commerce. Perhaps to an even greater degree than John Locke or Adam Smith, then, Hume looks to be the archetypal partisan of modern commercial civilization.[5]

Once we have noted this fact—as many before us have done—there is still the deeper question of causality. How, specifically, will the instrumental reason and self-interest of the marketplace polish away the "barbarity" and "ignorance" of premodern societies and the "superstition" and "enthusiasm" that have arisen with modern Christianity (Hume 1985t [1752b], 274)?[6] There is also the question of the kind of sociopolitical order that will likely result from the empire of commerce. Is this new commercial order of the ages compatible with traditional aristocratic manners and a monarchical political system? Or, as Hume suggests at many points in his *Essays* and his *History*, are the manners and political institutions of the traditional aristocracy, especially their disdain for commerce and industrious employment, themselves part of the "rudeness" that must be jettisoned in order to arrive at this new and uniquely democratic virtue of civility (Hume 1985i [1741i], 93)? We know from the eighteenth-century lexicon that a "civil society" is juxtaposed to the condition of "barbarism." But the specific moral attitudes that compose the practices of "civility" have yet to be fully unpacked by contemporary moral philosophers or historians of political thought. Put differently, simply "polishing" away "rude" or "barbarous" habits of senseless cruelty would seem to be the necessary but insufficient condition for behaving toward one another with what Hume, Smith, Ferguson, and others call "civility." So what is this nebulous virtue of civility, and how can one see Hume's defense of it arising from his writings on political economy?

In attempting to answer these questions this chapter will pursue three main lines of analysis. The first is to argue that, in contrast to aristocratic *noblesse oblige* or an exclusively "courtly" notion of politeness and manners, civility for Hume is imminently inclusive and substantively democratic. This is best seen in Hume's description of civility as a kind of "mutual deference" that allows those in the middle station of life to partake of the full range of moral sympathies (Hume 1985k [1742a], 126; 1985n [1742d], 546–47). This makes the virtue of civility something more than what John Rawls has recently described as a *modus vivendi*, that is, a minimal baseline of civil order allowing those with different comprehensive moral viewpoints to live peacefully alongside one another (Rawls 1993, 147–49, 166, 168). Civility does indeed serve this remedial function, and yet it is important to recognize how even this minimal sense of civility may prove more ennobling than the kind of "armed stalemate" derided by Rawls (1993, xxxix–xli).[7] As I will argue in the first section of this paper, civility is not only a *prudential*, but also an *intrinsic* moral good, valuable for its own sake rather than just for its functional contribution to ending factional and sectarian disputes. Hume's conspicuous focus on the former justification should not lead us to overlook the independent moral standing of the virtue of civility in his social and political theory. Second, this virtue of civility has important affinities for the commercial logic of the marketplace. Both the commercial economy and the virtue of civility presuppose a basic tolerance and respect for others that supersede whatever other differences might separate us. This affinity is evident in the different connotations of the word *commerce* in the eighteenth-century lexicon: *commerce* is a synonym not only for *trade*, but also for *sociability* or social interaction more generally, and the two are seen as connected (Hume 1985n [1742d], 547). Finally, the political economy of civility does more than just ameliorate cultural differences and transcend moral pluralism. It also and more importantly, like the division of labor, is foreseen as a way of turning those differences to the mutual benefit of all nations.

Civility Defined: Beyond *Modus Vivendi*

Our first step is to arrive at a satisfactory definition of *civility*. Civility is ordinarily discussed at an aggregate level, as in the familiar eighteenth-century distinction between "rude" or "barbarous" peoples, on the one hand, and those "civilized," "polished," and "enlightened" nations, on the other. Nations that have acquired civility are free from the bellicosity, rudeness, and cruelty of ancient republics: "When the tempers of men are softened as well as their knowledge improved, this humanity appears still more conspicuous, and is the chief characteristic which distinguishes a civilized age from times of barbarity and ignorance" (Hume 1985t [1752b], 274). Speaking of the early conquerors and rulers of England, Hume uses the adjective *civil* in opposition to *military*, such that "*civil* employments and occupations" are contrasted to a "perpetual attention to wars" whereby "violence universally prevailed" (Hume 1983 [1754–62], 2:262, 521–22).[8] Whether Hume distinguishes a "civil society" from the barbarism of the state of nature or the historico-anthropological condition of backwardness, civil society is first and foremost a moral rather than a taxonomical category (Boyd 2004b). Conspicuously lacking in the eighteenth-century language is the contemporary usage of *civil society* as merely the structural antithesis of the *state*, a distinction that emerged only belatedly in the wake of the nineteenth-century Marxian reappropriation of Hegel.[9]

Notwithstanding its possession by peoples, nations, or entire ages, civility is also—and I would submit, more importantly—a moral faculty of *individuals*. At a minimum, civility seems to be implied in the usual canon of liberal virtues such as tolerance, moderation, prudence, reasonableness, and peacefulness. These moral dispositions are necessary conditions for habits of civility to take hold, and it is absolutely essential for the peace and order of a free society that individuals should possess them. As Hume notes, "Laws, order, police, discipline; these can never be carried to any degree of perfection, before human reason has refined itself by exercise, and by an application to the more vulgar arts, at least, of commerce and manufacture" (Hume 1985t [1752b], 273). The "refinement" of human reason by its application to something as intrinsically uninspiring as the "vulgar arts ... of commerce and manufacture" has broader consequences for the peacefulness and order of society. By training individuals to attend to their instrumental reason or interests, rather than their unenlightened passions, commerce leads to the creation of civility. This in turn allows individuals to live peacefully alongside one another and to obey the minimal procedural justice imposed by the rule of law. In this respect, at least, Hume's defense of the importance of civility resembles the kind of *modus vivendi* described by John Rawls and others.[10]

The early-modern turn to civility is at least in part, as Rawls correctly noted, a response to pluralism. In a post-Reformation world torn apart by partisan and sectarian conflicts, the cultivation of civility was an important feature of the political theories of Hume, Smith, Ferguson, and other members of the Scottish Enlightenment. The vaunted "*civil* society" of which they all in some degree speak is not so much the structural antithesis of the state as the moral antonym of cruelty, fanaticism, persecution, intolerance, superstition, enthusiasm and, ultimately, civil war (Boyd 2000). In the wake of centuries of civil war and religious controversies, agreement no longer seemed possible about a single hierarchy of virtues, shared purposes, or principles of distributive justice. F. A. von Hayek has observed of modern pluralistic societies, "what makes agreement and peace in such a society possible is that the individuals are not required to agree on ends but only on means which are capable of serving a great variety of purposes and which each hopes will assist him in the pursuit of his own purposes." The discovery of such a "method of collaboration which requires agreement only on means and not on ends" is characteristic of what he and others have termed "civility" (Hayek 1976, 3). And, as Michael Oakeshott has similarly noted, it "is a characteristic (or what, from another point of view, may be called a virtue) of civility that, being independent of both rivalry and tender concern, it may subsist where the one is present or where the other is absent" (Oakeshott 1990, 123).

Nancy Hirschman has recently reminded us that the positive natural virtues of sympathy or compassion occupy a central place in Hume's moral and political theory (N. Hirschman 2000, 178–85; cf. Rotwein 1955, xcix–ci). Civility for Hume seems to have as much in common with these "natural virtues" of generosity, beneficence, empathy, and compassion as with the "artificial virtues" of justice, fidelity and allegiance that have developed over time as a way of dealing with the increasing scale and complexity of modern society.[11] And so we see the intermediary, puzzling nature of civility. It clearly partakes of a kind of "natural virtue" in the sense that it arises from a sentiment of beneficence or sympathy that is heartfelt. The ultimate sources of civility are to be found in "love, which when properly managed, is the source of all politeness and refinement" (Hume 1985q [1748a], 215). At the same time, however, it has some of the characteristics of "artificial virtues" like justice or prudence in that it is not properly speaking natural to us, but requires us to learn to overcome the self-regard that is the more ordinary lot of mankind.[12] Just as commerce accustoms us to behaving "justly" in our dealings with others—respecting their property and obeying abstract laws of title and transfer—it may also accustom us to treat others in ways that are "polite" or "civil" (Hume 2000a, 3.2.3.1–11).

Civility includes positive virtues of "humanity," "charity," and "generosity" that Hume associates with the condition of "manners" or "politeness" (Hume 1985t [1752b], 274, 280). These contribute not just to keeping the peace and assuaging social conflicts. They also and more importantly give way to the "easy and sociable manner" with which citizens meet and develop the "habit of conversing together, and contributing to each other's pleasure and entertainment" (271). So one of the things that seems to set civility apart from other liberal virtues like tolerance or moderation is that it supposes an active and positive moral relationship between the person who is civil and the one to whom this virtue is directed. The problem is to determine the nature of this moral relationship.

Hume sees civility as the product of a natural "propensity to company and society," which "makes us enter deeply into each other's sentiments." On the one hand, this propensity "causes like passions and inclinations to run, as it were, by contagion, through the whole club or knot of companions," which means that this sociability of man is a source of perpetual contention (Hume 1985q [1748a], 202). This very same love or sympathy may be responsible for the "parties of affection" or "personal factions" that Hume so laments (Hume 1985f [1741f], 56, 63). In contrast to those today who speak of "civil society" in the contemporary sense of a rich life of active and benign associational involvement, the Scottish Enlightenment was deeply ambivalent about the fanatical and sectarian tendencies of groups (Boyd 2000).

This is not to say, as did Thomas Hobbes, "that men have no pleasure, but on the contrary a great deal of grief, in keeping company when there is no power able to over-awe them all" (Hobbes 1994 [1651], 75). Hume, Smith, and other eighteenth-century thinkers are well aware of the importance, indeed the naturalness, of human society and sociability. However, the extent to which there is indeed great pleasure and delight to be found in the company of others hinges not so much, as it did for Hobbes, on whether this "commerce" takes place in the presence or absence of an overwhelming state power. It depends instead on whether the various parties respect one another through the practices of civility. For, "in order to render conversation, and the intercourse of minds more easy and agreeable, good manners have been invented, and have carried the matter somewhat farther" (Hume 1985k [1742a], 132). Without civility, which makes human companionship not only "easy," but also and more importantly "agreeable," there is only a disrespect of human equality whose consequences range from simple bad manners all the way down to those "gross vices, which lead us to commit real injury on others" (132). Being uncivil amounts to more than just bad manners, or what Hobbes described mockingly as "how one man should salute another, or how a man should wash his mouth or pick his teeth in front of company, and such other points of the *small* morals" (Hobbes 1994 [1651], 57).[13] At the extremes incivility may culminate in actual, physical cruelty.

First of all, being civil to someone else obviously communicates something about oneself. Through our civility we demonstrate that we are in possession of manners, politeness, or what Hume refers to as refinement in education or good breeding (Hume 1985l [1742b]). In that sense, and as many commentators have assumed, civility has some affinities with aristocratic honor, or what Hume describes as "gallantry" (Hume 1985l [1742b], 132–33). Civility is a self-imposed moral responsibility to which we subscribe because we have self-respect. We owe it to ourselves to be civil because to behave in ways that are uncivil brings shame or social opprobrium on us. So at one level, as Rousseau noted in his devastating critique of the emptiness of courtly and bourgeois manners, civility is other-directed insofar as it depends, at least in part, on our seeing ourselves through the eyes of others (Rousseau 1979 [1762], 221–24; Rousseau 1964b [1754], 132–34). The "commerce" of civility, however, goes in both directions. Like Rousseau's *pitié* or compassion, civility also requires us to put ourselves in the position of others.[14] At least as described by Hume it implies a consideration of their feelings. Civility is not just a standard, like aristocratic honor, to which we hold ourselves because of our inner sense of the exceptionality of our position or our fear of incurring disgrace. Civility is also and more importantly something that *other people deserve* because of the relevant ways in which we are their equals.

Hume confesses that in many cases we are able to behave in ways that are civil only because our natural self-regard has been conditioned by education. It is especially because "we are commonly proud and selfish, and apt to assume the preference above others" that "a polite man learns to behave with deference towards his companions, and to yield the superiority to them in all common incidents of society" (Hume 1985k [1742a], 132). This does not mean that civility is merely disguised condescension, however. Hume makes it clear that civility is a form of sympathy or affection directed toward another sensible being who is at the most fundamental level our equal. Like Smith's well-known artifice of the impartial spectator, the practice of civility rests on a cultivated ability to identify with another, to look past one's own partial interests, and to imagine oneself in her position (Smith 1982 [1759], 9–12, 25, 37–38, 204–8, 223–24).[15]

Civility: Aristocratic or Democratic?

The substance of civility, at least for Hume, bears little resemblance to aristocratic pretension, which creates invidious distinctions by means of an inscrutable code of courtly manners.[16] The moral core of civility consists of a kind of modesty or self-deprecation: "Among the arts of conversation, no one pleases more than mutual deference or civility, which leads us to resign our own inclinations to those of our companion, and to curb and conceal that presumption and arrogance, so natural to the human mind" (Hume 1985k [1742a], 126). Thinking about civility as a "*mutual* deference" that "curbs or conceals" self-regard and allows the natural virtues of sympathy and beneficence to express themselves brings to light the democratic core of what civility actually communicates. Presumably it is not just the "deference" of civility—which as a permanent condition can hardly be satisfying—but its "mutuality" that "pleases" us.

Hume's description of civility as a "studied display of sentiments," whereby we "curb and conceal" our true feelings, suggests that civility may be compatible with concealed disdain (132). Civility's ostensible inauthenticity has troubled critics from Rousseau onward. As Mary Wollstonecraft famously observed in her criticism of the hollowness and invidious distinctions lurking beneath the "polish of manners,"

> Manners and morals are so nearly allied that they have often been confounded; but, though the former should only be the natural reflection of the latter, yet, when various causes have produced factitious and corrupt manners, which are very early caught, morality becomes an empty name.
>
> (Wollstonecraft 1988 [1792], 4)

Hume's own examples of the "well-educated youth" who "redouble the instances of respect and deference to their elders"; the vulnerable "strangers and foreigners" who "are entitled to the first place in every company"; or the "studied deference and complaisance" of men toward the "inclinations and opinions" of the women whom Hume believes to be their natural inferiors—all are instances where civility thinly disguises a recognition of superiority (Hume 1985k [1742a], 132–33). There may, indeed, be something a bit condescending about civility, especially when it is evident that one is evincing the mere "*appearance* of sentiments different from those to which they naturally incline" (132).

However, we might wonder what the alternative to this would be. Would it be to behave so as to make another *more* conscious of such differences by refusing ever to defer to them in the course of everyday life, when these differences in power and status are, or at least ought to be, irrelevant?[17] Ideally, the kind of civility that Hume describes as appropriate to circumstances like these is not intended as a way of signaling one's natural or circumstantial superiority, which would exist whether or not one behaved politely. Instead, civility is intended in all these cases as a kind of "generous attention" or "deference" whose goal is to please, serve, and make comfortable the person with whom one is interacting (132). As such, it is based not on an assertion or communication of superiority, but out of an elemental consideration or sympathy for the feelings and vulnerability of the other to which our own vanity and self-interest would otherwise make us blind. To be sure, like any other virtue, civility has an undeniable ambivalence:

> No advantages in this world are pure and unmixed. In like manner, as modern politeness, which is naturally so ornamental, runs often into affectation and foppery, disguise and insincerity; so the ancient simplicity, which is naturally so amiable and affecting, often degenerates into rusticity and abuse, scurrility and obscenity.
>
> (Hume 1985k [1742a], 130–31)

Mary Wollstonecraft, too, in commenting on Hume's treatment of manners, distinguishes between the empty forms of manners and "that [true] reciprocation of civility which the dictates of humanity and politeness of civilization authorize between man and man" (Wollstonecraft 1988 [1792], 55).[18] By linking the "politeness of civilization" with "the dictates of humanity," Wollstonecraft suggests that civility entails some recognition of the moral equality "between man and man." Ideally, civility must be "reciprocal." The consequences of a disregard for this moral equality may also be seen in civility's antithesis, namely, barbarism. Eighteenth-century connotations of "rudeness" include both a lack of formal manners and a kind of barbarism that disposes us to cruelty. So a "rusticity" of manners, or a lack of "politeness," is connected not just with disrespect—whether for ourselves or for those with whom we engage in commerce. Failure to respect another human being enough to pay deference to his sensibilities is connected with a more basic moral disregard for his person and property. Rudeness is tied to a lack of humanity, which might culminate in cruelty, bellicosity, and bloodshed.[19] It is the most conspicuous feature of military peoples. Conversely, "When the tempers of men are softened as well as their knowledge improved, this humanity appears still more conspicuous, and is the chief characteristic which distinguishes a civilized age from times of barbarity and ignorance" (Hume 1985t [1752b], 274). It is rudeness then, and not civility, that falsely presumes the superiority of one human being over another.

We ordinarily think of civility as a formal and not a substantial moral relationship, if we indeed think about civility as a moral relationship at all. Being civil involves the respect of certain formal conditions—politeness or good manners, for example—that govern our interactions with others. In Michael Oakeshott's description, civility is "adverbial" in the sense that it involves certain moral conditions that govern the performance of one's self-chosen ends (Oakeshott 1990, 63–72, 113, 121–23, 158, 182). Civility means that regardless of what one says, one speaks "politely," "respectfully," or "modestly." With respect to the virtues constitutive of civility, then, the substance of *what* we say to one another is less telling than the *way in which we say it*. Whether we respectfully communicate our grievances or scream them angrily and insultingly would seem to distinguish "civil" disobedience from angry protest. Even theorists of civil disobedience like Aquinas are just as concerned about the ways in which we express our disagreements with the laws of our society as with the substance of those complaints. This is true at least to the extent that our ability to resist is contingent on our doing so in a way that is unlikely to produce what Aquinas calls "scandal and disorder" (Aquinas 1988 [1269–70], 55).

These emphases on the consequential dimensions of civility (or, in this case, incivility) may actually draw attention away from the intrinsic virtues of the moral relationship of civility, and especially its communicative functions. Speaking rudely to another communicates disdain, disrespect, and moral disregard. It conveys, in no uncertain terms, that I believe I am superior to you. This transgression against the basic postulate of moral equality is easier to recognize in extreme cases of incivility. Civility's importance is most vivid in its absence. However, its positive connection to the postulate of moral equality is also apparent—if more difficult to appreciate—in the practices of everyday life. Being polite to another communicates many things, ranging from respect to a sense of equality, and a basic sympathy toward others as fellow, sensible beings.

It may seem like an uphill battle to argue that civility is a democratic virtue. In our own day, especially, "civility" is laden with aristocratic or conservative overtones.[20] Hume himself seems to compound this difficulty by suggesting that civility is in fact a kind of "politeness of manners," "delicacy of breeding," or "polite deference and respect" that "arises most naturally in monarchies and courts." By way of contrast, republics are conspicuous for their "want of politeness," as in the case of the derogatory French expression cited by Hume, of one having "The good manners of a Swiss civilized in Holland" (Hume 1985k [1742a], 127–28). The implication seems to be that "civility" or "politeness" requires a kind of refined breeding that may be cultivated only in the few and lacking in the common mass of individuals. Steven Wallech has argued this most pointedly by suggesting that Hume's social and political thought presupposes "sharp lines of distinction between ranks in society," which make his political theory something less than wholly democratic (Wallech 1984, 213).

No doubt such orders, ranks, and distinctions founded in differences of property are represented as empirical facts in Hume's *Treatise of Human Nature.* "There are," Hume concedes, "certain deferences and mutual submissions, which custom requires of the different ranks of men towards each other" (Hume 2000a, 382). But Hume's acknowledgment of the *reality* of these distinctions need not imply that Hume is an apologist for a world where, in the words of Wallech, the upper orders "associate [only] with each other and deny their company to the poor" and the poor in turn "become isolated from their social superiors and insulated against the great distances that separate them from the top of society" (Wallech 1984, 214). First, Hume's language in this passage suggests that these "deferences and *mutual* submissions" are intended to take place *within* the various ranks of men, "*towards each other*," "even tho' they be our *equals*," or at least "where we are not very much distinguish'd above them" (Hume 2000a, 382; my emphasis). This is by no means a self-evident call for the poor to slavishly defer to the wealthy and well-born. Second, because "custom *requires*" such a deference toward our rough social equals, "*prudence*" alone may "suffice to regulate our actions in the particular." Hume says only that "'*Tis necessary*, therefore, to know our rank and station in the world, whether it be fix'd by our birth, fortune, employments, talents or reputation" (382).[21] This is a prudential admonition: one would be foolhardy to buck custom by unveiling the pride that is natural to us. Precisely because of the lamentable necessities and circumstances that drive the lower classes toward servility and make the upper classes prey to flattery, Hume's own preference is for the "middle station of life." As he notes, "I shou'd, therefore, chuse to ly in the middle Way, and to have my Commerce with my Friend varied both by Obligations given and receiv'd" (Hume 1985n [1742d], 547).[22]

Hume writes with nothing analogous to Edmund Burke's undisguised contempt for "servile employments" like hairdressers or candle-makers, which "cannot be a matter of honor to any person"; nor does Hume share Burke's generalized suspicion of the lower orders of society and the dangers of social mobility (Burke 1987 [1790], 35–44; Herzog 1998). Hume argues to the contrary that "a good-natured man, who is well-educated, practices this civility *to every mortal*, without premeditation or interest" (Hume 1985k [1742a], 126). So in an ideal world where this moral virtue were not so readily overshadowed by "presumption and arrogance," each individual would be indiscriminately civil to "*every mortal*," without an eye to his own interest. In the absence of this good nature, however, which may admittedly be rare, one must rely on a kind of artificial support for civility: "in order to render that valuable quality general among any people, it seems necessary to assist the natural disposition by some general motive." In a "civilized monarchy" this takes the form of a "long train of dependence from the prince to the peasant," which "is sufficient to beget in every one an inclination to please his superiors, and to form himself upon those models, which are most acceptable to people of condition and education" (126–27).

Critics have seen civility as a demeaning species of deference imposed by superiors on the lesser members of the political community (Keane 1998; Elias 2000). In Hume's words, manners are deemed "acceptable" (or unacceptable!) by "people of condition and education." And yet the very thing that makes civility so "pleasing" is the fact that it is "mutual," that is to say, that this "deference" or self-abnegation goes both ways. Despite the possibility of civility being encouraged by a great hierarchical chain of aristocratic dependency, Hume also notes that unthinking deference and "a rigid loyalty to particular persons or families . . . are virtues that hold less of reason, than of bigotry and superstition" (Hume 2000a, 359). Hume is clear that commercial societies, where industry and the arts and sciences have flourished, are most conducive to the polished habits of what one recent commentator has called a "polite and commercial" society (Langford 1988).

Moreover, civility seems only truly pleasurable—distinguishable from obsequiousness, on the one hand, and condescension, on the other—when we find ourselves at different moments occupying one or the other position of superiority or inferiority. Civility must be reciprocal. One of the strongest points that Hume makes on behalf of what he calls the "middle station of life" is that one is constantly in the position of being both benefactor and beneficiary of the full range of moral virtues: "The middle Station is here justly recommended as affording the fullest Security for Virtue, and I may also add, it gives Opportunity for the most ample Exercise of it, and furnishes Employment for every good Quality, which we can possibly be possest of" (Hume 1985n [1742d], 546). Rather than always being in the position of exercising "Patience, Resignation, Industry and Integrity," as are the lower orders of society, or constantly practicing "Generosity, Humanity, Affability, and Charity," as are the superior ranks, those in the middle station of life have the opportunity to experience the full range of moral virtues. "When a Man lyes betwixt these two Extremes, he can exert the former Virtues towards his Superiors, and the latter towards his Inferiors," and in so doing partake of the goods of reciprocity or "mutual deference" (Hume 1985n [1742d], 546; 1985k [1742a], 126).

This praise of the "middle station of life" is not confined to the essay by that same name that was omitted from editions of the *Essays* in Hume's own time. It is not the traditional aristocracy of birth and breeding, but the "tradesmen and merchants," the "middling rank of men," who by the increase of "commerce and industry" come to enjoy the "authority and consideration" that rightly marks them out as the "best and firmest basis of public liberty" (Hume 1985t [1752b], 277). Hume further underscores an essential tension between a commercial society where talents and industry are encouraged and respected and those "civilized monarchies" that Hume admits may enjoy some limited advantages over the purely republican form of government (Hume 1985k [1742a], 124–26). "Commerce," Hume notes, "is apt to decay in absolute governments not because it is there less *secure*, but because it is less *honourable*." Because "a subordination of ranks is absolutely necessary to the support of monarchy," in an aristocratic society of any sort, "Birth, titles and place, must be honoured above industry and riches." The real danger of this is that "all the considerable traders will be tempted to throw up their commerce, in order to purchase some of those employments, to which privileges and honours are annexed" (Hume 1985i [1741i], 93).[23]

Civility: Inclusive or Exclusionary?

A commercial society is uniquely, and for better or worse, one in which we are accustomed to deferring to a value in exchange for every other human being or object that is different from its use value.[24] This may very well lead to the problem identified by contemporary philosopher Michael Walzer, that capitalist societies rest on a single "dominant good" of money to which all other standards become subordinated and to which everyone slavishly defers (Walzer 1983, 10–12). And yet in an aristocratic society such as Hume's, "where Birth alone" exercises a kind of dominance, the introduction of the valuations and social mobility of the marketplace seems a step in the direction of creating another dominant good, albeit one that may be just as unequally distributed (Hume 1985n [1742d], 548). We escape a kind of hereditary dominion or subordination and begin to exercise a "mutuality" of deference where respect becomes a two-way street. Through the commerce of civility we may communicate our appreciation of human equality and become accustomed, as Hume notes, to exercising the full range of human virtues. The complete human type—one who has the experience of being recognized by others for his authority, and yet who also has the habit of acknowledging a similar authority in others—can exist only in a society in which all persons, at least in theory, can access the dominant good.

Critics like Alasdair MacIntyre have complained that Hume's procedural notion of justice and his rejection of Aristotelian virtue are more suitable for a modern, tolerant, and humane democratic society than for the more heroic possibilities of a Christian or classical polity (MacIntyre 1981). This is because Hume begins with the basic assumption of the givenness of pluralism, and of the need to readjust our moral expectations in light of this basic fact of modern pluralistic societies. Trying to organize political life around a shared conception of virtue or "ends" is in large measure what has led to the factional and sectarian controversies of the last several centuries. Instead, given such a world, what is most important is that citizens share a common agreement about the means most appropriate for them to use in the pursuit of their diverse, self-chosen ends.

To call this aspect of Hume's moral theory a "concession" is to suggest, along with MacIntyre and other critics of modern liberalism, that something vital to public life has been sacrificed in this moral transformation. And in fairness there is probably something to be said for the costs of the passing of aristocratic honor, classical "virtue," and the kinds of heroic public lives one might lead in a Christian commonwealth or a classical

Athens, Sparta, or Rome. However, Hume's endorsement of the new-modern virtue of civility as a surrogate for classical virtue also heralds a new possibility of inclusivity, of those with different ends and ethical visions abiding by a moral theory of civility that will allow them to interact peacefully with one another without any deeper expectation about shared purposes. Civility is, in this respect, an immanently inclusive moral theory—to be understood as the very antithesis of Christian moralism, republican virtue, aristocratic honor, or a conservative nostalgia for the manners of a bygone past. It anticipates a notion of "humanity."

Attending carefully to these democratic and inclusive aspects of Hume's account of civility allows us to disentangle the virtue of civility from the aristocratic and exclusionary overtones with which it has come to be associated by contemporary critics and defenders alike. For Aristotle, only the few could be truly virtuous; aristocratic honor was similarly confined to the well-born; and it was the unfortunate admixture of Christianity and philosophy that resulted in the most furious religious conflicts of the seventeenth century. But one of the most unique, if often overlooked, features of Hume's account of civility is that it is open to anyone who learns to practice it. Although some nations and peoples may heretofore have acquired a greater degree of civilization than others, the virtue of civility is potentially open-ended and inclusive. So long as one agrees to be bound by a respect for another as one's moral equal, the virtue of civility is at least in theory accessible to all races and peoples. Indeed for Hume civility seems a virtue uniquely suited to a modern world of deep moral complexity. Rather than nostalgic or conservative, then, Hume argues for civility as a virtue tailor-made for a modern world in which we have moved beyond any expectation that we will all share thicker, purposive values. His social and political theory rests on what E. J. Hundert has aptly termed the "psychological equality" of all individuals with respect to the basic motivations and incentives of a commercial society (Hundert 1974, 141–43).

The Civilizing Lessons of the Marketplace: Respecting Differences

After sketching out these virtues of civility, we must now consider how these democratic aspects of civility are intimately related to the properties Hume attributes to the market. The universality of commerce offers the first hints of the conventionality and arbitrariness of otherwise reified boundaries between nations, races, parties, religions, and civilizations. Commerce teaches us to "deconstruct" the apparent "naturalness" of these distinctions and to resolve differences (of skin color, religious doctrine, or ideological affiliation) into matters about which reasonable people might disagree without resorting to force or senseless cruelty. The fluid and communicative dimensions of commerce, the easy spontaneity with which it bridges or compromises seemingly intractable differences, are models for the democratic virtue of civility.

Commerce accomplishes this in at least two distinct ways: at the level of social habits and at the more fundamental level of value. First, the market accustoms individuals to look past such differences in the habits of everyday life. Hume's beloved middle station of life brings its members into "commerce"—both in the narrow sense of trade as well as the broader sense of communication—with an extraordinarily wide range of persons. Just as being civil obliges us to look past the different beliefs and identities that separate us from others, our prejudices against other nations, religions, or races should not interfere with our ability to engage in trade. Understanding national, ethnic, or religious differences as incidental or irrelevant to a more fundamental interest in buying low and selling dear amounts to a kind of education or strengthening of reason and tolerance.

It is helpful to think of the act of commerce as itself expressive of Hume's basic insights into the conventional or socially constructed nature of such differences. On the one hand, the market teaches us to look past prejudices of nationality, religion, or creed as nothing more than "species of ill-founded jealousies" or a "narrow and malignant opinion" about the mutually exclusive benefits of trade (Hume 1985ee [1758], 327–28).[25] These differences are no true barrier to commerce—social or economic—for "the domestic industry of a people cannot be hurt by the greatest prosperity of their neighbors; and as this branch of commerce is undoubtedly the most important in any extensive kingdom, we are so far removed from all reason of jealousy" (328). Such jealousies as exist are unreasonable, founded in unwarranted suspicion, ignorance and a lack of "enlarged and benevolent sentiments toward each other" (331). Indeed, rather than these differences being insurmountable barriers to commerce, such differences themselves are conducive to "emulation and novelty" under conditions "where an open communication is preserved among nations" (328–29).

One basic moral problem with which both Hume and Adam Smith are concerned is how to retain some element of sociability in an increasingly complex, anonymous, and extended market order. Much has been written about Smith's role as a civic moralist, and especially how his *Theory of Moral Sentiments* softens the capitalism of his *Wealth of Nations* (Phillipson 1983; Haakonssen 1981; Dickey 1986; Muller 1990; Griswold 1999). Less attention has been paid to Hume's reckoning with a parallel question: namely, how are modern individuals expected to cultivate sympathy and sociability when they are increasingly estranged from one another by the extended economic order and the division of labor?[26] There is, first and foremost, Hume's conspicuous concern with sociability and the creation of a public sphere. In contrast to the isolation and rudeness "peculiar to ignorant and barbarous nations," modern commercial societies are in fact distinguished by their sociability and urbanity: "They flock into cities; love to receive and communicate knowledge; to show their wit or their breeding; their taste in conversation or living, in clothes or furniture ... Particular clubs and societies are every where formed: Both sexes meet in an easy and sociable manner; and the tempers of men, as well as their behaviour, refine apace." As we have seen above, civility makes possible an "encrease of humanity, from the very habit of conversing together, and contributing to each other's pleasure and entertainment" (Hume 1985t [1752b], 271).

Beyond commerce providing what we might think of as the necessary structural preconditions or "easy subsistence" that makes this enlightenment and urbanity possible, there is also a more direct way by which commerce bridges gaps between individuals created by the division of labor (Hume 1985bb [1752i], 420). "In the infancy of society," Hume notes, different individuals, "being neighbours, are easily acquainted with each other's necessities, and can lend their mutual assistance to supply them" (Hume 1985v [1752d], 299). In an extended market order, however, producers and consumers are necessarily "wholly unacquainted" and utterly "ignorant of each other's necessities." Because "the difficulty of their intercourse encreases" in direct proportion as "the people encrease in numbers and industry," the different "ranks of men, so necessary to each other, can never rightly meet, till one man erects a shop, to which all the workmen and all the customers repair" (300; cf. Smith 1976 [1776], 433). So commerce itself provides a public setting for modern individuals of *different ranks and social stations* to meet and interact on terms more sociable than complete anonymity but less intimate than personal benevolence (cf. Ignatieff 1984). Even under circumstances far too remote for buyers and sellers to cultivate face-to-face relationships, "*merchants*, one of the most useful races of men," serve as "common benefactors," not only by increasing the rapidity with which industry and wealth circulate throughout the kingdom or the entire globe, but also by coordinating trade such that the industry of some benefits the unknown necessities of others (Hume 1985v [1752d], 300–301).[27]

We might lament the extent to which these increasingly impersonal relationships of the marketplace have come to dominate modern society. But there are salutary consequences associated with the translation of the infinity of human wants and desires into the common and fluid medium of money. Hume reminds us, first, that many of these new commercial relationships would never have taken place under the conditions of a face-to-face economy. Necessities would have gone unfulfilled, and the industry that ultimately goes into satisfying them would have been squandered. At a deeper level, however, the market renders these differences themselves commensurable by introducing a common scale of value or "interest" by which they might be respectively weighed and exchanged. The consequences of this commensurability of the market for social life as a whole are not altogether pessimistic, as some today have assumed (Walzer 1983; Anderson 1993). Indeed the fact that the market is indiscriminate—that it weighs people, works of art, and heartfelt principles according to a common scale of interest—may be something more than a small consolation in a world where incommensurable principles prevent people from living peacefully alongside one another. This pedagogical aspect of the marketplace can teach something valuable with respect to the problem of difference.

The concept of "interest" has an important function not just in domesticating the passions, or tutoring us to set aside our immediate and unlimited passions in the longer term "interest" of peace and order. Hume's deeper point seems to be an even more fundamental statement about the nature of economic value itself. The logic of the marketplace teaches us that differences are indeed commensurable. There exists a common scale of value or "interest" to which all preferences and necessities are ultimately reducible. That is not to say that this scalar does not beget differences or even exclusions of its own. Some goods are worth more than others, after all, and measuring everything by one Procrustean scale inevitably introduces invidious distinctions of rank, of more or less value according to price. However, the key innovation of the realm of interest is that distinctions such as "more" or "less" are qualitatively different from the realm of abstract principles, which are about "Truth" or "Falsity," and where the acceptance of my position entails the negation of yours. Because of this the realm of interest is uniquely suited to accommodate contradictory desires and human appetites, and indeed to render them "mensurable" (Hume 1980 [1779], 80).

Hume's model is that of "two men travelling on the highway, the one east, the other west" who "can easily pass each other, if the way be broad enough" (Hume 1985f [1741f], 60). Commerce is like this; the realm of abstract principles is not. Commerce renders "interest" mutual in a way that principles, which are either true of false, by their very nature cannot be. In the absence of such a common scale there is only the assertion of incommensurability and the eventual appeal to force. Moreover, as unappealing as the ideal of mutual self-interest (treating other people as a means) may appear from the perspective of a Kantian ethics of ends, that act of appealing to someone's interest does have the virtue of taking them seriously as a fellow human being. By way of contrast, appealing to force in order to impose one's beliefs or ideals on another is inherently degrading because it does not take seriously the other self as a being worthy of our respect.

Feminist and postmodernist scholars have recently been drawn to Hume because of the challenge his work presents to the fallacy of essentialism, which would suggest that there are certain fixed and immutable characteristics associated with different races, nations, or genders.[28] To such interpreters, Hume is among the first to recognize the socially constructed nature of such ostensibly essential characteristics as nationality, race, or gender. Or, at the very least, like Hobbes before him, Hume wants to show how political elites manipulate these differences, investing them with a moral intensity or political significance that they do not intrinsically possess. While feminist and postmodern scholars are most concerned with the power relationships and exclusions that are implicated in these social constructions of difference, Hume's own concern has more to do with how certain differences are constructed as commensurable or incommensurable, and thus as grounds for social conflict and political disorder.

Hume notes that "the civil wars which arose some few years ago in Morocco, between the *blacks* and *whites*, merely on account of the complexion, are founded on a pleasant difference" (Hume 1985f [1741f], 59). This difference is at least a "sensible and a real difference," if not necessarily one that individuals ought to invest with any kind of hostility. But how ridiculous must the European wars of religion seem to the ostensibly barbarous Moors, for these conflicts have invested deadly significance to "a few phrases and expressions, which one party accepts of, without understanding them; and the other refuses in the same manner" (59). The deeper point here is not so much to show the greater rationality of conflicts founded in "real differences" like skin color, which are comprehensible, and those founded in abstract "principles," which are "utterly absurd and unintelligible." Instead it is to show the irrationality of constructing *any* of these differences as sufficient grounds for moral disagreement. Hume's ironic deconstruction of the alleged "naturalness" of conflicts over skin color, personal affection, abstruse principles, or—at the height of absurdity, the color of uniforms!—intends to show the unique advantages of conflicts rooted in interest (57). Although these latter may represent "real" conflicts, they are also susceptible to compromise in a way that other more abstract disagreements of principle are not.

Hume notes, "The vulgar are apt to carry all national characters to extremes; and having once established it as a principle, that all people are knavish, or cowardly, or ignorant, they will admit of no exception, but comprehend every individual under the same censure" (Hume 1985q [1748a], 197). In contrast to this "vulgar" prejudice by which individuals are judged not on their individual capacities but in terms of their membership in a national collectivity, "men of sense" must "condemn these undistinguishing judgments" (197). This is in its essence a liberal democratic argument about the moral requirement, first, of judging each individual on his or her own merits, regardless of the alleged manners of a nation as a whole—generalizations about peoples or races in the aggregate that Hume confesses may be well-founded either in physical or moral causes (198–99). It also requires the cultivation of the liberal democratic habit of reserving judgments. Treating national character as determinative, especially in the biological sense, is a form of prejudice, which Hume opposes at least in theory, even if in practice he himself momentarily indulges unsavory prejudices about the distinguishing characteristics of race (208 n. 10).

There is also an important distinction at work here that separates Hume from many of his "Enlightenment" counterparts. In contrast to what has often been described as the "Enlightenment quest for uniformity," where traditional differences of customs and manners are acknowledged as artificial, and thus targeted for extirpation and replacement by a more "universal reason," Hume intends only to point out that these differences need not be sources of conflict or jealousy. He accepts these differences as a given. His goal of trying to render these differences commensurable must be seen as distinct from the parallel Enlightenment goal of trying to eliminate such differences altogether. Only a political economist could appreciate that the quest for uniformity is inefficient. Differences between nations allow each to benefit from specialization and natural advantages: "Nor need any state entertain apprehensions, that their neighbours will improve to such a degree in every art and manufacture, as to have no demand from them. Nature, by giving a diversity of geniuses, climates and soils, to different nations, has secured their mutual intercourse and commerce, as long as they all remain industrious and civilized" (Hume 1985ee [1758], 329).

We should note that this praise of socioeconomic diversity is conditional on the nation's possession of industry and civility. Cultural differences, without the admixture of industry and civility, may amount to mere barbarism (329). Hume has no interest in glorifying the "sloth and ignorance that prevails in Morocco and the coast of Barbary" (331). And yet rather than condemning some nations to a perpetual barbarism and backwardness, all that nations need to do in order to move forward is to apply industry toward cultivating that "diversity of geniuses, climates and soils" that set them apart from other nations. It has been insufficiently noted that these differences *between* nations serve much the same wealth-creating function for Hume as the division of labor *within* nations fulfills for Smith. Even so, Hume is not unaware of the latter's distinctive insight into the value of the domestic division of labor, noting the importance of specialization for trade: "Like many subordinate artists, employed to form the several wheels and springs of a machine: such [are] those who excel in all the particular arts of life." The task of the philosopher and statesman is to render these disparate attributes into a "just harmony and proportion" that leads to "true felicity as the result of their conspiring order" (Hume 1985l [1742b], 149). But in addition to these more overt cases, in which a philosopher or statesman must plan how to reconcile these differences, one of the miraculous features of the market is that it allows some nations and individuals to benefit from their specialized skills or natural advantages even in the absence of explicit coordination.

In contrast to the Enlightenment impulse to replace these differences altogether by the uniformity of reason, Hume's essays on commerce are premised on the value of respecting and preserving differences. Just as commerce allows apparently incommensurable goods—the proverbial "pushpins and poetry"—to be exchanged through a common medium or scale of value, and indeed for wealth to be created through such exchanges, the virtue of civility similarly allows us to transform incommensurable moral disagreements into "mensurable" interests while leaving the differences themselves unchanged. This basic respect for difference—and indeed, Hume's appreciation of the economic value of and interdependency beget by

differences—is yet another democratic feature of Hume's political economy. This requires, of course, that people become more tolerant of those
national differences (specializations) that are the ultimate sources of wealth
creation.

Here Hume follows Montesquieu's critique of the Enlightenment fetish
for uniformity, as though development presupposes one "rational" way of
life to which all peoples aspire. Not only does this Enlightenment vision fail to
take into account the full range of cultural diversities, but it also neglects to
appreciate how these diversities are susceptible to becoming specializations.
There is perhaps, then, a direct pathway between the original autocritique of
the Enlightenment fascination with rational uniformity and the development
of the science of political economy. Hume's political economy is "scientific"
in that he sought to derive certain uniform laws of supply, demand, and
capital flow that were relatively generalizable. This amounts to a "science"
of human nature. And yet at the same time he appreciates that the very
human and institutional factors of capital that lent constancy to these "laws"
were historically contingent and culturally variable. The progress of economic development requires not just "emulation, example and instruction,"
whereby one nation seeks to mimic the national industries of others (Hume
1985ee [1758], 331). It also demands imagination, diversification, and specialization, so that a nation does not find itself precariously dependent on a
single staple industry, like Britain, or in the position of being mere brokers
and traders of the goods created by others, like the Dutch (329–31). What
Hume seems to have in mind is for nations and industries to take an active
role in cultivating new needs and tastes in their neighbors; they will then for
a time enjoy a relative advantage in satisfying those desires. Hume under-
stands economics, then, not merely as the competition to satisfy some static
array of existing wants, but as the dynamic process of creating new refined
tastes in one's neighbors.[29] To put this in Hume's own terms: economic
development entails both "emulation and novelty" (328–29).

Conclusion

We have seen some of the diverse ways that civility and commerce are linked
in Hume's social and political theory. On the one hand, as many have
observed before, commerce encourages habits of reason and self-restraint that
are conducive to a *modus vivendi* and other minimal conditions of a civil
order. Without denying these functional justifications of civility, this chapter
has argued for the intrinsic importance of the virtue of civility in terms of the
greater humanity and sociability it yields in civilized societies (cf. Miller 1981,
124–25). Above and beyond the baseline of peace and order it makes possible, civility is a virtue deeply implicated in democratic ideals of social mobility, inclusivity, equal respect, and mutual recognition. In contrast to the many
critical portrayals of capitalism in the nineteenth and twentieth centuries,
Hume insists that commerce, like civility, promotes a basic respect for others

that supersedes more fundamental differences of nationality, race, or creed. Commerce reveals the conventionality of ostensibly "natural" differences. That accidental differences of race, religion, creed, or affiliation have been invested with controversy and enmity—as they are in nationalism, ethnocentrism, and sectarianism—is both profoundly unnatural and an affront to the basic norms of a democratic social order. This is surely not the end of the story, as subsequent critics of "bourgeois" civil society have complained: commerce may itself prove compatible with the creation of invidious distinctions, inequalities, and even, ironically, incivility. However, the full measure of commercial civilization cannot be taken without first reckoning with Hume's singular optimism about the transformational possibilities of the modern commercial economy.

Notes

1 Burke asks whether the improved physical condition of the laboring poor through "an increase of labor be on the whole a *good* or an *evil*." Burke declines to answer this question in the context of a tract defending the justice of free trade (1871, 134–36).
2 J. G. A. Pocock (1975, 462–67) has done much to draw attention to these themes, suggesting that eighteenth-century disagreements between defenders of classical republican ideals of antiquity and modern advocates of commerce were ultimately "dialectical."
3 For a more extended discussion of this point about Hume's comparative optimism, see Stephen Buckle (1991, 250–51) and Duncan Forbes (1975, 87–88).
4 On the more general issue, see Pocock (1985c, 130–31). Pocock's subsequent point about Hume's worries over excessive public debt is well taken (132–33). One wonders, however, if the corrupting effects of public debt are for Hume a *necessary* or a *contingent* feature of commercial society. A slightly different emphasis on the answer to this question may be found in John Robertson (1983, 154–60). Conversely, on Hume's worries about how commercial prosperity may lead to the equally undesirable outcome of universal empire, see Corey Venning (1976, 79–92). In contrast to subsequent nineteenth-century complaints about the failures and shortcomings of capitalism, the main worry in the eighteenth century seems to have been that commerce would in fact prove all *too* successful in the kinds of social transformations it ushered in.
5 For John Locke's ambivalence about commerce and his numerous complaints about luxury, see Richard Boyd (2002, 31–62).
6 James Farr (1988, 51–69) has explored this matter of the scientific or "enlightening" impetus of eighteenth-century thought in greater detail.
7 My argument parallels a similar discussion of toleration as a *modus vivendi* recently put forward by Andrew Murphy (2002).
8 Emphasis added. Interestingly, this usage of the adjective *civil* most emphatically distinguishes the civil from the military—as, for example, in the contemporary distinction between civilians and military combatants—rather than using *civil* as a synonym for *political* and the antonym of *ecclesiastical*, as did Hobbes, Locke, and countless other seventeenth-century authors. It should also be noted that Hume believes that this "civil" power of a trading nation is in and of itself a power no less important for national greatness than the classical emphasis on martial spirit. Compare with Christopher Berry (1994, 150–52).

9 Notable conceptual histories of the emergence of the concept of civil society include Adam Seligman (1992); Krishan Kumar (1993); Edward Shils (1991); and John Keane (1988). For detailed etymological analyses of the ways in which leading figures of the Scottish Enlightenment actually employed the term, see Christopher Berry (2003b) and Fania Oz-Salzberger (2001).

10 For a fuller account and defense of liberalism as a *modus vivendi*, see Charles Larmore (1987).

11 For a succinct treatment of this distinction between the "natural virtues" and "artificial virtues" in Hume, see David Fate Norton (1993b, 162–68). For a slightly different emphasis on the relative priority of these "natural" and "artificial" virtues, see Knud Haakonssen (1982, 212–13); cf. Frederick Whelan (1985, 224–27).

12 For a complementary discussion of how self-interest is the sole force capable of redirecting and channeling our natural avidity, see Andrew Skinner (1993, 227–29).

13 Emphasis in original. It should be noted here that Hobbes did not question the connection between manners and morals—he only insisted that the manners he described were points of *small* morals.

14 For a more extensive discussion of self-transcendence and the moral virtue of pity in Rousseau, see Boyd (2004a).

15 See also the treatment of Nicholas Phillipson (1983).

16 Mark Kingwell (1993, 363–87) has similarly argued for the democratic potential of politeness as the reciprocal "polishing" of individuals—in contrast to the merely formal aspects of manners, which create invidious distinctions, snobbery, and exclusion.

17 Nancy Rosenblum has defended a similar kind of "easy spontaneity" in our treatment of others in everyday life (1998, 351–54).

18 For a compelling hypothesis about why eighteenth-century moral ideals of politeness may have decomposed into merely formal notions of manners, see Kingwell (1993, 382–87).

19 Christopher Berry (1997, 138–39) has noted the etymological connection between *civility*, *civilization* and *city-dwelling*, or what we might think of as *urbanity*. Presumably it is this aspect of civility that contributes to increased humanity and sociability.

20 For examples of conservative deployments of civility as equivalent to traditional values, see Stephen L. Carter (1998). See John Keane (1998) for a prominent criticism of such conservative deployments of civility. Mark Kingwell has argued that the common objection against civility as necessarily politically conservative and supportive of the status quo is too facile (1995, especially chap. 7). Compare Boyd (2004b).

21 My emphasis. Cf. the inegalitarian interpretation of this same passage by David Miller (1981, 134–35).

22 On the difficulties of identifying this "middle station of life," see especially Duncan Forbes (1975, 176–80).

23 Original emphasis.

24 A distinction expressed already in the seventeenth century by John Locke (1988, 294).

25 For a more extensive discussion of Hume's arguments in the context of the problem of economic disparities between nations, see Hont (2005e [1983]).

26 For an excellent treatment of this problematic in both Smith and Hume, see Nicholas Phillipson (1983, 179–202).

27 For a more extensive discussion of the role of merchants and contracts in forging relationships between strangers, see Margaret Schabas (1994, 125–28, 131).

28 See, for example, many of the recent contributions to Anne Jaap Jacobson, ed. (2000).

29 Compare this emphasis on the dynamic aspects of the competitive economy to the writings of the early Chicago economist Frank H. Knight (1997 [1935]).

5 Hume's Framework for a Natural History of the Passions

*Till Grüne-Yanoff and
Edward F. McClennen*

> In pretending therefore to explain the principles of human nature, we in
> effect propose a compleat system of the sciences, built on a foundation
> almost entirely new, and the only one upon which they can stand with
> any security.
>
> (Hume 2000a, xvi)

1. Introduction

David Hume's concept of *passion*, as developed in *A Treatise of Human
Nature*, serves as the basic building block of his political economy. The
characteristics Hume ascribes to the passions in this work crucially shape
the viewpoint in his later essays. In particular, he argues that observed
behavior results exclusively from the passions, and that the passions are
original existences. Furthermore, to understand Hume's account of economic development and his policy recommendations, it is essential to grasp
not only the primary role of the passions but the fact that reason serves the
passions.

   This view of the passions as irreducible and not subject to rational correction seems at first sight to collide with Hume's historical outlook, which
strives to explain the *development* of commerce, borrowing habits, international trade, and so forth. In this paper, we show how his position on the
passions and his historical outlook come together in his political economy.
First, we investigate the mechanism by which, according to Hume, institutions and other situational conditions influence people's behavior. We
demonstrate that Hume construes these influences as a type of refinement—as
the formation of new passions based on the perception of new external
impressions. We also discuss Hume's account of the different ways in which
a newly formed passion interacts with existing passions—whether it eliminates the existence of contrary passions, overrules the effect of the existing
passions, or results in an altogether new effect. The combination of this
theory of predominant passions and the theory of refinement, we argue, is
the core of Hume's *natural history of the passions*; this dynamic framework

of passion change provides the basis for explaining the development of economic and political institutions.

We then turn to Albert Hirschman's thesis that Hume praises the rise of commerce as the rise of the benign passion of interest, which supposedly suppresses the more violent and disruptive motivations of which humans are capable. We counter Hirschman's view by showing that Hume's use of the concept *interest* is ambiguous. It appears both in the narrow sense of avarice and in a more expansive sense; and while he certainly maintains the connection between the development of commerce and the dominance of interest in the narrow sense, he insists on the disruptive nature of this passion. *Interest* in its wider meaning differs substantially from *interest* as mere avarice, in that it is the result of rational self-restraint. Within the dynamic framework of passion change discussed in this paper, we illustrate how to demystify this notion of rational self-restraint. Refinement—the formation of new passions through the perception of new impressions—is a process initiated not only by accidental historical developments, but also through rational mediation. Reason—when providing insight into the suboptimal quality of actions driven by momentary, selfish desires—allows for such a rational refinement. It introduces external restraints that can bring about the formation of new, dominant passions, which in turn result in more beneficial actions. Thus we conclude that Hume not only provides a dynamic framework of passion change, but also envisages a notion of rational self-restraint within this framework. Contra Hirschman, then, we show that Hume distinguishes two types of commercial developments: one, socially disruptive, that is based on avarice; and another, more beneficial, that is based on rational self-restraint.

2. Passions in Explanation and Policy Advice

Passions, according to Hume, are irreducible impressions that exhibit constant conjunctions with human actions.[1] Within his program of a "compleat system of sciences," the explanation of action enjoys a new foundation as the result of his elaboration of passions. A passion, like any impression, is an *original existence*, analogous to other physical states of a person.[2] That a passion arises through the mediation of an idea only specifies its origin; it does not mean that it can be reduced to other mentally represented components, like ideas or other impressions. In this sense, passions are primitive, irreducible entities of the mind. Nonetheless, Hume deems them worthy of an extended analysis.[3]

Further, the relation between passions and actions is just as constant as are connections between phenomena in the natural sciences. Just as observations of the natural world enable us to explain and predict physical phenomena, so too the presence or absence of a particular passion allows us to explain and predict an individual's every action.[4]

> [I]f we compare these two cases, that of a person, who has very strong motives of interest or safety to forbear any action, and that of another, who lies under no such obligation, we shall find ... that the only *known* difference betwixt them lies in this, that in the former case we conclude from *past experience*, that the person never will perform that action, and in the latter, that he possibly or probably will perform it.
>
> (Hume 2000a, 312)

Further, because Hume sees the passions as primitive, irreducible entities of the individual mind, he construes them also as the ultimate motivations for actions. In particular, Hume's conception of the passions limits the role of reason in motivating actions: because of the nature of human motives, reason never constitutes a motivating force *in itself*. For Hume, reason is a purely inferential faculty that allows and regulates the influence of arguments on our beliefs. What reason does not have is any representational faculty. Anything that is before the mind must be derived from the senses or from reflection; reason in itself is impotent to produce any such mental representation. In particular, therefore, reason cannot produce an impression of pleasure or pain by itself, or an idea with similar content.[5] Yet Hume identifies exactly those reflective impressions, the passions, as the motivational causes of behavior. Because reason cannot produce these impressions, it cannot by itself cause actions. Thus, reason does not constitute a motivating force in itself, but, as we will show in section 6, it can form a motivating force *in interaction* with the passions. This qualification has important implications for interpreting Hume's views on the limits of reason and his explanation of human action.

Hume, it can be concluded, sees the passions as the fundamental *explanans* of actions.[6] He expresses this conviction unequivocally in his essays on economics, as when he states that "our passions are the *only* causes for labor" (Hume 1985s [1752a], 261, emphasis added); when he declares that people's borrowing habits depend *solely* on their *temper* (1985v [1752d], 299); and when he invokes the notion of an *infallible attraction*, "arising from the interests and passions" to explain the drain of the surplus of specie from a richer to a poorer country (1985x [1752e], 313).

The irreducibility of passions and their resistance to rational manipulation also have consequences for Hume's discussion of policy formulation. There, he argues against the attempt to reign in contradiction to the desires and tastes of the majority of subjects. Any policy by the state that aims to manipulate people's passions is doomed to fail. Instead, leaders must cater their laws to the passions of their subjects:

> Sovereigns must take mankind as they find them, and cannot pretend to introduce any violent change in their principles and ways of thinking. A long course of time, with a variety of accidents and circumstances, are requisite to produce those great revolutions, which so much diversify the face of human affairs. ... It is best policy to comply with the

common bent of mankind, and give it all the improvements of which it is susceptible.

(1985s [1752a], 260)

Given the irreducibility of passions, and the inability of reason to be a motivating force in itself, the policymaker is advised to take the fundamental human passions as a given. The sovereign should not attempt to influence his subjects in any direct way, because it would be futile: he cannot manipulate the relevant causal laws. Instead, a leader should design institutions and implement policies that accommodate the basic passions, the "common bent," of individuals.

Thus Hume considers the passions as basic both in their functions as *explanans* and as parameters of policy advice. This aspect of his program is very much in accord with the idea, prominent in eighteenth-century thought, that human nature is to a large extent uniform. As Hume states, "It is universally acknowledged that there is a great uniformity among the actions of men, in all nations and ages, and that human nature remains still the same, in its principles and operations" (Hume 2000b, 150). The uniformity thesis, however, seems *prima facie* to collide with Hume's approach to social change. The principal aim of his economic essays, after all, is to clarify the principles behind a state's rising powers and the prospering of a nation. For this, he investigates the development of commerce and luxury consumption, the changes in the use of monetary means, and the progress of credit and international trade. His abundant use of historical examples in all of these essays reveals his interest in discovering the principles of change, of development, or—as one would say today—of evolution. Given the status of the passions as ultimate *explanans*, one might wonder how the uniformity thesis could be compatible with this historical outlook and historical method.

A correct understanding of the uniformity thesis dissolves the apparent incompatibility. It does not claim all humans share uniform and stable passions. Rather, the *relations* between passions and actions remain stable, while the actual passions vary between people.[7] Human nature is uniform in its "principles and operations," not in its actual motivations, as he expresses in the *Treatise*:

> Whether we consider mankind according to the difference of sexes, ages, governments, conditions, or methods of education; the same uniformity and regular operation of natural principles are discernible. Like causes still produce like effects; in the same manner as in the mutual action of the elements and powers of nature.
>
> (Hume 2000a, 401)

Once the thesis is understood this way, causal uniformity neatly fits together with the passions' irreducibility in Hume's historical framework. The passions are basic for Hume in the sense that they motivate action; and they are the

basic impressions social scientists and policymakers deal with when understanding people's actions and making recommendations. But this does not
imply that the passions are unchangeable. Instead, passions are subject to
changes in conditions. By manipulating a person's situation—that is, by con-
trolling for the "variety of circumstances and accidents" (Hume 1985s [1752a],
260) an individual might encounter—one can facilitate a gradual transformation of the passions. A systematic analysis of these environmental influences—
a *natural history of the passions*—discovers the regularities behind those
transformations.[8] On the basis of the causal uniformity thesis, however, the
relations between passions and actions remain constant; hence changes in
people's passions explain changes in their actions, which in turn feature as the
means to explain cultural and historical developments.

In his economic and political essays, Hume widely employs this framework of a natural history of the passions to explain an increase in the
industriousness of a nation's people. In particular, he applies this approach
to three phenomena: (1) the increased desire for luxury goods, which in turn
is caused by the increased provision of luxury goods through accelerated
foreign trade (1985s [1752a], 264); (2) the increased desire for art or musical
entertainment as a result of a refinement of taste, brought about through
increased exposure to art or music (1985dd [1757], 235); and (3) the desire to
apply oneself to one's employment as the result of the experience of pleasures derived from having an occupation in a professional society (1985v
[1752d], 300). All these examples pursue the explanation of institutional
change (the rise of luxury consumption, the emergence of a cultured society,
the rise of a new work ethic) by reference to a change in individual actions
based on a transformation of the motivating passions.

Nevertheless, while Hume's concept of the passions does not rule out their
change or even manipulation, it imposes severe restriction on any such process. A human being is neither able to conjure up a new passion out of
nothing, nor able to manipulate any of the existing ones. For that, it requires at
least another passion, that is, another impression of pleasure derived from a
new impression or idea. According to Hume, *any* transformation of passions
must come about through the interaction of passions themselves. Thus the
accounts of passion changes in his framework of a natural history of the
passions all employ the same underlying mechanism: to pit one passion
against another. The motivating impulse of a passion can only be counter-
balanced by a contrary passion: "Where two objects are contrary, the one
destroys the other" (Hume 2000b, 106n). John Immerwahr calls this Hume's
"theory of the predominant passion."[9] This mechanism needs clarification,
however, as Hume's notion of contrariness is quite complicated.

3. Influence of Contrariness on the Mental Appearance of Passions

Hume offers two accounts of contrariness: either it occurs directly between
passions, or between the causal effects of passions. Accordingly, that one

passion "counterbalances" or destroys another can be understood either as affecting the existence of the second passion, or as affecting only the causal effect of that passion. In the first case, the passions are "directly contrary in their sensation" (Hume 2000a, 330), as in the case between pride and humility or love and hatred. Hume does not elaborate on this rather vague notion, as he thinks, "this decision [whether two passions are directly contrary] we always pronounce at first sight, without any enquiry or reasoning" (ibid., 70).

In the second case, the causal influences of two passions, but not the two passions themselves, cancel each other out. That is, two passions are contrary if they produce *contrary impulses* (Hume 2000a, 415). My anger, for instance, might dispose me to shout at you, while my love and respect for you, being stronger, cancels out the causal power of my anger and makes me speak to you about our conflict in a calm fashion. Love, Hume would say, is contrary to anger in this case, by overriding its causal effect, without eliminating the presence of anger itself (ibid., 492). In this case of contrariness, the passions are not inherently contrary, but contrary only to the extent that their effects cannot both pertain at the same time.

Employing both notions of contrary passions, Hume distinguishes three different outcomes when contrary passions are opposed:

> 'Tis observable, that where the objects of contrary passions are presented at once, ... it sometimes happens, that both the passions exist successively, and by short intervals; sometimes, that they destroy each other, and neither of them takes place; and sometimes that both of them remain united in the mind.
>
> (Hume 2000a, 441)

Hume explains the different ways in which contrary passions interact by the difference in the relation between their objects—that is, the objects that causally trigger these passions.

If two different objects trigger contrary passions, these passions are experienced alternately, and do not have any effect on each other. If a political event fires my patriotism, for instance, and at the same time I am personally humiliated by failing an exam, then according to Hume, neither of the passions affects the other. Rather, I feel pride for my country, when I think of it, and I feel humiliated when I think of my poor intellectual performance. These sensations remain separate in the mind like "oil and vinegar" (Hume 2000a, 443), neither blending with nor affecting each other. Thus, the *prima facie* contrary passions are not contrary in either of the two notions Hume discusses.

If one and the same object arouses contrary passions, but the passions are not "directly contrary" and only contrary in their effects, then the stronger passion eliminates the effect of the weaker passion, without eliminating its existence. This happens in the case of my simultaneous love and anger for one and the same person. Both passions themselves continue to coexist within me (remain "united in the mind") such that I feel anger and love at the same time, but my action will be driven by only one of the two passions.

In some cases, in which one and the same object arouses contrary passions of equal intensity, these passions cancel each other out. For this to take place, two conditions have to be fulfilled: "Contrary passions are not capable of destroying each other, except when their contrary movements exactly rencounter,[10] and are opposite in their direction, as well as in the sensation they produce" (Hume 2000a, 442). Here, both types of contrariness have to be satisfied. For one, the causal effects of the passions have to be contrary. Exact opposition in this sense is attained only if the causal effects spring from one and the same object. Further, the passions themselves have to be contrary in their *direction*. Without being very clear on this notion, Hume seems to imagine passions as having a direction and intensity in their sensation, which can add up and cancel each other. Only then do contrary passions eliminate each other: "To excite any passion, and at the same time raise an equal share of its antagonist, is immediately to undo what was done, and must leave the mind at last perfectly calm and indifferent" (ibid., 278).

Hume thus explains the different possibilities resulting from a clash of two contrary passions by referring to the way their objects relate, and to the strength and direction of the passion aroused. In addition to this analysis, he points out two further ways in which contrary passions affect each other. The fourth scenario envisages a situation in which the mind is affected by the prospect of an event with uncertain outcomes. Here, the passions, arising from each of the uncertain outcomes, are fused into one new impression that is associated with the event.[11] Finally, in his *Dissertation on the Passions*, Hume discusses a fifth option, in which the weaker of the two contrary passions enhances the intensity of the stronger one.[12] For example, the pain and suffering a marathon runner experiences during a competition will not diminish his sense of triumph if he wins; rather, the suffering will intensify his feeling of pride and accomplishment.[13]

Altogether, passions have to satisfy three conditions to cancel each other: (1) they arise from the same object, (2) they have contrary directions, and (3) they are of the same intensity. Only then does the dynamic of passion have an effect on one's mental state—leaving the mind "calm and indifferent"; the passions cease to exist as impressions of the mind. The restrictive conditions Hume identifies for mutual cancellation make clear that the dynamics of passions are, for the most part, not driven by the tendency of the mind to come to rest by eliminating contrary passions. Rather, the opposite holds: human beings do not necessarily act on the basis of unanimous, coherent passions, but on a jumble of passions that push in contrary directions.[14] In fact, the persistence of contrary passions is a central element of Hume's concept of human nature, as he expresses most clearly in his essay "On Polygamy and Divorces":

These principles of human nature, you'll say, are contradictory: But what is man but a heap of contradictions! Though it is remarkable, that, where principles are, after this manner, contrary in their operation, they do not always destroy each other; but the one or the other may predominate on any particular occasion, according as circumstances are more or less favorable to it.

(Hume 1985m [1752c], 188)

Hume's concept of human motivation emphasizes diversity, conflict, and change. The mental states he employs as *explanans* and parameters for policy advice are not forced into the corset of consistency or coherence. For the most part, passions do not cancel each other out, but maintain their presence in the face of contrary passions. Hume therefore does *not* anticipate models of human motivation that are driven by logical principles and the overall consistency of the mind's content.[15] Nevertheless, in his framework of passion change, all of the different kinds of contrariness discussed here play a key role.

4. Refinement

The transformation of passions manifests as a change in the causal effects of the totality of an individual's passions. This change of causal effects occurs when one or more newly emerged passions "tip the balance," so to speak, of the totality of passions. The question then is which conditions give rise to new passions that effect such a change?

Within the passions, Hume distinguishes between the violent and the calm. Humans are "by nature" fitted with the violent passions, or passions in the narrow sense; the extent to which they are susceptible to these passions marks their tempers. Some people may naturally be endowed with the calm passions, and in particular an appreciation for aesthetic and moral beauty. The rest of us, however, can cultivate the ability to *feel*[16] aesthetic and moral beauty through experience of successively finer differentiations—such as the active practice of an art, or the regular contemplation of beautiful objects—leading to a refinement in our tastes. Hume defines "delicacy of taste" as the state "Where the organs are so fine, as to allow nothing to escape them; and at the same time so exact as to perceive every ingredient in the composition" (Hume 1985dd [1757], 235). Delicacy of taste depends on the subtlety and precision with which we can identify the features of our (external) impressions. The senses are like other bodily organs, whose regular employment leads to their heightened ability to perform an assigned task. But this enhanced ability to discriminate leads automatically, according to Hume, to an increase in the motivational force that comes with the appreciation of beauty: the desire to produce or to own a piece of art, or the desire to perform a good deed.

> This is a new reason for cultivating a relish in the liberal arts. Our judgment will strengthen by this exercise: We shall form juster notions

of life: Many things, which please or afflict others, will appear to us too frivolous to engage our attention: And we shall lose by degrees that sensibility and delicacy of passion, which is so incommodious.

(Hume 1985a [1741a], 6)

The cultivation of taste, then, leads to two separable effects. First, by increasing the sensitivity of the mind, new impressions widen the scope of passionate emotions. Objects and actions that may in the past have inspired indifference now create reflective impressions that can influence actions. Second, these newly acquired tastes have the power to counterbalance some of the violent passions. Refinement does not directly reduce the power of violent impressions; rather, through the mechanism discussed earlier, the new calm passions acquire greater force and dominate the causal effects of the violent passions:

> The emotions which they [the tastes] excite are soft and tender. They draw off the mind from the hurry of business and interest; cherish reflection; dispose to tranquillity; and produce an agreeable melancholy, which, of all dispositions of the mind, is the best suited for love and friendship.
>
> (Hume 1985a [1741a], 7)

But refinement is not restricted to the perception of art. Any sense that can provide pleasure can be refined. The pleasures of the palate, of providing "for friends, family, or every proper object of generosity or compassion," and of "ambition, study, or conversation" (Hume 1985t [1752b], 269), can be increased by a cultivation of the sense and taste for them.[17]

We conclude that the change of passions through refinement proceeds in three steps. First, exercise develops a dormant sense faculty, which leads to an increase in (primary) impressions. Second, these primary impressions lead to an increase in secondary impressions, namely, passions for or against certain primary impressions. Third, these new passions—if they are strong enough—cancel out the effects of passions contrary to them, which previously caused the individual's behavior. This is how refinement transforms the motivational dispositions of humans.

5. Passion and Economic Development

The mechanism of refinement together with the theory of predominant passions offers a foundation for Hume's political and economic thought. His natural history of the passions enables him to explain institutional changes, especially of economic institutions.[18] In particular, this framework provides the basis for his explanation of why the production and trade of consumption goods creates such an unstoppable dynamic of its own:

> [Foreign Trade] rouses men from their indolence; and presenting the gayer and more opulent part of the nation with objects of luxury, which

they never before dreamed of, raises in them the desire of a more splendid way of life than what their ancestors enjoyed.

(Hume 1985s [1752a], 264)

In this passage, it is exposure to luxury goods, rather than to works of art, that refines the taste. Seeing others indulging in luxury consumption, the observers themselves become sensitized and develop a taste for a "more splendid way of life." The desire for a better life in turn spurs industriousness.[19] Engaging in commercial activity in order to satisfy one's desires, one undergoes a second refinement, "craving ... for exercise and employment" (Hume 1985v [1752d], 300), the taste for pure engagement and challenge for mind and body, regardless of its potential to satisfy specific desires. This passion finds its expression in the amassing of money or other financial resources, which in turn makes future commercial activity possible. This new desire for money now stands as a passion contrary to the desire for luxury goods. Even though the desire for luxury goods precedes and triggers a desire for money, according to Hume, the desire for money ultimately dominates; hence, the spendthrift feudal landlord is replaced by the economically oriented bourgeois. "It is an infallible consequence of all industrious professions, to ... make the love of gain prevail over the love of pleasure" (Hume 1985v [1752d], 301).[20] One must be careful, however, not to read *refinement* as a positive evaluative term. What we described above (in section 4, "Refinement,") is a central mechanism of Hume's natural history of the passions; the result of such a transformation is not necessarily good. Nevertheless, Albert Hirschman has argued that Hume is an uncompromising apologist of the new exchange-oriented society. According to that reading, Hume not only explains how refinement processes lead to the rise of love of gain and hence to the increase of commercial activity, but he also endorses this development as desirable. Commenting on Hume's claim that "[i]t is an infallible consequence of all industrious professions, to ... make the love of gain prevail over the love of pleasure," Hirschman suggests that

Hume's statement can stand as the culmination of the movement of ideas that has been traced [in this work]: capitalism is here hailed by a leading philosopher of the age because it would activate some benign human proclivities at the expense of some malignant ones—because of the expectation that, in this way, it would repress and perhaps atrophy the more destructive and disastrous components of human nature.

(Hirschman 1977, 66)

Hirschman's thesis is that the modern age of commerce is ushered in as the result of the ascendancy of "interest" (understood as love of gain or "avarice, the spur of industry" (Hume 1985i [1741i], 93)) over love of pleasure and also over the more violent and disruptive passions. But Hume in fact takes a more ambivalent position regarding the love of gain, in that he allows that, in certain cases, it may prove to be most disruptive. In speaking of the love of gain, Hume is not always as approving as Hirschman presents him:

> All the other passions, besides this of interest, are either easily restrain'd, or are not of such pernicious consequences when indulg'd. ... This avidity alone, of acquiring goods and possessions for ourselves and our nearest friends, is insatiable, perpetual, universal, and directly destructive of society.
>
> (Hume 2000a, 491–92)

Love of gain, then, is sometimes a virtue, sometimes a vice. While it can counterbalance some of the passions that were traditionally seen as vicious (such as lust, gluttony, anger, and particularly sloth), as well as those that were viewed as especially disruptive (for example, glory and dominion), it can also lead to the suppression of passions that Hume regards as positive—namely, friendship, benevolence, love, and honor. To speak as Hirschman does of interest (in the narrow sense) as activating "some benign human proclivities at the expense of some malignant ones" is therefore a bit misleading. To be sure, the issue here is complicated. Hume does think that the love of gain is the driving force behind the development of commerce, and that the institutions of commerce in turn produce benefits for its participants. And again, as others have argued, Hume indeed hails specific aspects of commerce (for example, market contracts, uniform prices) as exerting such a beneficial influence.[21] But these results are beneficial *despite* the nature of interest in the narrow sense, not because of it.

Hume contrasts the narrow sense of the interested affection as "love of gain," or "avarice," with another, much more expansive meaning of "interest." Hirschman himself points to this other meaning, when he states: "[In] the late sixteenth century, its meaning was by no means limited to the material aspects of a person's welfare; rather, it comprised the totality of human aspirations" (Hirschman 1977, 32). Now, in the *Treatise*, the *Enquiries*, and the *Essays*, Hume typically uses *interest* in the more general sense Hirschman describes, namely, to refer to whatever is of concern to the individual (which may be a concern for oneself, or a concern for the well-being of others, such as family and friends).[22] This is especially the case whenever Hume speaks about the *true* interests of the individual. Hirschman, however, does not associate this more expansive concept of interest with Hume.[23] Instead he regards Hume as among those thinkers who *narrowed* the late-sixteenth-century concept of interest to mean essentially the desire for material gain.[24]

Hume does refer to this narrower concept, and he speaks of it as a "universal passion, which operates at all times, in all places, and upon all persons" (Hume 1985k [1742a], 113).[25] Note, however, that for Hume, interest in either the narrow sense (love of gain) or the broad sense (the sum total of aspirations of the individual) is a passion. Moreover, in either case, it is a *calm but strong* passion. How is it that love of gain or interest in the more general sense is a calm but strong passion? Hirschman's interpretation of the more general sense of interest is very useful here. It is a passion that involves, in some way or other, reason or reflection. We suggest that this is true of interest in the more narrow sense as well: reason is once again involved.

6. The Place of Reason

But just what role does reason play in regard to interest, in either its broad or narrow senses? The question is important, for the proper resolution of this has important implications for the first of the additional issues raised above, regarding whether interest (in some sense or other of that term) represses the more violent passions.

How, then, is this idea of a "reasoned" or "reasonable" interest to be understood? Much has been written about Hume's claim that "reason is, and ought to be, the slave of the passions, and can never pretend to any other office than to serve and obey them" (Hume 2000a, 415). But the sense in which, for Hume, reason *serves* the passions has not been sufficiently elucidated.

For Hume, reason clearly plays an important role in deliberation. To be sure, its role is not to establish what our ends should be, but to establish what we ought to do, *given* our ends (which are set by the passions).[26] But in this context reason functions clearly as more than just the *slave* of the passions, for Hume insists that it is unreasonable when, "in exerting any passion in action, we choose means insufficient for the design'd end" (Hume 2000a, 416). And reason, in this context, not only makes a judgment, but exerts a powerful influence: "The moment we perceive ... the insufficiency of any means our passions *yield to our reason* without any opposition" (ibid., emphasis added). Of course, reason does not dictate to passion. It simply makes clear what must be done if passions' objective is to be realized. This is true regardless of whether we are speaking about the very specific passion of love of gain, or the passion associated with the more general sense of the interests of the person.

Hume's commentators have also understood that reason does advise regarding the appropriate means to the ends that passions set. What has not been sufficiently emphasized is that, on Hume's account, reason has another function to perform, one in which it plays a more directly constraining role. In a number of places, Hume speaks of a passion that has been informed by reason as to the best manner in which to pursue it, namely, by *self-restraint* rather than impetuous, headlong pursuit. Hume develops this idea in one of the more remarkable passages of the *Treatise*:

> 'Tis certain, that no affection of the human mind has both a sufficient force, and a proper direction to counter-ballance the love of gain, and render men fit members of society, by making them abstain from the

> possessions of others. ... There is no passion ... capable of controlling
> the interested affection, but the very affection itself, by an alteration of
> its direction. Now this alteration must necessarily take place upon the
> least reflection; since 'tis evident, that the passion is much better satis-
> fy'd by its restraint, than by its liberty.
>
> (Hume 2000a, 492)[27]

How are we to understand Hume's remark that the alteration "must
necessarily take place upon the least reflection"? The question under reflection here is whether "the passion is much better satisfy'd by its restraint,
than by its liberty." But this reflection concerns a deliverance of instrumental reason—which is the one kind of reason Hume acknowledges as
playing a role in the choice of an action. Connecting this with Hume's
notion about refinements of a passion, we suggest that the natural way to
interpret these remarks is to understand Hume as putting forward a distinct
sense in which a passion can be refined, namely, by a reasoned reflection
that the passion is better served by its being restrained than by allowing it
to motivate action in an unrestrained manner. So interpreted, this is a form
of refinement in which reason, then, plays a central role. It is thus not
simply a matter of becoming more sensitized, as a more or less accidental
result of increasingly nuanced experiences. But this means that, even though
Hume is often characterized as denying the possibility of the rational criticism of the passions, certain kinds of passions—namely headlong or
unconstrained passions—*are* subject to rational criticism, precisely on the
grounds that when a passion is unconstrained it is less suited to achieve its
objective than when it is constrained.

Interestingly, Hirschman does not know what to do with this passage. He
suggests that counteracting a passion with itself is not "an easy operation to
perform" (Hirschman 1977, 25), and remarks with deprecation that

> One might of course quibble that to avow the need for some reason or
> reflection ... means to introduce an alien element (which, moreover, is
> supposed to be the "slave of the passions") into an arena in which only
> passion is supposed to fight with passion.
>
> (Hirschman 1977, 25)

But where is the flaw? Hirschman just is not clear about the role that reason
plays in Hume's account of the passions, and this misunderstanding leads
him to believe that only a passion can provide a countervailing force to
another passion, excluding reason completely from this arena. This, however, misses the significance of there being a distinct kind of refinement in
which reason plays a role.

Hume's account of the way that interest constrains itself is, indeed, puzzling. Returning to the last passage quoted, he states that self-restraint must
"take place upon the least reflection; since 'tis evident, that the passion is

much better satisfy'd by its restraint, than by its liberty." This remark seems to suggest that humans are capable of constraining themselves, and this by simply *resolving*, after due reflection, to take the more effective course of action—which is to constrain themselves to pursue their interest in a less headlong manner. However, it is hard to see how to fit this idea into his general account of the dynamics of the passions.

Somewhat later in the *Treatise*, Hume returns to this topic, and offers a different, and what many have taken to be a more plausible, account of self-restraint. He begins by noting that humans are subject to the infirmity of preferring their immediate interests to their greater, long-term interests. In so doing, they "act in contradiction to their known interest; and in particular ... prefer any trivial advantage, that is present, to the main-tenance of order in society" (Hume 2000a, 535). Moreover, and most importantly, this weakness will not be overcome by "the least reflection." Indeed, due to the particular nature of the passions and the restricted role of reason, it is difficult to overcome this infirmity:

> I may have recourse to study and reflection within myself; to the advice of friends; to frequent meditation, and repeated resolution: And having experienc'd how ineffectual all these are, I may embrace with pleasure any other expedient, by which I may impose a restraint upon myself, and guard against this weakness.
>
> (Hume 2000a, 536–37)

Reason, then, in this case cannot shape the motivating passion. That is, a rational insight into the ineffectiveness of a certain way of acting is not sufficient to persuade the agent to choose differently—to prefer long-term to short-term advantage. All reason can do is uncover the inefficiency and identify an "external" way to deal with it. What he recommends is the expedient to which Ulysses resorts when he ties himself to the mast:

> 'Tis evident such a remedy can never be effectual without correcting this propensity [to prefer the contiguous to the remote]; and as 'tis impossible to change or correct anything material in our nature, the utmost we can do is to change our circumstances and situation, and render the observance of the laws of justice our nearest interest.
>
> (Hume 2000a, 537)

This change of circumstances is to be accomplished by putting into place an external system of sanctions administered by magistrates, who serve at the pleasure of the citizens, and thus have an immediate interest in the execu-tion of justice and the maintenance of civil order. In turn, the threat of the application of such sanctions motivates persons to look to their greater, longer-range good. Hume elaborates the argument, with many ramifications, into a general account of the origin of government.[28] For our discussion, however, the important point is that, while the constraints are self-imposed and the passion that drives us to impose those constraints is interest itself, the constraints put into place are *external*. That is, a mental resolve to act in a certain way will not suffice.[29] There is, in all of this, a striking anticipation of how modern economics and game theory have chosen to deal with the issue of preference for short-term as opposed to long-term interests.[30]

Moreover, an intriguing question remains: Regarding the problem posed by our preference for the more contiguous over the more remote, why does Hume insist that intellectual insight into the problem does *not* suffice—that we require more than a mere act of will? His stance is especially puzzling considering his earlier insistence, in the case of restraining interest from pursuing its objective in a headlong fashion, that the refinement of a passion requires only reasoned reflection. In the interest of space, we will have to save this last question for future consideration. It does seem clear, however, that Hume's appeal, in the one case, to an act of will based on rational insight, and an appeal, in the other case, to an external device serves as a powerful reminder that we need a much more sophisticated account of practical reasoning, even within the Humean framework, than is captured in the simple idea of "choosing means sufficient to our ends."

7. Conclusion

In discussing Hume's dynamic framework of passion change, we have arrived at three main conclusions: First, passions are the basic *explanans* of human action, but their change is a result of historical developments. Second, the historical development of commerce is driven by the rise of interest, but contrary to Hirschman's thesis, Hume evaluates this passion ambivalently. Third, the version of interest that Hirschman neglects, but which is salient in Hume's work, is not identical to love of gain; instead, it includes interests of a much more general sort, and also includes rational self-control through both "internal" and "external" restraints.

In his effort "to explain the principles of human nature," Hume builds not on one foundation, but on two. On a first level, he sees the passions as basic, both in relation to explanation of human action and in policy advice. But on a second level, he develops a framework for the evolution of motivations, a natural history of the passions. For this framework, the mechanism of refinement and the theory of predominant passions are central. New passions emerge as a result of the development of one's senses, and these new passions interact with the existing passions, either canceling out each other or counterbalancing each other's causal influence on human action. This framework allows Hume to explain how situational changes regularly lead to changes in human action. In particular, it allows him to explain the rise of commerce as the rise of the love of gain, resulting from increased availability of consumption goods, the collapse of traditional concepts of the good life, and changed modes of production.

When he explains the rise of commerce as driven by interest (in the narrow sense), we argued that Hume is aware of the potentially disruptive consequences of the dominance of this interest so understood. By showing this, we sought to correct a view that, since the publication of Hirschman's *The Passions and the Interests*, many have accepted as a definitive statement of Hume's intellectual contribution to economics and political economy. According to this view, Hume endorses commerce, because the passion that spurns its development will repress and harness the more destructive and malignant of the human passions. Hirschman investigates the political justifications for the rise of commerce—and it is true that Hume engages in many arguments to that end—but Hirschman does not manage to connect with some of the most interesting and original aspects of Hume's theory. He gives the impression that Hume sanctions the love of gain's rise to dominance itself. In contrast, we argued that it is a different understanding of "interest"—also closely related to the rise of commerce—to which Hume more often than not draws attention.

Finally, we considered the ways in which reason can influence motivation. We argued that Hume assigns reason a constraining role, but that he appears to speak of two quite different ways in which reason can constrain a passion— by either "external" or "internal" devices. The operation of both constraints leads to the formation of new passions through the process of a refinement mechanism, which in turn cancels out or counterbalances some existing passion. Thus, however this process of rational constraint is interpreted, Hume clearly assigns to reason a greater role than many have supposed.

Notes

We wish to thank the editors of this volume, Joanne Grüne-Yanoff, and two anonymous referees for helpful comments on earlier drafts.

1 Hume himself often presents this relation between passions and actions as a causal relation. He argues, e.g., that "our passions are the only causes for labor" (Hume 1985s [1752a], 261). We think that this is not only an equivocal manner of speaking about causes and constant conjunctions, as Hume at times explicitly distinguishes mere correlation from true causal correlation: "we mistake, as is too usual, a collateral effect for a cause" (Hume 1985u [1752c], 290). However, we cannot argue for this position here with the necessary depth and detail and therefore adhere to a more cautious terminology.
2 "A passion is an original existence, or, if you will, modification of existence, and contains not any representative quality, which renders it a copy of any other existence or modification. When I am angry, I am actually possest with the passion, and in that emotion have no more a reference to any other object, than when I am thirsty, or sick, or more than five foot high" (Hume 2000a, 415).
3 It is important to repeat that, despite this analysis, which consists of a causal analysis and the comparison of similarities between the different passions, Hume thinks of *all* passions as simple and nonreducible. This interpretation is supported by Ardal: "A simple perception cannot be analyzed into distinct parts. Yet Hume thinks that it can be characterized by pointing out its similarity to other

simple perceptions or its difference from them. One can also state the conditions under which it is found to arise, or, in other words, its causal conditions. Thus, for Hume, a simple perception is not just something that can only be pointed to or given a name. Many things may be predicated to it. I shall, indeed, emphasize that the bulk of the second book of the *Treatise* is concerned with stating the causal conditions for the emergence of simple impressions, and indicating various similarities between them" (Ardal 1989, 12).

4 "As the union between motives and actions has the same constancy, as that in any natural operations, so its influence on the understanding is also the same, in determining us to infer the existence of one from the other" (Hume 2000a, 404).

5 For further discussion of Hume's concept of purely *inferential* reason versus the Cartesian notion of *representing* reason, compare Garrett (1997, 26–27).

6 Hume's program has often been described as a Newtonian science of the mind. In particular, the identification of a corpuscular unit (the perceptions, or for the theory of action, the passions), the specification of an observational method (introspection), and the employment of the principle of association have lent credibility to such a claim. See, for example, Penelhum (1993, 120–21); for a cautioning perspective, see Jones (1982).

7 Compare Forbes (1975, especially 113–21) for a discussion of this point. Forbes concludes that "the universal principles are to be regarded as abstractions from the concrete variety of human (= social) experience; Hume's 'general psychology' is concerned with the function and mechanism, not the content of mind, which is various and supplied by social and historical circumstances."

8 The term *natural history of the passions* was coined by Rotwein, who explains further that Hume "frequently ... sought to show that historical transformations in human behavior, e.g. in 'habits, customs and manners' were caused by the influence of various environmental changes on 'human nature,' or, in a word, could be couched in the form of 'laws' " (Rotwein 1976, 119).

9 Immerwahr (1994, 230).

10 To "rencounter" is "to meet, as in battle," "to skirmish," or "to duel."

11 "Impressions and passions are susceptible of an entire union; and like colors, may be blended so perfectly together, that each of them may lose itself, and contribute only to vary that uniform impression, which arises from the whole" (Hume 2000a, 366).

12 "An opposition of passions commonly causes a new emotion in the spirits. ... This new emotion is easily converted into the predominant passion, and in many instances, is observed to encrease its violence, beyond the pitch, at which it would have arrived, had it met no opposition" (Hume 1997, 176).

13 Compare Immerwahr (1994, 230).

14 Our conclusion here is in agreement with Baier, who writes that Hume "portrays opposed passions as mainly alternating, wheeling us about from love of undeserved praise to contempt for our flatterers, from disinterested benevolent love to a 'great partiality in our favour' (Hume 2000a, 321). Hume had written in Book 1 that 'if you wheel about a burning coal with rapidity, it will present to the senses an image of a circle of fire' (Hume 2000a, 35). The fiery circling of our successive passions allows many that threaten to extinguish each other to wheel together, without this threat being realised" (Baier 1991, 145).

15 Recently expressed views that claim Hume as a predecessor of modern economic theory do not sufficiently take into account these differences between Hume's notion of contrariness and the notion of consistency employed in modern microeconomics. For examples of such a claim, see Soule (2000, 153): "Hume's account of human nature does not conflict with modern economic theory; rather, it supplements it by explaining the source of preference"; or Diaye and Lapidus (2005). In Hume's framework, people's actions change not because they adjust

their passions according to a criterion of logical consistency of the sentences expressing these passions, nor to any other criterion of coherence of the passions. While this is one of the central tenets of contemporary microeconomics and decision theory, it is not central to Hume's psychological theory.

16 That we *feel* beauty—instead of perceiving it—is of course central to Hume's concept of moral and aesthetic sentiments: "Morals and criticism are not so properly objects of the understanding as of taste and sentiment. Beauty, whether moral or natural, is felt, more properly than perceived" (Hume 2000b, 210).

17 In an influential paper, Stigler and Becker (1977) have developed this mechanism of refinement for contemporary preference theory. Exposure to activities like listening to music, playing football, or consuming drugs increases our ability to derive satisfaction from such experiences, and thus our desire to continue or repeat them rises as well. Note that the authors speak of improved information, instead of speaking of the refinement of sense organs; the underlying idea is, however, similar.

18 This aspect of Hume's work inspires Skinner to compare Hume with the German Historical School and the American Institutionalists (Skinner 1993, 248).

19 In this particular explanation of the rise of industriousness, the difference between Hume and his close friend Adam Smith becomes quite obvious. Both Hume and Smith endeavored to combine a theory of the mind with a political and economic theory (Skinner 1979, 90–93; 1993, 246). But their respective cognitive models, on which they based their economic theories, are quite distinct. For Hume, the development of commerce begins with the increased desire for luxury goods. For Smith, however, the development starts with the increase in capital accumulation. One might therefore speak of a Humean "demand driven" and a Smithian "supply driven" history of economic development (Davis 2003, especially 273–76, 281–83, 295–96). It is thus largely correct to portray Hume as an antirationalist in relation to his model of institutional development, and to contrast this with Smith's rationalism, which allows reason to guide the self to choose prudent and frugal courses of action. However, the complexity of Hume's model needs to be stressed again. We emphasize the distinction between (i) direct and (ii) indirect manipulation—between (i) the concept that somehow reason itself can "take over" and motivate actions and (ii) the concept that agents are sometimes able to design their future environment in such a way that their own passions will motivate them to do what is in their long-term interest. In section 6 we will argue that Hume allows for the possibility of indirect change of passion. We thus show that rationality has a role in passion formation without Hume being a closet rationalist, and that Hume's and Smith's cognitive models indeed remain fully distinct.

20 A note of caution is necessary here. While the passage quoted from "Of Interest" seems unambiguous, a reading of the essay "Of Refinement in the Arts" raises some doubts. In the latter text, Hume expresses reservation about the dominance of any excessive desire: "The more men refine upon pleasure, the less they indulge in excesses of any kind: because nothing is more destructive to true pleasure than such excesses" (Hume 1985t [1752b], 271). If this passage is read as part of Hume's explanatory program, it contradicts his claim that the love of gain will ultimately prevail over the love of pleasure. Love of gain, if understood as the desire to exclusively use all gains for the sheer amassment of riches, can certainly be deemed excessive; and, since Hume contrasts it with the love of pleasure, it cannot generate more true pleasure than any other desire fulfilled. However, we think that the above passage should not be read as part of his explanatory program. "Of Refinement in the Arts" is a normative tract on the value of refinements of the passions, in which Hume argues that no passion can be judged vicious in itself. As part of that argument, he appeals to an Aristotelian

average principle, which identifies any excess as irrational. But even here he has to qualify the sense in which it is irrational: only for those seeking true pleasure is it irrational to indulge in excesses of any kind. However one defines this true pleasure, we are convinced that Hume here expresses a normative judgment, which ultimately does not touch on the question of explanation. The economical bourgeois might be an irrational miser; his actions are predictable nonetheless.

21 Compare Schabas (1994) and the essay by Richard Boyd in this volume.

22 See, in particular, the discussion about nearer and more remote interests in Hume (2000a, 534–39), and virtually all references to interests (e.g., self-interest, self-love) in the *Enquiry*. Of the more than 20 such references in the *Essays*, all invoke interest in the broader sense.

23 Hirschman may, of course, be correct that this more narrow view of interest was characteristic of the wider circle of thinkers in Hume's time, but it does not capture what is distinctive about Hume's own view.

24 This becomes clear when Hirschman discusses "the eventual identification of interest in its original broad sense with one particular passion, the love of money" (Hirschman 1977, 54) and points to Hume as the leading advocate of this development. His evidence for this claim, however, is meager; all he offers is to quote Hume speaking of avarice "without bothering to disguise it as 'interest'" (ibid.).

25 Hume sometimes refers to the love of gain as avarice (Hume 1985i [1741i], 93). But, in turn, he characteristically speaks of avarice as excessive love of gain, that is, as a vice (Hume 1985j [1741jj], 570). For interest as a matter of love of gain, see Hume (2000a, 491–92) and also Hume (1985a [1741a], 7).

26 "'Tis obvious, that when we have the prospect of pain or pleasure from any object, we feel a consequent emotion of aversion or propensity, and are carry'd to avoid or embrace what will give us this uneasiness or satisfaction. 'Tis also obvious that this emotion rests not here, but making us cast our view on every side, comprehends whatever objects are connected with its original one by the relation of cause and effect. Here then reasoning takes place to discover this relation; and according as our reasoning varies, our actions receive a subsequent variation. But 'tis evident in this case, that the impulse arises not from the reason, but is only directed by it" (Hume 2000a, 414).

27 See also Hume (2000a, 497, 521, 537, 543). Hume's idea of a reasoned self-restraint figures as well in a remark he makes about pleasure: "The more men refine upon pleasure, the less will they indulge in excesses of any kind; because nothing is more destructive to true pleasure than such excesses" (Hume 1985t [1752b], 271).

28 This is also the reason behind the origin of conventions more generally. Compare Hume (1998, app. 3).

29 It is interesting to note that this second way of thinking about self-restraint reflects a deep underlying connection between this part of the *Treatise*, and the earlier arguments in Hobbes's *Leviathan*. In the *Leviathan*, it does not suffice for men to grasp that the laws of nature are but theorems of prudence—and thus fully in their interest; they must be reinforced by the creation of a Sovereign Power, that is, the Leviathan itself. We are indebted to Tatsya Sakamoto for reminding us of this point.

30 We have in mind a large body of literature, starting with a watershed paper by Strotz (1956), which provoked further explorations by many important economists, including Hammond (1976), Yaari (1977), Kydland and Prescott (1977), and Elster (1984). More recently, Ainslie (1992) has offered a most interesting discussion.

6 An Artificial Virtue and the Oil of Commerce: A Synthetic View of Hume's Theory of Money

Carl Wennerlind

1. Introduction

David Hume's thinking on money is notoriously protean, frequently escaping our grasp and defying our best attempts to articulate it. This methodological pluralism—or inconsistency, to some—has given birth to a large and vibrant interpretive literature, in which scholars have tirelessly posited their versions of Hume's thinking. While one may feel momentarily confident about the validity of a particular interpretation after having read, for example, the essay "Of Money," the reading of a different text, say, "Of the Balance of Trade" or *A Treatise of Human Nature*, more often problematizes than corroborates one's intuition. Still, even though it may be difficult to make sense of Hume's monetary theory when we approach his oeuvre synthetically, such a reading is a necessary exercise, because it is only by seeking an understanding of Hume's economic thinking within his political philosophy and historical vision that we can begin to adequately grasp the complexity of his analysis and thus appreciate the weight of his contribution.

This article attempts to synthesize Hume's two major contributions to monetary theory: the philosophical treatment in the *Treatise* and the economic analysis in the *Political Discourses*. The inquiry is organized around a set of basic questions: What is money? Of what substance should money be comprised? What is the optimum quantity of money? What role should the government play in managing the monetary system? What is the relationship between Hume's ideas on money and those of his immediate predecessors? In addressing these questions a monetary theory emerges that can be briefly summarized in the following manner. For Hume, money is a medium and measure of exchange complementing private property and markets as the constitutive conventions of a modern commercial society. Money functions as a promise to redeem and a consequent claim on private property in market exchange. Money's most important quality is not its intrinsic material features but rather its capacity to ensure the promises made by its users. As such, in principle, any object can serve as money. Hume, however, ultimately claims that the monetary system must be centered around a metallic currency, as its scarcity provides a built-in discipline that facilitates the maintenance of confidence in the currency. In the absence of metallic money, the government is likely to fall victim to the temptation of artificially expanding the money supply—which Hume views as a distraction at best and a disaster at worst. That is, despite his acknowledging the benefits associated with trade-induced money inflows and supporting certain monetary measures (such as the prudent use of privately issued paper money and the occasional debasement or trade restriction), Hume adamantly opposes any attempt by the state to systematically engineer an artificial expansion of the money supply of the kind that John Law and George Berkeley had earlier advocated.

This reading further suggests that, while money is central to Hume's political economy, it is not so for the reasons frequently cited. Most discussions regarding Hume's treatment of money focus on his quantity theory of money, but few have recognized that his use of this theory was designed to convince legislators to *ignore* money. For Hume, the key feature of the wealth-creation process is the nation's people and their industry; a nation's money can safely be left alone to adjust automatically in proportion to each nation's output. Money matters, however, in Hume's discussion of the foundational conventions of a modern society. In this discussion, Hume claims that money, alongside property and markets, provides the basic framework within which social interaction is best facilitated. Only when these three conventions are present can a higher degree of civilization, economic development, and political liberty be achieved. Hence, for Hume, the monetization of society is absolutely necessary, but, once accomplished, the monetary system should be left alone.

2. What Is Money?

Hume subscribed to the common Enlightenment view that society evolves through four stages, from a savage and primitive era to a commercial modernity, in which civilization and justice approach their highest form.[1] The primary impetus for this civilization process is the recognition among people, through experience, that they have the capacity to organize their social institutions in ways that will bring greater individual benefits and conveniences. Through trial and error, a set of conventions emerge that coordinate social interactions in ways that facilitate the division of labor, technological progress, and trade. While the middling sorts are responsible for providing the foundation for this new set of institutions, gradually, either by becoming part of this expanding social class or by being instructed to comply with the new social rules, more and more people will join the conventions and thus contribute to the formation of the new commercial society.[2]

In Book III of the *Treatise,* Hume states that the primary conventions of a modern commercial society are private property, markets, and money.[3] In a world characterized by scarcity and avidity, Hume argues that these institutions effectively impose limits on people's selfishness, while at the same time promoting the best use of available resources. As people recognize that their personal interests are better served in the long run by committing themselves to these restraints, the conventions gradually congeal into a solid societal structure. That is, people do not curtail their quest for immediate gratification out of a sense of decency or concern for the common good, but rather do so in expectation of others doing the same, which ultimately ensures that the conventions provide individual benefits. While the motivation for this behavior is, quite simply, private gain, the fact that participation in the conventions necessitates the curtailment of one's immediate inclinations leads Hume to elevate this behavior to a virtue—a so-called artificial virtue. Since these artificial virtues are necessary to uphold the conventions, which in turn provide the fundamental structure of a civilized society, it follows that they constitute the very basis of justice in a commercial society.

For Hume, the security of private property is the first necessary condition for the establishment of a modern commercial society. Second, considering that possessions are rarely distributed in the proper mix to satisfy people's desires and that people's talents make them fit for different kinds of employment, Hume argues that "all this requires a mutual exchange and commerce ..." (2000a, [1739–40] 330). However, since barter is plagued by various inconveniences, some other way to engage in transactions in which goods and services are delivered in exchange for guarantees of future payments must be developed for people to fully benefit from an economy based on private property and exchange (ibid., 334). Since Hume believes that we can never fully guarantee anything with a promise, he argues that a convention has to emerge whereby people can signal their commitment to a system of deferred payments by using a standardized symbol (ibid., 335). By accepting a symbol in exchange, a person extends credit to the recipient of the goods delivered or services rendered. In an isolated exchange, this debt would have to be settled by a symmetric reciprocation. However, if an entire society agrees by convention to accept a symbol as a promissory note and redeem it with property when presented, then the symbol acquires the capacity to mediate any conceivable transaction and thus operates as a universal equivalent. Once fully developed, money serves as a medium and measure of exchange that allows market participants to share information in a way that resembles the workings of a linguistic system.[4] Hume in fact highlights this commonality by pointing out that, much like languages are "gradually establish'd by human conventions ... do gold and silver become the common measure of exchange..." (ibid., 315).

Although Hume regards the formation of the conventions as an organic process wherein people decide to participate out of their own long-term self-interest, he recognizes that human fallibility necessitates having a state that can protect the conventions. While violations of the conventions may be rare, "they are, however, never the less real for being remote; and as all men are, in some degree, subject to the same weakness, it necessarily happens, that the violations of equity must become very frequent in society, and the commerce of men, by that means, be render'd very dangerous and uncertain" (Hume 2000a, [1739–40] 343). It is therefore crucial that the state assumes responsibility for upholding the conventions by punishing trans-gressors. In fact, this was the full extent of the state's responsibility. The rather limited role that Hume prescribes to the state is based on the idea that the state should pass only those laws that are compatible with "the common bent of mankind" (1985s [1752a], 260) and that help people behave in ways that are ultimately in their own best interest. In the case of money, this means that the state's authority is used to ensure that people honor the implicit promises of reciprocation that participation in the monetary system requires.

3. Of What Substance Should Money Be Comprised?

In the *Political Discourses*, Hume claims that money is "the instrument which men have agreed upon to facilitate the exchange of one commodity for another" (1985u [1752c], 281) and that it functions as "the common measure of exchange" (ibid., 291). He views money as the "oil" of com-merce—a lubricant designed to make the "wheels of trade ... [turn] more smooth and easy" (ibid., 281). Money's capability to play this facilitating role is not attributed to its intrinsic value, as metallists would argue.[5] Instead, for Hume, money has "chiefly a fictitious value" (1985v [1752d], 297) that arises "from the agreement and convention of men" (632).[6] That is, much in the spirit of his elaboration in the *Treatise*, Hume argues that money is a rating-and-mediating mechanism that functions only insofar as people conventionally agree to accept it in exchange. Consequently, the solidity of the currency depends on the surety and solemnity of people's commitments, and the collective confidence therein, rather than the intrinsic value of the money object itself.

Hume's views on paper money further underscores the fact that he was not philosophically opposed to non-metallic money. He claims "the advan-tages of paper-credit and banks to be superior to their disadvantages" (Hume 1985x [1752e], 318) and thus believes that paper money has the capacity to function perfectly well in a commercial society alongside a metallic currency. He discusses the benefits to merchants of being able to discount their bills of exchange in banks and have access to bank-credit (ibid., 319)—a benefit not only to the merchants alone, but to the nation's trade in general. In the essay "Of the Populousness of Ancient Nations," Hume praises bills of exchange as being "extremely useful to the encour-agement of art [and] industry" (1985bb [1752i], 420). He also notes the benefits of the small-denomination currencies issued by the Sword Bank and Arms Bank in Glasgow (1985x [1752e], 320), as well as the potential advantages of state-issued securities, which during his time had become "a kind of money" (1985aa [1752h], 353). He argues that paper money has the capacity to mediate trade as effectively as gold and silver, as long as people are able to trust the issuer and its users and thus be assured, with a high degree of probability, that a note will command property as well as a coin. He illustrates the interchangeability between paper and silver money in the *Treatise*:

> Paper will, on many occasions, be consider'd as riches, and that because it may convey the power of acquiring money: And money is not riches, as it is a metal endow'd with certain qualities of solidity, weight and fusibility; but only as it has a relation to the pleasures and conveniences of life.
>
> (Hume 2000a [1739–40], 203)

Thus Hume believes there is no fundamental conceptual difference between paper money and metallic money—both are established by convention and function in proportion to the confidence people have in their continued ability to be exchanged.

However, even though Hume is favorably disposed to paper money, he ultimately concludes that, since paper money has a tendency to be over-issued, causing inflation at best and a destabilization of the entire monetary system at worst, only a monetary system grounded in a metallic currency can be functional in the long term. Overexpansion is of course not a problem facing a metallic currency as a metal's scarcity provides an inherent discipline. In a letter to André Morellet, Hume explores this issue:

> It is true, money must always be made of some materials, which have intrinsic value, otherwise it would be multiplied without end, and would sink to nothing.

He then gives an example of the American colonies, which

> for want of specie, used to coin a paper currency ... [which] passed in all payments, by convention; and might have gone on, had it not been abused by the several assemblies, who issued paper without end, and thereby discredited the currency.
>
> (Hume 1932, 2:204)

Additionally, Hume argues that a currency based entirely on paper is not feasible because it will leave the nation powerless in international affairs. Moreover, it will make the monetary system too precarious, since confidence in the paper currency is dangerously susceptible to political and economic shocks (Hume 1985x [1752e], 316–17). The scarcity of precious metals and the impossibility of multiplying them at will ensure that gold and silver are best suited to function as money. In sum, Hume favors a monetary system centered on metallic money, but fully allows for privately issued paper money to mediate commercial transactions, as long as it is strictly backed by good security.

4. What Is the Optimal Quantity of Money?

The preceding discussion suggests that Hume views money as an *artificial virtue* forming one of the crucial pillars of a modern society and as an *oil of commerce* providing a medium of exchange that facilitates economic development. He also proposes that the monetary system should be grounded in a metallic currency, as it provides a built-in check against overexpansion. These views raise some important questions: If, as Hume argues, money is only a mediation device, why would the monetary authority be tempted to expand the money stock? Are there actual benefits associated with an increasing quantity of money or is it preferable to have an inelastic money supply disciplined by the scarcity of metals and international trade flows? The next two sections will try to discern Hume's notoriously subtle views on these questions.

The common theme throughout Hume's discussion of the quantity of money, whether in the essays "Of Money" and "Of the Balance of Trade" or even as early as the 1749 letter to Montesquieu, is that money always gravitates to regions where commodities, industry, and skill abound in greater quantities. In the above-mentioned letter, he suggests that, much like water, money cannot "be raised or lowered anywhere much beyond the level it has in places where communication is open, but that it must rise and fall in proportion to the goods and labour contained in each state" (Rotwein 1955, 189).[7] The hydraulic device that ensures this adjustment is the specie-flow mechanism. It dictates that when a nation increases its industry additional commodities enter circulation, thus lowering domestic prices. Since gold now commands a greater number of commodities in the nation with enlarged industry, gold will naturally flow to this region until prices of all goods are equalized. As Hume points out in a letter to James Oswald, "the only way of keeping or increasing money is, by keeping and increasing the people and industry" (Hume 1932, 1:143). Thus, the optimal quantity of money is simply that which is proportional to a nation's industry and its marketable commodities.

Hume suggests that, in a world of open trade, the specie-flow mechanism ensures that the world's money stock is automatically distributed so that each nation ends up with the appropriate quantity of money. For that reason, the legislator or regulating authority should not concern itself too much with the size of the nation's money stock as it will adjust optimally on its own. However, the direction in which the money flows does matter. Hume points out that an inflow of money from trade triggers a positive multiplier process giving a nation's industry a further boost. The logic is as follows: during times of improvement in industry and the arts, the number of marketable commodities increases, forcing prices to fall.[8] If some of these commodities are suitable for exportation, the lower prices are likely to generate an increased flow of goods abroad and a consequent inflow of specie.[9] The additional revenues will be used by the receiving merchants to further increase their production at home.[10] Since the laborers employed by the exporting merchant have already expanded their productivity or diligence, it is unlikely they can be made to work much harder. Therefore, new workers have to be added in order to expand production. This extra demand for workers will eventually force merchants to pay higher wages, which will also lead to an increase in the prices the merchants charge for their finished products. At the same time, however, the increase in wages enables these workers to expand their consumption of other goods, thus stimulating additional industry among the vendors of these goods. This will, in turn, force these vendors to hire more workers, who eventually will enjoy higher wages as well. In this way, the multiplier effect gradually spreads throughout the economy:

> [The workman] carries his money to market, where he finds every thing at the same price as formerly, but returns with greater quantity and of better kinds, for the use of his family. The farmer and gardener, finding, that all their commodities are taken off, apply themselves with alacrity to the raising more; and at the same time can afford to take better and more cloths from their tradesmen, whose price is the same as formerly, and their industry only whetted by so much new gain.
>
> (Hume 1985u [1752c], 287)

As wages increase in each successive sector, commodity prices gradually rise. Eventually this process comes to a halt when the domestic price level is equal to that of other nations and the money stock is proportional to the now higher levels of industry (Hume 1985u [1752c], 286–87). The end result is that output is greater, wages are higher, and prices are back at the initial equilibrium level.[11] As such, the inflow of money is advantageous, as it gives a further boost to the nation's industry and wealth, and also generates an increase in wages, which Hume generally views as a favorable consequence.[12]

While increasing wages enhance "the happiness of so many millions," Hume notes that the English nevertheless "feel some disadvantage in foreign trade by the high price of labour" (1985s [1752a], 265). However, if the improvements in industry—which Hume defined as increases in skills, arts, attention, diligence, and alacrity—are permanent, then the higher wage levels do not constitute an inconvenience in international trade. The reason for this is that the labor cost per unit of output is the same in a nation with high wages and high productivity as in a nation with less industrious and less well paid people. Alternatively, if the improvements are transitory, the higher wages will generate less favorable terms of trade and thus trigger an outflow of gold or a gradual shift of manufactures to lower wage areas.[13]

Hume outlines the most plausible scenario in his letters to Oswald and Lord Kames, stating that the industrious nation is able to maintain its competitiveness in the manufacturing sectors "that require great stock or great skill," while the poorer nations' lower wages give them an edge in "the simple and more laborious" sectors (Hume 1932, 1:143, 1.143). Such a situation will generate an international division of labor wherein all nations derive advantages from trade and rich nations "will not be able entirely to annihilate or oppress [the poor]" (ibid., 1:271).[14]

While Hume most famously discusses this monetary dynamic in the essay "Of Money," he articulates similar ideas elsewhere. In the *History of England*, he argues that, barring two brief periods of rapid inflation (during the reign of Elizabeth and during the time Hume was writing), England's expanding industry "encreased as fast as gold and silver, and kept commodities nearly at a par with money" (Hume 1983a [1754–62], 4:381). In fact, during certain periods, England's "art, employed in the finer manufacturers, has even made some of these commodities fall below their former value" (ibid., 3.78). Hume also observed that the inflow of money has had a tendency to ignite additional industry. He writes, "while money thus flowed into England, we may observe, that, at the same time, and probably from that very cause, arts and industry of all kinds received a mighty encrease" (ibid., 5.39). Around the same time, in a letter to Oswald, Hume articulates an even more succinct formulation of the multiplier process: "[an] increase of money, if not too sudden, naturally increases people and industry, and by that means may retain itself" (Hume 1932, 1:143). In a letter to Lord Elibank, he expresses the same idea, writing that "The Encrease of the Money encreases the Demand; but if the Encrease of the Demand encreases as much the Industry, the Prices will remain the same" (Mossner 1962, 442).

In sum, when discussing the effects of an inflow of money from a trade surplus, Hume abandons the simple quantity theory of money he used when considering sudden, policy-induced changes in the money stock.[15] In its place, he proposes a more sophisticated version of the quantity theory in which money is endogenous, in that it adjusts to the levels of industry and prices, and non-neutral, in that an inflow triggers a positive multiplier effect. Hume argues that nations that abound with productivity and industry are given a further boost by the inflow of money, while nations that "lose their trade, industry, and people, ... cannot expect to keep their gold and silver" (1985x [1752e], 325) and thus will become even more impoverished through a negative multiplier process. Hence, the multiplier process rewards rapidly growing nations by further stimulating industry and penalizes stagnating nations by further reducing economic activity. This suggests that, rather than being a mere mediating device, money may actually have the capacity to create additional wealth. This, however, is not the case. Although Hume does indeed add layers to his discussion of money here,[16] his revision is slight and does not constitute a major alteration (or inconsistency) in his understanding of money. When we consider the actual process whereby an inflow of money stimulates further industry, we recognize that it is not money alone that triggers this process. It is rather the initial increase in industry and the ensuing wealth effect that spurs additional industry. While money is certainly an integral part of this process, it does not serve as its principal force or prime mover, but rather as a conduit transmitting the increase in industry throughout the economy.[17] Hence, money alone does not have the capacity to initiate the multiplier process; only an inflow of money caused by a preceding improvement in industry can systematically stimulate an expansion of output. In this sense, money remains a facilitator of exchange and not an instrument that by itself can create wealth.

5. What Role Should the Government Play?

It is notoriously difficult to derive a clear answer to this question from Hume's writings. He seems to argue, for the most part, that only increases in industry can generate a favorable increase in the money stock. But, at other times, he seems to suggest that other forms of monetary expansions may also prove favorable. Supported by Hume's suggestion that the magistrate should try to keep the money stock increasing at all times (1985u [1752c], 288), the latter view has become dominant. This interpretation provides a central role for the government to play in expanding the money stock, by issuing paper money or by generating trade surpluses through trade restrictions. I have challenged this view in detail elsewhere.[18] Here I will show briefly that Hume holds firmly to his position that only industry-generated trade surpluses are consistently favorable and, as such, he limits the role of the government to maintaining a legal system that provides proper incentives for commerce and industry.

As shown in the previous section, Hume argues that only improvements in industry can attract money and that only such trade surpluses can consistently trigger the multiplier process. As such, he believes that money is best left alone to adjust automatically in proportion to each nation's industry. Nevertheless, he considers various possibilities whereby the money supply could be artificially altered. First, he treats the use of privately issued paper money, such as bills of exchange and bank-credit. Since such mechanisms have the capacity to expedite the multiplier process by allowing a merchant to "coin his houses, his household furniture, the goods in his warehouse, the foreign debts due to him, [and] his ships at sea" (Hume 1985x [1752e], 319), Hume is favorably disposed toward them. In his comments on Lord Elibank's *Thoughts on Money, Circulation, and Paper Currency* (1758), he endorses fully backed paper-credit, suggesting that "Banks are convenient by the safe Custody & quick conveyance of money" (Mossner 1962, 441). However, while Hume was fully accepting of privately issued paper-money, he did not endorse the practice of using this form of money to expand the overall money stock. Regarding "the Multiplication of

Money," he wrote: "I question whether it be any Advantage either to an industrious or idle country" (ibid., 441). That is, in agreement with Lord Elibank, he argues that paper credit can be functional as long as it is backed by specie—or, at a minimum, bills of exchange payable in gold or silver. If banks are allowed to issue money beyond the gold and silver that would otherwise circulate, as in the proposals of Law and Berkeley, then the nation's competitiveness will be undermined by "encreasing money beyond its natural proportion to labour and commodities, and thereby heightening their price to the merchant and manufacturer" (Hume 1985u [1752c], 284). The only certain consequence of using such artificial means to expand the money stock would be to increase the price level, reduce net exports, and thus trigger a consequent outflow of money—negating the initial increase in the money supply (Hume 1985x [1752e], 311). Therefore, Hume concludes that an artificial increase in paper credit "can never be the interest of any trading nation" (Hume 1985u [1752c], 284).[19]

The second contrivance Hume considers for expanding the money stock is the circulation of state-issued paper money—or, more precisely, securities backed by the national debt, which had "become a kind of money" (1985aa [1752h], 353). He views this device as potentially beneficial because it provides merchants with a highly liquid interest-bearing asset, allowing them to trade on smaller profits, which consequently leads to lower prices and increased consumption. This in turn "quickens the labour of the common people, and helps to spread arts and industry throughout the whole society" (ibid., 353). Hume, however, ultimately opposes this form of paper money. The reason for his aversion is that, even though the money is backed by a security, the security does not provide a built-in discipline, since the national debt is likely to spiral out of control. To Hume, an expanding national debt can ruin the nation's fiscal health, while monetization of the debt has the capacity to destabilize the entire monetary mechanism.

The third possibility for expanding the quantity of money is through debasement. Hume actually believes that debasements may prove beneficial, as long as they are secret and slight so that people may be fooled into thinking that the extra money is the result of an inflow from trade (1985u [1752c], 288).[20] However, considering that he calls Edward VI's Great Debasement a "pernicious expedient" (Hume 1983a [1754–62], 3.370), it seems unlikely that he thinks debasements should be used systematically to expand the money stock. It is more likely he believes that when wear and tear has created a need for a general recoinage, the deflationary mistake of William III should be avoided and the mint should recoin with a smaller amount of metal in each coin, in order to slightly inflate the economy.[21]

The final method Hume considers whereby the money stock can be expanded artificially is through trade restrictions. Addressing the bullionist fear of experiencing a depletion of the money stock through international trade, Hume devotes most of the essay "Of the Balance of Trade" to demonstrating the shortsightedness of such views. He points out that while many nations have a jealous fear of losing their money, such concerns are groundless. He writes, "I should as soon dread, that all our springs and rivers should be exhausted, as that money should abandon a kingdom where there are people and industry" (Hume 1985x [1752e], 309). His aversion to trade restrictions designed to generate a favorable trade balance does not, however, rule out his support for occasional trade barriers—such as taxes on German linens—to protect certain strategic industries (ibid., 324).

Further evidence of Hume's view on the futility of artificial manipulations of the money stock is provided in the essay "Of Interest," in which he argues that an expansion of the money stock has no impact on the interest rate. Only improvements in industry may lower the interest rate, making any given quantity of real wealth smaller in relation to the now larger national stock, which consequently should make it less expensive to borrow. However, he points out that people have often misunderstood the causality at work in this scenario. Since an increase in industry also attracts more money, it appears as though the greater quantity of money causes a fall in the interest rate; while in reality, the increase in industry causes both the interest rate and the quantity of money to change. He calls the former view a fallacy, "where a collateral effect is taken for a cause, and where a consequence is ascribed to the plenty of money; though it be really owing to a change in the manners and customs of the people" (Hume 1985u [1752c], 294).

According to Hume, the only situation that merits state intervention in the monetary system is when a government is trying to expedite the transformation of a region from a "rude and savage" stage to a commercial and civilized society. As outlined in the *Treatise*, a society must have the proper set of conventions in order to make its transition toward order, prosperity, and liberty. In his view, a government interested in civilizing a colony or a remote region must facilitate and encourage the formation of private property, markets, and money. Not only will this generate more orderly exchanges and provide proper incentives for industry, but it will also make it easier to tax the inhabitants, who will now hold part of their wealth in a more liquid form. Roger Emerson, in this volume, and George Caffentzis (2001 and 2005), have convincingly argued that Hume's deliberation on the importance of monetizing a traditional society is specifically intended to serve as a policy prescription to Scottish legislators for how to deal with the unruly and rebellious Highlanders.

The preceding discussion suggests that Hume does not think that there are any monetary levers that the government can use to systematically stimulate industry in an already developed nation. This contradicts the long-standing view that Hume was an inflationist, a view that seems particularly indisputable in light of Hume's famous comment that "The good policy of the magistrate consists only in keeping [money], if possible, still increasing; because, by that means, he keeps alive a spirit of industry in the nation" (1985u [1752c], 288). However, as I have pointed out elsewhere, the reason why there seems to be a contradiction in Hume's thinking is because of a long-standing misreading of the above-quoted passage.[22] To correct this, we must consider both the context and wording of this passage. That it appears immediately *after* Hume argues that increases in the money supply are only favorable when generated by previous improvements in industry, and immediately *before* he argues that poor nations experience an outflow of money because of a lack of industrious people, suggests that this passage cannot reasonably be considered a proposition for an inflationist monetary or trade policy. Add to this that the eighteenth-century British magistrate had no direct influence over the money supply and the traditional reading of this passage becomes even more implausible. The magistrate, much like the Justice of the Peace, was responsible for upholding society's legal structure, while the Exchequer and the Bank of England were in charge of issuing paper money. Hume clearly makes this distinction throughout his writings. He uses the terms *banks* or *public banks* to describe the authority that issues paper money (ibid., 285), while the issuer of circulating public securities he refers to as the *public* or the *state* (Hume 1985aa [1752h], 353). In fact, he never uses the term *magistrate* when discussing the money-issuing authority, as his historical context dictated. Additionally, there is little textual support that Hume uses the term *magistrate* to refer to the legislative body in charge of Britain's trade policy, thus making it unlikely that Hume is calling for trade restrictions to induce an inflow of money.

This line of reasoning brings us to the conclusion that, although Hume favors an inflow of money as long as it results from improvements in industry, he does not support polices designed to artificially expand the money stock. Instead he instructs the legislator to focus on ways in which domestic skills and industry may be enhanced and suggests that the state should let the inexorable dynamic of the specie-flow mechanism operate without interruption.

6. How Do Hume's Ideas on Money Relate to His Immediate Predecessors?

Like any other seminal thinker, Hume did not develop his ideas in a vacuum, but drew on the pool of ideas available at the time he was writing. He revised, readjusted, and recombined various ideas from his predecessors in a way that constituted an original contribution to political economy. Some commentators hold that Hume's essays were conceived of and written as challenges to specific theoretical fallacies and that he was therefore one of the earliest liberal thinkers to bravely take on the mercantilist dogma. While there may be some validity to this claim, one should not over-emphasize the trail-blazing character of Hume's monetary analysis, because, as will be shown below, his thinking was firmly embedded in the monetary discourse that had already been established during the half-century preceding him by writers like Dudley North, John Law, George Berkeley, Jacob Vanderlint, Isaac Gervaise, and Richard Cantillon. That said, we should also be cautious of claims that Hume's analysis was entirely derivative[23] or that he gleaned his analysis from any one specific thinker.[24] Below I compare Hume's thinking to that of other mid-eighteenth-century writers on money and show how he rearranged existing ideas in a way that generated a novel and seminal contribution to monetary thought.[25] While I am neither seeking to trace the exact lineage of Hume's ideas nor proposing that Hume was directly influenced by any specific text, I will point to the presence of Hume's ideas in the contemporary discourse and, as such, suggest that he is likely to have encountered them in print or in conversation. In conclusion, I will reflect on what may constitute Hume's greatest contribution to eighteenth-century monetary thought.

First, let us focus on Hume's idea of money as a conventional sign mediating exchange. We can find similar notions in the works of Berkeley, Francis Hutcheson, and Montesquieu. In *The Querist*, Berkeley builds on the seventeenth-century notion of money as a representation or symbol of value. For Berkeley, the intrinsic value, or lack thereof, of a money object is of no importance; rather it is only by people agreeing to allow money to convey and record value that it serves as such. Money is a pledge that can be expressed through a counter or a ticket, the material of which is entirely inconsequential (Berkeley 1970 [1735], 127). Hence, while Berkeley and Hume ultimately disagree about how money affects the economy, they are in agreement regarding the symbolic character of money. In another discussion that in many ways resembles that of Hume's *Treatise*, Hutcheson's *A System of Moral Philosophy* examines the centrality of contracts in modern society and develops an analysis of money as a sign. Hutcheson proclaims that most important social relations are mediated by contracts and he makes exchange relations the focal point of his study. The essential element in these contracts, he suggests, is the fidelity of people's commitment to uphold them. As such, the same reasons that "show the necessity of a social life, show also the necessity of contracts and the obligation of faithfully observing them" (Hutcheson 1755, 2). He also warns that "violations of contracts ... were they frequent in society, must destroy all social commerce" (ibid., 3). Hutcheson elaborates on how these contracts are formulated. He claims that, while speech and writing are the best methods for two parties to express their intention and consent, it is also possible to express agreements "by any other signs previously agreed upon by the parties as evidences of consent" (ibid., 6). He then discusses the nature of obligations arising from contractual commitments before turning toward a treatment of money as a subset of symbols mediating social relations. Hence, much like Hume, Hutcheson views money as a symbol that allows people to communicate their intentions to deliver goods in the future, which in turn increases the likelihood that people will part with their goods today in return for such a promise of reciprocation. For both Hutcheson and Hume, money is a sign that mediates exchange relations and as such allows society to move beyond barter trade.

Another mid-eighteenth-century thinker who considered money as a sign was Montesquieu. In his *Spirit of Laws*, in the chapter "On the Nature of Money," he states that "money is a sign representing the value of all commodities" (1989 [1750], 399). While Montesquieu argues that silver is most frequently chosen to serve as money because its qualities make it particularly suitable for the task, he is open to the idea that paper may function as a substitute for silver. He reasons, much in the same way Hume does in the passage from the *Treatise* quoted above, that, "As silver is the sign of the values of commodities, paper is a sign of the value of silver, and when the paper is good, it represents silver so well that there is no difference in its effect" (ibid., 399). Hence, much like Hume, Montesquieu regards money as a sign whose most important feature is not its intrinsic properties, but its capacity to circulate widely. While supportive of the use of money substitutes, Montesquieu does not favor all forms of paper money. He distinguishes between different kinds of circulating paper depending on how they are secured. He considers (i) paper representing silver, (ii) paper "that is the sign of the profits a company has made or will make in commerce," and (iii) paper that "represents a debt" (ibid., 418), and concludes that "the first two are very advantageous to the state; [while] the third cannot be advantageous" (ibid., 418). Thus, like Hume, Montesquieu favors private credit instruments and paper fully backed by silver, but opposes publicly issued paper money backed by the national debt.

This brings us to Hume's discussion of the optimal quantity of money and the specie-flow mechanism. Here we can find variations of Hume's argument anticipated in the writings of Jacob Vanderlint, Isaac Gervaise, and Richard Cantillon.[26] In his tract *Money Answers All Things*, Vanderlint proposes a theory of money that emphasizes the self-balancing nature of international money flows. He firmly believes in the inexorable dynamic of the specie-flow mechanism and recognizes a direct relationship between the quantity of money and the general price level.[27] However, like Hume, Vanderlint still favors and proposes ways to maintain a favorable balance of trade in order to secure an inflow of money. He argues that the only way a nation can consistently export more than it imports is by expanding its domestic output, which will then allow it to undersell its neighbors. The added quantity of money will then provide the nation with a further boost to consumption and thus expand output and employment.

In a proto-physiocratic manner, Vanderlint argues that everything of value stems from the land. Consequently, the more land that is "improv'd and cultivated, etc. the greater will the Plenty of all things be, and the more People will it also imploy" (1914 [1734], 15). He continues, "And as the Produce will hence be increased, so will the Consumption of all Things increase too; and the greater the Plenty becomes this Way, the cheaper will every Thing be" (ibid.,

15). Considering that the price of labor is "always settled and constituted of the Price of Victuals and Drink" (ibid., 16) and that workers can now support themselves and their families with less money, Vanderlint claims that nominal wages are bound to fall throughout the entire economy. Since wages are the largest expense in manufacturing, it means that "all Manufactures will [now] be vastly cheaper" (ibid., 16). Such a situation yields multiple benefits. Not only will manufactured commodities become cheaper for the domestic population, but the nation can now "export our Manufactures at much lower Prices" (ibid., 16). As a result, an additional quantity of money flows into the nation[28] and provides a further boost to output, "because, where Money is plentiful, the People in general are thereby enabled, and will not fail to be as much greater Consumers of every Thing" (ibid., 16–17). Furthermore, in nations that maintain a competitive advantage and are able to undersell their neighbors, "people always increase greatly, and become generally happy" and they also "grow potent and formidable" (ibid., 17). Hence, for Vanderlint as for Hume, a growing economy tends to be self-reinforcing by attracting more money, improving people's manners and industry, and providing employment for its growing population.

After presenting his version of the specie-flow mechanism, Vanderlint clarifies that he is not in favor of artificial expansions in the money stock—either through credit money or trade restrictions. Nevertheless, he writes, "yet I must own, I am entirely for preventing the Importation of all foreign Commodities, as much as possible; but not by Acts of Parliament, which never can do any good to trade; but by raising such Goods ourselves, so cheap as to make it impossible for other Nations to find their Account in bringing them to us" (1914 [1734], 58). Like Hume, Vanderlint favors a trade surplus, partly because it is evidence of improvements in arts and industry and partly because it provides a further boost to industry. Then, much in the same spirit as Hume's essay "Of Jealousy of Trade,"[29] Vanderlint suggests that "I wish every Nation in the world would [produce more cheaply to undersell their neighbors] as much as ever they can; for then the Plenty of every thing would be so great, that all Mankind would be happy" (ibid., 58).

In comparing Vanderlint and Hume, we have seen that their versions of the specie-flow mechanism are in fundamental agreement. In addition, both of them support free trade, while at the same time indicating a preference for a trade surplus, which they agree can come only from a competitive advantage in the exporting manufacturing sector. According to Vanderlint, these advantages stem from lower agricultural prices, which in turn allow for lower wages in the manufacturing sector, whereas for Hume, improvements in arts and industry in the exporting sectors allow a nation to undersell its foreign competitors. Despite differing opinions on the dynamics of the specie-flow mechanism, both see the inflow of money as having its roots in increased domestic production and, as such, view an inflow of money as a real phenomenon rather than a monetary one. Furthermore, while Hume provides a more thorough elaboration on the multiplier effect, both he and Vanderlint seem to agree that the inflow of money is beneficial because it triggers additional consumption, which eventually will stimulate more output.

Some fifteen years before Vanderlint published his tract, another writer presented an analysis that also anticipated some of Hume's basic points regarding the specie-flow mechanism. In a short treatise, *The System or Theory of the Trade of the World*, Isaac Gervaise presents a theoretical elaboration on the specie-flow mechanism and argues that money will be distributed among nations in proportion to their relative levels of industry. He proclaims that "A Nation can naturally draw and keep unto itself, but such a proportion of the real Denominator of the World, as is proportion'd to the quantity of its Inhabitants, because the Denominator can be attracted but by Labour only" (Gervaise 1720, 3). He then proceeds to argue that artificial increases in the money stock through credit-money expansion "is of pernicious consequence to that Nation" (ibid., 8), as it raises prices, reduces exports, and thus results in an equal sum of money "in time be[ing] drawn off by the Labour of other Nations, in Gold and Silver" (ibid., 5). Like Hume and Vanderlint, he is an unwavering advocate of free trade, convinced that only under such circumstances will each nation end up with the appropriate quantity of money.

The precursor to Hume whose monetary theory has received the most attention, at least lately, is Richard Cantillon.[30] In his *Essay on the Nature of Commerce in General*, most likely written around 1730 but not published until 1755, Cantillon presents his systematic treatment of political economy. This contains a monetary analysis that in many ways resembles that of Hume, in particular, the latter's distinction between exogenous and endogenous increases in the money stock, and his views on credit money and the dynamics of monetary adjustments.

Cantillon considers two primary ways whereby the money stock may be altered: a discovery of new mines and a trade surplus.[31] In both the case of exogenous (mines) and endogenous (trade) increases, Cantillon's treatment is similar to (although more elaborate than) the dynamics proposed by Hume. In the case of a newly discovered mine inside a country, the increase in gold or silver prompts the owners, undertakers, and workers of the mine to expand their consumption. This group "will consume in their household more Meat, Wine, or Beer than before, will accustom themselves to wear better cloths, finer linen, to have better furnished Houses and other choicer commodities" (Cantillon 2001 [1931], 67). These added expenditures consequently generate more employment among the manufacturers of these goods, who "for the same reason will increase their expenses" (ibid., 68). The increase in demand then circulates throughout the economy, enabling those whose revenues have increased to expand their consumption. However, their demand for "Meat, Wine, Wool, etc. being more intense than usual, will not fail to raise their prices" (ibid., 68), which will consequently inconvenience certain other groups. Not only will landowners suffer during the term of their leases, but domestic servants and workers on fixed wages will also be seriously disadvantaged, by the increasing price level. Cantillon believed that the hardship generated by these price increases will compel a large number of people to emigrate. Additionally, as the increasing price level expands the demand for other nations' goods, "who makes them much more cheaply" (ibid., 68), an outflow of money ensues. This outflow of gold will continue as long as the mine is producing additional gold, "the great circulation of Money, which was general at the beginning, ceases: poverty and misery follow and the labour of the Mines appears to be only to the advantage of those employed upon them and the Foreigners who profit thereby" (ibid., 69). Hence, for Cantillon, the exogenous increase in the money stock, while providing benefits to some groups, ultimately hurts the nation's prosperity—much like Spain's actual experience in the sixteenth century (ibid., 69).

The sequence of events is different when the increasing quantity of money originates from a trade surplus. In this case, the additional money will "enrich a great number of Merchants and Undertakers in the State, and will give employment to numerous Mechanicks and workmen who furnish the commodities sent to the foreigner from whom the money is drawn" (ibid., 69). Similar to an exogenous increase, the additional money leads to an increase in consumption and a consequent increase in prices, which will likely spur emigration among those who do not experience proportional increases in their wages. Additionally, other nations will set up manufacturers in order to take advantage of their now relatively lower price and wage levels. Cantillon suggests, however, that this will not have an immediately detrimental effect on the nation's prosperity, as it will take a substantial period of time before other nations may be able to take advantage of their cost advantage and produce goods of similar quality. Furthermore, if the nation is a maritime state, the "cheapness of its shipping ... may compensate in some sort the high price of labour caused by the too great abundance of money; so that the work and Manufactures of this State, dear though they be, will sell in foreign countries cheaper sometimes than the Manufactures of another State where Labour is less highly paid" (ibid., 70). Hence, the inflow of money is not canceled out by a consequent outflow generated by the higher prices and wages,[32] therefore, the nation can retain its money and higher standards of living for a number of years. Cantillon here suggests that an inflow of money stemming from a competitive advantage not only stimulates additional industry, but also can be retained as long as the nation maintains its competitive advantage.

As might be obvious, there are significant similarities between Cantillon's and Hume's monetary analyses. Although Cantillon's discussion of the effects of an increase in the money stock is more elaborate and complex than Hume's, their multiplier analyses share common ground, in particular the emphasis on how consumption spreads from sector to sector. They also agree that an exogenous increase in the money supply hurts a nation's prosperity. While Cantillon's discussion of this matter was phrased in terms of new discoveries of mines, he also believes, like Hume, that "an abundance of fictitious and imaginary money causes the same disadvantages as an increase of real money in circulation, by raising the price of Land and Labour, or by making works and manufactures more expensive" (ibid., 125). Finally, they both believe that an inflow of money from a trade surplus is favorable and that a nation can retain the additional money as long as it maintains its competitive edge.

Hume's writings provided additional support to those, like Cantillon and Vanderlint, who challenged the idea that a nation could increase its quantity of money and thus stimulate greater industry by either using trade restrictions or by issuing paper money. Both of these strategies can be traced back to the mid-seventeenth century when political economists were trying to find a solution to the scarcity-of-money problem. In the eighteenth century, the trade-surplus strategy was still associated with Thomas Mun and the inflationist ideas were tied to Law and Berkeley. To Hume, these writers had failed to fully grasp the relationship between money and the economy. Instead of tracing the expansion of money to an increase in the nation's industry, these writers reversed the causality and claimed that an increase in money "stirreth up industry" (Berkeley 1970 [1735], 125). While Hume agreed with these writers that an increase in the money stock may be favorable, he argued strongly that this can only be the case when the money inflow is the result of previous increases in industry. Hence, for Vanderlint, Cantillon, and Hume, the extra boost provided by an increase in money is actually a transmission of productivity improvements through the economy, rather than a pure monetary phenomenon. This insight led them to prescribe the policy, here summarized by Hume, that the "government has great reason to preserve with care its people and its manufactures. Its money, it may safely trust to the course of human affairs, without fear or jealousy" (Hume 1985x [1752e], 326).

As we have seen, Hume's thinking on money had much in common with that of other prominent eighteenth-century political economists. In particular, Hume believed in the well-subscribed views that: (i) money is a symbol that mediates exchange; (ii) the specie-flow mechanism distributes money across the globe in proportion to each country's industry; (iii) only increases in the money stock that stem from improvements in industry or competitive advantages are favorable; while (iv) trade restrictions or paper money expansions are not capable of systematically generating a favorable increase in the money stock. We know that Hume was familiar with the writings of Berkeley, Montesquieu, Hutcheson, Vanderlint, and perhaps even Cantillon—making it highly likely that he studied their ideas about money.[33] In fact, it seems highly plausible that Hume drew heavily on the existing literature in developing his monetary thinking. Yet, I argue, there should be no doubt as to the novelty of his theory of money. Hume elaborated on the semiotics of money, the specie-flow mechanism, the quantity theory of money, and the politics of money in his own characteristic prose and from his own particular historical and philosophical per-spective. Not only is Hume's overall theory of money unique, but each component part of his theory has a distinct Humean signature. That said, however, when we discuss the originality of Hume's ideas, we should also keep in mind that Hume may not necessarily have been trying to be origi-nal. It is quite possible that, following in the tradition of polite essay writing (in the manner of *The Spectator* and *Cato's Letters*), Hume was more interested in writing about the economy and politics in order to educate people in how to best conduct their affairs and to persuade legislators to govern in a more informed manner.[34] In this effort he drew on all the available knowledge to gain the best possible understanding of his subject matter in order to be able to formulate the most convincing arguments. Distinguishing between his ideas and those of his contemporaries in order to stake out his claim on originality was not the primary purpose of his analytical project. Therefore, when we think about Hume's enduring con-tribution to eighteenth-century monetary thinking, we should not focus on the novelty—or lack thereof—of specific ideas, such as whether Hume *really* invented the specie-flow mechanism or the quantity theory of money; rather, I contend, we should focus more broadly on how he theorized money as a social relation embedded in a larger societal and political context. Hume's contribution cannot and should not be traced to any one specific idea or formulation. Instead we should look for the greatness of Hume's thinking on money in his systematic examination of the complex roles that money plays in the constitution and dynamics of the modern polity, society, and economy.

Conclusion

This paper makes the case for reading Hume's monetary theory synthetically. I argue that it is only when we recognize that Hume situated his monetary thinking within his political economy and political philosophy that we can fully appreciate the truly seminal facets of his contribution. Hume's monetary analysis plays an integral part in his political economy, in particular, in his discussion of economic growth and commercial modernization. He carefully examines how money operates domestically and internationally and he per-ceptively traces out how various public policies—from taxes to the public debt to usury laws—influence the workings of the monetary mechanism. He is always attentive to different kinds of monetary dynamics, while at the same time never exaggerating the role money plays. For Hume, money is central to the economy, but he frequently reiterates that it should not be too central in the minds of policymakers, as he believes that money, once established, best functions autonomously from the legislator. Money also plays a central role in Hume's political philosophy. As one of the three foundational conventions of the modern social form, Hume suggests that money is a necessary condi-tion for the establishment of a civilized, prosperous, and liberal society. Hume defines money as an artificial virtue that has to be observed in order for justice to be maintained. As such, he integrates money as a cornerstone to his political philosophy, in particular his discussion of civility, manners, politeness, justice, and virtue. In short, as Tatsuya Sakamoto (2003) has recently pointed out, Hume provides a sophisticated elaboration on how money relates to such diverse features as "industry, knowledge, and humanity." Indeed, it is his capacity to theorize the complex role that money plays in modern society that constitutes Hume's most enduring contribution to eighteenth-century monetary thought.

Notes

I would like to thank the participants of the 2003 Conference on David Hume's Political Economy at Barnard College. I am particularly indebted to George Caffentzis, Istvan Hont, Ian Simpson Ross, and Margaret Schabas for useful suggestions.

1 See for example Meek (1976) and Berry (1997).
2 For a detailed discussion of the evolutionary features of Hume's conventions in the *Treatise*, see Stewart (1963), Berry (1997), and Wennerlind (2002).
3 Most commentators read Hume as proposing that property, markets, and promises constitute the primary conventions. I have argued elsewhere that Hume's discussion of promises may be read as a treatment on fiduciary money (Wennerlind 2001b). For an additional discussion about the commercial features of the *Treatise*, see Schabas (1994) and Davis (2003).
4 For a discussion of money as a semiotic system, see Dyer (1989), Goux (1990), and Wennerlind (2001a).
5 According to Schumpeter (1986 [1954]), the metallists include Child, Petty, Locke, and Harris. Schumpeter also includes Hume in this category, a claim that is here challenged.
6 The last passage appears in the essay "Of Interest" from the 1752 edition to the 1768 edition.
7 In "Of Balance of Trade," Hume writes "wherever I speak of the level of money, I mean always its proportional level to the commodities, labour, industry, and skill, which is in the several states. And I assert, that where these advantages are double, triple, quadruple, to what they are in the neighbouring states, the money infallibly will also be double, triple, and quadruple" (1985x [1752e], 315).
8 Hume points out that "every thing must become much cheaper in times of industry and refinement ..." (1985u [1752c], 291).
9 Hume presents his argument in the context of England's trade with Spain, a nation with which England ran a substantial trade surplus when Hume was writing (Davis 1962, 243). This trade surplus led to many English ships returning home with gold and silver from Cadiz. Quoting William Osgodby, a merchant who commanded ships trading to Cadiz for twenty years, Ralph Davis informs us that in "every such voyage made by him ... he did receive silver and plate and pieces of eight and gold aboard his said ship lying in the Bay of Cadiz to be transported to England for account of English and other merchants" (230).
10 Hume clarifies that, "When any quantity of money is imported into a nation, it is not at first dispersed into many hands; but is confined to the coffers of a few persons, who immediately seek to employ it to advantage" (1985u [1752c], 286).

11 For a more detailed analysis of this process, see Wennerlind (2005) or, for slightly different interpretations, see Duke (1979), Berdell (1995), and Sakamoto (2003).

12 Hume suggests that workers ought to be allowed to "enjoy the fruits of their labour" (1985s [1752a], 265). As such, Hume challenges the utility-of-poverty argument that lower wages are preferable because they force the laborers to work harder (see Furniss 1920). However, at other places, Hume reveals that he favors lower wages (or higher taxes on the poor) as it teaches them frugality and industry.

13 Andrew Skinner notes that "an increase in productivity ... may give the developed economy an advantage in terms of the price of manufactures" (2003, 184). However, Skinner continues, Hume "recognized that advantages may be eroded, causing the loss in turn of particular industries, *unless care is taken to preserve them*" (ibid., 184).

14 As Istvan Hont (2005e [1983]) points out, this is likely to generate a sectoral adjustment wherein rich countries specialize in high-skill and capital-intense industries and poor countries focus on lower-skill and labor-intense production. For further discussion of these themes, see Hont in this volume.

15 When considering a situation in which "the money of Great Britain were multiplied fivefold in a night," Hume uses a simple quantity theory of money in which money is both exogenous and neutral. He suggests that prices would rise in exact proportion to the increase in the money stock, generating a trade deficit and a resulting outflow of money, in exact proportion to the initial increase in the money supply.

16 For a detailed discussion of the different layers in Hume's analysis of money, see Skinner (1993).

17 Whereas Hume primarily uses a hydraulic metaphor when considering money, Schabas (2001) has pointed out that he may actually have been thinking in terms of the conductivity of electric fluids, a phenomenon that was central in the minds of most scientifically inclined people in Edinburgh during the 1740s.

18 Wennerlind (2005).

19 While Hume seems to be more comfortable with the idea of expanding the money supply through the use of paper money in the essay "Of Balance of Trade", he still concludes that this is not a policy that can be systematically employed. He writes, "A good effect ... may follow too from paper-credit; but it is dangerous to precipitate matters, at the risk of losing all by the failing of that credit, as must happen upon any violent shock in public affairs" (Hume 1985x [1752e], 317).

20 Hume reached this conclusion after reading Melon's and Du Tot's discussions of Louis XIV's frequent debasements. While Melon (1738a) was in favor of debasements as a way to reduce the burden of the national debt, Du Tot (1974 [1739]) was firmly against it on the grounds that it would force an increase in prices and a consequent outflow of gold and silver. Hume, however, suggested that both Melon and Du Tot had overlooked a possible benefit of the debasement, namely that, if "all our money ... [were] recoined, and a penny's worth of silver taken from every shilling, the new shilling would probably purchase every thing that could have been bought by the old; the prices of every thing would thereby be insensibly diminished; foreign trade enlivened; and domestic industry ... would receive some encrease and encouragement" (1985u [1752c], 288).

21 For an alternative interpretation of Hume's discussion of debasements, see Caffentzis in this volume.

22 Wennerlind (2005).

23 Rashid (1984).

24 Friedrich A. von Hayek was convinced that Hume had read Cantillon's *Essai* in manuscript form. He wrote, "Better known is the somewhat shorter exposition of

the same idea which David Hume gave a little later in a famous passage of his *Political Discourses,* which so closely resembles the words of Cantillon that it is hard to believe that he had not seen one of those manuscripts of the *Essai* which are known to have been in private circulation at the time when the [Political] Discourses were written" (Hayek 1932, 9).

25 Adam Smith was in the process of developing his ideas on money around the same time as Hume. While we cannot be sure how much Smith and Hume learned from each other, a case can be made for a significant Humean paternity to Smith's monetary thinking (Wennerlind 2000).

26 For an alternative comparative reading of the monetary theories of Vanderlint, Gervaise, Cantillon, and Hume, see Sekine (1973).

27 Vanderlint suggests that "the Prices of Things will certainly rise in every Nation, as the Gold and Silver increase amongst the People; and, consequently, that where the Gold and Silver decrease in any Nation, the Prices of all Things must fall proportionably to such Decrease of Money" (1914 [1734], 14). He also adds that cash notes "hath the same Effect, as if there was so much more Cash really circulating" (ibid., 15).

28 For the reason that the "Nations that can work cheapest, must have the Money, as sure as they always will have the Trade" (1914 [1734], 13).

29 Hume writes "not only as a man, but as a British subject, I pray for the flourishing commerce of Germany, Spain, Italy, and even France itself. I am at least certain, that Great Britain, and all those nations, would flourish more, did their sovereigns and ministers adopt such enlarged and benevolent sentiments towards each other" (1985ee [1758], 331).

30 Cantillon's *Essai* was recently reissued and two books (Murphy [1986a] and Brewer [1992]) have been written about his work and life. In addition, a number of journal articles focusing on his monetary analysis have appeared (for example, see Sekine [1973] and Bordo [1983]).

31 Cantillon also considers an inflow of money brought in by travelers and ambassadors, as well as funds transferred from abroad for investment purposes.

32 "From all this," Cantillon concludes "that by doubling the quantity of money in a State the prices of products and merchandise are not always doubled. A River which runs and winds about in its bed will not flow with double speed when the amount of its water is doubled" (2001 [1931], 73).

33 Hume was closely familiar with the writings of Berkeley, Hutcheson, and Montesquieu by the time he formulated his theory of money. We also know that Hume was in possession of Vanderlint's book, although we cannot be sure when he obtained it. Regarding Hume's relationship to Cantillon, there has been a long-standing controversy as to what Hume's intellectual debt may have been. Since Cantillon's *Essai* (2001 [1931]) circulated in France prior to its publication, it is conceivable, though unlikely, that Hume encountered a copy during his travels.

34 For a discussion about Hume's attempts to influence the legislator, see Wennerlind (2006).

7   Temporal Dimensions in Hume's Monetary Theory

Margaret Schabas

David Hume comes at the end of a long and venerable tradition of monetary analysis harking back to Aristotle. It is not too much of a distortion of the historical record to maintain that after Hume's essays on the subject, money faded into the background of economic theory until the writings of Knud Wicksell, Irving Fisher and John Maynard Keynes in the first half of the twentieth century. This claim is not meant to imply that no one wrote about money during the second half of the eighteenth century, or throughout the nineteenth century. Many did, producing numerous treatises on banking, currency, and credit. But money was no longer the point of departure for economic theory as found in the many *Principles* texts produced with great regularity from James Steuart to Alfred Marshall.[1] As John Stuart Mill characteristically remarked in his *Principles of Political Economy*, there is no "more insignificant thing, in the economy of society, than money" (Mill 1965 [1848], 3:506).

Hume's essay "Of Money" commences with its denigration: "Money is not, properly speaking, one of the subjects of commerce" (Hume 1985u [1752c], 281). In his essay "Of Interest" he remarks that money has "chiefly a fictitious value" (Hume 1985v [1752d], 297). Hume was part of a broader movement that sought to discredit mercantilism, particularly its emphasis on a favorable balance of trade and the accumulation of specie. His intentions to promote the unrestricted trade of goods and money are clearly stated in his 1750 letter to James Oswald. He wrote "to prohibit the exportation of money, or the importation of commodities, is mistaken policy; and I have the pleasure of seeing you agree with me" (see Hume [1955], 199). Even if there had been no mercantilist doctrine to oppose, or advocates of protectionist measures, the demise of Spain and Portugal was lesson enough that hoarding gold and silver would only diminish wealth and power. Rather frugality, industry, and mercantile ingenuity were the traits that enabled one region of Europe, such as the Netherlands, to achieve commercial eminence. Merchants had become the heroes of the modern age. Unlike the landed gentry who tend to prodigality, the frugal and industrial merchants "beget industry, by serving as canals to convey it through every corner of the state" (Hume 1985v [1752d], 301). And while no single country could ever sustain its dominant economic position indefinitely, it could, once developed, sustain a high standard of living. As Hume observes in his later essay "Of the Jealousy of Trade," the Dutch have reason to fear that their neighbors will emulate their ingenuity as "the brokers, and factors, and carriers of others" and that their commerce might suffer due to the lack of land and "native commodities." Nevertheless, Hume believes they will continue to thrive on the economic development of neighboring states, and that their decline "may be warded off for many generations, if not wholly eluded." This leads Hume to argue that British commerce will flourish as the commerce of Europe grows in general, even in rival states such as France (Hume 1985ee [1758], 330–31).

A persistent theme throughout Hume's writings on political economy, both in his *Treatise* and in his *Essays*, is the distinction between a monetary veneer and the locus of wealth in a nation's industry and people. There is, in short, a nascent distinction between the nominal and the real in Hume, and while Hume was not the first to treat money as a veil, he undoubtedly wove into it several new strands.[2] The reason I claim the distinction was nascent is that Hume did not entirely segregate the monetary realm from the non-monetary. It is important to keep in mind that at times he treats money in the abstract, and at other times, within an historical framework of an emerging commercial order, and for that reason alone, he defies simple categorization. For example, it is only as commerce extends its reach across the globe, that money tends to become neutral. On the other hand, commercial growth enables if not demands the proliferation of kinds of money spurred on by clever bankers and other financial traders. These added layers of monetary issue imply that money is embedded even more deeply into the realm of production and distribution. It is for this reason that I see the nominal/real distinction in Hume as not fully developed or even fully intended. If Hume had in mind the treatment of money as a mere coating or veneer, it could not be entirely detached from the underlying state of commercial development.[3] As I hope to show here, the advent and rise of commerce and trade for Hume is a complicated tale of the interplay of human trust and deception, and money is part and parcel of this account as it unfolded over time. In sum, Hume ascribed properties to money that evolve over time. This dynamical account builds on the recent work of Carl Wennerlind (2002), specifically his emphasis on the long durée that frames Hume's account of commercial expansion.

For much of the century preceding Hume, economic tracts had maintained that a low interest rate, as in the Netherlands, pointed to flourishing trade and commerce (see e.g. Appleby 1978, Ch. 4). But it was still widely assumed that the interest rate was determined by the supply of money. Hume's essay "Of Interest" argues that the interest rate be viewed as a nonmonetary phenomenon, that variations in the money stock ought no longer to be treated as a proximate cause. This is true of both a feudal society, when usury prevailed, and of a fully developed commercial state, when interest rates became much lower. In both cases, the interest rate "depends on the habits and way of living of the people, not on the quantity of gold and silver" (Hume 1985v [1752d], 298). To make his point more forcefully, Hume considers a world devoid of merchants, first in a clever thought experiment, where an overnight doubling of the money stock would not alter the interest rate one whit, and then in his historical account where the landed interest takes hold and prodigality becomes more pronounced (see Hume 1985v [1752d], 298–99). Throughout, Hume assumes that the market for loanable funds serves the single purpose of supporting the luxurious spending of the landowning class. Perhaps he had in mind the eleventh or twelfth centuries when, as he observes in his *History of England*, "the improvements of agriculture were also much checked, by the immense possessions of the nobility, by the disorders of the times, and by the precarious state of feudal property; it appears, that industry of no kind could then have place in the kingdom" (Hume 1983a [1778], I:484). In more recent times, needless to say, merchants grew in sufficient numbers so as to channel funds into significant stocks and thus influence the market for lending and borrowing. Hume's point throughout is that it is the set of new habits, especially among the merchant class, that truly propelled the decline in the interest rate in countries such as Holland or England. In sum, a reduction in the interest rate "must proceed from an encrease of industry and frugality, of arts and commerce" (Hume 1985v [1752d], 299). Even more than his predecessors, Hume promotes the sense in which "interest is the barometer of the state, and its lowness is a sign almost infallible of the flourishing condition of a people" (Hume 1985v [1752d], 303).

Hume gives us a picture of economic development that stems first and foremost from the formation of new habits and customs, such as frugality and industriousness, which in turn foster manufacturing and commerce, which in turn promote a lower interest rate and a higher standard of living. But Hume also grasped that the causal path flowed, perhaps simultaneously, in the opposite direction. A lower interest rate enables commerce to spread more rapidly, by facilitating merchant loans and enterprises, and this in turn forges new habits and customs, for example more honesty and trust. "The freedom and extent of human commerce depend entirely on a fidelity with regard to promises."[4] This fuels more trade thereby increasing and intensifying the network of reciprocity among strangers. "When men's industry encreases, and their views enlarge, it is found, that the most remote parts of the state can assist each other as well as the more contiguous, and that this intercourse of good offices may be carried on to the greatest extent and intricacy" (Hume 1985v [1752d], 299–300; also see Ignatieff 1984 and Boyd this volume). As a result, there is greater civility: "*Nothing is more favourable to the rise of politeness and learning, than a number of neighbouring and independent states, connected together by commerce and polity*" (Hume 1985k [1742a], 119; italicized in the original).

While there are glimmers of optimism in Hume – the modern age is better than the ancient in many respects – mankind is also destined to repeat the same mistakes again and again (Hume 1985aa [1752h], 363). Persons in political office are tempted toward deceiving one another and hence must be more readily forgiven for their immoral actions than in the private sphere. Recall that for Hume the system of morals governing princes is freer than that for ordinary folk (Hume 2000a, 363). But duplicity and hypocrisy trickle all the way down. The poor hide their poverty out of a sense of humility and shame as much as the rich flaunt their wealth out of pride and vanity (Hume 2000a, 198–205). As with Bernard Mandeville's *Fable of the Bees* (1732) and Adam Smith's *Wealth of Nations* (1776), Hume paints a picture of a thriving if not benign commercial world that is replete with illusion and deception.[5]

Part of the illusion commences with the advent of money, which emerges innocently from ordinary barter but then takes on a life of its own. One region produces an excess supply of cheese and butter, the other bread and corn. It only takes one person to discern the gains from trade and to facilitate this, but once set in motion, merchants arise to facilitate more trade. Then "the business of the agency or merchandize becomes more intricate; and divides, subdivides, compounds, and mixes to a greater variety" (Hume 1985v [1752d], 300). The merchant is entitled to his share which "he will sometimes preserve in kind, or more commonly convert into money, which is their common representation" (Hume 1985v [1752d], 300). Note that the justification of money replacing barter is not the problem of the double coincidence of wants, but rather the preferability of a uniform measure of value as trade and industry become more "intricate." The theme of money representing and measuring goods is iterated by Hume in several other passages in his economic writings. Indeed, he credits Anacharsis with the original insight "that money is nothing but the representation of labour and commodities, and serves only as a method of rating or estimating them" (Hume 1985u [1752c], 285). Precisely because Hume weighs in on the function of money as a unit of account rather than as a store of wealth or a medium of exchange serves to promote his broader treatment of money as coating industry and trade.

In the *Treatise*, Hume also discerns certain parallels between the formation and evolution of language and the tacit promises that yield money (Hume 2000a, 315). Money is laden with convention, and is clearly something that humans created, but in the modern era it operates on a level that overrides human law and regulation. This was a point already made forcefully by Thomas Mun at the close of his popular tract, *England's Treasure by Forraign Trade*. Even were the crown to debase the currency, merchants would restore the rightful balance of money "by a Necessity beyond all resistance" (Mun 1986 [1664], 87). The same point was echoed by Hume, for example, that "all laws alone are ineffectual" in forcing the redistribution of money, even where communication is cut off, as in the case of China (Hume 1985x [1752e], 313). Likewise, he asks, "Can one imagine, that it had ever been possible, by any laws, or even by any art or industry, to have kept all the money in SPAIN, which the galleons have brought from the INDIES?" (Hume 1985x [1752e], 312). Illicit and ingenious actions thus trump any legal regulations.

Hume went further than Mun in granting money its own autonomy. I have argued elsewhere that Hume treats money as a natural force, drawing inspiration from the subtle fluid doctrine that was ascendant in experimental physics of the 1740s (Schabas 2001). That he appeals to ocean imagery too is highly relevant. The ebb and flux of money worldwide is much like the tides, specific to its local geography, but overall subject to the gravitational forces of the sun and the moon. And like all fluids, it must always reach a uniform level: "it is impossible to heap up money, more than any fluid, beyond its proper level" (see Hume 1985x [1752e], 312). For it is only when money has become universally diffused and kept in circulation, when "no hand is entirely empty of it," that its full force is felt (Hume 1985u [1752c], 294). Foreign money likewise has vitalizing effects: "in every kingdom, into which money begins to flow in greater abundance than formerly, every thing takes a new face: labour and industry gain life" (Hume 1985u [1752c], 286). So a domestic drift from barter to a monetized trade also benefits from international trade and the influx of foreign specie. The extent to which money works its way into every transaction, is "digest[ed] into every vein, so to speak," and above all keeps in circulation depends critically on foreign trade (Hume 1985u [1752c], 294). And the more the money is linked to global trade, the more it evolves away from its initial state and becomes subject to forces akin to those in nature. There is thus a tension throughout Hume's analyses of money, between his appreciation of the purely conventional and passive nature of money, and of its autonomy and efficacy as part of the fabric of human society if not the natural order. Hume, I submit, came closer than many to grasping the Janus-faced nature of money, and perhaps backed away from certain problems because he intuited their intractability.

A central leitmotif in Hume's essays is that the absolute level of money is irrelevant: "the greater or less plenty of money is of no consequence; since prices of commodities are always proportioned to the plenty of money" (Hume 1985u [1752c], 281). This he argues is true both domestically and internationally, since trade will determine that each nation has the appropriate quantity of money commensurate with its level of economic development. If the money stock is fixed in a nation, and its level of industry increased, then prices must fall since the money must now accommodate a larger number of goods and market transactions (Hume 1985u [1752c], 291). If the money stock is subject to international trade, then it too will adjust to the rightful level "proportionate to the art and industry of each nation" (Hume 1985x [1752e], 312). Hume uses this analysis to attack those who favored upholding a trade balance, or who sought to impose customs and duties to protect domestic industry. His conclusion is short and succinct: "a government has great reason to preserve with care its people and its manufactures. Its money, it may safely trust to the course of human affairs, without fear or jealousy" (Hume 1985x [1752e], 326).

As with most general maxims, however, Hume cannot resist some quali-fication. He observes, for example, that a "greater quantity of money, like the ROMAN characters [as opposed to the Arabian notation for numbers] is rather inconvenient, and requires greater trouble both to keep and trans-port it" (Hume 1985u [1752c], 285).[6] Plenty of money also results in higher prices and wages, which tend to inspire the consumption of imported goods. "The dearness of everything, from plenty of money, is a disadvantage, which attends an established commerce, and sets bounds to it in every country, by enabling the poorer states to undersel [sic] the richer in all foreign markets" (Hume 1985u [1752c], 284). Not only can an above-average quantity of money produce inconveniences or result in a reduction in domestic pro-duction, but a below-average quantity can also pose problems. Scarcity of specie engenders a situation whereby rents and taxes are paid in kind, which in turn limits the gains from trade. Austria suffers from this plight, not-withstanding the fact that it is "in general well peopled and well cultivated." The unfortunate result of a dearth of specie is that Austria can not garner taxes sufficient to mount a good army (Hume 1985u [1752c], 289). As per-sonal secretary to General St. Clair, Hume was acutely aware of the con-stant need for cash to maintain provisions and armaments, particularly when stationed abroad.[7] All of these qualifications would lead one to infer that the absolute level of money in a nation is indeed significant, that it cannot be either too high or too low.

Hume, moreover, is equivocal about the form that money takes. He insists at times that the kind of metal used is of no consequence, and even suggests mixing the gold or silver coins with baser metals: "they still serve the same purposes of exchange, whatever their number may be, or whatever colour they may be supposed to have" (Hume 1985u [1752c], 290). In a letter to the abbé Morellet of 1769, he appears to have changed his mind, insofar as he acknowledges that "money must always be made of some materials, which have intrinsic value, otherwise it would be multiplied without end, and would sink to nothing" (Hume 1955). He points to the existence of a French coin, the *billon*, that is composed of silver and copper. Because it is too "expensive and troublesome" to retrieve the silver, it cir-culates as essentially a base coin (Ibid., 214). Yet this is in contrast to the silver shilling and sixpence in Britain that are in principle convertible into valuable metal. The coins are so depleted by illegal filings, however, that they may be "twenty, thirty, or forty per cent below their original value" (Ibid., 214). Both the French and British coins circulate as legal tender, but because the British coins have some intrinsic net value, there is a differ-ence.

In other passages, Hume presents himself as a strong adherent to gold and silver as the only viable forms of money. One recent interpretation reads this as a belief that for practical purposes it is best to have a specific commodity, gold, permanently regarded as the monetary medium but that there is no theoretical basis for this commitment (see Caffentzis 2001, 303–4). Yet Hume also contemplates the complete annihilation of gold in England, with the claim that silver would serve just as well (Hume 1985v [1752d], 296). Hume also considers devaluing the shilling. Prices would remain the same but the added quantity of money would stimulate foreign trade and domestic industry. He makes this suggestion (that a penny's worth of silver be taken from every shilling) in opposition to Locke, who advised the recoinage of 1695 when clipped coins were reissued at par.

When it comes to paper money, Hume admits there is no definitive solution: "It must, however, be confessed, that, as all these questions of trade and money are extremely complicated, there are certain lights, in which this subject may be placed, so as to represent the advantages of paper-credit and banks to be superior to their disadvantages" (Hume 1985x [1752e], 318). There is reason to believe that when there is a considerable shortage of specie, paper notes might serve just as well. Hume suggested this as preferable to the iron coins used in ancient Sparta (Hume 1985x [1752e], 318). Hume knew about Benjamin Franklin's *A Modest Inquiry into the Nature and Necessity of a Paper Currency* (1729) and almost certainly read George Berkeley's *Querist* (1735–37), both of which championed the need for paper issue as a way to ameliorate the woes of America and Ireland, respectively.[8] Two scholars have made the case that in Volume Three of his *Treatise of Human Nature*, Hume appears to be more favorably disposed toward paper money (see Gatch 1996; Wennerlind 2001a). Hume also became more enthusiastic in later editions of his *Political Discourses*, starting with the 1764 edition (see Wennerlind 2000, 89, 92). As Robert Dimand demonstrates, this coincided with the period during which Hume oversaw the issuance of playing cards in Canada, as Secretary to the British Embassy in Paris (see Dimand, this volume). In any case, for all his protestations to the contrary, Hume recognized that the material form money takes was of some significance. Even more pertinent was the formation of sound policies by the monetary authorities, so as to coordinate the denomination and overall supply of money.

Carl Wennerlind argues persuasively that Hume cannot be characterized as an "inflationist" (Wennerlind 2005). His admonitions to the magistrate to keep the money supply ever increasing, once read in their proper context, are really about facilitating trade and inducing more entrenched patterns of commercial behavior. In fact, the magistrate was not in a position of authority to regulate the money supply, at least not directly. But it is also important to bear in mind that Hume may only have meant that money can be left to its own accord in a state where money is sufficiently, if not universally, disseminated because the habits of banking and commerce are fully developed. While people and industry are the real strength of a region, their full potential can only be actualized when money "enter[s] into every transaction and contract" and serves to foster "its universal diffusion and circulation"

(Hume 1985u [1752c], 294). In that respect, the magistrate could play a significant role insofar as he is able to reduce hoarding, either by promoting the security of the banks, or by encouraging the use of china plate rather than silverware.[9] A magistrate might also, at a local level, oversee improvements to the collection of taxes. In a 1749 letter to Montesquieu, Hume observes that the tax *fermiers*, motivated by profit, served a valuable preliminary role in England, by figuring out "a hundred thousand tricks and devices for dealing with fraud ... which the government collectors would never have dreamed of" (Hume 1955, 187). Once these are snuffed out, Hume submits, the *fermiers* can teach the government collectors and taxes can then be well administered by the state. It might be measures of this sort that a magistrate could control at the local level, but clearly Hume welcomes the day when money functions entirely at a global level and is no longer subject to the whims of individual authorities. There is temporal endpoint to Hume's vision of economic development, whereby the wheels of trade are highly differentiated and lubricated universally by the "oil" of money.

There are two insights in Hume that have received a disproportionate amount of attention from both historians and economists.[10] One is his recognition that money is not passive (or neutral in modern terminology). A sudden injection of specie from abroad can result in greater productivity in both the agrarian and manufacturing sectors. In other words, an unanticipated spurt of gold or silver in one port town can yield real-growth effects during the interval that ensues after the arrival of the money stock and before the consequent rise of domestic prices. The other insight, which has come to be called the specie-flow mechanism (although Hume never used this term), maintains that money is indeed passive and of no consequence. International trade, if unimpeded, will result in a global equilibration of the distribution of metallic money through price adjustments. As Hume put it in that same 1749 letter to Montesquieu, "if half the money which is in England were suddenly doubled, goods would suddenly become more expensive, imports would rise to the disadvantage of exports and our money would be spread among our neighbours. It does not seem that money, any more than water, can be raised or lowered ... that it must rise and fall in proportion to the goods and labour contained in each state" (Hume 1955, 188–9).

On first reading, Hume appears to be inconsistent, because his real-growth account is undercut by his specie-flow mechanism (see Rotwein 1970, lxiv–v). Surely the concomitant rise of prices will lead people to import cheaper goods from abroad and thus bring prices immediately back down to the initial situation? Would not the temporary spurt in output simply fall back to the previous level, or perhaps decline even further as imports supplant domestically-produced goods? Furthermore, the rise in wages that accompanies the rise in prices would attract immigrants and thus alter the demand for money per capita. James Oswald made this very objection in a letter of 10 October 1749. "If the price of labour still continued for a short time at a higher rate than that level, it would only serve, by attracting foreigners, to increase the number of useful inhabitants in proportion to the increased quantity of money" (see Hume 1955, 192).

Moreover, what about the fact that different goods have different "elasticities of demand"? Thomas Mun had discerned this phenomenon with respect to the sale of English cloth, that by underselling abroad they had managed to capture a larger share of the market (Mun 1986 [1664], 8). By the early eighteenth century, there was a widespread understanding from the work of Charles Davenant or Gregory King that the demand for corn is price inelastic, to use modern terminology (see Endres 1987, 623). Hume recognized that, in the case of duties on an imported good, revenues would increase by more than the reduction in the ostensive price. "If the duties on wine were lowered to a third, they would yield much more to the government than at present" (Hume 1985x [1752e], 324–25). He also recognized clear cases where a change in price results in a shift to a close substitute: "a tax on brandy encreases the sale of rum" (Hume 1985x [1752e], 324). Why then, as prices increase, does this not unleash a different domestic pattern of demand which could not in any clear sense result in global price uniformities?[11] One might argue that the pattern would remain intact in the case of a sudden overnight doubling of money. In the case of an influx of specie, however, Hume is explicit that it trickles into a few hands first, and that "it is easy to trace the money in its progress through the whole commonwealth" (Hume 1985u [1752c], 287). The scenario he provides suggests that prices rise unevenly, over the course of time, rather than *tout ensemble*. Otherwise, how could one trace their progress?

It is also unclear how an overnight addition of specie would lead to no changes other than the price level. Hume explicitly recognized that the existence of inventories might well result in a delayed effort by merchants to raise prices. In fact, the very crux of his argument that money can induce growth is that shopkeepers do not immediately raise prices when workmen increase their demand for goods. The artisan, being promptly paid, "carries his money to market, where he finds everything at the same price as formerly, but returns with greater quantity and of better kinds" (Hume 1985u [1752c], 287). Likewise, the farmer and the gardener "apply themselves with greater alacrity to the raising more; and at the same time can afford to take better and more cloths from their tradesmen, whose price is the same as formerly" (Hume 1985u [1752c], 287). As Michael Duke has argued in the case of Hume, prices appear to be "sticky" (see Duke 1979, 577). The critical fact of Hume's article is that additional coins in the pockets of artisans, and the additional demand of agrarian goods from artisans, spurs both the agrarian and artisanal sectors to increase the intensity of their labor before prices or wages actually increase. This is the source of the unanticipated economic growth.

Several scholars have maintained that this central inconsistency can be partly resolved if one differentiates between the short run and the long run for Hume (see Duke 1979; Cesarano 1998). In the short run, there are real-growth effects to an increase in the money stock, but in the long run, these wash out due to the global flow of specie. Alfred Marshall, while acknowledging the arbitrariness of his categories, proposed that we think of the short run as a few months up to a year, and the long run as several years (Marshall 1920 [1890], 314–15). Marshall based these measures partly on technological change and partly on market mechanisms. Of course, Hume did not know Marshall, but presumably when others ascribe these categories to Hume they have the Marshallian distinctions in mind. As I read Hume, however, there is no such clear distinction; to speak of short-run versus long-run adjustments is to succumb to an anachronism. For one, there is little indication in Hume that technological invention and innovation plays a role in economic development. He suggests that cloth-making and ship-building are good indicators of the advantages of modern life, but there are virtually no concrete references to technical improvements.[12] For another, while he allows that the real-growth effects only transpire in the "interval before matters be adjusted to their new situation," he never gives us a concise measure of that interval (Hume 1985u [1752c], 288). The closest he comes to a measure is when he observes that in the last year of Louis XIV (1715) the money stock rose by three-sevenths and the price level by one-seventh, but he never goes on to acknowledge that prices caught up to the increased money stock (ibid., 287).

In a different passage, Hume gives the impression that the interval remains open-ended indefinitely. The amount of gold and silver that has entered Europe since Christopher Columbus is considerably greater than the four-fold increase in the price level (Hume 1985u [1752c], 292). It is possible that within this stretch of time there were certain years whereby the price level rose commensurate to the specie influx, but Hume never indicates that this was what he had in mind. In one place he notes that the price of some goods will rise before that of others, and the diffusion of money itself will be gradual, but all he tells us is that it will take "some time" for the increase in the money supply to result in a uniform rise in prices (Hume 1985u [1752c], 286).

One might assume that he conceived of this interval as short-lived, and there is some evidence in a letter to Oswald to suggest this, but the only meaningful comparison would be his sense of a long run, which is for Hume incredibly long. In his essay "Of Money" his most prevalent temporal interval is two to three centuries. He compares the value of a crown in the reign of Henry VII to the present, a stretch of over two hundred years (Hume 1985u [1752c], 281), or the aggregate level of wealth in Germany to what it was three centuries before (Hume 1985u [1752c], 289). Hume also harks back to the European discovery of America, and suggests that "money is not more plentiful in CHINA, than it was in EUROPE three centuries ago" (Hume 1985u [1752c], 294). Yet if one juxtaposes those comparisons with the three times he refers back to ancient Rome (Hume 1985u [1752c], 282, 285, 294), then it might be more accurate to ascribe 300 years as the short run for Hume, and over 1,500 years as the long run. Hume even peers well into the future, conjecturing in his essay "Of Public Credit" that in 500 years servants and masters will have changed stations (Hume 1985aa [1752h], 357).

To impose a numerical measure on Hume's temporal sensibility is thus extremely difficult. With rhetorical flourish, he speaks at one point of manufactures "flying" to other countries in the wake of higher domestic wages, while having just maintained that they "gradually shift their places" (Hume 1985u [1752c], 283). Certainly when he points (in the same paragraph) to the "happy concurrence of causes in human affairs, which checks the growth of trade and riches," he could only have had several centuries in mind, if not the thousand-plus years that separated his day from the fall of Rome. Elsewhere, he compares the British level of industry from the present to a state two centuries ago (Hume 1985ee [1758], 328). If this is to be Hume's sense of a long run, it would take considerable massaging to impose it on the specie-flow mechanism. Eugene Rotwein and Andrew Skinner have rightfully emphasized the overarching framework of natural history in Hume's political economy (see Rotwein 1970, xxviii–xl; Skinner 1967). Paul Wood (1989) has argued persuasively that a central concern of the Scottish enlightenment was natural history and that nascent evolutionary thinking had already taken place. Hume's mildly irreverent stance toward the human condition, his many gestures toward the behavior of animals, and his own contributions to historical scholarship, all suggest an ability to gain a view of considerable detachment and historical neutrality.

As for the short run, Hume might have had in mind one year, since he mentioned that in his 1750 letter responding to Oswald's criticisms. To quote at length:

> You allow, that if all the money in England were increased four-fold in one night, there would be a sudden rise of prices; but then, say you, the importation of foreign commodities would soon lower the prices. Here, then, is the flowing out of the money already begun. But, say you, a small part of this stock of money would suffice to buy foreign commodities, and lower the prices. I grant it would for one year, till the imported commodities be consumed. But must not the same thing be renewed next year? No, say you; the additional stock of money may, in this interval, so increase the people and industry, as to enable them to retain their money. Here I am extremely pleased with your reasoning. I agree with you, that the increase of money, if not too sudden, naturally increases people and industry, and by that means may retain itself
> (Hume 1955, 1970, 197–98)

There are at least two points to be made. Hume is taking the one-year interval from Oswald; there is no reason to believe that it was part of his own original analysis. Moreover, he suggests that this would only address a small part of the newly arrived money, and engender a price adjustment necessarily. If Hume believed this estimate on Oswald's part to be accurate, presumably he would have incorporated it into his published account. But there is no reference to a time period of one year in the essay itself. More importantly, the one year refers only to the consumption of imported commodities. It is not clear from the passage that Hume intended that the real-growth effects would fully transpire in one year, only get underway. If anything, he implies that the growth would be sustained for much longer and perhaps spiral on indefinitely. All that Hume agrees to is that some portion of the additional stock of money would be retained if it stimulated growth in population and industry. He ends the passage with a supposition to make the point in a negative fashion:

> Suppose twenty million brought into Scotland; suppose that, by some fatality, we take no advantage of this to augment our industry or people, how much would remain in the quarter of a century? Not a shilling more than we have at present. My expression in the Essay needs correction, which has occasioned you to mistake it.
>
> (Hume 1955, 198).

The last line of this letter suggests that Hume has not changed his mind as a result of the correspondence, but realized the need to articulate his argument more clearly. Furthermore, he suggests that it might take up to twenty-five years for the sudden injection of money to drift out of the country through the purchase of imported goods. But that would only transpire if there was no economic growth whatsoever. One reasonable inference to draw from this supposition, which also did not appear in his published work, is that the potential for growth due to an injection of specie is at best twenty-five years. Yet even that is not self-evident from Hume's remarks in the letter to Oswald. The point is rather that, if the new specie stimulates growth, then some of it will be retained so as to accompany the increased transactions (industry and people). Prices are therefore not likely to return to their prior level.

A charitable reading might thus ascribe twenty-five years as the short run for Hume, and three hundred years as the long run. I do not think these ascriptions can be made, but even if they were, it makes something of a mockery of the instantaneous price adjustments that would be required for the specie-flow mechanism to work. A better way to resolve the inconsistency is to recognize that for the specie-flow mechanism, Hume has devised a thought experiment that strictly speaking never transpires in our actual world.[13] He uses the device of a thought experiment on several occasions and in each case it seems he is more bent on revealing an underlying propensity that could only manifest itself under the hypothetical scenario. In this thought experiment, Hume has isolated a relationship between global specie flows and price adjustments, but arguably they are never fully actualized. Indeed the empirical evidence he marshals to contrast the increase in bullion and the rise of prices in Europe since Columbus is a clear refutation of his so-called mechanism. The real-growth effects account, however, is something that can actually transpire, hence his more detailed account of gold and silver from Cadiz, of cloth merchants becoming better paymasters, and of farmers following their ploughs with greater vigor (Hume 1985u [1752c], 286–87). But it is also fully consistent with his account to allow this to take one year or more than two decades. Little is gained by drawing a temporal distinction between the short and long run.

Even if the two central tenets of Hume's monetary theory are not inconsistent, as Carl Wennerlind (2005) has recently argued, each has internal inconsistencies or incomplete trains of thought. I will first look at the growth account and then at the specie-flow mechanism. Exactly how an influx of money induces greater economic productivity remains, at its very core, a mystery. Money has vitalizing powers that induce workers to intensify their productivity. There is a brief allusion to the fetishism of money, mere "shining bits of metal" (Hume 1985v [1752d], 297). Elsewhere he remarks, "Nor can any thing restrain or regulate the love of money, but a sense of honour and virtue" (Hume 1985t [1752b], 276). Hume, like many of his age, observed the overriding bent among merchants toward frugality. "If the employment you give him be lucrative, especially if the profit be attached to every particular exertion of industry, he has gain so often in his eye, that he acquires, by degrees, a passion for it, and knows no such pleasure as that of seeing the daily encreases of his fortune" (Hume 1985v [1752d], 301). Hume extended this passion to laborers, to farmers and weavers, "their industry only whetted by so much new gain" (Hume 1985u [1752c], 287). His emphasis on the monetization of society, where money is universally diffused, is thus partly driven by the love of lucre.

The crux of the argument for economic growth depends on the recognition that in the eighteenth century, everyone lived on credit, whether running up a tab with the local shopkeeper or tailor, or incurring debt from a bank to run a business or line of trade. While the data to support this claim may always fall short of a concrete measure of the full extent of credit, straightforward comparisons of the quantity of coins in circulation and the levels of expenditure and volumes of trade point to the fact that credit was a critical means of taming the velocity of money.[14] Hume observed that in Scotland the specie could sustain one-third of the transactions; the rest were backed by lines of credit (Hume 1985x [1752e], 320). Moreover, the great shortage of small change meant that workers were less likely to be paid on time than merchants. As was already understood at the time, money served as a magnet for more. As one maxim ran: "A Man that gets a Hundred pounds a Year can better pay ten pounds, than a man with ten pounds can pay 10 shillings."[15]

Hence when Hume observes that the merchants receiving the Spanish specie from Cadiz become better paymasters, what is meant is that workers are paid on time and paid in full-bodied coins. With coins in their pockets, they can pay off their debts with local shopkeepers, leave with choicer cuts of meat and fresher ale, and this in turn inspires them to be more attentive and industrious workers. What is not required initially, and Hume is explicit about this, is an actual rise in wages. "If workmen become scarce, the manufacturer gives higher wages, but at first requires an encrease of labour; and this is willingly submitted to by the artisan, who can now eat and drink better, to compensate his additional toil and fatigue. He carries his money to market, where he finds every thing at the same price as formerly, but returns with greater quantity and of better kinds" (Hume 1985u [1752c], 287).

The availability of good coins explains why the artisan can purchase more goods at market without a rise in wages or a change in prices. Indeed, the expectations of the workers have been fulfilled by prompt payment in specie. "Here are a set of manufacturers or merchants, we shall suppose, who have received returns of gold and silver for goods which they sent to CADIZ. They are thereby enabled to employ more workmen than formerly, who never dream of demanding higher wages, but are glad of employment from such *good paymasters*" (Hume 1985u [1752c], 286–87; emphasis mine). The illusion eventually wears off, "by heightening the price of commodities, and obliging every one to pay a greater number of these little yellow or white pieces for every thing he purchases" (Hume 1985u [1752c], 286). Hume's language is carefully chosen here. If people regarded money as just "little yellow or white pieces" that facilitate trade they would not be inspired to work harder. It is the weight and sound of jangling coins in the pocket that induces greater productivity. Similarly, it is the payment for goods with bona fide specie that prompts the provisioner to offer better quality goods, and in turn to inspire the farmer to "follow his plough with greater alacrity and attention" (ibid., 286). And it is this process that still remains mysterious, the temporary succumbing to the illusory value of money itself.[16] To the best of my knowledge, no one has gone beyond Hume in unpacking this causal process. At least Hume, to his credit, acknowledges that "this is not easily to be accounted for" (ibid., 286).

In a different essay, "Of the Balance of Trade," Hume observes in a footnote that the same result might also be induced by paper-credit. He is wary of such a process, however, because of the dangers of a sudden collapse due to "any violent shock in public affairs" (Hume 1985x [1752e], 317n). As part and parcel of this trend, Scottish merchants in collaboration with the banks came to issue notes as low as 10 shillings, which could be used for almost any transaction, including the payment of "tradesmen's labour of all kinds." As result, "a stock of five thousand pounds was able to perform the same operations as if it were six or seven; and merchants were thereby enabled to trade to a greater extent, and to require less profit in all their transactions" (ibid., 320). This in turn tended to banish specie, as Hume witnessed in Scotland of his time, "notwithstanding the great encrease of riches, commerce and manufactures of all kinds" (ibid., 320). As long as the notes are legal tender and widely accepted, they have the same capacity to stimulate production and trade.

As for the specie-flow mechanism, Paul Samuelson does a hatchet-job on Hume, for overlooking the law of one price, the Marshall–Lerner conditions that attend to different price elasticities, and the distinction between transportable and nontransportable goods (see Samuelson 1980). Filippo Cesarano (1998) has argued, contra Samuelson, that Hume discerned the law of one price, but from my reading this is somewhat far-fetched. Hume certainly never articulated such a claim; Jevons appears to have been the first, or at least he wrote as if he was the first.[17] Moreover, Hume would not have observed uniform prices for any one good, either in Britain or in his travels to the Continent. On the contrary, newspapers and broadsides at the time that provided information about prices showed many regional variations (see Schabas 1994). As Hume remarked, "there is more difference between the prices of all provisions in Paris and Languedoc, than between those in London and Yorkshire" (Hume 1985aa [1752h], 354–55). This would make sense given the high costs of transportation, and the limited means for preserving perishable foodstuffs. And this in turn would make sense of the uneven distribution of money between cities like London and the countryside, such as Derbyshire (see Hume 1985x [1752e], 315n). Londoners were indeed experiencing a trend at the time toward uniform and fixed prices, with the advent of newspapers and advertisements, the clustering of shops, and the decline of haggling (see Schabas 1994). The prices of bread and beer were already regulated by the government, though this tended to induce a high variance in quality. But insofar as most consumers developed lines of credit with specific merchants, price discrimination was the rule rather than the exception.[18]

For the law of one price to hold, there must be an ample supply of arbitragers to eliminate observed price differentials. In Hume's day, middlemen tended to specialize, as drovers, crimpers, badgers or broggers (see Westerfield 1915). The very existence of a wide array of names for persons who specialized in a single task at the wholesale or retail level reminds us that opportunism was somewhat limited by tradition. Needless to say, some of the lines were becoming blurred, especially within the woollen trade (Westerfield 1915, 265). It is reasonable to assume there were persons who essentially sought out opportunities to arbitrage, and that Hume would have known of such persons even though the term *arbitrageur* had not been coined.[19] In his argument that motivates the strong correlation between the interest and profit rates, he points to "vigilant enterprising merchants, [who] will soon draw money to a state, if it be any where to be found in the world" (Hume 1985v [1752d], 303). In a different essay, he observes that one of the reasons Spain lost its gold is that on the other side of the Pyrenees prices were one-tenth what they were in Spain (Hume 1985x [1752e], 312). The implication is that merchants brought French goods to Spain to undersell the inflated goods on the market, though Hume never completes the thought. Because the export of specie was illegal, arbitrage could not be completed and hence the price discrepancy endured. Price convergence may have been observed among "money jobbers," those who dealt in the foreign currency markets. But then one had a clear case of a fungible good. Even insofar as Hume acknowledges the importance of large numbers of traders, and their efficacy in lowering prices, this is not the law of one price. That requires the added claim that for goods which appear to be the same, but have different prices, are in fact different goods, most likely because of their spatio-temporal attributes. This is not to be found in Hume. If anything, he was aware of a price spectrum for any one good, such as grain. Hence, while he depicts arbitrage-like actions, it is still a stretch to commit him to the law of one price.

One passage that might seem at first reading to link Hume with the law of one price (and that Cesarano does not cite) is found in a letter of 1766 to A. R. J. Turgot (see Hume 1955, 208–9). First, Hume acknowledges that wages depend on supply and demand and that in sectors subject to foreign competition, such as the market for cloth, wages cannot be raised because this will diminish the market share. This is even true, Hume claims, for domestic markets: "Neither can the Tradesmen who work in Cloath [sic] for home Consumption raise their Prices; since there cannot be two Prices for the same Species of Labour" (Hume 1955, 208). Hume then generalizes this to virtually all commodities: "This extends to all Commodities of which there is any part exported, that is, to almost every Commodity. Even were there some Commodities of which no part is exported, the Price of Labour employ'd in them, cou'd not rise; for this high Price wou'd tempt so many hands to go into that Species of Industry as must immediatly [sic] bring down the Prices" (Hume 1955, 208–9). What Hume implies here is that prices are governed by costs, specifically the cost of labour, and that there is some mobility in the labour market. Basic wages for specific trades had long been known if not posted, and the fact that there "cannot be two Prices for the same Species of Labour," while a cousin to the law of one price (insofar as wages are a price), was still not the law when it came to commodities.

Note that Hume has also acknowledged that some commodities can not be exported, and so Samuelson was wrong to suggest that Hume was ignorant either of price elasticities or the role of nontransportable goods even if they did not figure largely in his reasoning. Yet, the specie-flow mechanism would still falter when it came to the lack of fungibility, internationally, between paper and metallic money. Or so it would be reasonable to assume. In a thought experiment, Hume downplays these obstacles. He supposes a case in which a kingdom has 30 million in cash, 12 million of which circulates in paper form. Were the 12 million to be removed, it would promptly attract the equivalent in specie, until the nation was "full and saturate." "Whence would it have acquired that sum?" Hume asks. "From all the kingdoms of the world" (Hume 1985x [1752e], 317).

Again, Hume may well have sought to isolate a tendency of money to fill a vacuum, or of paper issue to be supplanted by specie and vice versa. Certainly, Hume recognized the many shades of money extant in his day, as well as the blurry line dividing money and credit. For example, because of the developed financial markets of London, merchants need not keep much money on hand, for it takes but 15 minutes, Hume observes, to transform stocks in the East India Company into bullion (Hume 1985aa [1752h], 353). Bonds also serve as good substitutes, and have the added advantage of earning steady interest: "our national debts furnish merchants with a species of money, that is continually multiplying in their hands, and produces sure gain, besides the profits of their commerce" (ibid., 353). Hume also extols the new procedure of deposit banking in Scotland whereby a merchant may convert his bank-credit into ready money and pay it back in modest installments, with an account reckoning the interest by the day (Hume 1985x [1752e], 319). Add to this the wide circulation of private merchant bills and public paper-notes, which Hume recognizes to be a permanent feature for "opulent kingdoms" (which after all do the most trading), and one cannot begin to approximate a world exclusively of metallic money (Hume 1985u [1752c], 284–85).

In sum, Samuelson is right to maintain that Hume (like all great thinkers) was inconsistent. There are numerous unresolved questions or inconsistencies in his account of the specie-flow mechanism, and in his real-growth account, and between the two. But this misses the point. Hume sought to isolate a causal tendency under the guise of a thought experiment, in a hypothetical scenario that can best be discerned by ignoring or distorting other factors and circumstances. And while Hume appeals to an array of temporal dimensions, ranging from 15 minutes to 1,500 years, for us to impose the contemporary distinction between the short run and the long run would seriously mislead. Wealth measured in terms of goods produced, land toiled, and persons raised to adulthood, are what most concern Hume and, for this reason, money as the surface noise of these broader human narratives is ultimately of little consequence.

My reading of the record suggests that Hume's account of money tugs in more than one direction. On the one hand, he has a predilection for treating money as a veil and thus as something that can be downplayed if not altogether ignored. And for the next 150 years or so, authors of the major texts in political economy tended to follow that lead. On the other hand, Hume weaves money right into the human condition. Money is a form of promise-keeping and thus serves the common good. It fosters and draws upon the social stock of trust. As Hume observes in his *Enquiry Concerning Human Understanding*:

> the mutual dependence of men is so great, in all societies, that scarce any human action is entirely compleat in itself, or is performed without some reference to the actions of others, which are requisite to make it answer fully the intention of the agent. The poorest artificer, who labours alone, expects at least the protection of the magistrate, to

ensure him the enjoyment of the fruits of his labour. He also expects, that, when he carries his goods to market, and offers them at a reasonable price, he shall find purchasers; and shall be able, by the money he acquires, to engage others to supply him with those commodities.

(Hume 2000b, 68)

But money is also the source of many false idols. It leads the miser astray (Hume 2000a, 204) but even in normal folk it arouses passions to emulate the rich that Hume finds unwarranted (ibid., 233). Money is always in some sense not what it seems: "Money implies a kind of representation of such [luxurious] objects, by the power it affords of obtaining them; and for that reason may still be esteem'd proper to convey those agreeable images, which may give rise to the passion" (ibid., 232).

Money thus evolves in step with habits and customs. It incites frugality and industry which in turn enables the spread of commerce and trade. When merchants "beget industry, by serving as canals" they are not simply coating the trade with money but enmeshing it with the very manners and passions that drive trade. Money is both part of the trust that enables commerce to thrive, and part of the deception and illusion that spurs its growth.

Notes

1 One could argue that there were no major texts before James Steuart and Adam Smith, with the exception of Richard Cantillon (1755), and there is only spotty evidence in support of the circulation of his manuscript. Money was a central topic for the pamphlet and essay literature of political economy circa 1600 to 1750, but as a result of the insights of Boisguilbert, Petty, Locke, and Hume, among others, sufficient laws and principles were discerned to motivate the full-scale texts that commence with James Steuart and Adam Smith. And the command of deeper mechanisms meant that money became more and more a veil.

2 The actual phrase "the veil of money" is of much more recent origin. See Patinkin and Steiger (1989) and Boianovsky (1993).

3 Loren Gatch also argues, but from a different standpoint, that the nominal/real distinction is not fully developed in Hume, namely that Hume was a metallist and thus, like Locke before him, clung to the view that "money must be a species of property" (Gatch 1996, 173).

4 Hume (2000a, 349). For more selective passages on these behavioral traits and their ties to the advent of modern commerce, see Hume (1985k [1742a], 132; 1985t [1752b], 272–73; and 1985u [1752c], 292–93). Also see Skinner (1993), Schabas (1994), and Wennerlind (2002).

5 As Edward Hundert points out, "Mandeville understood hypocrisy as the socially constituted ensemble of techniques necessary for the fabrication of disguises civilized persons don in order to conceal their avarice from one another" (1994, 178). Emma Rothschild's brilliant closing chapter, "A Fatherless World," brings out numerous similarities between Hume and Smith regarding the deceptive features of modern commerce (2001, ch. 8).

6 A good example of this is the Italian lira in the twentieth century, whose denominations became almost unmanageable. The advent of the euro is undoubtedly an improvement over that.

7 In the papers of General St. Clair (Scottish National Library), there are numerous letters in Hume's handwriting that were dictated by the general, including several from their stay in northern Italy after defeating the Austrians. St. Clair's letters are almost exclusively requests for more funds, bolstered by detailed lists of the provisions and salaries needed for his troops.

8 In his letter to Morellet, Hume refers explicitly to Franklin's account of paper bills in Pennsylvania, and recommends that Morellet meet up with Franklin during his visit to Paris (Hume 1955, 215).

9 Hume addresses the use of plate in estate homes and churches in his essay "Of the Balance of Trade" (Hume 1985x [1752e], 317). Also see Paganelli (2004).

10 About one-third of the entries to the volume on money of *The New Palgrave* pay tribute to Hume for his contributions to the quantity theory of money, the specie-flow mechanism, or the neutrality of money. See Eatwell, Millgate, and Newman (1987).

11 The Marshall–Lerner conditions, devised in the 1940s, partly account for the problem of price elasticities in assessing the global balance of payments.

12 Hume points to the contributions of the mathematician Christian Huygens on ship design during the mid-seventeenth century (Hume 1985cc [1752j], 513). Hume also observes that "progress in the arts is rather favourable to liberty" (Hume 1985t [1752b], 277). But only once does he refer to an engine (Hume 1985cc [1752j], 512). More often, when writing about cloth production or shipbuilding, there is no mention of technical improvements (see Hume 1985t [1752b]).

13 There is no definitive definition of a thought experiment, a term that was first devised by Ernst Mach in the 1890s. For two general assessments of the role of thought experiments, see Kuhn (1977 [1964]) and Horowitz and Massey (1991). Filippo Cesarano makes much the same argument, namely that the thought experiment was not meant to refer to an "actual adjustment process" (1998, 182). Istvan Hont (2005f [1993]) also refers to Hume's analysis of the public debt as a thought experiment.

14 On the many facets of credit in Hume's age, see Hoppit (1987) and Muldrew (1998).

15 Quoted in Appleby (1978, 211). For more on the understanding of the passion for frugality, see Hirschman (1977, 54–66). Also see Sargent and Velde (2002).

16 Michael Duke also locates this process within the human mind: "increased productivity which has been psychologically stimulated by the increase in money" (1979, 580).

17 Jevons named it the Law of Indifference: "In the same open market, at any one moment, there cannot be two prices for the same kind of article" (1957 [1871], 91). He also recognized the importance of the spatio-temporal dimensions of commodities, and defined markets as having perfect access to information, something much facilitated by the advent of the telegraph in the 1850s. To this end, he noted "Madsen's law," namely that there is a direct proportion between the volume of international trade and the number of international telegraphs (see Schabas 2000, 145).

18 Mandeville emphasized the need to assess the good character of the merchant in establishing a rapport for the purchase of goods on an on-going basis. This was also the advice of Reverend Trusler in his *London Advisor and Guide* (1786). He recommends against going to the shop with the lowest price, for unless one is a very good judge of the wares, the buyer will be deceived. This is discussed in Schabas (1994).

19 If the *Oxford English Dictionary* is to be trusted, the term *arbitrage* was only applied in the economic sense starting in the 1880s. As a more generic term for judgment, it dates back to the fifteenth century.

8 Fiction or Counterfeit?

David Hume's Interpretations of Paper and Metallic Money

C. George Caffentzis

People of Baetica, do you want to be rich? Imagine to yourselves that I am very rich and that you are too. Each morning put it into your head that your fortune has doubled during the night. Then arise, and if you have creditors, go pay them with what you have imagined and tell them to do some imagining of their own.

Charles-Louis Montesquieu, *The Persian Letters* (1961, 259)

This Office was not Constituted for Impossibilitys, nor to gratify wild imagination.

William Chetwynd, master of the Tower mint, to the British Treasury in 1745
(quoted in Dyer and Gaspar 1992, 411)

Hume against the Monetary Grain

The publication of up-to-date stock price lists and foreign exchange rates in London and Amsterdam newspapers played an influential role in the financial and monetary revolutions of the eighteenth century (Neal 1990). These revolutions, however, not only required the development of new information networks, but also called for the creation of suitable ways to conceptualize these bits of information and effective self-definitions of the agents who used them. Many of the major philosophers of the period invested considerable intellectual effort in creating categories and self-definitions in response to these revolutions. Some philosophers, like George Berkeley, did so enthusiastically. The Anglo-Irish bishop Berkeley viewed the increasing role of paper money—a central feature of the monetary revolution—as a chance for Ireland to escape a long-standing cycle of poverty (Caffentzis 2000). David Hume, from his vantage point in Scotland, held a much more nuanced and cautious interpretation of these revolutions.

Hume certainly witnessed a dramatic expansion of the use of nonmetallic forms of money in his lifetime. Between 1744 and 1772, the circulation of bank notes in Scotland increased 15-fold, 13 provincial banking companies opened, and the total bank assets rose from £329,000 to £3,100,000 (Whatley 2000, 67). But the banks were not the only sources of paper money in Hume's time. In order to circumvent the "shortage of specie" problem, manufacturers and merchants created paper money notes that served as substitutes for metallic coins. By 1764, there were at least 14 note issuers in Scotland in addition to the banks (Munn 1981, 18).

Another major source of paper credit instruments was the public debt. In the course of Hume's life, the British national debt increased from approximately £20 million to £140 million (Brewer 1990, 115). This national debt became the basis of a market in governmental securities that functioned as a means of exchange in large business transactions.

Hume was fully apprised of how public debt instruments functioned:

> Public securities are with us become a kind of money, and pass as readily at the current price of gold or silver...our national debts furnish merchants with a species of money, that is continually multiplying in their hands, and produces sure gain, beside the profits of commerce.
>
> (Hume 1985aa [1752h], 353)

He also was well-informed as to the growing use of bank notes as well as checking credit (or "bank-credit") in Scotland, as the following passage indicates:

> A man goes to the bank and finds surety to the amount, we shall suppose, of a thousand pounds. This money, or any part of it, he has the liberty of drawing out whenever he pleases, and he pays only the ordinary interest for it, while it is in his hands...As a man may find surety nearly to the amount of his substance, and his bank-credit is equivalent to ready money, a merchant does hereby in a manner coin his houses, his household furniture, the goods in his warehouse, the foreign debts due to him, his ships at sea.
>
> (Hume 1985x [1752e], 319)

Hence, Hume realized that a modern commercial economy gives rise to numerous money substitutes that constitute an elastic currency with the capacity to accommodate the demand for additional means of exchange as the economy expands. However, even though he had a sophisticated understanding of paper money, he was critical of its government-debt and private-bank sources. Paper money, he argued, inevitably tended to "banish gold and silver from the considerable commerce of the state" and "render all provisions and labour dearer than otherwise they would be" (Hume 1985aa [1752h], 355).

Hume cautioned his readers about the expansion of paper money and paper credit with these words:

> to endeavour *artificially* to increase [paper credit], can never be the interest of any trading nation; but must lay them under disadvantages, by encreasing money beyond its *natural* proportion to labour and

commodities, and thereby heightening their price to the merchant and manufacturer.

(Hume 1985u [1752c], 284, my italics)

Indeed, the kind of bank he deemed most "advantagious" was one, like the Bank of Amsterdam, that "locked up all the money it received and never augmented the circulating coin, as is usual, by returning part of its treasure into commerce." The advantage of such a bank is that it would result in the "low price of labour and the destruction of paper-credit" (Hume 1985u [1752c], 284–85). Thus, Hume only countenanced the most disciplined paper-money regime, that is, one that "destroys" other undisciplined uses of paper money and paper credit.

Hume's suspicion of "paper money," "paper credit," and the institutions of banks and public debt that supported them, though often qualified, was a lifelong disposition.[1] For example, one of his early criticisms in 1752 of public debt and its allied paper instruments is that they, "being a kind of paper-credit, have all the disadvantages attending that species of money" (1985aa [1752h], 355). Toward the end of his life, in 1776 to be precise, Hume delivered an apocalyptic critique (in the *History of England*) of public debt and, by implication, the paper instruments monetizing the debt:

Our late delusions have much exceeded any thing known in history, not even excepting those of the crusades. For I suppose there is no mathematical, still less an arithmetical demonstration, that the road to the Holy Land was not the road to paradise, as there is, that the endless increase of national debts is the direct road to national ruin. But having now completely reached that goal, it is needless at present to reflect on the past. It will be found in the present year, 1776, that all the revenues of this island north of Trent and west of Reading, are mortgaged or anticipated forever....So egregious indeed has been our folly, that we have even lost all title to compassion in the numberless calamities that are awaiting us.

(Hume 1850 [1754–62], 363)

One can find other, similarly critical, though qualified, passages concerning the use of bank notes and other forms of paper credit throughout his work.[2]

Hume clearly had a complex, ambivalent attitude toward paper money. He recognized it both as a product of "commercial modernization" and as its nemesis. For example, following two pages of harsh criticism of paper money, he tempered his attack:

It must, however, be confessed that, as all these questions of trade and money are extremely complicated, there are certain lights, in which this subject may be placed, so as to represent the advantages of paper-credit and banks to be superior to their disadvantages....But whatever advantages result from these inventions [like bank credit], it must still be allowed that, besides giving too great facility to credit, which is dangerous, they banish precious metals.

(Hume 1985x [1752e], 318, 320)

In a telling but paradoxical formulation of this attitude, he claimed in the *Political Discourses* (1752) that, although gold and silver money has "merely a *fictitious* value, arising from the agreement and convention of men" (Hume 1985v [1752d], 297), paper money is "*counterfeit*" (1985u [1752c], 284).[3] This was not a passing insight. Hume certainly emphasized the conventional or what he called the "fictional" character of metallic money throughout his life. For example, in his first published comments on money in book 3 of the *Treatise* (Hume 2000a [1740]), he claimed that both languages and metallic money developed as conventionally coordinated practices:

> In a like manner are languages gradually establish'd by human conventions without any promise. In like manner do gold and silver become the common measures of exchange, and are esteem'd sufficient payment for what is of a hundred times their value.
>
> (Hume 2000a, 315)

Nearly 30 years later, toward the end of his life, in a letter of 1769 to the abbé Morellet, he gently disagrees with his correspondent's anti-conventionalist view of "the establishment of [metallic] money" and argues that the conventionalist or fictional view of metallic money has "some foundation" (Hume 1955, 214; Caffentzis 2001, 326–27).

Why then did Hume choose to defend "fictions" (metallic money) over "counterfeits" (paper money), which, after all, are fictions as well? This was certainly a provocatively idiosyncratic way to make his point. It contrasted, for example, with the way a "theoretical metallist" like Richard Cantillon depicted the difference between metal and paper money in his *Essai sur la nature du commerce en général* (completed in 1734 and published in London in 1755) (Schumpeter 1986 [1954], 291). For Cantillon, paper money is "fictitious and imaginary" while silver money is "real." He writes:

> An abundance of fictitious and imaginary money causes the same disadvantages as an increase of real money in circulation, by raising the price of land and labour, or by making works and manufactures more expensive at the risk of subsequent loss. But this furtive abundance vanishes at the first gust of discredit and precipitates disorder.
>
> (Cantillon 1964, 311)

Hume, however, is cautious of binary contrasts like fictitious/real, for his philosophy reveals that there is much that is fictional in the "real" (and vice versa). Hence, Hume's "fiduciary theory of money" is a nuanced one.

In this paper I examine Hume's distinction between fiction and counterfeit in his pre-1752 writings, especially in *The Treatise on Human Nature*, in order to explore the philosophical motivation for his provocative formulation of the distinction between metallic and paper money. My essay contributes to a lively research program in recent Hume scholarship whose core hypothesis is that Hume's philosophical work (especially his *Treatise*) played a crucial role in the formulation of his "economics."[4] In particular, I locate the philosophical basis of the fiction/counterfeit contrast in Hume's distinction between *natural fictions*, which are arrived at unconsciously and universally through conventions, and *artificial fictions*, which are arrived at consciously and particularly and are expressed as promises. I argue that Hume applied his philosophical analysis of natural and artificial fictions in the formulation of his monetary-policy recommendations, including his "scandalous" support for the debasement of the coinage as a legitimate tool of statecraft.

Counterfeit and Fiction in Hume's Philosophy

A typology of the false, the fictitious, the fallacious, and the widely believed but unproved and, perhaps, unprovable permeates Hume's thought. This play with and revaluation of the many variations of falsehood gives his work a certain freedom and charm that is absent from most systems of truth piously announced in the history of philosophy.[5] Hume's interest in the varieties of falsehood arises from one of his central philosophical tenets: *truth is not explanatory.* That is, simply because a proposition such as "The Himalayan Mountains have existed for millions of years" is true does not explain how creatures like ourselves come to accept this proposition. The ironic Hume finds that fiction, fallacy, and illusion, not truth, provide a better explanatory road to comprehend human understanding.

Hume distinguished at least two kinds of fictions that, for want of better terms, can be called "natural" and "artificial" (parallel to Hume's distinctions between virtues) (Norton and Norton 2000, 576).[6] He was eager to legitimate natural fictions, including such central ideas as time, enduring sensible objects, ideal standards, substances, and the self. These fictions are cruxes for his thought since they seem both to be indispensable for everyday common life and to violate his crucial epistemological axiom that all ideas are ultimately "deriv'd" from impressions. Of course, Hume recognized an "exception" to the axiom from the start of the *Treatise*, with his famous and heavily commented on "shade of blue" counterexample (2000a, 10).[7] But the fictional creation of a previously inexperienced pseudo-impression, which Hume first treats as an oddity, becomes his model of a general process of the human mind. This process enables the mind to respond to moral and epistemological crises by creating vivid ideas, verging on impressions.

In this paper I can only briefly sketch this philosophical territory with full recognition that all the separate fictions in Hume's *Treatise* I discuss here have been commented on and debated about in a rich, ever-growing body of philosophical literature especially stimulated by the publication of Annette Baier's *A Progress of Sentiments* (Baier 1991).

Hume's first use of such a fictional analysis in the *Treatise* is his discussion of the origin of the idea of time. He argues that the idea of time or duration "is always deriv'd from a succession of changeable objects" (Hume 2000a), but this idea is also applied to objects that are unchanged or unchangeable. How is this possible? "Ideas always represent the objects or impressions, from which they are deriv'd, and can never without a fiction represent or be apply'd to any other" (ibid.,). Thus, the idea of duration can only be applied to unchanging or unchangeable objects with "a fiction." What is the source of that fiction? Hume locates it in a variety of universal experiences, the most prominent one being the "continual succession of perceptions in your mind" that gives us a sense of change even when observing unchanged objects. The idea of duration "deriv'd" from this internal machine of fancy is "by a fiction" applied to unchanged objects, without our noticing it. The timeless unchanged object is thus fictitiously, but naturally, drawn into time by our own inner agitation.

Another type of natural fiction is encountered in the process of constructing ideas of ideal (or fictional) standards. For example, we have rough-and-ready ideas of greater, lesser, and equal distances between objects that are often refined and corrected by the use of measuring instruments. This process of correction seems to have an ideal limit: the idea of "some imaginary standard of equality, by which the appearances and measuring are exactly corrected, and the figures reduc'd entirely to that proportion" (Hume 2000a, 36). This "standard is plainly imaginary," since it goes beyond any distinction an instrument or art can make. But such a "fiction however is very natural" (ibid., 1.2.4.24). Hume finds such an idealization process taking place in those involved in ever more exact measurements of time, in musicians who claim to have the idea of perfect pitch, in painters who claim to have an idea of a perfect color, and in the "mechanic with regard to motion" (ibid., 37). In other words, artists and artisans naturally tend to create ideal fictions by taking to the limit the everyday refinements they practice in their craft.

Hume's most prominent use of the notion of natural fiction is in his solution of Berkeley's conundrum concerning the continued existence of sensible objects. Surely, books, chairs, trees, and mountains are not sensed continually. On the contrary, the perception of such objects is often interrupted. But what gives "the unthinking and unphilosophical part of mankind (that is, all of us, at one time or another)" the belief that these objects continue to exist even though they do not continue to sense them? Hume appeals to a natural fiction to solve the puzzle:

> Here then we have a propensity to feign the continu'd existence of all
> sensible objects; and as this propensity arises from some lively impression

of the memory, it bestows a vivacity on that fiction; or in other words, makes us believe the continu'd existence of body.

(Hume 2000a, 138)

A similar operation takes place in the creation of the fiction of substance. For when we notice a unity of the qualities in objects, the imagination is obliged "to feign an unknown something, or original substance and matter," that might give the compounded object "a title to be call'd one thing, notwithstanding its diversity and composition" (Hume 2000a, 146). The ancient philosophers, of course, developed this natural fiction to unnatural levels. The peripatetic philosophers, for example, created a whole system of occult qualities and unintelligible chimeras of substance that "yet is deriv'd from principles as natural as any of those above explain'd" (ibid., 147).

Finally, and most radically, personal identity is based on a fiction as well, according to Hume:

> The identity, which we ascribe to the mind of man, is only a fictitious one, and of a like kind with that which we ascribe to vegetables and animal bodies. It cannot, therefore, have a different origin, but must proceed from a like operation of the imagination upon like objects.
>
> (Hume 2000a, 169)

Hume's argument for the fictionality of personal identity is more extreme than the one he produced for the continued existence of objects of perception, simply because the fictitious object in question must be a most intimate one to the reader. But Hume manages to "alienate" the self by using the tools of his proto-phenomenological impression/idea analysis, thus bringing into question the self's very existence. Once that is done, he then applies a procedure that reveals the self to be a fiction. But one arrives at this fiction by "feigning" the existence of an entity that unifies acts and perceptions. This "feigning" is not a conscious mental act, of course, though it is done by everyone, everywhere, and at all times.

Time, continued existence of objects, the self, substance, and ideal standards: all fictions! Hume's notion of natural fiction must bear a remarkable weight. Therefore it is important to determine what status Hume ascribes to it and its products. Does Hume mean that they do not exist in the same way that a fictional character (for example, Robinson Crusoe) does not exist? Or, is he claiming that the existence of these entities cannot be adequately proven (that is, their existence is not verifiable)? Or, is he claiming that the beliefs in their existence cannot be falsified? Annette Baier's characterization of these "non-truths" is more faithful to Hume's intentions:

> Hume calls them "fictions," and this is quite different from calling them false. What is provably false is to deny that they are fictions, and Hume

does think that we are prone to such falsehoods. Fictions are plausible stories we tell ourselves to organize our experience.

(Baier 1991, 103)

Baier's "plausible stories" are convincing, according to Hume, because they arise when the mind is tempted to apply a variety of useful mental mechanisms beyond their justifiable limits. Although these mechanisms are different in the case of time, self, body, substance, and standard, their fallacious but effective result can be described in Hume's words as the "propension to confound identity with relation" (Hume 2000a, 166). The texts of the *Treatise*, the *Enquiries*, and the *Essays* constitute an auto-biography of individual and collective "unconscious" mental tricks, dis-placements, and oblique transitions-without-reflection that conflate relations with identity.

Hume's quest, then, is for a set of criteria differentiating natural, involuntary fictions and artificial, consciously orchestrated ones. This quest is important to my argument, for it is exactly along this divide, I claim, that we will find the differentia of metallic and paper money and the philosophical motivation for Hume's monetary conclusions.

Natural fictions have an aura of dignity (or at least necessity about them), since they are the "feigned" though "natural" products of essential mental mechanisms. But what are artificial fictions? Are they just plain fantasies, manufactured illusions, or Machiavellian lies? To answer this question let us consider a small census of passages in the *Treatise* that deal with such fictions.

An early, but major reference to such fictions is the following comparison of belief and fiction: "an idea assented to *feels* different from a fictitious idea, that the fancy alone presents to us" (Hume 2000a, 68). The passage that includes this sentence is, of course, one of Hume's most important, for in it he distinguishes belief not on the basis of an internal feature of any idea or set of ideas, but on the *manner* in which the idea is conceived. Fictions of the fancy differ from beliefs assented to because the latter "are more strong, firm, and vivid, than the loose reveries of a castle-builder" (ibid.). In such discussions, ("idle," "loose") fictions (of the imagination and fancy) are evoked in contrast to beliefs, that is, ideas that surprisingly transform themselves back into semi-impressions due to the force and vivacity with which they are experienced.

This contrast between belief and artificial fiction, however, is not absolute, since almost any such fiction can become a belief (in someone, some-where, sometime) given the powers of passion and artifice. For example,

among the vulgar, quacks and projectors meet with a more easy faith upon account of their magnificent pretensions, than if they kept them-selves within the bounds of moderation. The first astonishment, which naturally attends their miraculous relations, spreads itself over the

> whole soul, and so vivifies and enlivens the idea, that it resembles the
> inferences we draw from experience.
>
> (Hume 2000a, 82–3)

This permeable, but at first glance mysterious, barrier between belief and artificial fiction is the basis of some of Hume's most entertaining philosophical exercises. For example, he observes that poets, "tho' liars by profession," always try to "give an air of truth to their fictions," otherwise their performances will not be entertaining. Similarly, he observes that those who always lie can never give satisfaction to the mind, since what they say is immediately dismissed and cannot have a hold on one's mind (Hume 2000a, 83).

Hence, according to Hume's philosophy of falsehood, artificial fictions must be presented in the context of "truth and reality" in order to be emotively effective. Poets often use historical settings and the names of real personages to make a deeper impression "on the fancy and affections" (Hume 2000a, 84). But even this is not always necessary, since such a context of "truth and reality" can be manufactured by the repetition of images and names (as in the case of propaganda). So there is a continual traffic between the judgment and fancy in literature. Inevitably, when the permeability between judgment and fancy increases sufficiently, poetical fiction ends and madness begins. For madness is a state where "every loose fiction or idea, having the same influence as the impressions of the memory, or the conclusions of the judgment, is receiv'd on the same footing, and operates with equal force on the passions" (ibid., 84). Poetical fiction, however, can hardly create genuine madness because it never generates a level of feeling beyond that of the lowest "species of probability" (ibid., 85).

Of course, many more artificial fictions, beyond the rather innocent literary ones I have mentioned, inhabit Hume's human cosmos, from philosophical ones (for example, "the state of nature") to political and economic ones. Hume (in)famously located many examples of artificial fiction in religious belief as well. He found that

> the conviction of the religionists, in all ages, is more affected than real,
> and scarce ever approaches, in any degree, to that solid belief and per-
> suasion, which governs us in the common affairs of life....They make a
> merit of implicit faith; and disguise to themselves their real infidelity, by
> the strongest asseverations and positive bigotry.
>
> (quoted in Bernard 1995, 231)

Conviction is often lacking because, according to Hume, there is no innate religious faculty. Consequently:

> a habit of dissimulation is by degrees contracted: And fraud and false-
> hood become the predominant principle. Hence the reason of that

vulgar observation, the highest zeal in religion and the deepest hypocrisy, so far from being inconsistent, are often or commonly united in
the same individual character.

(quoted in Bernard 1995, 233)

Hence, the field of artificial fiction is much broader than that of natural
fictions. The artificial fictions of religion, myth, art, and literature have an
infinity of possible linkages since they play with the inevitable surplus
energy of the imagination while the natural fictions of the understanding are
much more limited, since they depend on specific mechanisms of thought
(especially the unconscious ability of confounding "identity with relation"
through projection, inertia, or "feigning").

What, indeed, are the general differences between these "artificial" fictions and the "natural" ones that are at the foundation of our conceptions
of space, time, body, standards, substance, and self? David and Mary
Norton, in their recent edition of Hume's *Treatise on Human Nature*, sum
up the distinction in the following passage:

> In general terms, such natural fictions are ideas that, although they take
> us beyond experience, are nonetheless the involuntary result of experi-
> ence and the usual processes of the mind. In contrast, the fictions of the
> poet or the dramatist might be called artificial fictions, these arise
> voluntarily or, to use Hume's language, as the result of contrivance and
> design.

(Norton and Norton 2000, 440)

The accompanying table displays some of their specific differences.

Artificial fictions can be transformed into beliefs by being "counterfeited"
as ideas of memory or impressions through artful repetition or through
being placed in "truth-like" contexts or environments of excitement and
interest. As Hume points out:

> an idea of the imagination may acquire such a force and vivacity, as to
> pass for an idea of the memory, and counterfeit its effects on belief and

Natural Fictions	Artificial Fictions
universally believed	not universally believed
unconscious mechanisms of belief	belief involves conscious deception
difficult to doubt	overuse can lead to lack of conviction
without this belief a life of 'melancholy and delirium' (Hume 2000a, 175)	if not controlled, they lead to 'philosophical madness'
formed by mental mechanisms that turn 'relations to identities'	formed by the attachment of belief to a fancy
a precondition of a common life	a consequence of and parasitic on a common life

judgment. This is noted in the case of liars; who by the frequent repetition of the lies, came at last to believe and remember them, as realities.

(Hume 2000a, 60–1)

Natural fictions, on the contrary, become established in the mind through normal mental mechanisms operating beyond their standard range through a principle of ideational inertia. For example, the development of perfect standards brings the procedures of correction and comparison "beyond what we have instruments and art to make," for there is not "any thing more usual, than for the mind to proceed after this manner with any action, even after the reason has ceas'd, which first determin'd it to begin" (Hume 2000a, 36–7).

The "speculative politician," therefore, has two paths to follow, not one, in preparing the minds of the people for a fiction like money.

Money, Fiction, and Counterfeit

Given the importance of the distinction between natural and artificial fictions for Hume's philosophy, it should not be surprising that it enhances the explication of his controversial contrast between "fictitious" metallic money and "counterfeit" paper money. This apparent dichotomy is problematic simply because Hume recognizes that, in commerce, metallic money and paper money are often substituted for each other, and that banks often issue paper money "backed" by precious metals. Is Hume simply trying to steer his readers away from paper money *tout court* or is he calling for a more sophisticated understanding of the relation between the two?

Clearly, Hume does not denounce the directors of the Bank of Scotland or the officials of the British government as counterfeiters in the standard sense of the time, that is, those who make false resemblances of coin to fool the public and enrich themselves. Counterfeiters are the quacks and "professional liars" of the monetary world who deviously exploit the existence of a common metallic monetary system to trick the average person into accepting less valuable metallic copies (cf. Wennerlind 2002).

Indeed, eighteenth-century bankers who issued paper credit money (in contrast to those who issued stocks, bonds, and other speculative instruments) promised that their paper truly represented a certain amount of metallic coin and that this coin would be returned on presentation of the paper to the appropriate person. But the frequent experiences of bank failures and credit crises showed that bankers systematically broke this promise. Indeed, it was widely known that the amount of metallic money in the banks' vaults was usually only a fraction of the total paper money they issued. National government officials also falsely claimed that they could entirely pay off the national debt in specie even though they recognized that this was neither possible nor even undesirable (Brewer 1990, 123). Hence, the counterfeit aspect of paper money does not lie in the sensory resemblance of the paper to the metal, of course, but in its claim to symbolize (while actually falsifying) a higher-order feature of the monetary system: the monetary promise.

Still, Hume also claims that metallic money is a fiction as well. Of course, metallic money does not have the same status as natural fictions like time, enduring sensible objects, ideal standards, substances, and the self; but within the social realm it attains a status similar to language and justice. It is true that justice is an artificial virtue in Hume's philosophy, but in typical fashion he qualifies its status as such:

> as no principle of the human mind is more natural than a sense of virtue; so no virtue is more natural than justice. Mankind is an inventive species; and where an invention is obvious and absolutely necessary, it may as properly be said to be natural as anything that proceeds immediately from original principles, without the intervention of thought or reflection.
>
> (Hume 2000a, 311)

Similarly, the slow development of a monetary system (which presupposes justice and language systems, of course) has the same character as the property system: "it arises gradually, and acquires force by a slow progression, and by our repeated experience of the inconveniences of transgressing it" (Hume 2000a, 315).

To test this view of the correspondence of the natural fiction/artificial fiction distinction with the metal money/paper money distinction in Hume's philosophy, we should apply the oppositions in the previous table to the monetary realm. Metallic coinage has a claim to a universal belief based on unconscious conventions that are difficult to forgo. Once one is in a monetary economy any attempt to reject money makes it impossible to lead a common life and ends in "melancholy and delirium." With exposure to the world of exchange, coins are inevitably worn, clipped, and bagged; they gradually come to have a very different "intrinsic value" from what they had when they were originally coined; but these facts do not block the confounding of "identity with relation" during usage. On the contrary, the difference between judging coins by weight or by tale (that is, by the stamped official value) is an excellent example of how this confounding of "identity with relation" takes place, for, in the eighteenth century, as previously, there was a continual exchange of coins *as if* they were full weight when truly they were not (because of clipping and wear). This shifting from the material location of value (the weight and purity of the coin's metal) to the representation of value and back again is a conventional aspect of coinage that paper money (which represented, at best, an absent and abstract mass of metal) could not mimic.

Hume was conscious of the millions of unconscious acts in commercial exchange when underweight coins are treated "as if" they were up to the standard stamped on their sides. The dramatic deterioration of the British silver currency in Hume's lifetime certainly challenged this confounding of "identity with relation." For example, by 1777 government officials found that "£300 in silver, which ought to have weighted 1,200 ounces, weighed 624 ounces" (Thompson 1996, 135). This was similar to "[a]n experiment...made [in the preparation of the 1696 recoinage] which showed that £57,2000 sterling in silver coin, which should have contained 220,000 ounces of pure silver, contained only 141,000 ounces" (Caffentzis 1989, 20). That is, the average deterioration of the silver coinage in 1777 was 48 percent in contrast to the 1690s when the deterioration rate was "only" 36 percent. The margin of "fiction" in the British silver coinage of Hume's time was very wide indeed, but coined money still retained universal conviction because it was based on social conventions and mental mechanisms that created all natural fictions.[8]

Paper money did not generate a similar universal conviction. Certainly Hume was far from being the only paper-money skeptic of his time. On the contrary, he shared his suspicions with commentators from Massachusetts (William Douglass) to Naples (Ferdinando Galiani) because it was widely recognized that the issuing of paper money required conscious deception and its overuse could easily lead to a sudden loss of conviction in the monetary promises that gave paper its credit. But, even worse, if its audience did not quickly lose conviction in these promises, the continued issuing of paper money would lead to monetary bubbles, hyperinflations, and other social catastrophes (as in Law's "System's" and the South Sea Company's crises). The essence of paper money is that its attractiveness requires a specific but potentially fanciful belief that some bank, company, or government is, respectively, growing, profitable, or triumphant.

These were well-known objections to paper money. Hume, however, showed that the problem with paper money is not what it is made of but what it signifies. The crucial difference between paper and metal money manifests in the effects they have on their users and originators. While the paper signifier brazenly circulates in public, its signified is hidden either behind physical vaults or behind the even more mysterious vault of the future. Its referent is both "absent and general" and its functioning depends on an explicit promise from its issuers that it will be exchanged for specie at some specified time and place.

The functioning of metallic money does not depend on promises, since its referent, the coin in one's hand, is both "present and individual." Metallic money is rooted in a deeper, conventional layer of social life that arises from "a general sense of common interest; which sense all the members of the society express to one another, and which induces them to regulate their conduct by certain rules" (Hume 2000a, 314–315). Just as "even promises themselves...arise from human conventions" (ibid., 314), so too paper money (which depends on promises) arises from the ur-world of conventions supporting specie. Paper money is thus based on and is parasitic on a common monetary life; it cannot be the basis of such a life in the way that coinage can.

This is not to say, however, that for Hume paper money (like art, religion, and literature) did not have an important role to play in the development of commerce and civilization. This Humean theme was familiar to the many poets and writers of the eighteenth century who appreciated, criticized, and marveled over the connection between literature and paper money brought about by the so-called financial revolution. The many ironies, puns, and metaphors implicating the realm of paper money with writing in the work of Alexander Pope, Jonathan Swift, and Samuel Johnson, among others, make Hume's use of the trope "counterfeit" in characterizing paper money almost trite.[9] For example, Patrick Brantlinger quotes the famous lines from Pope's *Epistles*:

> Blessed paper-credit! last and best supply!
> That lends Corruption lighter wings to fly!
> Gold imp'd by thee, can compass hardest things,
> Can pocket States, can fetch or carry Kings....

Brantlinger then comments:

> Even more impressively (and impishly and impiously), Pope underscores the analogy between such "paper credit" and literature (or perhaps literacy—reading and writing in general—and therefore civilization in general). His own poetry is a sort of "paper-credit," imp'd, impowered or "empired" only by individual fantasy or genius to be, like Sibylline prophesy, scattering fates, fortunes, kings, queens, and nations to the winds (just as Britain was an island "Debtor to the Wind").
>
> (Brantlinger 1996, 63–64)

Hume also recognized that the imagination creates artificial fictions in literature as well as in the monetary sphere that are crucial for the development of a polite culture. However, unless the surplus energy of the symbolic realm in literature and money is restrained, it can become the basis of destructive passions and madness. The problem with paper money from Hume's perspective is that the "present and individual" restraint internal to coinage (the weight-versus-tale dialectic) does not exist for paper notes. Their referent is "absent and general" and any restraint on their iteration must be external, hence "political" (in a pejorative sense of that word).

Inevitably then, the divergent structures of use and verification presupposed by "natural" metallic and "artificial" paper money create a tremendous tension in a monetary system. It is no surprise that Hume would concern himself with this tension, for he lived on the cusp between two great and simultaneous monetary transformations in Britain. First, Britain was shifting from a dominant use of silver to that of gold coinage and, second, from specie to paper currency (Feavearyear 1963, 150–73). Paper money, as an artificial fiction or counterfeit, requires the dynamics of belief to function. The continued acceptability of its issuers' promises depends on artful repetition and on being placed in "truth-like" contexts or environments of excitement and interest. On the other hand, the conventions sustaining metallic money operate on the basis of the mind's inertial tendency to try, as much as possible, to feign the correspondence of a given perception with a standard (to confound "identity with relation"), even if it is known that the standard is never perfectly attained. Surely both kinds of money operate as fictions, but the coin's acceptance is based on mental mechanisms that are essential to the construction of nature and society while the paper note must continually depend on *external* reinforcements to keep up its force and vivacity so that it can counterfeit its face value. Thus, in the moment of greatest tension between these two radically different but interdependent systems of money in the mid-eighteenth century, Hume sided with William Chetwynd, the master of the mint and author of the second of this paper's epigraphs, in eschewing "wild imagination" as the arbiter of Britain's monetary life.

The Natural Limits of Monetary Manipulation

This investigation throws new light, I believe, on Hume's rejection of an absolute-quantity theory of money. In his essay, "On Money," he argues that "the alterations in the quantity of money...are not immediately attended with proportionable alterations in the prices of commodities" (1985u [1752c], 288). In the course of this discussion Hume gives his remarkable blessing to the debasement of the currency in France and recommends a similar one in Britain (the first since 1559, in Hume's later estimation) (Hume 1850 [1754–62], 364). In order to understand Hume's support for debasement we must consider the context of monetary discourse in Britain and France following the speculation "bubbles" of 1720.

The man who set the terms of the discourse was the infamous Scotsman, John Law, the object of Montesquieu's satire in this paper's first epigraph. This child of Aeolus, the god of winds, and a Caledonian nymph, called on French investors "to leave the country of base metals. Come to the Empire of the Imagination" (Montesquieu 1961, 258). This empire, of course promised ever-increasing riches to its investors. According to Sir James Steuart, when Law's System (also known as the Mississippi Scheme) collapsed, the French collectively decided "to bid a long farewell to credit and confidence; and to return to the old system of rent upon the town-house of Paris; and of coming at money in the best way they could" (Steuart 1966 [1767], 557). Antoin Murphy's late twentieth-century assessment echoes Steuart's, namely that, "The collapse of the System left a legacy of animosity towards financial innovation, which restrained and strait-jacketed the French economy under its control until the Revolution" (Murphy 1997, 333).

The British experienced the bursting of the South Sea Company Bubble almost simultaneously with the crash of Law's System in 1720. But the results were radically different. In France the Compagnie des Indes and the Banque Royale (the organizational vehicles of Law's System) were dissolved and most of the holders of bank paper lost everything. In Britain, as Niall Ferguson points out, the Bank of England and the South Sea Company were preserved and investors came off with "tolerable losses" (Ferguson 2001, 114). As a result, the British and French monetary systems dramatically diverged after the 1720 bubbles. The British—especially the Scottish—approach was to intensify the opening of private banks and the issuing of paper money notes. The French approach was to eschew paper instruments as much as possible and reestablish the reliability of and trust in metallic currency.[10]

Hume generally supported the post-1720 French monetary model:

> It is not to be doubted, but the great plenty of bullion in France is, in a great measure, owning to the want of paper-credit. The French have no banks: Merchants bills do not there circulate as with us: Usury or lending on interest is not directly permitted; so that many have large sums in their coffers: Great quantities of plate are used in their private houses; and all the churches are full of it. By this means, provisions and labour still remain cheaper among them, than in nations that are not half so rich in gold and silver. The advantages of this situation, in point of trade as well as in great public emergencies, are too evident to be disputed.
>
> (Hume 1985x [1752e], 317)

He also had a cosmopolitan admiration for many features of the French absolute monarchy, especially its ability to escape enslavement to the national debt (Hume 1985i [1741i], 96), which was a continual source of anxiety for Hume. The French king, according to him, can "make a bankruptcy when he pleases" (quoted in Forbes 1975, 173–74).[11] Moreover, Hume was certainly not convinced as to the general reliability of the monetary managers, private *and* public, in both England and Scotland (Caffentzis 2001; Caffentzis 1996).

Hume's support of the post-1720 French preference for coin over paper money included a suggestion that the oft-decried, but more oft-practiced art of debasement should be revived in Britain. After all, debasement was no stranger to the English mint from the seventh to the sixteenth centuries (Challis 1992). The practice ended in Britain due to the crisis ignited by the Great Debasement in the years 1544 to 1551, when minting activity was stimulated by "a substantial monetarization of plate and ornament from the suppressed religious houses" (Gould 1970, 33). The ambitious Henry VIII apparently was not content with the seigniorage from this monetization of the "Great Plunder." He embarked on a reckless debasement that dramatically reduced the silver content of English coins.[12]

After Henry VIII's death, Elizabeth I tried to reverse the effects of the currency vitiation in the first years of her reign. Moreover, a large critical literature on the Great Debasement sprang up to excoriate it. Just as the crash of Law's System put paper money instruments in retreat in France, the Great Debasement banished the strategy of debasement from the region of polite monetary conversation in Britain.

Hume's controversial support for debasement in Britain, approximately two centuries after the Great Debasement, clearly signals the importance of the distinction between metal and paper in his monetary politics. Hume recognized the stimulating effects of an expanding monetary area and supply and, at the same time, he was suspicious of the most available instrument of expansion, paper money, since he claimed, "I scarcely know any method of sinking money below its level, but those institutions of banks, funds, and paper-credit, which are so much practised in this kingdom" (1985x [1752e], 316).

He saw that debasement might answer the conundrum posed by this tension between the need for monetary expansion and paper money skepticism, *if* it was practiced in a way that recognized the natural fictionality of coin. Debasement, according to Hume, could be acceptable just so long as the operation is done "to preserve the illusion, and make [the new coins] be taken for the same [as the old coins]" (1985u [1752c], 288). We have here the exact formula for the natural fiction in Hume's terminology: the confounding of identity with relation. In effect, reasonable debasement only applies (and does not strain) the standard mental mechanisms required for the normal functioning of the conventions underlying the coinage. Hume's support for debasement, in effect, is his answer to any of his critics (like Smith) who might have charged him with monetary passivity. Hume approves of the right of monetary authorities to manipulate gold and silver money in a way that private bankers do with the issuing of paper bank notes, though with more limitations. The public authorities can deploy the natural fiction of money in order to excite industry, just so long as they do not disturb the conventions based on "the illusion" of identity between old and new coinage. But this illusion guarantees that the expansionary process has its own internal limit. The monetary authorities should have the right to use the self-reflexive dialectic between the "intrinsic" and "official" value of coins to "excite the industry of mankind," to use George Berkeley's phrase, for the nation's well-being, just as the private bankers can turn the semantic distance between paper money and the gold and silver in their vaults into a personal profit.

Hume sought to erase an economic hobgoblin, the Great Debasement, from the minds of his readers and to join the lively debate taking place in France and Italy on the effects of debasement. This debate had been initiated by Jean-François Melon's positive assessment of debasement in his *Essai*

Politique sur le Commerce (1734) (Monroe 1966, 236–40). To do so, Hume refers the reader to "the frequent operation of the French king on the money" and he points out that "augmenting of the numerary value [of the coinage] did not produce a proportional rise of the prices, at least for some time" (1985u [1752c], 287). The example he offers to clinch the point is the price of corn, which "is now sold at the same price, or for the same number of livres, [as] it was in 1683; though silver was then at 30 livres the mark, and is now at 50" (ibid., 287).

Hume presents, in an infamous footnote to this passage, a case for debasement in Britain by first referring to the work of Melon, Du Tot, and Pâris-Duverney on the issue. He then goes on to argue:

> Were all our money, for instance, recoined, and a penny's worth of silver taken from every shilling, the new shilling would *probably purchase* every thing that could have been bought by the old; the prices of everything would thereby be *insensibly diminished*; foreign trade enlivened; and domestic industry, but the circulation of a greater number of pounds and shillings, would receive *some encrease* and encouragement. In executing such a project, it would be better to make the new shilling for 24 halfpence, *in order to preserve the illusion,* and *make it be taken for the same.*
>
> (Hume 1985u [1752c], 288, my italics)[13]

Stealthy terms abound in this passage: "probably purchase," "insensibly diminished," "some encrease," "preserve the illusion," and "make it be taken for the same." The perfect Machiavellian political economist is at work, simultaneously preserving the conventional fiction of the coinage while secretly exciting the industry of mankind. Hume slyly suggests in this footnote that if the French can do it so can the British.

From Plate to Chinaware: Transcending the Metallic Stage?

Loren Gatch has argued that Hume's view of money could support an "entirely fiduciary circulation" system similar to our present one (1996, 185). Hume's defense of "the French solution," debasements and all, as a response to the crisis generated by the 1720 collapse, however, suggests a different interpretation. One might have thought, along with Gatch, that the most Deleuzean of eighteenth-century philosophers should have seen and even embraced the possibility of a monetary economy not founded on specie (Deleuze 1991). If all society was based on opinion, convention, and unconscious fictions, then why should money be eternally stuck in a metallic stage? Hume certainly had philosophical predecessors who pointed to the new monetary horizon. He was familiar, for example, with George Berkeley's *The Querist,* published 15 years before the *Political Discourses,* in which Berkeley suggested the complete substitution of a total paper-

money economy for gold and silver coinage (Caffentzis 2000). The historically minded Hume, however, seems to have been ambivalent at best to the
direction the money form actually took in the preceding two-and-a-half
centuries.

Why, then, did Hume not hypothesize the elimination of specie and the
institution of a completely paper money system in Britain as Berkeley proposed for Ireland, if gold and silver money was a fiction? After all, if,
according to Hume, the Dutch (among others) had completely substituted
chinaware, a "brittle commodity," for silver plate in their dining rooms
(1985x [1752e], 318), why could the British not rid their markets and pockets of specie with equal ease?

Some might claim that this limitation arose from a purely technical fact:
paper money could be infinitely iterated without a corresponding increase in
work while the iteration of coinage required a proportional productive
effort. But Hume recognized that this technical fact was not central to the
operation of metallic money. As he wrote to Morellet:

> It is true, money must always be made of some materials, which have
> intrinsic value, otherwise it would be multiplied without end, and would
> sink to nothing. But, when I take a shilling, I consider it not as a useful
> metal, but as something which another will take from me; and the
> person who shall convert it into metal is, probably, several millions of
> removes distant.
>
> (Hume 1955, 214)

For Hume, the difference between paper and specie is based on the different structure of relations the two monetary regimes impose on issuers
and users and on the users with themselves. Coinage shares with time, ideal
standards, substances, endurance of sensed objects, and the self a fundamental "pathos of identity," that is, every coin reflexively says of itself to
both buyer and seller that it has a certain intrinsic value. But this pathos is
based on a false but reflexive elision of perceptual fact and intrinsic value
that is indispensable for the creation of the conventions at the base of
commercial life. A coin's "use value" is determined by a seller's acceptance
of it in exchange for a particular commodity. This acceptance is based on
the condition that other sellers will accept the coin as equal or greater in
value to the commodities they are selling. Indeed, the magistrate in charge
of debasing the currency recognizes and depends on this eternally productive mistake, just as the wise philosophical ruler recognizes that it is essential to develop and strengthen unsupported confoundings of identity with
relation in order to guarantee individual and social stability. The key question about money is whether it is "something another will take from me" in
exchange, but Hume holds that there ultimately has to be a sensible external
something there to be taken as the object of a convention, not just a *promise*
of something.

Can there be a monetary system without specie? If the parallel between natural fictions/artificial fictions, on the one hand, and metallic money/ paper money, on the other hand, is at all convincing, then the Humean answer is that it is possible to have such a system, but only if its inhabitants are willing to live in a state of continual monetary "melancholy and delirium." Hume, I argue, would conclude that a complete antifoundationalism is ultimately unlivable in both the intellectual and commercial spheres, even though foundationalism is false in both.

Conclusion

My answer to the question, why does Hume call metallic money "fictitious" and paper money "counterfeit"?, is complex, since it requires that one apply to the problem both Hume's discussion of natural and artificial fictions and his thoughts on the differences between conventions and promises. From this perspective, paper money is not based on collective, "natural" conventions (like language), but is an artificial product of the promises of specific institutions: private banks, companies, and governments. Hence, it is prone to the secular superstitions of trust in individual institutions that can degenerate into epidemic madness (in the form of, for example, panics and bubbles). Metallic money is also a fiction, but it is a natural fiction that is based on resemblances eliding into identities. After long use of the coordinating conventions, coins give a sense of equal exchange even though this equality is not "really" there. This "natural fiction," however, puts equally "natural" limits on its possible abuse, whereas there are no such natural limits to warn the magistrates with paper-credit money.

According to Hume, then, a monetary economy is "fiduciary," that is, based on "opinion" (Wennerlind 2001b). But there is opinion and opinion. When the fate of a monetary economy is based on an "artificial" fiction—a fancy barely bound to a belief—then the bonding opinions, trust, and credit are vulnerable to being rapidly discredited, distrusted, and debunked. Therefore, Hume looked to France for a monetary system based on "natural" fictions, once it had thoroughly repudiated John Law's attempt to systematically defetishize gold and silver and eliminate metals from its circulatory system. Hume definitely had more confidence in the French system and he showed why it was even open to limited monetary activism through careful debasements.

Hume was committed to a *philosophical* distinction between metallic and paper money and not merely a technical one. This commitment is best reflected perhaps in the depth of the passion behind his dying apocalyptic footnote about the national debt and the implicit monetary use of public credit instruments in the *History of England* (see above; also Pocock 1985c, 125–41; Hont 2005f [1993]). But his prophecy was apparently mistaken. After all, "metallic" France had its revolution barely a decade-and-a-half after his death, whereas "paper" Britain has been able to defer it indefinitely.

Notes

1 Hume had a personal financial interest in national debt instruments and stocks, since he did not invest his substantial earnings in land. As E. C. Mossner writes: "While in London in 1761 he had invested in the public funds.... Having long declaimed against the stocks, Hume was now exposed to the many jokes of his friends. His rebuttal was that he had bought real stock and was not a jobber" (Mossner 1980, 409–10).

2 Indeed, these passages have been the basis of the mistaken view that Hume was a "theoretical metallist," to use Schumpeter's phrase (Wennerlind 2001; Caffentzis 2001).

3 The full phrase in the first seven editions of the *Essays* is "Money having merely a fictitious value, arising from the agreement and convention of men," while in the eighth and ninth editions it was replaced by the shorter, "Money having chiefly a fictitious value." For a discussion of counterfeiting in this period see Wennerlind (2002, 263–64).

4 Some important articles in this research program include Schabas (1994), Gatch (1996), Schabas (2001), Wennerlind (2001b), Wennerlind (2002), and Davis (2003).

5 Steven Shapin recruited Hume, along with Francis Hutcheson and Adam Smith, into the ranks of "Common Sense philosophers" who "agreed that social order was predicated on trust in others' truthfulness" (Shapin 1994, 12). Shapin seems to have missed Hume's "pseudological" side, i.e., for Hume, most of the "truths" basic to the social order are fictions.

6 There is a small body of literature on Hume's theory of fictions. Some early and more recent texts include Kemp Smith (1941, 133–37), Deleuze (1991), Streminger (1980), and McRae (1980). They have little to say about the artificial fictions, however.

7 In an often-puzzled-over passage in the *Treatise*, Hume provides a counterexample to one of his most cherished principles: ideas are copies of impressions. He asks the reader to imagine a person who has never seen a particular shade of blue. He then asks us to imagine such a person confronted with a series of colored patches from dark to light blue that does not include the particular unseen shade of blue. Hume claims that such a person should be able, simply on the basis of the imagination, to "raise up to himself the idea of that particular shade, tho' it never been convey'd to him by his senses" (2000a, 1.1.1.10). Cf. the following important articles on Hume's "shade of blue": Williams (1992), Fogelin (1984), and Losee (1992).

8 The gold coinage was also in peril by the 1770s. As Dyer and Gaspar point out, "[It] had been ravaged by 'the infamous and daring Practices of Coiners, Clippers, Seaters, &c.' With newly-minted, full-weight coins being hoarded, melted down or exported, the domestic circulation had become a sink for the worst coins; and there were fears that the country would soon be short of gold as it was of silver"(1992, 440).

9 A number of important studies on this theme include: Thompson (1996), Nicholson (1994), Sherman (1996), and Ingrassia (1995).

10 This is not to say that coinage was passé in Britain, for, after all, during Hume's lifetime most British foreign trade was transacted with gold and silver coinage. As Vilar observes, "Between 1733 and 1766, 65% of England's exports to Asia were in the form of silver bullion and, even more, of silver coin. The total value amounted to some £400 million sterling, as opposed to only £9 spent by France on such transactions" (Vilar 1976, 285). Indeed, it appeared that at least in foreign trade, Hume's pro-coinage views were vindicated at the end of his life (though without his tolerance of debasement). In 1774, one of the most important steps in the

development of the gold standard was taken by Lord Liverpool who ordered a full weight recoinage for gold coins and managed the passage of a law that "Firstly ... limited silver currency: for sums about £50 payment in silver might be refused and payment in gold could be demanded; this reduced silver to the role of small cash coin; and secondly, the law laid down that once gold was recast at full weight, coins would be allowed to deteriorate by only 1 39/39 grains a guinea, a tiny proportion" (Vilar 1976, 285). Vilar sums up the monetary developments in England: "far from being in opposition to one another, the move towards gold coin as the universal standard, and the development of banking and credit, took place simultaneously" (Vilar 1976, 286).

11 Echoing Hume's observation concerning an absolute monarch's ability to repudiate debt, Montesquieu notes a systematic opposition between absolute monarchs and banks, for "In a government of this kind [i.e., an absolute monarchy], none but the prince ever had, or can have, a treasure; and wherever there is one, it no sooner becomes great than it becomes the treasure of the prince" (Montesquieu 1966, 322).

12 Glyn Davies describes the Great Debasement in the following passage: "The process of physical debasement from the original pure sterling silver standard reached 75 per cent silver by March 1542, 50 per cent by March 1545, 33 1/3 per cent by March 1546, and reached its nadir of 25 per cent under the young King Edward in 1551. The mainly copper-alloy coins were, in order to improve their acceptability, 'blanched' from 1546 onwards, by applying a thin surface coating of purer silver, a subterfuge which quickly wore thin to show the red copper underneath—hence Henry VIII's well-earned nickname 'old copper-nose' " (1994, 199).

13 The sentence concerning the 1696 recoinage was included in the errata of the first edition. Was this a sign of Hume's hesitancy?

9   David Hume on Canadian Paper Money

Robert W. Dimand

The Scottish Enlightenment philosopher and historian David Hume is justly renowned as a monetary economist for his specie-flow mechanism of balance-of-payments adjustment and his analysis of the short-run non-neutrality of money. The memorable use of playing cards as the paper currency of New France (Norrie, Owram, and Emery 2002, 44; Lester 1939) is a commonplace of monetary economics, second only to the stone money of the island of Yap. The two resulting, extensive literatures have remained separate: writers on Hume's economics have concentrated almost exclusively on the essays he published in 1752 (to which he added "Of the Jealousy of Trade" in 1758), while the literature on Canadian monetary history has failed to identify Mr. Hume, the British chargé d'affaires in Paris who attempted a settlement of the outstanding paper currency of New France after the British conquest, as having been the eminent philosopher. Hume's draft memorandum of 25 September 1765 on the proposed settlement of the Canada Bills, together with the related correspondence, constitutes Hume's only known contribution to economics after his 1752 and 1758 essays (apart from brief passages in letters[1] and the passages in his *History of England* noted by Eugene Rotwein (1970 [1955], lxxix–lxxx)), and differs from his published economic essays in dealing with an applied problem of economic policy rather than theory. Taking account of Hume's involvement in the Canada Bills leads to no dramatic re-evaluation of his monetary theory (or of the history of the Canada Bills), but it serves to remind us of Hume's participation in practical affairs, which has been forgotten in the literature on Hume as an economist. Articles whose titles emphasize the practicality of Hume's economics or Hume on economic policy (Velk and Riggs 1985; Davlantes 1990; Soule 2000) consider Hume's economics as practical in the senses of rejecting utopian projects or of still remaining relevant, and consider the policy implications of Hume's theorizing, without mentioning his involvement in the practice of economic policy as well as its theory. Hume's protégé Gibbon reflected that the captain of the Hampshire grenadiers had not been useless to the historian of the Roman empire. The lasting reputations of Hume and Gibbon do not result from their participation in affairs of state; rather, such practical experience (Hume as diplomat and under-secretary of state, Gibbon in the county militia and Parliament) made their understanding of how the world works more insightful and more applicable to the issues facing the nation.

Carl Wennerlind notes that Hume, who in 1752 had been "vehemently opposed to paper money ... inserted his comments about the potentially favorable effects of paper money for the first time in the 1764 edition of *Political Discourses*," but does not mention what Hume was doing in 1764 or consider why he might have had occasion to reconsider the question of paper money (2000, 89, 92). In October 1763, following the Treaty of Paris, which ended the Seven Years War, Hume went to Paris as secretary to the earl of Hertford, who was then the British ambassador. Hume assumed the position of secretary of the embassy (with a salary of £1,200) on 3 July 1765, and served as chargé d'affaires from 21 July to 17 November 1765, between Hertford's departure (to become the lord lieutenant of Ireland) and the arrival of the duke of Richmond. The settlement of the Canada Bills was a central concern of the British Embassy, as is shown by the space they occupy in Hume's dispatches to the secretary of state for the Southern Department (Lieutenant General Henry Seymour Conway, Lord Hertford's younger brother) in London on 12 August, 23 August, 27 August, 3 October, 13 October, and 23 October 1765 (earlier dispatches would have been from Hertford rather than Hume) (Klibansky and Mossner 1954, 93–95, 99–100, 100–105, 122–23, 124, 125). The preoccupation is further revealed in Hertford's letters to Hume from 16 August to 20 September 1765 (Burton 1849 [1820], 112–18, cited by Klibansky and Mossner 1954, xxiv n). Hume departed for London on 4 January 1766 (accompanied by Jean-Jacques Rousseau). Raymond Klibansky and Ernest Mossner, the editors of an additional volume of Hume's letters, report that "The question of Canadian money was taken out of [Hume's] hands by the French Government," which sent the comte de Guerchy to London to negotiate the matter; and that "The affair was finally settled on 22 April 1766, after Hume's return to England, when Guerchy and Conway signed a convention[2] in London" (1954, xxiv–xxv). Klibansky and Mossner (see also Mossner 1954, 497) do not recall in this connection that Hume's return to England was promptly followed by Hume's appointment as General Conway's under-secretary of state,[3] or that Guerchy, who had been the French ambassador to England since 1763, took part in Hume's meeting at Compiègne with the duc de Praslin about the Canada Bills on 10 August 1765 (Hume to Conway, 12 August 1765, in Klibansky and Mossner 1954, 92). The location of the negotiations shifted, but the personnel were only partly changed.

The only reference I have found in the literature of the history of economics or of economic history to Hume's connection with Canadian paper money is a bare listing in Paul Sturges's *Economists' Papers 1750–1950* (1975, 47). Sturges notes that the National Library of Scotland has Hume's memorandum and two related letters of 1765. Yet these materials, like Poe's purloined letter, have long been hiding in plain view, for Hume's draft memorandum and a draft in French of the accompanying cover letter to the French foreign and colonial minister, the duc de Praslin, were published in *The Letters of David Hume*, edited by J. Y. T. Greig (Hume 1932, 2: app. J).

Why have scholars not taken notice? The modern literature on Hume as an economist began with,[4] and continues to rely heavily on, Eugene Rotwein's edition of Hume's *Writings on Economics* (Rotwein 1955) and on Rotwein's monograph-length introduction to that collection (Rotwein 1955). At least until the appearance of Skinner's article on Hume's political economy (1993), Rotwein's overview of Hume's economics remained without rival. The nine essays reprinted by Rotwein (eight from 1752, plus "The Jealousy of Trade," which Hume added to the 1758 edition) and Rotwein's selection of relevant extracts from letters to and from Hume have been accepted as the canon of Hume's economic writings. Rotwein extracted (and, when the original was in French, translated) seven of Hume's letters from the Greig edition (Hume 1932), but made no mention of Greig's appendix J. With rare exceptions, notably a quotation by Berdell (1995, 1,213) from a 1758 letter from Hume to Lord Elibank first published by Mossner (1962, 441–42), writers on Hume as a monetary economist have relied exclusively on Rotwein's 1955 variorum edition of Hume's economic essays or on the Liberty Fund reprint of Hume's essays edited by Eugene Miller (1985 [1741–77]). Scholars may have related Hume's 1752 economic essays to his *Treatise on Human Nature* (for example, Soule 2000, Wennerlind 2001b) or placed them in the context of writings on natural philosophy by Hume and his contemporaries (for example, Schabas 2001), but they have accepted Rotwein's edition of Hume (1955) as the definitive corpus of Hume's economic writings. Other Hume scholars, whose interests fall outside economics, have of course approached Hume's writings, including the correspondence edited by Greig, without Rotwein's intermediation. But these scholars have paid little attention to Hume's involvement with the Canada Bills for the same reason that they have not relied on Rotwein: their interests lie with Hume's philosophy, his biography, and his role in the Scottish Enlightenment, not his economics. As Arkin objected, "although Professor Mossner [1954] goes on to describe Hume as "a shrewd anticipator of Adam Smith, he can spare no more than two pages out of nearly 700 for an assessment of the economic writings in a work which purports to be a biographical consideration of Hume's intellectual activities" (1956, 208 n. 12).[5] Similarly, although Greig noted that Hume's dispatches to Conway about the Canada Bills and the Newfoundland fishery survived in the Public Records Office (Hume 1932, 2: app. J), he chose only to publish one about an alleged injustice to a British subject in France. (The dispatches were eventually published by Klibansky and Mossner [1954].)

Meanwhile, writers on Canadian monetary history appear not to have realized that "Mr. Hume," the British diplomat mentioned in three footnotes in Adam Shortt's *Documents Relatifs à la Monnaie* (1925, vol. 2), was the philosopher and economist David Hume. The draft memorandum of 25

September 1765 reproduced in the appendix to this essay, for example, is signed "Hume" and refers at its start to "Mr. H." (which would be expanded to "Mr. Hume" in the final memorandum), without giving a first name. Shortt appears not to have known much about Hume, for the index entry lists only "Hume, Mr., 957n, 1035n, 1037n," while entries for other individuals include much fuller biographical details, such as "Hocquart de Champerny, Giles (1694–1783), intendant 1729–48" (1925, 2:1112). Of Shortt's three footnotes, the first mentions Hume attending a meeting as a representative of the British holders of Canada paper, the second refers to "Mr. Hume, secretary to the Earl of Hertford," and the last states that

> Mr. Hume, then Chargé d'Affaires, in the absence of Lord Hertford, on 25th September 1765, on behalf of his government, submitted to the Court of France a memoir embodying the proposals of the British merchants interested in the Canada paper.
>
> (Shortt 1925)

The circulation of playing cards, signed by the governor or other officials, as currency in New France[6] has inspired commentary by many an economist, ever since Breckenridge wrote about the circumstance in the inaugural volume of the *Journal of Political Economy* (1893).[7] Later scholars have relied as heavily on the extensive and valuable documentation published and translated by Breckenridge, Stevenson (1875), and especially Shortt (1897–99; 1925; 1987) as scholars of Hume's economics have relied on Rotwein.[8]

Hume as a Monetary Economist

Writers on Hume as a monetary economist have concentrated on his 1752 essays "Of Money" (1985u [1752c]) and "Of the Balance of Trade" (1985x [1752e]). His quantity-theoretic thought experiment in "Of Money"—a consideration of what an economy's new equilibrium prices would be if four-fifths of its money supply vanished overnight—leads Mayer (1980) and Wood (1995) to consider the extent to which Hume was a precursor of monetarism. Hume's specie-flow mechanism for international monetary adjustment attracts much attention (for example, Viner 1937; Staley 1976), with Sekine (1973) weighing the relative contributions of Hume and such predecessors as Isaac Gervaise and Richard Cantillon, while Rashid (1984) expresses skepticism regarding the centrality of Hume's role. Duke (1979), Waterman (1988), and Berdell (1995; 2002) offer formalizations of the open-economy monetary dynamics of Hume's specie-flow mechanism. Fausten (1979), Humphrey (1986b [1981]), Laidler (1981), and Wennerlind (2000) consider both Hume's influence on Adam Smith's open-economy monetary economics, and what distinguishes their approaches. The consensus view (with Cesarano [1998] dissenting) holds that Hume's specie-flow mechanism relies on changes in the relative prices of foreign and domestic goods in a world economy that is not in long-run equilibrium, while Smith, like the modern monetary approach to the balance of payments, assumed the law of one price. Humphrey (1986c [1982]) considers Hume's analysis in "Of the Balance of Trade" of the short-run non-neutrality of money in the context of what became the Phillips-curve trade-off between inflation and real economic activity, but Perlman (1987) argues that Hume always emphasized long-run equilibrium and neutrality (see Dow 2002 on issues involved in the interpretation of such passages in Hume). This expanding and illuminating literature, however, treats Hume only as the theorist of the 1752 essays, without suggesting that he had any exposure to policy issues that might have occasioned reflection.

Hume on Paper Money

In his essay "Of the Balance of Trade," Hume dismissed the importance of paper money, arguing that it merely displaced specie in circulation:

> Before the introduction of paper-money into our colonies, they had gold and silver sufficient for their circulation. Since the introduction of that commodity, the least inconveniency that has followed is the total banishment of the precious metals. And after the abolition of paper, can it be doubted but money will return, while these colonies possess manufactures and commodities, the only thing valuable in commerce, and for whose sake all men desire money.
>
> (Hume 1985x [1752e], 318)

Hume contended that, through the specie-flow mechanism, the balance of payments would adjust the money supply in a country to the demand for money. Convertible paper would simply displace an equal quantity of gold and silver. Inconvertible (or doubtfully convertible) paper would not be acceptable in international payments:

> What pity LYCURGUS did not think of paper-credit, when he wanted to banish gold and silver from SPARTA! It would have served his purpose better than the lumps of iron he made use of as money; and would also have prevented more effectually all commerce with strangers, as being of so much less real and intrinsic value.
>
> (Hume 1985x [1752e], 318)

However, in the sixth edition of his essays, published in 1764, Hume inserted two qualifying paragraphs immediately after these remarks, and deleted the statement that "our darling projects of paper-credit are pernicious." In the new material, Hume acknowledges that "there are certain lights, in which this subject may be placed, so as to represent the advantages of paper-credit and banks to be superior to their disadvantages" (1985x [1752e], 318). He still emphasizes that the use of paper money in a country will displace precious metals from circulation, but now accepts that the increase of industry and credit, promoted by a proper use of paper money, can more than compensate for the displacement of specie and bullion. Bank credit, as provided by the banks of Edinburgh, is "one of the most ingenious ideas that has been executed in commerce," he observes, a contrivance whose advantages are manifold. A man might go to one of the banks in Edinburgh and offer surety for a line of credit of, say, £1,000, on which he will pay interest only to the extent that he draws on the line of credit:

> As a man may find surety nearly to the amount of his substance, and his bank-credit is equivalent to ready money, a merchant does hereby in a manner coin his houses, his household furniture, the goods in his warehouse, the foreign debts due to him, his ships at sea; and can, upon occasion, employ them all in payments, as if they were the current money of the country. If a man borrows a thousand pounds from a private hand, besides that it is not always to be found when required, he pays interest for it, whether he be using it or not: His bank-credit costs him nothing except during the very moment in which it is of service to him: And the circumstance is of equal advantage as if he had borrowed money at much lower interest.
>
> (Hume 1985x [1752e], 319)

In this passage, dating from 1764, Hume expressed a new appreciation for the possible "right use of paper-money" at a time when, as a diplomat, he was engaged in discussions with a committee of British merchants who had holdings of the paper money of New France. This circumstance is masked, however, by his citing only current Scottish experience, not the Canada Bills or the earlier Scottish proposals and French experiments of John Law.[9] Other possible influences on his economic views at that time include his interaction with French economists, especially A. R. J. Turgot; his continued contacts with Adam Smith,[10] who was in France from 1764 to 1766 as a tutor to the young duke of Buccleuch; and Benjamin Franklin, whom Hume mentioned, in a letter to the abbé Morellet dated 10 July 1769, as a source of information on Pennsylvania's issue of paper currency (Rotwein 1970 [1955], 215). In that same letter, Hume made clear that his appreciation of privately issued notes did not extend to approval of government issues: the assemblies in the British colonies in North America had "issued paper without end, and thereby discredited the currency" (ibid.). For Hume, the crucial distinction was the limitation of the note issue by convertibility-on-demand into metallic coin, the only legal tender. In an example that would inevitably occur to a Scot writing to a French correspondent, John Law's Banque Royale had prospered as long as convertibility-on-demand was required, but foundered through excessive note issue and loss of confidence once the notes themselves were made the only legal tender for payments exceeding 100 livres (A. Smith 1982, 515–19). Hume's heightened appreciation in 1764 of the possible "right use of paper-money" brought his views closer to those of a philosopher who would have been very familiar to him, George Berkeley, who reflected in *The Querist* on "Whether having considered the Conveniencies of Banking and Paper-Credit in some Countries, and the Inconveniencies thereof in others, we may not contrive to adopt the former, and avoid the latter?" (1910 [1735–37], 34).

Hume's disapproval, in his letter to Morellet, of the excessive note issue by the colonial assemblies and his opposition to granting paper money the status of legal tender set him apart from Benjamin Franklin (1764), who, writing in his capacity as London agent for Pennsylvania, protested against the Act of Parliament banning further colonial issue of legal-tender bills. Each year from 1764 to 1766, Franklin and Thomas Pownall proposed to the British government the establishment of a bank, based in England with a loan office in each American colony, with the power to issue legal-tender bills. The danger of excessive note issue would be avoided by making the bank subject to control by Parliament, rather than the colonial assemblies (Riddell 1930; Dorfman 1946, 188–90). As early as 1729, Franklin had praised the stimulating effect of issuing paper money; he was keenly aware of its stimulus to the printing trade, for he had received the printing contract for the note issue in 1729 (Dorfman 1946, 179–81). A few decades later, Franklin argued that the long-term economic interest of Britain and its American colonies lay in retaining Canada rather than Guadeloupe after the war, in contrast to Voltaire's dismissal of Canada as "quelques arpents de neige" (Colombo (1974 [1759], 616). Franklin was the London agent for the colony of Pennsylvania from 1757 to 1762 and again from December 1764 to March 1775. He met Hume on a visit to Scotland in 1759, and was Hume's guest in Edinburgh in 1771, but his visits to France in 1767 and 1769 (during which he met Quesnay, Mirabeau, and Turgot) came after Hume's return to Britain. It would be fascinating to know what discussions or correspondence Hume and Franklin might have had about paper money or Canada, but, unfortunately, when Franklin left Britain for France in 1775 at the start of the American War of Independence, he left his papers with Joseph Galloway, whose house was sacked by a mob during the war.

The Canada Bills

In 1685, Intendant Demeulle issued 39,000 livres of paper money by printing face values on playing cards and affixing his seal. This note issue was redeemed for cash in 1686 once a shipment of coins arrived, and was a temporary expedient to meet authorized expenses (payments to officials, soldiers, and suppliers), not meant to increase money in circulation. Nonetheless, frequent recourse to such expedients meant that 2 million livres of such card money was circulating in New France by 1714 (Trudel 1968, 186), when the French government proposed to retire the card money over five years by exchanging 1 livre in bills of exchange to 2 livres of cards. To compensate, bills of exchange would be payable in coin rather than bonds. However, the Naval Treasury was unable to make even the first payments on the bills of exchange in March 1715, and the colonial government again began to pay its current expenses by reissuing, at their full face value, playing cards it had redeemed for half that amount (McCullough 1984, 39). Playing-card money was made legal tender in 1705, and after 1729 was printed on playing-card stock rather than on actual playing cards. Shortt, Lester (1939), and Hamelin (1961) interpret the monetary problems of New France, which resulted in issues of assorted paper currencies, as a chronic shortage of currency due to persistent balance-of-trade deficits, but Robert Armstrong finds "no hard evidence that the recurring deficit in the overall balance of *trade* extended also to a regular deficit in the overall balance of *payments*. ... Temporary currency shortages undoubtedly occurred, but there is no evidence of a chronic deficiency in the aggregate money supply" (1984, 31–32). Angela Redish (1984) points out that such an alleged chronic shortage of specie (such as the shortage of media of exchange that Stevenson [1876–77, 1891–92], Breckenridge, and Shortt believed followed the withdrawal of the Army Bills after the War of 1812) runs counter to Hume's specie-flow mechanism, which holds that, under the gold standard, money will flow to where it is demanded. Her analysis concerns Canadian monetary history from 1796 to 1830 after the British conquest, but is also applicable to the French colonial era. Michener (1987) makes a similar argument concerning the British colonies in what is now the United States. Redish (1984) suggests that Gresham's law was at work: Lower and Upper Canada experienced a shortage of good-quality coin, with poor-quality coins (small silver coins that were frequently clipped) circulating and good-quality coins going into strong-boxes or trading at a premium. To adapt her argument to the French regime, good-quality coins would have been displaced from circulation in New France by various forms of paper money, rather than by poor-quality coins. Such displacement, rather than an external drain, would account for the colonial complaints of a chronic shortage of specie. The question whether a shortage of small-denomination coins (due to high production costs) stimulated recourse to paper money (which, as Redish notes, was posed by Hanson [1980]; see also Michener 1987) has recently been taken up in a Western European context by Sargent and Velde (1999; 2002).

At the census of paper money ordered in 1764 by General Murray, the British military governor of Quebec, holdings of 16,782,510 livres of paper money were declared: 3.8 percent in card money, 4.7 percent in certificates given to suppliers by the keepers of the government stores, 13.1 percent in *lettres de change* (bills of exchange) on the Naval Treasury, and 78.4 percent in *billets d'ordonnance*, promissory notes signed by the intendant on printed forms (Trudel 1968, 187; Shortt 1925, 2:1003). These figures marked a sharp decline from the estimated circulation of 30 million livres in 1759 and 49 million in 1763 (Armstrong 1984, 48). Ouellet (1980, 51) cites a *mémoire* of 1762 that estimated circulation of 80 million livres of paper money in the period 1757–60. The French government shipped 1 million livres in coins to New France in 1755 to pay for official expenses, and another million livres in coins in 1756. Issues of paper money to pay wartime expenses, the inability of the French government to send coin past the British Navy to New France after 1756, and the associated suspension of cash payments on the bills of exchange on 15 October 1759 (Shortt 1925, 2:929), accelerated the depreciation of the paper money against specie and goods. Montcalm, the French military commander, estimated that the colony's expenses rose from 4 million livres in 1755 (the last prewar year) to 36 million livres in 1759, and

> in April 1759 Montcalm noted that people were offering 36 livres and even 48 livres of paper for 25 livres of coin. Later in the year Bigot [the Intendant] was reduced to begging army officers for any coined money they had in order to purchase wheat; the habitants refused to accept paper money of any sort.
>
> (McCullough 1984, 51)

As early as November 1759, General Murray, the British military commander in Quebec after the death of Wolfe, banned the circulation of the French paper money, declaring only metal currency as legal tender. In the preliminary peace negotiations of November 1762 and in Article 4 of the Treaty of Paris in February 1763 (Shortt 1925, 2:973), France acknowledged responsibility for settlement of the outstanding paper money of New France. Already in 1762, English merchants who had acquired Canada Bills petitioned Lord Egremont, then secretary of state, to intercede for redemption (Short 1925, 2:967; Ouellet 1980, 62–63). General Murray tried to discourage as "public brigandage" the sale of Canada Bills by habitants to English speculators at 15-to-25 percent of face value, with the English merchants then demanding that the British government oblige the French government to redeem the bills at face value (Shortt 1925, 2:993), and conducted a census of paper money still in the hands of the colonists (ibid.: 2:1003). One London merchant, François Rybot, acquired 1,333,681 livres of Canada Bills, and others had substantial holdings (Ouellet 1980, 65).

Three *arrêts* of the French court on 29 June, 2 July, and 15 December 1764 called for registration of all outstanding Canada Bills, with terminal dates for their conversion. Bills of exchange acquired before October 1759 by their present possessors (that is, not resold to English merchants), and those declared and stamped bills of exchange that had been drawn in 1760 for provisioning of the armies, were to be paid in full; other declared and stamped bills of exchange would be redeemed only at half their nominal value (including those issued before October 1759 that were no longer in the hands of the original possessors); and *billets d'ordonnance*, certificates, and card money (together accounting for 87 percent of the total in Murray's 1764 census) were to be paid at one-quarter of face value, to reflect the depreciated value at which they had been acquired (Shortt 1925, 2:1005, 1013; Ouellet 1980, 66; Hamelin 1961; Petrie 1973). Indignant delegations of British speculators descended in 1764 on the earl of Halifax, Egremont's successor as secretary of state for the Southern Department, and in 1765 on his successor, General Conway (Klibansky and Mossner 1954, xxiv). Hertford and Hume were directed to intercede, resulting in the series of inconclusive meetings with French ministers and officials recounted in Hume's dispatches (in Klibansky and Mossner 1954) and in Hume's official memorial (Hume 1932, 2: app. J; and appendix below), which never received a formal response, although one was promised.

Far from improving on the announced settlement, Hume encountered great difficulty in inducing the French government to carry out its promises of 29 June 1764. The eventual convention signed by Conway and Guerchy in London in April 1766 (which included a bonus of 3 million livres on the whole settlement over and above the terms of 29 June 1764) pleased the London merchants sufficiently that they published an open letter of gratitude to Conway (Klibansky and Mossner 1954, xxiv). They were too hasty in doing so: France paid, not in coin, but in promissory notes bearing interest at 4.5 percent a year. In May 1766, these notes traded on the London market at 74 percent of their face value, but by 1771 they were repudiated and worthless (Ouellet 1980, 67; Armstrong 1984, 48). The deep discounts at which the bills had been bought from the colonists reflected the risk to the speculators (although those merchants who sold their notes promptly in 1766 made a profit). Robert Armstrong concludes that

> If paper money from the French regime had been prohibited without further ado by the British occupant, the burden of the Conquest would have fallen entirely upon the Canadian population. The French government, by promising compensation for colonial paper money, sustained false hopes for almost a decade and effectively redistributed a part of the burden to British merchants and speculators.
>
> (Armstrong 1984, 49)

The longer-term effect was to make Canadian habitants very reluctant to accept the paper currency of the invading Continental Army during the American War of Independence, and perhaps to delay subsequent use of paper money in Lower Canada.

Conclusion

The affair of the Canada Bills shows David Hume, the theorist of international monetary adjustment and the quantity theory of money, in an unfamiliar light as a diplomat engaged in negotiating an international monetary settlement. His involvement in negotiations concerning paper money coincided with a dramatic change in his published opinion of the usefulness of bank notes, in the 1764 edition of his essays, raising the possibility that his involvement in practical affairs of state led him to think further about the economic consequences of paper money. Although the relevant documents have long been in print in editions of his correspondence, Hume's involvement with the settlement of the Canada Bills has been overlooked both in the extensive literature on Hume as a monetary economist (which concentrates exclusively on his 1752 theoretical essays) and in the voluminous literature on the paper monies of New France, and receives a bit less than half a sentence in the standard biography of Hume by Mossner (1980). Discussions of Hume as an economist would do well to bear in mind that his theorizing was informed by his direct acquaintance with practical affairs and public policy. The Canada Bills would also be relevant to the literature on whether colonial North American experience shows that the value of paper money depends on its backing rather than its quantity, a literature that even when published in Canada (for example, B. Smith 1985) uses data only from the present United States.

Appendix[11]

Mémoire

Mr. H. has received Orders from his Court to lay before the Court of France the Proposals of the English Merchants concern'd in the Paper Money of Canada &c.

These Proposals are made by the English Merchants, in order to conform themselves, as much as possible to the Arret, issu'd by the Court of France. They still insist, however, that as that Arret was fram'd without consulting the Court of England, it is liable to great Objections, and exposes them to great Injustice. They insist that all the Paper Money of Canada ought to have been pay'd in full, because the Faith of the French Government is doubly plighted to that purpose both by their original Engagements in Canada, and by the strong Declaration annexed to the late Treaty.

They insist, that, even if a Reduction was to have place, the payment of 50 per cent for the Bills of Exchange preceding Octr 1759 was too low, as well as that of 25 per cent for the Cards & Billets of Ordonnance; because there was so considerable a Difference made between Paper and Money in Canada.

Allowing, that such a Difference had been made in Canada during the years 1759 & 1760; yet as the Arret of the French Court was not issued until July 1764, the Proprietors of the Paper Money had been great Losers, by so late a Payment.

This Hardship is greatly aggravated by the Terms of Payment: The very 25 per cent granted them cannot be disposed of but at 35 or 36 per cent

Discount, a Circumstance, which the Court of France itself, reasoning upon its own Principles, must allow to be a great Hardship & Injustice.

For all these Reasons, the English Merchants insist that besides the Payments required as above the Sum of 120.000 Pounds Sterling shall be pay'd them in four quarterly Payments as a Reparation of their Losses. This Sum is proposed to be distributed among the Proprietors of the cards & Billets d'Ordonnance. The Court of England, sensible of the Justice of this Demand, support it with the utmost Force, and demand, as soon as possible, a precise answer from the Court of France. If the Demand is comply'd with, as from the good Intentions of H. M. Christ Majesty[12] the former Court has reason to expect, she also offers to acquit the latter of all Claims, which the Canadians may have, for the unequal Taxations of Provisions made by the French Intendant and which the last Arret promis'd to redress. These Claims and many others of a like Nature are very considerable; and this Consideration is an additional Reason for yielding to the present Demand.

Paris 25 of Septr 1765

HUME

Notes

I thank Tom Velk, Glenn Hueckel, and other participants in the annual meetings of the Canadian Economics Association and the History of Economics Society for helpful comments. I am very grateful to Professor Douglas Mair of Heriot-Watt University for his research on my behalf at the National Library of Scotland. A short note related to this paper appeared in August 2005 in the *Journal of Money, Credit and Banking*. Permission to reprint in part is duly granted.

1 In a postscript to a recently discovered letter (now at Kwansei Gakuin University) to Adam Smith on 17 November 1772, Hume wrote, "You once asked me for an account of the Money imported into Spain: I send you the enclosed Scrawl, which is all I can find out about it! But I found at the time it concurd very exactly with an Account I had given of it, I know not where. It was Count Zinzendorf gave me this Account!" (in Smith 1987a, 415–16). The "enclosed Scrawl" has not been found.

2 A copy of the 1766 convention appears in Stevenson (1875). Ouellet reports of the negotiators only that "The British government and the businessmen sent H. S. Conway as a delegate to the Count of Guerchy, the French Ambassador in London" without further identifying Conway, not to mention Hume (1980, 67).

3 Conway and Hume transferred from the Southern to the Northern Department in 1766 (serving until 1768) when the duke of Grafton (a nephew of Lady Hertford) advanced from secretary of state for the Northern Department to prime minister and first lord of the Treasury (1766–70). The new secretary of state for the Southern Department was Sir William Petty (2nd earl of Shelburne, later prime minister and 1st marquess of Lansdowne), named for his ancestor, the political arithmetician. The Northern and Southern Departments were reorganized into the Home and Foreign Offices in 1782.

4 The first four volumes of the American Economic Association's *Index of Economic Journals*, covering articles published in English from 1886 to 1954, list no

articles on Hume under the classification 4.8: History of Economic Thought: Individuals. The fifth volume, for the period 1954–59, lists two: Arkin (1956), a review article about Rotwein's edition, and Vickers (1957), which was also occasioned by Rotwein's edition of Hume's essays. There were, of course, discussions in more general books, notably by Rotwein's teacher Viner (1937) (see Staley 1976), and, after his own study was largely complete, Rotwein discovered a 1902 volume in French on Hume's economics by A. Schatz, "an excellent analysis which, it appears, has suffered from serious neglect" (1955, xviii n).

5 In 1965, Mossner accepted the invitation of the Adam Smith Committee of Glasgow University to write a life of Smith to accompany the Glasgow Edition of Smith's works, but in 1971 illness obliged him to relinquish the project to Ian S. Ross (Smith 1987a, vii–viii). Presumably Mossner would have given more attention to economics in that work.

6 See McCullough (1984, 28) for reproductions of a 24-livre card of 1742 and a 3-livre card of 1749, and Trudel (1968, 186–87) for reproductions of cards from 1714 and from the last period of New France.

7 See also Heaton (1928), as well as Lester (1939), whose chapter 11, "Playing-Card Currency of French Canada," is the opening reprint in Neufeld (1964).

8 E.g., McCullough states, more than 50 years after Shortt's death, that "The standard bibliographic references cannot adequately acknowledge the debt which this volume owes to the late Dr. Adam Shortt. His published works, and more particularly the notes on monetary history in his papers in the Public Archives of Canada, have illuminated the more obscure corners of Canadian monetary history" (1984, 15).

9 See Law (1966 [1705] and 1994) for his Scottish proposals, and Lande (1982) for Law's reflections in Venetian exile.

10 A letter from Glasgow banker John Glassford to Smith in November 1764 reported a proposed bill by Scottish members of Parliament to repeal the "optional clause" allowing bank notes to be redeemed in cash or in notes of other banks (Smith 1987a, 105), drawing Smith's attention to the proper role of bank notes while Smith was in France.

11 The text of Hume's memorial in this appendix incorporates the additions and deletions made by Hume on the handwritten draft, now (together with the draft cover-letter) in the National Library of Scotland (MS 2618, fols. 53–54). See Hume (1932, 2: 405–6) for the nature of these additions and deletions.

12 His Most Christian Majesty, the King of France.

10 French "New Politics" and the Dissemination of David Hume's *Political Discourses* on the Continent, 1750–70

Loïc Charles

1. Introduction

Modern scholarship has shown that the rise of prominence of Adam Smith's *Wealth of Nations* was a slow process.[1] In England, it was not until the last years of Smith's life that his book progressively gained some influence at the policy level (Teichgraeber 1987). In Germany, too, the *Wealth of Nations* passed largely unnoticed before the 1790s (Tribe 1988, 133–48). In France, as in England, the Anglo-French commercial treaty of 1786 marked the beginning of a growing interest from both the public and the government.[2] This movement continued to gain strength during the last decade of the eighteenth century and, by the end of the Napoleonic wars, the *Wealth of Nations* had achieved canonical status in both countries. The delayed reception of Smith's political economy in Europe contrasts sharply with the quickness with which David Hume's *Political Discourses* penetrated the European public after its publication in 1752. The *Discourses* was republished no fewer than seventeen times in five languages in the next fifteen years.[3] The work raised a great deal of interest among English writers (Hont 2005e [1983]), and also gained a strong reputation in Continental Europe, in the "republic of letters," and in the policy debates of various countries.

In this article, I will investigate the context of the *Political Discourses'* success on the Continent. I will show that the reputation of the *Political Discourses* resulted, to a large extent, from one of its translations in French, by the abbé Jean-Bernard Le Blanc, published in 1754. Le Blanc's translation, with its extensive introduction, notes, and appendix, provided a context for reading Hume's political economy that appealed to the French and the European public. This edition highlighted Hume's Continental influences, in particular Jean-François Melon and Charles-Louis de Montesquieu, whose works were widely known and discussed. In his edition, Le Blanc also introduced to readers the works of French politico-economic writers from the circle of Vincent de Gournay. Thus, for its Continental readers, the *Political Discourses* appeared less as a contribution specific to its English-Scottish origins, despite its important discussions of pressing issues related to that context (for example, the public debt, and the rich country–poor country debate). Instead, the volume was read as a new voice in a European debate on commerce and luxury, and their role in modern politics. The reception of the *Political Discourses* in France and in Continental Europe is to be understood in this context.

I will argue that Le Blanc's translation corresponded with a cultural policy designed by a group of enlightened members of the French government led by Gournay. This policy aimed to implement "the new politics of the nations" pursued by England and the Netherlands in France, and to relieve both the French administration and the public from their prejudices about commerce. In this perspective, the interest among Gournay's associates for the *Political Discourses* was one-sided. On the one hand, they responded enthusiastically to Hume's general outlook on trade, luxury, and the role of each in modern politics, and they emphasized their common views with Hume on these issues. On the other hand, they either downplayed or dismissed what historians of political economy today consider Hume's main analytical achievements: his monetary theory, most notably the specie-flow mechanism, and his pioneering stance on free trade.

2. The "New Politics" of Vincent de Gournay

Jacques-Claude-Marie Vincent de Gournay left France at an early age.[4] At 17, he was in Cádiz, Spain, working for his father and his associates, Verduc and Villebarre. Gournay spent the next 15 years as a successful businessman there, rapidly gaining a leading position in the French community of traders. Around 1744, his career took a different course. He inherited his father's business when the latter died in 1744. He also began to work for the French government either as a negotiator in international affairs or as a secret agent, traveling in Germany, Holland, and England in the period 1745–47 to gather information for the Ministry of Foreign Affairs (Meyssonnier 1989, 169–74). When one of his associates, Villebarre, died in 1747, he married the man's widow, gaining by marriage the title of Marquis of Gournay. At this point, he decided to come back definitively to France and sought a position in the administration of trade; he obtained it in March 1751, becoming intendant of trade.[5]

His choice to enter royal government was not unexpected as his work and travels for the French Ministry of Foreign Affairs, combined with his wide experience as a merchant had persuaded him that the French kingdom was losing its preeminence in European politics. In 1748, Gournay was already thinking of ways to change this course. On the eve of the peace treaty of Aix-la-Chapelle (1748), he sent a memoir to his superior, the secretary of foreign affairs, in which he underlined a vast plan to counter this trend. At the root of this plan was the strong belief that trade was the key to political power (see Vincent de Gournay 1993, 3). He also detailed the various economic and trading policies the French government needed to restore French preeminence in Europe.[6] Many of the economic policies Gournay advocated were ones he had encountered in seventeenth- and eighteenth-century English pamphlets. He felt that these pamphlets explained why the English government was so keenly aware of the nation's political interest. In 1752, he wrote that "all these errors [regarding economic policy and legislation] and many others are as well received and established in our country as they were 80 years ago in England" [*] (Gournay in Child 1983 [1752], 36). However, the English government had since 1660 made much progress "in the science and maxims of commerce," whereas France's economic administration was still ruled by old prejudices. And Gournay explained that, "by following the maxims of M. [Josiah] Child, which have formed for 80 years, just as he had wished, the basis and the rule of English administration of trade," the English nation had overcome its prejudices (ibid., 43).

In the last section of his memoir of 1748, Gournay had already stated that the lack of commercial and economic culture was impeding France's economic success; in England and Holland trade was valued highly by the political elites and merchants had a role in the government, while in France merchants were excluded from political affairs and the nation's elites viewed trade as a despicable activity (Gournay 1993, 10–12). Consequently, while "these two nations do not know another interest besides those [of their trade], and never separate them from that of their State," this was not the case in France. Gournay concluded that it was important "that high nobility and the most distinguished men from legal nobility enlightened themselves on trade, and took interest in the trading business and dared to admit it publicly" (ibid., 12). Gournay linked this opposition to the French political elites' lack of economic knowledge. The nature and function of commerce was hardly known outside the community of professional traders, and it was the victim of prejudices in the public and the administration. Thus, not only was the political promotion of the trading interest important, whether by giving to the merchants more agency in the policymaking process or by turning noblemen into traders, but it was also necessary to publicize what he called the "science of commerce" [*science du commerce*].[7] In doing so, the economic ideas of English authors would become the basis of French administration of trade so as to turn "their own maxims against them [the English]" (Child 1983 [1752], 37). This desire led Gournay to translate and annotate two seventeenth-century English pamphlets in 1752, Josiah Child's *Treatise on Trade* and Thomas Culpeper's *Treatise against Usury*, to persuade his superior, Daniel Trudaine, to his economic ideas.[8] Although Trudaine endorsed his plea for freer trade, Gournay met strong opposition to economic reforms inside the administration. When he tried to publish his translation and notes on Child and Culpeper, his own patron inside the administration, Jean-Baptiste de Machault d'Arnouville, the controller general of finance, forbade him to do so.

Discouraged by the fate of his translation, Gournay looked for further political support inside the French government, as well as a way to present his program to a wider public. He formed a network of administrators prone to reforms, among whom Trudaine, father and son, and Chrétien-Guillaume Lamoignon de Malesherbes were the most dedicated; this group helped him to print books and pamphlets on trade and to recognize their authors.[9] Gournay also gathered a circle of young writers who wrote a host of essays, pamphlets, and translations. These aimed at changing the economic and political culture of French elites, an objective best summarized by the title of one of these writings: *Reflections on the Necessity of Including the Study of Trade into That of Politics.*[10] This effort crystallized into a campaign for political economy or, as Gournay put it, for a "science of commerce." Gournay's well-known effort to have pamphlets and treatises on trade published was part of a cultural policy he designed to initiate French political elites as well as French public into the "new politics of nations" (Morellet 1821, 64–65; Murphy 1986b, 299–320; Meyssonnier 1989, 179–81). In the introduction of the first translation made under his auspices and dedicated to Machault, François Véron de Forbonnais characterized the "new politics of nations" as such: "If the spirit of calculus has not corrected men's passion, if it has not destroyed ambition, it has reformed the plan of its politics. It is no more conquests, slaughters, and fright which decide the superiority of an empire; it is the happiness of its subjects. It is to trade, father of industry, that the world owes these happy changes. It populates the states, only it enrich them. . . . Therefore, the objective of the new politics of nations is but to attract [trade] by powerful means, to fasten it by constant preference" [faveurs constantes] (Ustariz 1753 [1742], iii–iv). It was this program that Gournay had in mind when he became intendant of trade and that he publicized, either inside or outside the French administration of trade, during the seven years he held this office.

3. The Place of Translations in the Cultural Policy of Gournay's Circle

Translations were an important part of Gournay's campaign for the "science of trade": they represented roughly one-fourth of the total output of the economic and political writings of Gournay's circle. However, translation is a word that should be treated carefully in this context: the translations made by Gournay and his circle were far from faithful to their originals. Of the thirteen "translations" made by Gournay's circle two were not translations at all, but fakes (Plumard de Dangeul 1754; Le Blanc [John Tell Truth, Pseud.] 1756). One was a translation of chosen extracts inserted in a larger text mainly written by the translator (Cary 1755 [1745]); and five had very long introductions, numerous notes from the translator, and included texts from at least one other author (Child 1983 [1752]; Decker 1757 [1744]; Hume 1754a; and King 1753 [1713–14]). Two others had notes and a significant introduction (Anon. 1760; Ustariz 1753 [1742]) or translated just a part of the original text (Tucker 1751 [1751]); only two were regular or "true" translations (Child 1754; Ulloa 1753 [1740]).

These irregularities should be understood in the context of the French state's politics of censorship during this period. Matters related to financial and political matters were severe as illustrated by Gournay's difficulty in publishing his notes on Child (see Félix 1999, 5–31; Ives 2003, 2–8). Likewise, most writings that discussed economic subjects or advocated economic reforms, particularly when they touched on religious and fiscal issues, were officially banned and their authors and publishers could be fined or even imprisoned. Even if the government seldom resorted to such harsh measures, it was not uncommon for the state to prevent a book from being sold for a lengthy period, a risk publishers had to take into account when they planned to publish writings that discussed political themes.[11] Numerous and ingenious tactics to escape censorship developed during the eighteenth century.[12] The most common was the use of tacit permission instead of the usual privilege to print. The government had created tacit permissions to grant foreign books the right to circulate and be commercialized in French territory. It progressively enlarged the scope of tacit permission to include French-made books for which it was willing to allow publication, but did not want to assume responsibility in case religious or legal authorities condemned a particular text.[13] Accordingly, a large and growing number of French books were released with tacit permissions and under false foreign addresses. A more elaborate tactic was to disguise an original text as a translation. This way the author/translator as well as the publisher of the book gained further protection from legal pursuits, since they could argue that they had merely presented the ideas of the foreign author of the book without endorsing them.

Gournay's circle used all these tactics. For example, one of the circle's most important writings, Louis-Joseph Plumard de Dangeul's *Remarques sur les avantages et les désavantages de la France et de la Grande Bretagne* was published under the pseudonym "John Nickolls" and it was only after it was translated into English that it became clear that it was a fake translation. Moreover, all the books emanating from Gournay's circle, with a few exceptions, were allegedly printed outside the French kingdom and circulated with tacit permissions.[14] Le Blanc, Hume's translator, assumed false authorship for *Le patriote Anglois* (1756), which was published under the name of John Tell Truth, a supposed member of the English parliament and an opponent of Prime Minister William Pitt's foreign policy. At that time, aware of the previous case of John Nickolls, the Parisian public was less prone to be fooled.[15] Other examples show the impertinence with which some of the members of Gournay's circle treated the original text in their translations. In the foreword to his translation of J. Cary's *Essay on the State of England*, Georges-Marie Butel-Dumont stated simply:

> It is important to observe that in this first volume, what we have taken from the English author amounts to no more than 43 pages of his book, and that the *Essay* of Cary is in fact only the outline of the

French *Essai*. The second volume owes even less to Cary. We have borrowed only its general plan and themes.

(Cary 1755 [1745] [1695], 1:16–17)

Clearly, Butel-Dumont had less interest in Cary's text per se than in the themes discussed in the *Essay*. Cary's writing was taken as a point of departure for a discussion on the recent and comparable evolution of the French and the English nations, which emphasized the role played by economic policies and political constitutions. Another fine example is given by Forbonnais, who chastised French translators for being too faithful (!) to the English originals when the authors' conclusions about public credit were obviously oriented by political prejudices (Forbonnais 1755b, 73). Hence, it is no wonder that in many cases the original text had been no more than the so-called translator's excuse to present Gournay's program of economic and political reforms.

Le Blanc's translation of Hume's *Discourses* contributed to Gournay's agenda of publicizing the "science of commerce." That Le Blanc signaled in advance that the translation of Child's *A Discourse of Trade* was soon to be published leaves no doubt of Le Blanc's involvement in Gournay's program (Hume 1754a, 2:393).[16] In fact, several elements put the Hume translation in a central position among the other translations. First, as Le Blanc himself and others pointed out, his translation of Hume's *Discourses* was a best-seller.[17] After the publication of the *Discourses*, Hume's other writings were translated into French and these translations were regularly republished.[18] The second element is simply the personality of the translator, the abbé Le Blanc. Although Le Blanc's fame had waned considerably since its peak in the eighteenth century, he was still a well-reputed man of letters.[19] Protected by the Marquis de Marigny, brother of Madame de Pompadour, Le Blanc was the author of an important and a successful work on the English nation in 1745; it went through several editions in three languages. From 1750, he worked for the French government, either writing essays and pamphlets (such as *Le Patriote anglais*) that favored French international policies, or working for French foreign affairs (for example, traveling to Germany in the period 1754–55). Le Blanc had previously lived a year-and-a-half in England (1737–38), which gave him a mastery of the English tongue few Frenchmen had at this time.[20] Moreover, he had been in close contact with Melon, a prominent forerunner of Gournay and author of the influential *Essai politique sur le commerce*; he also maintained a long-lasting friendship with Montesquieu that began in the mid-1730s.[21] Consequently, he was well-versed in the new political culture that emphasized commerce over sheer military power as the underlying rationale of the European political equilibrium.[22] This mastery manifests clearly in his *Lettres d'un Français*: Although Le Blanc was obviously trying to emulate Voltaire's *Lettres philosophiques* (1986 [1734]), he shows much more interest for issues of trade and politics and much less for those of religion and natural philosophy compared to Voltaire. The third element that distinguishes Le Blanc's translation is related to Hume's original text.

While the other works translated by Gournay's circle were second-rate literature, valued either for their contribution to economic or political theory or their artistic achievement, Hume's *Political Discourses* was obviously of a much higher standard, as Le Blanc pointed out in his introduction (Hume 1754a, 1:xv–xviii).[23] Moreover, some of the themes and the general outlook developed by Hume in the *Discourses* were perfectly in accordance with those of Gournay's circle.[24] Like Gournay, Hume was convinced that commerce played a major role in the " 'new politics of the nation' " and that trade and luxury had benevolent effects on the wealth and manners of nations—a view Albert Hirschman has described as the *doux commerce* thesis (1977).[25] The fourth element is the timing of the publication of Le Blanc's translation. The year 1753 saw the publication of the first translations by Forbonnais (two) and Dangeul (one), and, in the first months of 1754, programmatic works of Gournay's circle were presented to the public: Dangeul's *Remarques* in February and Forbonnais's *Élémens du commerce* in March.[26] When Le Blanc's translation of Hume came out in August of the same year, the time was ripe for consolidating these early successes.

In his introduction to Hume's text, Le Blanc called attention to the achievements of Forbonnais and Dangeul with much praise:

> I do not think that I should let the public ignore ... that we owe the main works of this catalogue [that is, the second appendix] to two authors ... whose friendship as well as parenthood reunited. I should add that they had proven the high capacity and zeal which moved both of them toward the welfare of their fatherland at an age at which few are able to collect as much knowledge and, moreover, to make such use of it.
>
> (Hume 1754a, 1:xxvii–viii)

The first appendix is a well-informed list of English works on trade. In the second appendix. which lists the "Works on trade, finance, etc., cited in the notes of the *Discourses* of M. Hume, and which have been published in France for the last two years," Le Blanc highly recommends all the works from Gournay's circle published thus far. By contrast, he criticizes the three books (out of twelve mentioned in this appendix) that were written outside Gournay's circle. Le Blanc's editorial efforts certainly influenced the French public's reading of Hume's work by identifying books that should complement it. As such, Le Blanc's labors were aimed at making Hume's *Political Discourses* part of Gournay's campaign for the "science of commerce."

4. Le Blanc's Contextualization of Hume's *Political Discourses*

Le Blanc begins his introduction along the lines set by Gournay in his note on Child, emphasizing the benevolent influence of the English constitution

on political power and the eminent role essays and pamphlets on trade
played in the process:

> It is not merely by the nature of the land Englishmen inhabit, which
> being an island is so favorable to navigation, but first and foremost by
> their political constitution that they had succeeded during the last cen-
> tury in gaining mastership on the seas. We can only praise them for
> their continuous awareness to preserve and even improve, if possible, a
> form of government to which they owe their liberty and wealth. Such is
> the purpose of these discourses, and of the great number of writings of
> the same kind, which are becoming a school of politics for the other
> European countries who had thrown off the yoke of ignorance and
> superstition.
>
> (Hume 1754a, 1:vii–viii)

That geography is not an explanation of England's superiority on the seas is
important from two viewpoints. First, the explanation of differences in
power and wealth purely in terms of political arguments was a genuine feature of the "new politics of the nations" advertised by Gournay.[27] Second, it
was a reverse of opinion for Le Blanc who had sustained the opposite idea
in his *Lettres d'un Français*, before he met Gournay (Le Blanc 1745, 1:4).
   In the rest of the introduction, Le Blanc builds up a case for considering
the *Discourses* as a product of a French tradition of economic and political
thought rather than that of an English one. Le Blanc begins by placing
Hume under the wing of the *Esprit des loix*, the ultimate authority in
French political discussions at that time (Hume 1754a, 1:xi–xiii). He continues by arguing that, although Hume had used some of the English sources listed in the first appendix, in contradistinction to these authors "he had
established his principles not as a prejudiced Englishman but as a political
philosopher," and

> nobody but him has shown more aptly that prejudices have more than
> once blinded the nation that pretends to be the most enlightened one,
> and that, by listening too much to its hatred for its neighbors, England
> has done more wrong to itself than to others.
>
> (Hume 1754a, 1:xiii–xiv)

Having disentangled the *Discourses* from the larger context of English political literature, Le Blanc introduces a more radical assertion—that Hume's
absence of prejudice was in fact evidence of the influence of *French* economic and political thought on him! To bolster his case, he identifies one
specific French writer, Jean-François Melon, to whom Hume had, according
to Le Blanc, an intellectual debt. Le Blanc eventually invokes his friendship
with Melon to give more weight to his claim. He suggests that it is his inti-
macy with Melon's *Essai* that has permitted him to uncover the intellectual

origins of Hume's writing.[28] The following passage reveals Le Blanc's rhetorical refinements:

> After having paid tribute to such a judicious writer [Hume], I care too much for the honor of my country and for the truth to obscure what M. Hume owes to a French work, which in the beginning was not sufficiently appreciated among us, but whose value the English, more applied to trade, were the first to understand. I want to speak of the *Essay* of M. Melon *on trade.*
>
> (Hume 1754a, 1:xiv–xv)

To understand what this passage may have suggested to French readers in 1754, it is worth recalling that Melon's *Essai politique sur le commerce* had gone through several editions in French since its publication in 1734.[29]

Le Blanc goes on to refine his interpretation of Hume's *Discourses.* Certainly, "Hume had better carried out the plan outlined by the French author," and "instead of following him step by step, he leaves him and even corrects him whenever he goes astray. He examines his principles, he develops these germs that the French author had only piled up" (ibid., 1:xv, xvii–xviii).[30] He even suggests that Hume's *Discourses* was only one of the several works inspired by Melon's *Essai*, although "the *Discourses* of M. Hume are of a higher order" (ibid., 1:xviii–xix). As I have noted earlier, Le Blanc gave special attention to Dangeul and Forbonnais. This mention of other French authors leads Le Blanc to describe the "science of commerce" as emerging through a forum of discussion among several French authors, a forum Hume has entered with the *Political Discourses* (ibid., 1:xx–xxii).

Le Blanc recreates such a discussion through the numerous and sometimes lengthy notes he adds to the original text. These notes were comments on Hume's statements and reasoning and are constructed on one or a few citations from other writings. Melon was the author most quoted by Le Blanc (twenty-three notes), but he quoted himself a few times (four notes) along with Forbonnais (eight notes), Plumard de Dangeul (four notes), and other writers, including Locke (three notes), Mun and Wallace (two notes), Montesquieu, Rousseau, and others (one note each). Through these notes, Hume's text is included in an ongoing conversation on the role of trade, economic and monetary policies, and national debt and political constitutions in international politics, to name but the most prominent issues that were debated in the writings of Gournay's circle. The quotations and comments provided by Le Blanc on trade and luxuries underlined the similarity of views on these subjects between Hume and the French economic writers he cited—Melon, Forbonnais, and himself (Hume 1754a, 1:23, 37, 40–41, 48–49, 52, 57, 60–61, 63, 75, 81–85, 87–88, 92). Likewise, the treatment of other issues, such as foreign-trade policies, was designed to highlight Gournay's proposals. For example, on the issue of the exportation of precious metals, Le Blanc gives repeated emphasis to Hume's critique of mercantilist policies of prohibition through citations to Melon (ibid., 1:182–83, 215) and to Ustariz (ibid., 2:193–94).[31]

The issue of grain trade was the most pressing policy debate at the time of the publication of Le Blanc's translation. Through Le Blanc's treatment of this issue we see most clearly how Hume's original text was inscribed in the French debates that Gournay sought to launch. In this endeavor, Le Blanc emulated Gournay's example. In the original texts that Gournay had translated and annotated, only two paragraphs discussed the legislation of grain trade.[32] Conversely, Gournay's notes had provided a detailed analysis between French and English grain-trade legislation to the exclusive advantage of the latter, and argued for a reform in France on this model (in Child 1983 [1752], 40–44, 106–23, 397–98). Commenting on the complaint by Culpeper that the French were exporting (in 1621) their corn in England, Gournay stated:

> Do we need a more powerful and impartial proof of the decay of our agriculture than the testimony of this author? In 1621 we were flooding, so to speak, England with corn, and for 50 years now, this nation furnishes us with wheat every five or six years at great expenses. How could such a dreadful revolution have occurred in such a relatively short time? What are its causes? The several laws that Englishmen have made [since that time] to encourage their agriculture.
>
> (Gournay in Child 1983 [1752], 397)

This statement was then taken up by several writers who belonged to Gournay's circle as well as outsiders such as François Quesnay in the article "Grains" (2005 [1757], 71).[33] Gournay had transformed circumstantial evidence from Culpeper into a decisive proof of the superiority of English legislation of grain trade over the French legislation such that this very passage was quoted authoritatively by a whole generation of French economic writers.

Le Blanc does something similar in his translation of Hume's *Political Discourses*. From one cursory sentence by Hume designed to illustrate the consequences of the wrong policies "of nations ignorant of the nature of commerce,"[34] he develops a whole case for free trade in grain:

> There is no author learned on this matter who does not agree with M. Hume, and on this issue theory is confirmed by experience. In England, a practice completely opposed to ours has saved it from the shortages that France often experiences: the law gives a reward to those who export grain as long as it does not exceed a given price. ... Whenever it exceeds this price, the reward is canceled, but free trade remains. It was in 1689 that the parliament of England made this wise legislation. Until that date, this nation had been subjected to the same ills as France, and often had to turn to foreigners for its subsistence.

Ever since, England has not endured any famine, while it exports large quantities of grain each year.

(Hume 1754a, 1:179–80)

Le Blanc also advertised the writings published by Gournay's circle on this issue—Forbonnais's *Élémens du commerce* and Dangeul's *Remarques*. He urged readers "who want to be completely aware of this matter" to "first and foremost consult the *Essai sur la police générale des grains* printed this year 1754," and he informed them that "copies of this book may be found in Paris, at Lambert's bookshop" (ibid., 1:181). He ended his long note by the remark that Herbert's work "merits all the attention of the government" (ibid.). The little game of cross-citations continued with the publication in 1755 of a revised edition of Herbert's *Essai*, in which the latter made this recommendation in a note on the subject of grain trade: "Read the *Political Discourses* of M. David Hume, lately translated by a clever author, who has often cleared its difficult passages, and whose remarks, as instructive as thoughtful, are an evident proof that he has understood well his author and his subject" (Herbert 1910 [1755], 188–89).[35] Again, the readers of Le Blanc's translation were reminded that Hume's *Discourses* should be read in the context of Gournay's "science of commerce." Consequently, aspects of Hume's text in translation assumed significance they did not have in the original. By contrast, some of the strongest and most genuine aspects of Hume's political economy were downplayed or openly criticized by Le Blanc and Gournay's circle because they were foreign or even opposed to their program of reforms.

5. Gournay's Circle and Hume's Theory of Paper Money and Public Credit

In this perspective, the subject that was most problematic to Gournay and the writers of his circle was Hume's position on public credit and his reflections on money related to it. They were strongly in favor of the institution of public credit in France on the English model (the Bank of England). For them, it was one of the keys to England's recent superiority over France.[36] Hume's position on public credit was irreconcilable with such an analysis. Le Blanc was clearly uneasy about this and, since he was less able to manage technical aspects of political economy than with its social and political sides, his strategy to reconcile Hume and French writers lacked coherence. First, Le Blanc tried to downplay somewhat their differences by remarking that Hume, Melon, and Forbonnais (and Gournay's circle) had a conventional theory of money (Hume 1754a, 1:105–6). Second, when forced to recognize the straightforward opposition between Hume and Melon, Le Blanc simply withheld his judgment.[37] Finally, he concluded the chapter by leaving the whole matter to others, that is, Dangeul and Forbonnais, who were more learned in this highly technical issue:

One will find in the work of M. of Dangeul the most instructive details on the cause and progress of English debts, and the wisest reflections on the abuses of national credit. The author of *Elémens du commerce* has also deepened these matters to the point that it seems to have left nothing unclear.

(Hume 1754a, 1:328–29)

Despite all his hesitations, Le Blanc did give his own explanation of Hume's position on public credit. He tied Hume's position on the subject to the English political context.[38] In addition to Hume's text "Of Public Credit," he translated Henry St. John Bolingbroke's "Some Reflections on the Present State of the Nation." In a note to the essay "Of Public Credit," Le Blanc said that, in his text, Bolingbroke displayed "the same principles, and the same language as that of M. Hume" (ibid., 1:311–12). Indeed, Le Blanc was persuaded that Hume was a Tory and when the latter forcefully rejected such an assertion, Le Blanc was very confused, as he expressed in a letter to Hume, dated 25 December 1754:

Your judgment on the posthumous works of Lord Bolingbroke is certainly just, although a bit rash. Nevertheless, as he had the same principles as you on paper-money, I believed that, in order to support your sentiment, it was necessary to add his *Reflections* to the discourse where you dealt with this matter, I shall delete it in the edition that is going to press.

(Monod-Cassidy 1941, 409–10)[39]

The exceptional success of Le Blanc's translation in France (as I will discuss in section 6) and the desire to implement a public credit forced Gournay and his circle to provide a deeper critique of Hume's analysis of paper money. In the mid-1750s, Forbonnais, an expert in monetary matters, wrote several memoirs to convince the French government of the necessity of a public credit.[40] His plan was tantamount to creating a bank modeled on the Bank of England in order to monetize the public debt and increase the financial means of the French state. In this work, which circulated widely in manuscripts at the summit of French trade administration, Forbonnais endeavored to show the technical flaws of Hume's reasoning. This aspect of Forbonnais's critique is particularly interesting since he had already discussed these subjects in detail and with great technical skill in a chapter of *Élémens du commerce* published the year before.

Forbonnais singled out two theoretical pillars on which Hume's reasoning rests: The specie-flow mechanism and the increase of prices due to an increase of the quantity of paper-money in circulation (Forbonnais 1755b, 143–44). Forbonnais attacked the famous thought experiment given by Hume in the essay "Of the Balance of Trade" (Hume 1985x [1752e], 311–12) by showing that Hume had simply ruled out the stickiness of prices and wages:

This reasoning of M. Hume is false in all its parts. If we suppose, according to his first hypothesis, that four-fifths of all the money of England is destroyed, the remaining fifth could not but pay a small part of the nation's labor, because it would be absurd to think that the price of labor would sink in proportion to the small amount of money that stood in the state, or as suddenly as the four fifth had disappeared.

(Forbonnais 1755b, 140)[41]

According to Forbonnais, the necessary period of deflation that would take place after part of the money supply disappeared would induce English producers to cut investments and wages and to fire some of their workers, causing a decrease in the global output of the nation. Therefore, the process that would restore the proportion between home prices and international prices would not be confined to an inflow of money through a positive balance of trade; instead it would gravely disrupt the previous level of employment and production. Moreover, the decrease in the output implied that English industry and agriculture would have fewer products to offer to foreign markets, creating in turn a decrease of its foreign trade and a further delay in the restoration of equilibrium between home and foreign prices (Forbonnais 1755b, 141–42).

Conversely, a rise in the money supply through the transformation of the debt in paper-money had not caused an equivalent rise in home prices and wages, which could have endangered the competitiveness of English trade on the international markets (Forbonnais 1755b, 141–42). Forbonnais explained that the increase in price is a tendency that other effects of money creation keep in check. First, the creation of money depresses the rate of interest, which in turn stimulates economic activity.[42] Second, an increase in activity means increased competition between economic agents, which limits the rise of prices and wages: "It is true that this multitude of workers and traders ensures that each private individual will win less, because of competition, but the gain of the nation in general is much more important" (ibid., 150). Forbonnais had already described the same kind of process in detail in the chapter "*De la circulation de l'argent*" in *Élémens du commerce*, which was then reprinted with corrections as the article "*Espèces*" in the fifth volume of Jean Le Rond d'Alembert and Denis Diderot's *Encyclopédie* (Forbonnais 1754a, 2:154–80; 1755c, 963–65). Forbonnais closed his refutation of Hume by opposing Melon to the latter (1755b, 150–51).

6. The Dissemination of the *Political Discourses* in Continental Europe

The very fact that Forbonnais felt obliged to discuss in detail Hume's position on public credit and dedicate a whole memoir to this point is a conclusive sign of the fame the *Political Discourses* was enjoying in the upper echelons of the French economic administration.[43] In the 1750s and in the next decade, Hume stood out as a major authority regarding the "science of commerce," not only in France but more generally in continental Europe. This reputation is related to the outstanding success of Le Blanc's translation as well as to the efforts of Gournay's associates to recast Hume's *Political Discourses* as a proponent of their program of reform. The dissemination of their version of Hume's political economy—one that insisted on its compatibility with Gournay's "science of commerce" at the expense of its monetary theory—was very wide in continental Europe, indeed.

The publishing history of another translation of Hume's *Discourses*—by Elézéar Mauvillon—further illuminates the influence of Le Blanc's translation. Mauvillon's version was the first translation into French of the *Discourses*, and a few copies of it appear to have circulated by the end of 1753.[44] Inspired by the success of the English edition in the English market (two editions in 1752), Mauvillon's translation was a commercial enterprise without the political overtones that characterized Le Blanc's translation.[45] Although Mauvillon's translation differs in a number of ways from Le Blanc's, the lack of *peritext*[46] is what distinguishes it most clearly from the latter. Mauvillon simply edited Hume's text and notes without adding further commentary. The success of Le Blanc's translation of Hume altered the fate of Mauvillon's edition to a large extent. At German book fairs, a traditional outlet for Dutch publishers, Le Blanc's version as well as a German translation of 1754 competed with Mauvillon's.[47] Le Blanc's version clearly outshone its competitors. Mauvillon's translation was not mentioned in the main French journals of the time and when Hume heard of it from Le Blanc he could not find a copy in London. Moreover, it seems that the publisher was not able to sell out the first edition, and so he reissued it in 1761 and 1767 with a different title page.[48] The Dutch publisher was not without resources. Confronted with the success of Le Blanc's edition and the poor reputation of his own, Schreuder tried to gain the favor of the public by emulating Gournay's cultural politics. Between 1756 and 1758, he constructed an enlarged edition according to the plan outlined by Le Blanc in his translation. The five volumes he edited as sequels of the original volume of *Political Discourses* were mainly made of pirated editions of works emanating from Gournay's circle (Tsuda 1979, 417–18). The second volume not only replicated Le Blanc's second appendix with some changes, but also contained an essay by Bolingbroke that Le Blanc had translated in his edition, two works by Forbonnais, and one by Pierre-André O'Heguerty, members of Gournay's circle.[49] Schreuder clearly designed the sequel to Hume's *Political Discourses* along Le Blanc's model—embedding Hume's text in a host of works, mostly French and related to the "new politics" of Gournay.

A new French translation of Hume's *Discourses* that appeared a decade later (1767a) also confirmed the significance of Le Blanc's interpretation of Hume. This new edition, which contained only the economic essays of Hume's original work, omitted "Of the Jealousy of Trade" whose cosmopolitanism was found to be too reminiscent of the physiocrats. The anonymous translator provided a detailed comment on the essays concerning the interest of money, taxes and public credit, themes of special interest for those who were faithful to Gournay's program of reform.[50] Thus, it is no surprise that Forbonnais was the only writer cited in this edition (Hume 1767a, 142), and that the translator criticized the physiocrats on taxes and Hume himself on public credit, drawing heavily on Forbonnais in each instance (see *supra* for Forbonnais's critique of Hume). Neither is it a surprise that this new translation was one of the books (indeed, the only foreign book) used by a journalist in the *Journal d'Agriculture, du Commerce et des Finances* to launch a direct attack on the physiocrats, nor that this journalist cited extensively Montesquieu, Forbonnais, and Melon on this occasion.[51] The journal's anonymous reviewer summarized Hume's monetary theory in three propositions that characterized well how Gournay's circle, and Forbonnais in particular, assessed his work:

> By this analysis of the system of M. Hume, it is clear that it can be reduced to these three propositions: 1) Money is useful only when it circulates; 2) Circulation follows necessarily from commerce and luxury; 3) The most wealthy and commercial states must lose their advantages through the very consequences of their commerce, whose growth increases the value of all kinds of necessaries, merchandise, and labour. It is surprising that M. Hume made this third proposition, since he gives himself the solution of the problems that have arisen from it.
>
> (Anonymous 1767 [March], 151–52)

Likewise, the reviewer had no words strong enough to criticize the essay "Of Public Credit" along lines delineated by Forbonnais a decade earlier (Anonymous 1767 [May], 148–71).

The case of Italian political economists also highlights Le Blanc's influence. Apart from Galiani, all the major Italian economists—Antonio Genovesi, Pietro Verri, and Cesare Beccaria—did not read English very well and they encountered English political economy through the French translations made by Gournay's circle (Robertson 1997, 675, 684–92; Groenewegen 1994b, 110–11).[52] Consequently, Italian economists read and discussed Hume's *Discourses* in the editorial context provided by Le Blanc, which presented Hume as a participant in a conversation between French political economists, among whom Melon, Montesquieu, and the writers of Gournay's circle figured prominently. This reading of Hume can be traced back to the reception of Le Blanc's translation by Italian journals in the mid-1750s. In 1755, the *Novelle letterarie*, the most important Tuscan journal at that time, reviewed the book and it "used the occasion to make the authors referred to by the translator ... known to his Tuscan readers" (Wahnbaeck 2004, 82). Then, it is no surprise that Italian economists followed the reading of it propounded by Gournay's circle; they were, according to the formula of one commentator, "anglophile[s] in French dress" (Robertson 1997, 688–89). The Neapolitan Genovesi, for example, did not respond well to Hume's critique of Melon's monetary theory or to his argument for free trade as a means for the economic development of poor countries (Robertson 1997, 690–93). In his discussion of Hume, Genovesi was quite faithful to the example set by Gournay's circle.[53] Likewise, Matteo Dandolo, in the introduction to his Italian translation of Hume's *Discourses* (published in Venice in 1767), argued for a restoration of the Venetian balance of trade through aggressive and protectionist commercial policies, a view that differed greatly from Hume's actual position on economic policies; conversely, Dandolo directly echoed Gournay's program for France (Venturi 1983, 351–53).[54] This example shows that the presentation of Hume by the Gournay circle as a supporter of Gournay's "science of commerce" even supplanted Hume's original text—which clearly dismissed the balance-of-trade theory—in the mind of its Continental readers.[55]

7. Concluding Remarks

The case of Hume's *Political Discourses* on the Continent underlines two aspects of how the displacement of an economic text in a different linguistic and cultural context, most notably through its translation, can result in a shift in the interpretation of the author's ideas. First, even when the text was not modified—Le Blanc's translation was unabridged and did not show a significant bias in its presentation of Hume's original text—the addition of a substantial *peritext* (introduction, notes, and appendices) modified the way this text was read and the way it was interpreted on the Continent. The interpretation and assessment of Hume's ideas depended, at least to some extent, on the media that conveyed them. Therefore, writing meaningful histories of political economy requires an understanding of the ways in which economic ideas have been translated and the context of their circulation. Second, Le Blanc's work belonged to a cultural policy designed by Gournay, one that was consistently pursued by his circle with the help of part of the French government during the 1750s. One aspect of this policy was the translation of several foreign political and economic texts that were edited to serve the political purposes of Gournay and his circle. Thus, Le Blanc's motivation for disseminating Hume's ideas differed from that of Mauvillon and his Dutch publisher Schreuder, who hoped to make a profit from the translation. In terms of transmission of Hume's ideas, Mauvillon's edition was value-free before he added sequels to the original volumes, whereas Le Blanc's was politically driven. The transmission of Hume's economic ideas into a different cultural context was not a simple and one-dimensional process of exchange but, on the contrary, carried with it political and cultural values that informed the contemporary reading and interpretation of them in Continental Europe.

Notes

This paper has benefited from the comments of the participants of the Conference on Hume's Political Economy organized by M. Schabas and C. Wennerlind (Columbia University, May 2003). I would also like to thank the *Groupe H2S*, C. Théré, Jennifer Barager, Monica Miller, and two anonymous referees for their corrections and suggestions.

*All translations of French sources are by the author unless otherwise indicated.
1 See Willis (1979), Rashid (1982), Teichgraber (1987), Tribe (1988), and Carpenter (2002).
2 The physiocrat Pierre-Samuel Du Pont de Nemours, who was the main French economic expert engaged in the preparation of the treaty, sent his book on the treaty to Smith with a cover letter, dated 19 June 1788, in which he praised Smith for having facilitated a "useful revolution" in the economic administration (Smith 1987a, 311–13). Du Pont also took the defense of Smith's *Wealth of Nations* in front of his fellow-physiocrat, the Marquis de Mirabeau. In a letter to Mirabeau dated 19 June 1788, Du Pont acknowledged that he had at first read only a few extracts of Smith's book and had a bad opinion based on this partial reading; a decade later, he took full measure of Smith's importance (Hagley Museum, Du Pont de Nemours Papers, group 2, series A).
3 This group included six reprints in English, six in French, two in German, two in Italian (one bilingual), and one in Swedish. This evaluation is based on Carpenter (1975) with a few additions (two French editions, 1754 and 1761; and one German, 1766).
4 On Gournay's life, the main source is still Schelle (1897). However, it should be complemented by Meyssonnier (1989, 168–88) and Tsuda Child (1983 [1752]) and Vincent de Gournay (1993).
5 There were four intendants of trade at that time. They acted as economic counselors to the controller of finance (a position equivalent more or less to economic prime minister). They had no power of decision but their advice had much influence in the administration. They were also in charge of the administration of trade and manufactures of specific areas, the southwest and Burgundy for Gournay, as well as of specific branches of industry, the stocking and hosiery trade in the case of Gournay (see Garrigues 1998).
6 On a general level, he pleaded for a navigation act similar to the English one, a lowering of the interest rate, and the freeing of colonial trade. He also proposed some specific advice and measures regarding trade with Portugal, Russia, and Spain, as well as trade in fishing (in particular, whale fishing) and tobacco (Gournay 1993, 4–10).
7 The "science of commerce" combined two aspects: On the one hand, it designated the savoir-faire necessary to be a successful individual tradesman; on the other hand, it referred to the study of the economic forces and welfare of nations, which was necessary to a wise legislator. Writers from Gournay's circle focused mainly on the second aspect in their writings.
8 See Gournay's letter to Trudaine dated 25 September 1752 (Vincent de Gournay 1993, 152–53). Trudaine was intendant of finances and Gournay's superior inside the administration; his son Trudaine de Montigny succeeded him in the 1760s.
9 Malesherbes as director of the Librairie controlled the censorship of French books. He brought to Gournay's circle a network of editors and journals that was essential to the publicizing of its ideas. My investigation into the Librairie's archives in the French National Library [Bibliothèque nationale] has convinced me of the major role he had in protecting the circle's writings from censorship.

For more on the composition of Gournay's circle and its political program, see Charles (1999a, 118–48; 2004).

10 Its author was François Véron de Forbonnais (1755d), the most prominent writer of Gournay's circle.

11 The *Lettres d'un Français* (on the English nation) by the abbé Le Blanc was held a whole year by the authority before it was finally released in 1745 (Monod-Cassidy 1941, 54). Another example from May 1754 concerning a writing emanating from Gournay's circle is recounted in the *Correspondance littéraire* (Grimm et al. 1966 1750–76, 2:350–51). Other examples exist in the archives of the French Librairie deposited in the manuscript division of the French National Library.

12 The more detailed account related to Gournay's circle is given in Murphy (1986a, 299–321). See also Perrot (1984) and Théré (1998).

13 It must be understood that by granting a privilege to a text, the French king not only authorized its publication but also assumed liability for it as was clearly stated in the legal text included in each book that bore a privilege. Therefore, when a book bearing a privilege fell under the fire of religious or legal authorities, it undermined the king's authority and could cause a severe political crisis (such as the case with Claude-Adrien Helvétius's *De l'esprit* and d'Alembert and D. Diderot's *Encyclopédie*).

14 The most usual false addresses were Amsterdam, Dresden, Leipzig, and London. The publications were in fact produced by Parisian publishers—Lambert, Duchesne, Estienne, and Guyllin. Two significant exceptions were Forbonnais's *Élémens du commerce*, a collection of articles that appeared in the *Encyclopédie* and also in a separate publication put out by the publishers of the *Encyclopédie*; and the second edition of Le Blanc's translation of Hume's *Political Discourses*, which was eventually published in Dresden (1755). Le Blanc traveled in Germany during 1755 and passed time in Dresden (Monod-Cassidy 1941, 99).

15 "It is not necessary to be clever to understand that this work has never existed in English," wrote Grimm in the *Correspondance littéraire* (Grimm et al. 1750–76, 3:225).

16 Another interesting detail is that Gournay had two copies of Le Blanc's translation of the *Discourses* (Meyssonnier 1988, 2: annex, 34).

17 "It is good to tell you that this translation sells like a novel which says it all," said Le Blanc to Hume in August 1754 (Monod-Cassidy 1941, 403). Le Blanc might have taken the expression from an anonymous review of his translation published in the *Affiches de province*: "This book … has been an astonishing success. Although profound and solid, he sells as well as the most agreeably frivolous; it looks as if it was the novel of the day" (Anon. 1754, 129).

18 For a description of the French translations of Hume's other writings and their context, see Mertz (1929, 658–61) and Price (1999).

19 Hume himself thought highly of Le Blanc's writings, as he expressed in a letter to Le Blanc dated 12 September 1754: "I must confess, that I cannot conceal my vanity, when I find an author, so justly celebrated for his own performances, deign to give the public a translation of works, so much inferior [to his]. I have often read *Les letres d'un François* [sic], with profit and pleasure" (Hume 1932, 1:194). Le Blanc's downfall is most certainly due to Grimm's numerous and scornful comments about him and his writings in the *Correspondance littéraire*, but Grimm's was not the general opinion of the time.

20 In his note to Child, Gournay lamented: "Foreigners by deluding us that the French tongue has become the universal tongue have caused us a real wrong: By using only our [tongue], we are always strangers out of our homeland. By the same reason, everything becomes difficult in foreign countries, and we only inform ourselves in the things we are most eager to learn only with much trouble

and often very imperfectly. On the contrary, foreigners who learn French from childhood cease, so to speak, to be strangers among us and easily succeed in learning the things that we would have interest to hide from them; therefore our knowledge soon becomes theirs whereas theirs becomes ours slowly and only with difficulty" (in Child 1983 [1752], 437).

21 In early 1734 Melon loaned one of his Parisian apartments to Le Blanc, who was facing money trouble at that time. Melon was then finishing his *Essai politique sur le commerce*, which Le Blanc read in manuscripts. They were close friends (Monod-Cassidy 1941, 198, 207, 253). Le Blanc had met Montesquieu in 1733, probably through Melon's intercourse, and dined with him several times in 1733 and 1734 (ibid., 183, 199, 210). They kept in contact after this period, and two long and important letters of his *Lettres d'un Français*, discussing political freedom, commerce, and English constitution, are addressed to Montesquieu.

22 See Paul Cheney's essay in this volume, which develops in detail the context of this new political culture in France in the first half of the eighteenth century.

23 Interestingly, neither Locke nor Petty were translated, although authors belonging to Gournay's circle certainly knew their writings: Locke and Petty figured in Le Blanc's "Notes on Some of the Leading English Writings on Commerce," which he included in the appendix to Hume's translation. There are also references to these writings, especially to Locke's pamphlets on money, in several writings of Gournay's circle. This point goes well with the idea defended here that Gournay and his circle were less interested by the genuine theoretical content of the texts they translated than by their adherence to Gournay policies.

24 For example, Forbonnais's *Élémens du commerce* shared several themes with Hume's *Political Discourses*. They both included 11 essays, five of them having very similar titles (Forbonnais's are presented in parentheses) and identical subject matter: "Of Commerce" ("Du commerce en général"), "Of Luxury" ("Du luxe"), "Of Money" ("De la circulation de l'argent"), "Of the Balance of Trade" ("De la balance du commerce"), and "Of Public Credit" ("Du crédit").

25 Le Blanc opened the chapter with a note underlining the fact that Forbonnais, "the learned author of the *Élémens du commerce*," shared completely Hume's position on luxury; in another long note, however, Le Blanc stressed his opposition to Rousseau on this peculiar subject (Hume 1754a, 1:81–84). See also John Shovlin's essay in this volume.

26 *Élémens du commerce* had three editions in two years (two in 1754 and one in 1755); Dangeul's *Remarques* went to three editions in 1754. Both Forbonnais's and Dangeul's works were praised and heavily quoted in French economic and political writings during the next decade. An implicit division of labor existed between the two books: Forbonnais's was limited to economic issues and had a more theoretical approach while Dangeul's focused more on political issues, describing thoroughly the functioning of English government, and detailing the reforms that needed to be made to French economic government and policies. Hence, Dangeul had to resort to a pseudonym to protect himself against the possibility of legal problems while Forbonnais could make his contribution public without risk.

27 At that time, the usual explanation of English superiority in trade and navigation was set in terms of geography, natural history (the theory of climates), or social psychology (the French were sanguine but versatile, while the English were sad but stubborn, etc.). Even Montesquieu retained some features of traditional explanations (the theory of climates), even if it played a somewhat marginal role in *De l'Esprit des loix*. Forbonnais criticized this aspect of Montesquieu's thinking in his commentary on *De l'Esprit des loix* (Forbonnais 1753a, 107–9).

28 "As I have more than any other to honor the memory of that citizen philosopher I had the good fortune to have as a friend, I have found a new pleasure in

translating in our tongue a work that justifies a part of his principles on trade, and that, from all appearances, his *Essai* brought about" (Hume 1754a, 1:xv).

29 Melon's *Essai politique sur le commerce* also sparked some interest in England, where a translation was made in 1738, and reprinted the next year (see Carpenter 1975, 14–15).

30 Although a full discussion of Le Blanc's general thesis is out of place here, it probably deserves some attention since Groenewegen in a recent article states that "Melon's book ... has been in great part the source of Hume's *Essays*" (1994a, 25). Groenewegen does not mention Le Blanc's introduction to his translation of Hume's *Discourses* and does not seem to have been aware of it.

31 Le Blanc quoted the French translation of Ustariz but seized this opportunity to praise once again Forbonnais's skills in economics: "The author of the *Élémens du commerce*, to whom we owe the translation [of Ustariz], has added notes to it that augment its value and prove that nothing regarding trade is foreign to him" (194).

32 One appeared in Child's *New Discourse on Trade* and one in Culpeper's *Treatise against Usury* (Child 1983 [1752], 98, 386–87).

33 I have provided a fuller discussion of this case in Charles (1999a, 163–64).

34 "And to this day, in France, the exportation of corn is almost always prohibited; in order, as they say, to prevent famines; though it is evident that nothing contributes more to the frequent famines that so much distress that fertile country" (Hume 1985x [1752e], 309).

35 Note how Herbert ratified Le Blanc's presentation and interpretation of the *Discourses*.

36 For example, Gournay stated that it was to public credit that England "owes the reduction of the rate of interest, the growth of agriculture and the navy, its most surprising efforts in the wars that have troubled Europe since the beginning of this [eighteenth] century, and its influence nowadays in public affairs [of Europe]; these advantages must make us feel all the more the necessity of a public credit, since, notwithstanding that it has produced all these good effects in England, it would produce even greater ones in France" (in Child 1983 [1752], 210–11).

37 "It is in the restriction of such [public] credit that lies the main danger of using paper money. For my part, I do not want to risk a judgment on such a difficult issue. I would only say that in their opposed opinions, the two authors seem to have taken the task of attacking the most received opinions in their respective countries" (Hume 1754a, 1:293).

38 Forbonnais also subscribed to this point of view (Forbonnais 1755b, 72–78 and 137); see Sonenscher (1997, 95).

39 Le Blanc did not keep his word and had the *Reflections* of Bolingbroke reprinted at the same place in the second edition.

40 The original manuscript dated 21 September 1755 belongs to the French National Library. It is dedicated to Moreau de Séchelles, who was controller general at that time. The manuscript is named "Mémoires pour l'établissement d'un crédit public" and is composed of eight memoirs plus a short introduction and a table of contents. There are at least two other copies at the Bibliothèque de l'Arsenal (MS 4591). One of these copies dates some of the memoirs as beginning in June 1751. This and the fact that the memoirs cover a wide area suggest that they were composed independently and reunited in 1755 with new materials, in particular the refutation of Hume's position, when Forbonnais, Gournay, and others from his circle tried to convince Moreau de Séchelles to implement a system of public credit.

41 At the end of the phrase, Forbonnais includes a note: "We have several examples, among which one M. Hume himself quotes. At the end of the last reign, the face value of money was increased by three-sevenths, and the price of goods by only

one-seventh; as a raise in the face value of money does not instantly cause an increase in the price of goods, likewise the sudden fall in the money supply will only bring about slowly and gradually the decrease of the price of work and goods." Hume includes this episode in "Of Money" (Hume 1985u [1752c], 287–88).

42 "One of the good effects of the abundance of money, when it is multiplied by a well-proportioned credit, is the easiness of borrowing. ... It is this small interest that ensures that ... nobody neglects the smallest profits, that everybody trades, undertakes, clears the land, cultivates, wins money, spends, is comfortably well off, and pays to the state two or three times what we do without bothering" (Forbonnais 1755b, 149–50).

43 Forbonnais began his critique of Hume's stance on paper money and public credit with these words: "The *Political Discourses* of M. Hume have impressed a lot of people here" (Forbonnais 1755b, 136). This is confirmed by Le Blanc who wrote to Hume (1 October 1754): "Our government is as satisfied [with his translation of the *Discourses*] as the public. M. the Count of Argenson, M. the Marshall of Noailles, in a word all those who are part of the government have talked about your work as one of the best that was ever made on these matters" (in Monod-Cassidy 1941, 407).

44 Commentators have sometimes blurred the distinction between Mauvillon's and Le Blanc's translation (e.g., Price 1999, 9–10; Carpenter 1975, 16), were published independently; and for different purposes (see below).

45 Schreuder was emulating another Dutch publisher, Schneider, who had published a French translation of Hume's *Essays, Moral and Political* in 1752. At the end of the 1750s, Schneider re-edited his translation with that of other philosophical writings of Hume as *Œuvres philosophiques de M. Hume*, an edition that he reprinted with additions several times up to 1788. Schneider had hoped to obtain the copyright of Mauvillon's edition but never succeeded: "One of my fellow-editor[s] had translated a volume [the *Political Discourses*] in French. I cannot have the copyright, but I hope to soon acquire it, to have it printed. The translation was made by M. Mauvillon in Dresden; M. the abbot Le Blanc had also made one translation of this volume which is much better than the other in my point of view" (Hume 1932, 2:344).

46 I borrow the word *peritext* from Carpenter (2002), who uses it to describe the textual apparatus surrounding the main text, that is, the foreword, introduction, notes, appendices, etc.

47 From Dresden, Le Blanc wrote to Hume: "I saw here the translation of your *Political Discourses* printed in Holland; it cannot be read. You would suffer, Sir, to see you altered in such a way. The translator whoever he is knows neither English nor French; it is probably one of these authors who works in the fair for Dutch publishers whose books, good or bad, are sold in the fairs of Leipzig and Frankfurt. The libraries of this country [Germany] are filled with French books that were never sold and would never be known in France" (quoted in Monod-Cassidy 1941, 410).

48 This was a current common practice in the book trade when an edition had difficulties selling; Carpenter (2002) offers various examples in the case of the French translation of the *Wealth of Nations*. In the case of Mauvillon's translation, various elements clearly point in that direction: The "new" editions were made available in the wake of an important editorial event—the translation of Hume's *History of England* in 1761 and a new edition of Hume's economic writings in 1767. The type-setting and page-setting are identical in all three editions; moreover, the last two editions amounted to a very small number of copies marketed (Tsuda 1979, 417–18). Carpenter propounded to call this kind of edition a "reissue" because only the title page was reprinted; the rest of the book was simply taken from the remaining stock of the 1754 edition.

The publisher of the German translation of the *Political Discourses* had also been forced to reissue its edition with a different title page in 1766 (Tribe 1988, 134).

49 Schreuder canceled the three works he published in the second volume from Le Blanc's list, namely, *Considerations on the Spanish Finances* (Forbonnais), *Essay on the Interests of Sea Trade* (O'Heguerty) and *The Political Testament of Lord Bolingbroke*. He added to the list the *Noblesse commerçante* by the abbé Coyer, another member of Gournay's circle (Tsuda 1979, 426–27). In addition to these writings, he also published a pirated edition of Cantillon.

50 After Gournay's death in 1759, his circle broke into two camps: One comprised Turgot, Abeille, Morellet and, to a lesser extent, Clicquot de Blervache, and moved toward the physiocrats; the other group challenged the physiocrats, especially in the *Journal d'Agriculture, du Commerce et des Finances*, when they had control over its content (1767–69). The latter group consisted of Dangeul, Forbonnais, Montaudoin de la Touche, Butel-Dumont and, to a lesser extent, Buchet du Pavillon.

51 There were no less than six articles, in total almost 200 pages, dedicated to this new translation in the *Journal d'Agriculture, du Commerce et des Finances*, from February to July 1767. At that time, Forbonnais was acting as one of the editors of the *Journal*, and he contributed to many articles attacking the physiocrats.

52 Some of the Italian translations of these English writings were made through their French translations, for example Cary's *Essay on the State of England*. Since Butel-Dumont, the French translator, claimed that only a small part of his two-volume translation was taken from Cary's original text, one wonders whether the Italian translation testifies to the influence of English thought or that of Gournay's "science of commerce" on Italian political economists.

53 See Genovesi (1769 [1765–67], 2:144–52 and ch. 7).

54 Another interesting point concerning this translation is that, like the French edition of 1767, it reproduced only the "economic" essays of Hume's *Discourses*.

55 It is all the more surprising in that case, since Dandolo's edition was bilingual—English and Italian.

11 Hume's *Political Discourses* and the French Luxury Debate

John Shovlin

> When one considers commerce as a merchant, I am not surprised that luxury should be praised. But why did M. Hume, a Philosopher and a Statesman, fall into this glaring error?
>
> Gabriel Bonnot de Mably, *Principes des négociations* (1757)

When David Hume traveled to France in 1763 to serve in the British Embassy, he was accorded an enthusiastic welcome in the Paris salons. "Those who have not seen the strange effects of modes," he wrote later, "will never imagine the reception I met with at Paris, from men and women of all ranks and stations" (Hume 1985, xxxix). Hume's reputation in France owed much to the success of his essays, particularly the *Political Discourses*, published in 1752. As Loïc Charles demonstrates in his contribution to this volume, during the 15 years after their initial publication in English, three different French translations of the *Political Discourses* were produced, the most influential published in 1754 by the abbé Jean-Bernard Le Blanc, author of the celebrated *Lettres d'un Français sur les Anglois* (1745). Le Blanc's *Discours politiques de Monsieur Hume* aroused a lively interest in the French reading public. The *Affiches de province*, an advertising sheet sold in provincial cities, likened public enthusiasm for the new work to the reception of "the latest novel," remarking that the *Political Discourses* was being "snapped up as fast as the most agreeably frivolous book" (Labrosse 1988). The *Année littéraire*, one of the leading literary reviews of the day, stated that, in translating the *Political Discourses*, Le Blanc had rendered a service to his country (Balcou 1975, 122).

A theme of the *Political Discourses* that was particularly significant for French readers, I will argue, was Hume's treatment of luxury. The second essay in the book, "Of Luxury" (a title changed to "Of Refinement in the Arts" in editions published from 1760), made a critical contribution to the eighteenth-century luxury debate. A spirited controversy about the benefits and drawbacks of luxury had agitated the French Republic of Letters since the Regency. At the simplest level, the disagreement was about whether spectacular consumption by the rich, and the middling and poorer sort's growing taste for fashionable clothing, colonial commodities, and other consumer goods, had positive or negative economic consequences.

Apologists for luxury argued that expenditure on frivolities by the rich created employment for the poor and stimulated their industry. Critics charged that such luxury drew labor away from more productive activities, or engendered a negative balance of trade by drawing expensive foreign imports into the country. But to assume that the debate was simply about the economic effects of consumption would be incorrect; the storm over luxury functioned to articulate deeper issues of social, moral, and political order.

One intimation of the luxury debate's complexity lies in the unending efforts to define the concept, none of them successful. At midcentury, Denis Diderot singled out *luxe* as emblematic of those terms whose uncertain meaning led to interminable and pointless intellectual wrangling (Diderot and d'Alembert 1751). *Luxury* could not be defined because it was one of that class of words whose meaning and power inheres in their capacity to evoke a wide range of ideas or feelings not contained in any formal definition. In contemporary terms, one thinks of words such as *science*, *nature*, *art*, or *racism* that have powerful legitimating or censuring functions but whose precise meaning will always be a matter of dispute. Indeed, arguments concerning the meaning of such terms are necessarily confrontations between worldviews rather than merely semantic deliberations (Skinner 1988). In an important sense, the luxury debate was generated by a philosophic effort to neutralize the powerful sense of disapproval conveyed by the term *luxury*. The *philosophes* were intensely aware that ordinary language was not a neutral medium for the communication of information but that, through the associative process analyzed by Locke, words became freighted with multiple deposits of meaning. The *philosophes* pursued a politics of language intended to redefine the word *luxury* and thereby sap its power.

The Enlightenment effort to redefine luxury was simultaneously an attack on the negative view of the passions that undergirded Christian asceticism, an assault on prejudices holding that aristocrats were superior to people of the middle rank, and a strike against the civic humanist view that economic modernity heralded a process of political, cultural, and moral degeneration. In Christian theology, Saint Augustine used the term *luxury* to signal the comprehensive sin of worldliness, while Thomas Aquinas emphasized that the luxurious man is unable to contain his passions, and is blinded by insatiable desires (Sekora 1977, 41–46). Such views continued to enjoy authority in early modern Europe, and were championed particularly by moralists in the Augustinian tradition such as Pascal, Pierre Nicole, and the duc de La Rochefoucauld. To redefine *luxury* as morally worthy or, at worst, morally neutral was to strike a blow against this gloomy morality so inimical to the Enlightenment view of the passions. The concept of luxury had also traditionally functioned to support an aristocratic vision of the social order that denounced upward social mobility conferred by money and sustained noble prejudices against merchants. The seventeenth-century antiluxury discourse, as Renato Galliani has noted, was the expression of a "noble ideology" aimed at reversing the process whereby a class of parvenus had come to compete with the ancient nobility for office and honor (Galliani 1989). The Enlightenment effort to redefine luxury was an attack on such "Gothic" attitudes. However, by the time Hume wrote, the most important question at issue in the debate on luxury was the political, cultural, and moral status of commercial modernity. What was at stake was whether the growth of modern wealth ought to be seen as a positive and progressive development or, as civic humanists held, the source of a process of moral, cultural, and political decline. The example of the ancient Roman Republic, which, according to Roman moralists, had been corrupted and ultimately destroyed by luxury, loomed large in the thinking of the critics of luxury (Berry 1994). They argued that luxury enervated and feminized men, sapping their capacity for military virtue; they claimed that luxury was a tool of potential despots who used it to weaken the commitment of their subjects to liberty and the public welfare; and they claimed that it made both rulers and their subjects corrupt and self-serving.

French writers immediately recognized Hume's apology for luxury as the single most powerful and compelling argument made to date in favor of *le luxe*. Apologists and critics alike singled out his views for applause or reproach. However, as I will demonstrate in this essay, Hume's views on luxury failed, in the final analysis, to settle the luxury debate in France. In fact, the criticisms the *Political Discourses* generated helped to catalyze a shift in the thinking of French Enlightenment writers toward a less complacent view of luxury. Ultimately, I suggest, the reason why Hume failed to persuade the French—even those committed to the philosophic defense of civilization and commercial modernity—was that the word had important additional resonances in the French context that Hume's analysis failed to capture. A representation of luxury that equated it with commercialization could not be adequate in France, where the system of taxation and public finance had long been regarded as a central source of luxury, and where the financiers and courtiers who benefited from this system were the prototypically luxurious classes. As concern grew in France during the 1750s and 1760s about the baneful effects of fiscalism on national prosperity and power, French critics found the word *luxury* too useful a stick with which to beat the financiers and their courtly allies to allow it to be transformed into a synonym for commerce, manufactures, and refinement in the arts.

1. Hume and the Enlightenment Apology for Luxury

Hume's essay in the *Political Discourses* was the culmination of a substantial eighteenth-century literature articulating a defense of luxury. The utilitarian argument in favor of luxury was expressed most trenchantly by Bernard Mandeville in his *Fable of the Bees*, published in 1714. Mandeville argued that a prospering powerful society depended on the selfishness, vanity, and self-indulgence of its citizens. If the people of a great state were suddenly to give up luxury, he suggested, the economy would disintegrate, population would collapse, and the state would be rendered vulnerable to foreign invasion (Mandeville 1988). In his *Persian Letters*, published in 1721, Charles-Louis Montesquieu had one of his characters—the Persian aristocrat Usbek—articulate a similar apology for luxury, disputing the received wisdom of antiquity that luxury saps the virtue of nations and renders them prey to conquest by simpler, less decadent peoples. A state that chose to abandon the arts and commerce, Usbek warns, would enfeeble itself: the revenues of individuals would dry up, and with them the revenues of the prince; social bonds based on exchange would languish, and population would collapse (Montesquieu 1993, 193–96). Perhaps the most important French contribution to the defense of luxury was that of Montesquieu's friend, the political economist Jean-François Melon. In his *Essai politique sur le commerce* (1734), Melon suggested that, if luxury harmed individuals, it nevertheless afforded wealth and security to states and was a spur to industry because it provided incentives for work (1734, 133–34). Melon's defense of luxury inspired Voltaire to launch his own apology for *le luxe* in two witty, polemical poems, "Le Mondain" (1736) and "Défense du Mondain, ou L'Apologie du Luxe" (1737). In these works, Voltaire represented consumption, refinement, and pleasure as allies of the arts and taste, and eulogized the "polish" of the worldly man. He vaunted civilization and refinement in place of asceticism and stoic control of the passions, and he celebrated the rise of new needs and new pleasures brought about by commercial prosperity and international trade (Morize 1970 [1909]).

If the apologists for luxury had enjoyed the upper hand in French intellectual life during the first half of the century, in the latter half of the 1740s the critics began to recover the initiative. In 1745, François-André Boureau-Deslandes published his *Lettre sur le luxe*, which criticized the Enlightenment apology for luxury and especially Melon's *Essai politique sur le commerce*. Two years later, Etienne de La Font de Saint-Yenne published his *Réflexions sur quelques causes de l'état présent de la peinture en France*, suggesting that luxury had caused the degeneration of painting—a position that ran directly counter to the philosophic view that commerce and luxury sustained the arts. In 1750, Jean-Jacques Rousseau caused a sensation with his *Discours sur les sciences et les arts*, which savaged the philosophic defenders of luxury and reiterated in trenchant terms the claim that *luxe* weakened polities by sapping the civic virtue of their citizens: "I know that our philosophy, always fertile in singular maxims, claims against the experience of all ages, that luxury is what underpins the splendor of a state," Rousseau chided, but would it deny "that good manners are essential to the duration of empires, and that luxury is diametrically opposed to good manners"? (Rousseau 1964a [1754], 43).

Though there is no evidence that Hume was aware of the resurgence of French criticisms of luxury, his statements about luxury in the *Political*

Discourses seem custom-made to refute them and, in the French context, were undoubtedly read as such. In "Of Luxury," Hume claims a position of moderation for himself by denouncing both "men of severe morals," who blame luxury for "all the corruptions, disorders, and factions, incident to civil government," and those "men of libertine principles"—namely, Mandeville—who "bestow praises even on vicious luxury, and represent it as highly advantageous to society" (1985t [1752b], 269). Hume's principal interest, however, was to criticize the severe moralists. He met these critics on their own terrain, claiming that luxury actually fosters a range of critical social virtues. He maintained that ages of luxury are also the most virtuous epochs, an argument that rests on his view that refinement in the mechanical and liberal arts stimulates sociability, and that sociability enlivens the sentiment of humanity. "Thus," he observes:

> *industry, knowledge,* and *humanity,* are linked together by an indissoluble chain, and are found, from experience as well as reason, to be peculiar to the more polished, and what are commonly denominated, the more luxurious ages.
>
> (Hume 1985t [1752b], 271)

Having established that luxury, far from undermining virtue, actually contributes to fostering it, Hume moves on to counter the charge that luxury undermines the power and stability of states. He affirms that industry, enlightenment, and humanity, which he celebrates, are not advantageous in private life only, but "diffuse their beneficial influence on the *public*, and render the government as great and flourishing as they make individuals happy and prosperous" (Hume 1985t [1752b], 272). Hume argues that modern kingdoms have grown prodigiously in power as a result of advancements in the arts and sciences. When Charles VIII of France invaded Italy, he notes, the 20,000 men he took with him nearly exhausted the resources of the nation, yet his descendant, Louis XIV, was able to maintain 400,000 men in arms over a period of 30 years (ibid., 273).

The chief conceptual innovation in Hume's political economic argument in favor of luxury is his claim that the artisans who are engaged in manufactures form "a *storehouse* of labour, which, in the exigencies of state, may be turned to the public service" (Hume 1985t [1752b], 272). Here he adverts to an argument he made at length in "Of Commerce," the essay preceding "Of Luxury" in the *Political Discourses,* and his only other substantive consideration of the benefits of luxury. In that essay, Hume concedes that ancient Sparta and Rome were incomparably more powerful than any modern societies of similar size, and argues moreover that their military prowess stemmed from their eschewal of commerce and manufactures (1985s [1752a], 257). He suggests, however, that for a modern state to follow the same policy would be foolhardy: "Though the want of trade and manufactures, among a free and very martial people, may *sometimes* have no other effect than to render the public more powerful," he states, "it is certain, that, in the common course of human affairs, it will have a quite contrary tendency" (ibid., 260). In most countries where agriculture alone is practiced, he argues, farmers easily win a subsistence for themselves and have no incentive to create a surplus (ibid., 260–61). When in time of war some of them are called for military service, the remainder "cannot encrease their skill and industry on a sudden" and their armies may have to "disband for want of subsistence" (ibid., 261). On the other hand, artisans employed in manufactures, who produce goods to exchange against an agricultural surplus, can be mobilized without any serious injury to the national economy.

Hume counters the charge that luxury sows venality and corruption, saps military virtues, and heralds the onset of tyranny. The art of government improves in ages of luxury and refinement, he argues: knowledge expands, superstitions are abandoned, and rulers act with more mildness and moderation. As a consequence, he holds, "factions are then less inveterate, revolutions less tragical, authority less severe, and seditions less frequent" (Hume 1985t [1752b], 274). Civilization does not lead to a loss of martial spirit, he argues, because honor takes the place of ferocity in the personality of the soldier. The bravery of the English and the French, he remarks, is as "uncontestable as their love of the arts, and their assiduity in commerce" (ibid., 275). He offers an alternative explanation of the decline and fall of Rome. What the ancients ascribed to the effects of luxury, Hume suggests, was really the fault of an "ill-modeled government, and the unlimited extent of conquests" (ibid., 276). "Luxury and refinement on the pleasures and conveniences of life has no natural tendency to beget venality and corruption," he affirms (ibid., 276, 631). The only factor that can be expected to restrain the love of money that abounds in all ages and all classes of people, Hume argues, is "a sense of honour and virtue," which, he claims, "will naturally abound most in ages of knowledge and refinement" (276). The progress of the arts in England, he notes, was accompanied by the expansion of liberty. Before the development of commerce and the arts, society was divided into two classes: lords and peasants. The former tyrannized the latter and feuded among themselves, creating a destructive political chaos. But the development of commerce and the arts enriched the peasantry and shifted the balance of power toward the middling ranks, "the best and firmest base of public liberty" (ibid., 277).

Hume sharply criticizes the author of the *Fable of the Bees*, while appropriating and integrating the most compelling features of his argument. In the final paragraphs of the essay, Hume considers what he calls "vicious luxury," that is, sensual indulgences that prevent a man from carrying out duties such as the education of his children, the support of his friends, and the relief of the poor. But if he allows that such extravagances can be vicious, he implies that this is a problem affecting the individual and his family rather that society or the polity. Hume also attacks Mandeville's

utilitarian claim that all consumption is morally equivalent because it stimulates circulation, industry, and employment. Though like Mandeville, he
discerns some benefit even in vicious luxury. Vicious luxury is a poison, he
says, but as "one poison may be an antidote to another," vicious luxury may
be a remedy for worse ills such as laziness and indolence (1985t [1752b],
279). He suggests that in *philosophical* terms Mandeville is wrong; one can
imagine a utopian society in which all vices have disappeared and people
are better off than in the quotidian world of the present. However, as a
political question, it is quite otherwise. The magistrate "aims only at possibilities" and

> very often he can only cure one vice by another; and in that case, he
> ought to prefer what is least pernicious to society. Luxury, when exces-
> sive, is the source of many ills; but is in general preferable to sloth and
> idleness.
>
> (Hume 1985t [1752b], 280)

Hume's divorcing of the apology for luxury from a Mandevillian position
was significant in two ways. In the middle decades of the eighteenth century,
Mandeville's extreme position was more a liability than a strength for
French defenders of luxury. His radical utilitarianism did not resonate with
the central tenets of French Enlightenment moralism (Hulliung 1994, 19). It
was associated with a deeply pessimistic, Jansenist moral framework that
was out of step with the moral optimism of the Enlightenment at mid-
century. Moreover, in one crucial respect, Hume's apology for luxury was
more comprehensive and radical than Mandeville's. The luxury of which
Mandeville approved was principally a luxury of the rich. He was much
more ambivalent about the possibility that luxury might function to stimulate the industry of working people. In remarks appended to editions of the
Fable of the Bees from 1714, he identified a strong leisure preference among
the lower orders and argued that the only means to sustain the diligence of
artisans was to keep them poor.

> Every Body knows that there is a vast number of Journey-men Weavers,
> Tailors, Clothworkers, and twenty other Handicrafts; who, if by four
> Days Labour in a Week they can maintain themselves, will hardly be
> persuaded to work the fifth. ... When Men shew such an extraordinary
> proclivity to Idleness and Pleasure, what reason have we to think that
> they would ever work, unless they were oblig'd to it by immediate
> Necessity?
>
> (Mandeville 1988, 1:192)

Hume's view was very different. As E. J. Hundert has pointed out, Hume
argued that the industry of the poor, just as much as any other class, could
be animated by the prospect of comforts and luxuries (Hundert 1974, 343).

2. The French Reception of Hume's Apology for Luxury

French writers recognized in Hume's *Political Discourses* the most coherent and powerful defense yet elaborated for *le luxe*. Indeed, almost from its first appearance, Hume's essay became a central point of reference for the French debate on luxury. Apologists for luxury drew on the Scot for support, and the most uncompromising critics of luxury singled out his argument for attack. Ultimately, however, Hume's resolution of the antinomy between wealth and virtue satisfied few French commentators. Even those, like the writers close to the intendant of commerce, J.-C.-M. Vincent de Gournay, who were attracted to Hume's claim that commerce fostered certain virtues, were unwilling to concede that vicious luxury was a purely private and individual problem. They continued to use *luxury* as a term of censure for the wealth associated with courtiers and financiers. Other critics of Hume, including the abbé de Mably and the marquis de Mirabeau, were skeptical about Hume's claim that commercial wealth was the foundation of the power of modern states. Decrying the "luxury" that Hume defended, they advocated a development strategy based on agriculture. I will suggest that some of Mably and Mirabeau's hostility to luxury also turned on an association between *le luxe* and financier interests.

What were these interests, and why did they loom so large in the thinking of French political economists in the second half of the eighteenth century? The provision of financial services to the state was one of the largest and most sophisticated businesses in eighteenth-century France, and perhaps the most lucrative. Contractors, known generically as financiers, handled most of the financial business of the royal administration—from collecting taxes, to paying troops, to managing public services—in return for an opportunity to make a profit. Syndicates of tax farmers, entrusted with the collection of indirect taxes, advanced sums of money to the Crown in return for the right to collect a particular tax over a specified period. Any difference between the amount of taxation collected and the monies advanced to the Crown constituted the tax farmers' profit, and those profits could be enormous (Matthews 1958, 263–66). The collection of direct taxes—the *taille*, the *vingtième*, and the *capitation*—was entrusted to the receivers general who, though technically royal officials, functioned no less as private entrepreneurs than the tax farmers did. As J. F. Bosher has noted, the office of a receiver was "a business investment to be exploited for maximum profit at the expense of the Crown and the general public. No cynicism and no exaggeration are necessary to draw the conclusion that in practice a royal accountant was engaged in a private enterprise" (Bosher 1970, 11). Finally, the Crown also depended on treasurers general, *traitans*, and *partisans* who undertook to advance money to supply the army and navy, purchase and transport public grain supplies, manage the postal service, or any number of other public services. This private enterprise in public finance, as Bosher characterizes it, was big business in the old regime, and the top stratum of financiers were among the richest men in the kingdom.

Financiers had played an important role in French politics and social life since the seventeenth century (Dessert 1984). But their power and social prominence grew in the eighteenth as the upper tiers of finance increasingly merged with the court nobility to form a plutocratic hybrid class. Marriages between the sons and daughters of financiers and those of court nobles became increasingly common in the eighteenth century. By midcentury, according to Guy Chaussinand-Nogaret, "There were hardly any great noble families who had not felt the attraction of financiers: integration between the two worlds was total, and irreversible" (Chaussinand-Nogaret 1985, 124). Links with the court nobility gave financiers and their relations broad access to office and honors. Many of the officials who served as controllers general in the 1750s—effectively royal ministers of finance— came from the financial milieu. Nothing symbolized the rise of financiers to positions of authority and eminence so powerfully as the accession of Madame de Pompadour to the position of royal mistress in 1745. As Louis XV's closest confidante for 20 years, the political influence of Madame de Pompadour was enormous. The new favorite could not have been more thoroughly a creature of *la finance*. Her family members were clients of the Pâris brothers, the most influential financier clan of the day; with their *protégée* installed as royal mistress, Pâris influence and prestige reached its apogee.

In addition to marriage ties, the court nobility and financiers were increasingly linked by shared investments. Court nobles benefited directly from the profits of tax farming through their ownership of *croupes*—shares in the investment capital of tax farmers that entitled them to a portion of the profits (Matthews 1958, 235; Chaussinand-Nogaret 1972, 49). Court influence, in turn, was indispensable in order to secure a place as a tax farmer (Durand 1971, 61). Financier-aristocratic joint ventures played an important role in the mercantile world. The shares of large-scale, privileged trading companies were owned almost exclusively by financiers and court nobles (Chaussinand-Nogaret 1972, 69). When it was first established, the capital of the Indies Company was raised primarily from members of the royal family, courtiers, and financiers, and, in the 1760s, the company was still dominated by court and financier capital. According to Guy Chaussinand-Nogaret, the period between 1748 and 1756 was the golden age of this "court capitalism." Taking advantage of the peace that followed the Treaty of Aix-la-Chapelle (1748), he argues, several major joint-stock companies were founded by financiers and court nobles to pursue opportunities for profit in international commerce. Similar patterns of investment prevailed in the privileged large-scale manufacturing sector.

Antipathy to financiers and their courtly allies animated the circle of young political economists who were linked to the reforming intendant of commerce, Vincent de Gournay, and his administrative allies; and it powerfully influenced their attitude toward luxury. Members of Gournay's circle generally took a positive view of luxury, and drew on parts of Hume's argument to establish the benefits of *le luxe*. They argued that well-distributed, general prosperity and high consumption of both basic goods and luxuries were the conditions of a flourishing economy and hence of a powerful state. In his *Considérations sur les finances d'Espagne*, François Véron de Forbonnais observes that a state "is not rich through the great fortunes of a few subjects, but when everyone ... is able to spend above real needs. It is in this sense that luxury is really useful in an Empire" (Forbonnais 1753b, 171–72). In his *Elémens du commerce*, Forbonnais comes close to identifying luxury with commerce and consumption, defining it as "the use made by men of the faculty of existing agreeably through the work of others" (Forbonnais 1754a, 2.291). Luxury, he suggests, generates a useful competition among men to be esteemed by others, a competition that drives them to work harder, making the state stronger and more prosperous. Forbonnais identifies in Hume's arguments a useful corrective to the moralized vision of the opponents of luxury. Citing the *Political Discourses* for support, Forbonnais claims that luxury "humanizes mankind, polishes their manners, softens their humors, spurs their imagination, perfects their understanding" (ibid., 299–300).

However, while the dominant thrust of Forbonnais's argument is that luxury is beneficial, he insists that the circumstances that bring luxury into being may more than counterbalance its advantages. If the source of luxury is not commerce—that is, implicitly, if it has its origins in the court of fiscalism—then its effects will be transitory, and will be experienced only by a few people. It will be confined to a small number of cities, or to just one; useless occupations will multiply while the most useful portion of society will languish; debauchery will be encouraged and depopulation worsened (Forbonnais 1754a, 2:302–4). The defenders of luxury are defending a paradox, Forbonnais argues, if they do not think such excesses are capable of sapping the vitality of a political body. "If luxury is not general," he insists, "if it is not the fruit of national affluence, one will see arise at the same time as it disorders capable of destroying the political body" (ibid., 2:308). These warnings were echoed by another member of Gournay's circle, Forbonnais's cousin, Louis-Joseph Plumard de Dangeul. "Well ordered luxury consumes," Dangeul argues, while "excessive luxury abuses and destroys." Great fortunes that do not arise from commercial or agricultural activity, Dangeul remarks, arise at their expense. Moreover, he argues, when wealth is very unevenly distributed, consumption is disrupted; 20 households with an income of 1,000 livres act as a far greater stimulus to production than one household disposing of 20,000. The baneful effects of such luxury are exacerbated, he argues, if the great fortunes are all concentrated in one place—as he says they are, in Versailles and Paris (Plumard de Dangeul 1754, 60–65).

If Dangeul and Forbonnais embraced a version of Hume's apology for commercial society, nuanced by criticisms of the malign luxury of plutocratic elites, Mably was much more pointedly critical of the Scotsman. "When one considers commerce as a merchant," he wrote in his *Principes des négociations*, "I am not surprised that luxury should be praised. But why did M. Hume, a Philosopher and a Statesman, fall into this glaring error?" (Mably 1757, 238). If the principal object of government in favoring commerce is to increase the strength of a nation, Mably argues, its efforts are misplaced; the money commerce brings into a state causes more harm than good because of its destructive effect on manners. It is agriculture rather than commerce, Mably argues, that deserves the attention of the legislator: "It is the commerce of cultivators which merits the principal attention of statesmen. If their industry is not encouraged, one may have several cities rendered flourishing by their manufactures, but the whole body of the nation will always be badly constituted. The majority of citizens will just get by, living in poverty" (ibid., 236–37).

Separating luxury conceptually from commerce, Mably denies that luxury is beneficial even to trade. He argues that "luxury, far from being favorable to commerce, is, on the contrary, a symptom of its imminent decadence" (Mably 1757, 239). He cites Richard Cantillon's *Essai sur la nature du commerce en général* (1755) as a "complete proof" of this thesis (ibid., 239n). Mably argues that luxury causes labor to become more expensive, thus raising the price of a country's merchandise, causing it to be undersold by poorer, cheaper competitors. "Since luxury destroys the commerce of which it is the fruit," he maintains, "instead of seeking whatever means one can to encourage it, would it not be better to examine whether it is possible to retard its progress?" (ibid., 239).

Mably's views on luxury are best seen as a component of a larger attack on Colbertist strategies of economic development, which, he implies, are geared toward increasing the fiscal revenues of the monarch rather than the prosperity of the people, and are, even in the former respect, ineffective. In a veiled remark on the relationship between commerce and fiscalism, Mably writes:

> I suspect that commerce ought not to be considered separate from finances, nor finances from commerce. Those wheels of the machine, ever united, ought to mesh with one another in order to produce only a single movement; and unfortunately, our books of commerce and of finance always have a different object; the former show only the means to make money enter the state, and the latter how to enrich the prince, or rather how to procure for him all the sums he demands.
>
> (Mably 1757, 237–38)

Does Mably here imply that a treatment of commerce separate from the fiscal purposes to which commercial development is harnessed must be misleading? If so, he is criticizing Hume for considering the effects of commercial development in the abstract, rather than in the context of actually existing political economic structures such as fiscalism and Colbertism. Mably saw commercial development in France as ineluctably tied to an economy of privilege. He opens the chapter with an attack on the practice of giving privileges to merchants who engage in international trade. Such privileges are always abused he claims, and give rise to monopolies. Manufactures are also inseparable from the apparatus of Colbertism that protects and sustains them. "A manufacture has only to invent new superfluities ... for the minister who protects it to be praised as a great man," Mably remarks acidly, when "perhaps he has merely opened a new wound in the state" (1757, 241).

I noted above that Mably thought Cantillon's *Essai sur la nature du commerce en général* provided powerful support for the view that luxury was pernicious. Cantillon seems to have been read in similar fashion by France's most important critic of luxury in the 1750s, the marquis de Mirabeau. Both Mirabeau and Mably appear to have seen in Cantillon a vindication of the classical political insight that all states degenerate due to luxury and are eventually surpassed by poorer neighbors (Wright 1997, 61). Whether this was Cantillon's own view is by no means clear; in general he seems to have used the word *luxury* in a narrow sense to refer to the acquisition of expensive commodities, regarding such consumption as disadvantageous to the extent that the luxury purchases are imports. But Mably and Mirabeau read Cantillon's argument about the long-term effects of an increase in the money supply as an argument about the way luxury will eventually weaken a state's ability to compete internationally. Cantillon argues that a sustained favorable balance of trade, by bringing money into a country, increases prosperity and enhances the capacity of a state to wage war. In the very long run, however, an increasing money supply will cause domestic prices and wages to rise, undercutting the competitiveness of the affected country in the international marketplace. Cantillon identifies several factors that slow this process, but eventually, in his view, a rich manufacturing nation can expect to be undersold by neighboring lands where money shortages will limit both wages and prices. At a certain point, the favorable flow of specie will reverse and the nation previously rich and powerful will become relatively less so until prices and wages rise among its competitors. This is hardly an argument about the degenerative effects of luxury on state power. However, Cantillon confuses matters by claiming that the Roman Empire was destroyed as a consequence of the specie-flow mechanism he analyzes. Through their success in arms, the Romans greatly increased the amount of specie in circulation, giving rise to luxury. Eventually, however, the rising price of Roman goods engendered a reverse in the flow of money and the Romans lost their specie, and along with it their power. Thus, according to Cantillon, "the Roman Empire fell into decline through the loss of its money before losing any of its estates. Behold what Luxury brought about and what it always will bring about in similar circumstances" (Cantillon 1964, 199). It is not entirely surprising that Mably and Mirabeau might have drawn civic humanist inferences from such statements.

Cantillon's *Essai* was a touchstone for Mirabeau in writing his *L'Ami des hommes, ou Traité de la population* (1756). The first draft of *L'Ami des hommes*, which is preserved among Mirabeau's papers, offers a paragraph-by-paragraph commentary on Cantillon's work (Weulersse 1968, 3). But Mirabeau's is a very different kind of work than Cantillon's. It can usefully be regarded as an effort by a moralist in the civic humanist tradition to appropriate elements of political economy to bolster a thesis about the destructive effects of luxury. *L'Ami des hommes* has three central and closely intertwined themes: that patriotic virtue is necessary to sustain the health of a polity; that agriculture is the true foundation of national wealth and power; and that luxury undermines the power and well-being of states. "I am going to finally prove," Mirabeau states in the foreword, "that luxury is ... the ruin of a large state even more so than of a small one" (1756, 1:iv). To sustain his thesis on luxury, Mirabeau thought it necessary to rebut Hume's argument; he described the Scot as "one of the cleverest men ... who has written on political subjects" (ibid., 2:125), and he devoted half of a lengthy chapter to refuting the argument on luxury articulated in the *Political Discourses*.

Mirabeau did not disagree with the substance of Hume's thesis on the benefits of commerce and refinement in the arts. Rather, he contested Hume's equation of such beneficent agencies with luxury. Mirabeau charged that what Hume analyzed was not *luxury* at all:

> from one end of his treatise to the other he confounds luxury with politeness, industry, and the arts. I remain in accord with him concerning all the good effects which he attributes to these; but in the sense I mean, this is not luxury at all.
>
> (Mirabeau 1756, 2:124)

For Mirabeau, a central aspect of luxury is consumption that disturbs the proper hierarchical arrangement of society. In his view, goods ought to make visible the social order; when they signify only wealth, the social order is threatened: "In their original institution," he observes, "these things were supposed to designate power; but from the point when they designate only wealth, from hence, I argue, luxury reigns" (1756, 2:106). In a military monarchy, he argues, birth and military services ought to constitute the first order of citizens, but, "it is the lowest classes who make pecuniary fortunes," and by the "apotheosis of gold" overthrow the proper order of society (ibid., 2:132). In the context of such luxury, Mirabeau complains, honor, prestige, and esteem are lavished on people according to their wealth, rather than birth or merit. The passion for honor draws men to pursue profit rather than to serve the public. He refers to this "consideration for money" as "an illness more redoubtable for a state than plague or famine" and affirms that it "reigns today without rival" (ibid., 1:97). Like Mably's critique of Hume, Mirabeau's claim seems to be that modern economic forces, *in the context of the French institutional order*, will have problematic effects that Hume's argument elides.

Not only should luxury not be equated with politeness, industry, and the arts, Mirabeau argues, but it actually damages these: "I said that politeness, industry and the arts were not at all [the same thing as] luxury. I say more, and I hold that luxury tends to destroy them entirely" (Mirabeau 1756, 2:125). Politeness "cannot be observed in a society composed of people who are all out of place" (ibid., 2:132), he contends, and, in general, the fine arts are damaged by luxury. When the taste of the nation tends toward trinkets, he suggests, art must necessarily degenerate (ibid., 2:131). According to the marquis, it is not industry that luxury animates so much as a rapacious desire for money, and this desire can actually be damaging to ordinary commerce and agriculture (ibid., 1:119–20). He concedes that luxury may excite the kind of industry that produces trifling things, but this variety of manufacture is evanescent and unstable: "A few years of a war, even if it goes well, deranges and throws into necessity half the artisans of Paris" (ibid., 2:134). Agriculture, in particular, suffers as a consequence of luxury. Mirabeau's central concern is that agriculture, which he regards as the true basis of national prosperity and power, has been sacrificed to the pursuit of a mercantile wealth that is at once illusory and destructive in its social, economic, and moral effects. False ideas of urbanity and politeness have made agriculture seem contemptible. The land is neglected also because there is too much greed for quick and easy wealth.

Mirabeau did not share Hume's confidence that social affections and private virtues would necessarily flourish in the conditions of commercial modernity. For Mirabeau, the fundamental problem facing any social order is to foster sociable impulses in human beings and to restrain their avarice. From sociability, he argues, follows attachment to one's near and dear, to one's friends, to "the public," and finally to "*la patrie*" (Mirabeau 1756, 1:5). Cupidity is the enemy of such social affections and the patriotism they sustain. It is manners, Mirabeau argues, that decide toward which of these tendencies—cupidity or sociability—human beings gravitate. To the extent that manners degenerate, he suggests, "the bonds of society slacken in proportion," and this process enervates and destroys the state (ibid., 2:58). By manners, Mirabeau means private virtues, principally qualities associated with the moral paradigms of sensibility and domesticity. These civil virtues, he suggests, form a kind of foundation for patriotism. For Mirabeau, luxury is the antithesis of sociable impulses. As the fruit of unrestrained interest, it destroys manners; sociability, on the other hand, is disinterested—a selfless disposition to care for others.

Mirabeau's themes resonated with the French reading public. For a brief period in the summer of 1757 the marquis became the most celebrated writer in France. It was rumored at court that the dauphin wanted him appointed preceptor to his son, the future Louis XVI. From Saint-Malo in Brittany, Mirabeau's brother reported that he was basking in the reflected glory of the "friend of mankind" (Loménie 1889, 2:169–70). In the three years following its initial publication, *L'Ami des hommes* appeared in 20 editions, and over the rest of the century seems to have enjoyed 20 more (Carpenter 1975). It appeared in nearly a quarter of the 500 private libraries inventoried by Daniel Mornet, suggesting that it was among the most widely disseminated books of the century (Mornet 1910). Certainly *L'Ami des hommes* did not win its enormous popularity based on its literary merits. The work is long, poorly organized, and written in an eccentric style. Friedrich-Melchior Grimm acknowledged as much when he criticized the quality of Mirabeau's writing but praised his principles, which he described as "the only ones that a wise government ought to follow" (Loménie 1889, 2:140).

3. The Reformulation of the Enlightenment Perspective on Luxury

In the 1760s, Enlightenment commentators began to recast their thinking on luxury. If an earlier generation of *philosophes* had viewed luxury with complacency, many of those writing in the three decades before the Revolution took a much more critical view. One aspect of the Enlightenment apology for luxury—the effort to represent commerce in a beneficent light—had proven a triumph. However, the second dimension—the attempt to change the meaning of the word *luxury* itself, to evacuate it of its negative valence—was less successful. In essence, writers like Mirabeau insisted that it was necessary to preserve the older, negative meaning of the word to capture and condemn those effects of economic modernity that could not be seen as positive. For Mirabeau, these effects included the weakening of social hierarchy, the spread of the mercenary personality, and the orientation of economy and culture away from the necessary and toward the trivial. For others, such as Mably or the writers associated with Vincent de Gournay, it was important to preserve *luxury* as a word of censure in order to denounce the effects of courtly and financier parasitism. This latter perspective, in particular, proved persuasive to *philosophes* in the 1760s. Such writers continued to hold to the view that the effects of commerce are positive, but they had to concede that, in the French context of privilege, monopoly, and fiscalism, economic modernity had also produced distinctly negative effects. They argued that the debility and corruption from which the nation seemed to be suffering was a product of the institutional order, not the fruit of commerce or luxury. If mobile wealth as it had actually developed in Europe was a source of corruption, critics argued, liberated from the monopolies, privileges, and fiscal expedients of the absolutist political order, it would function quite differently. Instead of undermining agriculture, it would foster it; instead of generating dangerous inequalities, it would permit moderate wealth for all and great fortunes for none. A commercial order severed from the institutions of the absolute monarchy would be a foundation for the virtue and patriotism of the nation, not its bane.

One of the most prominent expressions of the new approach was the marquis de Saint-Lambert's essay, "Luxe," published in the *Encyclopédie* in 1765. Saint-Lambert was quite critical of Hume; indeed the first paragraphs of the encyclopedia article constitute an ironic restatement of the opening lines of Hume's essay. Saint-Lambert criticizes both the moralists who have censured luxury with "more gloominess than enlightenment," and those "*politiques*" who have spoken about it "more as merchants or clerks than as philosophers or statesmen." This latter comment was a swipe at Hume, whom Mably had criticized in almost exactly these terms, while Saint-Lambert's formula, contrasting gloomy moralists with tradesman-like *politiques*, parallels the contrast Hume drew at the beginning of his own essay between "men of severe morals," and "men of libertine principles." Just as Hume distanced himself from the extreme position of Mandeville while borrowing some of its substance, so Saint-Lambert implicitly rejects Hume's argument while co-opting parts of it. Saint-Lambert lays out and refutes the positions of both the apologists for luxury and their critics. He denies that luxury always contributes to population, enriches states, facilitates circulation, softens manners, and improves the fine arts. In what seems to be another direct critique of Hume, he notes that the apologists have claimed "that luxury increases both the power of nations and the happiness of citizens." Saint-Lambert rejects this view, giving examples of ancient peoples who became luxurious and were conquered, and arguing that in luxurious modern states the great majority of ordinary people are not happy. However, he insists that the "censors of luxury are also contradicted by the facts" (Saint-Lambert 1765b, 764).

At the core of Saint-Lambert's argument is the claim that luxury is useful under a good government but becomes dangerous as a result of the ignorance or ill will of those in authority. Depopulation should not be attributed to the seductive luxury of cities, he remarks, but rather to fiscal policies that impoverish the inhabitants of the countryside. It is the forces of fiscalism, privilege, and monopoly, not luxury, he argues, that have driven country dwellers into the cities. Indeed, luxury is a partial palliative to these other scourges, softening and delaying their full impact. Nor will Saint-Lambert attribute to luxury the excessive inequality he believes characterizes modern states. Again, he argues, this ill is a consequence of bad government: "The extreme inequality of riches, supposedly due to luxury, finds a sufficient cause in the oppression of the rural population." The effects of such oppression have been amplified by other disastrous policies—the practice of privileging great trading and manufacturing enterprises, and of permitting scandalous profits to financiers:

> There are countries where the government has taken still other measures to intensify inequality of wealth: exclusive privileges have been

distributed or kept in force for the benefit of various manufacturers, of a few citizens who exploit the colonies, and of a few companies which hold the monopoly on a lucrative commerce. In other countries these mistakes have been compounded by rendering excessively lucrative those financial offices that it should have been an honor to hold.

(Saint-Lambert 1765b, 767)

According to Saint-Lambert, the root cause of these disastrous derange-ments of the political economic order is the system of public finance that has developed since the last decades of the reign of Louis XIV. "In France," he remarks, "luxury has exceeded acceptable limits only since the mis-fortunes of the war of 1700 brought disorder to its finances and caused some abuses" (Saint-Lambert 1765b, 770). Such abuses have created a class of financiers and monopolists, and it is for these that Saint-Lambert reserves his opprobrium. "The fortunes of the holders of a monopoly, of the administrators and collectors of public funds are the most despicable," he states, and "these men have been unjustly preferred to the majority of their fellow citizens whom they have prevented from making money." The other kind of wealth Saint-Lambert regards as pernicious are the *rentes* enjoyed by the creditors of the state. "In several countries of Europe there exists a type of property that demands from the owner neither investments nor upkeep," he observes. "I am speaking of the national debt," he continues, "and this type of property too is very liable, in the large cities, to add to the excesses that are the necessary effect of an extreme opulence combined with idleness" (ibid., 768).

Saint-Lambert's essay marks a critical moment in the history of the luxury debate because it captures the process whereby philosophic defen-ders of economic modernity came to terms with the fact that the poli-tical economy of modern France was not productive of power, prosperity, or virtue. Saint-Lambert's essay is ostensibly a defense of luxury. Defin-ing *luxe* as "the use that is made of wealth and industry to procure an agreeable existence" (Saint-Lambert 1765b, 763), he insists that "the desire to become rich and to enjoy one's riches forms part of human nature … [and] this desire supports, enriches, and gives life to every important society. Thus luxury is good and does no harm in itself" (ibid., 770). However, he breaks sharply with earlier apologists for luxury. He accepts virtually every aspect of Mably and Mirabeau's critique of French society, but denies that luxury is the direct cause of these calamities. Flawed institutions, he argues, account for all the derangements of the economic, social, and moral order that the critics of luxury underline. Through much of the essay, Saint-Lambert seems to wish to reserve the word *luxury* for the positive, vivifying effects of commerce and consumption, but in practice he is unable to do so, and slips occasionally into using the word in a negative sense.

220   *John Shovlin*

The complexity of Saint-Lambert's position on luxury was not generally appealing to later writers in the Enlightenment tradition. For example, Diderot—in a dialogue on luxury that he wrote in the late 1760s, with Grimm as the interlocutor—opted for the much simpler position that there are two kinds of luxury, one beneficial and the other destructive. The former is "born of wealth and general affluence," the latter "of ostentation and misery" (Diderot 1995, 78). Diderot's conception of the useful variety of luxury can be described as general, well-distributed prosperity, marked by a large consumption not just of necessaries but of aesthetic objects. Such beneficial luxury, he insists, is based on the generalized prosperity diffused by a thriving agriculture. Destructive luxury, on the contrary, is a consequence of defective government, which fosters venality and financiers. The Grimm character in the dialogue goes on to identify Colbertism, fiscalism, and public credit as the progenitors of a destructive luxury. Such luxury, he says, is the work of

> He who first advocated the superiority of industry, and its right to flourish on the ruins of agriculture. ... he who, after having degraded agriculture, encumbered free exchange with all kinds of fetters. ... he who created the first of the great extortionists and their numberless clan. ... he who facilitated the taking of ruinous loans by foolish, spendthrift sovereigns.
>
> (Diderot 1995, 76)

A similarly dualistic conception of luxury was offered by Alexandre Deleyre in his *Tableau de l'Europe* (1774). For Deleyre, the luxury generated by commerce and manufactures is unambiguously a social good. The taste for luxury and comforts, creates an appetite for work, which constitutes the principal strength of European states. However, he concedes there is also a destructive variety of luxury, connected with the activities of aristocrats and financiers. The economically active members of society are not the ones corrupted by commercial wealth; rather, it is the idle classes who are tainted by it. When a nation grows rich, Deleyre argues, those who hold the reins of power engross much of the benefits, giving themselves over to "luxury," "intrigue," and the "baseness that is called grandeur" (Deleyre 1774, 80). He criticizes the effects of public borrowing, arguing that it causes the fruits of industry to pass from those who work into the hands of the idle. Love of gain does not have to supplant virtue under a good government, he argues. However, under a government organized around the interests of one, or the few, it will always happen, as it will under arbitrary authority (Deleyre 1774, 156–57).

Hume himself may have shared in the rethinking that occurred around the category *luxury* during and immediately after the Seven Years War. One of the principal thrusts of the French critique of his argument was that, in identifying luxury with commerce, manufactures, and refinement in the arts, his theory did not adequately consider the baneful economic, moral, and political influence of plutocratic elites. Some of the remarks on luxury Hume made in other essays in the *Political Discourses* suggest that he was himself quite negatively disposed toward luxury when it was attached to aristocrats and profiteers in public finance. In "Of Public Credit," he adverts to the "stupid and pampered luxury, without spirit, ambition, or enjoyment" into which stockholders in the public debt can be expected eventually to fall (Hume 1985aa [1752h], 357–58). In "Of the Populousness of Ancient Nations," he refers to "the seats of vast monarchies" as places of "extravagant luxury, irregular expence, idleness, dependence, and false ideas of rank and superiority" (Hume 1985bb [1752i], 448).

Hume recognized the problem posed by financiers in the French context, but seems to have regarded it as less intractable than did his peers across the Channel. All that would be necessary to solve the problem, he argued in "Of Civil Liberty," was a far-sighted minister with the interests of the kingdom at heart. "The greatest abuses, which arise in FRANCE," he argued,

> proceed not from the number or weight of the taxes, beyond what are to be met with in free countries; but from the expensive, unequal, arbitrary, and intricate method of levying them, by which the industry of the poor, especially of the peasants and farmers, is, in a great measure, discouraged, and agriculture rendered a beggarly and slavish employment. ... The only gainers by it are the *Financiers*, a race of men rather odious to the nobility and the whole kingdom. If a prince or minister, therefore, should arise, endowed with sufficient discernment to know his own and the public interest, and with sufficient force of mind to break through ancient customs, we might expect to see these abuses remedied.
>
> (Hume 1985i [1741i], 95)

Hume was wrong, as the failure of Turgot's ill-fated ministry in 1776 would show. The odium of the financiers did not prevent them from building intimate and powerful alliances with the court aristocracy, and courtly allies could be depended on to unseat a dangerous minister. It was obvious to many in France as early as 1759 that no reforming minister was likely to be able to solve the problem of parasitic financiers and courtiers. In that year, the controller general, Etienne de Silhouette, who had attempted to retrench the profits of the farmers general, was unceremoniously driven from office after only six months (Marion 1914–27, 1:191–97).

It is possible that the French reaction to the *Political Discourses* persuaded Hume that it might be useful to retain the term *luxury* to criticize the harmful influence of parasitic aristocrats and financiers. After all, Hume changed the title of his essay on luxury to "Of Refinement in the Arts" for the 1760 and subsequent editions. He made another revision in a similar vein for the 1760 edition, changing the sentence "Luxury and refinement on the pleasures and conveniences of life has no natural tendency to beget venality and corruption" to "Refinement on the pleasures and conveniences of life has no natural tendency to beget venality and corruption" (Hume 1985t [1752b], 276). What does the excision of the word *luxury* from this sentence and from the title of the essay signify? Was Hume himself retreating from a full-blown defense of luxury? Had he come to the conclusion that luxury *did* have "a natural tendency to beget venality and corruption"? There is no evidence in Hume's published correspondence to decide the issue, but it is tempting to view the revisions as evidence that Hume modified his original position on luxury in response to the reception his argument on luxury met with in France.

12 Constitution and Economy in David Hume's Enlightenment

Paul Cheney

Introduction

In several of his essays and in the *History of England*, David Hume explored the relationship between the patterns of economic activity to be found in states from antiquity to the present, and the constitutions—or regime types, in modern parlance—that characterized them. In this respect, Hume did not differ from any number of eighteenth-century writers, including Adam Ferguson, James Steuart, Voltaire, Jean-Jacques Rousseau, and Charles-Louis Montesquieu, all of whom used constitutional form as an analytical grid for understanding issues of wealth and poverty. Hume's attempts to understand the relationship between constitutional forms and economic prosperity were part of a broader Enlightenment movement that was transforming older historiographical practices. By the eighteenth century, it was hardly original to use the Platonic (later Aristotelian and Polybian) typology of state forms—monarchical, aristocratic, and democratic—in order to trace patterns in the rise and decline of states. What was new, however, was to apply this typology to the task of coming to terms with the revolutionary consequences of the discovery of the New World and the expansion of European commerce that followed from this event. Hume himself argued that by dint of their regularity, impersonality, and sheer number, economic activities now enjoyed a privileged status in all scientific "political" inquiries: European history had become the history of commerce, and the study of this subject paved the way for the development of political economy.[1] From this point of view, Guillaume Raynal's best-selling *Histoire Philosophique et Politique des Etablissements et du Commerce des Européens dans les deux Indes* (1773–74) represents less a decisive shift in eighteenth-century historical writing than a culmination of trends well under way.

Eighteenth-century writers transformed established historiographical practice by integrating the economy into the very heart of a historical method that generally privileged regime type, or the constitution, as a basis for the analysis of the political and economic fortunes of ancient and modern states.[2] For the historian of commerce—a subtype of political economist whose existence goes largely unnoticed in present-day accounts of eighteenth-century political economy—constitutions and commerce existed in a dialectical relationship that was expressed in Montesquieu's dictum: "commerce has a relation with the constitution" (1989, bk. 20, ch. 4).[3] This relationship dictated first of all the relative power of European states within an increasingly competitive world economy. Which sorts of states, in short, were poised to take greatest advantage of the expansion of European commerce in all its forms? More gravely, however, it seemed that the newly privileged place of commerce in European society threatened those states whose constitutions did not seem propitious to commerce.

By the time Hume began writing on these issues in the 1740s, a firm bias had already been established against the monarchies of Europe. "Commercial republics" such as Holland and England dominated European trade, and seemed ready to overturn even the military and political superiority enjoyed by Europe's oldest and most powerful monarchies—Spain and France. Hume cut against the grain of received wisdom by arguing that the differences between monarchies and republics were actually *diminishing* with the rise of commerce; all "polite" European societies were converging around a shared set of legal and social norms: increasingly Europeans lived in orderly, well-regulated "civilized monarchies" whose functioning could not be readily distinguished from supposedly superior republican states. Hume's analysis undercut bitter Whig/Tory oppositions in Georgian England, but also spoke to a common social and political evolution in most European nations.[4]

In revisiting Hume's concept of *civilized monarchy*, situating it within his economic thought, and discussing the largely positive—but nevertheless qualified—reception that his treatment of this issue received in France, this essay has two aims. The first is to provide a non-British context for understanding Hume's economic thought. The second is to situate Hume's economic thought outside a rather canonic understanding of him as an enlightened but unsystematic "pre-Smithian" economist who may or may not have made useful contributions to nineteenth- and twentieth-century economic thought. After analyzing Hume's notion of *civilized monarchy*, this essay will explore the connections between Hume's writings of the 1740s and 1750s and earlier writings in France that analyzed the relationship between national constitutions and economies. This will provide us with a more precise sense of the cosmopolitan intellectual traditions out of which Hume's own thought developed and, finally, provide contextual insights into the way Hume's writings were received and transmitted by his first translator into French, the abbé Jean-Bernard Le Blanc.

Hume and the "Civilized Monarchies" of Europe

France's great gains in foreign trade during the eighteenth century, even after England was thought to have definitively consolidated its advantages in the Treaties of Utrecht (1713–14), forced a rethinking of economic theories that premised a genetic superiority of "republican" polities over their monarchical rivals. Paul Butel speaks of an eighteenth-century "golden age" for France's foreign trade, when rates of growth clearly exceeded those of Great Britain, at least until the malaise of the 1770s. During the period 1716–20 until the Revolution of 1789, France's overseas trade increased from 155 million *livres tournois* (Tournoise pounds) to 1,062 million, while England's grew over the same period from £325 million to £775 million (Butel 1993, 80–81). (This said, the value of overseas trade per capita remained superior in England over the same period.) Even if these figures merely demonstrate that France was catching up to Great Britain, the realities of international trade (American, East Indian, and intra-European) necessitated a revision of the dominant explanations of Anglo-Dutch economic superiority over the sixteenth and seventeenth centuries.

In this spirit, Hume attempted to move beyond a method of analysis that took constitutional form as dispositive of the prospects for commercial success in republics, monarchies, or mixed constitutions. What set Hume apart from his contemporaries was that he told an evolutionary story about how the decline of feudalism and the rise of commercial society rendered constitutional factors progressively less relevant. The majority of French writers, by contrast, feared that what they termed "les progrès du commerce" [the advances of commerce] were amplifying the differences between monarchical and republican governments. According to Hume, the strong claims of the constitution over the development of economic life (and much else) gradually cede, through the progress of commerce, to the more autonomous structures and operations of the market and civil society. This process, in Hume's terminology, is identified with the development of "civilized monarchy," not just in the England of Hume's *History*, but all over Europe. In sketching out this story, Hume adumbrated later and more explicit formulations—such as those of Adam Ferguson and Adam Smith—that placed the notion of civil society at the very center of a process that could be explained by the rise of commerce (Ferguson 1966 [1767], pts. 3 and 4; Smith 1976 [1776], bk. 2, pt. 3).

The "civilization" of modern absolutist governments was a cultural, material, and political process whose elements were "linked together by an indissoluble chain" (Hume 1985t [1752b], 271). While Hume describes in several essays how progress was driven by forces unique to the spheres of commerce, the arts, and government, a dialectic between the private and the public spheres pulled this chain, as a whole, in a progressive direction. Writing in "Of the Rise and Progress of Arts and Sciences" (1985k [1742a]), Hume emphasizes the public sphere's contribution to the private: "from law arises security." Security begets curiosity and curiosity, in turn, begets knowledge (Hume 1985k [1742a], 118–20). The enabling condition of this virtuous circle, law, is the "slow product of order and liberty," which insures the secure enjoyment of property and, hence, the progress of commercial life (ibid., 124). In "Of

Refinement in the Arts," Hume emphasizes, on the other hand, the contribution that private activities make to progress in public life: "[I]ndustry, knowledge, and humanity are not advantages in *private* life alone: they diffuse their beneficial influence on the *public* and render their government as great and flourishing as they make individuals happy and prosperous" (Hume 1985t [1752b], 272, emphasis added). If elsewhere Hume argues that liberty is necessary for material progress, here he emphasizes the other half of the equation: "progress in the arts ... has a natural tendency to preserve, if not produce a free government" (ibid., 277).

Commercial progress creates middling orders that "covet equal laws which may secure their property" (Hume 1985t [1752b], 278). As many eighteenth-century observers had occasion to note, commerce requires separate judicial institutions (for example, bureaus and councils of commerce, and customs houses). Beyond questions of efficiency, commercial classes impress on the minds of ignorant princes and ministers "the advantages attending an equitable administration" that will keep the wheels of commerce turning predictably and cheaply (Hume 1879 [1754–62], 1:543). Hume avoids the question of the political representation for mercantile classes, preferring to stress the protection their reclamations afford against "monarchical, as well as aristocratical tyranny" (1985t [1752b], 278).[5]

The growth of commerce, mercantile classes, and cities were long-term processes taking place in all European nations; the fundamental dynamics were the same everywhere, even if their effects sometimes spread unevenly under monarchical and republican regimes. This is why Hume could pose the question "whether there be any essential difference between one form of government and another" (Hume 1985c [1741c], 14). Although Hume appears to favor republican forms of government, in this essay he notes that provinces conquered by a monarchy generally fare better than those under a republic. Abroad, residents of a conquered province are more likely to enjoy the rule of law if subjected to a monarchy, while the constitution of a republic more consistently prevents "mal-administration" at home. In each case, the standard for measuring the performance of monarchies and republics is the check that their laws provide, in different contexts, against the "humours and tempers of men" (ibid., 16).

For all of these reasons, legal norms were converging between the republics and monarchies of Europe under the civilizing influence of commerce. Hume's historical thesis on the rise of commerce overturned the Manichaean logic that structured partisan debates between Whigs and Tories over the form of England's government at home, and over the nature of England's rivals abroad. Hume wrote: "It may now be affirmed of civilized monarchies, what was formerly said in praise of republics alone, that they are a government of Laws, not of Men." The rise of commerce engendered a set of changes "which in time will bring these species of civil polity still nearer an equality." Indeed, the example of France, a nation that produced "at once philosophers, poets, orators, historians, [and] painters," in addition to a flourishing commercial empire, proved that the subjects of an absolute government can become "[England's] rivals in commerce, as well as in learning" (Hume 1985i [1741i], 91–95).[6]

Hume's *History of England* gave a different reading of the transition from the "military despotism of Rome" cherished by Machiavelli and other republican historians to the gentle, predictable norms of modern commercial society. This discussion at once confirmed the European scope of Hume's *History* and *Political Discourses*, and softened the republican–monarchical dichotomy that structured so many histories of European commerce. Hume's central observation was that feudal government was similar in all European nations and that England's own feudal institutions derived from those of France (Hume 1879, 1:537).[7] These European states—so often at odds with each other—shared a common heritage in the improvisations of the post-Roman world, and Hume evidently relished the irony that "the seeds implanted by those generous barbarians" (ibid., 200) laid the basis for the "independence and legal administration which distinguishes European nations"—a condition Hume elsewhere saw as both the cause and effect of commercial expansion (ibid., 194).

How did this happen? Through the institution of the military fief "the idea of property stole in gradually" and the division of "the kingdom of Europe into baronies, and these into inferior fiefs" led to a pan-European resistance to monarchical power (Hume 1879 [1754–62], 1.526). Given this common heritage, the states of modern Europe, from commercial republics to supposedly "absolute" monarchies, were to be understood as treading a common path toward the "legal administration" that formed the institutional basis for commercial expansion and prosperity. This was true, however much outward differences of constitutional form may have obscured their common origins and destiny. The modern phenomenon of *civilized monarchy* only confirmed the underlying kinship among European nations.

History, Economic Theory, and the Limits to Convergence

Hume's historical theses on the convergence of European nations around a "civilized" set of norms that were propitious to commerce bore a striking similarity to the logic he employed in elaborating the specie-flow mechanism, perhaps his most oft-cited contribution to present-day economic theory. Hume reproduced the logic of his economic argument in his broader historical narrative, which indicates, from the point of view of Hume's economic methods and assumptions, the limits to the historical convergence addressed in the preceding pages.

The specie-flow mechanism was intended to demonstrate, *pace* the mercantilists, that regulating the amount of precious metals within a nation was futile. If four-fifths of England's monies were wiped out overnight, the prices of England's manufactures on the international market would fall accordingly by four-fifths; the logic of competition would send the lost specie flowing back to England as the fruit of competitively priced exports.[8] If, by contrast, a misguided policy prevented specie from being exported to other nations, then this "extra" bullion would only serve, *ceteris paribus*, to ratchet up the prices of England's manufactures, by the logic of the quantity theory of money. English consumers would then prefer cheap imports to expensive domestic commodities, and specie would flow out of England (Hume 1985x [1752e], 311–12). Although Hume admitted the odd case in which restrictive laws or extraordinary distances might prevent the operation of this economic law, he affirmed in general that money, like water, sought its own level: "We need not have recourse to a physical attraction to explain the necessity of this operation. There is a moral attraction, arising from the interests and passions of men, which is full as potent and infallible" (ibid., 313). The "moral attraction" of interests and passions also ensured the equalization of economic development between rich and poor nations, in contrast to the polarization of wealth feared by many. The "cheapness of provisions and labour" ensures that "manufactures, therefore, gradually shift their places, leaving those countries and provinces which they have already enriched, and flying to others" (Hume 1985u [1752c], 283).

For these reasons, Hume believed that commerce and its underlying economic laws constituted a universal and universalizing force. At the same time, the cultural and historical limits to this universal logic demonstrate the irreducibly "institutionalist" aspects of Hume's thought (Skinner 1993, 222–54, esp. 235).[9] For Hume, the operation of economic laws varied widely, depending on the manners, institutions, and climates of different nations. The progress of commerce ensured that some institutional changes affected most commercial nations; for example, the increasing industriousness of Europeans pushed the average rate of interest down by multiplying the lenders of capital. Beyond broad secular changes, however, Hume allowed for persistent and significant differences between nations. Hume argued that given an equal money supply, rates of interest would consistently differ between nations because variables dictated by manners and social structure such as distribution of wealth, patterns of consumption, and investment would finally determine the amount of funds that could actually be lent. In a state dominated by the landed interest or with an excessively unequal distribution of wealth, there would be relatively few lenders, and borrowers would bid up the rate of interest: "The prodigal landlord dissipates it, as fast as he receives it; and the beggarly peasant has no means, nor view, nor ambition of obtaining above a bare livelihood" (Hume 1985v [1752d], 298–99). By contrast, a nation of thrifty merchants (such as England and Holland) enjoyed an excess of lenders over borrowers, and hence a low interest rate. Even as Hume affirmed that the "moral attraction" of interest tended to ensure that the quantity of money found its proper level *between* nations, he ultimately concluded that this did not mean that each nation had an *equivalent* amount of money. Rather, the equilibrium, a relative "scarcity of money" between producing and exchanging nations, was determined by the "manners and customs of the people," their respective propensities to productive labor (Hume 1985u [1752c], 290). In the case of the "rich country–poor country debate," Hume argued that while the high price of labor in wealthy nations might favor the flight of certain manufactures to relatively underdeveloped ones—thus equalizing differences between them—rich nations were ultimately in a position to keep the upper hand. Cultural and institutional factors, which Hume termed "great stock and great skill," ensured a permanent advantage over poorer nations, however much the dynamics of international trade prevented complete economic polarization between them (Hont 2005e [1983], 270–2).

Hume's treatment of the relationship between climate and manners demonstrates the same pattern whereby commerce plays a role in erasing national differences, but only up to a point. In "Of National Characters" (1985q [1748a]) Hume denied that climate should have a role in explaining variations in national character and the institutions resulting from it. Adducing the sameness of manners between the varied climates within China's borders, Hume argued that national characters resulted from "moral factors," principally a combination of the form of government and the manners of its elites (ibid., 207). In Europe, commerce accomplished what a unified government could not: "Where several neighboring nations have a very close communication together, either by policy, commerce, or travelling, they acquire a similitude of manners, proportioned to the communication" (ibid., 206). Writing four years later in "Of Commerce," however, Hume invoked the effects of the climatic differences he had previously denigrated in order to explain the failure of the peoples occupying the "torrid zone" to "attain to any art or civility, or reach even any police in their government" (Hume 1985s [1752a], 267).[10] Warm climates did not impose the sort of necessity that made the development of the arts and sciences necessary.[11] A harsh climate, by contrast, had the effect of "sharpening men's wits by care" by forcing them into the production and exchange of the necessities of life; where this compulsion was lacking, in gentler climates, the arts and sciences did not progress and men remained autarkic (ibid., 267).

In each of these cases, we see that for Hume factors such as institutions, manners, and climate limit the ability of commerce to erase differences between nations. To state the issue in this way, however, risks falsifying Hume's thought by implying that in his writings culture or history are accidents that distort the universal and universalizing forms of behavior of *homo oeconomicus*. To the contrary, for Hume "commerce" never has any existence apart from the people that undertake this activity in specific contexts, which is why institutions and customs exert a profound influence on the practice of commerce in different nations; commercial activity has the power to render nations homogeneous only if it is itself the same in every nation. In Hume's history of commerce, the workings of the market are bound and directed by the irreducible differences between societies. The progress of commerce that draws nations into a community of shared arts, interests, and practices (what Hume calls "commerce" in its broadest sense) has very important limits. This is why, for all his insistence on the convergence of the social, intellectual, and political conditions of England with the absolute monarchies of Europe, and in particular that of France, Hume ultimately doubts that the development of civilized monarchy can efface all the differences between absolute monarchies and their mixed or republican analogues.

Like many French observers of state finances in monarchies, Hume concluded that while good administration could remedy a number of the defects inherent in absolutist government, other abuses were inherent in monarchy as a form of government. These included "the expensive, unequal, arbitrary, and intricate method of levying [taxes], by which the industry of the poor, especially of the peasants and farmers is ... discouraged." The form of France's government discouraged industry among the lower orders, and this was the effect of a more general problem: life in a society of orders posed something "hurtful to commerce, inherent in the very nature of absolute government, and inseparable from it." This harm was not, as many were inclined to believe, due to any insecurity of property. Civilized monarchy rendered France "the perfect model of a pure monarchy," and other absolutist governments were also nations of "laws, not of men." Rather, this malaise was a function of underlying attitudes toward commerce, which was bound to decay "not because it is there less *secure*, but because it is less *honorable*." Because "a subordination of ranks is absolutely necessary to the support of a monarchy," monarchical government in itself placed limits on the extent to which commerce, which had the notorious effect of confusing the ranks, could become the sole organizing principle of monarchical societies (Hume 1985i [1741i], 92–95).[12] This genre of observation would be particularly troublesome for Hume's translator, the abbé Le Blanc.

If commerce and the arts could only progress asymptotically in absolutist states toward the perfection they attained in republican polities, this was due to a more fundamental set of defects. Whatever perfection absolutist states attained due to the rise of commerce had its origin in the "force and energy" of free republics. Arts may have been easily transplanted to a "civilized monarchy," but "however perfect, therefore, the monarchical form may appear to some politicians, it owes all its perfection to the republican" (Hume 1985k [1742a], 125). What this meant as a historical thesis was that the rise of commerce, whose effects were communicated throughout Europe, was originally the province of the free cities of Europe. While the story Hume tells about the development of commerce and the rule of law is European in scope, its origin is much more historically and "constitutionally" specific.[13]

Hume's analysis and conclusions presented a mixed prospect for French observers: the thesis of historical convergence was on its face quite encouraging, and corresponded to a certain reality on the ground in early eighteenth-century Europe.[14] On the other hand, France's persistent financial woes and the disappointing performance of its overseas trading companies seemed to confirm the observation that, while the French monarchy could closely follow England's commercial lead, it would remain economically inferior. An examination of some French views of the relationship between the constitution and economy—views that predated the translation of the *Political Discourses*—demonstrates how pervasive this issue was before Hume's intervention. This provides a sense of the wider European context out of which Hume's thought developed, and makes Hume's reception in France more intelligible.

Administration versus Constitution

The French observed with a mixture of admiration and chagrin that the British constitution gave scope and force to the natural industry and intelligence of its inhabitants. Voltaire's panegyric to the English nation in his *Lettres philosophiques* (1733) was paradigmatic of a view that saw mixed government, like overseas trade itself, as a risky but often profitable venture. "Commerce," wrote Voltaire, "which has enriched English citizens, has helped to make them free, and this freedom in its turn has extended commerce, and that has made the greatness of the nation" (Voltaire 1980 [1733], 51; quoted in Roche 1998, 140). Etienne de Silhouette, who would eventually serve a short stint during the Seven Years' War as France's controller general, affirmed the basic pattern by citing the "spirit and principles" and the "constitution of [England's] government" as principal factors in its commercial preeminence. Significantly, in this influential memoir—a latter-day white paper written to inform diplomats charged with improving France's competitive position—Silhouette conceded that differences between their respective constitutions would make it difficult to adopt the English model *in toto* (French Ministry of Foreign Affairs 1747, 213v).[15]

While affirming the underlying rapport between constitutional structure and economic prosperity, other observers viewed the English constitution with suspicion, wondering on what terms the English model could be adopted.[16] While the United Provinces of the Netherlands were born during a heroic struggle with despotic Spain, Britain's maritime empire emerged from the brutal chaos of civil war; political instability and religious intolerance—not a love of liberty—provided the first impetus to Britain's commercial empire. In tracing the origin of the North American colonies, one observer from France's Ministry of the Navy remarked in 1738 that they were "at first nothing but a refuge for fugitives and the banished; the troubles of the Civil Wars sent a great number of Calvinists, Quakers and other types who started to inhabit this lengthy Colony" (French Ministry of the Navy 1738, f. 43).[17] If the Puritan colonies abroad were the result of royal intolerance and oppression, the Parliamentary faction that represented them at home was representative of the disorder inherent in most mixed regimes: "[The Parliament] is led by a party which imperceptibly gains superiority [and] which will sooner or later overturn all that remains of the monarchy. They cry louder than ever the memory of their hero Cromwell, and boast of certain revolutions." While Cromwell was universally praised for instituting the Navigation Acts of 1651—and making them stick—his legacy was also deeply suspect. Parliamentary rule, which Cromwell imposed by regicide and transformed into an irrevocable writ of British liberty, had an anarchic character unseemly to monarchic sensibilities: "The actions and convulsions of England's Government are so extraordinary that they are daily exposed to new incidents" (ibid., f. 46). Despite a permanent state of conflict between the Council of Commerce appointed by the king and that of the House of Commons, these bodies found "themselves always united about the Interest of Commerce; this is the only certain advantage that they draw from their mixed government" (ibid., f. 49). As much as he appeared to deplore the English system, the author agreed with Voltaire that parliamentary rule—however rowdy—had the virtue of representing commercial interests in a way that monarchy simply could not.

Whether anglophilic or anglophobic, French observers shared the widespread belief in the intimate link between the English constitution, its social structure, the manners of its inhabitants, and its commercial prosperity. But most of these authors were economic reformers, not revolutionaries; they would not have willingly traded the stability of monarchy for commercial prosperity if this meant, in turn, assuming the defects they imputed to mixed governments and excessively egalitarian societies. The hazards of the English example, along with their attachment to the institutions and manners of Old Regime France, led these writers to think of ways in which the apparent preeminence of the constitution in commercial questions could be transcended. In this connection, the writings of Charles-Irénée Castel, abbé de Saint-Pierre and Jean-François Melon provide a faithful guide to how these problems were faced, if not precisely resolved, in the economic literature of early eighteenth-century France.

Although he is now relatively obscure, the abbé de Saint-Pierre was a common eighteenth-century type: the well-connected graphomaniac who moved in interlocking circles of the literary salon and upper-echelon government ministers (Perrot 1992, 42–45). Saint-Pierre also wrote copiously on economic subjects, but his oeuvre ranged over history, theology, aphorisms, and social advice, as well as far-seeing and (some thought) utopian projects for pan-European political reform. Of all these projects, the most well-known was his "Project for Perpetual Peace," a scheme that was frequently dismissed by contemporaries as utopian, and which later influenced Immanuel Kant's writing on the same subject (1970). In praising him as "the most zealous Frenchman of his time for the public good," Gabriel Bonnet, the abbé of Mably, summed up contemporary judgments of the man and his work (quoted in Baker 1981, 253).[18] For the historian Jean-Claude Perrot,

Saint-Pierre's economic and political works were an exceptionally "precocious" expression during a period of relative quiet between the loss of confidence in Ludovician absolutism, and the full flowering of the French Enlightenment in the 1740s and 1750s (Perrot 1992, 40).[19]

Saint-Pierre's frequently cited *Project pour perfectionner le commerse de France* (1733) argued that overseas trade, and particularly that of the *Compagnie des Indes*, was the most beneficial for France. In this discussion, the negative example of Bourbon Spain loomed large. Like France, Spain had all the natural resources requisite of a wealthy nation, "but fortunately for their neighbors, they are lazy and their poorly constituted government does not encourage them to any commercial enterprise." Moreover, the Inquisition, so active in expelling commercially active Jews and Muslims living as "false Christians," had deprived Spain of its most useful citizens (Saint-Pierre 1733, 206–7).[20] In summing up these weaknesses, the abbé suggested that the French choose the example of the tolerant, thrifty, and industrious British. The implication of this recommendation was clear: France stood at a crossroads between two very different social and political systems: absolutism and moderate government, and had to choose correctly for the sake of its happiness and prosperity.

The abbé, in anticipating the qualms readers might have about his plan, advanced an apparently fatal objection: "you want to change [our military] constitution to make all of us into good Dutch merchants" (Saint-Pierre 1733, 225). This objection followed naturally from the received idea that "the republican constitution is even more favorable to commerce and maritime companies than the monarchical constitution" (ibid., 243). That the abbé felt obliged to parry this sort of objection shows how deeply engrained these beliefs were. His responses, in turn, are paradigmatic of the way that economic reformers tried to gently elide the question of the constitution and commerce, or even turn it to their advantage.

According to Saint-Pierre, the same objections had been made in England a century earlier, but it was discovered in short order that military prowess and commerce were complementary; commercial nations did not become pacific, but turned their warrior nobility to the ends of national enrichment. The abbé therefore concluded that the French "can, without disturbing [the] state's constitution, follow the example of the English nation, and succeed in equaling their commerce in less than thirty years" (Saint-Pierre 1733, 243). Saint-Pierre conceded that many monarchies had handled their colonies and overseas trading companies badly, but denied that their poor management was attributable to the inalterable characteristics of monarchies. Many skeptics believed that monarchies were condemned to poverty since taxes were ceded only grudgingly to monarchs by noble elites who persisted in the conceit that the king could "live of his own" domains, as the expression went. For these reasons, any royally sponsored trading company was apt to be regarded as a scheme for the king to plunder his subjects in order to pay debts. That state-sponsored finance and capitalization schemes (for example, national banks) could not work in arbitrary governments, where the sovereign could raid the coffers at will, was taken simply as an article of faith after the fall of John Law's system in 1720 (Montesquieu 1989 [1750], bk. 20, ch. 10; Jones 2002, 61–73; Kaiser 1991).

Constitutionally based objections could be muted if commerce and finances received what Saint-Pierre termed a "bonne administration." The possibility that *bonne administration* could trump constitutional differences occupied a central place in Saint-Pierre's argument, and was a motif that Hume played on later in arguing against party politics and for the rise of civilized monarchy in the England of his day. At the same time, while a constitutionally neutral *bonne administration* occupied such a central place of Saint-Pierre's reform project, it remained a hope, advanced more by assertion than by argument. It was a case that was continually undercut by the spectacle of France's finances and overseas trading monopolies, whose faults were systematically linked back to the nature of the French monarchy by critics and supporters alike. In this connection, Saint-Pierre's friend Jean-François Melon, a former secretary to John Law and a cofounder, along with Montesquieu, of the Academy of Arts and Sciences of Bordeaux, also evinced the ambiguities of constitutional economic thought within the context of a reform-minded monarchy.

Jean-François Melon's universally admired *Essai politique sur le commerce* (1734) is important not only because it echoes and amplifies Saint-Pierre's analysis but because it occupies an important nodal point in a dense Franco-Hibernian intellectual network. Hume's first translator, the abbé Jean-Bernard Le Blanc, salted his entire translation of Hume's *Political Discourses* with references to Melon's work, arguing at length in the footnotes that Melon was Hume's most important predecessor.[21] On the French side, Melon's *Essai politique* was written in the same year (1734) as his friend Montesquieu's *Considérations sur la grandeur des Romains et de leur décadence*. Definite proof of their collaboration is difficult to come by, but a common thread in both works, an analysis of the differential effects of the "spirit of conquest" versus the "spirit of conservation" in ancient and modern nations, suggests at the very least a shared concern over the weakness of the absolutist system.[22] In his *Réflexions sur la Monarchie Universelle* of the same year, Montesquieu meditated on the obsolescence of territorial empires dedicated to conquest in an age of commerce, which provides further confirmation of common concerns and, indeed, patterns of analysis (Pocock 1999–2003, 3.339).[23] Montesquieu would have ratified Saint-Pierre's own trenchant judgment: those who believe that in modern times monarchies should devote themselves to conquest instead of commerce are "frivolous minds . . . who have no knowledge of Europe's current situation" (Saint-Pierre 1733, 252).

Melon also viewed "conquest" and "conservation" as "mutually exclusive" from the point of view of national manners, and therefore for the development of commerce (Melon 1971 [1734], 688). In this analysis, Melon drew on the examples of Rome, Carthage, Egypt, Alexandrine Greece, and finally Spain. The Spaniards were admittedly "the conquerors of America," but unfortunately for them the New World "is a thousand times more beneficial to the nations that trade there than those who possess it." Melon, like Hume and Montesquieu, emphasized economic changes that transformed the ancient political calculus: the world had changed so much "since Europe has become commercial, that is to say since the discovery of the New World," that the disadvantages in this altered political landscape of the purely military constitution, then so intimately associated with Europe's monarchies, were only magnified (ibid., 690).

While Melon continued to emphasize the broadest context of laws, manners, and institutions when he opposed the sprit of conservation to the spirit of conquest, the very terms he used relativized, in the manner of Hume's later writings on the subject, the differences between monarchies and republics. Indeed, for Melon, the Roman republic and the despotic monarchies of Asia both pursued "military government" to the detriment of "commerce and police"—here *police* and *policé*, which have a common origin in the Greek word *polis*, are synonymous with *civilization* and *civilized*, whose Latin equivalent is *civitas*. Republican Rome pursued conquest, rather than "policing itself" and obtaining its subsistence in an "equitable" manner through commerce. The long-term consequences—in the form of the barbarian conquests—were fatal for the later empire. The monarchical despotism of the Turks, had they cultivated the "spirit of commerce and of police, which is inseparable from it," might have overwhelmed even a united Europe (Melon 1971 [1736], 690).

As in Hume, for whom *civilization* became synonymous with an orderly and prosperous society, no matter the form of government, Melon's discussion of a generic *police* was intended to displace sticky debates over the constitution. Thus, he observed, "the republican spirit counts with pleasure the faults of monarchies; the monarchical spirit counts those of republics, and the balance is just about the same." It was for this reason, Melon continued, that England and France managed their colonies "according to virtually the same principles" (Melon 1971 [1736], 679). Thus, Melon concluded,

> It is neither the monarchical government nor the republican government that sustains companies [that is, trading companies like the Dutch Verenigde Oostindische Companie (VOC) or the French Compagnie des Indes]; it is the solidity of their establishments; it is the wisdom of their administration, the capital they possess. Administrative corruption, personal interests of the directors ... all of this pertains to all sorts of governments, because it pertains to human nature.
>
> (Melon 1971 [1736], 684)

Despite Melon's confident recasting of the debate, cracks appeared everywhere in the edifice, if not the very foundation, of his argument. In analyzing the question of finances, Melon argued that since Holland had some debt repudiations in its history, "republican debts are no more assured than the others." At the same time, echoing Saint-Pierre, he conceded that only republics can establish "true" banks, and that countries without them would remain relatively poor (ibid., 751). Similarly, Melon affirmed the importance of Holland's strategic monopolies on certain goods, while arguing that France could do equally well, given similar initial conditions (for example, available capital and exploitable markets). This boast breezily ignored the question of how the initial conditions of Dutch superiority arose. Melon himself admitted that he sought to study the "political interests of Europe, since it has become commercial, that is to say since the discovery of the New World, *or rather the establishment of the Dutch Republic*" (ibid., 703, emphasis added). Like Hume, who conceded that modern monarchical states owed their commercial vitality to republican ones, Melon tacitly acknowledged that Europe's new order *did* have fundamentally republican origins. *Police*, like civilized monarchy, could not entirely replace the constitution as a category of analysis and comparison; for this reason Europe's republics and mixed monarchies continued to stand as a reproach to monarchies with commercial aspirations.

By 1754, when Hume's *Political Discourses* were published in French translation, diplomatic, administrative, and intellectual elites had been engaged in a long-running discussion on commerce in monarchical societies. This was a context that simultaneously informed Hume's discussion of civilized monarchy, and shaped the reception of his writings in France. Nowhere is this more evident than in the abbé Jean-Bernard Le Blanc's translation of Hume's work.

The abbé Le Blanc: Translating Hume

The abbé Le Blanc (1706–81) was the son of a Dijon notary, and thus a presumptive member of the petite bourgeoisie of the robe. While he received a solid education with the Jesuits that later stood him in good stead as a member of the Republic of Letters—and might have aided his local fortunes—his father visited on him the social misfortune of becoming the jailer of Dijon, a *déclassement* so severe that Le Blanc became a deracinated intellectual in order to overcome this social handicap (Monod-Cassidy 1941, 3–40). Thus, Le Blanc tried his luck first in Paris, and then in England, where he developed his interest in British manners, institutions, and literature. Le Blanc was hardly unique in his anglophilia; indeed, he capitalized on trends rather than creating them, and in his acute awareness of his tenuous social position, he preferred to "howl with the wolves," intellectually speaking, rather than venture out on his own (ibid., 11). Accordingly, in addition to translating Hume, he wrote art criticism after the abbé Jean-Baptiste Dubos's fashionable treaty on the subject, as well as works on education following the publication of Rousseau's *Emile*. If Le Blanc was not a particularly original mind, his work of serving up Hume to a French audience provides us with an accurate guide to the wider contours of Hume's reception.[24]

Both publicly and privately, what comes through most insistently in Le Blanc's appreciation of Hume is the latter's intellectual filiation with Montesquieu. Like many of his contemporaries, Le Blanc saw Montesquieu as the father of a new type of political discourse, and Hume as his heir apparent. Writing to Hume in 1757, Le Blanc remarked, "Your *Discours Politiques* are having the same effect among us as *De l'esprit des loix*" (quoted in Mertz 1929, 657). At the same time, a closer look at Le Blanc's introduction to Hume's work proves that he had something more specific in mind when he likened the geniuses of both men. Le Blanc believed that if manufacturing and commerce were increasingly contributing to mankind's happiness, only moderate systems of government could help nations hold these possessions securely by perfecting "the overall order of a Nation" (Hume 1754a, 1:xii). While the English regarded Montesquieu's *Spirit of the Laws* as the "finest system of political knowledge," Hume and Montesquieu both deserved the title of "benefactors of the human race" for their work as "Philosophes Politiques" (ibid., xiii).

The appellation "philosophes politiques" made Hume and Montesquieu into standard-bearers of *doux commerce* and Enlightenment. These thinkers spelled out the lessons of England's "continual attention to conserving, and even perfecting, if it is possible, a form of government to which they owe their liberty and their wealth. Such is the object of this discourse and of the great number of works of the same genre, which are starting to become a school of politics for other European countries that have shaken off the yoke of ignorance and superstition" (Le Blanc in Hume 1754a, 1:viii). For Le Blanc, Hume and Montesquieu's political economy served as a "school of politics" that instructed readers about the history of commerce; it gave them a rigorous analysis of the relationship between the "form of government" and liberty—or, in the case of France, the possibility of emancipation from prejudice and arbitrary government. The significance of Hume's and Montesquieu's ideas for Le Blanc, and more widely for eighteenth-century political economy, had little to do with their contributions to modern theories of value and distribution, and everything to do with enlightened narratives of progress.

Despite his admiration for Hume, Le Blanc did not simply offer an anglophilic paean to English institutions at the expense of the French. In his capacity as translator, Le Blanc provided a French response to Hume's work. In effect, he repackaged Hume's treatment of civilized monarchy, giving a specifically French polemical edge to his analysis of the relationship between constitutional form and commercial prosperity.

Le Blanc used Hume's text, for instance, as a sounding board, for his own concerns about commercial activity among French elites. Hume rejected the commonplace that people living under monarchical government turned away from commerce due to the insecurity of property that resulted from arbitrary laws. Hume, as we have seen, maintained that civilized monarchies and republics afforded property the same level of security. What, then, was the cause of the palpably diminished enthusiasm of French nobles for commerce? While quoting Hume directly on the subject ("Si le Commerce fleurit moins en ce Royaume, ce n'est pas qu'il y soit moins sûr, c'est qu'en effet, il y est moins honoré" (ibid., xlvi)), Le Blanc was also quick to point out—justly, as it happens—that it was not for lack of effort on the part of the crown that the nobility remained ambivalent toward commerce in France.[25] Rather, Le Blanc lamented—paraphrasing Montesquieu's famous dictum, "the empire of climate is the first of all empires"—that "the empire of prejudice is more powerful than that of laws and of kings" (Montesquieu 1989 [1748], bk. 19, ch. 14; Le Blanc in Hume 1754a, 1:xlvii). It was the French nobles, not the crown, who needed to be convinced that commerce was worthy of honor. In addressing this problem, Le Blanc, as others, hoped that commerce could be honored while maintaining the subordination of ranks necessary in a monarchical society (Le Blanc in Hume 1754a, 1:li).

Le Blanc's proposed solution recalls in certain respects that of Montesquieu, who wanted to combine the dynamism and liberty of modern, commercial nations with the civility and refinement more characteristic of monarchical nations. Montesquieu's backhanded compliment that "commerce produces in men a certain feeling for exact justice" (Montesquieu 1989 [1748], bk. 20, ch. 2) pointed to the philistinism and egotism of purely commercial societies, as opposed to the politesse of monarchical nations organized around the principle of honor: "Money is highly estimated [in England]; honor and virtue very little" (Montesquieu 1951, 878). Indeed, a closer reading of Montesquieu showed that while he admired the English in many respects, he was generally appalled by the manners he found among these cold, brutal, and reserved people. There, men were "confederates more than fellow citizens," and one found among these democratic souls "bluntness," "debauchery," "bashfulness and pride." In sum, while they enjoyed all the fruits of liberty and commerce, "they would be unhappy while having so many grounds not to be so" (Montesquieu 1989 [1748], bk. 19, ch. 27). Montesquieu, in retaining monarchy and the "subordination of ranks" within the context of commercial modernity, sought to effect a synthesis that compensated for the shortcomings of both constitutions (Spector 2000, 14–19).[26]

Le Blanc's own solution was considerably less nuanced, but his reaction to Hume's *Political Discourses* reveals some of Montesquieu's typically French misgivings about the (alleged) leveling of orders in commercial societies. Hume denied many of the differences between monarchies and republics in an age of civilized monarchies, but, at the same time, he asserted the final superiority of the republican constitution. Like Hume, Le Blanc recognized some differences, but claimed either that these differences had no social and economic relevance, or that they could be overcome easily. Thus, in arguing that the profession of arms should be "the most, but not the only, honored" profession in a monarchy, Le Blanc ignored the "empire of prejudice"—the necessary, if artificial, stratification into orders—on which monarchical societies were built. Like those who called for *bonne administration* against the defects of monarchical financial management, Le Blanc simply restated the problem in the form of a solution.

Similarly, Le Blanc's entire reading of Hume's *Political Discourses* displays a hypersensitivity to any suggestion of the superiority of the republican constitution to the monarchical, even though it is clear that the main thrust of Hume's analysis was to relativize these differences. The rise of commercial republics such as Venice and Genoa, which Hume praised, took place during "centuries of ignorance," but now monarchies had caught up: "What advantages doesn't France have to support and extend its own [commerce] ... ? I don't hesitate to argue now that whatever the English might say, thanks to the excellence of our government, the goods, the estate and the life of subjects here are just as sure as they are in England" (Hume 1754a, 2:xlv–xlvi). This was, of course, precisely the point that Hume himself made, but Le Blanc's reading of Hume tended in a much different direction, one that would become the *idée fixe* of theories of enlightened despotism: "Monarchy, under a good king, is the most perfect of all governments" (Le Blanc in Hume 1754a, 1:xviii). In those passages where Hume seemed to say that absolute monarchy was a second-best sort of affair, as in his memorable discussion of the "euthanasia" of the British constitution, Le Blanc eagerly leaped on Hume's tergiversations and "exposed his contradictions" (Hume 1985e [1741e], 47–53; Le Blanc in Hume 1754, 2:371n). So eager was Le Blanc to deny the meaning of these ostensibly "republican" passages that he advanced a theory of esoteric meaning—a sort of Straussianism *avant la lettre*—to explain them: "among the best authors ... normally one neither says all one thinks, nor does one believe [*pense*] everything one has said; one wants of course to be guessed at [*deviné*], but one doesn't want to compromise oneself" (Le Blanc in Hume 1754a, 2:374n).

Conclusion

Le Blanc's careful framing and qualifications point to the problem of naturalizing Hume's economic writing for a French context. Indeed, the literal meaning of "to translate," "to bring across" (the Channel, in this case), describes the problem well. Hume argued from the other side of the Channel that the European monarchies were becoming increasingly civilized under the impress of commerce. For this reason, his arguments were bound to find an eager audience in France, as the reception of Hume's work demonstrates. At the same time, despite the related benefits of *civilized monarchy* and *doux commerce*, the limits to the convergence between European states remained striking and, in the case of Le Blanc, required considerable—perhaps excessive—finesse. France's perception of itself as a second-class commercial power had profound cultural, economic, and political ramifications, since such talk implied that France might have to adapt to the ways of its competitor. As we have seen, Le Blanc was not alone: administrators, diplomats, and independent citizens of the "Republic of Letters" all wrestled with the issue of how to accommodate the peculiarities of France's state and society—its constitution—to the new realities of a commercial Europe. Le Blanc and others were reluctant to draw the fullest consequences of this analysis for the reform of France's "constitution politique," and derided as dangerous utopianism the prospect of reforming monarchical governments, possibly beyond all recognition (Le Blanc in Hume 1754a: 2:372–73n).[27]

The recurrence over the course of the 1730s through the 1750s of the question of France's constitution—despite attempts to settle it by means of other categories such as *police*, civilization, and administration—is indicative of a larger issue. Writers like Melon, Silhouette, Saint-Pierre and, finally, Le Blanc did not return to the question; rather the question persistently returned to them, and indeed anybody who attempted to think seriously about France's economy in the eighteenth century. Neither Hume nor his predecessors had a ready answer for the conundrums that their analyses raised; here, as elsewhere, the uncomfortable relationship between aristocratic societies, with their characteristic constitutional form, and the sometimes unwonted modernity thrust on Europe by its commercial expansion, came brutally to the fore.

Notes

The author would like to thank Roger Emerson, Tamara Griggs, the editors of the present volume, and an anonymous reader for Routledge for their helpful comments. All translations from the French are by the author, unless otherwise indicated in the bibliography.

1 On the privileged status of the history of commerce in Hume, see J. G. A. Pocock (1999–2003, 2:184; 3:374) and Carl Wennerlind (2002, 247–48 et passim).
2 Chantal Grell (1995) traces the permutations and political stakes in the debate over classical (and particularly classical "republican" antiquity) in eighteenth-century France. See especially part 2, sections 6 and 8.
3 Cited also by Larrère (2002, 319) in her illuminating discussion of Montesquieu as a historian of commerce.
4 This thesis was a distinctive aspect of Duncan Forbes's scholarship on Hume; see Forbes (1975, 297; 1978, 57–60). See also Teichgraeber (1986, 106) cited by Skinner (1993) and Pocock (1999–2003, 2:179–80).
5 Notably absent from Hume's account of the manner in which commerce curbed the pretensions of the sovereign was another eighteenth-century commonplace: in an age of mobile capital, sovereigns could ill-afford to persecute the merchants and financiers from whom they regularly borrowed money. This omission was due, of course, to Hume's very strongly held views on the odious political effects of national debt. See "Of Public Credit" (Hume 1985aa [1752h]) and Istvan Hont's article on the subject (2005f [1993]).

6 Many of the same observations are reinforced in "Of the Rise and Progress of the Arts and Sciences" (Hume 1985k [1742a]).

7 Hume drew on Montesquieu's *Spirit of the Laws*, in particular, books 28, 30, and 31, as an authority.

8 This is the logic behind "competitive devaluations" of currency. For a seventeenth-century version of the specie-flow argument, see also Appleby (1978, ch. 7).

9 Some of the examples in the following paragraph were suggested by Skinner's essay.

10 Hume makes something of the same point in "Of National Characters" (1985q [1748a], 215).

11 Still later, in "Of Jealousy of Trade," Hume affirmed that the "diversity of geniuses" was given by Nature herself (1985ee [1758], 329). Also cited in Hont (2005e [1983], 293).

12 For a skeptical discussion of the British gentry and its vocation for commerce, see Thompson (1989) and Weiner (1981).

13 This tension between Hume's narrative of convergence and the latent superiority of the "republican" form is fully evident in Hume's "Idea of a Perfect Commonwealth." While Hume's Harringtonian ideas are of course republican, he also allows that "Even under absolute princes, the subordinate government is commonly republican" (1985cc [1752j], 528). As in the case of commerce, Hume draws our attention to how social developments mitigate or complement constitutional arrangements.

14 See, for instance, a diplomatic memoir of 1740, "Commerce d'Angleterre," which observed that their American colonies were on the verge of rebellion, their sugar production was in decline, state debts were increasing, and France had a positive balance of trade with them (French Ministry of Foreign Affairs 1740, 188v–189r).

15 Silhouette wrote his memoir on a diplomatic mission to London during the War of the Austrian Succession (1740–48) (Clément 1872, 25–28). Widely copied and circulated, it was ultimately printed as "Observations sur les Finances, la Navigation, and le Commerce d'Angleterre" (1760).

16 For a discussion of this problem in relation to Britain's debt, see Robertson (1993) and Hont (2005e [1983]).

17 The archive of the Department of the Navy is a large and varied collection relating to the administration of France's colonies. This long (100-page) anonymous memoir was devoted, like so many others, to analyzing the English, Spanish, and Dutch trading empires and comparing them to France's own establishment.

18 Jean-François Melon, Du Tot, and Voltaire also cited him copiously. Saint-Pierre was a regular guest in the Salon of Mme Dupin, whose husband Claude was an officer in the finance ministry and an important writer on economics in his own right.

19 Lionel Rothkrug (1965) links the emergence of the French Enlightenment with the efflorescence of critical models of political economy during the discontented final years of Louis XIV's reign.

20 The reference to the expulsion of Protestants in the wake of the revocation of the Edict of Nantes (1685) would have been only too obvious to readers.

21 For further discussion of the abbé Le Blanc, see below. Also see the contributions of Charles and Shovlin to this volume. Although this does nothing to discredit the connections that Le Blanc drew, it should be acknowledged that Hume did go out of his way to discredit the ideas of Melon and Du Tot in his essay "Of Public Credit" (1985aa [1752h]).

22 The surviving exchanges between Montesquieu and Melon in the former's correspondence are rare and disappointingly superficial. Melon's correspondence has not been recovered.

23 While these two works were initially published in the same year, Montesquieu had the *Réflexions* pulled from circulation for "certain reasons" [des raisons] (Shackleton 1963, 150). An examination of Melon's commentary on the Romans—in particular his claim that they "had only a commerce of necessity" and that their city was "more a camp than a city" (Melon 1971 [1736], ch. 7)— reinforces this impression. Compare these comments, in particular, to chapter 1 of Montesquieu's *Considérations*.

24 John Shovlin's piece in this volume discusses Le Blanc's work through the prism of the luxury debate—an important node of eighteenth-century political economy that is left aside in this essay.

25 The Conseil du Commerce proclaimed in 1701 that nobles could engage in the wholesale trade, and some merchants were even ennobled by the king. This stipulation was repeated throughout the eighteenth century, but prejudices remained toward commerce (Sutcliffe 1982, 239). Even without derogation laws, nobles could (and did) easily skirt them through legal dodges if they chose (Roche 1998, 415–19). Despite these lingering prejudices against commerce, Roche (1998, 412), drawing heavily on the scholarship of Chaussinand-Nogaret (1985), argues that "the nobility was not united in either rejection or participation [of commerce]. What seems clear is that noble status remained linked much more solidly to landed wealth."

26 Céline Spector (2004, 22–35 et passim) furnishes an excellent account of this synthesis in Montesquieu's *oeuvre*. Spector sees in Montesquieu two complementary models of the "heterogeneity of ends," or the "autoregulation" of selfish passions and interests for social benefit: honor and commerce. Because these models are not perfectly self-sustaining, the combination of the logics of honor and commerce furnishes the basis—beyond a simple model of *laissez faire*—for the development of civil society.

27 Le Blanc registered this fear even more vividly in the preface to his 1755 edition of Hume's work, which he wrote and published during his stay in Dresden (Hume 1755).

13 The "Rich Country–Poor Country" Debate Revisited

The Irish Origins and French Reception of the Hume Paradox[1]

Istvan Hont

1. The Rich Country–Poor Country Debate: Hume and Tucker

Hume's "rich country–poor country" argument, although almost forgotten in the history of economic and political thought, generated huge interest among his contemporaries. In the third paragraph of his essay "Of Money," first published in his *Political Discourses* in 1752, Hume offered a striking comparative assessment of the economic future of rich and poor nations (Hume 1985u [1752c], 283–84).[2] Rich nations, he declared, had virtually unbeatable advantages over their backward competitors. Their Achilles heel, however, was in their high wage costs. Consequently, in order to preserve their competitiveness, manufacturing industries often relocated from high to low wage areas. This industrial migration, Hume claimed, gave a welcome boost to the economies of latecomer nations. Its beneficial effects, however, only lasted until wages in the new location also rose to uncomfortably high levels, forcing the same industries to migrate to countries of yet lower wage levels. Hume regarded his native Scotland as a poor country. His appraisal of the low-wage advantage of poor nations and the corresponding weakness of rich ones had a decisive influence on his stance on key issues of economic policy, including his assessment of the impact of foreign trade on the economy and the inflationary consequences of credit creation. It was his lifelong interest in the economic future of poor countries that made him a Scottish political economist.

Hume's few sentences on the economic futures of rich and poor nations in "Of Money" stirred up an unusually focused and intense debate with the leading English political economist of the day, the Reverend Josiah Tucker (Tucker 1774b). Like many of Hume's Scottish contemporaries, Tucker read Hume as expressing a menacingly negative vision of Britain's economic prospects. He classified it as an atavistic remnant of the belligerent economic thinking of the past, which encouraged rather than rejected Britain's dangerous propensity to remain mired in "jealousy of trade." He saw Hume's thesis as supportive of the mercantile system. In the unfinished second part of his *Elements of Commerce* (Tucker 1755a, 1755b), Tucker listed the most damaging "vulgar prejudices" that plagued British political economy. He linked Hume's rich country–poor country argument in "Of Money" to three vulgar errors:

1. that rival nations cannot all flourish at the same time;
2. that poor nations will draw away trade from rich;
3. that low wages create cheap manufactures.

> (Tucker 1755b in Clark 1903, 239)

Tucker insisted that Hume was wrong on all three counts. Market hegemony required skill, good organization and the abundance of capital. Poor countries had none of these. Specialization and the division of labor required access to extensive markets which allowed progressive economies of scale. In a rich country, Tucker explained,

> where the demands are great and constant, every Manufacture that requires various processes, and is composed of different Parts, is accordingly divided and subdivided into separate and distinct Branches; ... whereas in a poor Country, the same Person is obliged by Necessity ... to undertake such different Branches, as prevent him from excelling, or being expeditious in any.

> (Tucker 1774b 33–34)

Wage rates did not straightforwardly determine the sale price of products. The easiest thing, in fact, was for rich countries to acquire cheap labor through immigration. In reality, however, it was cheaper to pay 2s 6d to a skilled worker than to pay 6d to an "awkward bungler" (ibid., 34). This principle also applied to agriculture. Growing corn, Tucker pointed out, required considerable skill. Accordingly, English corn was cheaper than Scottish, although the first was a rich country, the latter poor. Hence, he concluded, "the manufacturing Counties of England ... Sheffield and Birmingham are in the Possession of the Trade, and will ever keep it, unless it be their own Faults." The existing wealth of rich countries "will promote still greater Industry, and go on, for anything that appears to the contrary, still accumulating." (ibid., 40).

Poor countries, Tucker conceded, would not remain poor forever. They were bound to get their share of the spoils of modern economic growth. While rich countries would manufacture all the high-skill or "*operose*" products, poor ones could specialize in the "ruder arts." They could then trade these goods in reciprocal exchange. This way both rich and poor countries would grow, but the gap between them, Tucker hoped, wouldn't close. Rich nations like England, he insisted, could sustain their lead over latecomers practically indefinitely. European countries had every reason to be optimistic about the future of their economies. Why should one suppose, Tucker wrote, that

> our Children cannot as far exceed us as we have exceeded our Gothic Forefathers? And is it not much more natural and reasonable to suppose, that we are rather at the Beginning only, and just got within

the Threshold, than that we arrived at the *ne plus ultra* of useful Discoveries?

(ibid., 31)[3]

Most observers thought that Tucker was an optimist and Hume a pessimist about the future of rich countries. What puzzled Hume's readers, however, was his description of the competitive advantages of low-wage nations as a "happy concurrence of causes in human affairs." Was Hume asserting that the migration of industries from rich to poor nations was part of some kind of providential plan? Even Hume's Scottish compatriots agreed with Tucker that Hume sounded very much as if he were predicting the necessary decline of all rich economies. The Aberdonian David Skene, for example, summarized the author "Of Money" as saying that, "Trade has its natural limits beyond which it cannot pass, it circulates from one nation to another and poverty and industry continually draw it from Wealth." Skene then concluded:

If this is a just representation of things, I cannot forbear calling it uncomfortable. I must regret the lot of Humanity, where principles seemingly opposite are so nearly connected as to be productive of each other; where every advance towards wealth is likewise a step to Poverty and where the destitution of Trade is the immediate consequence of its perfection.

(Skene n.d [c.1758]., 95–96)[4]

This was no mere philosophical issue. England was the wealthiest country of the time and Hume's theory seemed to foretell the inevitable catastrophe that awaited it. Skene, of course, knew that Hume was not English. Hume wrote "Of Money" as a North-Briton, as a Scot living in the composite state of the United Kingdom. Since Scotland's fate became inexorably tied to England's, the economic decline of its southern sister nation would have been exceedingly bad news for the Scots. To wish for it would have been practically suicidal. Nothing, in fact, was further from Hume's mind than predicting Britain's economic demise. His correspondence reveals his real agenda that remained largely hidden in his published essays.

To his Scottish friends Hume presented the issue in terms of making good the economic promise of the 1707 Union of England and Scotland. His own country, although part of mighty Britain and twinned with gloriously wealthy England, remained poor. True, Scotland benefited from Britain's colonial trade. But it was only fair, Hume claimed, that it should also be able to share some of England's manufacturing wealth. This was possible, he contended, only by exploiting the one competitive advantage Scotland's poverty offered, its low wages. Hume's strategy for economic development had a dual aim. He envisaged a system of inter-regional and inter-national division of labor wherein poor provinces and nations specialized in those simple but labor intensive manufacturing industries in which low wage costs alone could ensure reasonable competitiveness. Developed economies, Hume suggested, had no reason to continue with these rather crude economic activities. Instead, they should shift their manufacturing toward the production of complex and innovative luxury goods. Producing them well, or at all, required skill, capital and affluent markets, all of which existed in rich countries alone. By insisting that rich and poor nations should specialize in industries of different complexity and then exchange the products through reciprocal trade, Hume implied, in essence if not by name, a non-competitive trade policy based on "comparative advantage" and "product cycles."

In a previous study, entitled "The Rich Country-Poor Country Debate in the Scottish Enlightenment" (Hont, 2005e [1983c]), I described the Hume–Tucker debate in detail, together with the broader eighteenth-century Scottish controversy over Hume's rich country–poor country argument, in which Adam Smith, Sir James Steuart, John Millar, Dugald Stewart and Lord Lauderdale all participated. This essay extends the earlier discussion. It broadens it historically and adds two further contexts to the origional Scottish one. The first additional context is similar to the original Scottish one, insofar that it also directly relates to the post-Glorious Revolution construction of the British state. It is focused on late seventeenth- and eighteenth-century debates on Anglo-Irish commerce. This brief history of the Irish rich country–poor country debate is divided into two parts. The first covers the period before the Anglo-Scottish Union of 1707 and then the period up to the publication of Hume's essay "Of Money" in 1752. It was in Ireland that the rich country–poor country issue was given its first articulation, in the hugely defensive response of English theorists and politicians to the commercial challenge presented to them after the Glorious Revolution by the Protestant colonists of Ireland. Previously, in the seventeenth century, the central issue for England was winning the price competition against the country's major European competitors, mostly rich nations, some of them even richer than England. After the Glorious Revolution, the political economy of creating the new British state formation, however, produced a different kind of competition problem for England.

Ireland's demand for free trade in the wake of the Glorious Revolution helped to focus English attention on the special properties of economic competition between rich and poor nations. Ireland was no mighty Holland or France. Its national poverty, however, could easily be identified as the cause of its low price and wage levels. In isolation this did not matter. If a poor country, however, could contrive to enter into international market competition, its low prices could undermine the market positions of richer countries, whose wage levels were substantially higher. The first part of the Irish section of this study describes the near hysterical English response to this challenge. The next section bifurcates the argument. It traces the impact of the late seventeenth-century Anglo-Irish free trade debate in the period that immediately followed. On the one hand, the Irish debate transmogrified into a Scottish debate and set both the tone and underlying pattern of the commercial and economic controversies that surrounded the Anglo-Scottish Union of 1707. In the Scottish Union debate, both the rich country–poor country argument and the justifications given for the English legislative suppression of Irish free trade were widely and expertly discussed. It was this Scottish version of the original Irish argument about the potential competitiveness of poor nations that constituted the historical origin of Hume's rich country–poor country argument.

The next section considers English responses to international price competition in the era immediately after the brutal clampdown on Irish trade. English theorists continued to look for new economic policies that would allow rich countries to escape from the pressure of price competition, coming from both more efficient and affluent producers and from poorer, low-wage nations. Three adaptive strategies were suggested. The first was outsourcing, using low-wage areas in Asia as a platform for an aggressive import drive into Europe, including England. The second strategy focused on the use of labor-saving machinery and new organizational modes of production that allowed the use of an unskilled labor to manufacture complex products. The third option was industrial restructuring in such a way that England would become less vulnerable to rivalry from low-wage competitors. This implied moving economic activity away from those areas of production where less developed nations were able to compete and opening up new ones in which poor nations had no skill or resources to mount an effective challenge. The suppression of the Irish economy in the name of English reason of state was effective but had little intellectual relevance for competition with non-dependent nations. These three policy responses to the challenge of price competition, on the other hand, had a rather long shelf life. Later in the century they became the backbone of the arguments that Hume's opponents leveled at him in the rich country–poor country debate. They clearly influenced both Josiah Tucker and Adam Smith.

The middle section of this study, which separates the discussions of the earlier and later Irish debates, focuses on the reception history of Hume's rich country–poor country argument in France. The French context is as important for any properly historical assessment of Hume's statement as the Irish one. Franco-British rivalry was an ever present influence on political and economic arguments in both countries throughout the eighteenth century, particularly in the period of the Seven Years' War, when the Hume–Tucker debate took place and Hume was read avidly by practically all French political and economic thinkers. Economic competition, including straightforward price competition, played a central role in this great power rivalry. As a consequence, the rich country–poor country argument became a fashionable topic in French international relations theory. Eighteenth-century Scottish political economy cannot be studied fruitfully in isolation from the great French policy and theory debates of the age. Both Hume and Smith regarded Paris as the intellectual power house of the world. On certain issues, the dialectic between Scottish and French debates is directly relevant to understanding their thought. One can also use the ideas of their French contemporaries to construct a comparative framework for the study of the rich country–poor country debate. Both approaches are deployed in the French section of this essay, which starts with the work of Jean-François Melon, whose *Political Essay upon Commerce* was the most important European book on political economy in the 1730s and 1740s.

Melon publicized the merits of a neo-Colbertian economic strategy that was designed to take on England's commercial might by copying the competitive policies that England had used with such signal success. Melon's work is then contrasted to the thought of Montesquieu, who deployed a version of the Irish argument about the self-canceling wealth of rich countries in order to demonstrate that England's commercial hegemony over Europe couldn't conceivably last. He probably derived this idiom from a manuscript by Richard Cantillon, an Irish banker who was familiar with the Anglo-Irish debates that had taken place earlier in the century. Hume's readers in the French Enlightenment recognized the similarity between Cantillon's views and Hume's rich country–poor country idiom. In France, Cantillon's argument was well known from the manuscript version of his work, which was written twenty years before the publication of Hume's essays. A number of important thinkers gave priority to Cantillon over Hume in this debate and some continued to prefer Cantillon's version of the argument to Hume's over several decades.

When Hume's political discourses were translated into French in 1754, Hume acquired an instant and influential intellectual presence in French debates on political economy. His contribution, however, was seen as deeply ambiguous. Was he arguing like Melon or like Cantillon or Montesquieu? Was he advocating English strategies of commercial growth, or was he arguing that England's huge wealth would cancel itself and collapse under its own weight? The difficulty of Continental European readers with Hume was captured unusually clearly by the Swiss republican writer Jean-Jacques Rousseau in his *Confessions*:

> [Hume] had acquired a great reputation for himself in France and above all among the Encyclopaedists from his treatises on Commerce and Politics ... I was persuaded, based on what I had been told about him, that M. Hume associated a very republican soul with the English paradoxes in favour of luxury.
>
> (Rousseau 1995 [1770], 527)

This study tracks the various responses by French political economists and international relations theorists to Hume's apparently paradoxical mixture of views. Hume's French translator tried to recruit Hume to the newly formed Gournay group of political economists which continued Melon's advocacy of an English style commercial, industrial and agricultural strategy as the best way to restore French grandeur. Gournay and his associates, however, had difficulty with the rich country–poor country argument. They welcomed Hume's emphasis on the benign consequences of the arts and sciences on social development, but found his critique of all designs for establishing a world commercial hegemony, whether British or French, disturbing. They noticed that Hume failed to give support to the neo-Colbertist celebration of the division of labor and labor-saving machinery. Hume's opposition to any linkage between commerce and war, to public credit and to monetarist strategies of boosting economic growth, also deeply troubled the Gournay group. The very same ideas, however, were welcomed by French critics of modern power politics and commercial society. The marquis de Mirabeau, the Gournay group's chief opponent, welcomed some of Hume's ideas far more warmly than the Gournay group did. But Mirabeau objected to the tone of Hume's support for luxury. His own work on political economy and international relations in fact represented a far more radical departure from the spirit of Hume's economic essays than the views of Melon's and Gournay's followers.

Virtually none of the French thinkers who addressed the issue appreciated the Scottish aspect of Hume's rich country–poor country argument.[5] Nonetheless, their various comments influenced European political theory debates deeply in the decades before the French Revolution. Understanding the futurity of wealthy nations was one of the most important topics on the agenda of political, economic and moral theory in the second half of the eighteenth century. As Rousseau surmised, Hume was a critic of certain negative consequences of commerce. Nonetheless, Hume wanted a world with more commerce, rather than less. French reflections on this apparently paradoxical position were sometimes uncomprehending or hostile, but they also contained very interesting insights into the stability conditions of modern politics and the dangerous synergy between economic competition and international power rivalry.

The second section dealing with the eighteenth-century Irish rich country–poor country debate picks up the thread after 1776, the year in which Hume died and both Condillac and Adam Smith published their magisterial contributions to political economy. The Irish Union debate, unlike the Scottish one, lasted for a whole century, way into the period when Hume in Scotland was a rather lonely voice in pleading the case of the commercial advantages of low-wage countries. Unionism in Ireland was seen as a creative solution to the rich country–poor country problem, because by merging competitor countries, price wars could be converted from an international into a purely domestic trade issue. Many in Ireland aspired to the solution that Scotland actually achieved in 1707. Some of the confusion about the strategical purposes of Hume's rich country–poor country argument arose from the fact that it revived the Irish pattern of debate at a time when the Union of England and Scotland had already been in place for half a century and Scottish independence was no longer a viable possibility. Hume's readers were puzzled, because prevalent economic thinking suggested that jealousy of trade could not apply to trade between the provinces of the same country. This kind of ambiguity, however, did not apply to the continuing Anglo-Irish debate. The rich country–poor country debate re-emerged in Ireland with a vengeance when the Union negotiations finally got underway in the last quarter of the eighteenth century.

Adam Smith, who disagreed with Hume on this issue, was consulted by the British government, and Josiah Tucker, Hume's chief opponent, wielded considerable influence over both the British and some of the Irish political leadership. Since the immediate issue was the repeal of the late seventeenth-century prohibitions against Irish free trade and its replacement with a modern liberal regime, attention focused on the purely economic arguments that had been developed earlier concerning the competitiveness or otherwise of poor nations. Adam Smith, Edmund Burke, Arthur Young and Josiah Tucker all argued that England needed no protection against Irish competition, because Irish low-wage competitiveness was a mere myth. Close attention to the history of the late eighteenth-century Irish Union debate also explains why and how Hume's ideas were revived temporarily in support of the Union, leading to the publication of some of his private correspondence that finally revealed his intentions behind the 1752 essay, making it easier to see those of his underlying arguments that had remained relatively unclear in his published writings.

The concluding section of this study develops further the comparison of Smith's and Hume's views on the role of low wages in competitive international trade. It aims to bring Hume's theoretical stance more into focus. Hume wished the Scottish economy to grow at the expense of some of England's manufacturing industries, but he clearly wished to see healthy economic growth in both countries. He readily acknowledged England's superiority and therefore looked for a pattern of trade in manufactured goods between the two nations that sidestepped any direct competitive rivalry. He did not work out this idea in any great analytical detail. Nonetheless, as the concluding section argues, Hume developed the kind of insights that later produced such theorems of international trade theory as "comparative advantage" and "product cycles." If this view is correct, then the apparent contradictions in Hume's rich country–poor country argument can be resolved not only historically, but also analytically.

2. The Case of Ireland and English Reason of State

The antecedents of Hume's line of reasoning can be found in Irish economic debates of the immediate post-Glorious-Revolution period. Using the rhetoric of liberty established in England after the revolution, the Protestant colonists of Ireland called for the right of free trade between themselves and the mother country. As Francis Annesley, a young associate of William King, Bishop of Derry and later a most influential Archbishop of Dublin (Kelly 1980, 34–35), explained eloquently, Irish Protestant patriots were not contending for Power or great Riches; they neither trade to the East-Indies, Turky or Africa; they have neither Hamborough, Hudson-Bay, Greenland or Russia Companies; they have no Fleets or Plantations; they ask only the common benefits of Earth and Air. They desire only to change their native Commodities for those they want, and to manufacture a small part of their own Product, which is a liberty seems to be allowed them by the Law of Nature, and which I don't find hath been denied by the most severe Conquerors.

(Annesley 1698, 8, reprinted Annesley 1740)

Despite occasional English encouragement of Irish wool production, Irish theorists and politicians had long concluded that it was elementary prudence to avoid direct economic competition with England. William Temple had cautioned the Irish against competing with England in the wool trade (Temple 1814 [1680], 3:12–13) and William Petty was equally adamant that Ireland should form a union with England and then transfer some of its population there rather than attempt to compete commercially (Petty 1899 [1687], 2:545–621). John Locke, writing as a member of the newly formed Board of Trade of England, was no less adamant that direct economic competition between Ireland and England was a foolish idea. He recommended that "the exportation of all sorts of woollen manufactures out of Ireland should be restrained and penalized," for Irish export of wool-based textiles could not but end up in "very ill consequences" to England (Locke 1876 [1697]; of Molyneux (1696), 5:704; Locke (1976–89 [1697]), 6:7; Laslett 1957).

As the country party agitation against the Irish woolen trade gathered strength in England, a number of Ireland's leading intellectual figures realized that the political status of the English Protestant colonists of Ireland had to be radically reconsidered (Kearney 1959; Kelly 1980). The frustration of the Anglo-Irish patriots was set out most prominently in a hastily written but vigorous pamphlet by William Molyneux, scion of an important Protestant Dublin family, philosopher and Irish MP. Molyneux challenged his friend John Locke, demanding the opinion of "the author of the Two Treatises on Government" on the central argument of *The Case of Ireland's Being Bound by Acts of Parliament in England Stated* (Molyneux 1698). In his dedication to the King, Molyneux claimed that the rights and liberties established by the Glorious Revolution ought to apply to Protestants in Ireland as much as to the King's English subjects, including the right to trade.[6] His book, however, was condemned by the English and Irish parliaments and gave rise to a spate of refutations, first by John Cary (Cary 1698b, 1698c), the Bristol merchant and John Locke's favorite English trade theorist, and later by others, including the increasingly influential Charles Davenant (Hont 2005d [1990]; Multamäki 1990).

Davenant regarded Ireland as part of the English empire and trusted that the metropolitan center could always dominate the commerce of its provinces without direct intervention. Once, however, Ireland claimed the right of free trade, its competition with England could become a threat.[7] Davenant quoted prominently from a pamphlet of Simon Clement, *The Interest of England with Relation to the Trade of Ireland*, a work that specifically targeted the claims of Francis Annesley. Clement warned that "if any one offers his goods cheaper than the usual price, that will then become the market price; and every one else must sell at the same, or keep his goods" (Clement 1698, 7; cf. Davenant 1771c [1699], 253). Davenant seconded this view: "All that have either writ or spoke upon this subject agree that the whole controversy turns upon this single point, whether they can make the same woolen goods cheaper there than here" (ibid., 252). England and Ireland had the same natural advantages and traded in the same goods. Hence, Ireland's low wages presented a deadly competitive threat. Davenant estimated that food represented half of a worker's subsistence costs, hence "the cheapness of provisions" enabled the Irish "to afford their commodities cheaper than England can do in foreign markets" and sell wool "a third cheaper" than England (ibid., 252).

Others, however, insisted that the alleged advantages of Irish poverty were negligible and also difficult to exploit in practice. Lack of skill and work discipline made the real cost of Irish workmanship difficult to estimate. Ireland suffered from a shortage of highly skilled workers. Also, the wages of skilled workers were generally much higher in poor countries than in rich ones. In addition, such critics argued, the wage advantages of backward regions were bound to be transitory. Once the country became successful, Irish wages would rise quickly. The low wages of poor countries were helpful only in the transitional phase of ramping up exports. During this period general skill levels would develop rapidly, while wages would still remain relatively low since "a great many artists will be instructed before the multitude of inhabitants can render provisions dear in such a place as Ireland" (ibid., 252). During this crucial time lag, however, Ireland's high-wage competitors could suffer a heavy blow and be thrown "into more disorders, than the most knowing man in England can readily describe" (ibid., 253).

In assessing Ireland's economic chances, Davenant assumed that there was considerable international mobility of labor:

> Where there is plenty of material, which, manufactured, yields a good price, hands will be soon invited over to work it up. ... But this holds more strongly, where not only the material, but all sorts of provisions are cheap; and in countries which have not been yet improved, where every new comer hopes to make a sudden fortune.
>
> (ibid., 251)

The lure of high profitability was a magnet for foreign investors and there were no reasons to believe that the entrepreneurs of rich countries would behave like good patriots:

where the prospect of gain is certain, money never fails to come ... foreigners will carry stocks to an improving place, where they may reasonably expect many more advantages than what shall arise from this manufacture. As for example, to lay out money upon good securities, at 10 per cent. interest, to buy land capable of great melioration at 10 years purchase; and to have almost all the necessaries of life half as cheap again as in other parts; are not all these circumstances sufficient to invite thither, not only foreign stocks, but very much of our own money, and a great number of our workmen, where their industry will turn to a better account than it does here.

(ibid., 253–54)

To prevent the migration of industry from England, Davenant saw no other option but the suppression of the Irish wool textile trade by legislation. His reasoning rested on the demands of national security. Being a wealthy and powerful nation suddenly seemed the source of severe danger because it implied that the country became expensive, which amounted to a serious disadvantage in market competition. Far from guaranteeing stability by providing ample financial resources for national defense, trade committed wealthy nations to a permanent price war and to the endless adaptation of their manufacturing industries to changing international market conditions. As an act of self-defense, Davenant argued, Ireland had to be denied "a capacity to ruin England" (ibid., 250). It was "the right of England ... that the legislative authority ... should, upon all emergencies, make such regulations and restrictions, relating to Trade especially, as shall be thought for the weal-public of both countries" (ibid., 250–51). Ireland's bold attempt to "undersell" the English, he wrote, was adequate grounds for a "reasonable jealousy of state." Davenant counseled the "severe wisdom" of a pre-emptive strike, for it was "not only prudent, but just ... to interrupt the too sudden growth of any neighbor nation" (ibid., 254) as a simple matter of self-defense. England's legislative and political onslaught convinced Irish Protestants that if they wanted free trade they had no choice but to form a common market with England. Under the circumstances, this was possible only through entering into a full political union of the two countries.

3. The Case of Scotland and the Union of 1707

The "rich country–poor country" controversy in the Scottish Enlightenment, in which Hume was the main protagonist, was a continuation of these Anglo-Irish debates of the turn of the seventeenth and eighteenth centuries (MacInnes 2001). In 1707 Scotland entered into a full parliamentary union with England, ending separate English and Scottish sovereignty. The coalescence of these two states was the first instance of modern state formation in which considerations of competitive trade played a major part (Hont 2005d [1990], 2005b; Robertson 1987, 1995b). By the Union, England gained national security and the Scots entered into a free trade area. For a brief period Scotland dabbled with the old, Machiavellian and post-Renaissance, route of external expansion. On the advice of William Paterson, the founder of the Bank of England, the Scots embarked on an audacious project of taking control of the trade between the Atlantic and Pacific Oceans by placing a trading colony at Darien, approximately at the location of today's Panama Canal (Dalrymple 1788, 1:95, 132). As an attempt at empire building, the project was ingenious. Darien required no occupation of substantial territory or high administrative costs to operate, in contrast to traditional conquest. This was not a project to exploit Darien's natural resources, or use cheap colonial labor to win market wars in England and Europe. Its aim was to establish a Scottish-owned cosmopolitan trading hub on the Dutch model, an entrepôt center for future inter-oceanic trade that would generate a plentiful income for Scotland by virtue of its strategic location (Hont 2005d [1990]; Armitage 1995, Armitage 2000a). This visionary project, however, failed because it transgressed the rules of international power politics. It directly challenged Spanish hegemony in and around its American colonies. England's objective was to maintain peace with Spain, more than to support Scottish mercantile adventurism in Meso-America. Darien was destroyed by the logic of war, not trade. It was at this juncture that a Union with England for economic reasons was conceived. After the Darien debacle Scottish supporters of the idea of transforming Scotland into a trading nation began to follow the Irish agenda, accepting that market access required a political union with England.

The alternatives were either to remain semi-independent from England, which implied the continuation of English hostility to Scottish trade, or the renunciation of national trading ambitions altogether. The latter option was proposed by Andrew Fletcher of Saltoun, the leader of the opposition to the Union in the Scottish Parliament. His opponents borrowed the Irish argument concerning the advantages of low wages in competitive trade. Fletcher, in turn, savaged this idea in his complex and elusive pamphlet entitled *An Account of a Conversation Concerning the Right Regulation of Governments for the Common Good of Mankind*, published in 1704. In the pamphlet Fletcher cited the unionist earl of Cromarty, who tried

> by many arguments to show that our country would be the place, where all manufactures, as well of the use of the whole island, as for exportation, would be made by reason of the cheapness of living, and the many hands that Scotland could furnish.
>
> (Fletcher 1997b [1704], 191)

The Union, Fletcher retorted, was unlikely to favor the development of Scotland's economy. Lacking productive skills and having a pre-modern social structure that was an obstacle to modernization, poor countries inevitably buckled under the pressure of competition with wealthier nations (Dickey 1995). The wage advantages were no match for these hindrances. To demonstrate his point, Fletcher pointed at the continuing poverty and stagnation of Wales, centuries after its political incorporation under the English Crown (Fletcher 1997b [1704], 193). Further, Fletcher raised the stakes in his argument, even if Scotland's low wages worked as magically as hoped, the outcome was bound to be political disaster. The casual brutality of the English destruction of the Irish woolen industry a few years earlier demonstrated this beyond dispute. Were Scottish economic success to hurt the English national interest, England's rulers would not hesitate to crush the valiant efforts of Scottish producers. The case of Ireland, Fletcher claimed, had shown convincingly that rich countries like England were pre-pared to override all considerations of morality and justice if they believed that the economic endeavors of their poorer neighbors presented an exis-tential threat to them (ibid., 201–2). To form a Union with England, so far from guaranteeing rising commercial prosperity and enhanced popular well-being in Scotland itself, would place the Scottish people at the mercy of the English state interest and destroy their economy, culture and capacity for autonomous political and social initiative (ibid., 191).

Without independent political authority to protect the country's interests, Fletcher claimed, Scotland would find itself at the mercy of savage market pressures, which it could do nothing to alleviate. Fletcher's analysis, just like Davenant's earlier, represented a fusion of an economic and political ana-lysis of domestic problems with a keen understanding of the changing structure of international relations in modern Europe. It was this combina-tion of internal and external issues that explains the intensity with which Fletcher opposed the Union and his stubborn search for an alternative fra-mework of international relations. As Fletcher insisted, Scotland's grim national prospects were simply a stark and revealing illustration of the harsh logic of military and commercial conflict between rival European great powers fighting for the domination of world trade. As one of Fletch-er's English interlocutors explained in the *Conversation*:

> We must not rely too much upon our own speculations, or think the world can ever be rightly governed; but must take things as they are, and consider the interest of the society in which we live. And if any profitable trade be in the possession of our neighbours, we may endea-vour to dispossess them of that advantage for the good of our own society.
>
> (ibid., 201)

Commerce had assumed the shape of war, insisted the English politician, because it had ceased to be a mere civilian vehicle to obtain foreign luxuries or to make the common people more prosperous. It had become the foundation of military greatness and modern national glory. This transformation placed new demands upon the political imagination. Commerce could be kept peaceful only if it was understood in terms of mutual national interests, the interest of the European community of nations and finally the interest of mankind. Politics, on the other hand, implied the defense of the national interest of particular and distinct societies. The logic of reason of state provided no means, as Fletcher came to see it very clearly, to take into account the rights, virtues and interests of others. The needs of international society and the interest of mankind were simply beyond the horizon of modern political thought:

> Not only those who have ever actually formed governments, but even those who have written on that subject, and contrived schemes of constitution have, as I think, always framed them with respect only to particular nations, for whom they were designed, and without any regard to the rest of mankind. Since, as they could not but know that every society, as well as every private man, has a natural inclination to exceed in everything, and draw the advantages to itself, they might also have seen the necessity of curbing that exorbitant inclination, and obliging them to consider the general good and interest of mankind, on which that of every distinct society does in a great measure depend. And one would think that politicians, who ought to be the best of all moral philosophers, should have considered what a citizen of the world is.
>
> (ibid., 209)

Fletcher had no doubt of the prospective fate of a world in which each state's interest and politics were determined without any regard to the general good of mankind. A world divided between violent, unjust, unnatural governments, following the dictates of their optimal 'advantage' in trade, was not a world of *doux* commerce but of intensified 'universal wars' that would engulf Europe, America and most of Asia and Africa (ibid., 205). Only a comprehensive reconstitution of the domestic political order and foreign policy of European states could rescue international trade from the malignancy which the geopolitical struggles of Europe's great powers had endowed it.[8] Fletcher was not utopian enough to project a complete cessation of present and future military aggression. He suggested, however, that peace could be established and preserved only if European nations were reorganized into a number of federalized military alliances of roughly equivalent size and power. The military resolution of commercial conflicts could be avoided only if no nation could hope to gain lasting advantage through aggression, if military conquest was made impossible. Fletcher was not naïve. He did not imagine that the differences between poor and rich nations would thereby disappear. Within a carefully balanced European state system, however, rich countries would not be able to exclude their poor competitors from foreign trade. Instead, international trade would return to its original Godly design of connecting and serving the needs of people living under different climates and possessing different natural resources.

4. English Competition Strategies: Davenant and Martyn

For the English, the issue of competitive trade and the problems of high wages remained of cardinal importance even after the Irish wool threat was dealt with by brutal suppression and the Scottish problem solved by an incorporating Union. The thinking of Charles Davenant, for example, remained focused on the dilemmas of price competition and the underlying link between prices and wages throughout his long career. Davenant saw England's high wage levels as a monstrous competitive encumbrance in every respect. He looked at Britain's domestic economy in great detail, searching for policies of lasting competitiveness. Importantly, he also searched for a solution in foreign trade and empire, hoping to find innovative ways of capturing external resources to improve England's precarious market position. Davenant's interest lay not in bringing back exotic products from colonies, or even gold and silver, but in seeking external assistance in keeping labor costs down. Indian textiles, he noticed, were cheaper than their European equivalents, because by European standards Indian wages were ridiculously low. It made sense therefore to go out to Asia and borrow, as it were, India's underpaid labor force and then use it to crack open European markets. England was a sea power and as James Harrington asserted a generation earlier, those who controlled the seas would give law to the rest of the world (Harrington 1977 [1656], 160). In Davenant's hands the Harringtonian control of the high seas amounted to Britain's exclusive access to India's low-wage economy (Davenant 1771b [1696], 94, 123). As he saw it, Indian wages and Indian textile technology were weapons, very effective weapons indeed, for destroying the textile industries of England's European competitors (Hont 2000d [1990]).

It was clear that England itself would also suffer a serious bout of de-industrialization if its home market was exposed to the price competition of Indian-sourced textile products. In his ruthless pursuit of commercial "reason of state," however, Davenant was willing to submit England's own textile industries to the ravages of cheap Indian imports. He ruled out any kind of protectionism and accepted that under free trade domestic prices had to follow the trend of world prices. There was also a broader political dilemma. England's high wage levels made the country very uncompetitive. The nation's political freedom required that wages must not be cut by force or administrative measures. Mere market pressures, however, were not proscribed by traditional notions of political or civil liberty. They were accepted as part and parcel of modern commercial realities, as a concomitant effect of modern freedom. To counter the negative effects of marketization, Davenant suggested not defensive regulation but proactive economic policies, such as the increase of agricultural output, the lowering of the price of

English wage goods and the redirection of the unemployed toward low waged jobs. He also proposed the restructuring of English manufacturing industry. Even in the wool textile sector, which was England's staple trade, it was advisable to abandon the lower end of the price spectrum and let it be taken over by poorer and leaner competitors. England, Davenant argued, had to utilize the accumulated skills of its work force and use it for the manufacturing of high-value-added products, such as premium wool garments, both for export and the domestic markets. England's advantages were greatest at the top, rather than the bottom, of the market, where competition involved quality and design rather than mere price comparisons.

Davenant's concerns with wages were shared by another supporter of the East India Company, Henry Martyn (Hont 2000d [1990]; MacLeod 1983, Maneschi 2002). He developed this line of thought even further. In order to compete with the Dutch shipbuilding industry, Martyn suggested, England should establish a new kind of production system of fishing vessels in its West Indian colonies. Colonial slave labor, even if totally unskilled, could be an effective weapon in price competition if the skills and experience necessary for Dutch-style shipbuilding could be substituted by mass production techniques:

> To single Parts of Ships, single Negroes might be assign'd, the Manufacture of Keels to one, to another Rudders, to another Masts; to several others, several other Parts of Ships. Of which, the variety wou'd still be less to puzle and confound the Artist's Skill, if he were not to vary from his Model, if the same Builders wou'd still confine themselves to the same Scantlings and Dimensions, never to diminish nor exceed their Patterns. And of Ships for the same kind of Trade, and for ordinary and common use; when once a good Model can be found, why shou'd the same be often chang'd? ... And, thus a way is shewn to build in our Plantations by the hands of Negroes, to render a Work of such variety plain and easie, to enable Negroes to build with as much skill as those in Holland.
>
> (Martyn 1701, 116–17)

The other way of winning in price competition was by the introduction of machines. The pressures of competitive trade, Martyn claimed, inevitably led to technological change and the invention of machinery. They saved labor costs, reversing the weak position of high-wage countries in international price competition. Although this solved the apparent contradiction between economic success and high wages, Martyn recognized that the advantage obtained through the deployment of machinery could not last for long. Competitors, Martyn suggested, would leapfrog each other in technological innovation until the market place, whether national or international, became a level playing field. Competition in technological innovation didn't doom the survival chances of early entrants or require a reduction in wage levels. It did, however, impose a national necessity to remain in the race forever. Once, Martyn wrote,

> things are successfully invented to do a great deal of work with little labour of Hands, every Man must be still inventing himself, or be still advancing to farther perfection upon the invention of other Men; if my Neighbour by doing much with little labour, can sell cheap, I must contrive to sell as cheap as he. So that every Art, Trade, or Engine, doing the work with labour of fewer Hands, and consequently cheaper, begets in others a kind of Necessity and Emulation, either of using the same Art, Trade, or Engine, or of inventing something like it, that every Man may be upon the square, that no Man may be able to undersel his Neighbour.
>
> (ibid., 67)

Despite persistent English efforts to dismiss the notion that poor countries could successfully win the price competition against rich ones by virtue of their low-wage advantages, Ireland clung to this idea for decades, if not more. It became something like the Irish Protestant economic credo. Hume's Scottish contemporaries were familiar with the history of the Irish trade prohibition debates and even more with the Scottish Union controversy. In 1752, they recognized that Hume had repeated the "Irish" argument for political and economic union between rich England and its poorer sister kingdoms in the British Isles. In his economic essays, however, Hume went further than merely reiterating the key arguments of 1707. He also actively sought to destroy alternative projects to the low-wage strategy, rejecting all other Scottish and Irish schemes that were adumbrated in the early part of the century and retained significant followings in both countries. In this respect, Hume faced a problem. The low-wage strategy was severely discredited, because after half a century of Union, Scotland's backwardness was still palpable. The alternative schemes, however, had never really been tried properly and hence retained their shine. Hume rejected Andrew Fletcher's dream of a semi-closed agrarian economy that was patterned after the apparent rural idyll of republican Switzerland. More importantly, Hume categorically discarded, just as Fletcher did in the Union debate, the inflationist or monetarist alternative of creating national economic flourishing, which was based on John Law's original idea of credit creation by a land bank (Law (1994) [1703–4]) that Law hoped to use for the rapid creation of a viable and growing Scottish economy without English help.

Law's project was originally presented to the Scottish parliament in 1705 (Law 1705) as a deliberate alternative both to Fletcher's republican vision and to the Irish "rich country–poor country" argument. Subsequently, Law had the unique opportunity to experiment with his ideas on a large scale in post-Louis XIV France (Murphy 1997; Kaiser 1991; Sonenscher 1998, 2002). The experiment turned out to be a total disaster. The causes of France's spectacular economic collapse, due to the mishandling of Law's "system" by the Regency, were widely debated in Scotland throughout the eighteenth century, as indeed in the whole of Europe, and, of course, particularly vehemently in France. In Scotland and Ireland there remained plenty of adherents to Law's principles if not to his institutional methods (Adam Smith and Sir James Steuart being among them). Hume, on the other hand, was emphatically against Law's economics and politics in any shape or form. In the late 1730s, Law's ideas enjoyed a renaissance in Ireland. Bishop Berkeley, Ireland's leading philosopher, popularized the idea of a national bank in his *Querist* (Berkeley 1910 [1735–37]; Caffentzis 1997) in a form that was designed to correct the failings of Law's French project, and hailed it as the "philosopher's stone" of political economy (Berkeley 1910 [1735–37], 93; cf. 9, 11, 21, 51, 61, 80–82, 91, 94; Hont 2006, 401–4). By reiterating the older Irish low-wage competition arguments as the best chance for generating economic growth in a poor country, Hume effectively rejected Berkeley's influential praise of banking and paper money (as well as its crypto-Jacobite political connotations) as not the best but the worst way of launching a development project in an underdeveloped nation (Seki 2003).

In the mid-eighteenth-century Irish context (Kelly 2000b; Rashid 1988), Hume also encountered a different kind of intellectual competitor. In 1738 a Dublin edition of Jean-François Melon's *Political Essay upon Commerce* appeared. This was very markedly not an English but an Irish edition of this important French book. It was translated by David Bindon, one of the many minor economic pamphleteers of Ireland in this period. Bindon was a fluent user of the competitive advantages of low-wages argument[9] and was very interested in Anglo-Irish competitive trade strategies. He saw Melon's treatise as a far superior version of the older Irish tradition he had inherited. In a substantial introduction, and also in long notes, he contextualized Melon's arguments for Ireland (Melon 1738 [1734]; Bindon 1738a). France, he noticed, had shown distinct signs of recovery from the debacle of Louis XIV's wars and from Law's failed banking project. With Melon, Bindon argued, France was returning to the developmental path first laid out by Colbert (Bindon 1738a, iv). A great French economic revival, he insisted, was definitely on its way. Bindon urged his compatriots to learn from these new French efforts. France regarded itself as a competitor to England. Ireland, obviously, was in a similar situation. Bindon, like Berkeley and others, wanted to find a way to escape from the terrible legacy of the prohibitions England imposed on the Irish economy at the end of the seventeenth century. When Hume published "Of Money" in 1752, he found his own advocacy for the development of poor economies, like Scotland and Ireland, in direct competition with Melon's political economy, as adopted by Bindon and others in Ireland. Therefore, he found himself in direct competition not only with English, Scottish and Irish, but also with French versions of the rich country–poor country problem. Competing with Melon raised Hume's game substantially.[10] In Europe, and in Ireland, everybody wanted to know how far he would succeed.

5. The Case of France: Melon versus Montesquieu and Cantillon

The rich country–poor country debate in France in the second half of the eighteenth century followed a dialectic that in many ways reproduced the vicissitudes of the British, Irish and Scottish version. France, of course, was not a poor country, not in the sense that Ireland and Scotland were. Rather, it was England's chief economic and military rival in Europe, even if increasingly losing the race for hegemony. Hence prophecies of England's inevitable decline, caused by the inner logic of its own economic development, were welcomed by French patriotic politicians and philosophers of all hues. They saw the "rich country–poor country" dynamic as having the potential to end English aspirations to global trade monopoly. The most influential and coherent work setting out France's economic options for an economic recovery in the mid-century, as David Bindon in Dublin correctly noticed, was Jean-François Melon's *Political Essay of Commerce* (1734, 1736, 1738 [1734], 1739 [1734]; see Megnet 1955). Melon wanted to get rid of Louis XIV's terrible legacy. He asserted that states had to choose between two different kinds of foreign policies, one guided by the spirit of conquest and one by the spirit of commerce (Hont 2006, 409–11).[11] The two were incompatible (Melon 1738 [1734], 136). He unhesitatingly chose the latter and developed a novel commercial strategy to accompany it (Meyssonnier 1989; Larrère 1992). He wanted to delineate France's options precisely. Therefore, in the brilliant theoretical introduction to his book, entitled "Principles" (Melon 1738 [1734], 1–12), Melon distinguished between three basic models of international trade.[12]

He drew up a model that described trade between three islands of equal territory and population, each of which was restricted to the production of a single product, such as corn, wool, etc. These island economies were complementary and therefore could barter with each other peacefully. Next, Melon assumed that one island would become diversified and hence be self-sufficient in all important respects, while the other two would still remain purveyors of a single commodity. The newly diversified country remained the monopoly producer of its original staple produce, but was no longer dependent in any way on the other islands. Given French perceptions of England as a rising monopolist, this was an evocative case. Melon maintained that a war declared on a commercial monopolist by vulnerable nations would be a just war, because it would be dictated by necessity. Enforcing the fairness and reciprocity of trade, he wrote, was "the natural and primitive Right of Nations, according to which, the Right of one particular Nation, giveth way to the Right of other Nations taken together" (ibid., 3). "Wool"

(England) as a monopolist could be defeated, because its product was not essential for the functioning and survival of its attackers. But if "Corn" turned into a monopoly, it would be practically invincible. Without food no nation could fight. "The power of its [Corn's] product alone would subdue them"(ibid.). "Corn" (France) would be able to dominate all other nations. This was not, however, Melon's strategic choice. He wanted all nations, not only France, to become self-sufficient in food, for "corn is the basis of trade, because it is the necessary support of life."

Melon's political economy rested on a three-stages theory of the natural progress of commerce (ibid., 188; Melon (1983b) [1724], 515, Melon (1983c) [1725], 531; Melon (1983d) [1727], 651).[13] First things first, he suggested, which was why agriculture enjoyed absolute precedence. Subsequent stages were possible only if there was a surplus of food and basic goods. Next local manufacturing and trade could develop. Only in the third stage, when its domestic economy functioned properly, could a nation embark on foreign trade. An extension of this activity was commercial rivalry. If all rivals, however, conformed to the natural progress of opulence and did not break the sequence or jump a stage, then only the quality of their trade policies could separate them. Countries that made many policy mistakes were left behind, while the one with the best policy could achieve competitive superiority. The losers could opt for war to repair the resulting imbalance in access to markets, but their chances of winning were slim. The war was bound to be protracted and required a high level of solidarity among the allies. In the meanwhile the superpower could increase its economic lead by attracting economic migrants seeking higher living standards. The economic hegemon could also initiate a Machiavellian policy of divide and rule and "support the trade of those islands from which she hath nothing to fear and destroy the trade of the other islands whose competition may alarm her" (Melon 1738 [1734], 10).[14] Its economy and military power would go from strength to strength, while its enemies would be exhausted by a hopeless war. The "tranquillity," that is the national security of such a mighty state, Melon claimed, would then "become equal to her Power"(ibid.). It was this scenario that Melon touted as the alternative to Louis XIV's failed attempt to lead Europe by establishing a "universal monarchy," that is by a combination of the spirit of commerce and the spirit of conquest. In other words, he advised France to challenge England at its own economic game and win.

Melon offered a competitive strategy whose central planks were industry, mechanization, free trade and democratic luxury. He denounced the admirers of Sparta and early Rome just as much as ancient constitutionalist eulogies of Merovingian France (he ridiculed the abbé Vertot's idea that the luxury-free life of the early middle ages was comparable to the healthy existence of the Iroquois and the Hurons) (ibid., 166–68 cf. Vertot 1722 [1720]). Melon also poured scorn on the sumptuary laws of modern European republics. "Luxury" was the greatest incentive for economic growth, provided it trickled down to the working classes. Luxury was a perfect "Spur for the Multitude," for the "expectation of being in a condition to enjoy an easy, voluptuous Life" was not a disincentive for labor as anti-modern theorists claimed (Melon 1738 [1734], 174). It was idleness that needed to be legislated against. Melon reformulated the relationship between the "necessary" and the "superfluous," the two concepts that were traditionally used to define luxury (cf. Voltaire 1901 [1738]; Hont 2006). All "commerce," he claimed, was "the Permutation of what is superfluous or superabundant, for what is necessary" (ibid., 8). Hence luxury, the producing and trading of "superfluity," was a positional or relational phenomenon, a necessary stage in the development of the economy. It was "an extraordinary Sumptuousness, proceeding from the Riches and Security of a Government" and it was "attendant upon every well-governed Society" (ibid., 174). The crucial leap forward toward luxury, Melon argued, was the invention of tools, which opened up a "Progress of Industry" that "hath no Bounds." It created a virtuous circle of "new Wants" and "new Skill and Industry" that satisfied them (ibid., 145). In competitive trade the nation that used better tools and machines was bound to be the winner (ibid., 4, 12, 146). By "employing fewer Men" to produce the same quantity of goods, it could sell its goods more cheaply than others. True, the introduction of machines caused unemployment. But it was a mistake, Melon claimed, to formulate policies with the express aim of avoiding the collateral damage caused by technological development. Changes in fashion had similar effects on employment, but it would be totally foolish, he pointed out, to try to save jobs in fashion industries, like the silk industry of Lyon, by legislation. It was better to retrain workers and redeploy their valuable skills: "the same Skill that serves for one," Melon wrote, "may, with ease, be turned to another, without the Legislatures having Occasion to intermeddle therein" (ibid., 148–49).

Melon's Bordeaux friend, Montesquieu (Shackleton 1961), offered a different vision (Larrère 2001). He also declared that military government and a Roman type of universal monarchy were both impossible and undesirable in modern Europe (Rahe 2005; cf. Pincus 1995). The idea of a lasting military superiority by any nation in Europe, Montesquieu claimed in his *Reflections on Universal Monarchy* (a book that was typeset but never distributed), was an obsolete idea (Montesquieu 2000b [1735]). For four hundred years, Montesquieu remarked, no nation had succeeded in changing Europe's political map through war. Thus French elites had no need to stoke the fire of military supremacy, since economic growth was a sufficient vehicle for achieving national greatness. French fears of a lasting English commercial hegemony were also misplaced, Montesquieu explained, for such a phenomenon was an impossibility:

Europe today has the commerce and shipping of the entire world, and the power of states augments and diminishes according to their share in them. It is in the nature of things that they are always changing, due to thousands of accidents and first of all according to the wisdom of governments. ... It is a peculiar property of powers founded on commerce and industry that their prosperity limits itself. If a country possesses a huge quantity of silver and gold, then everything becomes dear, the workers want to pay for their luxury and other nations can sell their goods cheaper.

(ibid., 341–42)

Prospective monopolist countries like England were bound to fail because poorer nations would eventually undersell them. Montesquieu's scenario was probably the first borrowing in France of the "Irish-style" argument about the high-wage problems of rich countries. It never became a prominent public doctrine attached to Montesquieu's name (Robertson 1993, 365–67) because he censored his own text, not once but twice. *Universal Monarchy* was withdrawn in the mid-1730s because it was politically far too risky. Montesquieu retrieved his rich country–poor country argument from *Universal Monarchy* and repositioned it in its sister work, the *Considerations on the Causes of the Greatness of the Romans and their Decline* (Montesquieu 2000a [1735, 1748], Montesquieu 1968 [1735]), which he re-issued in 1748 in a second edition as a companion volume to the *Spirit of Laws*. He wanted his critique of the commercial version of European hegemony to appear in this second edition as the new Chapter 4 of the book.[15] But the ideas in this particular chapter were again deemed to be too inflammatory for publication in the days when France signed a compromised and humiliating peace treaty at the conclusion of the Austrian War of Succession (Browning 1995, 327–63).

Montesquieu did not indicate any source for his view, but he may have had in mind an argument that had been set out in manuscript form by the Irish banker Richard Cantillon (Murphy 1986a), a former member of the circle of Lord Bolingbroke, who, like Montesquieu, was a member of the famous late-1720s foreign policy debating club, the *Entresol* (Childs 2000).[16] In Part II of this long manuscript, in the discussion of the relationship between the quantity of money in circulation and the economic performance of the nation, Cantillon teased out the implications of Locke's quantity theory of money for the economic fortunes of competitive trading nations (Cantillon 1964 [1933], 161). He described, just as Montesquieu did, Spain's economic decline as the consequence of the ballooning of its money supply following the colonization of South America (ibid., 163–67). He then investigated the inflow of money in nations that earned their income from successful foreign trade. (Brewer 1988, 1992). Although the mechanism whereby prices and wages increased was different (Cantillon 1931 [1755], 171–81), the outcome eventually was the same as in countries that, like Spain, received money directly from their colonial silver and gold mines. Developed and rich economies, Cantillon argued, had vast advantages over poorer ones. This was particularly true in the case of maritime nations with low shipping costs. Low transport costs could often compensate for "the high price of labour caused by the great abundance of money; so that the work and manufactures of this State, dear though they be, will sell in foreign countries cheaper than the Manufactures of another State where Labour is less highly paid" (ibid., 169–71, 185).

Turning to the case of poorer nations, Cantillon noted that "where money is rare ... everything is cheap" (ibid., 169). Hence, rich countries were always tempted by the cheap products of their poor neighbors, exposing their own vulnerability. The low wages and food prices of poor countries, Cantillon wrote, "naturally cause the erection of Manufactories," even if at first the quality of their products "will not be so perfect nor so highly valued" as of those of established suppliers (ibid., 169). However, well before these countries could become internationally competitive, they already began to consume their own products and hence stop the imports of the more expensive goods of rich countries (ibid., 183). The consequent loss of export markets would then push rich countries to the brink of a recession. Industries would migrate from rich to poor nations, wrote Cantillon, since unemployment would force "Workmen and Mechanicks who see labour fallen off leave the State to find work in the countries with the new Manufacture" (ibid.). In the meanwhile, he noted, the upper stratum of society would continue its spending on luxury products with abandon, oblivious to the grave economic crisis already looming on the horizon. This would, Cantillon diagnosed,

> gradually impoverish the state and cause it to pass from great power into great weakness. When a state has arrived at the highest point of wealth (I assume always that the comparative wealth of states consists principally in the respective quantities of money which they possess) it will inevitably fall into poverty by the ordinary course of things. The too great abundance of money, which so long as it lasts forms the power of states, throws them back imperceptibly but naturally into poverty.
>
> (ibid., 185)

Prevention would have required reining in the money supply in time:

> it would seem that when a state expands by trade and the abundance of money raises the price of land and labour, the Prince or the Legislator ought to withdraw money from circulation, keep it for emergencies, and try to retard its circulation by every means except compulsion and bad faith, so as to forestall the too great dearness of its articles and prevent the drawbacks of luxury.
>
> (ibid.)

This policy, Cantillon thought, was politically very difficult to implement, because it had to be done in advance. Instead, governments often acted evasively. Their first method was the creation of public debt that attracted foreign investment. The other method followed the time honored example of ancient military empires, mainly Rome, based on the belief that economic resources could be acquired by conquest and the formation of tributary empires. Both these schemes, Cantillon wrote, were bound to end in catastrophe. Rome's decline, due to its luxury, proved the utter futility of the military solution. As a critic of John Law, Cantillon also denounced paper money and debt experiments as the quickest way to push a state into bankruptcy. Both methods, he pointed out, concealed the underlying economic malady, thereby turning the recession into decline.

Nonetheless, a recovery, conforming to a cyclical pattern of rise, decline and rise again, was always possible. By historical standards, Cantillon asserted, modern economic cycles were relatively short in duration. The rise of modern trading economies could take place in a few decades, not centuries (ibid., 187). Equally, decline due to competitive pressures could be remarkably fast. "An able minister," Cantillon argued, could reverse this kind of decline and "make to recommence" the cycle upwards. This was possible, however, only in states with significant resources and population. "No ministers can restore the Republics of Venice and Holland to the brilliant situation from which they have fallen," Cantillon argued, "but as to Italy, Spain, France, and England, however low they may be fallen, they are always capable of being raised by good administration to a high degree of power by trade alone" (ibid., 195). The recovery had to exploit the sole virtue associated with the decline in a country's money supply when hitting competitive trade barriers in international markets. In a recession national and personal incomes took a dive, followed by a sharp fall of prices. This was a misfortune with a silver lining to it. The dramatically reduced wages and prices could restore competitiveness, provided the actual industrial capacity to export had survived:

> To revive a state it is needful to have a care to bring about the influx of an annual, a constant and a real balance of trade, to make flourishing by Navigation the articles and manufactures which can always be sent abroad cheaper when the state is in a low condition and has a shortage of money.
>
> (ibid., 193)

Cantillon, like Melon, argued that winning in European competition required more farsighted economic policies than those deployed by one's competitors (Liggio 1985; Tarascio 1985). Even then, regaining leadership was only possible if the deflationary crisis was confined to one nation. If all nations applied the same deflationary policy at the same time, and hence all regained their price competitiveness, then none gained price advantages over the other. In this case, wrote Cantillon, European trade would simply revert to a pattern where the ability of exporting goods had to be anchored in natural endowment advantages. However, even in the more positive case, if the competitiveness of a nation could be regained, Cantillon foresaw that the tendency to decline due to high wages would recur. "States who rise by trade do not fail to sink afterwards" (ibid., 235), was Cantillon's dictum. This was the same conclusion Montesquieu arrived at.

6. Hume and the Melon–Gournay School: Le Blanc, Plumard and Forbonnais

Hume's *Political Discourses* puzzled his French readers because they could not neatly pigeonhole the author within the grid provided by the earlier French debates between Melon's followers on the one hand and Cantillon's and Montesquieu's on the other. Hume seemed both to endorse foreign trade and highlight its self-defeating character. He seemed to praise luxury, but to take the opposite, anti-commercial, side over a number of closely related issues. The reception of Hume's political economy in eighteenth-century France was the history of the various French ways of coping with Hume's perceived ambiguity. The *Political Discourses* had three French translations before the French revolution. The first was a commercially motivated enterprise in Holland. It simply presented Hume's text in serviceable French (Hume 1754a). The third, in the 1760s, offered some interesting commentary and was aimed at bolstering the opposition to Physiocracy (Hume 1767a). The most important and influential translation, however, was the second one, by the abbé Le Blanc (Hume 1754b), because this was the one which explicitly exposed the Hume paradox. Le Blanc's edition was no simple translation, but a determined attempt to position Hume's book directly in the matrix of the French policy debates of the mid-1750s. The text of Le Blanc's French Hume was festooned with a long introduction (Le Blanc 1754a), ample footnote commentary and two bibliographies, the first listing other notable English works of political economy (Le Blanc 1754b) and the other offering a bibliography of recent new French translations and writings in the same area (Le Blanc 1754c). Most of these works were cited in Le Blanc's footnotes as the optimal context for the French reception of Hume's thought. Today we know, as only a select few knew at the time, that the new French works on political economy and the new translations, most of them accompanied by long commentaries, were orchestrated by Vincent de Gournay, one of France's four intendants of commerce (Guerrigues 1998).

Shaken by France's poor performance in the Austrian War of Succession, Gournay conceived the idea of restoring France to its former glory through a new and better commercial policy grounded in a better understanding of the causes of England's notable success in this area (Vincent de Gournay *c.* 1748; 1993 [*c.* 1748]; 1983b [1752]; 1983c [1752]).[17] In his translation project he went back to English writings of the 1690s and the early eighteenth century, which he regarded as the foundational period of England's rise to great power status (Le Blanc 1754b).[18] Gournay's publishing enterprise also included a number of original new French works that synthesized English approaches to political economy with current French political and economic perspectives (Le Blanc 1754c). Two of these major new works appeared in 1754, only months before Le Blanc's Hume volume was published. The first was the *Élémens du Commerce* by François Véron de Forbonnais (Forbonnais 1754a), the second was Plumard de Dangeul's *Remarques sur les avantages et les désavantages de la France et de la Gr. Bretagne par rapport au commerce et autres sources de la puissance des États* (Plumard 1754a), which masqueraded as a translation and was published under an English pseudonym. Most members of the Gournay circle, like Forbonnais and Plumard, were young and ambitious authors. Le Blanc belonged to a different generation. He was an older man and well-known author on English affairs whose most famous work was his *Lettres d'un François*, a wide-ranging, clever but often critical, and even satirical, survey of English politics (Le Blanc 1747 [1745]), scientific achievements and culture, and was widely read (including by Hume).

In Le Blanc's Hume translation, Gournay's name remained in the shadow. The leading lights of the new school were named as Forbonnais and Plumard. In fact, Le Blanc suggested that it was Jean-François Melon who was the originator of modern French political economy. He was one of Melon's last surviving personal friends and was eager to promote Melon's reputation. The *Political Essay on Commerce*, Le Blanc thought, had been unjustly forgotten and needed revival (Le Blanc 1754b, xv; cf. Melon 1754). Thus, for French readers of Hume, the Gournay school was presented as a progeny of Melon. To make the Melon–Hume convergence plausible, Le Blanc described Hume as a political philosopher without national animosity. In the "Introduction," he summarized key points of some of Hume's earlier political essays. In particular, he paraphrased the central contention of Hume's 1742 essay "Of Civil Liberty" (Hume 1985i [1741i]), namely that while Machiavelli and Renaissance authors failed to make trade an important political issue, in modern politics, as exemplified by the rise of Holland and England, commerce had become an "affair of state" (Le Blanc 1754a, xliv–xlv). Le Blanc was wary about over-promoting an English author to a French audience. He restricted his praise of England's achievement to one cardinal point, namely to the island nation's exemplary recognition of the importance of commerce to modern politics. He also extolled Hume for arguing that commerce was the foundation of not only modern politics, but the entirety of modern civilization. Commerce, therefore, was not an English policy, but the modern approach to politics in general. In this context Le Blanc depicted Melon as the Bacon of the new political economy, which for him was an exceedingly high praise (ibid., xviii–xix, xxiii). Hume, he suggested, continued, and in parts even imitated, Melon's approach in a more well-digested and superbly polished form.

This picture of the Hume–Melon convergence couldn't be sustained beyond a certain point. Hume failed to subscribe to important tenets of Melon's thought, namely to the Frenchman's support for public debt and monetary devaluation. Melon had become discredited in France, and in Europe, for precisely these views. Le Blanc acknowledged that Melon's most important French critic, Du Tot (Du Tot 1738, 1739 [1738]), had already effectively criticized Melon for this (ibid., xxi–xxii),[19] but Hume had clearly gone even further, by attacking not only Law's famous banking project, but all other experiments in inflationary policy and the introduction of paper money into modern economies. In the light of Hume's stern critique, Melon now appeared as a "man of system" (ibid., xxii). For Le Blanc, Hume's diametrical opposition to Melon's views on paper money (Hume 1754a, 1:211) appeared as paradoxical, because Hume's underlying theory of money, as he saw it, was a sort of "quantity theory," like that of Locke and a number of French authors, including that of Forbonnais (ibid., 1:105–6). Ultimately, however, Le Blanc could not ignore Hume's acerbic critique of the modern public debt system and its threat to national survival. When commenting on the paragraph in "Of Public Credit" where Hume explicitly criticized the magical notion of "circulation" upheld by Law, Melon and Du Tot (the latter two were also deeply involved in Law's project), he conceded that there was an irreconcilable difference between Hume's and Melon's opinions (Hume 1754a, 1:293).

Le Blanc excused this by arguing that both Melon and Hume argued their case against the fashionable doctrines in their respective countries, explaining the difference by relating these views to different national contexts (Hume 1754a, 1:196–97). Hume's opposition to public debt only made sense as an expression of English domestic partisanship. Le Blanc long held the view that party politics was the cancer of England (Le Blanc 1747 [1745], 1:195–99, 351–59; 2:123–29, 366–72, 400–412). In his bibliography of recent French books he listed a work (Magnières 1754; Le Blanc 1754c, 408–9) that demonstrated that in England the Whigs were the party of war and public debt and the Tories the opposite. To reinforce this association between Hume and the English country party opposition to the modern debt regime, Le Blanc translated Bolingbroke's critique of public debt (Hont 2005f [1993]; Sonenscher 1997) and positioned it at the end of the first volume of his translation of Hume's *Political Discourses*, just after Hume's "Of Public Credit" (Bolingbroke 1754a, 1754b, 1754c, cf. Bolingbroke 1755; Hume 1754a, 1:212). The purpose was to detach Hume's opposition to credit and paper money from his other doctrines and present Hume's quasi-republicanism in matters of debt and paper money as an instance of English Toryism. Forbonnais recognized that Hume's essays, and his rallying call against public debt, had become fashionable in France, and followed the path of Le Blanc's exercise in damage control. Keen to protect his own plans for the reform of the French public debt following the English model, that is by establishing a French version of the Bank of England, Forbonnais urged French government officials in a private memorandum to discount Hume's critique of debt finance as mere Tory-party political rant (Forbonnais 1755a, 181; Sonenscher 1997, 95; cf Forbonnais 1755b). Unsurprisingly, when Hume saw the inclusion of Bolingbroke's work in the French version of his own *Political Discourses*, he was livid (Hume 1932 [1754], 1:208). This was not an association that he welcomed. Le Blanc's feeble defense (Monod-Cassidy 1941, 411), i.e., that he genuinely saw Hume's and Bolingbroke's advocacy of patriotic public bankruptcy as very similar,[20] just poured oil on Hume's fire.

In this skirmish over the public debt issue Le Blanc passed over silently the rich country–poor country" argument, despite Hume's clear statement in the essay "Of Money" that it was the main source of his skepticism concerning inflationary credit-creating policies. Hume's French readers were not alerted in any obvious fashion to the importance of his argument, nor were they offered corrective views from Melon, Forbonnais or Plumard. Le Blanc's silence is surprising, since he had access to both Melon and Montesquieu precisely in the period when they were completing the *Political Essay* and the *Réflexions sur la monarchie universelle*, respectively. He could and probably did understand what was at stake. His young friends were less reticent in bringing up the issue openly. Le Blanc directed his readers to Plumard for understanding the history of the British public debt (Hume 1754a, 1:328–29). In the last chapter of his *Remarks*, Plumard did indeed discuss the relationship between inflationary pressures and the loss of export competitiveness. Money, he wrote, using the alias of Sir John Nickolls, was a precondition of national power.[21] Countries without gold and silver mines had to trade to become rich. "Amongst nations rivals in trade," Plumard continued, "every thing else being equal, that nation which sells cheapest will carry on the greatest trade" (Plumard 1754b, 232). Inflation could cause havoc in trading nations by pricing them out of their export markets.

Plumard's argument shadowed Hume's ideas uncannily. The influx of money earned through successful foreign trade was not a problem, just the opposite. The trickling down of trading profits took time and could create healthy economic growth in the interval before prices went up. Just as Hume argued in "Of Money," Plumard denounced the folly of nations that multiplied "to excess the representative signs of gold, and silver, and has raised the price of its commodities, and materials of trade" (Plumard 1754b, 234). The meteoric rise of English public debt, Plumard-Nickolls claimed, had just this effect. By creating paper credit instruments faster than the economy could absorb them, England inflated its commodity prices to levels that made exports difficult. Plumard also followed Hume's critique of Melon as a misguided author "who pretends that the national debt is nothing: that it is the right-hand which owes to the left-hand" (ibid., 239). Even if this were somehow true, the public debt system was bound to create huge inequalities, raise taxation to exorbitant heights and blunt international competitiveness. The debt system also undermined the political constitution, Plumard-Nickolls wrote, and it could be restored only by a patriot king.

Forbonnais, Plumard's cousin, was a much more formidable political economist and the author of important articles for Diderot's and d'Alembert's *Encyclopédie*, such as "Colony," "Commerce," "Commercial Company," "Competition," "Agriculture" and "Specie" (Fleury 1915; Meysonnier 1995; Sonenscher 2007; Forbonnais 1753c, 1754b, 1755c). He did not underestimate Hume's challenge to the practice of public debt and to paper money. While Plumard ostensibly presented the argument about the inevitable loss of competitiveness in rich countries as the view of Sir John Nickolls, an oppositional English politician, Forbonnais tackled the argument head on. In the *Élémens du Commerce,* Hume was recruited as an important ally on the issue of luxury. Forbonnais cited Hume's famous statement that "we cannot reasonably expect, that a piece of woollen cloth will be wrought to perfection in a nation, which is ignorant of astronomy, or where ethics is neglected" (Hume (1985t [1752b]), 270–71; Forbonnais 1754a, 2:238). But he was hostile not only to Hume's critique of the public debt, but also to Hume's famous theorem of an "automatic international specie flow mechanism," as we call it today. Forbonnais and Hume agreed that it was income earned from foreign trade that stimulated economic growth. Because price and wage rises lagged behind, trading profits could create a pull effect that might facilitate an economic take off and subsequent growth. Like Hume, Forbonnais investigated the case of Spain, where the huge monetary inflow from South America failed to stimulate the productive economy and led to decline (cf. Forbonnais 1753b). He denied, however, that paper money and public credit would produce the Spanish syndrome. Instead, he sought to demonstrate that its beneficial effects were similar to those that accrued from the income flows generated by foreign trade.

Like Hume's English critics, Forbonnais attacked Hume's eye-catching method of rejecting the paper money option as far too slick and unrealistic. Hume, in his essay "Of the Balance of Trade," sought to prove that any increase in the money supply that failed to generate corresponding economic growth created mere inflation and demonstrated this through two thought experiments in which he imagined that a country's money supply was either increased or decreased by four fifths overnight (Hume 1985x [1752e], 311–13). Forbonnais argued that the same stickiness of prices and wages that one saw under normal trading conditions would still apply, providing space and time for economic stimulation (Forbonnais 1755a, 182–83, 186–99). Hume obviously meant to signal a strict *ceteris paribus* condition, while Forbonnais sought to show that such framing conditions did not exist in reality. In the background of Hume's argument there was an ultimate distrust in the human ability to control the money supply during expansionary credit-creation experiments and he pointed at the failure of John Law's famous project. Forbonnais, on the other hand, was recommending safe methods for running a public debt system for the French administration, denouncing the outcome and the conduct of Law's project but not its underlying principles (Forbonnais 1754a, 2: 164; 1758, 1: 9, 58; 2: 574–644). Forbonnais rejected Hume's deceptive presentation of the futility of credit and paper money as inherently dangerous and denounced this view as either wrong or the product of confused patriotism. He recommended Melon to the French ministry as an author who was "more judicious and more sincere than Hume" (Forbonnais 1755a, 201–2).

Forbonnais understood that Hume went for the jugular of Melon's political economy, trying to destroy arguments that also became the doctrinal basis of the Gournay group. In his article "Commerce" in the *Encyclopédie*, also reprinted in the *Élémens du Commerce*, he provided an extended interpretation of the principles embodied in Melon's 'excellent' *Political Essay* (Forbonnais 1965 [1753], 82). The word commerce, he began his dictionary entry,

> signifies, in its most general meaning, a "reciprocal communication." It is used in particular for the communication by which men exchange the products of their land and their industry. Infinite Providence, the creator of nature, intended to make men dependent on each other through the diversity of this nature. The Supreme Being forged the bonds of commerce in order to incline the peoples of the earth to keep peace with each other and to love each other, and in order to gather to himself the tribute of their praise.
>
> (Forbonnais 1965 [1753], 49)

The subsequent history of mankind, Forbonnais contended, had destroyed this initial Godly promise. Commerce could have remained peaceful and sociable, but private property, inequality and the division of labor turned it into a viciously competitive activity. The power of modern states depended on income from trade and in trade the winners were those who sold their wares cheaper than others. To achieve this, he pointed out, nations had to foster competitiveness both domestically and externally by introducing labor-saving machines, lowering transport costs and reducing interest rates (Ibid., 72). In order to become champions, Forbonnais emphasized, nations had to expand trade far beyond the mere selling of their native products and commit themselves to international competition in every branch of the economy (Forbonnais 1755d). Failing to do so could render countries dependent on other nations and therefore being dominated by them. Inconveniently, Hume's rich country–poor country argument undermined this vision.

On the one hand, Hume's "happy concurrences in human affairs," caused by the migration of manufacturing industries from high-wage to low-wage nations, was good news for French political economists because it suggested that England's economic superiority could not last indefinitely.

On the other hand, it also emasculated the efforts of Melon's followers in the Gournay group to replace England by France as Europe's economic hegemon through copying English policies. For Forbonnais, trade was a constitutive part of modern power politics and the fostering of economic competitiveness a national duty (Forbonnais 1753a; cf. Krause 2002). In comparison, Hume's perspective appeared as supra-national, cosmopolitan and contrary to the economic patriotism of Melon, Vincent de Gournay and their younger followers. Forbonnais was a devoted national economist and patriot (cf. Dziembowski 1998; more generally Hont 2005b, 2005i [1994]) and explicitly criticized *cosmopolisme* (Forbonnais 1767, 1:69; cf. Heuvel 1986). In his 1755 memorandum to the French ministry, he explained the implications of Hume's rich country–poor country argument as follows:

> this amounts to saying that one might, in this respect, abandon every-thing to Providence whose wisdom restores everything in turn to a general and immutable order which it has established and that it has been something of a mistake for the various states to have gone to such lengths to acquire an advantage in the balance of trade because, for all their care, that same advantage will, sooner or later, revert to the other side, so that no-one will have gained or lost anything.
>
> (Forbonnais 1755a, 184)

Despite his opposition to Hume's prophecy, Forbonnais acknowledged that foreign trade that generated significant money inflows had a self-canceling tendency. Domestic living standards were not in danger, but the new money made exporting goods difficult. "It would seem," Forbonnais conceded Hume's point,

> that foreign trade, whose object is to attract a continuing new supply of money, works towards its own destruction in proportion to the progress that it makes in trade of this kind, so that the state comes to be deprived of the very benefit attributed to circulation.
>
> (Forbonnais 1754a, 2:121)

The simplest and neatest solution was withdrawal from foreign trade. This implied no economic collapse, because entering into self-imposed isolation did not damage the productive assets and labor skills of the country. Closed trading states could possess a vigorous domestic economy. Forbonnais saw withdrawal from foreign trade as a theoretical projection that might become reality only after many centuries of successful trading. Nonetheless, he decided to draw out its logic fully. A rich country that ceased foreign trading, he claimed, would by then have amassed a huge amount of excess capital, which could only be made to earn profit if it was lent out at a high interest rate to poorer countries that needed capital to promote their own economic development. The rich country's external income would then consist not of trading profits but regularly repatriated interest payments. If interest rates were kept high, Forbonnais explained, poorer states would in practice become abjectly dependent on richer ones:

> the workers of the debtor people would be no more than slaves allowed to retain the earnings of a few days of work in every year, in order to cover the costs of their mediocre subsistence; the rest would belong to the master; and the tribute would be exacted scrupulously, whether that subsistence was comfortable or miserable.
>
> (ibid., 2:129–30)

The foreign lending of rich countries in their post-foreign trade phase amounted to the creation of an informal empire. By monopolizing capital supply, rich nations could make poorer ones their tributaries. Without engaging in arduous and risky price competition, rich countries could retain their economic superpower status and even increase the gap between themselves and poorer countries. Hence the loss of manufacturing competitiveness, Forbonnais insisted, didn't necessarily cause economic deprivation. From the proceeds of their foreign lending rich countries could afford to import all the goods they needed for their high levels of luxury and comfort. Thus, Forbonnais claimed, rich countries could forestall their decline. Even if Hume was not entirely mistaken, his insights into the rich country–poor country problem were limited. The capacity of rich nations to export their commodities might have been finite, but this didn't mean that modern wealth as such was necessarily self-limiting.

7. Against Luxury and State Rotations: Mirabeau and Mably

The precise opposite of Forbonnais's vision was expressed eloquently in a hugely successful book published by the marquis de Mirabeau at the beginning of the Seven Years' War, entitled *L'ami des hommes, ou Traité de population* (Mirabeau 1756).[22] Mirabeau's tome also contained a very prominent criticism of Hume's essay "Of Luxury." Le Blanc immediately alerted Hume and wondered whether Hume wished to write a reply to Mirabeau that could appear in the next French edition of the *Political Discourses*. Le Blanc described Mirabeau as a patriotic writer, who praised agriculture and despised modern finance (Monod-Cassidy 1941, 417). This placed Mirabeau, as Le Blanc well knew, not so much in an opposition to Hume, but rather to Melon, and by implication to Forbonnais and the rest of the Gournay group. Indeed, Mirabeau carefully registered Hume's ambiguity about luxury (ibid., 2:102). He also praised the "judicious" and impartial Hume several times in the book (Mirabeau 1756, 1:30, 109, 114–16; 3:114), and approved Hume's critique of the moral damage caused by "overgrown" cities (ibid., 1:13–16; 2:107–8; Hume 1985bb [1752i], 401) and their tendency to limit population growth. He specifically endorsed Hume's "specie flow mechanism," adapting it to an analysis of the likely effects of a European-wide system of free trade in grain. Hume, he wrote, was right in stating that money, like water, would always find its "level" under such circumstances.[23] The same applied to grain (ibid., 3:24). Finally, when discussing the issue of public debt, Mirabeau, like Hume, dismissed Melon's claim that it amounted to no more than a transfer of money from the left hand to the right (ibid., 2:192; cf. 2:29–30).

Mirabeau objected to Hume's conflation of luxury with the development of the arts and sciences (ibid., 2:124–25). Whether in response to Mirabeau or to others who pressed him in the same direction, Hume changed the title of the essay in the 1760 edition of his *Essays and Treatises* from "Of Luxury" to "Of Refinement in the Arts." In the luxury chapter of the *L'ami des hommes,* Mirabeau's real target was Melon and he leveled at him the same kind of criticism that English authors had first pioneered against Mandeville. Luxury was not the use, but the abuse, of wealth. To attribute the positive impact of a flourishing manufacturing industry to luxury ignored the total havoc that the abundance of money and the proliferation of luxury consumption played with the *moeurs* of French society (ibid., 2:100–124). Mirabeau did not dwell on Hume's rich country–poor country argument. For him this idea belonged to Cantillon, who first presented it two decades before the publication of Hume's *Political Discourses.* In keeping with the careful study and detailed summary that Mirabeau made of Cantillon's *Essai* while it was still circulating in manuscript form only, *L'ami des hommes* praised Cantillon as the best theorist of population growth and its impact on the power and wealth of modern states (Higgs 1889; Weulersse 1910, 2).

Mirabeau's entire book was an answer to the specter of decline that Cantillon saw coming as the fate of all rich countries. The creation of an advanced foreign trade system in France, Mirabeau maintained, was no answer to the country's problems even if it succeeded in its own terms. The inevitable increase in the money supply that would accompany success was bound to create huge price rises. Hence, in international competition the winners were doomed as much as the losers. It was a mistake to imitate the policies of the maritime powers, Holland and England, who wished to dominate the whole world (Mirabeau 1756, 2:10; 3:7). Mirabeau borrowed his corrective policy not from Melon, Gournay and Forbonnais, but from Cantillon. The Irishman suggested that the loss of its exporting capabilities would not only stop the flourishing of a rich country, but would lead to a recession and a steep drop in both prices and wages. However, this sad outcome could also precipitate the beginning of a recovery. The newly acquired low-wage advantage of the once rich and flourishing country would make it yet again a successful export competitor. Mirabeau, like Cantillon, turned this insight into a positive policy. He singled out the case of Spain. The huge influx of precious metals and confused economic policies led to the country's decline. But a remedy was still possible. Following Cantillon's suggestion, the government could reduce the money supply and use the consequent price drop to restart the country's formerly flourishing export trade.

> Manufactured goods made in a very populous nation which has very little money would be infinitely less expensive than anywhere else in the rest of a Europe flooded with gold and they would rush to get hold of them to resell them at a profit elsewhere.
>
> (ibid., 2:11)

Having shown that a restart of foreign trade was possible, Mirabeau also wanted to know whether the second time round it might be possible to prevent the rise in wages that pushed successful trading countries into crisis previously. Success in trade was bound to lead to a new influx of money and hence to high prices yet again. Then, as Cantillon suggested, the rest of the previous cycle would also follow. Mirabeau's book offered a plan to prevent this cyclical pattern. He followed the prescriptions of Archbishop Fénelon, the most well-known opponent not only of Louis XIV's wars, but also of Colbert's policies (Rothkrug 1965). In his political novel, *The Adventures of Telemachus, Son of Ulysses,* (Fénelon 1994 [1699]) originally written as a tutorial for Louis's grandson and expected heir, the duc de Bourgogne, Fénelon suggested a complete reversal of Colbert's policy of luxury (cf. Cole 1939) by radical economic restructuring. He wished to restore agriculture as the foundation of prosperity, allowing only as much manufacturing industry as the needs of agriculture warranted. This was a plan of balanced growth, without any inflation or luxury. In *Telemachus* this radical reform was implemented by force, using the power of the absolute monarchy (Hont 2006, 383–87). Mirabeau, however much he admired Salentum (the imagined location where the creation of a new virtuous economy took place in Fénelon's novel), could not advocate such a violent plan (Mirabeau 1756, 2:141–42; cf. 1:62; Sonenscher 2007, 193–199). Instead of power, he put his faith in the built-in psychological and political advantages of agriculture over commerce.

Mirabeau's promotion of patriotic agriculture was different in kind from the similarly fervent calls for agricultural improvement by Melon and the Gournay group. The latter saw a flourishing agricultural sector as a strategic asset that secured France's food supply in times of war and as a source of cheap wage goods to boost commercial competitiveness. But once the agricultural foundations were laid, they wanted France to transform itself into a leading industrial and trading power. For Mirabeau, on the other hand, agriculture was the source of an entire political culture and civilization, a psychological barrier to the destructive passions that commerce and finance generated. He wanted the French people to love their agriculture and cherish the genuine use-value it created. He expressed this idea in a famous metaphor of the state as a "tree, agriculture its roots, population its trunk, arts and commerce its leaves." The leaves, manufacturing and trade, were the tree's least durable part, but they were renewable. "If, however, some unfriendly insect attack the roots, then in vain do we wait for the sun and the dew to reanimate the withered trunk. To the roots must the remedy go, to let them expand and recover. If not, the tree will perish" (Mirabeau 1756, 2:7). Agriculture, Mirabeau claimed, would increase sociability and inhibit the poisonous spread of cupidity, the cancer of modern political culture. If agriculture could be made into the rock-solid foundation of a new kind of economic patriotism, then the deflationary policy of cutting back the money supply would not only restore commercial competitiveness temporarily, but permanently prevent the recurrence of the sort of commercial crisis that hitherto afflicted all rich and luxurious commercial countries. Renewed France would be rich, but not luxurious. Instead of repeatedly falling back into crisis, it would step out of the vicious circle of trade competition in which victory was both arduous and ultimately ruinous. For Mirabeau, Forbonnais's vision of the future of France as a rich rentier nation was nonsense. It could only lead to France falling victim to a kind of master–slave dialectic, in which the increasingly effeminate masters become first imperceptibly and then openly dominated by their hardy and energetic slaves. If real production took place somewhere else, the lender nation would be really weak and corrupt in every sense but in terms of its illusionary monetary wealth. Such a rentier nation would be destroyed by its hardy enemies. Even if the abundance of money could support a formidable military machine, such a force would be a mere mercenary army, lacking in true patriotism. It would buckle under sustained and determined attack.

Mirabeau's theory of the modern "agricultural and commercial monarchy" faced yet another problem, the problem of population growth, as indicated by the book's subtitle. Mirabeau saw luxury as "homicidal" (ibid., 1:13; 3:15; 172). Equally, without international laws governing foreign trade, commercial rivalry was even more of a threat to society than living with "tigers and lions" (ibid., 2:6). Even if France could establish a well-balanced economy that was based on agriculture and the control of luxury and the money supply, it would still have to contend with the fact that the power struggle of commercial nations became an inescapable fact of European life. Mirabeau had no doubt that England aspired to a universal monarchy of the seas and generally behaved as a nasty commercial monopolist (ibid., 2: 10, 12, 14, 93–96; 3:96). Hence, reforming France required a reconstruction of European international relations by war, if necessary. This was another facet of Mirabeau's return to Fénelon's vision of Salentum as a pacific and luxury-free monarchy (Fénelon 1720; Hont 2006). If France assembled a coalition against England and destroyed the political underpinnings of European commercial rivalry (ibid., 3:99), it wouldn't be just following its own interest, but rendering a valuable service to the entire European continent. After victory, reason of state, both military and commercial, could be eliminated. Victorious France could then introduce and enforce free and fair trade and become a Friend of Mankind, *l'ami des hommes* (ibid., 2:33; 3:97, 103, 157, 162). With all the protectionist obstacles to trade having been removed by force, the nations of the world would share the fruits of commerce together and the progress of the arts and sciences peacefully and equitably (ibid., 3:103–10). This dream of a "universal confraternity of commerce" (ibid., 3:98, 103), Mirabeau claimed, was not a Platonic utopia but a practicable vision of the actual future of mankind. On its establishment, but only then, could the threat of self-canceling wealth, the inevitable migration of industries from rich to poor countries, be finally laid to rest.

Others were thinking along parallel lines, but came to somewhat different conclusions. The abbé Gabriel Bonnot de Mably, France's most important exponent of the urgent need of adapting the politics of the ancients, particularly the politics of the Greek and Roman republics (Mably 1749, 1751, 1766; c. Schleich 1980, 1981) to modern circumstances, and a leading expert on international relations, asked questions similar to those that Mirabeau raised (Wright 1992; cf. Sonenscher 2006, 2007). For Mably, modern commercial empires were fated to decline, just as the conquering military empires of the past had perished. Over-extended trade, he claimed, was just like over-extended empire. Like Melon and Montesquieu, he dismissed the spirit of conquest. Seeking old-style Roman dominance over Europe was dangerous (Mably 1794–95b [1757], 5:48–72). Great powers, Mably claimed, should aim at conservation. Lesser powers, he advocated in Machiavellian fashion, should refrain from challenging the greater ones and should, instead, seek alliances with richer nations (ibid., 5:83–84). National self-preservation depended not on fostering more and more commerce and luxury in the vain hope of winning the international trade wars, but on restraining these phenomena. Mably here echoed the well-known lessons of the fall of the Roman Republic. Luxury was not a sign of national greatness but the harbinger of decadence and eventual decline. Rather than returning to the ideas of Colbert, Mably claimed, one had to set one's eyes on the policies of the duc de Sully, the virtuous minister of Henri IV, and his support of agriculture rather than manufacturing and trade (ibid., 5:202). Instead of watching the balance of trade, Mably recommended, one must pay attention to agriculture and population growth. With these critical ideas Mably turned against his former self. In his first book, the *Parallèle des romains et des français* (Mably 1740), he had once celebrated, in the manner of Voltaire and Frederick's *Anti-Machiavel* (Frederick and Voltaire (1996) [1740], Frederick and Voltaire 1981 [1740]), modern European commerce and luxury as the guarantors of future peace (Hont 2006, 412–16).

In the chapter that surveyed commercial treaties in his *Principles of Negotiations* (Mably 1758 [1757] 191–99), Mably contrasted the ideas of

Hume and Cantillon and followed the Irishman's description of how the abundant money supply of rich nations undercut their commercial competitiveness, and hence their national power. Merchants, seeking their own profit, were blind to long-term perspectives. "But how could Mr. Hume," Mably asked,

> who a philosopher and politician, fall into this gross of errors? If the principal object which a government proposes to itself by favouring commerce be, and ought to be the increase of the nation's strength, by which it puts itself in a condition to defend its laws and its possessions against its enemies, how can it be doubted that luxury is not contrary to this end?
>
> (Mably 1758 [1757], 196)

As the Seven Years' War progressed and France's defeat became clear (Riley 1986), Mably became agitated about finding a solution to the dilemmas raised by Cantillon. He returned to the issue of the self-canceling properties of commercial greatness first in a work entitled *Phocion's Conversations: or the Relation between Morality and Politics* (Mably 1794–95c [1763], Mably 1769 [1763]), which appeared in the guise of a recently discovered set of Greek dialogues and soon won a prize in republican Switzerland. A year later, he repeated his ideas in the 1764 edition of his treatise on international law, entitled *Le droit publique de l'Europe* (Mably 1794–95d [1764], 6:515–16; that was first published in 1746 (Mably 1746). In these texts Mably qualified his earlier praise of Cantillon, because, as Mirabeau had already pointed out, the Irishman had failed to offer a method of proper and lasting crisis management.[24] Mably dismissed Cantillon's advice about exploiting the trade cycle as not addressing the underlying problem. Cantillon emphasized that the deflation caused by the rich country's economic crisis would facilitate a return to competitiveness. But he also admitted that the resumption of a steady inflow of commercial income would inevitably rekindle luxury. "The state," Cantillon wrote, "will fall into decadence a second time." This then necessitated a second rescue. "An able minister," Mably cited Cantillon, "has it always in his power to renew the rotation" (Mably 1769 [1763], 296; Mably (1794–95d [1764], 6:519–20).

Mably now emphasized that Cantillon grossly underestimated the damage caused by an economic downturn to a country's morale and national security. Cantillon's advice was no "master-piece" of the modern political art. Returning to foreign trade was not the only mode of re-acquiring wealth and power (Mably 1769 [1763], 296–98). It was a self-defeating policy that would cause repeated cycles of rise and decline, with each European state "necessarily passing through perpetual revolutions; falling from luxury to poverty, and rising from poverty and luxury" (ibid., 296; Mably 1794–95d [1764], 6:620–21). The task was not to muddle through repeated trade crises, but to learn the hard lesson from the demise of ancient commercial states and from the more recent decline of Spain and Holland. "Let us not be surprised,"

Mably declared, to find that "commerce is a kind of monster that is destroyed by its own hands" (ibid., 6:515). Patriotic prudence dictated that the only permanent solution to the "rotation" or "gyration" of modern states was the abandonment of foreign trade and the establishment of a closed trading state.[25]

Mably demanded a comprehensive reform of the European state system, but not through a virtuous war against the current European hegemon, as proposed by *L'ami des hommes*. His ideas rather resembled Andrew Fletcher's thinking in early eighteenth-century Scotland. Patriotism, Mably pointed out, could mitigate luxury within a national culture, but it was an impotent force in the arena of state rivalry (Mably 1769 [1763], 129–70). Worse, patriotism could all too easily turn into jealousy of trade. The world needed a new kind of politics in which the interest of mankind was also considered alongside the patriotically conceived interest of individual countries (ibid., 271–84). The love of mankind, *l'amour de l'humanité*, had to trump the love of country, *l'amour de la patrie*, in the heart of every individual (ibid., 136). To exorcise the mad and destructive economic race between nations, Mably further suggested, Europe must re-establish the sort of federal state that existed under Charlemagne (Mably 1794–95b [1757], 120; 1794–95e [1776], 287–89). Until that happened, Mably stated with resignation, the economic lessons of history had to be studied. Seeking grandeur and national security through economic growth was a chimera (Mably, 1794–95d [1764], 6:534; cf. Galliani 1975).

8. Democratic and Patriotic Luxury: Helvétius, Saint-Lambert and Schmid

It may be surprising to find that the famous *De l'ésprit* by Claude Adrien Helvétius (Helvétius 1758, 1759 [1758]) was also an important contribution to the discourse of luxury and to the rich country–poor country debate. Although it largely focused on the psychological foundations of politics, it was also a political treatise in a direct sense. Helvétius opposed Mirabeau's vision of agriculture providing an antidote to the Manichean struggle between sociability and cupidity that characterized modern politics (Mirabeau 1756, 1:6, 137; 2:49–50). Mirabeau denounced Epicureanism as the most dangerous doctrine in politics (2:141; 3:195). The *De l'ésprit*, on the other hand, became scandalous, because it offered a revised Epicurean alternative, utilizing the one philosophical tradition that was unacceptable for most social critics in the eighteenth century, not just for Mirabeau (Rosen 2003, 15–28, 82–96). Helvétius discussed luxury and its consequences at the beginning of the book, in a chapter entitled "Of ignorance," whose purpose was to demonstrate that we err in our political judgments not simply because our passions carry us away, but because we fail to study complex phenomena comparatively, that is by looking at them from more than one angle. Helvétius offered a spirited defense of moderate and egalitarian luxury, while maintaining the view that luxury based on inequality could never be a source of happiness, either for individuals or for the state. Commercial progress was beneficial only if it concentrated, as Mirabeau and Mably also suggested, on the necessities rather than the luxuries of life (Helvétius 1759 [1758], 13).

Helvétius pressed the rich country–poor country argument in the service of this thesis. He emphasized that luxury could be replaced by a healthier economy through the international economic rotation process implied by the idea of self-canceling growth. Instead of referring to Cantillon, he attributed the argument to Hume. The wealth and advantage of rich states were "as Mr. Hume observes, only transitory." Due to this transitoriness of wealth, Helvétius added, prosperity could become globalized: "riches, like those seas which successively forsake and overflow a thousand different tracts of land, must successively travel through a thousand climates." It was the relentless expansion of commerce that gave poor countries a chance to compete with rich ones. At first poor countries could "clandestinely procure some manufactures out of this rich nation" and copy them, making them more cheaply than the original inventors because "the price of goods, workmanship, and labor, will necessarily fall among those impoverished people." Even if these were somewhat inferior imitations, poor countries "may, by degrees ... supply themselves at a lower price with those goods, which they before imported from their rich neighbours." As a consequence rich countries gradually lost their export markets, which slowly "impoverished" them. The decline was difficult to arrest, Helvétius added, for "no sooner is the want of money perceived in a state accustomed to luxury than it becomes contemptible" (ibid.).

Helvétius, like Mirabeau and Mably, had to make sure that the same inflationary price mechanism that destroyed luxurious states won't destroy his healthy and democratic economy of "national luxury" too. He acknowledged that it was impossible to counterbalance the deleterious effects of rising mercantile income forever, even if the economy virtuously focused on the production and consumption of the right kind of goods (ibid., 1:120–21; cf. Helvétius 1759, 13). But the crisis could be delayed for a long period. It was manufacturing wealth, mainly operating at the luxury end of the market, which was particularly prone to self-canceling. "It is very different, however, with regard to the wealth flowing in from the commerce of goods immediately necessary" (ibid.). In a well-ordered poor country, like Switzerland, wages could be high, because citizens were stakeholders in the national economy and out of pure self-interest could resist the temptation of adopting seemingly attractive, but in reality self-destructive, pricing policies. Also, agrarian economies were much less exposed to competition from poor nations. Industries could relocate internationally without too much trouble, for "an art or a manufacture easily passes from one country to another." It was difficult, however, to copy complex agricultural practices:

To overcome the ignorance and sloth of peasants, and prevail on them to undertake the culture of a new commodity in a country is attended with great trouble and expence, by which the advantages of trade will almost ever incline to that country which produces this commodity naturally; and where it has, for a long time been cultivated.

(ibid.)

This new reading of Hume's message was widely noticed.[26] One highly audible echo appeared in the article "Luxury" of the *Encyclopédie* (Saint-Lambert 1764, 1765a, 1965 [1765b]; cf. Moureau 1968), which was first commissioned to Forbonnais, but was later reassigned by Diderot to Helvétius' friend (Saint-Lambert 1797–1801 [1777]), the marquis de Saint-Lambert. As Saint-Lambert presented it, luxury was not merely an economic phenomenon, but the central moral and political issue of modernity. He started off from the definition supplied by Forbonnais (Forbonnais 1754a, 1:221): Luxury is "the use which we make of riches and industry, in order to procure an agreeable existence" (Saint-Lambert 1766 [1765b], 1). This implied that "luxury" was a constitutive part of "self-love" and a direct offspring of human instinct. Saint-Lambert further described it as being caused by "dissatisfaction with our condition, that desire of bettering it, which is and ought to be in all men." This latter aspect of his definition is most familiar for us today from Adam Smith's *Wealth of Nations* as the "desire of bettering our condition, a desire which, though generally calm and dispassionate, comes with us from the womb, and never leaves us till we go into the grave" (Smith, 1976 [1776], 1:341). Saint-Lambert wanted to show off self-love in a positive light, and to counter Christian and republican moral asceticism. In his *Encyclopédie* articles on "Interest" and "Legislation" (Saint-Lambert 1765b, 1765c; cf. Grimsley 1985) he ferociously attacked the Jansenists and the libertines of the seventeenth century (Nicole, Pascal and La Rochefoucauld) for making "self-love a principle that is always vicious," and for finding "no virtue in us because self-love is the principle of our actions." Instead, Saint-Lambert aligned himself with the third earl of Shaftesbury, not as a theorist who counted "self-love in man for nothing" as he was often miscast, but as an innovative philosopher who regarded "benevolence, love of order, and even the most complete self-sacrifice as the effects of our self-love" (Saint-Lambert, 1765b, 8:818).

Saint-Lambert positioned himself between the two extremes of the luxury debate. For its critics luxury was the product of extreme inequality, the sacrifice of the countryside for the cities, the cause of depopulation, the nemesis of courage, honor and love of country. For its defenders, luxury was an engine of population growth, higher living standards, the circulation of money, good manners, the progress of the arts and sciences, and, last but not least, the power of nations and the happiness of citizens (Saint-Lambert 1766 [1765], 2–6). Saint-Lambert, like Melon, had no truck with radical anti-luxury reforms, or the cult of ancient military states. For him, it was better for a people "to obey frivolous Epicureans, than warlike savages, and to maintain the Luxury of voluptuous and intelligent knaves, than that of heroic and ignorant robbers" (ibid., 80). The real problem was to make modern economic growth politically and morally benign. World history, "the examples of the Egyptians, the Persians, the Greeks, the Romans, the Arabians, the Chinese, &c." proved that as nations and empires "increased in greatness," the concomitant luxury made them lose both "their virtues and of their power" (ibid., 12). This historical lesson, Saint-Lambert claimed, trumped all arguments in favor of luxury. Hume appeared in this context not as an apologist of unfettered luxury, but as a sage who foretold its demise. As Saint-Lambert explained,

> the prevailing opinion at present is, that to draw nations out of their weakness and obscurity; to give them a degree of strength, of consistency, of opulence, that shall raise them above other nations, Luxury is absolutely necessary: and that Luxury should proceed continually increasing, for the advancement of arts, of industry, and of commerce, and so bring nations to a point of maturity.
>
> (ibid., 12–13)

But at some point luxury had to stop. For the "vertical" point of the luxury of rich countries was

> necessarily followed by their old age, their decrepitude, and at length by their destruction. This is an opinion at present generally received, and that of Mr. Hume himself is not very distant from it.
>
> (ibid., 13)

Saint-Lambert dissolved the Hume paradox into a stages history of luxury whose trajectory resembled the biological life cycle. Hume, he claimed, approved luxury in the ascending stage and decried it in the descending one. Saint-Lambert, like Mirabeau, Helvétius and Mably, was interested in finding the tipping point and between rise and decline by looking at the cultural and political antidotes to luxury. He desired a "well-ordered" and patriotic luxury that could resist the threats involved in the rich country–poor country argument. Luxury sprung up from the private sphere (from the institution of private property, which was the source of inequality) and its selfish implications undermined the "*ésprit de communauté*" (ibid., 32; cf. Saint-Lambert 1765c, 9:357–58). It was this individualism that led to the catastrophic outcome of decline, because only "public spirit" could stop luxury from being harmful. Good or patriotic luxury had to be based not on individualism but on national communal feeling. Its establishment required a kind of monarchical equivalent of Rousseau's general will, a supervision of "patriotic luxury" by a pacific "pastoral king" as described by Fénelon and Mirabeau (Mirabeau 1756, 3:102, 206, 211; Saint-Lambert 1766 [1765], 60–75). Despite his rapport with Forbonnais in the definition of luxury and in the evaluation of England's merits (Saint-Lambert 1776 [1765], 76), Saint-Lambert disapproved of Melon's and Forbonnais' preference for commercially competitive states. On the other hand, he also rejected the idea of virtuous poverty, promoted by the Jansenists and Mably. Although he shared Helvétius' taste for Swiss-style patriotic economics, Saint-Lambert vehemently attacked his Epicureanism and replaced it with Shaftesbury as a moral guide. This eclectic philosophical repositioning of the entire luxury debate had a noticeable impact on how Hume was seen in its context.

Hume could now be depicted as a qualified supporter of luxury who also saw the fatal consequences of its abuse. This view was presented very clearly in the work of Georg Ludwig Schmid d'Auenstein, a Swiss writer in the service of the Prince of Weimar.[27] When Frederick the Great's Prussian armies chased Schmid back to Switzerland, he composed a series of philosophical and economic studies in French. The first volume of his essays, which included his thoughts on agriculture, commerce, and luxury, was noticed with interest in France (Schmid 1760a, 1760b; cf. with the less successful second volume, Schmid's 1763) as a clever synthesis of contemporary opinion with a fascinating Swiss gloss. Schmid's essay on agriculture was also published concurrently in the first number of the publications of the newly established Economic Society of Bern (Schmid 1760c; Strahm 1946; Kapossy 2002, 2006, 121–45), the most visible agency for the dissemination of republican economics in this period. In this important piece Schmid unmasked the patriotic mystique that surrounded French *agronomie* in the writings of the Gournay circle. The new French fashion for agricultural improvement, he claimed, was not a road to virtue, but to the restoration of France to great power status. Agriculture was promoted by French writers as a strategic necessity (Schmid 1772 [1760], 281–84). The true home of modern agriculture was England; hence *agronomie* was part and parcel of the new French strategy of directly copying the achievements of their neighbor island nation (ibid., 287–88). Schmid distanced himself from this route. He presented himself as a dedicated opponent of modern commercial wars, public debt and other experiments with paper money that were supposed to boost economic growth (ibid., 220–21, 226–27; cf. 78).

In order to prevent commercial wars and the economic self-destruction of rich nations, Schmid tried to locate the dividing line between good and bad luxury, between positive and corrupt economic development (Schmid 1772 [1760], 159, 203; cf. 209, 218–19, 249). On the one hand, just as Le Blanc had done earlier in his introduction to his Hume translation and Forbonnais in his *Élémens du Commerce*, Schmid cited Hume's famous dictum (the English translation actually adding Hume's name):

> that a people, who do not understand astronomy, cannot make a piece
> of cloth of a certain degree of beauty: a saying full of meaning, and of

which the inverted sense will hold equally good; namely, that astronomy will make but a poor figure in a country, where the people do not know how to make cloth in perfection. All holds together; and the progress of the human mind requires a gradation from the simple to the compound. A neglect of the mechanic arts would be an omen far from favourable to the fine arts and sciences.

(ibid., 205)

On the other hand, Schmid also recalled Hume's views on the inevitable decline of rich commercial nations. Too much money in a rich country raised wages, destroying export competitiveness (ibid., 201). This, Schmid explained, became a blessing for poor competitors. At first, they would feel injured, because their customary luxury imports from rich countries would be gradually priced out of their reach. Later, however, this loss could turn into a blessing in disguise. Feeling deprived, Schmid claimed, poor nations, had no choice but to set up their own manufacturing industry. This was the moment when the undoing of rich countries began. Normally, it was very difficult for poor countries to gather the necessary psychological and economic energy to launch a successful program of economic improvement. But now they "were obliged to exert themselves" because they missed the imported goods they became addicted to (ibid., 223). Of course, once they set up their own production facilities, their low wage levels made their new industries very competitive:

The rich people will even find their account in buying cheap of the poor. But if they buy more than they sell, the signs will soon follow their natural course, and pass into the hands of the poor nations.

(ibid.)

The result would be a spectacular collapse of the work ethic of rich nations:

The faculty of buying cheaper than their own productions cost them, will make the rich people neglect their industry: they will become poor in return. Such is the fatal circle which all commercial states have run through, as history testifies; and which they must of necessity go through.

(ibid.)

This kind of decline was not the natural outcome of trade as such, Schmid pointed out, but the result of the political misconception of seeing money as the sinews of power. It was international power politics that led to an over-promotion of commerce as the vehicle of achieving national greatness (ibid., 208). Schmid too had no doubt that England's intent was to acquire a world trade monopoly and recognized that this development called for some sort of response (ibid., 209; cf. 197). He searched for the key to England's success and discovered it in the agricultural projects of the country's republican period: "England owes her progress in good husbandry to the instructions and example of Milton's friend, Hartlib" (ibid., 79). It was this Cromwellian and Restoration boost to agriculture that prepared England's economic victory in the next century. "A single citizen," Schmid commented, "cemented the grandeur of his country" (ibid.; cf. 281). The French and most Europeans, he claimed, only saw the success of England's trade and industry and were seduced into imitating them as the best and only way to achieve great power status in the modern world (ibid., 207). In their mad scrambling for commerce the Europeans neglected agriculture and lost the competition with England. The correction, however, had to be more fundamental than a belated economic sprint to quickly improve agriculture, as in France in the 1750s. Instead, Schmid suggested, the entire modern project of coupling wealth and power had to be revised and perhaps abandoned.

Commerce and industry often needed special support, but only to such a degree that assured that they could never again charge ahead of the growth of agriculture. At first domestic trade, rather than exports, had to be promoted and excess population had to be channeled to agricultural employment rather than urban job opportunities. Schmid didn't recommend waging a holy war for free trade, as Mirabeau did. But, like Mirabeau, he wanted to roll back the pathological competitiveness of modern states and redirect their energies toward seeking patriotism and honor rather than economic profit (ibid., 252–62). Then free trade could flourish and generate all those benefits of commercial civilization that Hume had so eloquently described. In this light even Colbert could be partially rehabilitated:

> The utility of Colbert's projects, for establishing the arts and commerce in France, was not limited to the state for which they were made. All Europe reaped their fruits; and that great men may be truly said to have contributed more than any other to bring about the enlightened times in which we live. He roused the industry of all nations: an industry, which gave us that ease and luxury, without which there never will be either knowledge and politeness. The revocation of the edict of Nantes completed the dispersal in the north that seed which Colbert had intended only for the soil of France.
>
> (ibid., 77)

If politics were reformed and commerce were firmly brought under psychological and moral control, then the industrial migration mechanism underpinning Hume's rich country–poor country argument, instead of being a threat, would turn into a blessing. If trading nations kept to the path of a commercial golden mean, "trade ... will then prove the happiness of nations, and will re-establish the natural level of the riches of the world" (ibid., 267).

9. More Benign Gyrations: The New Hume Translation and Condillac

Due to these views, George Ludwig Schmid became a welcome guest in Parisian salons in the 1760s, making friends with Mably, Mirabeau and many others (Seifert 1987; cf. English translations, Schmid 1772 in England and Schmid 1791 in America, see also the later Schmid 1776; cf. Becagli 2004). Most of his conversation partners were also pondering the true character of Hume's rich country–poor country argument. The issue was pushed in the limelight when in 1767 a new translation of Hume's economic essays appeared (Hume 1767a). Hume's text, yet again, was carefully con-textualized for French audiences. The commentary supplied by the anon-ymous translator was anti-physiocratic, defensive of the centrality of foreign trade for economic growth and critical of Hume's opposition to the public debt. Forbonnais was the only writer he cited by name (Hume 1767a, 142). This time, however, the translator did not repeat Le Blanc's mistake of silently passing over Hume's disturbing prophecy of the decline of all rich nations. "Of Money" now received ample critical commentary, starting with the declaration that the contradiction generally perceived in Hume's views on commerce and luxury in his essay "Of Money" was illu-sory and an artifact of his elliptical way of writing (ibid., 78). Careful reading, the commentator insisted, could reduce Hume's essay to three propositions:

1   Money is useful only when it circulates;
2   Circulation follows necessarily from commerce and luxury;
3   The most wealthy and commercial states must lose their advantages through the very consequences of their commerce, whose growth increases the value of all kinds of necessaries, of merchandise, and of labour.

(ibid.)

The third proposition, the commentator explained, might look paradoxical until one noticed that Hume himself had resolved it. He did not go so far as to claim that Hume had somehow clarified the issue in the text of "Of Money" itself. Rather, he made the same point that some of Hume's oppo-nents had already developed in England. Josiah Tucker argued in the introduction to the first of his *Four Tracts*, written specifically against Hume's rich country–poor country argument, that in his *History of England* the Scottish author had recanted his earlier views (Tucker 1774a). In his series of special chapters on England's social and economic condition, Tucker noticed, Hume presented long-term price trends and concluded that in rich countries, such as England, the price of manufactured goods tended to decrease, rather than increase, over time.[28] The French translator did not refer to Tucker, but his point was the same as that of the English author.

The translator followed Forbonnais's earlier suggestion that the effects of the influx of money into a trading economy had to be studied realistically, rather than via imagined experiments presupposing a miraculously sudden rise or fall in the money supply. Since the new money was first spent by the upper strata of society on luxury products, the price level of basic goods, and hence wage rates, lagged behind the prices of luxury goods and could even fall (ibid., 85–86). Machines could also raise productivity enormously (ibid., 87). Hume, the translator claimed, had proven these conjectures in his *History of the Stuarts* (Hume 1766 [1754]) by supplying the necessary data. In order to substantiate this point, a translation of the relevant passages from the *History* was appended to the commentary on "Of Money" (ibid., 89–91; cf. Hume 1983a [1754–62], 5:138–40).[29]

It now appeared that Hume and Forbonnais were quite close to each other in their thinking. Rich countries had not experienced the sort of secular increase in the price of their wage goods that would have made them uncompetitive. Nor did they price themselves out of international markets by some automatic monetary correction mechanism. Therefore the key argument that was customarily leveled against a national economic strategy advocating the expansion of foreign trade turned out to be groundless. Foreign trade did not necessarily lead to ruin. Rather, commerce could be shown to be a blessing for all, because its inbuilt reciprocity mechanism ensured that wealth and high living standards were eventually reached by the entirety of mankind:

> Hence, the large quantity of gold and silver that commerce brings into a state is not harmful to that very commerce. Far from increasing the price of necessaries, of merchandise and of labour, it diminishes their value; its principal effect is thus to distribute the precious metals amongst all nations of this earth and, by making them rich in species, to engage them to participate themselves in a commerce which increases the pleasures and commodities of men and reduces the ills of which most of them are affected.
>
> (Hume 1767a, 88–89)

This was similar to the conclusion that Schmid and others had arrived at earlier. In this instance, however, there were no carefully constructed provisos against vicious international rivalry that moral and economic critics of the modern symbiosis between commerce and power invariably insisted on. It seemed, instead, that Hume had changed his spots. His credentials as a trusted supporter of commercial civilization were upheld and he could be removed from the Forbonnais group's list of paradoxical authors.

There were also interesting developments in the other side of the French rich country–poor country debate. The argument that high wages put a damper on international competitiveness in all rich nations received its fullest exposition in France in 1776, in a monograph entitled *Commerce and Government Considered in Their Mutual Relationship* (Condillac 1776; Condillac 1997 [1776]), which the author, the philosopher Étienne Bonnot de Condillac (Knight 1968) and Mably's brother, described as an introductory textbook (Eltis and Eltis 1997). In it Condillac criticized, just as Mably had, the corruption caused by France's entanglement in the commercial aspects of modern international politics (Lebeau 1903). He stridently complained about the envy of European nations regarding each other's wealth:

> European trade is not an exchange of works in which all nations will each find their advantage; it is a state of war in which they only think of how to plunder each other. ... In perpetual rivalry they only work at hurting each other. There is not one of them that would not wish to destroy all others; and not one of them considers ways to make its real strength grow.
>
> (Condillac 1997 [1776], 202)

Condillac focused on repairing the damage that Louis XIV and Colbert had caused to French agriculture, and reconsidered the policies of promoting luxury and the freedom of the grain trade. He was particularly emphatic in condemning competitive trade in manufactured goods. As "a new manufacturing process establishes itself in one nation," Condillac wrote, "each nation wants to establish it" (ibid., 201). Complementary trade was natural and true to the providential design of the world. There was, however, simply no need for every country and province to emulate the others in producing the same goods for export.

Condillac praised Cantillon, but did not refer to him when discussing the dangers facing rich nations. Rather, in a chapter entitled "The Circulation of Wealth When Trade Enjoys Complete Freedom" (ibid., 223–28) he offered a version of the rich country–poor country argument that seems to show that he had read Hume's version in "Of Money." In order to demonstrate that lasting competitive advantage in manufacturing was a chimera, Condillac presented an elaborate argument concerning the self-canceling nature of growth in manufacturing industries. Instead of assuming the international antagonism of rival nations, as his brother did, he stipulated a complete freedom of trade (the absence of borders and protectionism) since principles, he claimed, could only be discussed properly if the analytical premises were simplified (ibid., 213–14). To give his argument a realistic feel, he assumed not separate countries competing, but a set of industrial and agricultural provinces within the same nation.

Condillac passionately defended free trade and emphasized that under its aegis all trade had to be reciprocal, rendering protectionism a futile policy (Orain 2003). Under conditions of completely free trade, he emphasized, free from the distortions of political or military power, no nation or province could ever establish a competitive monopoly (ibid., 221). Initially, as industrial regions increasingly profited from their trade and got richer, they acted as magnets for transferable resources (manpower and goods). This migration of resources, Condillac assumed, was bound to lead to both the relative and absolute impoverishment of agricultural regions (ibid., 224). This monopolistic tendency of manufacturing, however, checked itself, because the newly successful centers of industry became not only opulent but also very expensive. To compensate for this loss of competitiveness, individual manufacturers were tempted to transfer production to low wage areas, where they would return to profitable trading (ibid., 225–26). At this point Condillac faithfully reproduced Hume's argument from "Of Money," including its clumsy metaphor of commerce apparently flying all over the globe, passing on the benefits of industry from province to province, and nation to nation. Registering the flight of productive assets and manpower from rich regions, however, was not the end of Condillac's analysis. He borrowed an argument from his brother Mably's earlier interpretation of Cantillon and asserted that trading economies always gyrated in a revolving motion. When "the high price of labor starts to make manufactures decay," Condillac wrote, "the low price will raise them up again in another" (ibid., 227). But the moral and political lessons the two brothers drew from this diverged quite sharply. According to Condillac, instead of leading to an endless series of destabilizing revolutions, the trade cycles of rich nations contributed to the birth of a better world.

As industrial production migrated from country to country across the world, international inequality would disappear. Eventually no country would be "too rich, so none will be poor" (ibid.). Therefore the world could avoid the sort of poisonous instability, which Mably feared so much, in which countries living in "wretchedness" and in "opulence" coexisted without remedy. With the help of the self-leveling process of industrial migration, Condillac hoped, all nations would eventually possess industry and agriculture in a balanced mix. Under the blissful auspices of genuine free trade, he wrote, commerce will not resemble anymore an ebbing and flowing tide, but it would be "like a river that divides into a host of channels, to water all lands in succession" (ibid.). Further developing Hume's metaphor for the specie-flow argument as of water finding its own level, Condillac argued that the never ending rotation of commercial states would be a benign one because it would operate without violence. "Wealth," he wrote, "will flock back continuously" from one province to another, "following the different gradients that trade will make them take" (ibid.). "Freedom," Condillac stated the political corollary of his argument, "has thus the benefit of guaranteeing them all against poverty, and the same time checking the advance of wealth in each, when excess of this kind could be harmful" (ibid., 227–28). In other words, the more the rich country–poor country dynamic was allowed a free rein in the world, the better it was for the future of mankind.

Condillac recognized that Hume's argument, which earlier was used to destroy the idea of commercial world monopoly, could also be used to provide an escape from the limitations of the views of his brother, who advocated the abandonment of the very idea of a world based on foreign trade. The menacing problem of rich countries losing trade to poor ones remained on Mably's mind when America achieved its independence and its leaders were actively searching for the most appropriate constitutional principles. In the fourth letter of his *Remarks Concerning the Government and the Laws of the United States of America, in Four Letters Addressed to Mr. Adams* (Mably (1794–95ff.) [1784], Mably 1785 [1784]) he warned the new republican state of the mortal danger it would face if it imitated Europe's commercial development. He relied still on Cantillon to demonstrate the danger for rich countries, but this time he formatted the issue of self-canceling wealth in a way that paid attention to the fact that the competition came from poor countries. His new view resembled the positions of Helvétius and Schmid, and of Condillac (and through Condillac, Hume). Commerce, Mably repeated Cantillon's message, produced no more than "momentary and transient power" in every nation. As America developed, it would become rich; hence prices and wages would rise. Mably, however, on this occasion didn't draw the picture of a future America locked into a deadly struggle with the European powers for external markets. Instead, he focused on the difficulties America would face if it did become a rich nation and a great power.

In a rich America, he warned, prices would rise, while the response of profit-conscious American merchants would be anything but patriotic. As domestic producers gradually priced themselves out of the market, Mably wrote, American "traders [would] abandon their own merchandise to hunt after the manufactures of an impoverished people, among whom the price of workmanship is cheap" (Mably 1785 [1784], 194). An employment crisis would inevitably follow, and eventually even war. That part of the population that suffered from the practice of outsourcing most would then petition the government to stop industrial decline. Their plea, however, would be in vain, for it was simply not in the government's power to protect them. Rich nations, Mably wrote, were invariably arrogant when their economy was flourishing. They despised their neighbors and competitors and, at the height of their growth, rushed into various financial schemes, like public debt and paper money. But when decline sets in, these "imaginary riches" disappear into thin air. At this point, Mably predicted, rich nations would become desperate and would try "to re-animate commerce by the assistance of the sword" (ibid., 196). This kind of policy, he warned, had always been based on a disastrous miscalculation concerning the cost of modern warfare. Wars consumed more resources than even the most flourishing trade could earn for a nation. Hence, wars for markets were bound to cause not the enrichment, but the impoverishment and hence the eventual decline of the mighty American state.

10. The Case of Ireland after 1776 and the Commercial Propositions

Hume died in 1776, in the year when Condillac published his *Commerce and Government* and Adam Smith's long awaited *Inquiry into the Nature and Causes of the Wealth of Nations* finally appeared.[30] The debate about international competition between nations of varying levels of economic development continued unabated. It flared up with a vengeance in its original Irish setting (Black 1969) in the two decades of controversy and discussion that preceded the Irish–British parliamentary union of 1801. In the *Wealth of Nations* Smith did mention, however briefly, the issue of Irish free trade. He recommended that Ireland should be allowed free trade in exchange for the extension of English taxation, both customs and excise, to Ireland (Smith 1976 [1776], 2:934–35). He surmised, however, that Ireland would probably have to pay a higher price. The precondition of receiving the right of free trade with England was likely to be a full political union between the two countries. He encouraged the Irish to see this as a worthwhile bargain. A Union was likely to deliver more important benefits than trade liberalization itself. It could usher in major social and political changes. Smith described Ireland as experiencing a simmering civil war between Protestants and Catholics and prophesized that without a Union "the inhabitants of Ireland" would never be able to "consider themselves as one people" (ibid., 2:944).

It took another quarter of a century and the long crisis of the French Revolution and the subsequent Continental war for the Union of Ireland and Great Britain to be consummated (Black 1950). The process, however, started soon after the publication of the *Wealth of Nations*. As America achieved its independence, Ireland slipped into a post-war economic depression, which caused serious political and social discontent (Powell 2003). The relaxation or outright abolition of the late seventeenth-century trade prohibitions against Ireland became an urgent issue. At first, compromises of a lesser order were sought, without as yet attempting to negotiate a full Union. Lord North, the Prime Minister, started the process in 1778. As his overtures failed to stop the unrest, the Viceroy in Dublin began to consult the Irish political elite in the spring of 1779, in order to measure the strength of feeling about Irish demands for free trade (O'Brien 1923–24). The definitive political answer was received on 12 October, when the Irish Parliament resolved to call for the liberalization of the country's trade. By that time a new Viceroy was nominated, Lord Carlisle, who was supported by the capable and proactive William Eden as his Chief Secretary. Eden decided to clear the air by publishing a number of open letters to Carlisle, in which he offered a candid analysis of the problems that Ireland faced in the wake of America's independence (Eden 1779a, 1779b, 1780a, 1780b). Eden's fourth letter to Carlisle concerned Irish free trade. Before finalizing it he solicited Smith's views through intermediaries such as Henry Dundas and Adam Ferguson. Dundas (Willis 1979; Teichgraeber 1987), one of the most influential Scottish politicians and effectively Scotland's political manager, expressed liberal views about Irish commercial progress and criticized the special interest lobby in England for their demand for protection. He was still worried, however, about the rich country–poor country issue. In his letter to Smith he advocated the creation of a new regulatory regime to prevent "the people in Ireland being able to undersell us in foreign mercates from the want of Taxes and the Cheapness of labour" (Smith 1987, 240).[31]

Smith dismissed these fears, claiming that there was no need for legislative prohibitions to hold back Irish aspirations. He had three arguements. First, he clained, England had overwhelming competitive superiority over Ireland:

> I cannot believe that the manufactures of G.B. can, for a century to come, suffer much from the rivalship of those of Ireland, even tho' the Irish should be indulged in a free trade. Ireland has neither the Skill, nor the Stock which could enable her to rival England; and tho' both may be acquired in time, to acquire them compleatly will require the operation of little less than a century.
>
> (Smith 1987d [1779], 240)[32]

Second, Smith indicated that the issue wasn't anymore competition in the wool industry, as in 1698, but rivalry in modern manufacturing. At the eve of the industrial revolution what mattered was the availability of cheap fuel. For "the progress of Great Manufactures" (Smith 1987e [1779], 243) Ireland's natural endowment was poor:

> Ireland has neither coal nor Wood. The former seems to have been denied to her by nature; and tho her soil and climate are perfectly suited for raising the latter; yet to raise it to the same degree as in England will require more than a century.
>
> (Smith 1987d [1779], 240–41)

Third, in his next letter on the subject, addressed to Lord Carlisle directly, Smith also offered the same broad social and political analysis concerning Ireland that he had already adumbrated in the *Wealth of Nations*. Economic growth required good government and a liberal and tolerant political environment. Ireland, Smith pointed out,

> wants order, police, and a regular administration of justice both to protect and to restrain the inferior ranks of people, articles more essential to the progress of Industry than both coal and wood put together, and which Ireland must continue to want as long as it continues to be divided between two hostile nations, the oppressors and the oppressed, the protestants and the Papists.
>
> (Smith 1987e [1779b], 243–44)

It would be madness not to allow the Irish to practice free trade, Smith claimed. International trade was not a zero-sum game, but a process of increasing overall wealth:

> Should the Industry of Ireland, in consequence of freedom and Good Government, ever equal that of England so much the better would it be, not only for the whole British empire, but for the particular province of England. As the wealth and industry of Lancashire does not obstruct, but promote that of Yorkshire; so the wealth and industry of Ireland, would not obstruct, but promote that of England.
>
> (ibid., 244)

There was not even a hint in Smith's vision of the kind of roller-coaster ride in the economic fortunes of provinces and nations, rising and falling as industrial competition between poorer and richer countries developed, that so many of his contemporaries, in Europe, America and Britain, feared and prophesied. Those who still insisted on such views, Smith suggested, were monopolists and the defenders of their own sectional interests against the national one. The government, Smith told Dundas, should deal with the issue through tactful pressure and persuasion.

Smith's advice must have reached Eden in time,[33] for he relied on it heavily in composing his own open letter to Lord Carlisle. Eden recapitulated Smith's taxonomy of the degrees of free trade Ireland might aspire to (Smith 1987 [1779], 241; Eden 1779b, 17–18). At the end, he also neatly summarized Smith's description of Ireland's competitive disadvantages. He did not refer to Smith. He had already paid a handsome compliment to the author of the *Wealth of Nations* in his third letter, which dealt with issues of taxation and the public debt.[34] Rather, Eden invoked Hume's authority in support of Smith's point. Any economic gain to Ireland, Eden emphasized, was also England's gain. He freely acknowledged that Ireland's troubles were caused by England's oppressive policies and he went out of his way to denounce Davenant's narrow-minded views on Irish free trade and the dangers it represented for the security of the British state. He denounced the special interests that asked for protection, conceding no more than the need of infant industries for a temporary shelter. It was at the end of his letter, that Eden paid special attention to the dangerous logic of the rich country–poor country argument. He made a valiant effort to dispel English fears about the competitive advantages of poor countries like Ireland.

It was ridiculous to fear, Eden wrote, that a "people should suddenly run away with an extensive commerce, because they are admitted to a participation of its advantages" (ibid., 27). There was no need for the knee-jerk response of jealousy of trade. Rather, Eden recommended a cautious and pragmatic approach to the Irish problem. "Theorems of trade, however plausible they may appear on paper" (ibid., 20, 25), had to be contextualized and verified first. He also deemed the notion that England would not allow the Irish free trade without a full political Union as "rash." Free trade could be managed without political unification, because poor countries like Ireland were not really competitive. Economic decline, Eden pointed out, was often swift. Economic improvement, on the other hand, was always slow and tortuous. To prove this point, Eden invoked David Hume's authority and quoted the first half of Hume's rich country–poor country argument from the 1752 essay "Of Money":

> The change is more difficult from indolence to industry, than it is from labour to ease; and it is forcibly observed by Mr. Hume, that "when one nation has got the start of another in a trade, it is very difficult for the latter to gain the ground which she has lost, because of the superior industry and skill of the former, and the greater stock of which its merchants are possessed, and which enables them to trade for much smaller profits."
>
> (ibid., 27–28)

Readers of Hume would have remembered that the rich country–poor country argument did not end here and would have registered Eden's irony in truncating Hume's paragraph. Clearly, Eden could not continue to cite the second half of Hume's statement, about the huge drawback of high prices in rich countries and the equally important advantage of low wages in poor nations. This was the point he wished to defeat, not to assert. Instead, Eden replaced it with his concise summary of Ireland's economic and political predicament, drawn from Smith's letter. The melancholy estimate of a "century" that might elapse before Ireland might become competitive did not appear, but Eden nonetheless enlisted the formidable obstacles that Ireland faced. This was not the moment, he wrote, for visionary prophecies and impatience:

> Amidst the difficulties which time, and the fostering attention of this country, alone can enable Ireland to overcome, it deserves remark, that she has little coal, is ill provided with wood, and is also without inland navigations.—In short, the constitution and establishment of a flourishing commerce imply a well-regulated order through the nation, a steady and effective police, habits of docility and industry, skill in manufactures, and large capitals in trade; all which can be the result only of a continued and gradual progress, aided by a combination of other favouring circumstances.
>
> (ibid., 28)

Eden and Smith were not alone in their dismissal of Ireland's competitive threat. Other leading politicians and intellectual heavyweights in political economy, such as Josiah Tucker, Edmund Burke and Arthur Young, expressed the same view. The protracted negotiations between Britain and Ireland were complex, for an elaborate regime of tax arrangements and commercial regulations needed to be negotiated. Throughout, the really big and divisive issue, however, was the rich country–poor country problem. The unfair and punitive regulatory regime of 1698 had long been justified by English fears that if Ireland allowed free trade it would simply snatch away English markets. Ireland would "undersell" England, it was claimed, by virtue of its low wages and food prices. This debating position had not changed much, if at all, over eighty years. The government feared and expected that the merchant and manufacturing interests would raise the old complaints about Irish "underselling" again, as they had done at every stage of legislative intervention since the Glorious Revolution. The government's fear proved to be justified (see Manufacturers 1785; cf. Kelly 1992, 114–18). To pre-empt this mischief, successive Prime Ministers, Lord North, Lord Shelburne and Pitt, aggressively argued the case for the overwhelming competitive superiority of rich countries like England over poorer nations like Ireland.

Josiah Tucker reminded his Irish readers of his earlier refutation of Hume's argument and claimed that everything he said about poor Scotland applied to Ireland as well (Tucker 1785, iv–vi). Edmund Burke, who faced up to the lobbying of the Merchant Venturers of Bristol for Irish trade prohibition (Mahoney 1960), just as aggressively argued in 1785 as it was in 1698, did not mince his words:

> The Irish will be able to follow the English at equal distance, in every stage, both in the outset and in the continuance, but they will never be able to accelerate their motion in order to overtake them. The lowness of labour is a nugatory argument; for until the instant that price of labour is equal, the superiority of manufacture will remain with the English. The price of labour rises with the growth of manufacture, and is highest when the manufacture is best. The experience of every day tells us, that where the price of labour is highest, the manufacturer is able to sell his commodity at the lowest price.
>
> (Burke 1991 [1778], 522)

Arthur Young cited both Tucker and Burke approvingly (Young 1785, 267–68) and set his sights on destroying the case for the English manufacturing interest's pleas for protection altogether. He thought that Ireland needed at least a half century to reach a moderately competitive position. He dismissed the assumption that England's industries might migrate, which he took to be the assumed migration of both capitalists and their workers, to Ireland:

> The emigration of great stocks, great skill, and a great manufacture from a rich country to a poor one! I will venture to assert, that the whole world cannot give a single instance of it.
>
> (ibid., 267)

Young marshaled a century of respectable Irish argument, from Petty and Temple to the eighteenth century, to show that the price of wage goods had to be high, in order to provide an incentive for the development of a kind of work ethic that was necessary for industrial achievement. Basing itself on low food prices and low wages, Ireland was doomed. Despite its high wages, Young observed, England produced textiles from Irish yarn cheaper than the Irish could. "The clearest proof in the world," he concluded, that "the *dear and wealthy* country will, in almost every competition, get the better of the *cheap and poor* one" (ibid., 273). Arguments of this kind were not addressed to an Irish audience, but to the English special interest lobby. Hence the dismissal of the rich country–poor country argument was meant as an expression of expressly liberal sentiments, based on the most up-to-date understanding of market forces. They were arguments for free trade. As Eden explained in his letter to Carlisle, the aim was "to convey essential benefits to Ireland, without any permanent disadvantage to Great Britain" (Eden 1779, 28).

The first round of English concessions, in 1780–82, allowed Ireland free trade with third parties, including England's colonies, but not with England itself. As the discontent continued, in 1785 Pitt tried to liberalize even this last bastion of the old commercial system. In his famous Commercial Propositions he offered unrestricted Anglo-Irish commercial relations in exchange for Ireland accepting a customs and excise regime that contained special provisions for an Irish contribution toward the finance of the British navy. Pitt was anxious to safeguard the English government from any accusation that they were selling out British industry by exposing it to the vicious rivalry of a poor and low-wage nation. (Pitt 1808a [1785] and 1808b [1785]). He acknowledged that the 1698 regulations were illiberal, unjust and amounted to a "system of thraldom" or "commercial subserviency" (Pitt 1808b [1785], 136). He also made two determined efforts to dismiss the rich country–poor country argument substantially following the line of reasoning that Tucker developed against Hume in the late 1750s and early 1760s (Semmel 1965, 759, 766). Low wage rates paid for simple or "rude" work, he claimed, were irrelevant in the modern age. Low wages did not entail cheap labor and cheap products. Rather, competitive success depended on the skill and productivity of poor countries, in which skilled work was very expensive and capital shortages were often debilitating. Establishing new production facilities required a long time and if they did take root, they were bound to generate wage rises, thereby canceling Ireland's competitive advantages (Pitt 1808b [1785], 143). England, Pitt claimed, had beaten Ireland on price in almost every sector of the economy, even in domestic Irish markets. Ireland's low taxation, Pitt added, didn't convey great advantages either. A rich country could bear a ten times higher tax burden than a poor one and still remain competitive. Ireland had a few price-competitive products, Pitt conceded, but this was no reason for jealousy of trade. Rather, it had to be looked at benevolently, for it allowed,

Pitt claimed, at least some mutual trade to continue between the two nations (Pitt 1785b [1785], 193–95).

11. Hume and arguments for the British–Irish Union of 1801

Due to the diverging interests of Britain and Ireland and to party political squabbles on both sides, the Commercial Propositions were rejected in 1785 (Schweitzer 1984; Kelly 1975 and especially Kelly 1992). Eden, who a year later negotiated a pioneering trade agreement between Britain and France, denounced Pitt as a free trade dogmatist. The principles Pitt pursued, Eden argued, "were suitable enough in theoretical essays, but calamitous when made applicable to the complicated state of this great kingdom" (Eden 1785, 964–65). Pitt's strategy was careless. He managed to neutralize some of the English and Scottish special interest groups, although not his party political opponents like Charles James Fox (Semmel 1965, 765–66). In the meanwhile he totally disappointed his Irish partners. Not only hopes and illusions were dashed, their arguments were also undermined. Pitt's Commercial Propositions failed because the Irish, not the British Parliament, refused to ratify them. Pitt insisted that Ireland's competitive situation was practically hopeless and thereby devalued free trade as a bargaining chip in the process of forging a political compromise. The consequences of this Irish disenchantment with a free trade regime that was likely to be dominated entirely by England's industrial might became painfully clear when the actual and final Union negotiations were launched in the late 1790s, under the pressure of the French Revolution and the ensuing war (Bolton 1966; Geoghegan 2000). The trade controversy aspect of the Union debate (cf. McCormack 1996) reached its rhetorical apex when the Speaker of the Irish Parliament, John Foster (Malcolmson 1972, 1978), reminded the Irish nation of Pitt's debating points in 1785. In 1799 Pitt tried a new tack. He wooed Ireland with the prospect that under the aegis of a Union Ireland's low wages would lure English capital there to build up a highly competitive export trade, delivering goods both back to Britain and also to Europe and the rest of the world. In response, Foster reminded Pitt of his previous paean of English competitive superiority in the face of any kind of low-wage-based challenge (Foster 1799a [1785] in Pitt 1799; Foster 1799b).

A comparison of Pitt's 1785 and 1799 speeches, Foster claimed, revealed either bad faith or a blatant contradiction in the British negotiating position. Pitt's promise of the "diffusion of British capital" to Ireland (Foster 1779b, 73) was false. If modern industry was indeed based on labor-saving machines, then Ireland's low wages became unimportant. Why should English firms migrate to Ireland, Foster asked, if their competitive superiority was assured anyway? Like Smith and Eden in 1779, Foster maintained that Ireland was poorly endowed with material resources for modern industry.[35] Hence, British capital would most likely stay put at home and swamp the Irish and world markets with superior products directly from its home base.

The gap between English and Irish competitiveness was so great that unrestricted free trade with Britain would simply destroy Ireland's economy. Therefore, Foster concluded, Ireland must not enter into a Union with Britain for commercial reasons.

Among others (Longueville 1799, 8–11), it was Hume's authority that was wheeled in by unionists to undermine Foster's judgment.[36] Lord Shelburne hailed Josiah Tucker as a countervailing authority in support of the Union. But in economic terms Tucker was Pitt's inspiration and the wrong weapon against Foster. In his first Irish tract (Tucker 1785), Tucker described Ireland as a free land unencumbered by the mercantile system in which England became hopelessly mired. Ireland was therefore Tucker's shining hope for developing a truly free commercial economy of the kind that England could have become after the Glorious Revolution but never did. A free Ireland could act as a magnet for capital both from England and Europe, as well as to entrepreneurial talent and skilled labor. Ireland, Tucker imagined, was to become Europe's new industrial base and the hub of its entrepôt trade. After the failure of Pitt's Commercial Propositions, Tucker immediately started his campaign for a Union. His views on the subject were published posthumously in 1799, extracted from his private correspondence and accompanied by a commentary by his closest Irish companion in the 1780s, Thomas Brooke Clarke (Tucker 1799a, 1799b).

It was this joint product of Tucker's and Clarke's views (Clarke 1799a, 1799b) that Shelburne praised (Clarke 1799c, title page). In it Clarke rebutted Irish skepticism about the Union and announced that Ireland was destined to become the pivot of the world economy if it joined forces with England. To achieve this, Ireland had to transform itself into a patriotic economy. An Irish economy had to get rid of Dublin as a bloated and corrupt capital city (Clarke 1799b, 22, 36–37) and follow the logic of the natural progress of opulence. First an "Agricultural System" had to be put in place that could produce cheap wage goods, alleviate poverty and abolish unemployment. Next domestic commerce had to be developed (ibid., 11–14) and finally foreign trade. With such sound foundations, Ireland could happily merge with Britain as the world's leading economic and naval power and receive its fair share of the spoils of England's world economic leadership while also sheltering safely under the world's best national security umbrella:

> For, she who commands the Commerce, commands the Wealth; and she who commands the Wealth of the World, must command the World itself. To an Union of this nature then Ireland is called.
>
> (ibid., 32)

Instead of jealousy of trade, Clarke argued, there would be a division of labor between the two countries:

> One nation will pursue that manufacture which it can fabricate with most profit; and buy from the other what it can render cheaper. The communication between their respective markets will be encouraged by a mutual preference; and consolidated and united they will soon out-rival all the strangers of the universe.
>
> (ibid., 41–42)

Clarke had confidence in Pitt's "diffusion of British capital" argument. If Ireland clearly shared Britain's political, military and economic aims, British capital would come to Ireland confidently and exploit the country's low wages. By availing itself of Ireland's low wages, Britain's world economic leadership would rest on even safer foundations than before:

> In the establishment of all manufactures, and to which we look through the security of Incorporation, there are two leading objects. The first is, cheapness as to provision and labour, and that is in Ireland: the next is near, sure, and extensive market, and that is England. Consequently, with a good climate, equal natural powers, cheaper food, and lower labour, the skill and capital of England will find its way to Ireland, in order to sell to England: and with superior situation, and Ports for Commerce, the skill and capital of England will find its way to Ireland to sell to, and undersell the world.
>
> (ibid., 41)

This was precisely the thesis that Foster wanted to undermine. Shelburne found Clarke's pamphlet congenial because it reflected many of the political and economic beliefs that he and the group of political thinkers and political economists around him had already developed in the previous decade. Shelburne was an acquaintance of both Smith and Tucker. More importantly, he was the patron of a number of more radical thinkers, such a Richard Price and Jeremy Bentham, and a friend of Benjamin Franklin. Tucker's relationship with Shelburne was ambiguous. His last published writing was directed against Shelburne's patronage of pro-revolutionary politics, denouncing his radical patriotic connections and refuting the Lockean–Dissenter–American politics that accompanied it (Tucker 1783; cf. Fitzmaurice 1875).[37] However, Clarke's own pamphlet, far more than Tucker's underlying draft, flirted with the Shelburne group's idea of a new commercial system (Clarke 1781; cf. Sheridan 1779), grounded in free trade but also aiming to put an end to international rivalry and jealousy of trade. The Fénelonian and Physiocratic overtones of Clarke's pamphlet (dismantling great cities and establishing an agricultural system) came from this quarter, as did his toying with the idea that Britain, when reinforced with the low-wage advantages of Ireland, could become a world dictator of free trade. This was a kind of British version of Mirabeau's *L'ami des hommes*, based of course on purely commercial hegemony rather than war. Hume was revered in this circle for his opposition to jealousy of trade. The manifesto of the Shelburne circle (Dickey 2002; Hamilton 2004), entitled *New and Old Principles of Trade Compared: or a Treatise on the Principles of the Commerce between Nations*, authored by Benjamin Vaughan (Vaughan 1788, 1789 [1788]; on Vaughan see Murray 1989; Hamilton 2004), concluded its majestic denunciation of nationalism and international economic rivalry by citing Hume's essay "Of the Jealousy of Trade":

> Mr. Hume who considerably favors the liberal system, and considers the others as founded in "narrow and malignant politics," concludes his short *Essay on the Jealousy of Trade* with a declaration, which I shall not be afraid of making the conclusion of the present: "I shall therefore venture to acknowledge that not only as a man, but as a British subject, I pray for the flourishing commerce of Germany, Spain, Italy, and even France itself!"
>
> (Vaughan 1788, 41, 1789 [1788], 55)[38]

Had he lived in 1799 Hume presumably would have also enlisted Ireland as a country whose flourishing commerce all Britons should wish for. Whatever Pitt's sins may have been in allowing the Union debate to become a squabble about the benefits or otherwise of free trade, in the eyes of Shelburne and his followers Foster's patriotic separatism and protectionism was the wrong response. Encouraged by Shelburne's approval of the "Union or Separation" pamphlet, Clarke thus set out to demolish Foster directly in his *Misconceptions of Facts, and Mistatements of the Public Accounts, by the Right Hon. John Foster, Speaker of the Irish House of Commons, Proved & Corrected"* (Clarke 1799d). Clarke then recruited Hume to support the commercial clauses of the Union and rehabilitated the second half of Hume's rich country–poor country argument, which Tucker always opposed and Eden had deliberately suppressed in his intervention into the Irish debate in 1779. Clarke was in a difficult position. He had used Tucker heavily for supporting the Union on general grounds, but in the rich country–poor country context Tucker was a liability and could not easily be paired with Hume. At this point Shelburne rode to Clarke's rescue. He released the private correspondence that took place between Tucker and Hume, via Lord Kames, in 1758 and authorized Clarke to utilize it in the service of the unionist cause.

Clarke announced that he obtained the "corroborative support" of "the authority of two of the first men of our age" to prove "what I before maintained against Mr. Foster's arguments, as not being founded upon true principles" (ibid., 32). The letters had shown that Hume's rich country–poor country argument was double edged in a way that was not entirely clear from reading Hume's original essay. First, Clarke cited Hume's acknowledgement that Tucker was entirely correct in assuming that rich nations had vast competitive advantages. Emphasizing this point repeated

Eden's invocation of Hume on the rich country side of the argument in 1799. Using the correspondence, however, allowed Clarke to go further and cite Hume's point about the Achilles heel of rich countries. Their high wages allowed poor countries to compete against them. In Hume's words, as cited by Clarke:

> Among the disadvantages, we may reckon the *dear price of provisions* and *labour*, which enables the *poorer* country to rival them, (the rich,) in Hume's words as cited by Clarke: first in the coarser manufactures, and then in those which are more elaborate.
>
> (Clarke 1799d, 32)

"Can an opinion more pointed or more weighty be given in favour of an Union?" Clarke concluded enthusiastically (ibid.). He also used the correspondence to demonstrate Hume's motivation for putting forward this opinion. Hume was not an English industrialist or Bristol merchant who feared Irish competition and used the low-wage advantage argument to whip up support for the continued suppression of Irish trade. Rather, Hume was a patriot who hailed from a poor country. As the letter demonstrated, Hume expressed the hope that "we in Scotland also possess *some advantages*, which may enable us to share with them (the people of Britain) in wealth and industry." (ibid., 33) This was an impeccably liberal patriotic sentiment. Clearly, if Hume was right the Union wouldn't just be a one-way affair to Britain's economic advantage. Clarke could now defy Foster's view of "the radical impossibility of extending the Irish trade." (ibid., 27) "Get capital, therefore," he confidently advised the Irish, "by *uniting* with the first partner in the world, in opulence, character and commerce" (ibid., 31). As he already explained it in the earlier pamphlet on *Union or Separation*:

> Under Incorporation, new repose and widely extended Trade must arise, with a whole system of industry, encouragement, and happiness, blessing and exalting the Nation. Incorporation is the angular stone of its greatness.
>
> (Clarke 1799b, 13)

The Union was concluded in 1801 and Clarke published the Tucker–Kames–Hume correspondence in its entirety in the same year (Clarke 1801, 20–27). He included the letters in a book, entitled *A Survey of the Strength and Opulence of Great Britain,* which had only a tangential Irish dimension. Clarke still hoped to prove that the Irish did not bet on the wrong horse in the Union (ibid., v) by demonstrating that Britain was robust and rich enough to see off the challenge of the new "Colossus" of Europe, Napoleon's military empire. But his polemical target shifted away from Ireland and he no longer wished to present Hume's rich country–poor country argument as an exploration of the possibility of an economically equitable

Union between the richer and poorer parts of the British Isles. Rather, he probed the implications and likely outcome of Anglo-French economic and power rivalry (Clarke 1799c, 71–80; Clarke 1799e). Despite its huge war effort, Clarke claimed, Britain was not facing economic or military decline. Like many British and French thinkers in the previous seventy years, Clarke argued that the British case was different from the Spanish. Spain's problems stemmed from its failure to convert its colonial income into a spur to genuine domestic economic growth. This was manifestly not Britain's predicament (Clarke 1801, 37). Nonetheless, in the shadow of the Napoleonic threat, "Mr. Hume's speculative theory of self-destructive greatness" (ibid., 38), as Clarke now called it following Tucker, was totally unwelcome.

History, Clarke claimed, had disproved Hume's alarmism. Before the Seven Years' War Britain's commerce grew threefold. But since the time of the Hume–Tucker correspondence, Britain's commerce grew a further thirteenfold and was still going strongly[39] (ibid., 27–28, 207). Hume was also proved wrong about the public debt (ibid., 209). His analogy between the life-cycle of physical bodies and the trajectory of moral entities, like peoples and states, was philosophically as well as politically hazardous (ibid., 209–10). Britain not only survived the debt crisis Hume had feared of, Clarke claimed, but also managed to avoid, unlike the French, a destructive political and social revolution. This was because Britain was a new kind of free commercial state. Its empire was a also a commercial one, not an instance of conquering military barbarism. Unlike earlier empires, Britain's modern commercial empire was not prone to traditional corruption by its wealth (ibid., 207, 215). As Clarke wrote in answer to Lucien Bonaparte, Napoleon's republican brother, the British case was different from recent French conquests:

> The stains upon the bloody swords of conquerors are thus wiped off by commerce. It converts riches into a blessing, which would otherwise be a curse; it forms them into an instrument of public morality and strength, instead of being ministers of vice and downfall.
>
> (ibid., 215)

Clarke could not have expressed a more Humean sentiment. Nonetheless, he dismissed Hume's "self-canceling greatness" thesis by lumping it with traditional views of the moral critique of luxury. Thereby he reproduced the Hume paradox that Rousseau wrote about several decades earlier. Clarke's French readers, an enemy target in this case, could recognize this kind of "Hume." Clarke's book, including the Hume–Kames–Tucker correspondence, was quickly translated into French, as a direct contribution to the then raging European debate about the consequences of the commercial rivalry between England and revolutionary France for the future of the European state system.[40] While Shelburne authorized Clarke to publish the correspondence to lay bare Hume's impeccably patriotic Scottish motivations, the moment of truth had passed with the successful conclusion of the Irish Union debate. The Humean view that Clarke presented in his book in 1801 was virtually indistinguishable from Cantillon's earlier thesis about self-canceling wealth and of the use Mably and Mirabeau made of the Irishman's arguments.

12. Hume and Smith Disagree: The Long Shadow of the *Wealth of Nations*

There is today often talk about the political economy of the "Scottish Enlightenment," as if the phrase implied some sort of substantive and reasonably unified "Enlightenment" position, rather than a particularly active period in the intellectual and civic life of the Northern province of the United Kingdom of Great Britain in the second half of the eighteenth century. What would be then "the Scottish Enlightenment" position on the rich country–poor country issue? No-one wanted Scotland to be poorer, and very few wanted Scotland to opt out of modern economic development. Beyond this, however, there was not much of a monolithic common position to be found. Rather, there was heated debate and substantial disagreement. One therefore needs to conceive the "Enlightenment" as a multi-polar conversation and controversy among a broad spectrum of "enlightened" Scottish thinkers. William Eden's move in his 1779 pamphlet is highly indicative in this respect. He dreaded the idea that Hume's rich country–poor country argument might be used by the protectionist English special interests in their campaign to obstruct Irish trade liberalization. Hence, his move was pre-emptive, by showing that Hume's argument had another side. His tacit closing the gap between Hume and Smith was clever, but it swept their disagreement about the theoretical merits of the Irish–Scottish rich country–poor country argument under the carpet. This has regrettably contributed to the rise of a long-standing illusion of a unified "Scottish Enlightenment." For there can be no doubt whatsoever that on this major issue the two friends, Hume and Smith, had sharply opposed each other.

In the *Wealth of Nations* Smith was pessimistic even about Scotland's immediate development prospects, but he didn't disagree with Hume's long-term vision that economic development would eventually spread evenly around the world. He asserted, very vocally, that such global well-being could be best achieved not by abandoning aggressive international price competition, as Mirabeau, Rousseau, Mably and many other moral critics of the new commercial world suggested, but by pursuing it further in a reformed manner. International rivalry had negative and positive versions. The bad one was fuelled by national animosity, i.e. nationalism in modern parlance, and used the state as its instrument. The good one was expressed through national emulation, i.e. international economic competition without national envy and without any entanglement in military power struggles. In this respect Smith's vision was not that far from the thinking of Shelburne or Richard Price. There existed forms of economic competition that were instances of noble rivalry. Emulation was the motor of modern civilization for the good of mankind (Hont 2005b, 111–23; Shovlin 2003; Kapossy 2006, 103–72). Smith knew that the late eighteenth century was frenzied by jealousy of trade, creating ever more virulent forms of nationalism (Hont 2005b, 111–25). It was, however, this jealousy and national envy, not the underlying pattern of emulation that had to be suppressed. This was clearly also Hume's view.

Nevertheless, when weighing up the advantages of low wages in international economic competition Hume and Smith parted ways. Like many of the British and French contributors to the rich country–poor country debate, Smith formed his views on the subject in the era of the Seven Years' War. In the early 1760s, before he traveled to France, he lectured on jurisprudence and political economy at the University of Glasgow and penned, or dictated, the text that today is rather misleadingly described as the "Early Draft" of the *Wealth of Nations*. The "Early Draft" shows Smith as fully engaged with the political economy literature of the 1750s and early 1760s. He was acquainted with Melon's work (he owned both editions). He not only noticed, but was deeply preoccupied with the issues that Hume and Tucker were debating. Smith chose Tucker's side against his Scottish friend. It was "vulgar prejudice and superficial reflection," Smith echoed Tucker, to regard it as a paradox that "in an opulent and commercial society labor becomes dear and work cheap." On the contrary, "these two things were evidently very consistent," he explained, "as the improvement of arts render things so much easier done that a great wage can be afforded to the artisan and the goods still be at a low price" (Smith 1978c [*c.* 1762–63], 566–67). In Smith's view trading nations did not have to pay for their successful foreign trade by sacrificing the high wages and hence the well-being of their workers.

It was a central tenet of the *Wealth of Nations* that historically high living standards for entire nations were compatible both with significant inequality in property ownership and with the dictates of international price competition. The wealth of modern nations was not self-destructive but often self-reinforcing. If sustained wealth creation failed, Smith wrote, "some other cause, we may be assured, most have concurred." The cause of decline was more likely to be in the inadequate grasp by policymakers of the science of legislation, which included political economy, rather than in some inherent catch in the economics of innovation and growth. If there was a recession, or signs of impending decline, Smith concluded, "the rich country must have been guilty of some error in its police." Had Eden, Burke, Pitt and Shelburne known this early text of Smith, they would have found it as useful for their purposes as Tucker's virtually identical formulations:

> The more opulent therefore the society, labour will always be so much dearer and work so much cheaper, and if some opulent countries have lost several of their manufactures and some branches of their commerce by having been undersold in foreign markets by the traders and artisans of poorer countries, who were contented with less profit and smaller wages, this will rarely be found to have been merely the effect of the opulence of one country and the poverty of the other.
>
> (Smith 1978c [c. 1762–63], 567; cf. Smith 1978a [1762–63], 343–44;
> Smith 1978b [1763–64], 490–91)

The *Wealth of Nations* was written to prevent these kinds of major errors in the political economy of rich countries. In the final text of 1776 the language of the 1750s—opulence, rich and poor countries and so forth—became submerged. The original meaning, however, was not only preserved but even amplified. Smith began the *Wealth of Nations* by zooming in on the issue of industrial productivity. The division of labor and the use of machinery, as Smith demonstrated graphically through the example of the pin factory, allowed for the coexistence of high wages and low prices even in the richest of nations. The book stridently advertised the benefits of a new mechanized system of mass production that was able to beat comprehensively, both in quality and price, many of the old artisan industries. Smith pushed a two-pronged strategy, combining arguments about introducing ever deeper and finer specialization in the production process with the use of machines to save labor costs. Many of Smith's contemporaries took pride in the skill and flexibility of the labor force of advanced nations. Smith fully realized, however, that his own recommendations inevitably led to the de-skilling of the labor force of rich countries. He lamented this fact and tried to offset the cultural damage by demanding better elementary schooling for working-class children before they entered the adult world of industrial labor. But he didn't change his advocacy.

The *Wealth of Nations* depicted the world as highly competitive and offered rich countries a "one strategy wins all" competition policy. What was peculiar about the *Wealth of Nations*, particularly if seen in a French perspective, was that it took over Melon's neo-Colbertist strategy of industry-led growth, but dropped every other element of Colbertism, including the originally Machiavellian idea of aggressively chasing avenues of external growth by means of projecting power. Not only did Smith dismiss conquest as a brutal and futile idea of the past, as did Melon and Montesquieu, he also dismissed colonization, monopolist trading companies and virtually all kinds of protectionism. Smith understood all too clearly that the external growth of Europe at the expense of other regions of the globe was possible only because of Europe's military advantage. In this context he subscribed to the view that trade generates benign forces that would lead to the diminution of uneven development over the globe. Europe's domination of other continents would come to an end, Smith wrote, once global commerce enriched those regions too and supplied them with all the fruits of modern development, including military might. If Britain were to keep its North American dependencies by admitting them into a restructured British federal state,[41] Smith fully expected that the new entity would be governed from North America once the huge growth potential of that vast country became realized.[42] As Smith knew all too well, power followed property. In due time, America was bound to become a significantly richer country than Britain. Smith in fact offered a similar political and taxation deal to Ireland as to America, a federal union, but he knew that neither the size, nor the politics of Ireland, favored economic growth to any degree comparable to the huge potential of North America.

Smith's strategy resembled the aggressive free trade ideas of Davenant, Martyn and Melon, except for Smith Britain's wealth had to be anchored squarely to the competitive achievements of its own domestic economy. He suggested no exploitation of cheap foreign labor, as Davenant and Martyn did, and viewed commercially motivated imperialism as stupid and short-sighted, an evasion of the laws of the market. Rich countries could inadvertently engineer their own decline, and imperialism for Smith was the one strategy that virtually guaranteed this outcome. Empire, commercial or otherwise, could not last, and would turn out to be enormously costly if implemented. If Britain ever lost its distant dependencies, as it was bound to, it would have to rely on its own resources and industry, that is on the economy of a medium-sized European country that had fallen behind its European competitors who never had the luxury to exploit captive colonial markets to the same degree as the British did.

The *Wealth of Nations* rejected the political legacy of "Machiavellianism," but Smith did not lose sight of the positive core of Machiavellian ideas of *grandezza*, namely that flourishing political communities had to be able to grow. He insisted that the most flourishing nations were not the richest, but the ones that grew the fastest, indicated by rapidly rising wage levels (a message that was not lost on some of his Irish readers). As an alternative to the Renaissance pattern of growth by war, empire and long-distance trade, Smith advocated the full conversion of the entire world to competitive trade. His impatient pleading for more free trade and full commercial reciprocity was anchored in his confident insistence that rich nations could retain their economic status if they pursued a farsighted and relentless policy of productivity growth. Having rejected all the traditional alternatives, he hardly had any other choice. He left himself only one master argument for securing the future of rich nations. Although he rejected protectionism, he did suggest, like many of his European contemporaries, that nations that were consistently losing in certain sectors of trading ought to contemplate withdrawing from it. Like Tucker, Smith regarded the theory of self-canceling economic greatness not as an argument for peace, but as an incitement to war and imperialism, or both. When added to jealousy of trade, it could lead to a feeding frenzy of national envy and animosity. The *Wealth of Nations*, with its celebration of productivity, division of labor and machinery, was meant to destroy the idea that modern national wealth, like its ancient and early modern forerunners, could not last. With it, however, the book also destroyed the one grand economic argument that European thinkers, chiefly in France, had used against the incipient threat of England becoming a commercial Rome, a trading superpower that ruled the world by dominating the seas and hence international markets.

There was nothing in the *Wealth of Nations* that lent any explicit support for the image of England as a world trade monopolist. What it did maintain was that England's national wealth could be preserved by implementing an economic strategy of mass production, supported by mechanization and constant technological innovation. Smith, like Melon, suggested that it was technology and the organization of production, rather than wage rates, which determined international competitiveness. This undermined the argument that wage differentials, more specifically the wage differentials between nations of varying level of economic and social development, could and would determine the future pattern of global economic development, for if wage levels mattered at all its effects were bound to be transitory. Henry Martyn already had a similar focus on mechanization at the very beginning of the eighteenth century. In 1776 Smith gave a full expression of Martyn's early insights. He well understood the mechanism whereby ever newer innovations made nations constantly leapfrog one another, eventually creating a level playing field of international competition, just as Martyn had predicted. Smith knew that it was easier to copy machines than to create highly skilled human capital. He emphasized that designs could be exported, imported or simply smuggled across borders. The suggested portability of mechanical ideas was also well understood by Smith's French readers. The pin factory was, after all, not some Scottish invention. Its mode of operation was perfectly well illustrated in the detailed graphical plates attached to the *Encyclopédie* and in other contemporary sources (Peaucelle 2006).

13. The End of the Hume Paradox: Toward a Theory of Comparative Advantage

This survey of the Irish origins and the later French and Irish polemical context of Hume's rich country–poor country argument can instruct us in various ways. It demonstrates without doubt that this was one of Hume's most widely noticed statements in political economy. Not only was it regularly remarked on in England, Ireland and Scotland, but also in France, Germany, Holland, Sweden and Naples. Its French reception shows that it was regarded as an important doctrine of modern international relations. For many, it also served as a powerful critique of the modern commercial state system. Rousseau was correct in reporting that Hume looked paradoxical to practically everybody, even if the reasons for the judgment varied quite radically. Hume could reconcile the English advocacy of luxury with republicanism, because he promoted the growth of the arts and sciences in order to create a commercial civilization, but criticized all attempts, including British ones, at establishing a world commercial monopoly. He also opposed linking commerce to warfare, to the new system of public credit and to monetarist strategies of boosting the economy of individual nations. Le Blanc could claim Hume to be a disciple of the neo-Colbertist views of Melon. But Hume differed from the Melonists and the followers of Gournay in one other crucial respect. Not only was he uncompromisingly against the legacy of John Law, he also failed to join in the neo-Colbertist celebration of the division of labor, technical innovation and the use of labor-saving machines. Lastly, Hume objected to the view that rich nations should keep poor countries in economic subservience.

From a French perspective Adam Smith could be pigeonholed into pre-existing political and economic traditions more easily than Hume. Smith came across as an author who developed Melon's neo-Colbertism to a higher level. He advocated an economic policy specifically designed to win in international competition, and supported the policy most often associated with Colbert, namely the support for urban centers and industry, complemented with the division of labor and machinery. Smith also gave qualified support to Law's ideas. On the other hand, Smith rejected the "mercantilist" element in the Melon–Gournay advocacy of the competitive empowering of nations; he was against the idea of the various India Companies and other institutional vehicles for enhancing national competitiveness, such as imperialism. Substantial parts of the *Wealth of Nations* also originated from the pre-Physiocratic period of the 1750s. Even if Smith learned a great deal from the Physiocrats later on, he thought that they grossly overstated their case. In his crucial chapter dealing with the "agricultural system" he accepted that "if the rod be bent too much one way... in order to make it straight you must bend it as much the other." The Physiocrats, Smith claimed, "who have proposed the system which represents agriculture as the sole source of the revenue and wealth of every country, seem to have adopted this proverbial maxim." They bent the rod the opposite way to Colbert: "in the plan of Mr. Colbert the industry of the towns was certainly overvalued in comparison with that of the country; so in their system it seems to be as certainly undervalued" (Smith 1976 [1776], 2:664). Smith not simply chose the golden middle. He regarded Colbert as a more acceptable guide to modern commercial policy than the Physiocrats. Colbert's system, Smith argued,

> by encouraging manufactures and foreign trade more than agriculture, turns a certain portion of the capital of the society from supporting a more advantageous, to support a less advantageous species of industry. But still it really and in the end encourages that species of industry which it means to promote. Those agricultural systems, on the

contrary, really and in the end discourage their own favourite species of industry.

(ibid., 2:686–87)

No contemporary could mistake Smith's message. They understood that Smith wanted Colbert without étatism (cf. Minard 1998; Minard 2000), without his constant bureaucratic interventions, and without Louis XIV's war policies. Also, agriculture had to be put back in the core of Colbertist political agenda, as Melon had already suggested. In the *Wealth of Nations* Smith offered a viable and improved Colbertism that could be realized within a system of natural liberty, by using only a few laws and no instruments of power politics. This also fitted well with Melon's insistence that governments should keep out of the administration of the economy. The correspondence with the free trade advocacy of Gournay was also remarkable, and Smith's repeated insistence on the crucial importance of agriculture was precisely the sort of encouragement that was the hallmark of the Gournay group in the 1750s and later. In a French perspective, Smith was a rescuer of the neo-Colbertist strategy, reviving this style of thought in political economy precisely when Physiocracy went into terminal decline as a political force after Turgot's prime ministership ran into trouble in 1775. Hume could be rightfully understood as also having supported some of the key features of this program. But Smith fitted the needs of French political economy more closely, because the *Wealth of Nations* took Melon's side on most of the issues that divided Hume from Gournay's followers.

For fifteen years Melon's *Political Essay* was the most visible modern work on political economy in Europe. Everybody studied Melon, even if most disagreed strongly with one or another of his tenets. In Scotland, both Hume and Smith definitely read him closely. Their disagreement stems from their diverging assessment of the fulfillment of the economic promises of the Anglo-Scottish Union of 1707. Hume accepted the Irish argument about the advantages of low wages in trade and rejected the monetarist alternative originating from John Law. The same Irish–Scottish angle also distanced Hume from his French counterparts in the neo-Colbertist Melon–Gournay tendency. When Hume wrote to Tucker in 1758, during the Seven Years' War, he sounded not just like a supporter of Scottish or Irish economic improvement but also very much like the French critics of England's ambition to world economic supremacy: "The question is," he wrote,

> whether these advantages can go on, increasing trade in *infinitum*, or whether they do not at last come to a *ne plus ultra*, and check themselves, by begetting disadvantages, which at first retard, and at last finally stop their progress. Among these disadvantages, we may reckon the dear price of provisions and labour, which enables the poorer country to rival them, first in coarser manufactures, and then in those which are more elaborate. Were it otherwise, commerce, if not

dissipated by violent conquests, would go on perpetually increasing, and one spot of the globe would engross the art and industry of the whole.

(Hume 1932 [1758] 1:271)

Cantillon, Montesquieu or Mably could have easily written this. Nonetheless, when Hume railed against the bullish English perspective of Josiah Tucker and claimed that no "one nation should be the monopoliser of wealth," his conclusions were different from that of most French authors. Patriotic political economists, in France, wanted to replace English hegemony with a French one. Hume hated this idea. That is why in 1799 Clarke could cite Hume in support of a British–Irish union as a friend of unification and a foe of continuing rivalry. "I am pleased when I find the author [Tucker] insist on the advantages of England," Hume wrote to Lord Kames,

and prognosticate thence the continuance and even further progress of the opulence of that country, but I still indulge myself in the hopes that we in Scotland possess also some advantages, which may enable us to share with them in wealth and industry.

(Hume 1932 [1758], 1:273)

Hume could be held up as a model for Irish free trade patriotism. But neither Scotland nor Ireland were aspiring great powers. Instead of aiming at hegemony, Hume envisaged a system of inter-provincial or inter-national division of labor: "It is certain," he wrote, "that the simpler kind of industry ought first to be attempted in a country like ours." This was not a perspective that applied easily to either England or France. France fought England as an equal or indeed superior nation that had fallen behind its island competitor for no other reason but a series of catastrophic policy blunders since the age of Louis XIV. Melon elaborated the rich country, not the poor country side of Hume's vision. He wished to sustain the flexibility of France's highly developed textile industry in order to preserve its world leadership in fashion fabrics and he reckoned that France's sophisticated population could adapt to the constant undulations in international textile markets without state intervention. Hume seconded these arguments. However, he also claimed that he represented the point of view of poor and underdeveloped economies.

Hume's analysis of the predicament of rich countries was almost invariably read without realizing its Scottish flavor. As we have seen, in a simplified form his message suited those who rejected English ambitions for economic supremacy. This critique could then be extended to an evaluation of similar French ambitions. But what these moral critics, like Mably, wanted was not an opportunity for poorer nations to join the ranks of rich commercial societies, but rather the arrest, or perhaps even the reversal, of the forward march of modern commerce. Had they understood Hume's position better, seeing it not as a sign of a moral contradiction but as a call for the joint and simultaneous development of both poor and rich nations, they might not have unequivocally welcomed it. Hume failed to support any kind of anti-commercial moralizing. Most critics of the warlike dynamics of international trade advocated the idea of a closed trading state, a morally motivated exit of rich nations from international trade altogether. Closed trading states were not liable to fall victim to competition either from rich or poor countries. Hume, unmistakably, was an enemy of this idea. From the viewpoint of poor nations, a closed trading state, the cessation of practically all trade links with the outside world, was the worst, not the best, answer to the terrifying problems of the modern commercial age. From the point of view of poor countries it was a clear cut expression of the selfishness of rich nations.

Hume looked at England and Scotland, a rich and a poor country, jointly and asked questions about the best mode of their commercial interaction. He constructed a framework that clearly displayed some of the key intuitions of what later came to be called the theory of comparative advantage in international trade (Chipman 1965). The nineteenth-century term "comparative advantage" is a clumsy phrase, which is usually attributed to David Ricardo (Ricardo 1951 [1821], 128–49, see Ruffin 2002, 2005) although the terminology probably originates from John Stuart Mill (Mill 1967 [1844], 233; Mill 1965 [1848], 3:589).[43] It is confusing for lay readers because it does not mean at all the advantage or superiority of one country over another in unrestricted competition. This was "absolute" advantage. Rather, it suggests avenues of trade between two countries when one of them is superior to the other in practically all respects, which is often the case in trade between rich and poor countries. This is the kind of commerce Hume envisaged. "Comparative advantage" does not compare nations. It refers to the relative or comparative efficiency of industries within each nation. Ricardo's theory stipulated that mutually profitable reciprocal trade could be generated between economically unequal partners if the nation which had absolute advantage in several sectors was prepared to abandon those ones in which its own productivity was relatively low (Maneschi 1998a, 1998b, 2004). These could be taken over by poorer or less efficient nations. The first country could henceforth acquire these goods through import, while concentrating on its own high productivity activities.

By optimizing their trade profiles according to their domestic scale of efficiency, both parties could achieve more and the aggregate volume of their trade could grow as well. Poor countries could take over less-skill-intensive activities, where their low wages gave them genuine advantage, while rich nations could concentrate on the best possible use of their highly skilled workforce and sophisticated production techniques. This was the point Hume pursued in his model of "cyclical economic growth" in "Of Money." If turned into a sequential phenomenon that spread through the whole world, as depicted in Hume's presentation, industrial transfer mechanisms of this kind could generate a pragmatic and benign model of economic globalization. Instead of prophesizing the inevitable economic decline of rich nations, Hume predicted that certain kind of productive activities would be regularly outsourced from high-wage to low-wage regions, greatly benefiting the poorer regions of the world. Hence, Hume's allegedly "pessimistic" (England versus Scotland and Ireland) and Ricardo's vaunted "optimistic" case (Britain versus Portugal) of international trade were in fact practically identical, both in intent and in predicted outcome.

Hume did not presage the inevitable economic decline of rich nations. Rather, he foresaw the inevitability of product cycles. Today we understand product cycles as a kind of stages theory of industrial competitiveness, which helps us to understand the dynamics of comparative advantage (Vernon 1966). In this view product cycles occur when a rich country, which used to manufacture and successfully export certain goods, loses its export market to poorer competitors that imitate the production technology and produce the goods cheaper. Hence the rich country becomes an importer of the products that it used to sell. Product cycle theory suggests that rich countries, and eventually all countries, live in constant economic flux. They have to both acquire and retain a genuine capacity for flexible specialization and technological innovation, or they face decline. Hume recommended that rich nations constantly shift their production profile toward the design and sale of ever more refined and value-added goods. His emphasis was on human capital and its flexibility, not on the increasing of productivity through a technical division of labor and the deployment of labor-saving machinery. For him, luxury, or refinement in arts, was the key economic phenomenon that allowed these upward economic shifts to happen. Habits of "luxury" created artificial new "needs." Satisfying these wants gave the scope for practically infinite product innovation and hence the creation of employment. Poor nations could undermine the competitiveness of developed economies through aggressive price competition, but only in certain types of goods. Melon deployed both of these arguments, emphasizing both the labor-saving effects of machines and also the flexible production patterns of skilled workers in luxury trades. He defined man as a tool-making animal and urged countries to practice constant innovation in machinery. This contention became the master argument of the *Wealth of Nations*. Hume has never denied or criticized this argument. Nonetheless, he never asserted it either, in contrast to so many of his contemporaries. His omission is quite conspicuous.[44]

There is never only one kind of history of political or economic thought. Political theorists or economists who construct such histories can legitimately pursue many different interests. It may well be worthwhile reconstructing Hume's theory of money, trade, or taxes etc. by pursuing each analytical category through tunnels bored through Hume's writings, looking for signs of hesitation or inconsistency. This paper, however, suggests that it is necessary to discern the national, institutional and policy environments Hume was operating in, and to consider his views not as "theories" but as strategy choices for his nation and his epoch. Hume was a very fine philosopher and was particularly adept in highly abstract modes of analysis and sophisticated taxonomic argumentation. He didn't often commit elementary methodological mistakes. He was highly interested in how "money" could best be defined and wanted to deploy his "theory of money" as plausibly and correctly as possible. But even if money was a single kind of entity, whose properties could be defined unambiguously and captured in a single theory, Hume realized all too clearly that human beings and their societies, the users of money, were far more complex formations. The way money affected an economy depended on many factors, among others, on the level of development, the entry point of money into the economy, the ability of the economy to absorb it, plus a number of purely moral and political factors (cf. Sakamoto 2003; Wennerlind 2000). Depending on circumstances, institutional arrangements, or stages of development, the influx of money had different effects on a society or economy. There is no reason to believe that Hume would have seen a contradiction in his rich country–poor country argument. Nor is it plausible to assume that he would have been unable to rectify it had he spotted it himself or if others called it to his attention. In fact, just such a proposition was put to him many times by an assortment of his Scottish, English and French friends, who all claimed in one way or another that his thoughts were "paradoxical." Hume, however, stuck to his position throughout his life and conceded very little. Like Smith, he put all his policy eggs into one basket.

Smith argued that an aggressive manufacturing export economy could be sustained without the institutional support of the "mercantile system," which, he claimed, hindered rather than supported its development. The plea of the *Wealth of Nations* for free trade and commercial reciprocity would have been almost meaningless had it not been accompanied by Smith's robust reassurance that rich nations should not fear for their wealth and status if they pursued a policy of constant productivity growth (cf. West 2000). Without its first two sections (Books I and II) and its single-minded emphasis on the technical division of labor and the use of machinery, Smith's book would have been shapeless and unconvincing. Hume, on the other hand, hoped for a foreign trade-led path of development for poor countries along the lines suggested by the theory of comparative advantage, which assigned to rich nations their high skills, and to poor countries their low wages as decisive factors in calculating their advantages. Smith, in turn, accused Hume of being a sort of mercantilist, because by fiercely opposing what he had wrongly thought were erroneous conceptions of monetary stimulation to economic growth, his friend had unwittingly perpetuated the notion that money, and hence price and wage levels, are the most important factor in the working of an economy.

Behind this disagreement lay a disparity in Hume's and Smith's evaluation of the "Irish" argument that "where the Necessaries of Life are cheap, there also will Labour and Art be cheap" (Browne 1729 [1728], 11, cf. 24–25; cf. Browne 1728). Although this statement was questioned a long way before David Hume appeared on the scene,[45] Hume's political economy was largely governed by his belief that in some important respects the economics of the Irish position were true. When his Scottish friends tried to convince him about the faults of this view, Hume unhesitatingly pointed to the general relevance of his argument for the entire political economy of Europe. Poor countries could "undersell" their high-wage rivals and snatch away some of their trade. The low-wage nations of Asia, he pointed out, could one day take over much of Europe's economy. His example was not India, as it was for supporters of the East India Company, like Davenant and Martyn. Hume had China in mind. As he explained to his Scottish friend, James Oswald of Dunnikier:

> The distance of China is a physical impediment to the communication, by reducing our commerce to a few commodities; and by heightening the price of these commodities, on account of the long voyage, the monopolies and the taxes. A Chinese works for three-halfpence a day, and is very industrious. Were he as near us as France or Spain, every thing we use would be Chinese, till money and prices came to a level; that is, to such a level as is proportioned to the numbers of people, industry, and commodities of both countries.
>
> (Hume 1955, 198, 1932 [1750], 1:144)[46]

Characteristically, Smith challenged this view. In his Glasgow lectures on jurisprudence he agreed with Hume on the facts of Chinese price competitiveness: "The cotton and other commodities from China would undersell any made with us, were it not for the long carriage and other taxes that are laid upon them" (Smith 1978b [1763–64], 491). But, he argued, Hume was wrong in believing that the Chinese case supported his assessment of Scotland's economic chances. China, Smith claimed, didn't show that poor countries can "undersell" rich ones (ibid.). Low wages, Smith conceded, were a huge advantage in price competition. But China exemplified the kind of competition that typically developed between rich and developed countries that had differential wage rates. Chinese wages were not low because the country was undeveloped. China was not an oriental version of Scotland or Ireland (cf. Pomeranz 2000).

In the *Wealth of Nations* Smith expanded on this argument. China was a very developed and immensely rich country with a long history in skill formation, longer than that of modern Europe. It had low wages because its economy had reached a "stationary state." It was China's immense population growth that depressed its wages. Provided that Chinese products could reach Europe in sufficient volume, their low prices, determined by low wage costs, could easily make China a competitive champion. China's low wages,

Smith added, were not a sign of China's decline. True, in China the urban poor were significantly poorer than even the most hard-up laborers of any European country. However, in China's "stationary state" the money supply was tightly controlled and price inflation was kept at bay, therefore the purchasing power afforded by China's low wages was higher than an equivalent income in Europe (Smith 1976 [1776], 1:30, 89–90). Similarly low wages in a rich European country would have signalled both economic collapse and moral decline. In some European states that were in decline, Smith claimed, the unemployed faced unspeakable deprivation and starvation, conditions much worse than the lot of China's working urban poor. For European countries, not yet in a stationary state but still very much growing, adopting a low-wage strategy in order to fend off Chinese competition would have spelt disaster. The Chinese threat at this point, of course, was still a hypothetical case. Rather, Smith's conclusions related to competition much closer to home. Rich European countries, he wished to assert, had no reason to fear competition from their poor European neighbours. Smith, like his French readers, focused on the rivalry between rich European countries rather than between rich and poor ones.

Hume opposed monetary boosts to the economy, public credit creation and protectionism, because these policies could easily cancel the advantages of low-wage nations. Only money earned through trade and ploughed back to generate further trade, he wrote, could stimulate genuine economic development. In the Anglo-Scottish union debate of 1707, Andrew Fletcher of Saltoun argued that if poor countries like Scotland had indeed possessed a significant competitive advantage due to their low wages, then rich nations like England would strangle those economies before they could harm their own national interest. International competition, Fletcher insisted, was a matter of power as well as price and wage differentials. Hume, of course, knew this very well and opposed commercial power politics with every possible argument at his disposal. Rich countries that wished to monopolize world trade, he thought, were following a futile and self-destructive strategy. Allowing poorer nations their place in the sun was a better approach and more conducive to peace. This alternative, however, required taking the high road of commerce and "refinement in the arts." Eighteenth-century critics of commercial society saw this as a brazen promotion of "luxury" and thought that in moral terms it was paradoxical. Although their view is understandable, it missed Hume's point.

The same applies to the various alleged paradoxes in Hume's theory of money. They are perplexing only if Hume's argumentative purposes are disregarded. This is not purely a matter of historical truthfulness. By recognizing the centrality of the rich country–poor country debate in Hume's political economy we can appreciate the dialectic of the Hume–Tucker and Hume–Smith controversies better. It is also important to realize that this debate, in a real way, is still with us. We know certain outcomes that Hume and Smith were only predicting. Scotland is still not as rich as

England and Ireland's catching up did indeed take centuries. The cost of transport between China and Europe (and the USA) is now reduced and we can see its consequences today in very much the way Hume and Smith described them. For some time it seemed that Smith's mass production and mechanization strategy would work well for rich countries. Today it looks like Hume's insights have been more valuable in the long run and that skill, human capital and flexibility hold the key to the survival of rich nations. Poorer countries still attract certain kinds of industries because of their lower wage advantage, by utilizing imported capital and technology. In poor countries the Irish low-wage arguments are still alive. Nationalist politicians and economists in rich countries can still be as alarmed by the threat of low-wage competition as their predecessors in the eighteenth century. The French Enlightenment debate remains indicative of the complex political and moral worries of rich nations needing to correct past errors in national economic policy in order to arrest and possibly reverse decline. Finally, the ideas of Hume and Smith can still be introduced into modern debates (cf. Krugman 1998; Cawthorne and Kitching 2001; Arrighi 2007) with considerable force. The debate between them concerning the causal explanation of Chinese competitive advantage offers an enduringly interesting perspective on China's recent economic success at the end of the twentieth and the beginning of the twenty-first centuries, and the value of the Chinese case for understanding the development options open for countries that are genuinely poor. In Hume's and Smith's time Japan and China were regarded as closed trading states. Today they are seen as examples of the benefits of aggressive foreign trade. David Hume's political economy dealt with long-term strategic issues of this kind. Paradoxically, studying its eighteenth-century context, by exploring the Irish origins and French reception of his Scottish rich country–poor country argument, makes our understanding of his thought not only more accurate but more interesting and more relevant for today.

Notes

1 I am very grateful for the two editors, Margaret Schabas and Carl Wennerlind, for their comments on this paper and for their persistent encouragement. I would like to thank Michael Sonenscher, Béla Kapossy and Ze'ev Emmerich for their patient reading of earlier drafts. I have discussed issues in eighteenth-century French political economy with Michael Sonenscher for over a decade. My debt to him is considerable.

2 It was in relation to this passage in "Of Money" that Eugene Rotwein introduced the rich and poor countries terminology to describe Hume's position (Rotwein in Hume (1955), 194n, 189n). The label "rich country–poor country issue" was invented by George Davie (Davie 1967a, 295–96). Elsewhere he described the argument as "David Hume's economic question as to whether backward Scotland, under the free-trade conditions provided by the Union, could ever catch up with the immense superiority of her predominant partner" (Davie 1967b: 33). The first substantial account of the eighteenth-century Scottish debate, in a

pioneering article by Joseph Low in the early 1950s, did not use the "rich country–poor country" terminology but defined the debate as a general controversy
over "the theory of economic progress of an internationally trading community"
(Low 1952, 311–33). Henry Spiegel presented Hume's argument as "a law of the
migration of economic opportunity" (Spiegel 1971, 210). The Rotwein–Davie
terminology was reintroduced and consolidated by Hont (2005e [1983c]) with
reference to Hume's own vocabulary. For subsequent accounts, accepting this
terminology, see Rostow 1990, Elmslie 1995, Dickey 1995, Berdell 2002, Maneschi 2006.

3 On Tucker's pronounced Christian providentialism see Urquhart (1995), Young
(1996) and Dickey (2002).

4 For an acceptance of Hume's argument see another Aberdonian, Alexander
Gerard, who thought that the difference between rich and poor countries was
self-corrective. Once a nation enriched itself wages started to rise; thus "its
Poorer Neighbours can undersell it, and by this draw back to themselves the
Advantages of Commerce" (Gerard 1758–59, 487–88).

5 A rare counter example is the agronomist Henry Pattullo who writes about
Hume as a Scottish author (Pattullo 1758, 218–19). Pattullo was a collaborator
of Quesnay, see Charles 1999b.

6 For the general background see Pincus, on the Irish political-constitutional context see, Kelly 1987, Kelly 1988, Smyth 1993, 1995, Hill 1995, Kelly 2000a,
Armitage 2000b.

7 John Cary, who was in the forefront of the campaign against Irish free trade,
argued in a similar fashion even earlier (Cary 1695). The strident passages in his
Essay on the State of England in Relation to Its Trade which demanded that Ireland is reduced to a regular colony in its trading rights were reprinted separately
(Cary 1696). He expressed even more candid views in a Bristol electioneering
pamphlet (Cary 1698a, 3–4).

8 Fletcher borrowed most of his argument concerning the "interest of mankind"
from Harrington's *Oceana* (Harrington 1977 [1656], 171–72). Harrington grounded it in the sociability of the human race, and referred to the authority of
Grotius, among others, in his effort to counter Hobbes's sceptical theory of the
state of nature. For Harrington and Fletcher the rebuttal of reason of state was
not a matter of rights and jurisprudential argument, but rather of establishing the
correct form of government. In this kind of republican cosmopolitanism only
republics could be peaceful, thanks to their unique ability to reconcile the
national interest with the interest of other republics.

9 See this example in a pamphlet attributed to Bindon that is exactly contemporary
with his Melon commentary: "every wise Nation will encourage Agriculture and
Fishing as much as they can … rather with a view to render Provision cheap
among their Manufacturers, than with View to get by Exporting the Produce of
either Foreign Nations; for the cheaper Provisions are in any Country, the more
able will their Manufacturers be to undersell Foreigners in every sort of Manufacture" (Bindon 1738b, 5).

10 The Irish Union debate gathered momentum (see Magennis 2001) precisely at the
time of the publication of Hume's *Political Discourses*, mostly in the 1751–59
period. It started with a pamphlet by Lord Hillsborough (Hillsborough 1751)
and was seconded by Dobbs, whose work Hume was familiar with (Hume 1948,
II: 24; Dobbs 1731–32). Dobbs joined the campaign in 1751–52 and drafted a
proposal for a Union along the time-honoured Irish argument praising the economic advantages of Irish low wages (Dobbs *c.*1752a) (*c.* 1752b). This particularly clear and assertive version of the rich country-argument, however, was
drafted later than Hume's essay. (Oswald 1883–85 [1749]; Hume 1732 [1750];
Hont 1983 (2005d)). For a later Scottish use and development of Melon's ideas in

comparison with Hume, see the interpretation of Thomas Reid's political economy in Nagao (2003).

11 Melon's first book was a short novel conceived vaguely in the style of Montesquieu's *Persian Letters*, entitled *Mahmoud le Gasnévide* (Mahmud of Ghazni), which offered a parable depicting the choice between peaceful and military methods of achieving national greatness through the example of a Muslim emperor in Afghanistan who conquered and plundered Persia and the Punjab (Melon 1729, esp. 69–72; cf. Melon 1983b).

12 It is often claimed that Melon's support for luxury was his most influential idea, particularly on Voltaire. Voltaire's copy of Melon's essay, however, has marginalia for Chapter 1 "Principles" only, see Zinsser 2002; cf. Voltaire 1901 [1738].

13 For a connection with Adam Smith's "natural progress of opulence" and his four-stages theory of history, see Hont (2005g [1989]) and Hont (2005c) [1986]).

14 Melon's Irish translator, David Bindon, insisted "that Ireland is in the Condition of one of the impoverished Islands mentioned by our Author" (Bindon 1738a, xv). He recommended that Ireland should start its recovery by concentrating on its agriculture (ibid., vii–ix). A similar reading of Melon was offered in Naples (Robertson 2005, 340–47, 363–64).

15 See Henri Barckhausen's reconstruction in Montesquieu (1900) [1735], 181–85; for comment see Larrère and Weil 2000 and especially Mason 1996, 61–87.

16 Friedrich A. von Hayek in the introduction to his wife's German translation of Cantillon's *Essai* (Cantillon (1931) [1755]) regarded Hume as an inferior copyist of Cantillon, based on the assertion that Hume covered a range of topics in monetary analysis that appeared in Cantillon (cf. Bordo 1983) and that some of his solutions also resembled some of Cantillon's positions. (Hayek 1985 [1931], 238–39, 247; cf. Rothbard 1995, 343–63). This assertion, more brusquely, was repeated in the same year as Hayek's famous *Prices and Production* (Hayek 1931, 9). Hayek's only textual support refers to an item (Section III, note 2) in Hume's "Early Memoranda" (Hume 1948, 503), which cites from a source a numerical example also mentioned by Cantillon. It is more likely that they used the same source. The idea itself was almost a commonplace, for an example see Cary 1695, 22: "as Clockwork, wherein we sell nothing but Art and Labour, the Materials therefore being of small value." Despite Hayek's erudition in the introduction to Cantillon, his surmise that the young Hume could have seen Cantillon's manuscript hasn't been substantiated in the seventy-five years since he wrote. Cantillon had Jacobite connections and if anywhere, Hume could have acquired access to a copy of Cantillon's manuscript when in touch with the circle of Andrew Michael Ramsay, better known as the Chevalier de Ramsay, in Rheims. Ramsay was the tutor of the sons of the exiled Stuart king, aka the Pretender, who was rumoured to have the Cantillon manuscript (Thornton 2005). In general, however, this current study suggests that there were many possible sources that led eighteenth-century political economists in this kind of direction, among whom one can count Irish and early eighteenth-century English and Scottish writings, of which Cantillon, an Irishman, could easily avail himself. Hume, of course, was not averse to hide his sources. One of the central arguments of his essay "Of Civil Liberty" was drawn from Nicholas Barbon's *A Discourse of Trade* (Barbon 1690) without any hint to the source. Hume's "Early Memoranda," however, makes it virtually certain that Barbon was Hume's source, see Hume 1985i [1741i] (originally published as "Of Liberty and Despotism"), 87–88; Barbon 1690, p. A3r-v; Hume 1948, 508. For commentary see Hont (2005b), 8–9.

17 On Gournay, the most spectacular account is still Turgot's *Éloge* (Turgot 1977 [1759]). Schelle 1897 and Weulersse 1910 are informative, for interpretation see Tsuda 1983, Murphy 1986b, Meysonnier 1989, 1990a, Larrère 1992. This study

does not extend to the study of the Physiocrats and Turgot. Useful contemporary studies for mapping the relationship between the Gournay circle and the Physiocrats is Charles and Steiner 1999, Charles 2000, Sonenscher 2001, Steiner 2002, Sonenscher 2007.

18 The republication of late seventeenth-century and early eighteenth-century economic pamphlets in the middle of the eighteenth century was not unique to the Gournay circle. Such works were regularly reprinted in both England and Ireland. In Scotland the Foulis Press of Glasgow, which had a close connection to the University, reprinted texts from Thomas Mun, William Petty, Josiah Child, William Paterson, John Law and Josiah Gee in the early 1750s. Similarly, the Gournay circle translated Josiah Child, John Cary, Charles King, and Matthew Decker, as well as the newly published work of David Hume. The Gournay group also translated two Spanish writers, Uzrariz and Ulloa. The former was translated into English at the same time.

19 For a good summary of Du Tot's criticism of Melon's views on money see Harsin (1935), 1:xvi–xxvii.

20 Hume's thoughts on patriotic voluntary bankruptcy as the termination of the public debt system were very popular in the eighteenth century. In France, however, those who thought that they had followed Hume often conflated it with Bolingbroke's version and his idea of a "patriot king" (Bolingbroke 1998 [1746]; Sonenscher 1997).

21 The design of Plumard's book was based on Josiah Tucker's *A Brief Essay on the Advantages and Disadvantages Which Respectively Attend France and Great Britain, With Regard to Trade* (Tucker 1749, 1753). Tucker approved it and welcomed the insights it offered on French economic difficulties (Tucker 1758, 13–14). Tucker was evidently on the same wavelength as the Gournay group. He recommended his readers to consult the works of Sir Josiah Child. It is not clear whether he knew of the new French translation of Child's book, sponsored by and commented upon by Gournay. His own pamphlet about the English naturalization debate was translated by Turgot (Tucker 1755b [1751]), who was at the time a member of the Gournay group. Both the Child and Tucker translations were listed in Le Blanc's bibliography (Le Blanc 1754b).

22 For a broader and highly illuminating comparative study of Forbonnais and Mirabeau see Chapter 3 "Morality and Politics in a Divided World" in Sonenscher 2007, 173–252.

23 For the scientific background of this notion see Schabas 2001.

24 Mably's use and interpretation of Cantillon caught the interest of the political economist Jean-Joseph-Louis Graslin, who cited the entire long passage relating to Cantillon's theory of self-cancelling wealth in *Phocion*, with added commentary in his *Essai analytique sur la richesse* (Graslin 1767, 365–84). On Graslin see Vatteville 1971, Orain 2006.

25 This tradition, which was widely discussed in the late eighteenth century, was worked out most assiduously by Fichte 1800. For background and interpretation see Müller 1801, Bloch 1973 [1959], Krause 1962, Verzar 1979, Gray 2003.

26 Helvétius wrote a defense of *L'esprit*, under the title *De l'homme* (*Treatise on Man*) that was published posthumously in 1773 (Helvétius 1773). In it Helvétius renamed the luxury of necessary goods as "national luxury," in contradistinction to any luxury based on inequality. He re-stated the rich country–poor country argument in Section VI, Chapter XV, under the title, "Of the period at which riches retire of themselves from an empire" (Helvétius 1778 [1773], 2: 120–22).

27 On Schmid see Venturi 1959, Venturi 1971, 206–7, Seifert 1988, Stüssi-Lauterburg 1989.

28 Tucker's detailed attack on Hume wasn't published until 1774. However, Tucker first claimed that Hume's *History* had proven that its author abandoned the rich country–poor country argument in December 1763; see his letter to Lord Kames in Tytler 1807, 2: Appendix 16–17; for commentary see Hont 2005e [1983], 295–96. Hume and Tucker subsequently met in France in the summer of 1765 while Hume was stationed in Paris as a British diplomat and they formed an amicable relationship (Shelton 1981, 170). It is possible that the news of Tucker's claim of having converted Hume reached the editors of the new French translation of Hume's *Essays*. If so, the French translator's comment would be the first printed version of Tucker's celebrated conversion claim. Hume's *History of the Stuarts* was a very popular book in France. Mably liked it and it was the only work of Hume that Rousseau ever had a glance at.

29 Tucker's claim of Hume's conversion referred to the entire run of Hume's socio-economic chapters in the *History*, not just to the "Appendix to the Reign of James I." The last volumes of the *History* that Hume published just before Tucker's letter to Kames in 1763 were the two volumes on *The History of England from the Invasion of Julius Caesar to the Accession of Henry VIII* in 1762. Two sections, the "Miscellanous transactions during this reign [Henry III]" (Hume 1983b [1778], 65–72) and the "Miscellaenous transactions during this reign [Edward II]" (ibid., 174–81) also contained important remarks about prices and wages that had a bearing on the interpretation of the rich country–poor country argument. For commentary see Hont 2005e [1983], 295–96. In a letter to Kames in 1764 Tucker mentioned issues from "Mr Hume's History of the Anglo-Saxons," see Shelton 1981, 170. The French translation of Hume's *Histoire d'Angleterre, contenant la maison de Plantagenet* was published in 1769 (Hume 1769 [1761]), two years after the publication of the new French translation of Hume's economic essays. In fact, the first segment of Hume's *History* that appeared in French translation was his *History of the Tudors*, in 1763 (Hume 1763 [1758]), followed by Hume's *History of the Stuarts* (Hume 1766 [1754]).

30 Isaak Iselin, the leading Swiss political economist, compared the two books that were published almost at the same time and reviewed both. He preferred Smith to Condillac, but he recognized Smith's debt to earlier writers and regretted that Smith failed to acknowledge "his teachers"; see his letter to Friedrich Nicolai, the German literary critic and the editor of the *Allgemeine Deutsche Bibliothek*, in April 1777 (Holger 1997, 458).

31 Although Dundas's rhetoric was liberal and Smithian in some respects, his views in this letter did not exhibit "a confident grasp of what is nowadays called the theory of comparative advantage," as Michael Fry claims (Fry 1992, 63). For a similar conflict between the views of Dundas and Smith see Fleischacker 2004, 261–62.

32 As if a "century" wouldn't be enough, in his letter that was addressed directly to Lord Carlisle, Smith corrected the expected time span of Ireland's rise to rich country status to "centuries" (Smith 1987e [1779], 243).

33 Dundas asked Smith for his advice on Eden's behalf on 1 November 1779. Smith answered, in some haste, on the same day. Eden's open letter to Carlisle is dated, in the printed version, 4 November 1779. Smith's letter to Carlisle, written in less haste, a few days after he had received Carlisle's request for help via Adam Ferguson, is dated 8 November 1799. Bernard Semmel (Semmel 1965, 766) assumed that Eden's pamphlet was written under the influence of Josiah Tucker, not Smith. Tucker's suggestion, however, that poor countries might consider defending themselves through aggressive protectionism, does not fit well with either Smith's or Eden's views (Tucker 1758, 5).

34 See Smith's response to Eden's query concerning the best options for introducing new taxation to defray the public debt in his letter to Eden on 3 January 1780 (Smith (1987 [1780]), 244–46).

35 For Foster's views in 1779 see O'Brien 1923–24, 95–102. Foster's attempt to alleviate English fears of Irish low-wage competitiveness, generated by the rich country–poor country argument, are on pp. 97–99. For an attempted refutation of the argument that the high price of fossil fuel would overwhelm Irish low-wage advantages see Douglas 1799, 86.

36 Bernard Semmel claims (Semmel 1965, 767–68) that the veteran Irish patriot politician Henry Flood deployed the poor country side of Hume's rich country–poor country argument in the Westminster Parliament debate about Pitt's and William Eden's British-French commercial treaty in 1787 (Henderson 1957; Ehrman 1962; Kelly 1989). This reference, however, is misleading. Flood (*Parliamentary History* 25 (1816) [1786–1778], 425–38, esp. 428–32, 438–39) did not refer to Hume, nor was his oratory in London following Hume in spirit. In foreign trade, Flood argued, always "that nation would have the advantage which was the poorest and the most abstemious"(ibid., 431) and suggested that since a "poorer nation would always drain from the richest in all commercial inter-courses, France must ultimately diminish our specie and increase of her own" (ibid., 432). But Flood's purpose was to attack Pitt by claiming that the anti-Irish arguments deployed in 1785 in the Irish Commercial Propositions debate should have been applied to Anglo-French rivalry too (ibid., 435). While England trea-ted Ireland as a dangerous rival, in the French case it was willing to forget about old animosities and suspend its traditional jealousy of trade. Flood's economic claim rested on the argument that "two bordering countries can seldom supply each other with advantage" (ibid., 434). Since both England and France were manufacturing countries, they had no reason to exchange goods in this sector. Instead, England would import French luxury goods, mainly food, wine and fashion accessories, and pay for it with cash, thereby suffering a net outflow of specie (ibid.,430). His argument, however, alluded not to France's low-wage advantage, but to its natural endowment advantages and to the damage caused by the irresponsible luxury consumption of wealthy nations like England. In some ways Flood prefigured John Foster's arguments in 1799; on Flood's poli-tical views see Kelly 1998, on Flood's role in Irish politics and his conflicts with Henry Grattan see York 1994, 131–40.

37 Tucker's *Letters to Shelburne* followed the arguments of his *A treatise concerning civil government* a year earlier (Tucker 1781); for an analysis of the latter see Pocock (1985d). On Shelburne's economic reform program, whose political implications Tucker criticized, see Norris 1963, 99–131, 255–56.

38 For a discussion of some tentative links between Vaughan's political economy and Hume's rich country–poor country argument see Hamilton 2004, 197–207. Note, however, Vaughan's declaration: "Much is said of the beauties of Fénelon's *Telemachus* and little of its precepts, which contain the seeds of all the senti-ments, if not all the doctrines of modern political economy" (Vaughan 1788, vii). These sentiments, of course, were not Humean. It was precisely the mixing of them with Hume's ideas in the French Hume reception that led to the Hume paradox mentioned by Rousseau.

39 Clarke's argument was close to Lord Lauderdale's rebuttal of Hume's rich country–poor country argument in his *Inquiry into the Nature and Origin of Public Wealth* of 1804 (see Lauderdale 1804, 298–99), although the specific emphasis on the role of machinery was missing. For commentary see Hont 2005e [1983b], 320.

40 See the debate between the comte Alexandre d'Hauterive (Hauterive 1800b, 1801; cf. 1800a) and Friedrich von Gentz (Gentz 1801, 1804). For background

see Forsyth (1980), Kronenbitter (1994), Rothschild (2005). It is worth noting that Gentz, who wrote in support of British policies and was in the pay of the British government, was a *protégé* of William Eden. Following the book that contained the Hume–Tucker correspondence (Clarke 1801, Clarke 1802), Clarke also published a direct attack on d'Hauterive (Clarke 1803). His knowledge of Europe was extensive. He was one of Britain's leading experts on Germany (Clarke 1790).

41 Smith's plea for the Irish Union was considered irrelevant after the early 1880s, because Ireland did achieve most of its free trade demands without surrendering its political identity. It was also noticed that the Americans spurned Smith's call for a union; see *Pro and Con* [Anon.] (1800), 35.

42 This was a view by no means unique to Smith. For a Scottish view see Jackson 2003, 123, 134. Tucker 1774e, 151–24, esp. 164–96, surveyed all the alternatives and 1776c Dickey 2002, 305–8. (See also Tucker 1776b). Smith raised the issue again a year later in Smith 1987 [1777], 377–85.

43 It was John Stuart Mill who introduced the names absolute and comparative costs in Essay I "Of the Laws of Interchange Between Nations; and the Distribution of the Gains of Commerce among the Countries of the Commercial World," in Mill 1967 [1844], 233 and repeated it in Book 3, Chapter 17, sect. 2 "Of International Trade," in Mill 1965, 3:589; see also Thweatt 1976, 207–34 on the efforts in this direction of John Stuart Mill's father, James Mill. Ricardo used the case of trade between England and Portugal to illustrate his case of comparative advantage and it is interesting to note in this light the history of trade conflicts between Ireland and Portugal in this period; see Lammey 1986 and Kelly 1990.

44 Hume never used the phrase "division of labor" either in the context of the "rich country–poor country" debate or in any other of his writings. For a single use of a parallel expression, "partition of employments," see the jurisprudence section of the *Treatise of Human Nature*, 3.2.2 (Hume 2000a [1739–40], 311–12).

45 In the copy of Browne's pamphlet held by the Cambridge University Library that was once owned by Jonathan Swift he added the following marginalia: "This is disputed." See also Swift 1962, 256.

46 Hume repeated his argument in print, with a slight variation, in "Of the Balance of Trade" (Hume (1985x [1752e], 312)).

Bibliography of David Hume's Works Cited in this Volume

Hume, David (1752) *Political Discourses*, Edinburgh: A. Kincaid and A. Donaldson.

——(1753) *Essays and Treatises on Several Subjects*, 4 vols. London: Andrew Millar.

——(1754a) *Discours politiques de monsieur Hume*, l'abbé Jean-Bernard Le Blanc (trans.), 2 vols. Amsterdam [Paris]: Lambert.

——(1754b) *Discours politiques de M. David Hume*, Elézéar Mauvillon (trans.), in Schreuder (ed) (1756) vol.

——(1755) *Discours politiques de monsieur Hume*, abbé Jean-Bernad Le Blanc (trans.), 2 vols., M. Groell (ed.) Dresde: n.p.

——(1763 [1758]) *Histoire d'Angleterre contenant la maison de Tudor*, (trans.) Octavie Du Rey de Meynières, dame Belot, 6 vols., Amsterdam: n.p.

——(1766 [1754]) *Histoire de la maison de Stuart sur le Trône d'Angleterre*, (trans.) Antoine François Prévost, London: n.p.

——(1767) *Essais sur le commerce; le luxe; l'argent; l'intérêt de l'argent; les impôts; le crédit public, et la balance du commerce*. Lyon and Paris: n.p.

——(1769 [1761]) *Histoire d'Angleterre, contenant la maison de Plantagenet*, (trans.) Octavie Du Rey de Meynières, dame Belot, Amsterdam: n.p.

——(1772) *Essays and Treatises on Several Subjects*, 2 vols. London: Thomas Cadell; Edinburgh: Alexander Kincaid and Alexander Donaldson.

——(1792 [1754–62]) *The History of England from the Invasion of Julius Caesar to the Revolution in 1688*, 8 vols. Edinburgh: George Mudie et al.

——(1894 [1754–62]) *History of England*, 3 vols. London: George Routledge.

——(1932; reprinted 1969, 1983) *The Letters of David Hume*, 2 vols., J. Y. T. Greig (ed.), Oxford: Clarendon Press.

——(1948) "Hume's Early Memoranda, 1729–40: The Complete Text," E. C. Mossner (ed.) *Journal of the History of Ideas*, 9: 492–518.

——(1955; reprinted 1970) *David Hume: Writings on Economics*, Eugene Rotwein (ed.), Madison, WI: University of Wisconsin Press; Edinburgh: Nelson.

——(1978 [1739–40]) *A Treatise of Human Nature*, edited with an analytical index by L. A. Selby Bigge, 2nd edn., with text revisions and variant readings by P.H. Nidditch, Oxford: Clarendon Press.

——(1980a) "My Own Life" (18 April 1776), in Ernest Campbell Mossner, *The Life of David Hume*, 2nd edn., Oxford: Clarendon Press, pp. 611–15.

——(1980b [1779]) *Dialogues Concerning Natural Religion*, Richard Popkin (ed.) Indianapolis, IN: Hackett Publishers.

——(1983a [1754–62]; 7th ed. [1778]) *The History of England, from the Invasion of Julius Caesar to the Revolution in 1688*, 6 vols., W. B. Todd (ed.) Indianapolis, IN: Liberty Classics.

——(1983b [1954]) *New Letters of David Hume*, Raymond Klibansky and Ernest C. Mossner (eds.) New York: Garland Publishers; Oxford: Clarendon Press, 1954.

——(1985 [1741–77]) *Essays: Moral, Political, and Literary*, Eugene F. Miller (ed.) Indianapolis, IN: Liberty Classics [henceforth *Essays*].

——(1985a [1741a]) "Of the Delicacy of Taste and Passion," in *Essays*, pp. 3–8.

——(1985b [1741b]) "Of the Liberty of the Press," in *Essays*, pp. 9–13.

——(1985c [1741c]) "That Politics May Be Reduced to a Science," in *Essays*, pp. 14–31.

——(1985d [1741d]) "Of the First Principles of Government," in *Essays*, pp. 32–36.

——(1985e [1741e]) "Whether the British Government Inclines More to Absolute Monarchy, or to a Republic," in *Essays*, pp. 47–53.

——(1985f [1741f]) "Of Parties in General," in *Essays*, pp. 54–63.

——(1985g [1741g]) "Of Parties in Great Britain," in *Essays*, pp. 64–72.

——(1985h [1741h]) "Of Superstition and Enthusiasm," in *Essays*, pp. 73–79.

——(1985i [1741i]) "Of Civil Liberty," in *Essays*, pp. 87–96.

——(1985j [1741j]) "Of Avarice," in *Essays*, pp. 569–73.

——(1985k [1742a]) "Of the Rise and Progress of the Arts and Sciences," in *Essays*, pp. 111–37.

——(1985l [1742b]) "The Stoic," in *Essays*, pp. 146–54.

——(1985m [1742c]) "Of Polygamy and Divorces," in *Essays*, pp. 181–90.

——(1985n [1742d]) "Of the Middle Station of Life," in *Essays*, pp. 545–51.

——(1985o [1742e]) "A Character of Sir Robert Walpole," in *Essays*, pp. 574–76.

——(1985p [1742f]) "Of Essay Writing," in *Essays*, pp. 533–37.

——(1985q [1748a]) "Of National Characters," in *Essays*, pp. 197–215.

——(1985r [1748b]) "Of the Original Contract," in *Essays*, pp. 465–87.

——(1985s [1752a]) "Of Commerce," in *Essays*, pp. 253–67.

——(1985t [1752b]) "Of Refinement in the Arts," in *Essays*, pp. 268–80.

——(1985u [1752c]) "Of Money," in *Essays*, pp. 281–94.

——(1985v [1752d]) "Of Interest," in *Essays*, pp. 295–307.

——(1985x [1752e]) "Of the Balance of Trade," in *Essays*, pp. 308–26.

——(1985y [1752f]) "Of the Balance of Power," in *Essays*, pp. 332–41.

——(1985z [1752g]) "Of Taxes," in *Essays*, pp. 342–48.

——(1985aa [1752h]) "Of Public Credit," in *Essays*, pp. 349–65.

——(1985bb [1752i]) "Of the Populousness of Ancient Nations," in *Essays*, pp. 377–464.

——(1985cc [1752j]) "Idea of a Perfect Commonwealth," in *Essays*, pp. 512–29.

——(1985dd [1757]) "Of the Standard of Taste," in *Essays*, pp. 226–49.

——(1985ee [1758]) "Of Jealousy of Trade," in *Essays*, pp. 327–31.

——(1985ff [1777a]) "Of the Origin of Government," in *Essays*, pp. 37–41.

——(1985gg [1777b]) "Of Suicide," in *Essays*, pp. 577–89.

——(1994) *Political Essays*, Knud Haakonssen (ed.) Cambridge: Cambridge University Press.

——(1997) *Four Dissertations*, Bristol, UK: Thoemmes Press.

——(1998 [1751]) *An Enquiry Concerning the Principles of Morals*, Tom L. Beauchamp (ed.) Oxford: Oxford University Press.

——(2000a [1739–40]) *A Treatise of Human Nature*, David Fate Norton and Mary J. Norton (eds.) Oxford: Oxford University Press.

——(2000b [1748]) *An Enquiry Concerning Human Understanding*, Tom L. Beauchamp (ed.) Oxford: Oxford University Press.

——(2001) *Essais moraux, politiques et littéraires et autres essais*, Edition intégrale, Gilles Robel (trans.), Paris: Presses Universitaires de France.

——(2004 [1748]) *A True Account of the Behaviour and Conduct of Archibald Stewart, Esq., Late Lord Provost of Edinburgh: In a Letter to a Friend*, Mark Box, David Harvey, and Michael Silverthorne (eds.) *Hume Studies*, 29: 223–66.

Bibliography

Anonymous (1754) "Review of Hume's Discours politiques," in *Annoncés, affiches et avis divers*, provincial edn., Paris, pp. 118, 129.

——(1757) *Discours pour et contre la réduction de l'intérêt naturel de l'argent, qui avait été prononcés en 1737, dans la chambre des communes de la Grande-Bretagne*, Jean-Paul de Gua de Malves (trans. and ed.) Wesel.

——(1760) *Acte du parlement d'Angleterre, connu sous le nom de l'acte de navigation passé en 1660*, Georges-Marie Butel-Dumont (trans. and ed.).

——(1767) "Review of Hume's Essais sur le commerce; le luxe; l'argent; l'intérêt de l'argent; les impôts; le crédit public, et la balance du commerce," *Journal d'Agriculture, du Commerce et des Finances*, février–juin.

——(1800) *Pro and Con: being an Impartial Abstract of the Principal Publications on the Subject of a Legislative union Between Great Britain and Ireland, in which the Arguments for and Against that Measure...are fairly Contrasted...* Dublin: R. Marchbank.

Addison, Joseph and Richard Steele (1982) *Selections from* The Tatler [1709–11] *and* The Spectator [1711–12], Angus Ross (ed.) Harmondsworth, UK: Penguin.

Ainslie, George (1992) *Picoeconomics: The Strategic Interaction of Successive Motivational States within the Person*, Cambridge: Cambridge University Press.

Amoh, Yasuo (2003) "The Ancient–Modern Controversy in the Scottish Enlightenment," in Tatsuya Sakamoto and Hideo Tanaka (eds.) *The Rise of Economy in the Scottish Enlightenment*, London: Routledge, pp. 69–87.

Anderson, Elizabeth (1993) *Value and Ethics in Modern Economics*, Cambridge, MA: Harvard University Press.

Annesley, Francis (1740 [1698]) *Some Thoughts on the Bill Depending before the Right Honourable the House of Lords for Prohibiting the Exportation of the Woollen Manufactures of Ireland to Foreign Parts. Humbly offer'd to their Lordships, Written in the year 1698*, 2nd edition, Dublin: S. Powell, for G. Faulkner.

Appleby, Joyce Oldham (1978) *Economic Thought and Ideology in Seventeenth-Century England*, Princeton, NJ: Princeton University Press.

Ardal, Pall S. (1989) *Passion and Value in Hume's Treatise*, 2nd edn., Edinburgh: Edinburgh University Press.

Aristotle (1900) *Ethika Nikomacheia*, J. Burnet (ed.), London: Methuen.

——(1976) *The Ethics of Aristotle: The Nicomachean Ethics*, J. A. K. Thomson (trans.), Harmondsworth: Penguin.

——(1977) *Politics*, H. Rackham (trans.), Cambridge, MA: Harvard University Press.

Arkin, Marcus (1956) "The Economic Writings of David Hume: A Reassessment," *South African Journal of Economics*, 24: 204–20.

Armitage, David (1995) "The Scottish Vision of Empire: Intellectual Origins of the Darien Venture," in Robertson (ed.) *A Union for Empire*, pp. 97–118.

——(2000a) *The Ideological Origins of the British Empire*, Cambridge: Cambridge University Press.

——(2000b) "The Political Economy of Britain and Ireland after the Glorious Revolution," in Jane H. Ohlmeyer (ed.) *Political Thought in Seventeenth-Century Ireland*, Cambridge: Cambridge University Press, pp. 221–43.

Armstrong, Robert (1984) *Structure and Change: An Economic History of Quebec*, Toronto: Gage.

Arrighi, Giovanni (2007) *Adam Smith in Beijing – Lineages of the Twenty-First Century*, London: Verso.

Ashley, John (1735) *Some Observations on a Direct Exportation of Sugar from the British Islands*, London: n.p.

Ashton, Thomas Southcliffe (1959) *Economic Fluctuations in England, 1700–1800*, Oxford: Clarendon Press.

Baier, Annette (1991) *A Progress of Sentiments*, Cambridge: Cambridge University Press.

Baker, Keith Michael (1981) "A Script for a French Revolution: The Political Consciousness of the abbé Mably," *Eighteenth-Century Studies*, 14(3): 235–63.

Balcou, Jean (1975) *Fréron contre les philosophes*, Paris and Geneva: Librairie Droz.

Baldi, Marialuisa (1983) *David Hume nel Settecento italiano: filosofia ed economia*, Firenze: La Nuova Italia Editrice.

Bannister, Saxe (1968) "Introduction" to S. Bannister (ed.) *The Writings of William Paterson, Founder of the Bank of England*, 2nd edn., 3 vols., New York: A. M. Kelley.

Barbon, Nicholas (1690) *A Discourse of Trade*, London: Thomas Milbourn.

Barfoot, Michael (1990) "Hume and the Culture of Science in the Early Eighteenth Century," in M. A. Stewart (ed.) *Studies in the Philosophy of the Scottish Enlightenment*, Oxford: Clarendon Press, pp. 151–90.

Becagli, Giorgio (2004) "Georg-Ludwig Schmid d' Auenstein e i suoi *Principes de la legislation universelle*: oltre la fisiocracia?," in Manuela Albertone (ed.), *Fisiocracia e proprieta terriera, Studi Settecenteschi*, 24: 215–52.

Berdell, John F. (1995) "The Present Relevance of Hume's Open-Economy Monetary Dynamics," *Economic Journal*, 105: 1205–17.

——(1996) "Innovation and Trade: David Hume and the Case for Freer Trade," *History of Political Economy*, 28(1): 107–26.

——(2002) *International Trade and Economic Growth in Open Economies: The Classical Dynamics of Hume, Smith, Ricardo and Malthus*, Cheltenham, Edward Elgar.

Berg, M. and E. Eger (eds.) (2003) *Luxury in the Eighteenth Century*, Basingstoke: Palgrave.

Berkeley, George (1901) *Works*, 4 vols., Alexander Campbell Fraser (ed.), Oxford: Clarendon Press.

——(1910 [1735–37]) *The Querist*, reprint, Jacob H. Hollander (ed.), Baltimore: Johns Hopkins Press.

——(1970 [1735]) *The Querist*, reprinted in J. Johnston, *Bishop Berkeley's Querist in Historical Perspective*, Dundalk, Ireland: Dundalgan Press.

Bernard, Christopher (1995) "Hume and the Madness of Religion," in M. A. Stewart and John P. Wright (eds.) *Hume and Hume's Connexions*, University Park, PA: Pennsylvania State University Press, pp. 224–38.

Berry, C. J. (1994) *Idea of Luxury: A Conceptual and Historical Analysis*, Cambridge: Cambridge University Press.

——(1997) *Social Theory of the Scottish Enlightenment*, Edinburgh: Edinburgh University Press.

——(1999) "Austerity, Necessity and Luxury," in J. Hill and C. Lennon (eds.) *Luxury and Austerity*, Dublin: University College Press, 1–13.

——(2003a) "Sociality and Socialisation," in A. Broadie (ed.) *Cambridge Companion to the Scottish Enlightenment*, Cambridge: Cambridge University Press, pp. 243–57.

——(2003b) "The Scottish Enlightenment and the Idea of Civil Society," in A. Martin (ed.) *Separata da Sociedade Civil: Entre Miragen e Oportunidade*, Coimbra, Portugal: Faculdade de Letras, pp. 99–115.

Bindon, David (1738a) "The Preface," in Melon (1738 [1734]), pp. iii–xxiv.

——(1738b) *A Letter from a Merchant who has left off Trade to a Member of Parliament. In which the Case of the British and Irish Manufacture of Linnen, Threads, and Tapes, is Fairly Stated*, London: R. Willock.

Black, R. D. Collison (1950) "Theory and Policy in Anglo-Irish Trade Relations, 1775–1800," *Journal of the Statistical and Social Enquiry Society of Ireland*, 18: 312–26.

——(1969) *A Catalogue of Pamphlets on Economic Subjects Published between 1750 and 1900 and now Housed in Irish libraries*, New York: A.M. Kelley.

Blaug, Mark (1978 [1962]) *Economic Theory in Retrospect*, Cambridge: Cambridge University Press.

——(ed.) (1991) *David Hume (1711–1776) and James Steuart (1712–1780)*, Aldershot, Hants: Edward Elgar.

——(ed.) (1995) *The Quantity Theory of Money from Locke to Keynes and Friedman*, Aldershot, Hants: Edward Elgar.

Bloch, Ernst (1973 [1959]) "Fichtes geschlossener Handelsstaat oder Produktion und Tausch nach Vernunftrecht," in Bloch, *Das Prinzip Hoffnung*, Frankfurt am Main: Suhrkamp, pp. 642–47.

Boianovsky, Mauro (1993) "Böhm-Bawerk, Irving Fisher, and the Term 'Veil of Money': A Note," *History of Political Economy*, 25:725–38.

Bolingbroke, Henry St. John, Viscount (1998 [1746]) *The Patriot King*, in Bolingbroke *Political Writings*, David Armitage, (ed.), Cambridge: Cambridge University Press.

——(1754a) "Some Reflections of the Present State of the Nation, Principally with Regard to her Taxes and her Debts, and on the Causes and Consequences of them," in David Mallet, (ed.), *The Works of the late Right Honourable Henry St. John, Lord Viscount Bolingbroke*, 4 vols., London, n.p., vol. 3, pp. 143–79.

——(1754b), *Testament Politique de Milord Bolingbroke, Écrit par lui-même; ou Considerations sur l'État Present de la Grande-Bretagne, Principalement par Rapport aux Taxes & aux Dettes Nationales, Leurs Causes & Leurs Conséquences*, London: n.p.

——(1754c) "Réflexions Politiques sur l'État Present de l'Angleterre, Principalement à l'Égard de ses Taxes et de ses Dettes, et sur Leurs Causes et Leurs Consequences," in Hume (1754a), 1:221–86.

——(1756) "Réflexions Politiques sur l'État present de l'Angleterre, Traduites de l'Anglais de Mylord Bolingbroke," Elézéar Mauvillion (trans.) in Schreuder (ed.) (1756–1758), vol. 2, pp. 251–314.

Bolton, Geoffrey Curgenven (1966) *The Passing of the Irish Act of Union: A Study in Parliamentary Politics*, Oxford: Oxford University Press.

Bongie, Laurence L. (1952) "Hume en France au XVIIIe siècle," unpublished thesis, University of Paris, Sorbonne.

——(1977) *Diderots Femme Savante*, in *Studies on Voltaire and the Eighteenth Century*, vol. 166. Oxford: Voltaire Foundation.

Bonolas, P. (1987) "Fénelon et le luxe dans le Télémaque," *Voltaire Studies*, 249: 81–90.

Bordo, Michael (1983) "Some Aspects of the Monetary Economics of Richard Cantillon," *Journal of Monetary Economics*, 12: 235–58.

Bosher, John F. (1970) *French Finances 1770–1795: From Business to Bureaucracy*, Cambridge: Cambridge University Press.

Bourdieu, Pierre (1979) *La Distinction: Critique sociale du jugement*, Paris: Minuit.

Boureau-Deslandes, François-André (1745) *Lettre sur le luxe*, Frankfurt: J.-A. Vanebben.

Bourne, Henry Richard Fox (1876) *The Life of John Locke*, 2 vols., London: King.

Boyce, D. George, Robert Eccleshall, and Vincent Geoghegan (eds.) (1993) *Political Thought in Ireland since the Seventeenth Century*, London: Routledge.

——(2001) *Political Discourse in Seventeenth- and Eighteenth-Century Ireland*, Basingstoke: Palgrave.

Boyd, Richard (2000) "Reappraising the Scottish Moralists and Civil Society," *Polity*, 33: 101–25.

——(2002) "The Calvinist Origins of Lockean Political Economy," *History of Political Thought*, 23: 31–62.

——(2004a) "Pity's Pathologies Portrayed: Rousseau and the Limits of Democratic Compassion," *Political Theory*, 32: 519–46.

——(2004b) *Uncivil Society: The Perils of Pluralism and the Making of Modern Liberalism*, Lanham, MD: Lexington Books.

Box, Mark, David Harvey, and Michael Silverthorne (2003) "A Diplomatic Transcription of Hume's 'volunteer pamphlet' for Archibald Stewart: Political Whigs, Religious Whigs, and Jacobites," *Hume Studies*, 29: 223–66.

Brantlinger, Patrick (1996) *Fictions of State: Culture and Credit in Britain, 1694–1995*, Ithaca: Cornell University Press.

Braudel, Fernand (1990) *The Identity of France*, vol. 1, *History and Environment*, Siân Reynolds (trans.), Perennial Library, New York: Harper and Row.

Breckenridge, Roeloff M. (1893) "The Paper Currencies of New France," *Journal of Political Economy*, 1: 406–31.

Brewer, Anthony (1988) "Cantillon and Mercantilism," *History of Political Economy*, 20: 282–95.

——(1992) *Richard Cantillon: Pioneer of Economic Theory*, London: Routledge.

——(1997) "An Eighteenth-Century View of Economic Development: Hume and Steuart," *European Journal of the History of Economic Thought*, 4(1) 4.1: 1–23.

——(1998) "Luxury and Economic Development: David Hume and Adam Smith," *Scottish Journal of Political Economy*, 45.1: 78–98.

Brewer, John (1990) *Sinews of Power: War, Money, and the English State, 1688–1783*, Cambridge, MA: Harvard University Press.

Brewer, John and Eckhart Hellmuth (eds.) (1999) *Rethinking Leviathan: The Eighteenth-Century State in Britain and Germany*, Oxford: Oxford University Press.

Brown, John (1758 [1757]) *An Estimate of the Manners and Principles of the Times*, 7th edn., 2 vols., London: Printed for L. Davis and C. Reymers.

Browne, Sir John (1728) *An Essay on Trade in General; And, On that of Ireland in Particular*, Dublin: S. Powell and George Ewing.

——(1729 [1728]) "Seasonable Remarks on Trade. With some Reflections on the Advantages that might accrue to Great Britain by a Proper Regulation of the Trade of Ireland. Wrote in London, but now First Publish'd in Dublin as a Preface to Other Essays on the Trade and Manufacturers of Ireland," in *Collection of Tracts, Concerning the Present State of Ireland with Respect to Riches, Revenue, Trade and Manufactures*, London: T. Woodward and J. Peele, pp. 1–46.

Browning, Reed (1995) *The War of the Austrian Succession*, New York: St. Martin's Press.

Bruni, Luigini and Robert Sugden (2000) "Moral Canals: Trust and Social Capital in the Work of Hume, Smith and Genovesi," *Economics and Philosophy*, 16(1): 21–45.

Buckle, Stephen (1991) *Natural Law and the Theory of Property: Grotius to Hume*, Oxford: Clarendon Press.

Burke, Edmund (1871) "Thoughts and Details on Scarcity," in *The Works of the Right Honorable Edmund Burke*, vol. 5, Boston: Little, Brown.

——(1991 [1778]) "Speech on Irish Trade, House of Commons, 6 May 1778," in *The Writings and Speeches of Edmund Burke*, Paul Langford, (ed.), vol. 9,: Oxford: Clarendon Press, pp. 519–23.

——(1987 [1790]) *Reflections on the Revolution in France*, Indianapolis, IN: Hackett Publishers.

Burton, J. H. (ed.) (1849 [1820]) *Letters of Eminent Persons Addressed to David Hume*, London and Edinburgh.

——(1846) *Life and Correspondence of David Hume*, 2 vols., Edinburgh: William Tait.

Butel, Paul (1993) *L'Economie Française au XVIIIe siècle*, Paris: SEDES.

Caffentzis, George (1989) *Clipped Coins, Abused Words, and Civil Government: John Locke's Philosophy of Money*, Brooklyn, NY: Autonomedia.

——(1996) "On the Scottish Origin of 'Civilization," in Silvia Federici (ed.) *Enduring Western Civilization: The Construction of the Concept of Western Civilization and Its "Others*," Westport, CT: Praeger.

——(2000) *Exciting the Industry of Mankind: George Berkeley's Philosophy of Money*, Boston: Kluwer Academic Press.

——(2001) "Hume, Money, and Civilization: Or Why Was Hume a Metallist?" *Hume Studies*, 27(2): 301–35.

——(2005) "Civilizing the Highlands: Hume, Money, and the Annexing Act," *Historical Reflections*, 31(1): 169–94.

Campbell, Archibald (1758) *Catalogus Librorum A.[rchibald] C.[ampbell] D.[uke of] A.[rgyle]*, Glasgow: Robert and Andrew Foulis.

Cantillon, Richard ([1755]) *Essai sur la nature du commerce en général, traduit de l'angloais*, London: F. Gyles.

——(1931 [1755]) *Abhandlung über die Natur des Handels in allgemeinen*, Hella Hayek (trans), Friedrich A. von Hayek, (introduction and notes) Sammlung sozialwissenschaftlicher Meister: Vol. 25, Jena: Fischer.

——(1931 [1755]) *Essai sur la nature du commerce en général*, Henry Higgs (trans.), New York: Augustus M. Kelley.

——(2001 [1931]) *Essay on the Nature of Commerce in General*, Henry Higgs (trans.), Anthony Brewer (new introduction), New Brunswick: Transaction Publishers.

Capaldi, Nicholas (1989) *Hume's Place in Moral Philosophy*, New York: Peter Lang.

Cardoso, José Luís and António Vasconcelos Nogueira (2005) "Isaac de Pinto (1717–87): An Enlightened Economist and Financier," *History of Political Economy*, 37(2), 263–92.

Carpenter, Kenneth E. (1975) "The Economic Bestsellers before 1850," *Bulletin of the Kress Library of Business and Economics*, 11.

——(2002) *The Dissemination of the* Wealth of Nations *in French and in France, 1776–1843*, New York: The Bibliographical Society of America.

Carswell, John (1993) *The South Sea Bubble*, 2nd edn., London: Alan Sutton.

Carter, Stephen L. (1998) *Civility: Manners, Morals, and the Etiquette of Democracy*, New York: Basic Books.

Cary, John (1695) *An Essay on the State of England in Relation to Its Trade, Its Poor, and Its Taxes*, Bristol, UK: W. Barry (reprinted several times up to 1745).

——(1696) *An Essay Towards the Settlement of National Credit, in the Kingdom of England*. n.p.: n.p.

——(1698a) *To the Freeholders and Burgesses of the City of Bristol*, Bristol: n.p.

——(1698b) *An Answer to Mr. Molyneux his Case of Ireland's Being Bound by Acts of Parliament in England, Stated: and his Dangerous Notion of Ireland's Being under no Subordination to the Parliamentary Authority of England Refuted; by Reasoning from his own Arguments and Authoritie*, London: Richard Parker.

——(1698c) *A Vindication of the Parliament of England, in Answer to a Book, written by William Molyneux of Dublin, Esq; intituled, The case of Irelands being Bound by Acts of Parliament in England, stated*, London: Freeman Collins, Samuel Crouch and Elizabeth Whitlock.

——(1755 [1745]) *Essai sur l'état du commerce d'Angleterre*, 2 vols., Georges-Marie Butel-Dumont (trans. and ed.), London: n.p.

Cawthorne, P. and G. Kitching (2001) "Moral Dilemmas and Factual Claims: Some Comments on Paul Krugman's Defense of Cheap Labor," *Review of Social Economy*, 59: 455–66.

Cesarano, Filippo (1998) "Hume's Specie-Flow Mechanism and Classical Monetary Theory: An Alternative Interpretation," *Journal of International Economics*, 45(1): 173–86.

Challis, C. E. (1992) *A New History of the Royal Mint*, Cambridge: Cambridge University Press.

Chamley, Paul E. (1975) "The Conflict between Montesquieu and Hume: A Study of the Origins of Adam Smith's Universalism," in Andrew S. Skinner and Thomas Wilson (eds.) *Essays on Adam Smith*, Oxford: Clarendon Press. pp. 274–305.

Charles, Loïc (1999a) "La liberté du commerce des grains et l'économie politique française (1750–70)," unpublished thesis, University of Paris, Sorbonne.

——(1999b) " 'Le masque et la plume': la contribution négligée de F. Quesnay à *l'Essai sur l'amélioration des terres*," *Économies et Sociétés*, Série PE 29: 29–59.

——(2000) "From the *Encyclopédie* to the *Tableau économique*: Quesnay on Freedom of Grain Trade and Economic Growth," *European Journal of the History of Economic Thought*, 7: 1–21.

Charles, Loic and Philippe Steiner (1999) "Entre Montesquieu et Rousseau: la physiocratie parmi les origines intellectuelles de la Revolution Française," *Etudes Jean-Jacques Rousseau*, 11: 83–159.

Chaussinand Nogaret, Guy (1972) *Gens de finance au XVIIIe siècle*, Paris: Bordas.

——(1985) *The French Nobility in the Eighteenth Century: From Feudalism to Enlightenment*, William Doyle (trans.), Cambridge: Cambridge University Press.

Checkland, Sydney (1975) *Scottish Banking: A History, 1695–1973*, Glasgow and London: Collins.

Child, Josiah (1690) *A Discourse about Trade*, London: n.p.

——(1754) *Traités sur le commerce et sur les avantages qui résultent de la réduction de l'intérêt de l'argent, avec un petit traité contre l'usure, par Thomas Culpeper*, Georges-Marie Butel-Dumont (trans.), Amsterdam: J. Neaulme.

——(1983 [1752]) *Traité sur le commerce de Josiah Child avec les remarques inédites de Vincent de Gournay*, Takumi Tsuda (ed.), Tokyo: Kinokuniya Company.

Childs, Nick (2000) *A Political Academy in Paris, 1724–1731. The Entresol and its Members*, Oxford: Oxford University Press.

Chipman, J. S. (1965) "A Survey of the Theory of International Trade. Part 1: The Classical Theory," *Econometrica*, 33: 477–519.

Clark, Walter Ernest (1903) *Josiah Tucker, Economist*, New York: Columbia University Press.

Clarke, Thomas Brooke (1781) *An Essay on the Powers of Parliament, the Right of Making Laws, and the Individual Declarations of this Kingdom. Written by Thomas Brooke Clarke ... and now addressed to the Right Honourable the Earl of Carlisle*, Dublin: W. Hallhead.

——(1790) *A Statistical View of Germany in Respect to the Imperial and Territorial Constitutions, Forms of Government, Legislation, Administration of Justice and Ecclesiastical State, with a Sketch of the Character and Genius of the Germans*, London: C. Dilly.

——(1799a) *Dean Tucker's Arguments on the Propriety of an Union between Great Britain and Ireland; Written some years since, and now first published in this tract upon the same subject. By the Rev. Dr. Clarke*, Dublin: printed for J. Milliken.

——(1799b) *Union or Separation. Written some Years since by the Rev. Dr. Tucker, ... and Now First Published in this Tract upon the Same Subject. By the Rev. Dr Clarke. ... In this Work, the Great Objections Urged at a Meeting of the Irish Bar, are Distinctly Considered and Confuted*, London: printed for J. Hatchard & J. Wright; Clarke & Rivingtons.

——(1799c) *The Political, Commercial, and Civil, State of Ireland. By the Rev. Dr. Clarke, ... Being an Appendix to "Union or Separation,"* London: John Hatchard, J. Wright Clarke and Rivington.

——(1799d) *Misconceptions of Facts and Mistatements [sic] of the Public Accounts by the Right Hon. John Foster of the Irish House of Commons Proved & [sic] Corrected According to the Official Documents and Authentic Evidence of the Inspector General of Great Britain in a Letter to Wm Johnson Esq. Member of the Irish Parliament from the Rev. Dr Clarke Secretary for the Library and Chaplain in Ordinary to his Royal Highness the Prince of Wales*, London: John Hatchard.

——(1799e) *A Letter to the Right Hon. Earl Cholmondeley on the Civil Policy of the Ancients. By the Rev. Dr. Clarke, ... To which is Prefixed an Enumeration of the Confiscations, &c. of the French Nation, Extracted from Official Documents. Translated from the German*, 2nd ed. London: W. Clarke.

——(1801) *A Survey of the Strength and Opulence of Great Britain: Wherein it is Shewn, the Progress of its Commerce, Agriculture, Population, &c. Before and since the Accession of the House of Hanover*, London: T. Cadell and W. Davies.

——(1802) *Coup d'Oeil sur la Force et l'Opulence de la Grande-Bretagne ... par le Docteur Clarke. On y a Joint une Correspondance Inédite du Doyen Tucker et de David Hume avec le, Lord Kaims, Concernant le Commerce. Ouvrage publié à Londres, en 1801*, J. Marchena (trans.), Paris: Levrault frères.

——(1803) *An Historical and Political View of the Disorganization of Europe: Wherein the Laws and Characters of Nations, the Maritime and Commercial System of Great Britain and other States, are Vindicated against the Imputations and Revolutionary Proposals of M. Talleyrand and M. Hauterive, Secretaries of State to the French Republic*, London: T. Cadell and W. Davies.

Clément, Pierre (1872) *M. de Silhouette Bouret: les dernières fermiers généraux*; *e'tudes sur les financiers du xviile siècle*, Paris: Didier et Compagnie.

Clement, Simon (1698) *The Interest of England, as it Stands with Relation to the Trade of Ireland, Considered; the Arguments against the Bill, for Prohibiting the Exportation of Woollen Manufactures from Ireland to Forreign Parts, fairly Discusst, and the Reasonableness and Necessity of Englands Restraining her Colonies in all Matters of Trade, that may be Prejudicial to her own Commerce, clearly Demonstrated. With short Remarques on a book, Entituled, Some Thoughts on the Bill depending before the Right Honourable the House of Lords, for Prohibiting the Exportation of the Woollen Manufactures of Ireland to Forreign Parts*, London: John Attwood.

Clerk, Sir John (1892) *Memoirs of the Life of Sir John Clerk of Penicuik, Baronet, Baron of the Exchequer, Extracted by Himself from His Own Journals, 1676–1755*, Publications of the Scottish History Society series, vol. 13, Edinburgh: Scottish History Society.

Coats, A. W. (1958) "Changing Attitudes to Labour in the Mid-Eighteenth Century," *Economic History Review*, 11: 35–51.

——(1992) "Economic Thought and Poor Law Policy in the Eighteenth Century," *On the History of Economic Thought*, vol. 1, London: Routledge, pp. 85–100.

Cole, Charles Woolsey (1939) *Colbert and a Century of French Mercantilism*, 2 vols. New York: Columbia University Press.

Colombo, John Robert (1974) *Colombo's Canadian Quotations*, Edmonton: Hurtig.

Condillac, Étienne Bonnot abbé de (1776) *Le Commerce et le Gouvernement, Considérés Rélativement l'un à l'autre, ouvrage élémentaire*, Amsterdam and Paris: Jombert & Cellot.

——(1997 [1776]) *Commerce and Government considered in their Mutual Relationship*, Walter and Shelagh Eltis (trans.), Cheltenham: Edward Elgar.

Cunningham, Andrew S. (2005) "David Hume's Account of Luxury," *Journal of the History of Economic Thought*, 27(3): 231–50.

Dalrymple, Sir John (1788) *Memoirs of Great Britain and Ireland, from the battle off La Hague till the capture of the French and Spanish fleets at Vigo*, 2 vols., Edinburgh: Bell, Creech, Strahan, and Cadell.

Davenant, Charles (1771a) *The Political and Commercial Works of that Celebrated Writer Charles D'Avenant, LL.D. Relating to the Trade and Revenue of England, the Plantation Trade, the East-India Trade, and African Trade*, Sir Charles Whitworth, ed., 5 vols., London: R. Horsfield and others.

——(1771b [1696]) *An Essay on the East-India-Trade. By the Author of The Essay upon Wayes and Means*, in Davenant (1771a), vol. 1.

——(1771c [1699]) *An Essay upon the Probable Methods of Making a people Gainers in the Ballance of Trade. Treating of these heads, viz. Of the people of England. Of the* land of England, and its product. *Of our Payments to the Publick, and in What Manner the Ballance of Trade may be thereby Affected. That a Country cannot Increase in Wealth and Power but by Private Men doing their Duty to the Publick, and but by a Steady course of Honesty and Wisdom, in Such as are Trusted with the Administration of Affairs. By the Author of The essay on Ways and Means*, in Davenant (1771a), vol. 2.

Davie, George (1967a) "Anglophobe and Anglophile," *Scottish Journal of Political Economy*, 14: 295–96.

——(1967b) "Hume, Reid and the Passion for Ideas," in George Bruce (ed.) *Edinburgh in the Age of Reason*, Edinburgh: Edinburgh University Press, pp. 23–39.

Davies, Glyn (1994) *A History of Money from Ancient Times to the Present Day*, Cardiff: University of Wales Press.

Davis, Gordon F. (2003) "Philosophical Psychology and Economic Psychology in David Hume and Adam Smith," *History of Political Economy*, 35: 269–304.

Davis, Ralph (1962) *The Rise of the English Shipping Industry in the Seventeenth and Eighteenth Centuries*, London: Macmillan.

Davlantes, Nancy (1990) "The Eminently Practical Mr. Hume or Still Relevant After All These Years," *Hume Studies*, 16: 45–56.

Decker, Matthew (1757 [1744]) *Essai sur les causes du déclin du commerce étranger de la Grande Bretagne*, Jean-Paul de Gua de Malves (trans. and ed.), n.p.

Deleule, Didier (1979) *Hume et la naissance du liberalism économique*, Paris: Aubier Montaigne.

Deleuze, Gilles (1991 [1953]) *Empiricism and Subjectivity: An Essay on Hume's Theory of Human Nature*, Constantin V. Boundas (trans.), New York: Columbia University Press.

Deleyre, Alexandre (1774) *Tableau de l'Europe, Pour servir de supplément à l'Histoire philosophique & politique des établissements & du commerce des Européens dans les deux Indes*, Maastricht, The Netherlands: J. E. Dufour.

Dessert, Daniel (1984) *Argent, pouvoir et société au Grand Siècle*, Paris: Fayard.

Devine, T. M. (1975) *The Tobacco Lords*, Edinburgh: John Donald Publishers.

Diaye, Marc-Arthur and André Lapidus (2005) "A Humean Theory of Choice of Which Rationality May Be One Consequence," *European Journal of the History of Economic Thought*, 12: 89–11; 119–26.

Dickey, Laurence (1986) "Historicizing the 'Adam Smith Problem'," *Journal of Modern History*, 58: 579–609.

——(1995) "Power, Commerce and Natural Law in Daniel Defoe's Political Writings 1698–1707," in Robertson (ed.) *A Union for Empire*, pp. 63–96.

——(2002) "Doux-Commerce and Humanitarian Values: Free Trade, Sociability and Universal Benevolence in Eighteenth-Century Thinking," *Grotiana*, new ser., 22–23:

Dickson, P. G. M. (1967) *The Financial Revolution in England: A Study in the Development of Public Credit*, London: Macmillan.

Diderot, Dénis (1995) *Diderot on Art*, vol. 2, *The Salon of 1767*, John Goodman (trans.), New Haven, CT: Yale University Press.

Diderot, Denis and Jean le Rond d'Alembert (1751) "Encyclopédie," *Encyclopédie, ou Dictionnaire raisonné des sciences, des arts et des métiers*, vol. 5, Paris: Briasson.

Dobbs, Arthur (1729–31) *An Essay on the Trade and Improvement of Ireland*, 2 vols. Dublin: A. Rhames, J. Smith and W. Bruce.

——(c. 1752a) "A Short Essay to shew the Expediency, if not Political Necessity of an Incorporating Union betwixt Britain and Ireland." (cover short title: *"An Essay on the Expediency of a Union betwixt Britain & Ireland"*) Alexander Thom Collection, MS 1, National Library of Ireland.

——(c. 1752b) "A Short Essay to shew the Expediency, if not Political Necessity of an Incorporating Union betwixt Britain and Ireland." (cover short title: *"An Essay on the Expediency of a Union betwixt Britain & Ireland"*), with dedication to Prime Minister Henry Pelham, MS in Kress Library of Business and Economics, Harvard University, 08759.1

Dorfman, Joseph (1946) *The Economic Mind in American Civilization 1606–1865*, New York: Viking.

Dow, Sheila (2002) "Interpretation: The Case of David Hume," *History of Political Economy*, 34.2: 399–420.

Duke, Michael (1979) "David Hume and Monetary Adjustment," *History of Political Economy*, 11(4): 572–87.

Durand, Yves (1971) *Les Fermiers généraux au XVIIIe siècle*, Paris: Presses Universitaires de France.

Durie, Alastair (1979) *The Scottish Linen Industry in the Eighteenth Century*, Edinburgh: John Donald Publishers.

——(ed.) (1996) *The British Linen Company, 1745–1775*, Edinburgh: Scottish History Society.

Du Tot, Charles de Ferrère (1738) *Réflexions politiques sur les finances et le commerce, ou l'on examine quelles ont été sur le Revenus, les Denrées, le Charge étranger, et conséquemment sur notre Commerce, les influences des Augmentations et des Diminutions des valeurs numéraires des Monnoyes*, The Hague: Fréres Vaillant and N. Prevost.

——(1739 [1738]) *Political Reflections on the Finances and Commerce of France, shewing the causes which formerly obstructed the advancement of her trade : on how much better footing it stands now than it did under Lewis XIV, with several expedients for raising it still to a greater heighth : containing, among many other curious things, an account of the proportions of gold and silver in the several coins of Europe ... a curious plan for enabling her to keep up a very powerful fleet with the greatest oeconomy and advantage*, London: A. Millar.

——(1754 [1738]) *Réflexions politiques sur les finances et le commerce*, 6th edn., 2 vols., The Hague: Vaillant and N. Prevôst.

——(1974 [1739]) *Political Reflexions on the Finances and Commerce of France*, Clifton, NJ: A. M. Kelley; reprint edition (no trans) London: Andrew Millar.

Dyer, G. P. and P. P. Gaspar (1992) "Reform, the New Technology and Tower Hill, 1700–1966," in Challis (ed.) *A New History of the Royal Mint*, pp. 398–606.

Dziembowski, E. (1998) *Un Nouveau Patriotisme Français, 1750–70. La France Face à la Puissance Anglaise à l'Époque de la Guerre de Sept Ans, Studies on Voltaire and the Eighteenth Century*, vol. 365, Oxford: Voltaire Foundation.

Eatwell, John, Murray Milgate, and Peter Newman, (eds.) (1987). *The New Palgrave: A Dictionary of Economics*, London: Norton.

Eden, William (1779a) *Four Letters to the Earl of Carlisle ... On Certain Perversions of Political Reasoning; and on the Nature, Progress, and Effect of Party Spirit and Parties. On the Present Circumstances of the War between Great Britain and the Combined Powers of France and Spain. On the Public Debts, on the Public Credit, and on the Means of Raising Supplies. On the Representations of Ireland respecting a Free-trade*, London: Printed for B. White.

——(1779b) *A Letter to the Earl of Carlisle, from William Eden, Esq. on the Representations of Ireland, Respecting a Free Trade*, Dublin: R. Marchbank.

——(1780a) *A Fifth Letter to the Earl of Carlisle, from William Eden, Esq. on Population; on Certain Revenue Laws and Regulations ... and on Public Oeconomy*, London: B. White and T. Cadell.

——(1780b) *Four Letters to the Earl of Carlisle, from William Eden, Esq. ...* 3rd edn, (To which is added a fifth letter, on population,) London: B. White and T. Cadell.

——(1785) "Speech to the Committee of the Whole House on the Commercial Regulations Proposed to be Adopted between Great Britain and Ireland, House of Commons, July 25, 1785," in *Parliamentary History* 25 (1816 [1785–86]), pp. 962–65.

Ehrman, John (1962) *The British Government and Commercial Negotiations with Europe, 1780–93*, Cambridge: Cambridge University Press.

Elias, Norbert (2000) *The Civilizing Process*, Oxford: Blackwell.

Elibank, Patrick Murray, Baron (1758) *Thoughts on Money, Circulation, and Paper Currency*, Edinburgh: Hamilton, Balfour, and Neill.

Elmslie, Bruce (1995) "The Convergence Debate between David Hume and Josiah Tucker," *Journal of Economic Perspectives*, 9(4): 207–16.

Elster, Jon (1984) *Ulysses and the Sirens*, Cambridge: Cambridge University Press.

Eltis, Shelagh and Walter Eltis (1997) "The Life and Contribution to Economics of the abbé de Condillac," in Condillac (1997 [1776]), pp. 12–18.

Emerson, Roger (1990) "Science and Moral Philosophy in the Scottish Enlightenment," *in Studies in the Philosophy of the Scottish Enlightenment*, M.A. Stewart (ed.) Oxford: Oxford University Press, pp. 11–36.

——(1973) "The Social Composition of Enlightened Scotland, 1754–64," *Studies on Voltaire and the Eighteenth Century*, 114: 291–329.

——(1979) "The Philosophical Society of Edinburgh, 1737–47," *British Journal for the History of Science*, 12: 154–59.

——(1997) "Hume and the Bellman, Zerobabel MacGilchrist," *Hume Studies*, 23: 9–28.

——(2004) "The Select Society of Edinburgh," in H. C. G. Matthew and Brian Harrison (eds.) *The Oxford Dictionary of National Biography*, Oxford: Oxford University Press, 49: 705–8.

Emmett, Ross B. (ed.) (2000) *Reactions to the South Sea Bubble, the Mississippi Scheme, and the Tulip Mania Affair*, 3 vols., London: Pickering and Chatto.

Endres, A. M. (1987) "The King–Davenant 'Law' in Classical Economics," *History of Political Economy*, 19: 621–38.

Epictetus (1928) *The Encheiridion Epictetus II*, W. A. Oldfather (trans.), Loeb Classical, Library Cambridge MA: Harvard University Press.

Farr, James (1988) "Political Science and the Enlightenment of Enthusiasm," *American Political Science Review*, 82: 51–69.

Fausten, Dietrich (1979) "The Humean Origin of the Contemporary Monetary Approach to the Balance of Payments," *Quarterly Journal of Economics*, 93: 655–73.

Feavearyear, Sir Albert (1963) *The Pound Sterling: A History of English Money*, Oxford: Clarendon Press.

Félix, Joël (1999) *Finances et politique au siècle des Lumières. Le ministère L'Averdy, 1763–1768*, Paris: Comité pour l'histoire financière de la France.

Fénelon, François de Salignac de La Mothe (1720) "Sentiments on the Ballance of Europe," in *Two Essays on the Ballance of Europe*, London: n.p.

——(1962 [1699]) *Les aventures de Télémaque*, J. L. Goré (ed.), Firenze: Sansoni.

——(1994 [1699]) *The Adventures of Telemachus, Son of Ulysses*, Patrick Riley, (ed.) Cambridge: Cambridge University Press.

Ferguson, Adam (1966 [1767]) *An Essay on the History of Civil Society*, Duncan Forbes (ed.) Edinburgh: Edinburgh University Press.

Ferguson, Niall (2001) *The Cash Nexus: Money and Power in the Modern World, 1700–2000*, New York: Basic Books.

Fichte, Johann Gottlieb (1800) *Der geschlossne handelsstaat: Ein philosophischer entwurf als anhang zur rechtslehre, und probe einer künftig zu liefernden politik*, Tübingen: J.G. Cotta.

Fieser, James (ed.) (2001) *Early Responses to Hume's Moral, Literary, and Political Writings*, 2 vols., Bristol, UK: Thoemmes Press.

Fitzmaurice, Edmond George Petty-Fitzmaurice, Lord (1875) *Life of William Earl of Shelburne, Afterwards First Marquess of Lansdowne: With Extracts from his Papers and Correspondence*, 3 vols. London: Macmillan.

Fleischacker, Samuel (2003) "The Impact on America: Scottish Philosophy and the American Founding," in Broadie (ed.) *Cambridge Companion to the Scottish Enlightenment*, Cambridge: Cambridge University Press, pp. 316–37.

——(2004) *On Adam Smith's "Wealth of Nations": A Philosophical Companion*, Princeton: Princeton University Press.

Fletcher, Andrew (1979 [1698]) *A Discourse of Government with Relation to Militias*, David Daiches (ed.), Edinburgh: Scottish Academic Press.

——(1997a) *Political Writings*, John Robertson, (ed.) Cambridge: Cambridge University Press.

—(1997b [1704]) *An Account of a Conversation Concerning the Right Regulation of Governments for the Common Good of Mankind. In a letter to the Marquiss of Montrose, the Earls of Rothes, Roxburgh and Haddlington, From London the first of December 1703* [1704], in Fletcher (1997a), pp. 175–215.

Fleury, Gabriel (1915) *François Véron de Forbonnais: Sa Famille, Sa Vie, Ses Actes, Ses Oeuvres, 1722–1800*, Le Mans: A. de Saint-Denis.

Flynn, Michael (ed.) (1977) *Scottish Population History*, Cambridge: Cambridge University Press.

Fogelin, Robert (1984) "Hume and the Missing Shade of Blue," *Philosophy and Phenomenological Research*, 45: 263–72.

Forbes, Duncan (1975) *Hume's Philosophical Politics*, Cambridge: Cambridge University Press.

——(1978) "The European, or Cosmopolitan, Dimension in Hume's Science of Politics," *British Journal for Eighteenth-Century Studies*, 1: 57–60.

Forbonnais, François Véron de (1753a) *Extrait du livre de l'Esprit des Lois, chapitre par chapitre, avec des remarques sur quelques endroits particuliers de ce livre, et une idée de toutes les critiques qui en ont été faites.* Amsterdam: Arkstée and Merkus.

——(1753b) *Considérations sur les Finances d'Espagne*, Dresde: n.p.

——(1753c) Articles "Colonie," "Commerce", "Communauté (comm.)," "Compagnie de commerce," "Concurrence," in *Encyclopédie ou dictionnaire raisonné des sciences, des arts et des metiers, par une société de gens de lettres; mis en ordre & publié par M. Diderot, ... & quant à la partie mathématique, par M. D'Alembert*, vol. 3 "Cha–Conjonctif," Paris: Briasson.

——(1754a) *Élémens du commerce*, 2 vols., Leiden and Paris: Briasson.

——(1754b) Articles "Crédit", "Culture des terres," in *Encyclopédie ou dictionnaire raisonné des sciences, des arts et des metiers, par une société de gens de lettres: mis en ordre & publié par M. Diderot, ... & quant à la partie mathématique,* par M. D'Alembert, vol. 4 "Conjontif–Discussion," Paris: Briasson.

——(1755a) "Réfutation de quelques articles des discours politiques *de M. David Hume, traduits de l'Anglois l'année dernière 1754,*" Bibliothèque de l'Arsenal, Paris, MS. 4591, fols. 181 ff. and 284 ff.

——(1755b). *Mémoires pour l'établissement d'un crédit public,* Bibliothèque Nationale de France, Département des Manuscrits, Nouvelles Acquisitions Françaises, n° 4295.

——(1755c). Article "Espèces (comm.)" in *Encyclopédie ou dictionnaire raisonné des sciences, des arts et des metiers, par une société de gens de lettres: mis en ordre & publié par M. Diderot, ... & quant à la partie mathématique,* par M. D'Alembert, vol. 5, "Discussion–Esquinancie," Paris: Briasson.

——(1755d) *Réflexions sur la nécessité de comprendre l'étude du commerce et des finances dans celle de la politique,* Dresde. n.p.

——(1755e) *Considérations sur les finances d'Espagne, seconde édition, augmentée de réflexions sur la nécessité de comprendre l'étude du commerce et des finances dans celle de la politique,* Dresde and Paris: Frères Estienne.

——(1758) *Recherches et considérations sur les finances de France depuis l'année 1595 jusqu'à l'année 1721,* 2 vols. Basel: Frères Cramer.

——(1767) *Principes et observations oeconomiques,* 2 vols., Amsterdam: M.M. Rey.

——(1965) [1753] Article "Commerce," in N.S. Hoyt and T. Cassirer, (eds.) *Encyclopedia-Selections,* Indianapolis: Bobbs-Merill, pp. 48–83.

Forsyth, Murray (1980) "The Old European States-System: Gentz Versus Hauterive," *Historical Journal,* 23: 521–38.

Foster, John (1799a [1785]) *Speech of the Right Honourable William Pitt, in the House of Commons, Thursday, January 31, 1799, on Offering to the House the Resolutions which he Proposed as the Basis of an Union between Great Britain and Ireland, to which are Added the Speeches of the Right Honourable John Foster, on the 12th and 15th of August, 1785, on the Bill for Effectuating the Intercourse and Commerce between Great Britain and Ireland, on Permanent and Equitable Principles, for the Mutual Benefit of Both Kingdoms,* Dublin: J. Exshaw.

——(1799b) *Speech of the Right Honorable John Foster, Speaker of the House of Commons of Ireland, Delivered in Committee, on Thursday, the 11th day of April, 1799:* Dublin, J. Moore.

Frankin, Benjamin (1906 [1764]) *Remarks and Facts Concerning the American Paper Money,* London; reprinted in Benjamin Franklin, *The Writings of Benjamin Franklin,* vol. 5, A. H. Smyth (ed.), New York: Macmillan.

——(1959 [1729]) *A Modest Inquiry into the Nature and Necessity of a Paper Currency,* Philadelphia: Franklin; reprinted in Benjamin Franklin, *The Papers of Benjamin Franklin,* L. W. Labaree and W. J. Bell Jr. (eds.), New Haven, CT: Yale University Press, 1: 139–57.

——(1967 [1760]) *The Interest of Great Britain Considered with Regard to Her Colonies and the Acquisition of Canada and Guadaloupe to Which Are Added Observations Concerning the Increase of Mankind, Peopling of Countries, &c,* London; reprinted in Benjamin Franklin, *The Papers of Benjamin Franklin,* vol. 9, L. W. Labaree and W. J. Bell, Jr. (eds.), New Haven, CT: Yale University Press.

Frederick II of Prussia and Voltaire, François Marie Arouet de (1981 [1740]) *The Refutation of Machiavelli's Prince or Anti-Machiavel*, trans. P. Sonnino, Athens, OH: Ohio University Press.

——(1996 [1740]), *Anti-Machiavel*, W. Bahner and H. Bergmann (eds.), in Voltaire, *Oeuvres complètes de Voltaire*, Ulla Kölving (ed.), vol. 19, Oxford: Voltaire Foundation.

Frenkel, Jacob and Harry Johnson (eds.) (1976) *The Monetary Approach to the Balance of Payments*, London: Allen and Unwin.

Friedman, Milton (1987) "Quantity Theory of Money," in J. Eatwell, M. Milgate, and P. Newman (eds.) *The New Palgrave Dictionary of Economics (Money)*, London: Macmillan.

Fry, Michael (1992) *The Dundas Despotism*, Edinburgh: John Donald.

Furniss, Edgar (1920) *The Position of the Laborer in a System of Nationalism*, Boston: Houghton Mifflin.

Galliani, Renato (1975) "L'abbé Mably, le luxe, le commerce, les manufactures et les ouvriers," *Revue d'Histoire Economique et Sociale*, 53: 144–55.

——(1989) *Rousseau, le luxe et l'idéologie nobiliaire: Etude socio-historique*, *Studies on Voltaire and the Eighteenth Century, vol. 268*, Oxford: Voltaire Foundation.

Garrett, Don (1997) *Cognition and Commitment in Hume's Philosophy*, New York: Oxford University Press.

Garrigues, Frédéric (1998) "Les intendants de commerce au XVIIIe siècle," *Revue d'histoire moderne et contemporaine*, 45: 626–61.

Gatch, Loren (1996) "To Redeem Metal with Paper: David Hume's Philosophy of Money," *Hume Studies*, 22: 169–91.

Gee, Joshua (1730) *Trade and Navigation of Great-Britain Considered*, London: n.p.

Gelderen, Martin van and Quentin Skinner (eds.) (2002) *Republicanism: A Shared European Heritage*, 2 vols., Cambridge: Cambridge University Press.

Gellner, Ernest (1994) *Conditions of Liberty: Civil Society and Its Rivals*, New York: Allen Lane.

Gentz, Friedrich von (1800) *The French and American Revolutions Compared*, John Quincy Adams (trans.), Philadelphia: Asbury Dickins and H. Maxwell.

——(1801) *Von dem politischen Zustande von Europa vor und nach der französischen Revoluzion, eine Prüfung des Buches De l'État de la France à la fin de l'an VIII*, Berlin: H. Frölich.

——(1804 [1801]) *On the State of Europe before and after the French Revolution: being an Answer to the Work entitled De l'état de la France à la fin de l'an VIII*, John Herries, (trans.), London: J. Hatchard.

Geoghegan, Patrick M. (2000) *The Irish Act of Union: A Study in High Politics, 1798–1801*, Basingstoke: Palgrave Macmillan.

Gerard, Alexander (1759) "Gerard's Lecture 'Of Commerce,' Philosophy Lectures, written by Robert Morgan, Marischal College, Aberdeen, 1758–59," Edinburgh University Library, De. 5. 62, fols. 487–88.

Gervaise, Isaac (1720) *The System or Theory of the Trade of the World*, London: H. Woodfall.

Gibson, A. J. S. and T. C. Smout (1995) *Prices, Food, and Wages in Scotland, 1550–1780*, Cambridge: Cambridge University Press.

Gleeson, Janet (2000) *The Moneymaker: The True Story of a Philanderer, Gambler, Murderer … and the Father of Modern Finance*, London: Bantam Books

Gould, J. D. (1970) *The Great Debasement: Currency and the Economy in Mid-Tudor England*, Oxford: Clarendon Press.

Goux, Jean-Joseph (1990) *Symbolic Economies: After Marx and Freud*, Ithaca: Cornell University Press.

Graslin, Jean-Joseph-Louis (1767) *Essai Analytique sur la Richesse et sur l'Impôt, où l'on Réfute la nouvelle Doctrine Économique, qui a Fourni à la Société Royale d'Agriculture de Limoges les Principes d'un Programme qu'elle a Publié sur l'Effet des Impôts Indirects*, London, n.p.

Gray, Richard T. (2003) "Economic Romanticism: Monetary Nationalism in Johann Gottlieb Fichte and Adam Müller," *Eighteenth-Century Studies*, 36: 535–57.

Grell, Chantal (1995) *Le dix-huitième siècle et l'antiquité en France: 1680–1789*, Oxford: Voltaire Foundation.

Grice-Hutchinson, Marjorie (1952) *The School of Salamanca; Readings in Spanish Monetary Theory, 1544–1605*, Oxford: Clarendon Press.

——(1993) *Economic Thought in Spain: Selected Essays*, Laurence Moss and Christopher Ryan (eds.), Brookfield, VT: Elgar.

Grimm, Melchior, et al. (1966 [1750–76]) *Correspondance littéraire, philosophique et critique*, 16 vols., Maurice Tourneux (ed.), Nendeln, Liechtenstein: Kraus.

Grimsley, Ronald (1985) "Saint-Lambert's Articles in the Encyclopédie," in R.J. Howells, A. Mason, H.T. Mason and D. Williams (eds.) *Voltaire and His World: Studies Presented to W.H. Barber*, Oxford: Voltaire Foundation, pp. 293–306.

Griswold, Charles (1999) *Adam Smith and the Virtues of Enlightenment*, Cambridge: Cambridge University Press.

Groenewegen, Peter D. (1994a) "La French connection: influences françaises sur l'économie politique britannique," *Dix-huitième siècle*, 26: 15–36.

——(1994b) "Pietro Verri's Mature Political Economy of the *Meditazioni*: A Case Study in the Highly Developed International Transmission Mechanism of Ideas in Pre-Revolutionary Europe," in M. Albertone and A. Massaro (eds.) *Political Economy and National Realities: Papers Presented at the Conference Held at the Luigi Einaudi Foundation*, Turin: Fondazione Luigi Einaudi.

Haakonssen, Knud (1981) *The Science of a Legislator: The Natural Jurisprudence of David Hume and Adam Smith*, Cambridge: Cambridge University Press

——(1982) "What Might Properly Be Called a Natural Jurisprudence?" in R. H. Campbell and Andrew S. Skinner (eds.) *The Origins and Nature of the Scottish Enlightenment*, Edinburgh: John Donald, pp. 205–25.

——(1994) "Introduction," to *Hume, Political Essays*, Kund Haakonssen (ed.) Cambridge: Cambridge University Press, pp. xi–xxx.

Hamelin, Jean (1961) "À la recherche d'un cours monétaire Canadien, 1760–77," *Revue Historique de l'Amérique Française*, 15: 24–34.

Hamilton, Andrew J. (2004) "Atlantic Cosmopolitanism and Nationalism: Benjamin Vaughan and the Limits of Free Trade in the Eighteenth Century," PhD. Dissertation, University of Wisconsin at Madison.

Hamilton, Henry (1963) *An Economic History of Scotland in the Eighteenth Century*, Oxford: Clarendon Press.

Hammond, Peter J. (1976) "Changing Tastes and Coherent Dynamic Choice," *Review of Economic Studies*, 23: 159–73.

Hanson, John R. II (1980) "Small Notes in the American Colonies," *Explorations in Economic History*, 17: 411–20.

Harrington, James (1977 [1656]) "The Commonwealth of Oceana," in J.G.A. Pocock (ed.) *The Political Works of James Harrington*, Cambridge: Cambridge University Press, pp. 155–359.

Harsin, Paul (1935) "Introduction," in Du Tot, *Réflexions politiques sur les finances et le commerce*, Paul Harsin (ed.), 2 vols., Paris: E. Droz, 1: xvi–xxvii.

Hauterive, Alexandre-Maurice Blanc de La Nautte, comte d' (1800a) *Résultat de la politique de l'Angleterre dans ces dernières années*, Paris: Les Marchands des Nouveautés.

——(1800b) *De l'état de la France à la fin de l'an VIII*, Paris: Henrics.

——(1801 [1800]) *State of the French Republic at the End of the Year VIII*, Lewis Goldsmith (trans.), London: J. S. Gordon.

Hayek, Friedrich A. von (1932) *Prices and Production*, with a foreword by Lionel Robbins, New York: Macmillan.

——(1968) "The Legal and Political Philosophy of David Hume" in Vere Claiborne Chappell (ed.) *Hume: A Collection of Critical Essays*, Garden City, N.Y.: Doubleday, pp. 335–60.

——(1976) *The Mirage of Social Justice*, in Hayek, *Law, Legislation, and Liberty*, vol. 2, Chicago: University of Chicago Press.

——(1985 [1931]) "Richard Cantillon: Introduction and Textual Comments Written for Hella Hayek's 1931 German Translation of Richard Cantillon's *Essai*," Micheál Ó Súilleabháin (trans.), *Journal of Libertarian Studies*, 7: 217–47.

Heaton, Herbert (1928) "The Playing Card Currency of French Canada," *American Economic Review*, 18: 649–62.

Helvétius, Claude-Adrien (1758) *De l'Esprit*, Paris: Durand.

——(1759 [1758]) *De l'esprit: or, Essays on the Mind, and its Several Faculties*, n.p. [London]: n.p.

——(1773) *De l'homme, de ses facultés intellectuelles et de son éducation: ouvrage posthume*, 2 vols., London: Société Typographique.

——(1778 [1773]) *A Treatise on Man, His Intellectual Faculties and His Education: A Posthumous Work of M. Helvetius*, W. Hooper, (trans.) 2 vols. London: B. Law and G. Robinson.

Henderson, W.O. (1957) "The Anglo-French Commercial Treaty of 1786," *Economic History Review*, 2nd ser. 10: 104–12.

Herbert, Claude-Jacques (1910 [1755]) *Essai sur la police générale des grains, sur leurs prix et sur les effets de l'agriculture*, E. Depitre (ed.), Paris: Paul Geuthner.

Herzog, Don (1998) *Poisoning the Minds of the Lower Orders*, Princeton, NJ: Princeton University Press.

Hill, Jacqueline (1995) "Ireland Without Union: Molyneux and His Legacy," in Robertson (ed.) *A union for Empire*, pp. 271–96.

Hillsborough, Wills Hill, Earl of (1751) *A Proposal for Uniting the Kingdoms of Great Britain and Ireland*, London: n. p.

Himmelfarb, Gertrude (1984) *The Idea of Poverty: England in the Early Industrial Age*, London: Faber.

Hirschman, Albert (1977) *The Passions and the Interests: Political Arguments for Capitalism before Its Triumph*, Princeton, NJ: Princeton University Press.

——(1986) "Rival Views of Market Society," in *Rival Views of Market Society and Other Essays*, Cambridge, MA: Harvard University Press, pp. 105–41.

Hirschman, Nancy J. (2000) "Sympathy, Empathy, and Obligation: A Feminist Rereading," in Anne Jaap Jacobson (ed.) *Feminist Interpretations of David Hume*, University Park: Pennsylvania State University Press, pp. 174–93.

Hobbes, Thomas (1994 [1651]) *Leviathan*, Edwin Curley (ed.), Indianapolis, IN: Hackett Publishers.

Holger, Jacob-Friesen (ed.) (1997) *Profile der Aufklärung. Friedrich Nicolai-Isaak Iselin: Briefwechsel (1767–1782)*, Bern: Haupt.

Hont, Istvan (1994) "Commercial Society and Political Theory in the Eighteenth Century: the Problem of Authority in David Hume and Adam Smith," in W. Melching and W. Velemaed, *Main Trends in Cultural History*, Amsterdam: Editions Rodopi, pp. 54–94.

——(2005a) *Jealousy of Trade: International Competition and the Nation State in Historical Perspective*, Cambridge, MA: Belknap Press of Harvard University Press.

——(2005b) "Jealousy of Trade: An Introduction," in Hont (2005a), pp. 1–156.

——(2005c [1986]) "The Language of Sociability and Commerce: Samuel Pufendorf and the Foundations of Smith"s Four Stages Theory," in A. Pagden (ed.) *Languages of Political Theory in Early Modern Europe*, Cambridge: Cambridge University Press, pp. 253–76; reprinted in Hont (2005a), pp. 159–84.

——(2005d [1990]) "Free Trade and the Economic Limits to National Politics: Neo-Machiavellian Political Economy Reconsidered" in John Dunn (ed.) *The Economic Limits to Politics*, Cambridge: Cambridge University Press, pp. 41–120; reprinted in Hont (2005a), pp. 185–266.

——(2005e [1983]) "The 'Rich Country-Poor Country' Debate in Scottish Classical Political Economy," in Hont and Ignatieff (1983), pp. 271–316; reprinted in Hont (2005a), pp. 267–323.

——(2005f [1993]) "The Rhapsody of Public Debt: David Hume and Voluntary State Bankruptcy," in N. Phillipson and Q. Skinner (eds.) *Political Discourse in Early Modern Britain*, Cambridge: Cambridge University Press, pp. 321–48; reprinted in Hont (2005a), pp. 325–53.

——(2005g [1989]) "The Political Economy of the 'Unnatural and Retrograde' Order: Adam Smith and Natural Liberty," in *Französische Revolution und Politische Ökonomie*, Schriften aus dem Karl-Marx-Haus, vol. 41, Trier: Friedrich-Ebert-Stiftung, pp. 122–49; reprinted in Hont (2005a), pp. 354–88.

——(2005h [1983]) "Needs and Justice in the *Wealth of Nations*: An Introductory Essay", in Hont and Ignatieff (eds.) (1983), pp. 1–44; reprinted in Hont (2005a), pp. 389–443.

——(2005i [1994]) "The Permanent Crisis of a Divided Mankind: 'Contemporary Crisis of the Nation State' in Historical Perspective" in John Dunn (ed.) *The Contemporary Crisis of the Nation State*, Oxford: Blackwell, pp. 166–231; reprinted in Hont (2005a), pp. 447–528.

——(2006) "The Early Enlightenment Debate on Commerce and Luxury," in M. Goldie and R. Wokler (eds.) *The Cambridge History of Eighteenth-Century Political Thought*, Cambridge: Cambridge University Press, pp. 379–418.

Hont, Istvan, and Michael Ignatieff (eds.) (1983) *Wealth and Virtue: The Shaping of Political Economy in the Scottish Enlightenment*, Cambridge: Cambridge University Press.

Hoppit, Julian (1987) *Risk and Failure in English Business, 1700–1800*, Cambridge: Cambridge University Press.

Horowitz, Tamara and Gerald J. Massey (eds.) (1991) *Thought Experiments in Science and Philosophy*; Savage, MD: Roman and Littlefield.

Houston, R. A. (1994) *Social Change in the Age of the Enlightenment: Edinburgh, 1660–1760*, Oxford: Oxford University Press.

Hulliung, Mark (1994) *The Autocritique of Enlightenment: Rousseau and the Philosophes*, Cambridge, MA: Harvard University Press.

Humphrey, Thomas (1974) "The Quantity Theory of Money: Its Historical Evolution and Role in Policy Debates," *Federal Reserve Bank of Richmond Economic Review*, 60: 2–19.
——(1986a) *Essays on Inflation*, 5th edn., Richmond, VA: Federal Reserve Bank of Richmond.
——(1986b [1981]) "Adam Smith and the Monetary Approach to the Balance of Payments," in Humphrey, *Essays on Inflation*, 5th edn., pp. 180–87.
——(1986c [1982]) "Of Hume, Thornton, the Quantity Theory, and the Phillips Curve," in Humphrey, *Essays on Inflation*, 5th edn., pp. 128–33.
Hundert, Edward J. (1974) "The Achievement Motive in Hume's Political Economy," *Journal of the History of Ideas*, 35(1):139–43.
——(1994) *The Enlightenment's Fable: Bernard Mandeville and the Discovery of Society*, Cambridge: Cambridge University Press.
Hutcheson, Francis (1755) *A System of Moral Philosophy*, London: A. Millar.
Hutchison, Terence (1988) *Before Adam Smith*, Oxford: Basil Blackwell.
Ignatieff, Michael (1984) *The Needs of Strangers*, London: Chatto and Windus.
Immerwahr, John (1992) "Hume's Revised Racism," *Journal of the History of Ideas*, 53(3): 481–86.
——(1994) "Hume's Dissertation on the Passions," *Journal of the History of Philosophy*, 32: 225–40.
Ingrassia, Catherine (1995) "The Pleasure of Business and the Business of Pleasure: Gender, Credit, and the South Sea Bubble," in Carla H. Hay and Syndy M. Conger (eds.) *Studies in Eighteenth-Century Culture*, 24:191–210.
Irwin, Douglas (1996) *Against the Tide: An Intellectual History of Free Trade*, Princeton, NJ: Princeton University Press.
Ives, Robin J. (2003) "Political Publicity and Political Economy in Eighteenth- Century France," *French History*, 17: 1–18.
Jackson, Clare (2003) "Revolution Principles, *Ius Naturae* and *Ius Gentium* in Early-Enlightenment Scotland: The Contribution of Sir Francis Grant, Lord Cullen (c. 1660–1726)," in T.J. Hochstrasser and P. Schröder (eds.) *Early Modern Law Theories: Contexts and Strategies in the Early Enlightenment*, Dordrecht: Kluwer, pp. 123–34.
Jacobson, Anne Jaap (ed.) (2000) *Feminist Interpretations of David Hume*, University Park, PA: Pennsylvania State University Press.
Jevons, William Stanley (1957 [1871]) *The Theory of Political Economy*, 5th edn., London: Macmillan.
Johnson, E. (1937) *Predecessors of Adam Smith*, London: P. King.
Jones, Colin (2002) *The Great Nation: France from Louis XV to Napoleon, 1715–1799*, New York: Columbia University Press.
Jones, Peter (1982) *Hume's Sentiments: Their Ciceronian and French Context*, Edinburgh: Edinburgh University Press.
Kaiser, Thomas E. (1991) "Money, Despotism and Public Opinion in Early Eighteenth-Century France: John Law and the Debate on Royal Credit," *Journal of Modern History*, 63: 1–28.
Kant, Immanuel (1970) "Idea for a Universal History with a Cosmopolitan Purpose (1784)," in Hans Reiss (ed.) *Kant's Political Writings*, Cambridge: Cambridge University Press, 41–53.
Kapossy, Béla (2002) "Neo-Roman Republicanism and Commercial Society: The Example of Eighteenth-Century Berne," in M. van Gelderen and Q. Skinner (eds.) *Republicanism*, 2 vols., Cambridge: Cambridge University Press, 2: 226–47.

——(2006) *Iselin Contra Rousseau: Sociable Patriotism and the History of Mankind*, Basel: Schwabe.

Keane, John (1988) "Despotism and Democracy: The Origins and Development of the Distinction between Civil Society and the State: 1750–1850," in John Keane (ed.) *Civil Society and the State: New European Perspectives*, London: Verso, pp. 35–71.

——(1998) *Civil Society: Old Images, New Visions*, Stanford, CA: Stanford University Press.

Kearney, H.F. (1959) "The Political Background to English Mercantilism, 1695–1700," *Economic History Review*, n.s. 11.

——(1990) "The Irish Trade Dispute with Portugal 1780–87," *Studia Hibernica*, 25: 7–48.

——*Prelude to Union: Anglo Irish Politics in the 1780s*, Cork: Cork University Press.

——(1998) *Henry Flood: Patriots and Politics in Eighteenth-Century Ireland*, Dublin: Four Courts Press.

Kelly, James (1989) "The Anglo-French Treaty of 1786: the Irish Dimension," *Eighteenth-Century Ireland*, 4:93–112.

——(1992) *Prelude to Union: Anglo-Irish Politics in the 1780s*, Cork: Cork University Press.

Kelly, Patrick (1980) "The Irish Woollen Export Prohibition Act of 1699: Kearney Re-visited," *Irish Economic and Social History*, 7: 22–44.

——(1988) "William Molyneux and the Spirit of Liberty in Eighteenth-Century Ireland," *Eighteenth-Century Ireland*, 3: 133–48.

——(2000a) "Recasting a Tradition: William Molyneux and the Sources of *The Case of Ireland … Stated* (1698)," in Jane H. Ohlmeyer (ed.) *Political Thought in Seventeenth-Century Ireland*, Cambridge: Cambridge University Press, pp. 83–106.

——(2000b) "The Politics of Political Economy in Mid-Eighteenth-Century Ireland," in Sean J. Conolly (ed.) *Political Ideas in Eighteenth-Century Ireland*, Dublin: Four Courts Press, pp. 105–29.

Kelly, Paul (1975) "British and Irish Politics in 1785," *English Historical Review*, 90: 536–63.

Kemp Smith, Norman (1941) *The Philosophy of David Hume: A Critical Study of Its Origins and Central Doctrine*, London: Macmillan.

Kindleberger, Charles Poor (2000) *Manias, Panics, and Crashes: A History of Financial Crises*, 4th edn., New York: John Wiley and Sons.

King, Charles (1753 [1713–14]) *Le négociant Anglois, ou traduction libre du livre intitulé*, 2 vols., François Véron de Forbonnais (trans. and ed.), Dresden: n.p.

Kingwell, Mark (1993) "Politics and the Polite Society in the Scottish Enlightenment," *Historical Réflections / Réflexions Historiques*, 19: 363–87.

——(1995) *A Civil Tongue: Justice, Dialogue, and the Politics of Pluralism*, University Park, PA: Pennsylvania State University Press.

Klibansky, Raymond, and Ernest Campbell Mossner (eds.) (1983 [1954]) *New Letters of David Hume*, New York: Garland Publishers.

Knight, Frank H. (1997 [1935]) *The Ethics of Competition and Other Essays*, Richard Boyd (ed.), New Brunswick, NJ: Transaction Publishers.

Knight, I.F. (1968) *The Geometric Spirit: The abbé de Condillac and the French Enlightenment*, New Haven, CT: Yale University Press.

Kozanecki, Tadeusz (ed.) (1963) "Dawida Hume'a Nieznane Listy W Zbiorach Muzeum Czartoryskich (Polska)," *Archiwum Historii Filozofii I Mysli Spolecznej*, 9: 133–34.

Kramnick, Isaac (1968) *Bolingbroke and His Circle: The Politics of Nostalgia in the Age of Walpole*, Cambridge, MA: Harvard University Press.

Krause, Sharon (2002) "The Uncertain Inevitability of Decline in Montesquieu," *Political Theory*, 30: 702–27.

Krause, Werner (1962) "Fichtes ökonomische Anschauungen im Geschlossenen Handelsstaat," in Manfred Buhr (ed.) *Wissen und Gewissen: Beiträge zum 200. Geburtstag Johann Gottlieb Fichtes 1762–1814*, Berlin: Akademie Verlag, pp. 232–33.

Kronenbitter, Günther (1994) *Wort und Macht: Friedrich Gentz als politischer Schriftsteller*, Berlin: Duncker and Humblot.

Krugman, Paul (1998) "In Praise of Cheap Labour," in Krugman *Accidental Theorist and Other Dispatches from the Dismal Science*, New York: W.W. Norton, pp. 80–86.

Kuhn, Thomas S. (1977 [1964]) "A Function for Thought Experiments," in Kuhn, *The Essential Tension*, Chicago: University of Chicago Press.

Kumar, Krishan (1993) "Civil Society: An Inquiry into the Usefulness of an Historical Term," *British Journal of Sociology*, 44: 375–95.

Kyd, James Gray (1975) *Scottish Population Statistics Including Webster's Analysis of Population, 1755*, Edinburgh: Scottish Academic Press.

Kydland, Finn. E. and Edward C. Prescott (1977) "Rules Rather Than Discretion," *Journal of Political Economy*, 85: 473–90.

Labriolle-Rutherford, M. (1963) "L'Evolution de la notion Luxe jusqu'à la Révolution," *Voltaire Studies*, 26: 1025–36.

Labrosse, Claude (1988) "Réception et communication dans les périodiques Littéraires (1750–60)," *La Diffusion et la lecture des journaux de la langue française sous l'ancien régime: Actes du colloque international, Nimègue 3–5 juin 1987*, Amsterdam: APA-Holland University Press.

La Font de Saint-Yenne, Etienne (1970 [1747]) *Réflexions sur quelques causes de l'état présent de la peinture en France*, Geneva: Slatkine Reprints.

Laidler, David E. W. (1981) "Adam Smith as a Monetary Economist," *Canadian Journal of Economics*, 14: 185–200.

Lammey, D (1986) "The Irish–Portuguese Trade Dispute, 1770–90," *Irish Historical Studies*, 97: 29–45.

Lamoine, Georges (1990) "Commerce et les relations humaines dans les essays économiques de Hume," in Suzy Halimi (ed.) *Commerce(s) en Grande-Bretagne au XVIIIe Siècle*, Paris: Publications de la Sorbonne.

Lande, Lawrence M. (ed.) (1982) *The Rise and Fall of John Law 1716–1720*, Montreal: Lawrence Lande Foundation for Canadian Historical Research and the McLennan Library of McGill University.

Langford, Paul (1989) *A Polite and Commercial People: England 1727–1783*, Oxford: Oxford University Press.

Larmore, Charles (1987) *Patterns of Moral Complexity*, Cambridge: Cambridge University Press.

Larrère, Catherine (1992) *L'Invention de l'économie au XVIIIe siècle: Du droit naturel à la physiocratie*, Paris: Presses Universitaires de France.

——(2001) "Montesquieu on Economics and Commerce," in D.W. Carrithers, M.A. Mosher and P.A. Rahe (eds.) *Montesquieu's Science of Politics: Essays on the Spirit of the Laws*, Lanham, MD: Rowman and Littlefield, pp. 335–73.

——(2002) "Montesquieu et l'histoire du commerce," in C. Volpilhac-Auger (ed.) *Le Temps de Montesquieu*, Geneva: Droz, 319–35.

——and Françoise Weil (2000) "Introduction" to Montesquieu, *Réflexions sur la monarchie universelle en Europe* in *Oeuvres Complètes de Montesquieu*, vol. 2, Oxford–Naples: Voltaire Foundation and Istituto Italiano per gli Studi Filosofici.

Laslett, Peter (1957) "John Locke, the Great Recoinage, and the Origins of the Board of Trade, 1695–1698," *William and Mary Quarterly*, 14: 370–402.

Lauderdale, James Maitland, Earl of (1804) *An Inquiry into the Nature and Origin of Public Wealth and into the Means and Cause of its Increase*, Edinburgh: Constable.

Law, John (1720) *Money and Trade Consider'd with a Proposal for Supplying the Nation with Money*, London: n.p.

——(1966 [1705]) *Money and Trade Considered, with a Proposal for Supplying the Nation with Money*, Edinburgh: Andrew Anderson; reprinted New York: A. M. Kelley.

——(1994 [c. 1702–5]) *John Law's "Essay on a Land Bank,"* Antoin Murphy (ed.), Dublin: Aeon Publishing.

Lebeau, Auguste (1903) *Condillac économiste*, Paris: Guillaumin.

Le Blanc, abbé Jean-Bernard (1745) *Lettres d'un François sur les Anglois*, 3 vols., The Hague: Jean Neaulme.

——(1747 [1745]) *Letters on the English and French Nations; Containing Curious and useful Observations on their Constitutions natural and political; Nervous and humorous Descriptions of the Virtues, Vices, Ridicules and Foibles of the Inhabitants; Critical Remarks on their Writers; Together with Moral Reflections interspersed throughout the Work*, 2 vols., London: n.p.

——(1754a) "Préface du traducteur, a monsieur le docteur Lami, professeur a Florence," in Hume (1754a) *Discours politiques de monsieur Hume*, pp. v–lviii.

——(1754b) "Notice de quelques-uns des principaux ouvrages anglois sur le commerce," pp. 250–59.

——(1754c) "Ouvrages sur le commerce, les finances, etc. cites dans les notes sur les discours de M. Hume, & qui ont paru en France depuis deux ans," pp. 260–75.

——(trans. and ed.) (1755) *Discours politiques de monsieur Hume traduits de l'anglois*, 2 vols., Amsterdam: Lambert.

——[John Tell Truth, pseud.] (1756) *Le patriote anglois ou réflexions sur les hostilités que la France reproche à l'Angleterre, et sur la réponse de nos ministres au dernier mémoire de sa M. T. C.*, Geneva: n.p.

Lecercle, Jean-Louis (1963) "Utopie et Réalisme Politique chez Mably," *Studies on Voltaire and the Eighteenth Century*, 26: 1049–70.

——(1972a) "Introduction," in Mably, *Des droits et des devoirs du citoyen*, Jean-Louis Lecercle (ed.) Paris: Marcel Didier, pp. ix–1.

Lerner, Ralph (1987) "Commerce and Character," in *The Thinking Revolutionary: Principle and Practice in the New Republic*, Ithaca, NY: Cornell University Press.

Lester, Richard A. (1939) *Monetary Experiments*, Princeton, NJ: Princeton University Press.

Levy, David M. and Sandra J. Peart (2004) "Sympathy and Approbation in Hume and Smith: A Solution to the Other Rational Species Problem," *Economics and Philosophy*, 20(2): 331–49.

Liggio, Leonard P. (1985) "Cantillon and the French Economists: Distinctive French Contributions to J.B. Say," *Journal of Libertarian Studies* 7: 285–304.

Lipsius, Justus (1586) *De Constantia Libri Duo*, Londini: Impersis Geor. Bishop.

Littré, Émile (1889) *Dictionnaire de la langue française*, 4 vols. and supp., Paris: Hachette.

Livy (1934) *Ab Urbe Condita (History of Rome)*, E. Sage (trans.), London: Loeb Library.

Locke, John (1692) *Some Considerations of the Consequences of the Lowering of Interest, and Raising the Value of Money*, London: Awnsham and John Churchill.

——(1854) *Essay Concerning Human Understanding*, J. St John (ed.), London: Bohn.

——(1876 [1697]) "Irish Trade Proposal for the Board of Trade", Accepted August 24, 1697, in Bourne, *Life of John Locke* (1876), 2: 263–72.

——(1976–89) *The Correspondence of John Locke*, E.S. De Beer, ed., 8 vols., Oxford: Clarendon Press.

——(1988 [1689]) *Second Treatise of Government*, Peter Laslett (ed.), Cambridge: Cambridge University Press.

——(1991) *The Clarendon Edition of the Works of John Locke—Locke on Money*, vol. 1, Patrick Hyde Kelly (ed.), Oxford: Clarendon Press.

Loménie, Louis de (1889) *Les Mirabeau: Nouvelles études sur la société française au XVIIIe siècle*, 3 vols., Paris: E. Dentu.

Longueville, Viscount R. Longfield (1799) *Observations on that Part of the Speaker's Speech, which Relates to Trade*, Dublin: T. Burnside.

Losee, John (1992) "Hume's Demarcation Project," *Hume Studies*, 18(1): 51–62.

Lucas, Robert (1996) "Nobel Lecture: Monetary Neutrality," *Journal of Political Economy*, 104: 89–101.

Luttrell, Clifton (1975) "Thomas Jefferson on Money and Banking: Disciple of David Hume and Forerunner of Some Modern Monetary Views," *History of Political Economy*, 7(2): 156–73.

Mably, Gabriel Bonnot de (1740) *Parallèle des romains et des françois, par rapport au gouvernement*, 2 vols, Paris: Didot.

——(1746) *Le droit public de l'Europe, fondé sur les traités conclus jusqu'en l'année 1740*, 2 vols. The Hague: Jean Van-Duren.

——(1749) *Observations sur les grecs*, Geneva: Compagnie des Libraires.

——(1751) *Observations sur les romains*, Geneva: Compagnie des Libraires.

——(1757) *Des Principes des négociations, pour servir d'introduction au droit public de l'Europe, fondé sur les traités*, The Hague: n.p.

——(1758 [1757]) *The Principles of Negotiations: Or, an Introduction to the Public Law of Europe founded on Treaties, etc.*, London: J. Rivington and J. Fletcher.

——(1766) *Observations sur l'histoire de la Grèce, ou des causes de la prospérité et des malheurs des Grecs.* Geneva: Compagnie des Libraires.

——(1769 [1763]) *Phocion's Conversations: or, the Relation between Morality and Politics, Originally translated by abbe Mably, from a Greek Manuscript of Nicolas*, William Macbean (trans.) London: W. Macbean and Dodsley.

——(1785 [1784]), *Remarks Concerning the Government and the Laws of the United States of America, in Four Letters Addressed to Mr. Adams*, London: J. Debrett.

——(1794–95a) *Collection Complète des œuvres de l'abbé de Mably*, 15 vols., Paris: Desbrière.

——(1794–95b [1757]) *Principes des négociations, pour servir d'introduction au droit public de l'Europe, fondé sur les traités*, in Mably (1794–1795a), vol. 5.

——(1794–95c [1763]) *Entretiens de Phocion, sur le rapport de la morale avec la politique*, in Mably (1794–1795a), vol. 10.

——(1794–95d [1764]) *Le droit publique de l' Europe fondé sur les traités*, in Mably (1794–1795a), vol. 6.

——(1794–95e [1784]) *Observations sur le gouvernement et des lois des États Unis d'Amérique*, in Mably (1794–1795a), 8: 338–85.

MacInnes, Allan (2001) "Union Failed, Union Accomplished: The Irish Union of 1703 and the Scottish Union of 1707," in Dáire Keogh and Kevin Whelan (eds.) *Acts of Union: The Causes, Contexts and Consequences of the Act of Union*, Dublin: Four Courts Press, pp. 67–94.

MacIntyre, Alasdair (1981) *After Virtue*, Notre Dame, IN: University of Notre Dame Press.

Mackillop, Andrew (2000) *"More Fruitful than the Soil": Army, Empire, and the Scottish Highlands, 1715–1815*, East Linton, Scotland: Tuckwell Press.

MacLeod, Christine (1983) "Henry Martin and the Authorship of Considerations upon the East India Trade," *Bulletin of the Institute of Historical Research*, 222–29.

Magennis, Eion (2000) *The Irish Political System 1740–1765: The Golden Age of Undertakers*, Dublin: Four Courts Press.

Magnières, Pierre-André O'Héguerty, Comte de (1754) *Essai sur les Intérêts du Commerce Maritime*, par M. D**, The Hague: n.p.

Mahoney, T.H.D. (1960) *Edmund Burke and Ireland*, Cambridge, MA: Harvard University Press.

Malcolmson, A.P.W. (1972) "John Foster and the Speakership of the Irish House of Commons," *Proceedings of the Royal Irish Academy*, 72C, pp. 271–303.

——(1978) *John Foster: The Politics of the Anglo-Irish Ascendancy*, Oxford: Oxford University Press.

Mandeville, Bernard (1988 [1732]) *The Fable of the Bees or Private Vices, Publick Benefits*, 2 vols., F. B. Kaye (ed.), Indianapolis, IN: Liberty Classics.

Maneschi, Andrea (1998a) *Comparative Advantage in International Trade: A Historical Perspective*, Cheltenham: Edward Elgar.

——(1998b) "Comparative Advantage With and Without Gains from Trade," *Review of International Economics*, 6: 120–28.

——(2002) "The Tercentenary of Henry Martyn's *Considerations upon the East India Trade*," *Journal of the History of Economic Thought*, 24: 233–49.

——(2004) "The True Meaning of David Ricardo's Four Magic Numbers," *Journal of International Economics*, 62: 433–43.

——(2006) "Globalization and Economic Development: Some Eighteenth-century Views," *Fiftieth Anniversary Conference of the Graduate Program in Economic Development*, Vanderbilt University: n.p.

Mankin, Robert (2005) "Can Jealousy be Reduced to a Science? Politics and Economics in Hume's *Essays*," *Journal of the History of Economic Thought*, 27(1): 59–70.

Manufacturers (anon.) (1785) *A Summary Abstract of the Evidence given by the Manufacturers, before the Committee of the House of Lords of Great Britain against the Irish Propositions. Being a Continuation of the Minutes of the Evidence Given before the House of Commons*, Dublin: P. Byrne.

Marcy, Peter Torrey (1972) "Eighteenth-Century Views of Bristol and Bristolians," in McGrath (ed.) *Bristol in the Eighteenth Century*, Newton Abbot: David and Charles.

Marion, Marcel (1914–27) *Histoire financière de la France depuis 1715*, 6 vols., Paris: A. Rousseau.

Marshall, Alfred (1920 [1890]) *Principles of Economics*, 8th ed., London: Macmillan

Marshall, M. G. (2000) "Luxury, Economic Development, and Work Motivation: David Hume, Adam Smith, and J.R. McCulloch," *History of Political Economy*, 32(3): 631–48.

Martyn, Henry (1701) *Considerations Upon the East-India Trade*, London: A. and J. Churchill.

——(1720) *The Advantages of the East-India Trade to England Consider'd Wherein all the Objections to that Trade ... are Fully Answer'd: With a Comparison of the East-India and Fishing Trades*, London: J. Roberts.

Mathias, Peter (1979) *The Transformation of England: Essays in the Economic and Social History of England in the Eighteenth Century*, London: Methuen.

Matthews, George T. (1958) *The Royal General Farms in Eighteenth-Century France*, New York: Columbia University Press.

Mayer, Thomas (1980) "David Hume and Monetarism," *Quarterly Journal of Economics*, 95(1): 89–102.

Maxwell, Robert (ed.) (1743) *Select Transactions of the Honourable the Society of Improvers in the Knowledge of Agriculture*, Edinburgh: Paton, Symmer, and Gordon; Hamilton and Balfour; Sands, Kincaid, Drummond.

Maza, S. (1997) "Luxury, Morality and Social Change: Why There Was No Middle-Class Consciousness in Prerevolutionary France," *Journal of Modern History*, 69: 199–229.

McCormack, W.J. (1996) *The Pamphlet Debate on the Union Between Great Britain and Ireland, 1797–1800*, Blackrock, Co. Dublin: Irish Academic Press.

McCullough, A. B. (1984) *Money and Exchange in Canada to 1900*, Toronto and Charlottetown, PE: Dundurn Press.

McGee, Robert W. (1989) "The Economic Thought of David Hume," *Hume Studies*, 15: 184–204.

McGrath, Patrick (ed.) (1972) *Bristol in the Eighteenth Century*, Newton Abbot UK: David and Charles.

McLeod, W. R. and V. B. McLeod (eds.) (1979) *Anglo-Scottish Tracts, 1701–1714: A Descriptive Checklist*, Lawrence: University of Kansas Publications.

McNally, David (1988) *Political Economy and the Rise of Capitalism: A Reinterpretation*, Berkeley and Los Angeles: University of California Press.

McRae, Robert (1980) "The Import of Hume's Theory of Time," *Hume Studies*, 6(2): 119–32.

Meek, Ronald (1976) *Social Science and the Ignoble Savage*, Cambridge: Cambridge University Press.

Melon, Jean-François (1729) *Mahmoud le gasnévide: histoire orientale, fragment trad. de l'arabe*, Rotterdam: J. Hofhoudt.

——(1734) *Essai politique sur le commerce*, n.p.: n.p.

——(1736) *Essai politique sur le commerce. Nouvelle édition, augmentée de sept chapitres, & où les lacunes des éditions précédentes sont remplies*, n.p.: n.p.

——(1738 [1734]) *A Political Essay Upon Commerce. Written in French by Monsieur M*** Translated, with some Annotations, and Remarks*, David Bindon (trans.) Dublin: Philip Crampton.

——(1739 [1734]) *A Political Essay Upon Commerce. Written in French by Monsieur M*** Translated, with some Annotations, and Remarks*, David Bindon (trans.) Dublin and London: T. Woodward and T. Cox.

——(1754) *Essai politique sur le commerce, nouvelle édition, revue & corrigée*, Amsterdam: F. Changuion.

——(1842 [1736]) *Essai Politique sur le Commerce*, in E. Daire (ed.) *Collection des pincipaux economists, vol. 1, Économistes Financiers du 18ᵉ Siècle*, Paris: Guillaumin, pp. 701–826.

——(1971 [1842][1736]) *Essai politique sur le commerce*, in E. Daire (ed.) *Économistes financiers du dix-huitième siècle*, Geneva: Slatkine, pp. 665–778.

——(1977) *Opere II, Scritti Editi*, Onofrio Nicastro and Severina Perona (eds.) *Studi sull'Illuminismo* 7, Siena: Stamperia dell'Universita di Siena.

——(1983a) *Opere I*, Onofrio Nicastro and Severina Perona (eds.) *Jacques e i Suoi Quaderni*, no.1, 2vols. Pisa: Libreria Testi Universitari.

——(1983b [1724]) "Mémoire sur la Compagnie des Indes, fait en mai 1724," in Melon (1983a), pp. 504–525.

——(1983c [1725]) "Mémoire présenté au mois de mai 1725 sur le Défaut de Circulation," in Melon (1983a), pp. 530–534.

——(1983d [1727]) "Mémoire sur la situation présente des affaires," in Melon (1983a), pp. 651–659.

Mertz, Rudolf (1929) "Les amitiés françaises de Hume et le mouvement des idées," *Revue de littérature comparée*, 9:644–713.

Meyssonnier, Simone (1988) *La genèse de la pensée libérale en France au XVIIIe siècle*, unpublished thesis, Paris: École des Hautes Études en Sciences Sociales.

——(1989) *La Balance et l'Horloge: La genèse de la pensée libérale en France au XVIIIe siècle*, Montreuil, France: Editions de la Passion.

——(1990a) "Vincent de Gournay (1712–59) et la 'Balance des hommes'," *Population*, 45: 87–112.

——(1990b) "Deux Économistes sous la Révolution: François Véron de Forbonnais et l'abbé Morellet," in Faccarello, G and P. Steiner (eds.) *La Pensée Économique Pendant la Revolution Francaise*, Grenoble: Presses Universitaires de Grenoble, pp. 109–22.

——(1995) "Deux négociants économistes: Vincent de Gournay et Véron de Forbonnais," in D. Roche and F. Angiolini (eds.) *Cultures et Formations Négociantes dans l'Europe Moderne*, Paris: EHESS, pp. 513–53.

Michener, Ronald (1987) "Fixed Exchange Rates and the Quantity Theory in Colonial America," *Carnegie-Rochester Conference Series on Public Policy*, 27: 233–308.

Mill, John Stuart (1965 [1848]) *Principles of Political Economy* in J. M. Robson (ed.) *Collected Works of John Stuart Mill*, Toronto: University of Toronto Press, vols. 2–3.

——(1967 [1844]) "Essays on Some Unsettled Questions of Political Economy," in J.M. Robson, (ed.) *Collected Works of John Stuart Mill*, Toronto: University of Toronto Press, vol. 4.

Miller, David (1981) *Philosophy and Ideology in Hume's Political Thought*, Oxford: Oxford University Press.

Minard, Philippe (1998) *La Fortune de Colbertisme. État et Industrie dans la France des Lumières*, Paris: Fayard.

——(2000) "Colbert Continued? The Inspectorate of Manufactures and Strategies of Exchange in Eighteenth-Century France," *French Historical Studies*, 23: 477–496.

Mirabeau, Victor Riqueti, marquis de (1756) *L'Ami des hommes, ou Traité de la population*, 3 vols., Avignon, n.p.

Mitchison, Rosalind (1989) "North and South: The Development of the Gulf in Poor Law Practice," in R. A. Houston and I. D. Whyte (eds.) *Scottish Society, 1500–1800*, Cambridge: Cambridge University Press, pp. 199–224.

Molyneux, William (1696) "Letter to John Locke, September 26 1696," in Locke (1967–1989), vol, 5.

——(1698) *The Case of Ireland's Being Bound by Acts of Parliament in England, Stated*, Dublin: Joseph Ray.

Monod-Cassidy, Hélène (1941) *Un Voyageur philosophe au XVIIIe siècle: L'abbé Jean-Bernard le Blanc*, Cambridge: Harvard University Press.

Monroe, Arthur Eli (1966) *Monetary Theory before Adam Smith*, New York: Augustus M. Kelley.

Montesquieu, Charles-Louis (1748) *L'Esprit des loix*, Geneva: Barrillot.

——(1951) "Notes sur l'Angleterre," in R. Caillois (ed.) *Oeuvres complètes*, vol. 1, Paris: Gallimard 875–84.

——(1961 [1721]) *The Persian Letters*, J. Robert Loy (ed. and trans.), Cleveland: World.

——(1966 [1748]) *The Spirit of the Laws*, Thomas Nugent (trans.), New York: Hafner.

——(1989 [1748]) *The Spirit of the Laws*, Anne M. Cohler, Basia Carolyn Miller, and Harold Samuel Stone (trans. and eds.), Cambridge: Cambridge University Press.

——(1993 [1721]) *Persian Letters*, C. J. Betts (trans.), Harmondsworth, UK: Penguin.

——(2000) *Considrations sur les causes de la grandeur des Romains et de leur décadence*, Francoise Weil et al. (eds.), *Œuvres Complètes de Montesquieu*, 18 vols., Oxford: Voltaire Foundation, vol. 2.

Morgan, Kenneth (1993) *Bristol and the Atlantic Trade in the Eighteenth Century*, Cambridge: Cambridge University Press.

Morize, André (1970 [1909]) *L'Apologie du luxe au XVIIIe siècle et "Le Mondain" de Voltaire: Etude critique sur "Le Mondain" et ses sources*, Geneva: Slatkine Reprints.

Mornet, Daniel (1910) "Les Enseignements des bibliothèques privées 1750–80," *Revue d'histoire littéraire de la France*, 17: 449–96.

Morrisroe, Michael, Jr (1973) "Did Hume Read Berkeley? A Conclusive Answer," *Philological Quarterly*, 52: 314–15.

Moss, Laurence S. (1991) "Thomas Hobbes's Influence on David Hume: The Emergence of a Public Choice Tradition," *History of Political Economy*, 23(4): 587–612.

Mossner, Ernest Campbell (1944) "Hume's Epistle to Dr Arbuthnot, 1734: The Biographical Significance," *Huntington Library Quarterly*, 7: 135–52.

——(1948) "Hume's Early Memoranda, 1729–40: The Complete Text," *Journal of the History of Ideas*, 9(4): 492–518.

——(ed.) (1958) "Hume at la Flèche, 1735: An Unpublished Letter," *Studies in English*, 37: 31–33.

——(ed.) (1962) "New Hume Letters to Lord Elibank, 1748–76," *University of Texas Studies in Literature and Language*, 4(3): 431–60.

——(1980) *The Life of David Hume*, 2nd edn., Oxford: Clarendon Press.

Moureau, François (1968) "Le manuscrit de l'article *luxe* ou l'atelier de Saint-Lambert," *Recherches sur Diderot et sur l'Encyclopédie*, 1: 71–84.

Muldrew, Craig (1998) *The Economy of Obligation*, New York: St. Martin's Press.

Müller, Adam von (1801) "Ueber einen philosophischen Entwurf von Hrn Fichte, betitelt: Der geschloßne Handelstaat [sic]," *Neue Berlinische Monatsschrift*, 6: 436–38.

Muller, Jerry Z. (1990) *Adam Smith in His Time and Ours*, New York: Basic Books.

Mun, Thomas (1986 [1664]) *England's Treasure by Forraign Trade*, New York: August M. Kelley Reprint.

Munn, Charles W. (1981) *The Scottish Provincial Banking Companies 1747–1864*, Edinburgh: John Donald.

Murphy, Andrew (2002) *Conscience and Community: Revisiting Toleration and Religious Dissent in Early Modern England and America*, University Park: Pennsylvania State University Press.

Murphy, Antoin (1986a) *Richard Cantillon: Entrepreneur and Economist*, Oxford: Clarendon Press.

——(1986b) "Le Développement des idées économiques en France (1750–56)," *Revue d'Histoire Moderne et Contemporaine*, 33: 521–41.

——(1997) *John Law: Economic Theorist and Policy-Maker*, Oxford: Oxford University Press.

——(1998) "The Enigmatic Monsieur Du Tot," in Gilbert Faccarello (ed.) *Studies in the History of French Political Economy: From Bodin to Walras*, London: Routledge.

——(2000) "Einleitung zu Isaac de Pintos Traité de la circulation et du crédit," in Arnold Heertje (ed.) *Vademecum zu einem niederlandischen Pionier des Denkens über die Staatsverschuldung*, Düsseldorf: Verlag Wirtschaft und Finanzen, pp. 55–83.

Murray, Craig Compton (1989) *Benjamin Vaughan (1751–1835): The Life of An Anglo-American Intellectual*, Ph.D. dissertation, Columbia University.

Nagao, Shinichi (2003) "The Political Economy of Thomas Reid," *Journal of Scottish Philosophy*, 1: 21–33.

Neal, Larry (1990) *The Rise of Financial Capitalism: International Capital Markets in the Age of Reason*, Cambridge: Cambridge University Press.

Neufeld, Edward P. (ed.) (1964) *Money and Banking in Canada: Historical Documents and Commentary*, The Carleton Library series 17, Toronto: McClelland and Stewart.

Nicholson, Colin (1994) *Writing and the Rise of Finance: Capital Satires of the Early Eighteenth Century*, Cambridge: Cambridge University Press.

Nijenhuis, Ida J. A. (1992) *Een Joodse Philosophe: Isaac de Pinto en de ontwikkeling van de politieke economie in de Europese Verlichting*, Amsterdam: NEHA Series III.

Norrie, Kenneth, Douglas Owram, and J. C. H. Emery (2002) *A History of the Canadian Economy*, 3rd edn., Toronto: Thomson/Nelson.

Norris, John (1963) *Shelburne and Reform*, London: Macmillan.

Norton, David Fate (1993a) *The Cambridge Companion to Hume*, Cambridge: Cambridge University Press.

——(1993b) "Hume and the Foundations of Morality," in Norton (ed.) *The Cambridge Companion to Hume*, Cambridge: Cambridge University Press, pp. 148–181.

Norton, David Fate and Mary J. Norton, (1996) *The David Hume Library*, Edinburgh: Edinburgh Bibliographical Society.

——(2000) "Annotations" and "Glossary," in David Hume, *A Treatise of Human Nature*, David Fate Norton and Mary J. Norton (eds.), Oxford: Oxford University Press.

Oakeshott, Michael (1990) *On Human Conduct*, Oxford: Clarendon Press.

O'Brien, George (1923–24) "The Irish Free Trade Agitation of 1779," *English Historical Review*, 38: 564–81; 39: 95–109.

Orain, Arnaud (2003) "Decline and Progress: the Economic Agent in Condillac's Theory of History," *European Journal of the History of Economic Thought*, 10: 379–407.

——(2006) " 'Equilibre' et Fiscalité au Siècle des Lumières——L'Économie Politique de Jean-Joseph Graslin," *Revue Économique*, 57: 955–82.

Ouellet, Fernand (1980) *Economic and Social History of Quebec, 1760–1850*, The Carleton Library series 120, Toronto: Gage.

Oz-Salzberger, Fania (2001) "Civil Society in the Scottish Enlightenment," in Sudipta Kaviraj and Sunil Khilnani (eds.) *Civil Society: History and Possibilities*, Cambridge: Cambridge University Press.

Paganelli, Maria Pia (2006) "Hume and Endogenous Money," *Eastern Economic Journal*, 32(3): 533–47.

Palter, Robert (1995) "Hume and Prejudice," *Hume Studies*, 21(1): 3–23.

Pâris-Duverney, Joseph and F. M. C. Deschamps (1740) *Examen du livre intitulé Réflexions politique sur les Finances*, 2 vols., The Hague: Vaillant and N. Prevôst.

Parliamentary History 25 (1816 [1785–86]) *The Parliamentary History of England from the Earliest Period to the Year 1803, from which Last Mentioned Epoch it is Continued Downwards in the Work Entitled "The Parliamentary Debates," vol. 25 1 February 1785 to 5 May 1786*. London: T.C. Hansard.

Parliamentary History 26 (1816 [1786–88]) *The Parliamentary History of England from the Earliest Period to the Year 1803, from which Last Mentioned Epoch it is Continued Downwards in the Work Entitled "The Parliamentary Debates," vol. 26 15 May 1786 to 8 February 1788*. London: T.C. Hansard.

Paterson, William (1968 [1859]) *The Writings of William Paterson, Founder of the Bank of England*, 2nd edn., 3 vols., Saxe Bannister (ed.), New York: A. M. Kelley.

Patinkin, Donald and Otto Steigler (1989) "In Search of the 'Veil of Money' and the 'Neutrality of Money': A Note on the Origin of Terms," *Scandinavian Journal of Economics*, 91: 131–46.

Pattullo, Henry (1758) *Essai sur l'amelioration des terres*, Paris, Durand.

Peaucelle, Jean-Louis (2006) "Adam Smith's use of Multiple References for his Pin Making Example," *European Journal of the History of Economic Thought*, 13: 489–512.

Penelhum, Terence (1993) "Hume's Moral Psychology," in Norton (1993), pp. 117–147.

Perlman, Morris (1987) "Of a Controversial Passage in Hume," *Journal of Political Economy*, 95: 274–89.

Perrot, J.-C. (1984) "L'économie politique et ses livres," in R. Chartier and H. J. Martin (eds.) *Histoire de l'édition française*, Paris, 2:240–57.

——(1992) *Une Histoire intellectuelle dé l'économie politique*, Paris: Presses Universitaires de France.

Petrie, A. E. H. (1973) "Documents Relating to Currency, Exchange and Finance in Canada, 1765–67, from the Adam Shortt Papers in the Public Archives of Canada," *Transactions of the Canadian Numismatic Research Society* 9: 1–25.

Petty, William Sir (1899 [1687]) "A Treatise of Ireland," in Petty, *The Economic Writing of Sir William Petty*, C H. Hull (ed.), Cambridge: Cambridge University Press, vol. 2, pp. 545–621.

Phillipson, Nicholas (1983) "Adam Smith as a Civic Moralist," in Hont and Ignatieff (eds.) *Wealth and Virtue*, pp.179–202.

——(1989) *Hume*, New York: St. Martin's Press, pp. 179–202.

Pincus, Steven (1995) "The English Debate on Universal Monarchy," in Robertson (1995a), pp. 37–72.

——(1998) "To Protect English Liberties: the English Nationalist Revolution of 1688–89," in Ian McBride and Tony Claydon (eds.) *Protestantism and National Identity: Britain and Ireland, c. 1650–c. 1850*, Cambridge: Cambridge University Press.

Pinto, Isaac de (2000 [1771]) *Traité de la circulation et du crédit*, Amsterdam: Marc Michel Rey; and Düsseldorf: Verlag *Wirtschaft* und Finanzen.

——(1774) *An Essay on Circulation and Credit, in Four Parts; and a Letter on the Jealousy of Commerce*. S. Baggs (trans.), London: James Ridley.

Pitavy-Simoni, Pascale (1997) "Vincent de Gournay, or 'Laissez-faire without Laissez Passer'," in James R Henderson, (ed.), *The State of the History of Economics: Selected Papers from the History of Economics Society Conference 1995*, London: Routledge, pp. 173–94.

Pitt, William (1799) *Speech of the Right Honourable William Pitt, in the House of Commons, Thursday, January 31, 1799, On Offering to the House the Resolutions which he Proposed as the basis of a Union between Great Britain and Ireland, to Which are Added the Speeches of the Right Honourable John Foster, on the 12th and 15th of August, 1785, on the Bill for Effectuating the Intercourse and Commerce between Great Britain and Ireland, on Permanent and Equitable Principles, for the Mutual Benefit of Both Kingdoms*, Dublin: J. Exshaw.

——(1808a) *The Speeches of the Right Honourable William Pitt, in the House of Commons*. 2nd edn, 3 vols, London: Longman, Hurst, Rees, and Orme.

——(1808b [1785]) "Speech to the Committee of the Whole House on the Commercial Regulations Proposed to be Adopted between Great Britain and Ireland, House of Commons, February 22, 1785," in Pitt (1808a), vol. 1, pp. 132–48.

——(1808c [1785]) "Speech to the Committee of the Whole House on the Commercial Regulations Proposed to be Adopted between Great Britain and Ireland, House of Commons, May 12, 1785," in Pitt (1808a), vol. 1, pp. 183–98.

Pluche, abbé Noël-Antoine (1732–51) *Le Spectacle de la nature*, 8 vols., Paris: La Veuve Estienne.

Plumard de Dangeul, Louis-Joseph (1754a) *Remarques sur les avantages et les désavantages de la France et de la Grande Bretagne, par rapport au commerce, aux autres sources de la puissance des Etats: Traduction de l'anglois du Chevalier John Nickolls*, 2nd ed., Leiden: n.p.

——(1754b) *Remarks on the Advantages and Disadvantages of France and Great-Britain with Respect to Commerce, and to the other Means of encreasing the Wealth and Power of the State. Being a (pretended) Translation from the English, written by Sir John Nickolls, and printed at Leyden 1754*, London: T. Osborne.

Pocock, J. G. A. (1975) *The Machiavellian Moment: Florentine Political Thought and the Atlantic Republican Tradition*, Princeton, NJ: Princeton University Press.

——(1981) "The Machiavellian Moment Revisited: A Study in History and Ideology," *Journal of Modern History*, 53: 49–72.

——(ed.) (1985a) *Virtue, Commerce, and History: Essays on Political Thought and History, Chiefly in the Eighteenth Century*, Cambridge: Cambridge University Press.

——(1985b) "Virtues, Rights, and Manners," in Pocock (1985a), pp. 37–50.

——(1985c) "Hume and the American Revolution" in Pocock (1985a), pp. 125–141.

——(1985d) "Josiah Tucker on Burke, Locke, and Price: A study in the Varieties of Eighteenth-Century Conservatism," in Pocock (1985a), pp. 157–92.

——(1999–2003) *Barbarism and Religion*, 3 vols. Cambridge: Cambridge University Press.

Pomeranz, Kenneth (2000) *The Great Divergence: China, Europe, and the Making of the Modern World Economy*, Princeton: Princeton University Press.

Popkin, Richard Henry (1970) "Hume and Isaac de Pinto," *University of Texas Studies in Literature and Language*, 11: 417–30.

——(1974) "Hume and Isaac de Pinto, II. Five New Letters," in William B. Todd (ed.) *Hume and Enlightenment: Essays Presented to Ernest Campbell Mossner*, Edinburgh: Edinburgh University Press; and Austin, TX: Humanities Research Center, pp. 99–127.

——(1987) *Isaac La Peyrère (1596–1676): His Life, Work, and Influence*, Leiden, The Netherlands: Brill.

Powell, Martyn J. (2003) *Britain and Ireland in the Eighteenth-Century Crisis of Empire*, Basingstoke: Palgrave Macmillan.

Price, Jacob (1973) *France and the Chesapeake*, 2 vols., Ann Arbor: University of Michigan Press.

Price, John Vladimir (1999) "Préface," in *Hume Essais moraux, littéraires et politiques*, Paris: Editions Alive.

Quesnay, François (2005 [1757]) "Grains," in INED (ed.) *Œuvres économiques complétes et autres texts*, Paris: INED, 1:161–212.

Rahe, Paul (2005) "The Book That Never Was: Montesquieu's Considerations on the Romans in Historical Context," *History of Political Thought*, 26: 43–89.

Ramsay, Allan (1951–74) *Works*, Burns Martin, John W. Oliver, et al. (eds.), 6 vols., Edinburgh: Scottish Text Society.

Rashid, Salim (1982) "Adam Smith's Rise to Fame: A Re-Examination of the Evidence," *The Eighteenth Century*, 28: 263–84.

——(1984) "David Hume and Eighteenth-Century Monetary Thought: A Critical Comment on Recent Views," *Hume Studies*, 5(2): 156–64.

——(1988) "The Irish School of Economic Development 1720–50," *Manchester School of Economic and Social Studies*, 56: 345–69.

Rawls, John (1993) *Political Liberalism*, New York: Columbia University Press.

Raynal, Guillaume-Thomas (1773–74) *Histoire Philosophique et Politique des Etablissements et du Commerce des Européens dans les deux Indes*, 10 vols., Amsterdam: n.p.

Raynor, David (1984) "Hume's Abstract of Adam Smith's *Theory of Moral Sentiments*," *Journal of the History of Philosophy*, 22: 51–79.

——(1998) "Who Invented the Invisible Hand?," *Times Literary Supplement*, 14: 2.

Redish, Angela (1984) "Why Was Specie Scarce in Colonial Economies? An Analysis of the Canadian Currency, 1796–1830," *Journal of Economic History*, 44: 713–28.

Ricardo, David (1951 [1817]) *On the Principles of Political Economy, and Taxation*, in *The Works and Correspondence of David Ricardo*, Piero Sraffa and Maurice Dobb (eds.), 11 vols., Cambridge: Cambridge University Press, vol. 1.

Richards, Eric (1982) *A History of the Highland Clearances*, London and Canberra: Croom, Helm.

Riddell, W. R. (1930) "Benjamin Franklin and Colonial Money," *Pennsylvania Magazine of History and Biography*, 54: 60–63.

Riley, James C. (1986), *The Seven Years War and the Old Regime in France: the Economic and Financial Toll*, Princeton, NJ: Princeton University Press.

Robertson, John (1983) "The Scottish Enlightenment and the Civic Tradition," in Hont and Ignatieff (eds.) *Wealth and Virtue*, pp. 137–178.

——(1987) "A. Fletcher's Vision of Union," in R.A. Mason (ed.) *Scotland and England, 1286–1815*, Edinburgh: John Donald, pp. 203–225.

——(1993) "Universal Monarchies and the Liberties of Europe," in N. T. Phillipson and Q. Skinner (eds.) *Political Discourse in Early Modern Britain*, Cambridge: Cambridge University Press, pp. 349–72.

——(ed.) (1995a) *A Union for Empire, Political Thought, and the British Union of 1707*, Cambridge: Cambridge University Press.

——(1995b) "An Elusive Sovereignty: The Course of the Union Debate in Scotland 1698–1707," in Robertson (1995a), pp. 198–227.

——(1997) "The Enlightenment above National Context: Political Economy in Eighteenth-Century Scotland and Naples," *The Historical Journal*, 40: 667–97.

——(2000) "The Scottish Contribution to the Enlightenment," in Paul Wood (ed.) *The Scottish Enlightenment*, pp. 37–62

——(2005) *The Case for the Enlightenment: Scotland and Naples 1680–1760*, Cambridge: Cambridge University Press.

Roche, Daniel (1993) *La France des Lumières*, Paris: Fayard.

——(1998) *France in the Enlightenment*, Arthur Goldhammer (trans.), Cambridge, MA: Harvard University Press.

Rosen, Frederick (2003) *Classical Utilitarianism from Hume to Mill*, London: Routledge.

Rosenblum, Nancy (1998) *Membership and Morals: The Personal Uses of Pluralism in America*, Princeton, NJ: Princeton University Press.

Roseveare, Henry (1969) *The Treasury: The Evolution of a British Institution*, New York: Columbia University Press.

——(1991) *The Financial Revolution 1660–1760*, London/New York: Longman.

Ross, E. (1976) "Mandeville, Melon and Voltaire: The Origins of the Luxury Controversy in France," *Voltaire Studies*, 155: 1897–1912.

Rostow, W.W. (1990) *Theorists of Economic Growth from David Hume to the Present: With a Perspective on the Next Century*, Oxford: Oxford University Press.

Rothbard, Murray N. (1995) *An Austrian Perspective on the History of Economic Thought*, Aldershot: Edward Elgar Hants, vol. 1.

Rothkrug, Lionel (1965) *Opposition to Louis XIV: The Political and Social Origins of the French Enlightenment*, Princeton, NJ: Princeton University Press.

Rothschild, Emma (2001) *Economic Sentiments, Adam Smith, Condorcet, and the Enlightenment*, Cambridge, MA: Harvard University Press.

——(2005) "Language and empire, c.1800," *Historical Research*, 78: 208–29.

Rotwein, Eugene (1955; reprinted 1970) "Introduction" to *David Hume: Writings on Economics*, Rotwein (ed.), Madison, WI: University of Wisconsin Press; Edinburgh: Nelson.

——(1976) "David Hume Philosopher-Economist," *Southwestern Journal of Philosophy*, 2: 117–34.

——(1987) "David Hume," John Eatwell, Murray Milgate, and Peter Newman (eds.) *The New Palgrave: A Dictionary of Economics (The Invisible Hand)*, London: Macmillan.

Rousseau, Jean-Jacques (1964a [1750]) *Discours sur les sciences et les arts*, François Bouchardy (ed.), Paris: Gallimard.

——(1964b [1754]) *Discourse on the Origins of Inequality*, Roger Masters (ed.), New York: St. Martin's.

——(1979 [1762]) *Emile, or On Education*, Allan Bloom (ed.), New York: Basic Books.

——(1995 [1770]) *The Confessions*, Christopher Kelly, Roger D. Masters, and Peter G. Stillman, (eds., trans.) Christopher Kelly, in Rousseau, *The Confessions and Correspondence, Including the Letters to Malesherbes, The Collected Writings of Rousseau*, vol. 5, Hanover, NH: Dartmouth College and University Press of New England.

Ruffin, Roy J. (2002) "David Ricardo's Discovery of Comparative Advantage," *History of Political Economy*, 34: 727–48.

Saint-Lambert, Jean-François de (1764) *Essai sur le luxe* n.p.: n.p.

——(1765a) "Intérêt", in *Encyclopédie ou dictionnaire raisonné des sciences, des arts et des métiers, par une société de gens de lettres; mis en ordre et publié par M. ****, vol. 8 "H-Itzehoa," Neufchatel: S. Faulche, p. 818.

——(1765b) "Luxury," in *Encyclopédie ou dictionnaire raisonné des sciences, des arts et des métiers, par une société de gens de lettres; mis en ordre et publié par M. *** vol. 9, "Ju-Mamira,"* Neuchatel: S. Faulche, pp. 763b–71a.

——(1765c) "Législateur," in *Encyclopédie ou dictionnaire raisonné des sciences, des arts et des métiers, par une société de gens de lettres; mis en ordre et publié par M. *** vol. 9 "Ju-Mamir,"* Neufchatel: S. Faulche, pp. 357–58.

——(1765d) "Luxe," in Diderot, Denis and Jean le Rond d'Alembert (eds.) *Encyclopédie, ou dictionnaire raisonné des sciences, des arts et des métiers*, vol. 9, Paris: Briasson.

——(1766 [1765b]) *An Essay on Luxury* [*written originally in French, by Mr. Pinto*], London: T. Becket and P.A. De Hondt.

——(1965 [1765b]) "Luxury (Moral Science and Philosophy)," in N.S. Hoyt and T. Cassirer (eds.) *Encyclopedia-Selections*, Indianapolis: Bobbs-Merill, pp. 203–32.

——(1797–1801 [1777]) "Essai sur la vie & les ouvrages de M. Helvetius," in *Oeuvres philosophiques de Saint-Lambert*, 6 vols., Paris: H. Agasse, vol. 5.

Saint-Pierre ábbé de, Charles Irénée Castel (1733) *Project pour perfectionner le commerse de France*, in *Ouvrajes de politique*, Rotterdam: Jean Daniel Beman, vol. 5, 197–316.

Sakamoto, Tatsuya (1995) *David Hume's Civilized Society—Industry, Knowledge and Liberty*, Tokyo: Sobunsha (in Japanese).

——(2003) "Hume's Political Economy as a System of Manners," in Tatsuya Sakamoto and Hideo Tanaka (eds.) *The Rise of Political Economy in the Scottish Enlightenment*, London: Routledge, pp. 86–102.

——(2004) "Hume's 'Early Memoranda' and the Shaping of His Political Economy," unpublished manuscript.

Sallust (1930) *De Coniuratione Catilinae*, W. Summers (ed.), Cambridge: Cambridge University Press.

Sally, Razeen (1997) *Classical Liberalism and International Economic Order*, London: Routledge.

Samuelson, Paul (1980) "A Corrected Version of Hume's Equilibrating Mechanism for International Trade," in John Chipman and Charles Kindleberger (eds.) *Flexible Exchange Rates and the Balance of Payments: Essays in Memory of Egon Sohmen*, Amsterdam: North Holland.

Sargent, Thomas J. and François R. Velde (1999) "The Big Problem of Small Change," *Journal of Money, Credit and Banking*, 31: 137–61.

——(2002) *The Big Problem of Small Change*, Princeton, NJ: Princeton University Press.

Schabas, Margaret (1994) "Market Contracts in the Age of Hume," in Neil De Marchi and Mary Morgan (eds.) *Higgling: Transactors and Their Markets in the History of Economics*, Durham, NC: Duke University Press. pp. 117–134.

——(2000) "The Jevonian Revolution Reappraised," in A. Murphy and R. Prendergast (eds.) *Contributions to the History of Economic Thought: Essays in Honour of R.D.C. Black*, London: Routledge, pp. 141–53.

——(2001) "David Hume on Experimental Natural Philosophy, Money and Fluids," *History of Political Economy*, 33(3): 411–35.

——(2005) *The Natural Origins of Economics*, Chicago: University of Chicago Press.

Schama, Simon (1988) *The Embarrassment of Riches: An Interpretation of Dutch Culture in the Golden Age*, Berkeley and Los Angeles: University of California Press.

Schatz, Albert (1902) *L'oeuvre économique de David Hume*, Paris: A. Rousseau.

Schelle, Gustave (1897) *Vincent de Gournay*, Paris: Guillaumin.

Schleich, Thomas (1980) " 'Der zweitbeste Staat.' Zur Sicht der Antike bei Gabriel Bonnot de Mably," *Der Staat*, 19: 557–82.

——(1981) *Aufklärung und Revolution: Die Wirkungsgeschichte Gabriel Bonnot de Mablys in Frankreich (1740–1914)*, Stuttgart: Klett-Cotta.

Schliesser, Eric (2003) "The Obituary of a Vain Philosopher: Adam Smith's Reflections on Hume's Life," *Hume Studies*, 29(2): 327–62.

Schmid, Georg Ludwig (1760a) *Traités sur divers sujets intéressants de politique et de morale*, n.p.: n.p.

——(1760b) *Essais sur divers subjets interéssants de politique et de morale*, n.p.: n.p., vol. 1.

——(1760c) "Reflexions sur l'Agriculture," in *Recueil de memoires concernants l'oeconomie rurale par une société établie à Berne en Suisse*, No. 1: 5–100.

——(1763) *Essais sur divers subjets interéssan de politique et de morale*, vol. 2, n.p.: n.p.

——(1772 [1760]) *Essays Moral, Philosophical, and Political*, John Mills (ed.), London: S. Hooper.

——(1776) *Principes de la législation universelle*, 2 vols., Amsterdam: Marc-Michel Rey.

——(1777–78) *Principi della legislazione universale*, Cosimo Cennini 4 vols. (trans) Paris and Siena: La Vedova.

——(1791) *Of Commerce and Luxury*, John Mills (trans.), Philadelphia: T. Lang.

Schmidt, Claudia (2003) *David Hume: Reason in History*, State College: Penn State University Press.

Schreuder, J. (ed.) (1756–1758) *Discours Politiques*, 5 vols., Amsterdam: J. Schreuder and P. Mortier.

Schumpeter, Joseph (1986 [1954]) *A History of Economic Analysis*, New York: Oxford University Press.

Schweitzer, D.R. (1984) "The Failure of William Pitt's Irish Trade Propositions, 1785," *Parliamentary History*, 3: 129–45.

Seifert, Hans-Ulrich (1987) "Banquets de philosophes: Georges Louis Schmid chez Diderot, d'Holbach, Helvétius et Mably," *Dix-huitième Siècle*, No. 19: 223–44.

——(1988) "Ein vergessener Schweizer Aufklärer: Georg Ludwig Schmid," in *Lenzburger Neujahrsblätter 1988*, Lenzburg: Kommissionsverlag Buchhandlung E.C. Otz, pp. 110–27.

Seki, Gentaro (2003) "Policy Debate on Economic Development in Scotland: the 1720s to the 1730s," in Sakamoto and Tanaka (eds.) *The Rise of Political Economy in the Scottish Enlightenment*, London: Routledge, pp. 22–38.

Sekine, Thomas (1973) "The Discovery of International Monetary Equilibrium by Vanderlint, Cantillon, Gervais and Hume," *Economia Internazionale*, 26: 262–82.

Sekora, John (1977) *Luxury: The Concept in Western Thought, Eden to Smollett*, Baltimore, MD: Johns Hopkins University Press.

Seligman, Adam (1992) *The Idea of Civil Society*, New York: Free Press.

Semmel, Bernard (1965) "The Hume–Tucker Debate and Pitt's Trade Proposals," *Economic Journal*, 75: 759–70.

Seneca (1932) *Epistulae Morales*, R. Gummere (ed.), Cambridge, MA: Harvard University Press.

Shackleton, Robert (1963, reprinted 1963) *Montesquieu: A Critical Biography*, Oxford: Oxford University Press.

Shapin, Steven (1994) *A Social History of Truth: Civility and Science in Seventeenth-Century England*, Chicago: University of Chicago Press.

Shaw, John Stuart (1983) *The Management of Scottish Society, 1707–1764*, Edinburgh: John Donald Publishers.

Shelton, George (1981) *Dean Tucker and Eighteenth-Century Economic and Political Thought*, London: Macmillan.

Sher, Richard B. (2000) "The Book in the Scottish Enlightenment," in Paul Wood (ed.) *The Culture of the Book in the Scottish Enlightenment*, Toronto: Thomas Fisher Rare Book Library, pp. 40–60.

Sheridan, Richard Brinsley (1779) *A Letter to William Eden, Esq; On the Subject of His to the Earl of Carlisle; The Irish Trade*, Dublin: M. Mills Smith.

Sherman, Sandra (1996) *Finance and Fictionality in the Early Eighteenth Century: Accounting for Defoe*, Cambridge: Cambridge University Press.

Shils, Edward (1991) "Sir Henry Sumner Maine in the Tradition of the Analysis of Society," in Alan Diamond (ed.) *The Victorian Achievement of Sir Henry Sumner Maine*, Cambridge: Cambridge University Press.

——(1997) *The Virtue of Civility and Other Essays*, Steven Grosby (ed.), Indianapolis, IN: Liberty Press.

Shortt, Adam (1897–99) "Canadian Currency and Exchange Under French Rule," *Journal of the Canadian Bankers Association*, 5: 271–90, 385–401; 6: 1–22, 147–65, 233–47.

——(1987) *Adam Shortt's History of Canadian Currency and Banking: 1600–1880*, Don Mills, ON: Canadian Bankers Association.

Shovlin, John (2000) "The Cultural Politics of Luxury in Eighteenth-Century France," *French Historical Studies*, 23: 577–606.

——(2003) "Emulation in Eighteenth-Century French Economic Thought," *Eighteenth-Century Studies*, 36: 224–30.

Sidney, A. (1990 [1698]) *Discourses Concerning Government*, T. West (ed.), Indianapolis, IN: Liberty Press.

Sigmund, Paul (ed.) (1988) *St. Thomas Aquinas on Politics and Ethics*, New York: W. W. Norton.

Skene, David (n.d. [*c.* 1758]) "Extracts from Wallace's *Considerations on the Present Political State of Great Britain*," in Skene (ed.) "Literary Essays: Dr. D. Skene," Aberdeen University Library, MS 475 fols. 95–96.

Skinner, Andrew S. (1967) "Natural History in the Age of Adam Smith," *Political Studies*, 15: 32–48.

——(1979) "Historical Theory," in A. Skinner (ed.) *A System of Social Science: Papers Relating to Adam Smith*, Oxford: Clarendon Press, pp. 76–108.

——(1993) "Hume: Principles of Political Economy," in Norton (ed.) *The Cambridge Companion to Hume*, Cambridge: Cambridge University Press, pp. 222–254.

——(2003) "Economic Theory," in Alexander Broadie (ed.) *The Cambridge Companion to the Scottish Enlightenment*, Cambridge: Cambridge University Press, pp. 178–204.

Skinner, Quentin (1988) "Language and Social Change," in James Tully (ed.) *Meaning and Context: Quentin Skinner and His Critics*, Oxford: Oxford University Press.

Smith, Adam (1976–2001) *The Glasgow Edition of the Works and Correspondence of Adam Smith*, 7 vols., A. Skinner (ed.), Indianapolis, IN: Liberty Fund.

——(1976 [1776]) *An Inquiry into the Nature and Causes of the Wealth of Nations*, 2 vols. Roy H. Campbell, Andrew S. Skinner, and William B. Todd (eds.), Oxford: Clarendon Press.

——(1980) "Contributions to the *Edinburgh Review* of 1755–56, in W.P.D. Wightman and J.C. Bryce (eds.) *Adam Smith: Essays on Philosophical Subjects*, Oxford: Oxford University Press.

——(1982) *Lectures on Jurisprudence*, R. L. Meek, D. D. Raphael, and P. G. Stein (eds.), Indianapolis, IN: Liberty Fund.

——(1984 [1759; 6th ed. 1790]) *The Theory of Moral Sentiments*, A. Macfie and D. Raphael (eds.), Indianapolis, IN: Liberty Press.

——(1987 [1977], 2nd ed.) The *Correspondence of Adam Smith*, E.C. Mossner and I.S. Ross (eds.), Oxford: Clarendon.

Smith, Bruce D. (1985) "American Colonial Monetary Regimes: The Failure of the Quantity Theory and Some Evidence in Favour of an Alternate View," *Canadian Journal of Economics*, 18: 531–65.

Smyth, Jim (1993) " 'Like Amphibious Animals': Irish Protestants, Ancient Britons," *Historical Journal*, 36: 785–97.

——(1995) "Anglo-Irish Unionist Discourse, *c.* 1656–1707: From Harrington to Fletcher," *Bullán: An Irish Studies Journal*, 2: 17–34.

——(2000) "The Act of Union and 'Public Opinion'," in Smyth (ed.) *Revolution, Counter-Revolution and Union: Ireland in the 1790s*, Cambridge: Cambridge University Press, pp. 146–160.

——(2001) *The Making of the United Kingdom, 1600–1800: State, Religion and Identity in Britain and Ireland*, Harlow: Longman.

Sombart, Werner (1913) *Luxus und Capitalismus*, München: Duncker and Humblot.

Sonenscher, Michael (1997) "The Nation's Debt and the Birth of the Modern Republic: The French Fiscal Deficit and the Politics of the Revolution of 1789," *History of Political Thought*, 18: 64–103 and 267–324.

——(1998) "Fashion's Empire: Trade and Power in Early 18th-Century France" in Robert Fox and Anthony Turner (eds.) *Luxury Trades and Consumerism in Ancien Régime Paris: Studies in the History of the Skilled Workforce*, Aldershot UK: Ashgate, pp. 231–54.

——(2001) "Physiocracy as Theodicy," *History of Political Thought*, 23: 326–39.

——(2002) "Republicanism, State Finances and the Emergence of Commercial Society in Eighteenth-century France—or from Royal to Ancient Republicanism and Back," in van Gelderen and Skinner (eds) *Republicanism*, vol. 2, pp. 275–91.

——(2006) "Property, Community and Citizenship," in M. Goldie and R. Wokler (eds) *The Cambridge History of Eighteenth-century Political Thought*, Cambridge: Cambridge University Press, pp. 465–96.

——(2007) *Before the Deluge: Public Debt, Inequality and the Intellectual Origins of the French Revolution*, Princeton: Princeton University Press.

Soule, Edward (2000) "Hume on Economic Policy and Human Nature," *Hume Studies*, 26: 151–68.

Spector, Céline (2004) *Montesquieu: pouvoirs richnese et sociétes*, Paris: Presses Universitaires de France.

Spiegel, Henry (1971) *The Growth of Economic Theory*, Englewood Cliffs, NJ: Prentice Hall.

Staley, Charles E. (1976) "Hume and Viner on the International Adjustment Mechanism," *History of Political Economy*, 8: 252–65.

Steiner, Philippe (2002) "Wealth and Power: Quesnay's Political Economy of the 'Agricultural Kingdom'," *Journal of the History of Economic Thought*, 24: 91–110.

Steuart, Sir James (1966 [1767]) *An Inquiry into the Principles of Political Oeconomy*, A. Skinner (ed.), Chicago: University of Chicago Press, vol. 2.

Stevenson, James (1875) *The Card Currency of Canada During the French Domination*, Quebec: Middleton and Dawson.

——(1876–77) "The Currency of Canada After the Capitulation," *Transactions of the Literary and Historical Society of Quebec*, 12: 109–34.

——(1891–92) "The Circulation of Army Bills with Some Remarks upon the War of 1812," *Transactions of the Literary and Historical Society of Quebec*, 21: 1–79.

Stewart, Dugald (1982 [1811]) "Account of the Life and Writings of Adam Smith, LL D," I. S. Ross (ed.), in Adam Smith (1982 [1795]), *Essays on Philosophical Subjects*, William Persehouse, Delisle Wightman, and John C. Bryce (eds.), Oxford: Clarendon Press.

——(1994 [1855–56]) *Lectures on Political Economy*, in Dugald Stewart, *The Collected Works of Dugald Stewart*, Sir William Hamilton (ed.), Edinburgh and Bristol: Thoemmes Press, vols. 8–9.

Stewart, John B. (1992) *Opinion and Reform in Hume's Political Philosophy*, Princeton: Princeton University Press.

——(1963) *The Moral and Political Philosophy of David Hume*, Westport, CT: Greenwood Press.

Stewart, M. A. (2000) "The Dating of Hume's Manuscripts," in Paul Wood (ed.) *The Scottish Enlightenment: Essays in Reinterpretation*, Rochester: University of Rochester Press, pp. 267–314.

Stigler, George J. and Gary S. Becker (1979) "De Gustibus Non Est Disputandum," *American Economic Review*, 67: 76–90.

Stockton, Constance Noble (1976) "Economics and the Mechanism of Historical Progress in Hume's *History*," in Donald W. Livingston and James T. King (eds.) *Hume: A Reevaluation*, New York: Fordham University Press, pp. 296–320.

Strahm, Hans (1946) "Das Gründungsprogramm und die ersten Veröffentlichungen der Ökonomischen Gesellschaft," *Der Schweizerbauer 1846–1946: Festschrift zur Hundertjahrfeier*, Bern, pp. 1–19.

Streminger, G. (1980) "Hume's Theory of Imagination," *Hume Studies*, 6(2): 91–118.

Strotz, R. H. (1956) "Myopia and Inconsistency in Dynamic Utility Maximization," *Review of Economic Studies*, 23(3): 165–80.

Stroud, Barry (1977) *Hume*, London: Routledge.

Sturges, R. Paul (1975) *Economists' Papers, 1750–1950: A Guide to Archive and Other Manuscript Sources for the History of British and Irish Economic Thought*, Durham, NC: Duke University Press.

Sturn, Richard (2004) "The Sceptic as an Economist's Philosopher? Humean Utility as a Positive Principle," *European Journal of the History of Economic Thought*, 11(3): 345–75.

Stüssi-Lauterburg, Barbara (1989) "Von Thalheim nach Brugg: Briefe von Georg Ludwig Schmid d'Auenstein an Johann Georg Zimmermann," in *Brugger Neujahrsblätter 1989*, Brugg: Buchdruckerei Effingerhof, pp. 141–55.

Sugden, Robert (2005) "Why Rationality is *Not* a Consequence of Hume's Theory of Choice," *European Journal of the History of Economic Thought*, 12(1): 113–18.

Sutcliffe, Frank Edmund (1982) "The Abbé Coyer and the Chevalier d'Arc," *Bulletin of the John Rylands Library Manchester*, 65(1): 235–45.

Swift, Jonathan (1962) *Miscellaneous and Autobiographical Pieces, Fragments and Marginalia*, Herbert Davis (ed.), Oxford: Blackwell.

——(1983) *The Complete Poems*, Pat Rogers (ed.), London: Penguin Books.

Tarascio, Vincent C. (1985) "Cantillon's *Essai*: A Current Perspective," *Journal of Libertarian Studies*, 7: 247–57.

Taylor, Charles (1989) *Sources of the Self*, Cambridge: Cambridge University Press.

Teichgraeber, Richard F. III (1986) *"Free Trade" and Moral Philosophy: Rethinking the Sources of Adam Smith's* Wealth of Nations, Durham: Duke University Press.

——(1987) "'Less Abused than I Had Reason to Expect': The Reception of *The Wealth of Nations* in Britain, 1776–90," *The Historical Journal*, 30(2): 337–66.

Temple, William Sir (1814 [1680]) "An Essay upon the Advancement of Trade in Ireland," in Temple (ed.), *The Works of Sir William Temple, bart.*, 4 vols., London: F.C. and J. Rivington, vol. 3, pp. 1–28.

Tertullian (1951) *De Cultu Feminari*, J. Marra (ed.), Torino: Parania.

Théré, Christine (1998) "Economic Publishing and Authors, 1566–1789," in G. Faccarello (ed.) *Studies in the History of French Political Economy*, London: Routledge, pp. 1–56.

Thompson, Francis Michael Longstreth (1989) "Aristocracy, Gentry and the Middle Classes in Britain, 1750–1850," in A. M. Burke (ed.) *Bürgertum, Adel und Monarchie: Wandel der Lebensformen im Zeitalter des bürgerlichen Nationalsismus*, Munich: K. G. Saur.

Thompson, James (1996) *Models of Value: Eighteenth-Century Political Economy and the Novel*, Durham, NC: Duke University Press.

Thornton, Mark (2005) "The 250th Anniversary of the Discovery of Economics," Ludwig von Mises Institute, Auburn, AL: Mises.org.

Tierney, Brian (1959) *Medieval Poor Law*, Berkeley: University of California Press.

Todd, William B. (1974) "David Hume: A Preliminary Bibliography," in W. B. Todd (ed.) *Hume and the Enlightenment: Essays Presented to Ernest Campbell Mossner*, Edinburgh: Edinburgh University Press; Austin, Texas: Humanities Research Center, pp. 189–205.

Tomaselli, Sylvana (1989) "Moral Philosophy and Population Questions in Eighteenth-Century Europe," in Michael Teitlebaum and Jay M. Winter (eds.) *Population and Resources in Western Intellectual Traditions*, Cambridge: Cambridge University Press.

Trenchard, John and Thomas Gordon (1995 [1720–23]) *Cato's Letters, or, Essays on Liberty, Civil and Religious, and Other Important Topics*, 2 vols., Ronald Hamoway (ed.), Indianapolis, IN: Liberty Fund.

Tribe, Keith (1988) *Governing Economy: The Reformation of German Economic Discourse 1750–1840*, Cambridge: Cambridge University Press.

Trudel, Marcel (1968) *Introduction to New France*, Toronto: Holt, Rinehart, and Winston Canada.

Trusler, Reverend (1786) *The London Advisor and Guide*, Kress Library Manuscripts, Harvard University.

Tsuda, Takumi (1979) "Etude bibliographique sur l'*Essai* de Cantillon," in T. Tsuda (ed.) *Essai sur le commerce en général*, Tokyo: Kinokuniya Company.

——(1983) "Un économiste trahi, Vincent de Gournay (1712–59)," in Child (1983 [1752]), pp. 445–85.

Tucker, Josiah (1749) *A Brief Essay on the Advantages and Disadvantages which Respectively Attend France and Great Britain, With Regard to Trade. With Some Proposals for Removing the Principal Disadvantages of Great Britain*, London: T. Trye.

——(1753) *A Brief Essay on the Advantages and Disadvantages which Respectively Attend France and Great Britain with Regard to Trade. With Some Proposals for Removing the Principal Disadvantage of Great Britain. In a New Method.* 3rd ed. Corrected with addition. London: T. Trye.

——(1755a) *The Elements of Commerce and the Theory of Taxes*, n.p: private edition of the author.

——(c. 1755b) 'Marginal Notes to *Elements of Commerce*, retitled as *The Moral and Political Theory of Trade and Taxes*, in presentation copy of Tucker (1755a) to Thomas Secker, Archbishop of Canterbury, Astor Division of the New York Public Library, reprinted in Clark (1903), "Appendix: Skeleton of Tucker's Great Work," pp. 233–40.

——(1755c [1751]) *Questions importantes sur le commerce à l'occasion des oppositions au dernier bill de naturalisation*, Anne-Jacques-Robert Turgot (trans.), London: F. Gyles.

——(1758) *Instructions for Travellers*, Dublin: William Watson.

——(1774a) *Four tracts on political and commercial subjects*, Gloucester: R. Raikes and J. Rivington.

——(1774b) "The great Question resolved, Whether a rich Country can stand a Competition with a poor Country (of equal natural Advantages) in raising of Provisions, and Cheapness of Manufactures? With suitable Inferences and Deductions," in Tucker (1774a), pp. 9–48.

——(1776a) *Four Tracts on Political and Commercial Subjects*, 3rd edn., Gloucester: R. Raikes and T. Cadell.

——(1776b) "Tract V. The Respective Pleas and Arguments of the Mother Country and of the Colonies Distinctively Set Forth" in Tucker (1776), separately paginated.

——(1776c) 'Tract V. The Respective Pleas and Arguments of the Mother Country and of the Colonies Distinctively Set Forth' in Tucker (1776a), separately paginated.

——(1779) *Thoughts on the Present Posture of Affairs, July 24, 1779. By the Dean of Gloucester*, [London?]: n.p.

——(1781) *A Treatise Concerning Civil Government, in Three Parts. Part I. The Notions of Mr. Locke ... Examined and Confuted. Part II. The True Basis of Civil Government set Forth ... Part III. England's Former Gothic Constitution Censured and Exposed*, London: T. Cadell.

——(1785) *Reflections on the Present Matter in Dispute between Great Britain and Ireland; and on the Means of converting these Articles into mutual Benefits to both Kingdoms*, London: T. Cadell.

——(1799a) *Dean Tucker's Arguments on the Propriety of a Union between Great Britain and Ireland; Written Some Years Since, and Now First Published in this Tract upon the Same Subject. By the Rev. Dr. Clarke*, Dublin: printed for J. Milliken.

——(1799b) *Union or Separation. Written some Years Since by the Rev. Dr. Tucker, ... and now First Published in this Tract upon the Same Subject. By the Rev. Dr. Clarke, ... In this Work, the Great Objections Urged at a Meeting of the Irish Bar, are Distinctly Considered and Confuted*, London: sold by J. Hatchard & J. Wright, Clarke, and Rivingtons.

——(1755 [1751]) *Questions importantes sur le commerce à l'occasion des oppositions au dernier bill de naturalisation*, Anne-Jacques-Robert Turgot (trans. and ed.) London.

Turgot, Anne-Robert-Jacques (1963 [1770]) *Reflections on the Formation and the Distribution of Riches*, New York: Augustus Kelley.

Ulloa, Bernardo de (1753 [1740]) *Rétablissement des manufactures et du commerce d'Espagne*, Louis-Joseph Plumard de Dangeul (trans. and ed.), Amsterdam: n.p.

Urquhart, Robert (1995) "David Hume and Josiah Tucker: Pagan and Christian Political Economy," *History of Economic Ideas*, 3: 1–33.

Ustariz, Geronimo (1753 [1742]) *Théorie et pratique du commerce et de la marine*, F. Véron de Forbonnais (trans. and ed.), Paris: Veuve Estienne.

Vanderlint, Jacob (1914 [1734]) *Money Answers All Things*, Baltimore, MD: Johns Hopkins Press.

Vatteville, Eric (1971) "La pensée fiscale de J.J.L. Graslin (1717–90)," *Revue d'Histoire Économique et Sociale*, 49: 325–42.

Vaughan, Benjamin (1788) *New and Old Principles of Trade Compared; or a Treatise on the Principles of Commerce between Nations; with an Appendix*, London: J. Johnson and J. Debrett.

——(1789 [1788]) *Nouveaux & Anciens Principes du Commerce, Comparés: ou Traité sur les Principes du Commerce entre les Nations: avec un Appendice*, London: Galabin.

Velk, T. and A. R. Riggs (1985) "David Hume's Practical Economics," *Hume Studies*, 11(2): 154–65.

Venning, Corey (1976) "Hume on Property, Commerce, and Empire in the Good Society: The Role of Historical Necessity," *Journal of the History of Ideas*, 37(1): 74–92.

Venturi, Franco (1959) "Su alcune pagine d'antologia," *Rivista Storica Italiana*, 71: 321–25.

——(1971) *Europe des Lumières: recherches sur le 18è Siècle*, Paris: Mouton.

——(1983) "Scottish Echoes in Eighteenth-Century Italy," in Hont and Ignatieff (eds.) *Wealth and Virtue*, Cambridge: Cambridge University, pp. 345–62.

Vernon, Raymond (1966) "International Investment and International Trade in the Product Cycle," *Quarterly Journal of Economics*, 80: 190–207.

Vertot, René Aubert, abbé de (1722 [1720]) *A critical history of the establishment of the Bretons among the Gauls, and of their Dependence on the Kings of France, and Dukes of Normandy*, 2 vols., London: W. Taylor, J. Pemberton, E. Symon, W. Chetwood, J. Lacy, and J. Clarke.

Verzar, Andreas (1979) *Das autonome Subjekt und der Vernunftstaat: Eine systematisch-historische Untersuchung zu Fichtes Geschlossenem Handelsstaat von 1800*, Bonn: Bouvier.

Veyne, Paul (1976) *Le Pain et le cirque*, Paris: du Seuil.

Vickers, Douglas (1957) "Method and Analysis in David Hume's Economic Essays", *Economica*, 24: 225–34.

——(1959) *Studies in the Theory of Money, 1690–1776*, London: Peter Owen.

Vilar, Pierre (1976) *A History of Gold and Money, 1450–1920*, London: New Left Books.

Vincent de Gournay (1983a [1752]), *Traité sur le commerce de Josiah Child avec les remarques inédites de Vincent de Gournay*, Takumi Tsuda (ed.), Tokyo: Kinokunya.

——(1983b [1752]) "Remarques sur quelques endroits de la Préface de Mr. Child," in Takumi Tsuda (ed.) *Traité sur le Commerce de Josiah Child avec les Remarques Inédites de Vincent de Gournay*, Tokyo: Kinokunya, pp. 24–44.

——(1983c [1752]) "Conclusion des Remarques sur le Traité du Commerce de Josias Child," in Takumi Tsuda (ed.) *Tsucer* pp. 416–38.

——(1993) *Mémoires et lettres de Vincent de Gournay*, Takumi Tsuda (ed.) Tokyo: Kinokuniya Company.

——(1993 [1748]) "[Untitle] Mémoire," in T. Tsuda (ed.) (Memoires 1993), pp. 3–12.

Viner, Jacob (1937) *Studies in the Theory of International Trade*, New York: Harper.

Voltaire, François Marie Arouet de (1901 [1738]) "[On John Law, Melon, and Du Tot]: On Commerce and Luxury, Money and the Revenues of Kings," in *The Works of Voltaire: A Contemporary Version*, notes by Tobias Smollett, rev. and modernized; new translations by William F. Fleming, 43 vols., Akron, OH: Werner, vol. 38, pp. 211–15.

——(1980 [1733]) *Letters on England*, Leonard Tancock (trans.), London: Penguin Books.

——(1986 [1734]) *Lettres philosophiques*, F. Delolfre (ed.), Paris: Gallimard.

——(2003 [1736]) *Le Mondain*, H. Mason (ed.), in *Oeuvres Complètes*, Oxford: Voltaire Foundation.

Wahnbaeck, Till (2004) *Luxury and Public Happiness: Political Economy in the Italian Enlightenment*, Oxford: Clarendon Press.

Wallech, Steven (1984) "The Elements of Social Status in Hume's *Treatise*," *Journal of the History of Ideas*, 45: 207–18

Walzer, Michael (1983) *Spheres of Justice: A Defense of Pluralism and Equality*, New York: Basic Books.

Waterman, Anthony (1988) "Hume, Malthus and the Stability of Equilibrium," *History of Political Economy*, 20: 85–94.

——(1998) "David Hume on Technology and Culture," *History of Economics Review*, 28: 46–61.

Weiner, Martin (1981) *English Culture and the Decline of the Industrial Spirit, 1850–1980*, New York: Cambridge University Press.

Wennerlind, Carl (2000) "The Humean Paternity to Adam Smith's Theory of Money," *History of Economic Ideas*, 8: 77–97.

——(2001a) "Money Talks, but What Is It Saying? Semiotics of Money and Social Control," *Journal of Economic Issues*, 35(3): 557–74.

——(2001b) "The Link between David Hume's *A Treatise of Human Nature* and His Fiduciary Theory of Money," *History of Political Economy*, 33(1): 139–60.

——(2002) "David Hume's Political Philosophy: A Theory of Commercial Modernization," *Hume Studies*, 28(2): 247–70.

——(2005) "David Hume's Monetary Theory Revisited: Was He Really a Quantity Theorist and an Inflationist?" *Journal of Political Economy*, 113(1): 223–37.

——(2006) "David Hume as a *Political* Economist," in Alistair Dow and Sheila Dow (eds.) *The History of Scottish Economic Thought*, London: Routledge, pp. 46–70.

West, Edwin G. (2000) "Unilateral Free Trade versus Reciprocity in the *Wealth of Nations*," *Journal of the History of Political Thought*, 22: 29–42.

Westerfield, Ray B. (1915) *Middlemen in English Business, Particularly between 1660 and 1760*, New Haven: Yale University Press.

Weulersse, Georges (1910) *Les manuscrits économiques de François Quesnay et du Marquis de Mirabeau aux Archives Nationales (M. 778 à M. 785), Inventaire, extraits et notes*, Paris: P. Geuthner.

——(1910) *Le movement physiocratique en France de 1756 à 1770*, 2 vols., Paris: G. Alcan.

——(ed.) (1968) *Les Manuscrits économiques de François Quesnay et du Marquis de Mirabeau aux Archives Nationales (M. 778 à M. 785)*, New York: B. Franklin.

Whatley, Christopher A. (2000) *Scottish Society 1707–1830*, Manchester, UK: Manchester University Press.

Whelan, Frederick (1985) *Order and Artifice in Hume's Political Philosophy*, Princeton, NJ: Princeton University Press.

Williams, William H. (1992) "Is Hume's Shade of Blue a Red Herring?," *Synthèse*, 92(1): 83–99.

Willis, Kirk (1979) "The Role in Parliament of the Economic Ideas of Adam Smith, 1776–1800," *History of Political Economy*, 11(4): 505–44.

Wilson, Charles (1971) *England's Apprenticeship, 1603–1763*, London: Longman.

Winch, Donald (1978) *Adam Smith's Politics*, Cambridge: Cambridge University Press.

——(1998) "The Political Economy of Public Finance in the 'Long' Eighteenth Century," in J. Maloney (ed.) *Debt and Deficits: An Histon: Perspective*, Aldershot, UK: Elgar.

Wollstonecraft, Mary (1988 [1792]) *A Vindication of the Rights of Women*, New York: Norton.

Wood, Geoffrey (1995) "The Quantity Theory in the 1980s: Hume, Thornton, Friedman and the Relation Between Money and Inflation," in Mark Blaug (ed.) *The Quantity Theory of Money: From Locke to Keynes and Friedman*, Aldershot: Edward Elgar.

Wood, John P. (1791) *A Sketch of the Life and Projects of John Law of Lauriston*, Edinburgh and London: n.p.

Wood, Paul (1989) "The Natural History of Man in the Scottish Enlightenment," *History of Science*, 28:89–123.

Wood, Paul (ed.) (2000) *The Scottish Enlightenment: Essays in Reinterpretation*, Rochester: University of Rochester Press.

Wootton, David (1993) "David Hume, 'the historian'," in David Fate Norton (ed.) *The Cambridge Companion to Hume*, Cambridge: Cambridge University Press.

Wright, John P. (2003) "Dr. George Cheyne, Chevalier Ramsay, and Hume's Letter to a Physician," *Hume Studies*, 29(1): 125–41.

Wright, Johnson Kent (1992) "Conversations with Phocion: The Political Thought of Mably," *History of Political Thought* 13: 391–45.

——(1997) *A Classical Republican in Eighteenth-Century France: The Political Thought of Mably*, Stanford, CA: Stanford University Press.

Yaari, Menachem E. (1977) "Endogenous Changes in Taste: A Philosophical Discussion," *Erkenntnis*, 11: 157–96.

York, Neil L. (1994) *Neither Kingdom nor Nation: The Irish Quest for Constitutional Rights, 1698–1800*, Washington, DC: Catholic University of America Press.

Young, Arthur (1785) "Observations on the Commerical Agreement with Ireland," in Young (ed.) *Annals of Agriculture, and Other Useful Arts*, vol. 3, London: Printed for the editor, and sold by H. Goldney, pp. 257–90.

Young, Jeffrey T. (1990) "David Hume and Adam Smith on Value Premises in Economics," *History of Political Economy*, 22(4): 6.

Youngson, A. J. (1973) *After the Forty-Five: The Economic Impact on the Scottish Highlands*, Edinburgh: Edinburgh University Press.

Manuscript Sources

Du Pont de Nemours, Pierre-Samuel and His Two Wives, Papers, Manuscript Division, Hagley Museum and Library, Wilmington, DE.

French Ministry of the Navy. Archives de la Marine (1738) Untitled memoir, series B^{III} 436, Archives Nationales, Archives de France, Paris.

French Ministry of Foreign Affairs. Ministère des Affaires Étrangères (1740) "Commerce d'Angleterre," Mémoires et Documents, Angleterre, vol. 68, Paris: Quai d'Orsay.

——(1747) "Observations sur les finances, le commerce, et la navigation d'Angleterre," Mémoires et Documents, Angleterre, vol. 68, Paris: Quai d'Orsay.

Hume, David (1746–47) Notebooks, National Library of Scotland, Edinburgh: Hume Papers, MSS. 25687–91.

St Clair, Lieutenant General James', Papers, National Library of Scotland.

Linlithgow Manuscripts, Hopetoun House, South Queensferry, Scotland.

South Sea Company Papers, British Library, London: MS. 25544.

The Select Society of Edinburgh Papers, National Library of Scotland, Edinburgh.

(c. 1742) Unpublished manuscript (MS GD18\1144), National Archives of Scotland.

Index

LaVergne, TN USA
06 November 2009
163285LV00002B/27/P